Second Edition

FUNDAMENTALS OF CONSTRUCTION ESTIMATING AND COST ACCOUNTING

WITH COMPUTER APPLICATIONS

KEITH COLLIER

Douglas College
New Westminster, B.C.

PRENTICE-HALL, INC., Englewood Cliffs, NJ 07632

Library of Congress Cataloging-in-Publication Data

Collier, Keith
  Fundamentals of construction estimating and cost
accounting.

  Bibliography
  Includes index
  1. Building—Estimates. 2. Construction industry—
Accounting. 3. Building—Estimates—Data processing.
4. Construction industry—Accounting—Data processing.
I. Title.
TH435.C72 1987   692′.5   86-18652
ISBN 0-13-335613-2

Cover design: *20/20 Services, Inc.*
Manufacturing buyer: *John Hall*

dBASE II® is a registered trademark of Ashton-Tate.
dBASE III® is a registered trademark of Ashton-Tate.
Lotus® and 1-2-3® are registered trademarks of Lotus Development Corporation.
SuperCalc® is a registered trademark of Sorcim/IUS MicroSoftware, a
  Division of Computer Associates International, Inc.
VisiCalc® is a registered trademark of Software Arts, Inc.
Microplan is the trademark of Digital Research.
Multiplan is the trademark of Microsoft.

Printed in the United States of America

10 9 8 7 6 5 4

ISBN 0-13-335613-2 025

PRENTICE-HALL INTERNATIONAL (UK) LIMITED, *London*
PRENTICE-HALL OF AUSTRALIA PTY. LIMITED, *Sydney*
PRENTICE-HALL CANADA INC., *Toronto*
PRENTICE-HALL HISPANOAMERICANA, S.A., *Mexico*
PRENTICE-HALL OF INDIA PRIVATE LIMITED, *New Delhi*
PRENTICE-HALL OF JAPAN, INC., *Tokyo*
PRENTICE-HALL OF SOUTHEAST ASIA PTE. LTD., *Singapore*
EDITORA PRENTICE-HALL DO BRASIL, LTDA., *Rio de Janeiro*

This book is dedicated to
Pauline Collier

CONTENTS

9 MEASUREMENT EXAMPLES AND EXERCISES

10 PRICING WORK: GENERAL

11 PRICING WORK: PARTICULAR

* Drawings marked with an asterisk are included in the standard full-page size, and also in double full-page size for clarity.

It is suggested that working copies of the drawings be made. However, no other copying, other than by the purchaser of the book in making working copies, is allowable under the copyright law.

PREFACE
TO THE SECOND EDITION

A new approach to estimating construction costs is needed: one that is designed for computer systems. Neither hardware nor software will ever completely replace the skilled and experienced estimator, but an estimator needs computer systems to produce better estimates. Estimators have always had to handle large masses of data and information, and existing estimating methods are in large part the result of this fact. That is why construction work is measured as it is, with similar but different items grouped or added together and, as a result, with much of the useful information about the work obscured by the estimating process.

Costs are increasingly critical. Estimating and bidding creates construction costs (within the constraints of a market), while accounting only sorts and allocates them. For a contracting company, therefore, estimating is more critical than accounting; except that the law requires a certain minimum standard of accounting.

So far, it seems that all the computer software developed for construction estimating assumes the estimating methods established centuries ago. No software I have seen says: Now that we have microcomputer power let us find new and better methods of estimating construction costs that use the full power of microcomputer systems.

This second edition takes a first step in that direction: a step toward a new method of measurement and pricing, and from there to a new contracting method.

Producing a second edition of a long-established text and reference book on construction estimating and cost accounting is a great opportunity to aim at new goals, because it enables us to keep one foot on the familiar while exploring new ground, as in this edition.

The first edition of this book was published in 1974, and it has been widely accepted and used. (The seventh printing was in 1984.) The example of a mainframe computer application to estimating and cost accounting in the first edition is still current; but mainframe computers are no longer needed because of the great advances in microcomputer technology, especially in their speed and capacity. And generally, software development has followed close behind to utilize the growing microcomputer capability—except software for estimating and cost accounting for construction. There are thousands of software packages for general accounting, and prices are still falling; but it is not the same with software for construction estimating and cost accounting.

Actually, there is a lot of estimating software

around, but most of it has not been marketed. Of that in the market, not much appears innovative let alone radical. Most of it is slow, clumsy, and obsolescent because it is based on existing estimating methods now redundant. Also, almost none of the existing software deals effectively with measurement. Pricing is easy with a computer, but for the measurement of work little software exists that is effective. A new approach to measurement is needed, and a new approach to measurement is introduced in this second edition.

In this second edition we go from the familiar to the innovative; from general principle to particular application. We discuss the fundamentals, and many illustrative examples of estimates are included. Redundant material has been removed from the first edition, and some additional estimating examples and exercises included. A new chapter introduces microcomputers and offers suggestions on selecting a system for estimating and cost accounting and for other construction management applications. The Glossary, the Bibliography, and the Index have been completely redone.

For estimating, now is the time to use microcomputers; but in making the change we should take the opportunity to develop better estimating methods to replace the old. In 1974, the first edition of this book introduced estimating by computers. Now it introduces a new approach to estimating that eventually will help to fully utilize the great speed and memory of that marvelous product of American technology: the microchip.

Finally, a few facts about this second edition: In some instances, references in the first edition have been retained because I think a point originally made is still valid, given the variety of estimating practices and methods still used, even though new editions of cited publications (e.g., methods of measurement; especially the Canadian, now in metric) have changed.

Metric measurement is used in only about half the construction jobs in Canada, it appears; so I have not "gone metric" in this edition except for a few minor examples. In any case, metric measurement changes nothing fundamental to estimating, and the period of change will probably be a long one. Measurement of work is, however, the primary concern of this text, especially in this new edition, in the light of microcomputer use.

If you are already using a microcomputer (for any purpose), I urge you to begin the changeover to computerized estimating. You will need lots of time, so it is not too early to start even if only in a small way: that is, by changing your measurement methods as suggested here and by "thinking computers." If you are not using a computer at all, even so, I urge you: Make a start, no matter how small your company and no matter how small the start; but do take the first step. Buy a personal computer. Of course it will be "out of date" in a year or so, in that there will be faster and more powerful models available; but buying a computer is like buying a car: You do not have to have the latest model to find it useful; but you do need a car if you want to drive. And, as with a car, it is only by owning and practicing often that one becomes proficient.

KEITH COLLIER
Construction Management Program
Douglas College
New Westminster, B.C.

1986

PREFACE
TO THE FIRST EDITION

I have assumed that whoever studies construction estimating has already learned something about building construction because that is the proper order; and I have not written about the science of building construction except to illustrate examples of estimating practice. Besides, there is more than enough to say about estimating, and for this reason it has been necessary to make a distinction between fundamentals and variables. Consequently, I have left it to the periodicals to more ably provide current cost data for estimators in different areas; and I have left it to the readers to obtain their own reference material on contracts and construction materials. Much of this reference material can be obtained free, or for a nominal charge, from original sources, and its reproduction here would not be worthwhile. Some useful material is listed in the Bibliography, and students should start to collect a reference library as soon as they can.

Construction estimating and building economics have a universal application, and I have tried to show the fundamental things that underlie them and how they apply to the building construction process, particularly in conjunction with that most neglected aspect of construction management—cost accounting. Good construction management is not possible without estimating and cost accounting; and although building economics has yet to be formalized and made into a discipline, cost accounting will be one of the means by which this is accomplished.

In places, I have used abbreviations of construction terms because this is commonly done in construction estimates; and those abbreviations used are listed before the first chapter. The text also includes certain terms in *italics*, and they are listed in the Glossary, at the end. The terms in *italics* are generally common words; but they are also *key words* in the text with special meanings that are explained in the Glossary. Some are terms specially coined for this text to convey certain concepts, and this usage is elaborated in a preamble to the Glossary.

The immediate acknowledgments I should make follow; others are not diminished because they are not included, nor are these by their brevity; G. Berkenpas, assistant master, BCIT: for all the figures and drawings; G. M. Hardie, FRICS, MCIQS, chartered quantity surveyor and associate master, BCIT: for reading the manuscript, for his assistance in checking some of the examples, and for his useful suggestions; R. Ochotorena, for typing the manuscript; G. E. Parsons, FRICS, MCIQS, chartered quantity surveyor, for reading the manuscript, for his suggestions, and for his aid and counsel over many years; and F. Wools,

FRICS, chartered quantity surveyor, for his good instruction.

Special acknowledgment is made to the following persons for their permission to reproduce the building drawings for this text: The Residence, H. E. Kuckein, architect, Vancouver, B.C.; The Warehouse, Dominion Construction Co., Ltd., Vancouver, B.C.; and The Apartment Block, W. Ralph Brownlee, architect, Vancouver, B.C.

Finally, I should acknowledge my debt to the Royal Institution of Chartered Surveyors, and to the Canadian Institute of Quantity Surveyors, for permission to quote from the Methods of Measurement and other documents that they publish, and for the general debt that all members owe to their professional institutes.

KEITH COLLIER
British Columbia
1973   *Institute of Technology*

LIST OF ABBREVIATIONS

Abbreviations are widely used in describing *work*[1] in construction estimates and on drawings. With some abbreviations there is a customary format, whereas others are written according to personal inclination. As a step toward standardization, I have used those formats that I believe to be the most common and the most easily understood, and I have been guided by general quantity surveying practice, and by other writers, particularly by Wass,[2] who rightly advocates the use of open punctuation with abbreviations. However, a few abbreviations make other words, as in the case of inch–in. To avoid confusion in such cases punctuation is used.

NOTES ON ABBREVIATIONS

1. Add the letter "g" for "ing" (i.e., ct–coat; ctg–coating).

2. In the absence of a standard abbreviation, the best method of abbreviation is to eliminate vowels other than those required to avoid ambiguity.

3. The well-known, standard abbreviations that are in general use, including titles of societies, associations, and the like, and those abbreviations found in trade manuals and dictionaries, are generally not included here.

A	area
a.b	as before
AG	asphalt and gravel
agg	aggregate
avg	average
B	breadth
b.f	both faces
BF	board feet
bk	brick
bkwk	brickwork
bldg	building
blk	block
blkwk	blockwork
bm	beam

---

[1] Terms listed in the Glossary are indicated by a ^G when they first appear, or whenever the reader's attention should be drawn toward a precise meaning.

[2] Alonzo Wass, *Manual of Structural Details for Building Construction* (Englewood Cliffs, N.J.: Prentice-Hall, Inc., 1968). List of Abbreviations, pp. XIII–XIV.

brd	board		**fbm**	feet board measure
brgdg	bridging		**FF**	first floor
brr	bearer		**fin**	finish(ed)
b/s	both sides		**flr**	floor
btm	bottom		**flrg**	flooring
b/up	built up		**flshg**	flashing
b/w	both ways		**fmwk**	formwork
			fnd	foundation
			frmg	framing
CA	cost accounting		**ftg**	footing
C & W	cutting and waste			
CF (cf)	cubic feet		**Ga**	gauge
c/flshg	counter-flashing		**galv**	galvanized
chy	chimney		**GF**	ground floor
CI	cast iron		**gnd**	ground
CIQS	Canadian Institute of Quantity Surveyors		**grd**	grade
circ	circle, circular			
clg	ceiling		**H (h)**	height (high)
CM (cm)	cubic meters		**Hdwd**	hardwood
cmt	cement		**hlw**	hollow
col	column			
conc	concrete		**incl**	include, including
constr	construct(ion)		**insul**	insulation
cont	continuous		**intl**	internal
cors	course		**intr**	interior
ct	coat		**inv**	invert
CY (cy)	cubic yards			
			jst	joist
			jt	joint
D	depth, deep			
dbl	double		**L**	length, angle (steel)
Ddt	deduct		**lab**	labor
desc	describe, description		**lam**	laminated
dia	diameter		**LF (lf)**	linear feet
dim	dimension		**l & m**	labor & material
do	ditto		**LS**	lump sum
dpf(g)	damproof(ing)		**LY (ly)**	linear yards
dtl	detail			
dwg	drawing		**M**	thousand
			м (m)	meter
			mat	material
ea	each		**max**	maximum
e.f	each face		**MBF**	thousand board feet
elev	elevation		**meas**	measure
E.O	extra (cost) over		**m.g**	make good
e.w	elsewhere		**min**	minimum
e/w	each way		**misc**	miscellaneous
excav	excavation		**mldg**	molding
extg	existing		**mm**	millimeter
extl	external		**MM**	method of measurement
extr	exterior			

MP	mean perimeter
m.s	mild steel
m/s	measured separately
mtr	mortar
n.e	not exceeding
No	number (enumerated)
n.w	narrow width
o/a	overall
o.c	over centers, on center
opng	opening
o/s	one side
P.C	prime cost
P cmt	portland cement
pcs	pieces
perim	perimeter
pl	plate
pr	pair
proj	projection, projecting
ptn	partition (wall)
pvg	paving
rad	radius
RC (& W)	raking cutting (and waste)
R conc	reinforced concrete
rebar	steel reinforcing bars
reinf	reinforced, reinforcement
RICS	Royal Institution of Chartered Surveyors
rnd	round
SF (sf)	square feet
SFCA	square feet contact area

sht	sheet
shthg	sheathing
sof	soffite
specs	specifications
Sq	square (100 square feet)
s.q	small quantities
std	standard
str	straight
super	superficial (area)
surf	surface
susp	suspended
SY (sy)	square yards
t & g	tongued-and-grooved
temp	temporary
th	thick
trwld	troweled
UF	upper floor
u/s	underside
V	volume
VB	vapor barrier
W	waste
wd	wood
wdw	window
WF	wide flange (section)
wi	with
wpf(g)	waterproof(ing)
wt	weight
X brgdg	cross-bridging

1

WHY ESTIMATE CONSTRUCTION COSTS?

To answer this question it is necessary to look at the ways in which buildings are designed and built, at the persons involved, and at the relationships among them. The construction industry is unique for reasons that have existed ever since man began to build.

Buildings are part of the land on which they stand because of the nature of buildings and because of their physical connection with the land beneath them.

The early laws of property recognized the difference between "movables" and "immovables."

> The only natural classification of the objects of enjoyment, the only classification which corresponds with an essential difference in the subject matter, is that which divides them into Movables and Immovables.[1]

Land and buildings are immovables, and they are called "real property" as distinct from "chattels," which are movables or "personal property." Buildings are legally part of the land because they are fixed to it; and, in a more fundamental sense, because of how they are constructed. This was more apparent in the past when buildings were built from simple materials. Cottages, castles, and churches all contained the same basic materials: earth, stone, and wood, and the differences among them involved only size and shape and the work and degree of skill in building and decorating them. Their common source was the land, and this ancient and natural relationship between buildings and land is still reflected in the laws of property.

Today, most building materials are manufactured by complex processes. Many building components are preassembled, and some buildings are completely prefabricated. Developments in technology have obscured or diminished the original relationship between buildings and the land. Nevertheless, this lasting relationship remains the primary reason why the construction industry is unique.[2]

Each piece of land is unique and may differ from every other in many ways; in soil and water conditions, substrata, topography, altitude, and aspect. Or the

---

[1] Sir Henry Maine, *Ancient Law* (Everyman's Library; London: J. M. Dent & Sons Ltd.; New York: E. P. Dutton & Co. Inc.).

[2] Other reasons include: (1) the history and nature of the traditional building trades; (2) construction is essential to all other industries, and largely dependent on them; (3) governments use the construction industry as an economic control; (4) the construction industry is made up of many small and a few large companies.

differences may be few and sometimes there may be only a difference in location. But this principle of difference is invariable; only the degree of difference varies. Because of the close relationship between land and buildings, the principle of difference applies also to the buildings fixed to the land. And to the extent that buildings are fixtures on land, so are they unique. The antithesis of this is the mass-produced mobile home with only a slight connection to the land. But until all buildings are mobile, and until that historical relationship between buildings and land disappears, the construction industry will remain unique and each building will be unique in at least one respect: its fixed location on the land.

Each site requires a building on it to be specially designed to suit the site's unique characteristics. In addition, buildings are different because of an owner's requirements; because of a desire for individual expression or for commercial reasons. Suburban estates of mass-produced houses are no exception to this principle of difference if the estate (and not the house) is regarded as the unit of construction. Usually this principle is not too difficult to detect because such houses are usually more or less identical, and the main difference is between one estate and another, often only because of a different location and a different arrangement of the houses on the site.

THE PERSONS INVOLVED
IN CONSTRUCTION

The *owner*[G] is the initiator of construction.[3] He may also be known as a *developer*.[G] He may want to develop land by building a residence for himself, or he may want to build an office building or a warehouse for business purposes. He may want to make an investment in a development to produce an income by renting building space to tenants. Or he may want to develop land with the intention of selling the land and its buildings (improvements) for a profit. The owner may be an individual person, a company, or a public body such as a school board. Anyone with rights to land who exercises those rights by having construction work[G] done on the land is an owner in the contractual sense.

If an owner is a company specializing in property development, the company may be equipped to carry out all stages of the development from land purchase to rental or sale of the developed property. In most cases, however, an owner is not equipped with either the staff or the experience for such an undertaking,

---

[3] A superscript [G] indicates words and terms explained in the Glossary.

and most owners require the services of a *designer*.[G] The designer makes a contract with the owner to provide certain services in return for a fee, and these services might include:

1. Schematic building designs and plans of land utilization
2. Developing the design drawings and site plans
3. Preparing the documents (drawings and specifications) required for the construction work
4. Negotiating with or obtaining bids from construction companies for the construction work
5. Inspecting the construction work in progress
6. Settling the final account for the work.

A designer's services to an owner may include some or all of these items, together with other services related to building and real property development. The role of the designer is changing, and the subject of professional services is complex. Further reading can be selected from the Bibliography.

The designer's consultants[G] are specialists in various aspects of the design and construction industry. Few designers can be expert in so many fields, and consultants are hired by a designer to assist him in providing all the services required by an owner. As the need for larger and more complex buildings and for environmental controls has increased so has specialization in design and construction. Such fields of specialization include:

Engineering	Planning and design
Structures	Hotels and theaters
Soils	Kitchens and
Acoustics	restaurants
Mechanical services	Educational buildings
Electrical services	Laboratories
	Industrial plants
Management	Parking and traffic
Financing	Parks and landscaping
Feasibility studies	Town planning and
Costs and economics	almost any class of
Scheduling	building and property
	development.

The number and variety of consultants retained by a designer is determined by the owner's requirements for the building and the site and the designer's need for specialized assistance.

The *contractor*[G] is the builder and the construction

expert who does construction work for payment and who enters into a contract with an owner for this purpose. He is sometimes called a *general contractor*[G] to distinguish him from the various specialist *subcontractors*[G] described below. In the past a general contractor employed a variety of tradesmen to do everything from concrete and masonry to glazing and painting. Mechanical work, such as heating and plumbing and gas and electrical services, was often done by subcontractors, or by tradesmen employed by the general contractor. Later, more was done by specialist firms and less by the general contractor, who became a manager and a coordinator of specialist subcontractors, although still doing a portion of the work himself; usually the foundations and the structure.

A subcontractor is a specialist who has a contract with a contractor to do work and who is responsible to the contractor for its proper execution. The contractor is in turn responsible to the owner for the subcontractor's work. The contract between a subcontractor and the contractor arises out of and is subsidiary to the primary contract; hence the name, subcontract.[G] Subcontractors often have contracts with others who may be called *sub-subcontractors*,[G] because they contract for part of the work of a subcontract. A subcontractor is responsible to the contractor for the work of a sub-subcontractor in the same way that the contractor is responsible to the owner for the work of a subcontractor.

Persons involved in design and construction are shown diagramatically in Fig. 1-1, and the parties to the several contracts are shown connected by double-headed arrows to indicate their contractual relationships. These are the usual relationships among an owner, his agent the designer, and a contractor. Other contractual arrangements are possible. A designer may be an employee of an owner if the owner is a public body or a government department, and in some cases a designer may be employed by a contractor.

If a designer is employed by the contractor, the owner may have what is commonly called a package deal,[G] and instead of being party to two contracts (one with the designer and one with the contractor) the owner is party to only one contract for the provision of both design and construction. An owner may also purchase the land together with these services from one company and enter into a turnkey project[G] through which the owner has only to state his requirements and pay to be able to "turn the key" and enter a completed building.

CONSTRUCTION CONTRACTS

This text cannot offer a complete explanation of the nature of contracts, but some reference to them is necessary because construction contracts are one of the primary reasons for construction estimates.

Civil law in the United States of America, Canada, Britain, and many countries in the British Commonwealth has a common origin in British common law. Consequently, contract law in these countries is basically the same, although specific laws vary from place to place. (Civil law in Quebec and Louisiana is based on French law.) The student of construction estimating should have a practical working knowledge of the law of the area in which his company does work. The nature of a contract is such that it binds contracting parties together in an exclusive relationship, referred to as "privity of contract" (see Fig. 1-1.) Contracts are essential and commonplace in modern society, and a good contract that benefits the contracting parties also benefits society at large. All technical specialization depends on contracts as the means through which a specialist can apply his knowledge and practice his skill in return for payment.

After the designer has approval of the design from the owner and local authorities and has obtained the owner's instructions to proceed, he prepares the *contract documents*,[G] which will be known as the *bidding documents*[G] until a contract is made. The designer then arranges for *bids*[G] to be submitted to the owner by construction companies, usually from selected construction companies (through selective bidding) or from any qualified company (through open bidding) in the case of public works. These bids are offers to do work according to the requirements of the bidding documents.

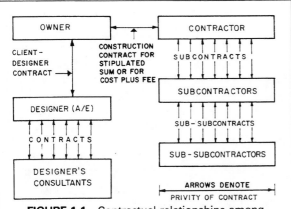

FIGURE 1-1 Contractual relationships among persons involved in the design and construction of a project, in which the *owner* has one contract for design services and one contract for construction.

Alternatively, and depending on the type of construction contract required, a designer may enter into negotiations with one or more construction companies on an owner's behalf so as to arrange a construction contract between the owner and a contractor for executing the work.[4]

A contract must have certain ingredients to be valid. These may be described as:

1. Mutual agreement   4. Capacity
2. Consideration   5. Genuine intention
3. Lawful object

Some texts use different terminology but they all refer to the same things. Not all construction contracts have to be in writing to be valid, but an oral contract is potentially a source of disputes and may be difficult to enforce. Therefore, all construction contracts should be in writing and certain construction contracts are required by statute to be written, usually including contracts for public works and contracts of more than one year's duration.

Mutual agreement is expressed in the offer (bid) made by a construction company and in the acceptance of the offer by the owner. The offer and its acceptance must be unqualified; that is, without terms and conditions. The basis of mutual agreement is the bidding documents, which become the contract documents when an offer to do the work as described in the documents is accepted.

Consideration in a construction contract, on the one hand, consists of the work performed by the contractor for the owner, and, on the other hand, of the payment made by the owner to the contractor for the work done. The law is not concerned with the amount of the consideration; only that it have some value. If a contractor makes an offer that is accepted, he cannot abandon the contract and not complete the work because he finds that his offer was too low and the payment insufficient. It is here that we begin to see the importance of estimating.

Lawful object is not usually a problem in construction contracts because of their nature and because of the preliminary procedures involving development approvals and building permits. A contract to construct a building for an illicit purpose would presumably be invalid, if a certain nineteenth-century legal case is a precedent. In that case, a fashionable lady refused to pay for a new carriage and was taken to court by the carriage-maker. Her defense was that the carriage-maker knew her trade and reputation and knew that the carriage would be used for illicit purposes; therefore, she claimed, there was no valid contract. The judge found in her favor.

Capacity refers to the capacity of the parties to make a legal and valid contract. To do so, they must not be sentenced criminals, lunatics, enemy aliens (during war), or infants (minors). However, minors can make valid contracts to obtain certain "necessaries" such as food and education.

Genuine intention means that a real and genuine offer and acceptance have been made and that both parties truly and willingly intend to enter into a contract. If one party's intention is not genuine, the contract may be invalid. Invalidation could be the result of one of the following:

1. A mistake, such as in regard to subject matter or identity
2. Misrepresentation of facts by one of the parties (without intent)
3. Fraud by one of the parties (with intent)
4. Duress, such as a threat of violence
5. Undue influence, such as is exerted by an educated person over an illiterate person.

The legal aspects of construction contracts are many and varied, and only the briefest outline has been given so that construction estimating can be seen in proper context. A contract is based on mutual agreement, which is expressed by offer and acceptance; and an offer to construct a building for a certain payment cannot be made without first making an estimate of the costs.

TYPES OF CONSTRUCTION CONTRACTS

There is always a risk in classifying things, because most things do not neatly fit into a few classifications. At the same time, classifications are useful in helping to identify and to compare, so long as we remember that classifications are made for our convenience and that they are not part of reality.

The design and construction industry uses three basic types of construction contracts, and others that are modifications. The types of construction contracts to be examined here are:

Basic types of contracts	Other types of contracts
1. Stipulated sum contracts	

---

[4] Further reading on the nature of construction contracts and bidding procedures can be selected from the Bibliography, including *Construction Contracts*, 2nd ed. (Keith Collier, Englewood Cliffs, N.J., Prentice-Hall, Inc., 1987).

2. Cost-plus-fee
   contracts
4. Unit price
   contracts

3. Target figure
   contracts

5. Management
   contracts

Types 1 and 2 are examined first, followed by an examination of type 3, a modification of and a development from the first two. The unit price contract is examined next, and finally management contracts, which are really not a type of contract but rather an arrangement of several different contracts.

Stipulated Sum Contract[G]

Few people will make a purchase before they know the price. Hence, the seller is required to establish and indicate the price at which he is prepared to sell; and such is usually the case when the purchaser is an owner and the seller a contractor. In the majority of construction contracts, there is a *contract sum,*[G] (or *contract amount*) which is the amount of the payment to be made by the owner to the contractor for the work to be done. This amount is first stipulated by the contractor in his offer to the owner, somewhat in this form:

> *"We offer to perform all the work shown on the drawings and described in the specifications for the sum of $. . . ."* (The sum is stipulated in the bid.)

By receiving several such bids, or offers, an owner expects to get a competitive price; and if he accepts an offer (usually the lowest), he expects to get the construction work done for that price. He may endeavor to further secure proper performance of the work by requiring a performance bond[G] from a third party who will guarantee that the contractor will perform the contract.

It will be apparent that to be able to stipulate a firm price for work a contractor must know exactly what the work includes. This kind of contract, therefore, requires the designer to prepare detailed bidding documents before invitations to bid for the work are extended. From the drawings and specifications that make up the bidding documents bidders must then make detailed estimates of the *costs of work*[G] as a basis for their bids to the owner.

In order for a bidder to make an accurate estimate of the costs of the work, adequate information about the work must be given in the bidding documents. He also must have knowledge of the conditions at the site

and experience in construction so as to be able to judge the probable costs. His knowledge can never be absolutely complete because site conditions are always unique and changing. His experience can never be totally adequate because no two construction projects are ever identical. And in this inevitable inability to foresee all costs lies much of the risk a contractor always takes, for there is always some risk of financial loss. But as long as the risk is not unreasonable a contractor is prepared to take it in return for the anticipated profit that he includes in his estimate of the costs and in his bid. Of course, he cannot overinsure against the risk of a loss by including an excessive profit,[G] because then his bid may no longer be competitive.

Bidders may not be able to make a reasonable estimate of the costs of work and thus may not be able to make firm and competitive bids to an owner if the bidders' knowledge of the site conditions is inadequate, and if: (1) the site is such as to make it impossible to ascertain these conditions in advance (because of location, substrata, or soil conditions, for example); (2) the bidders' experience does not include work such as that required by the owner; or (3) the information about the work is incomplete because of the owner's or the designer's inability to make an immediate decision about the work, for any reason. If all or most bidders find themselves in such a position, an owner may not be able to obtain competitive bids and a stipulated sum contract. Or, if any or all of the above conditions exist, any bids made for a stipulated sum contract may be inordinately high because all the bidders have included a high mark-up for profit and also allowances for contingencies to cover the risk they are unable to assess.

A designer should foresee if the nature of work or the conditions of a site are such as to make it impossible for the owner to get competitive stipulated sum bids, and he should then advise the owner that another type of contract is necessary.

Cost-Plus-Fee Contract[G]

In its simplest form, this type of contract may be made by accepting an offer worded essentially as follows:

> *"We offer to perform all the work for all costs (as defined in the agreement) and a fixed fee of $. . ."* (or, . . . *a fee of X percent of all costs*). Only the amount of the fee is stipulated.

This kind of contract need not eliminate competitive bidding. If "costs" are fully defined in the documents, the "fee" portion of the contract can be the basis of competitive bids. But this kind of contract is "open ended," and an owner does not know what his total costs will be until the work is finished. Therefore, the owner carries most of the risk.

Costs are usually defined in these contracts as all construction costs, except: certain job overhead costs,[G] all operating overhead costs,[G] and the profit,[G] which together are all covered by the fee. It is imperative that the costs are explicitly defined and that there is proper mutual agreement about them. One method requires the contract to explicitly state which costs are to be paid by the owner and to define the fee as including all other costs. Some *standard forms of contracts*[G] define costs as "reimbursable costs."[G] The "nonreimbursable costs"[G] are also defined, and they include any costs not included under "reimbursable costs" and they are covered by the fee.

The fee may be a fixed percentage of the costs as defined in the contract, or it may be fixed within certain limits of cost beyond which the percentage fee varies. Or the fee may be a fixed amount, or it may be fixed within certain limits of cost beyond which the fee varies pro rata, or according to a fee scale included in the contract. Many variations are possible, but the theme is always the same: Certain defined costs are paid periodically by the owner as they are incurred, whereas other costs of work[G] (primarily the operating overhead costs and the profit) are paid for as a fee to the contractor, usually in installments, pro rata to and at the same time as the periodic payments of the costs. Sometimes the fee is paid in installments related to specified stages of completion of the work.

This all becomes more easily understood by noting that the costs paid by an owner are costs directly chargeable to the work being done, for such tangible

and visible things as construction materials, workmen's payroll, the use of construction equipment, and for temporary services and offices on the site. The fee paid by the owner to the contractor, on the other hand, is for less tangible things *and for things over which the owner and the designer have no control*; namely, the contractor's operating overhead costs and profit. Therefore, the fee is determined in the first instance by the contractor according to his business needs and policies, even though he may subsequently negotiate for it with the owner or bid for it in competition.

Target Figure Contract[G]

If we imagine the two kinds of contracts just examined to be at the two poles of a "scale of risk," with the *stipulated sum contract* at one end, with most of the risk with the contractor, and with the *cost-plus-fee contract* at the other end, with most of the risk with the owner (as shown in Fig. 1-2), we can place between these two poles any number of different contracts composed of elements from both kinds of basic contracts at the poles, each with a different distribution of risk between owner and contractor. Chromatically speaking, with black at one end and white at the other, there are any number of shades of gray in between.

Standard forms for stipulated sum and cost-plus-fee construction contracts are published and sold, but almost all contracts based on a standard form of contract require some supplementary conditions and some changes to be made in the standard forms to suit some particular requirements. As developments and projects become larger and more complex, it often becomes necessary to make contractual arrangements that are different, and a better contract and a better arrangement

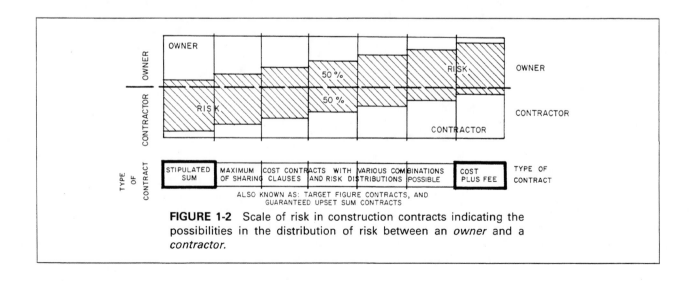

FIGURE 1-2 Scale of risk in construction contracts indicating the possibilities in the distribution of risk between an *owner* and a *contractor*.

for both parties may sometimes be achieved by a more even distribution of risk and by a more suitable form of contract.

The *stipulated sum contract* is essentially inflexible. Detailed requirements of the work must be determined and set down in the documents before contracting companies can be invited to make firm offers. Subsequent changes in the work, although usually permitted by the conditions of the contract, are contrary to the fundamental nature of a stipulated sum contract. Often they are a nuisance to the contractor, or of an unreasonable cost to the owner. At the same time, the contractor has little opportunity to use his full expertise and ingenuity because the work has of necessity already been designed to the last detail, which often helps to perpetuate the unnecessary redesigning of building components (the proverbial wheel) that might otherwise be standardized. The main advantage of this kind of contract is that the owner obtains a fixed price at the outset through competitive bidding; an advantage that is dissipated by any changes made in the work by the owner (or the designer) during the contract's execution because the costs of such changes are, for the most part, determined by the contractor. Attempts by designers to draw up stipulated sum contracts to obtain better control of the costs of changes usually succeed only insofar as they are able to introduce elements of other kinds of contracts[5] into the stipulated sum contract.

The *cost-plus-fee contract* is above all flexible, and the owner can make decisions and changes during the contract's execution, although this often creates extra costs. There is little or no incentive for the contractor to be economical or efficient, and the general result of this kind of contract is that the owner usually ends up spending more than he intended. The main advantages are: (1) the work can be started before complete documents have been prepared by the designers; (2) the work can be designed as it proceeds, and (3) the contractor's knowledge can be utilized by the designer.

The *target figure contract* is made like a stipulated sum contract and administered like a cost-plus-fee contract. The bids to the owner are worded essentially as follows:

"We offer to perform all the work shown on the drawings and described in the specifications for a maximum cost (as defined in the agreement) of $. . . and a fixed fee of $. . .". The wording is similar to the bids for stipulated sum contracts,

except that instead of one stipulated sum there are two sums in the bid; the maximum cost and the fixed fee.

In target figure contracts, bidders have to be provided with documents describing the work required so that they can estimate the probable maximum cost and the fee. With sufficient information, but lacking many of the details, a bidder can in effect say: *"It can be done for not more than $. . ., possibly for less,"* and he makes his offer on that basis. This means, of course, that the contractor in this kind of contract must have some part in making subsequent decisions about the work.

Up to the point of making a target figure contract, the owner has obtained the primary advantage of the stipulated sum contractual method; namely, competitive bidding and a fixed price. In the contract's performance, the owner obtains certain advantages found in the cost-plus-fee contractual method; namely, flexibility in making decisions and changes and the opportunity to utilize the contractor's expertise when decisions are made. As changes are made by the owner and the designer in a target figure contract, the contractor is asked to estimate the amount by which the change should alter the "target figure" stated in the contract. When this amount is approved by the designer and the order to make the change is issued, the target figure in the contract is changed accordingly.

The target figure contract usually contains what is called a "sharing clause" through which any savings made in the total cost of the work are shared between the owner and the contractor according to prescribed proportions. Savings occur when the actual total costs paid by the owner (excluding the contractor's fee) are less than the stipulated maximum cost. The usual proportions appear to be 75 percent of the total savings for the owner and 25 percent for the contractor, more or less. On the other hand, if the total costs exceed the maximum cost (adjusted for any changes as explained), under the terms of the contract the contractor usually has to complete the work at his own expense. The owner usually pays no more than the maximum cost plus the fee.[6]

The sharing clause creates an incentive for a

---

[5] Namely, unit price and cost-plus-fee contracts.

[6] For purposes of general discussion the terms "target figure" and "maximum cost" are here taken to mean the same. However, if the terms of a contract establish an absolute maximum cost to the owner, the term "maximum cost" (and "maximum cost-plus-fee contract") is more descriptive. Whereas, if the terms of a contract require the owner to pay part of any costs over the amount stated in the contract, the term "target figure" (and "target figure contract") is better. The difference lies mainly in the sharing clause.

contractor to be efficient and economical, in addition to the incentive created by the maximum cost in the contract for which the work must be completed. It appears that a 25 percent share of any savings for a contractor is reasonable and effective in contracts performed under conditions that would not normally deter the contractor from bidding on a stipulated sum contract. In other words, under conditions that might be classed as "normal," and under which a contractor would reasonably be able to estimate probable costs, given all the necessary information about the work, a sharing clause that provides the contractor with a 25 percent share of any savings made in the contract appears to be acceptable to most bidders.

Under less favorable conditions, such as would make an accurate cost estimate impossible and a stipulated sum contract undesirable to a contractor (even with the provision of complete and detailed bidding documents), it is unlikely that the 75/25 percent sharing of any savings would be very attractive to a construction company. Under such conditions, contracts are more likely to be made by negotiation rather than by the usual bidding procedures. After all, a designer cannot prescribe the terms of a contract and call for bids if the conditions affecting the work are such that he cannot predict what might be generally acceptable terms to bidding construction companies; although selective bidding for contracts with prescribed terms might be possible following preliminary discussions with selected companies to determine acceptable terms.

Looking at Fig. 1-2, a model of a target figure contract theoretically could be constructed exactly halfway between the two poles of the contractual scale shown. In such a contract, the target figure and the fee would be arrived at by a fairly detailed estimate to make it realistic, but not with the same detail that would be required in a stipulated sum contract. This would mean that reasonable design solutions would have been found for the primary components and major elements of the building, but that other solutions would be possible and might be more economical. The sharing clause would prescribe any savings to be shared 50/50 percent between owner and contractor, whereas any losses (excess of actual costs over the stipulated "target figure") would also be shared 50/50 percent. The model is theoretical, and such a contract might never be practical. Nevertheless, it does indicate how this type of contract can be used to stipulate terms to suit conditions.

The target figure contract may be viewed as a hybrid of the two basic types of contracts previously examined. It has many variations and names, including "maximum cost plus fee" and "guaranteed upset sum." The essential features are a stipulated "target figure," or "maximum cost," a "fixed fee," and usually a "sharing clause." The target figure contract may be awarded on the basis of competitive bids made up of the "target figure," or "maximum cost," and the "fixed fee," and therefore is similar to a stipulated sum contract in this respect. But once the contract has been made, it has to be operated like a cost-plus-fee contract, because the actual costs must be controlled and known so that the difference between actual costs and the stipulated maximum cost in the contract (which is increased or decreased by mutual agreement as changes are made in the work) can be determined and the sharing clause applied.

Unit Price Contract[G]

In North America this basic type of contract is more familiar in heavy construction and highway construction than in building construction. In Britain, and in other Commonwealth countries such as Australia, New Zealand, and countries in Africa and Asia where the quantity surveying profession is established and where the "quantities method" of bidding and contracting is used, this type of contract and the method related to it are widely used in building construction.[7]

Generally, a contractor's estimate prepared prior to making a bid for a stipulated sum contract consists of two primary parts:

1. The measured quantities of work
2. The prices of work.

For example, such an estimate might include this item:

(a)	(b)	(c)	(d)	(e)	(f)
033101	Concrete (3000 psi) in continuous footings	200	CY	$70.00	$14,000.00

(a) Code number (for identification).
(b) Description (abbreviated from specifications).
(c) Quantity (measured from drawings).
(d) Unit of measurement (cubic yards).
(e) Unit price (per cubic yard).
(f) Cost of item of work (cost = quantity × unit price).

and the estimator measures all the work in this way and prices it, item by item, with general items for temporary services, site offices, and supervision also included in the estimate.

In the bidding documents for a unit price contract there is a *schedule of unit prices*[G] prepared by the designer (or by a designer's consultant) that contains

---

[7] The quantity surveying profession is discussed in Collier, *Construction Contracts*, 2nd ed.

the measured quantities for all the items of work in the contract, as in columns (a), (b), (c), and (d) of the above example. The bidder does not have to measure the work: he only has to estimate the *unit prices*,[G] apply them to the quantities provided, and compute the total costs. *Overhead costs*[G] and *profit*[G] are usually allowed for in each unit price, but some overhead items and their costs may be entered separately in the schedule of unit prices.

The primary reason for using unit price contracts in heavy construction and highway construction is the difficulty in determining in advance the exact *quantities of work*[G] required to be done in these types of construction, which depend so much on ground conditions. Some of the decisions that determine such things as the amount of excavation necessary, or the amount of fill required, can only be made once the work is underway. Consequently, it is impossible for construction companies to make accurate estimates of costs and to submit firm bids. It would be possible for an owner to enter into a cost-plus-fee contract for this kind of work, and this is sometimes done. But most owners insist on a contract that gives them a tighter control of the costs, and this may be obtained through a unit price contract. Changes in the *quantity of work* are easily made in this type of contract. But changes in the actual *items of work* required are no easier to make than in a stipulated sum contract, although such changes are less frequently necessary in heavy construction, which often involves relatively few items of work compared with those in building construction.

As the contractor completes sections of the work in a unit price contract, the quantities of work are measured at the site by both the contractor and the designer, or their representatives, so that mutual agreement about the amount of work done is reached and the agreed amounts are recorded. The contractor is then paid for the actual quantities of work done at the unit prices in the contract. If quantities of work vary beyond specified limits, the contract may require the parties to agree to adjustments in the unit prices or the contract may provide for such adjustments.

In Britain, and in other countries where *quantity surveyors*[G] are employed by owners, *bills of quantities*[G] are used for the majority of major building projects. Because the items of work in the *superstructures* of buildings can usually be accurately measured from the drawings by the quantity surveyor, and because the measured quantities will accurately represent the actual quantities of work done by the contractor, it is not usually necessary to remeasure the work in the superstructure of a building at completion. In these building contracts, only the work in the *substructure* (below ground) is usually remeasured, because this

work is so often subject to variations owing to varying subsurface conditions. Nevertheless, any changes ordered in the work, and any discovered or suspected errors in the bills of quantities are cause for measuring at the site any or all items of work as required by either the contractor or the owner's quantity surveyor. Payment for the work is made on the basis of the unit prices in the contract, and if changes involve new items of work for which there are no unit prices in the contract, the method of payment will be as set down in the contract, usually on the basis of negotiated unit prices or on a "cost plus fee" basis.

Any type of contract can provide for items of work to be done on a different contractual basis from the others. This is frequently the case with extra work[G] ordered during a contract, but it can also apply to items of work prescribed in the original contract. For example, a stipulated sum contract may contain some work described and measured in a schedule of quantities to be done at unit prices. This provision gives the designer some latitude and flexibility in deciding on the quantity, location, and arrangement of such items as fixtures and movable partitions, or other items of work included in a schedule for this purpose.

Construction Management Contracts[G]

The term "construction management contract" has become popular in the last 20 years. So often, new terms for old commonsense methods become fashionable for a time, but often such terms are not properly understood and they mean many things to many people. A construction management contract may have many different features, but common to most of them are the following:

1. There are two agents of the owner, instead of one as before; namely:
   a. The *designer*, primarily responsible for the design
   b. The *construction manager*,[G] primarily responsible for translating the design into reality
2. There is not one contractor responsible for all the work, but instead several *specialist contractors*[G] all of whom have separate contracts with the owner for parts of the work required.[8]

The designer and the construction manager may

---

[8] Strictly speaking, the term "construction management contract" is imprecise as it refers to an arrangement of contracts which can be of any kind.

work together in both designing the project and in seeing that it is built according to the owner's requirements. Ideally, both are appointed by the owner at the outset so that they can complement each other's skills and experience. In this respect, this arrangement is not unlike the package deal[G] that has been available to owners for some time. But whereas the package deal is offered for the most part by designer-builders for commercial development the management contract is used in both commercial developments and in institutional developments, such as universities. It is often initiated by an owner who sees the advantage in having two agents with complementary skills but with different responsibilities and interests.

The increasing complexity of technology and construction processes has brought us to the point where designer and contractor cannot be responsible to the owner for all the specialized work of several subcontractors. For example, (in a stipulated sum contract) how can a contractor effectively take responsibility for the work of an elevator subcontractor when the contractor and the designer have only a superficial knowledge of elevator installations and their operation? Obviously, the better procedure is for the elevator specialist to have a contract with and a direct contractual responsibility to the owner. Hence, the practice in management contracts is for all persons doing parts of the work to have a contract directly with the owner. These contractual relationships are shown in Fig. 1-3.

The first function of a construction manager is to provide economic and technical knowledge during the design stages of the project, although the design is the primary responsibility of the designer. His next function is to recommend the type of contract to be undertaken for each part of the work. The primary responsibility of the construction manager is to organize and manage the work at the site in the best interests of the owner. A construction manager usually prepares cost estimates at various stages of the design and of the work in progress, and it is his responsibility to see that the work is completed within the budget established at the outset.

In some contracts, the construction manager may be required or subsequently requested to provide certain site facilities, or to undertake certain parts of the work. In other words, he then fulfills (at least in part) the function of a traditional general contractor. It is questionable that this is either necessary or desirable if the construction manager is to properly fulfill the function of an agent of the owner, as described above; and it is obviously not in an owner's interests to lose any advantage by awarding work to someone in a preferred position. From an owner's position, it is far better for his construction manager to have no investment or other similar financial interest in the work so that his responsibilities are clearly defined. Alternatively, an owner can get a package deal from a designer-builder, as indicated in Fig. 1-4.

The package deal has the great advantage of simplicity in that the owner enters into only one contract for what can include everything from the sale of land for the building site to the building complete and ready for occupation. Hence, the other name for this kind of arrangement: the turnkey project. One has only to turn the key and walk into a completed building. But, of course, first the key has to be paid for, and some criticize these contracts because an owner, in dealing

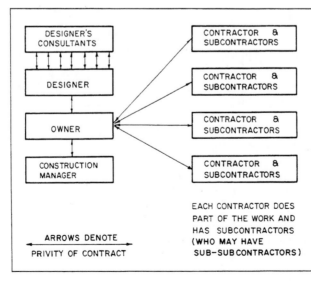

FIGURE 1-3 Contractual relationships among persons involved in the design and construction of a project in which the *owner* has one contract for design services, one contract for construction management services, and several other contracts for construction services covering all the *work* in the project.

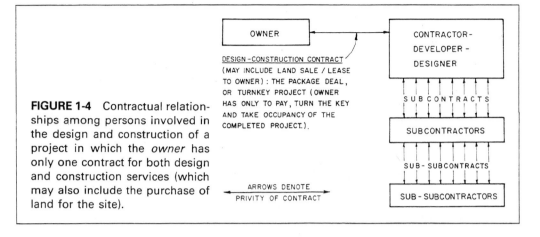

FIGURE 1-4 Contractual relationships among persons involved in the design and construction of a project in which the *owner* has only one contract for both design and construction services (which may also include the purchase of land for the site).

with one person only, may not have the expert advice he needs to guide him in matters of quality and costs. Others say that many of the firms offering design-and-build packages employ architects and engineers, and that these firms can be as reliable as any. Some owners have found that they should retain the services of an independent *cost consultant*[G] to advise them in making this kind of contract.

In another arrangement, sometimes called a *management contract*,[G] a *management contractor*[G] is employed by an owner. The variations are many; the terminology not standard.

ESTIMATING FOR BIDS
FOR CONSTRUCTION CONTRACTS

All kinds of contracts made as a result of competitive offers require the bidders to make estimates of costs before they can make an offer. Even the cost-plus-fee contract requires a proper understanding and consideration of costs as defined in the bidding documents, and a computation of the *fee* accordingly.

If a contract is the result of negotiations rather than of competitive bidding, the negotiations must be based on knowledge of the work, and this again requires an estimate. As we shall see, there are other reasons for making estimates, but the primary and fundamental purpose is *to make an offer to do construction work.*

Some estimates are very analytical and detailed, such as an estimate made as the basis of a competitive bid for work to be done for a stipulated sum. Other estimates are less detailed, such as an estimate made to determine the approximate cost of a project as the basis for determining the amount of the fixed fee required to do work within a cost-plus-fee contract. Nevertheless, the primary purpose is always the same: to obtain a knowledge of the costs of work so as to be

able to enter into an agreement for its execution. The various kinds of estimates are examined in Chapter 2.

ESTIMATING FOR OTHER PURPOSES

Estimates are made for several other purposes, other than for bidding, including estimates for:

1. Establishment of budgets for construction and development
2. Feasibility studies of proposed developments
3. Control of costs during the design phase of construction
4. Selection of alternative design proposals (based on costs and economics)
5. Corporate mergers and purchases
6. Appraisals of building assets based on construction costs made for many purposes.

Some such estimates are done by methods that are ineffective and inaccurate; the better estimates of this class are done by the estimating methods explained here for bidding purposes, which are the only sound basis for estimates intended for other than for bidding. There is no better way except to measure work and price it as explained here. For estimates other than for bids, and for estimates for which the estimator has incomplete design information, the best estimating methods are essentially those described in this book and its first edition's sequel.[9] Some less effective methods are described briefly in the next chapter.

---

[9] Keith Collier, *Estimating Construction Costs: A Conceptual Approach* (Reston Publishing Company, 1984).

QUESTIONS AND TOPICS FOR DISCUSSION

1. What is the essential difference between real and personal property?

2. Why are all buildings unique?

3. What similarity exists between *subcontractors* and *designer's consultants*, and what are the reasons for their presence and importance in the design and construction industry?

4. What are the *five* ingredients of a valid construction contract?

5. What information does a bidder need to be able to submit a satisfactory bid for work to be done in a *stipulated sum contract*, and why?

6. How can competitive bids be made for work to be done in a *cost-plus-fee contract*?

7. Explain how a *target figure contract* can contain major features and advantages of both a *stipulated sum contract* and a *cost-plus-fee contract*.

8. Explain the meaning of the term *unit price*.

9. Explain the meaning of the term *item of work*.

10. Name all the persons who have contracts with the owner in the arrangement commonly called a *construction management contract*.

11. What kind of estimate is needed to be made by a *construction manager*?

12. How can owners in *package deals* know that they will get value for their money?

2

WHAT IS AN ESTIMATE?

An estimate involves calculating the cost of work on the basis of probabilities. The calculations are of several kinds,[1] relative to the two primary parts of an estimate: (1) *measurement*, (2) *pricing*. The kinds of calculation used are relatively simple, and because they are simple they are often not given the attention they deserve. All measurement is approximate, and this fact should be remembered as it is invariable. Only the degree of approximation is variable, and an acceptable degree of accuracy depends on the purpose and methods of the measurement. Since all estimates start with the measurement of work,[G] it follows that all estimates are approximate to a variable degree in their first part, *the measurement*. In the second part of an estimate, *the pricing*, the degree of approximation is even greater because of the difficulty in predicting all the probabilities of such things as labor productivity and site conditions. The ability to predict probabilities largely depends on the information and data[G] available from past experience and the estimator's intuition.

All cost information and data is acquired from experience. If an estimator does not have cost data from his own experience, he must use data from another's experience.[2] For this reason, estimators' price books and handbooks are helpful to the novice and sometimes a useful guide to an experienced estimator. These handbooks contain data from the collected experiences of others. This is better than no data, but much less valuable than that from an estimator's own experience. These books sometimes make a wrong impression on the novice: that prices and productivity rates are facts applicable to all estimates at all times. But all prices are subject to economic conditions, and they fluctuate continuously. Labor productivity is even more variable, because it is subject to so many more conditions, some of which are reviewed in Chapter 3. The most valid and useful data for estimating is that acquired by an estimator from his own experience and from the contracting experience of the company for which he works. Not only is this data the most relevant to the future work done by that company, but also such data can best be analyzed and understood by those who have been involved in the work that produced the data.

The more valid data the estimator has available,

---

[1] Mostly, mensuration and arithmetic. Sometimes it is necessary to use geometry, trigonometry, and algebra. Statistical methods are also used in construction economics and in more complex applications.

[2] Notice that *information* precedes *data*; they are different things. However, at times, for brevity's sake, *data* refers to both.

the better he will be able to estimate the probabilities of costs arising from such things as:

Site, location, and accessibility
Soil and subsurface conditions
Time and season
Climatic conditions
Wage agreements
Strikes and lockouts
Market prices of basic materials
Availability of money
Demand for construction
Political and economic climates

and the innumerable other things that are continually changing and affecting the economics of construction.

Engineering science is governed by immutable laws, such as the law of gravity, which give a designer a sound basis on which to design a structure. The force of gravity can always be relied on; hence, it is a law. Construction costs are governed by economics, politics, and social conditions, and they are like the sea; fluid, moving, and never still, never the same from one moment until the next. Therefore, estimating cannot be a pure science, but in estimating scientific methods should be employed.

Estimating should be a part of the cyclical management process illustrated in Fig. 2-1, in which estimating is shown as one of several parts of construction management, each one interdependent with the others. Each part, or function, is discussed in detail in Chapter

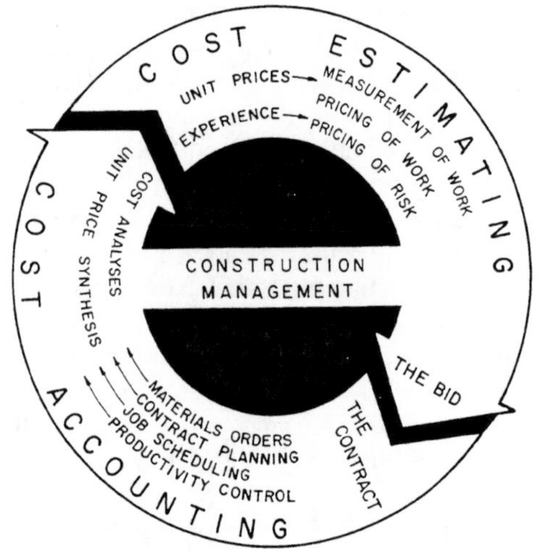

FIGURE 2-1 Cyclical process of cost estimating and cost accounting.

4, and in other chapters, but for the moment it can be seen from the cyclical diagram that *estimating* relies on *cost accounting*[G] to provide cost data, because it is only through cost accounting that data from past jobs can be acquired and recorded for use in future estimates.

Costs of construction work[G] are classified and examined in Chapter 3 under the following headings:

1. Materials costs[G]
2. Labor costs[G]
3. Plant and equipment costs[G]
4. Overhead costs and profit.[G]

Data on all of these costs are required to make an estimate and to calculate costs in an estimate:

$$\text{cost} = \text{quantity} \times \text{unit price}$$

The two parts of an estimate, (1) measured quantities and (2) prices, cannot be viewed separately because each is a function of the other. In Example 1 labor costs are $1,800.00 and the quantity of work is 150 CY of concrete in footings.

$$\text{unit price of labor} = \frac{\text{total costs of labor}}{\text{number of units}}$$

$$= \frac{\$1,800.00}{150 \, \text{CY}} = \$12.00 \, \text{per CY}$$

The unit price[G] for "labor placing concrete" in this job will not be known to the contractor until he has placed all the concrete and has accounted for all the labor costs. The first few yards of concrete probably will cost more than $12.00 per CY to place, and the last yards of concrete will probably cost less than $12.00 per CY to place. *The unit price is, therefore, an average price per unit of measurement.*

The *unit price for an item of work*[G] will vary with each job. The odds against an absolutely identical unit price occurring for the same item on two jobs are high because of the large number of variables involved, and this is sometimes presented as an argument against a scientific approach to estimating. But because accuracy is relative, and because the units of measurement and pricing are relatively large, practical accuracy in estimating and cost accounting can be achieved. Nevertheless, it is proper for estimators to keep in mind that every item of work in every construction job is unique, that it is done under unique conditions, and that, therefore, accuracy in estimating is relative.

The question might be asked, Why is it necessary

EXAMPLE 1[3]

Description of item: Ready-mixed portland cement concrete (3000 p.s.i. × 1½″ max size aggregate) placed in continuous footings:

Material	Quantity	Unit Price	Cost
Concrete, as specified	150 CY @	$50.00 per CY	$7,500.00
Labor			
Place concrete in footings	150 CY @	$12.00 per CY	$1,800.00
Material and labor costs	150 CY @	$62.00 per CY	$9,300.00

EXAMPLE 2

Description of item: Ready-mixed portland cement concrete (3000 p.s.i. × ¾″ max size aggregate) placed by crane in roof slabs:

Material	Quantity	Unit Price	Cost
Concrete, as specified	200 CY @	$50.00 per CY	$10,000.00
Labor			
Place concrete	200 CY @	$16.00 per CY	$ 3,200.00
Equipment	30 hr @	$50.00 per hr	$ 1,500.00
Material, labor, and equipment costs	200 CY @	$73.50 per CY	$14,700.00

to calculate unit prices, and why cannot an estimator simply estimate the total costs required to carry out each part of the work? Why does he need to divide costs by quantity to obtain the unit price when all he needs is the total costs of each item? Students of estimating often ask this question, and the answer lies in what has been said before about the estimator's need for cost data. The ability to predict probabilities largely depends on data from past experience. Cost data can be expressed by unit prices.

To estimate the costs of an item of work, an estimator may rely entirely on recorded cost data from past jobs; and the most convenient way of recording cost data is in the form of unit prices and unit rates.[G] To say that the labor costs for placing 150 CY of concrete in footings were $1,800.00 is (for the estimator) to immediately divide cost by quantity and to reflect on the validity of a unit price of $12.00 per CY for this item. Or if the current cost of labor is $16.00 per hour, to reflect on the validity of a unit rate of $0.75 manhours per CY. To estimate the costs of major and

important items in a job, an estimator may determine the required crew size and the total time the crew will probably require to complete an item of work. From this he can calculate the labor costs; but only by taking another step, by calculating the unit price (the average cost of a unit of work), can the estimator compare the price he has just estimated with the costs of similar items in past jobs; and by calculating the unit rate he can compare the productivity achieved.

CONTRACTOR'S ESTIMATE

To submit a competitive bid for a stipulated sum contract, a bidder must make as accurate an estimate of costs as possible and, if the offer is accepted, the sum stipulated in the bid becomes the contract sum[G] for which the work must be done. Similarly, in a maximum cost-plus-fee contract,[G] a bidder largely determines the costs of the work to the owner, even though the "maximum cost" may be subject to modification by changes in the work and by a sharing clause in the contract. *The contractor's estimate is the basic estimate in the design and construction process, and all other estimates are either subsidiary to it or try to anticipate it.* A contractor more or less establishes the price for

---

[3] These examples are given to show the function of unit prices in an estimate. The unit prices themselves are meaningless unless the location, date, conditions, and specifications of the work are known.

the work through his estimate, depending on the type of contract within which the work is done.

The contractor's estimate may be viewed in four parts:

1. Estimate of the costs of work to be done by the contractor with his own forces
2. Estimates of costs of work to be done by subcontractors (and prepared by them for bids to the contractor)
3. Estimate of costs of general requirements for all the work provided by the contractor
4. Estimate of overhead and profit required by the contractor for doing work with his own forces, for supervising and taking responsibility for the work of his subcontractors, and for providing the general requirements.

The meaning of the term work[G] should be recalled. It includes labor, materials, equipment, and all other services required by the contract and provided by the contractor.

Bidding contractors and bidding subcontractors essentially use the same estimating methods in respect to the work they propose to do with their own forces. A contractor receives sub-bids from subcontractors and combines the most favorable sub-bids[4] for each part of the work to be done by a subcontractor with his own estimate of parts 1 and 3. To this he adds estimated allowances for overhead and profit (4) to make up the total estimated costs and the amount of the bid. The integration of the subcontrators' sub-bids and the estimate of the work to be done with the contractor's own forces is often one of the most difficult parts of preparing a bid. Part of this difficulty arises from the variations in scope and content of subcontractors' bids. A contractor has to ascertain that each of the sub-bids he includes in his estimate and bid is for a known specific part of the total work, *no more and no less*, so that all parts of the work are included, but only once.

Because "mutual agreement" (expressed in the "offer and acceptance") is essential to a good contract, it follows that it is essential that a contractor's estimate is based on precisely the same facts and requirements as are contained in the contract, which comes about as a result of the owner's acceptance of the contractor's offer. In other words, contract documents must be identical to the bidding documents. Addenda to bidding documents[G] issued to bidders during a bidding period must be prepared and issued in such ways that there is nothing that can detract from the mutual agreement necessary to the contract. Anything a contractor is required to do as part of the contract must have been reasonably foreseeable by the contractor while making his estimate.[5]

For a cost-plus-fee contract, in which there is no maximum cost stipulated, the contractor's estimate will usually be an estimate of the "fee" portion only; and this will primarily include overhead and profit,[G] without the need for measurement and pricing of work. Nevertheless, mutual agreement is still essential to the contract and the same precepts apply. For complete mutual agreement in a cost-plus-fee contract, and in a maximum cost-plus-fee or target figure contract, it is essential that "cost" and "fee" be clearly defined. Lack of distinction between "cost" and "fee" is a common cause of incomplete "mutual agreement" and of misunderstandings that lead to disputes between owner and contractor. Standard forms of contracts[G] provide only general guidelines for properly defining these two important terms. Contract documents, particularly the articles of the agreement and the conditions of the contract, must be specially prepared for each unique contract.

Those who say that *standard forms of contract*[G] should always be used but should never be amended do not understand construction contracts. Standard forms are sometimes abused, and this may be a reason for some of the criticism of their use in amended form. For the sake of clarity, standard forms of contract should be incorporated in total by a specific reference to the entire standard form in a project's specifications. Any amendments, omissions, or additions should then be made in the specifications immediately after the reference. Made in this way, changes in standard forms are quite clear and easily understood.

The practice of copying the whole or parts of a standard form into specifications together with amendments is to be deplored because, made in this way, the amendments are not apparent and may be overlooked.

An estimator should always be aware of the fact that complete mutual agreement is essential to a good contract. If bidding documents are ambiguous, or if they are not complementary one to another, or if they are inequitable in their requirements, the estimator should try to get them changed by a written *addendum*[G]

---

[4] Usually, the lowest and most competitive bid. Sometimes, the lowest bid is not used because it is incomplete or because it is qualified by certain conditions, or because it is from a firm with whom the contractor does not wish to do business.

[5] This is not to say that the contractor may not overlook something and omit it from his estimate, but simply that all terms and requirements of the contract should be reasonably capable of being seen by the contractor while making his estimate.

from the designer. Failing that, he should decline to make an offer, or calculate and allow for and take the forseen risk. Silent acceptance of deficient documents by bidders leads only to disputes and more deficient documents.

One maxim for the specification writer is: *be fair*. Do not specify requirements that are inequitable or unreasonable. Do not require bidders to accept an incalculable risk by writing so-called *weasel clauses*.[G] Despite the efforts of the construction specification institutions, such clauses still appear in specifications and continue to hamper the workings of the construction industry because they create bad contracts.

An estimator should be aware of the fact that an estimate is more than simply a means of making a bid. If his bid is accepted, the result is a contract; and proper management requires information for purchasing, planning, controlling, and for cost accounting. It is essential that an estimate be made with all these objectives in mind, and this aspect of the estimator's work and the use of his estimate is explained in Chapter 4.

SUBCONTRACTOR'S ESTIMATE

Although a subcontractor's estimate is for only part of the work, the subcontractor is responsible to a project's contractor for that part in the same way that the contractor is responsible to the owner for the entire work. This also applies to the sub-subcontractor who bids to a major subcontractor, such as a mechanical contracting company, who may be responsible to a contractor for up to 50 percent of a project's total work.[6]

The contractual relationship between subcontractor and contractor (and sub-subcontractor and subcontractor) should reflect in details the contractual relationship between contractor and owner. If it does not, it is probably because the contractor (or subcontractor) has failed to make it do so, and he may carry unnecessary and additional risks if he has not delegated risks and responsibilities to his subcontractors (or sub-subcontractors) through contract documents that contain the same requirements as are contained in the contract documents between owner and contractor.

That which already has been written about a contractor's estimate can generally also apply to subcontractors' estimates. However, with many subtrades a large part of their work is done in a factory or a shop and not at the site, which means that the estimating technique for some subcontractors is similar to those estimating techniques used in manufacturing industries wherein work is done in factories and mass production and controlled work conditions prevail.

Another aspect of subcontractors' estimates and bids is the practice called *bid peddling* or *bid shopping*[G] in which some general contractors play off one sub-bidder against another by offering a subcontract to one firm for a lower price than that submitted by the firm's competitor. Consequently, *bid depositories*[G] have been established in many places in an effort to prevent this bid peddling and to regulate bidding procedures.

A bid depository requires an independent place where all sub-bids so designated by a bidding authority[G] (the owner or designer) must be deposited and recorded by a certain time. Bidders can then collect the sub-bids made to them from the bid depository, say, twenty-four hours after the closing time for sub-bids. Bidding documents prepared by a designer usually have to stipulate the requirements for depositing bids and, in particular, require that all bidders must use deposited sub-bids for those trades designated for bid depository, because only the designer calling for bids has the power (as agent of the owner) to require sub-bids to be deposited. The bid depository system reduces but does not eliminate bid peddling.

Contractors find bid depositories an advantage in that they are ensured of receiving deposited sub-bids by some specified time before their bids must be submitted to the owner. This helps to reduce the frenetic rush that so often precedes the completion of an estimate and the submission of a general bid.

It should be pointed out that bid depositories cannot change contractual principles. A bidding sub-trade is not obliged to deposit sub-bids for all bidding contractors, and he may make different sub-bids to different contractors. The fundamentals of "genuine intention" and "mutual agreement" must exist for a legal and valid contract, and these cannot be induced by any external agent. Bidders are always free to bid or not to bid however and to whomever they please.

Some bid depositories have been scrutinized for possible infractions of the law and, in some cases, their methods of operation have been questioned because they appeared to restrict competition. It can be argued that in some cases they do reduce competition; in fact, if not by intent. If only one sub-trade bid is deposited for a particular section of work, and bidders can use only deposited bids, there is not much incentive for a bidder to seek out a more competitive sub-bid, because he knows his competitors also must use the one and only sub-bid submitted. So each bidder can use that sub-bid without fear of competition, knowing

---

[6] The mechanical work (including plumbing, heating, ventilating, air conditioning, gas supply, and other mechanical systems) may include as much as from 40 to 50 percent of the total work in some kinds of construction, such as hospitals.

that if he is awarded the contract there is a good chance of realizing greater profits by shopping later for a more competitive sub-bid.

Some hypocrisy often accompanies formal practices, and terms such as "the sanctity of bidding" are used by some in explaining the purpose of bid depositories. Yet it always takes two to peddle bids; and if all subcontractors refused to peddle, no contractor seeking to increase his profits at the expense of others could force them into subcontracts for lesser payments. A subcontractor's greatest strength is his right to withhold his offer from those with whom he does not want to contract.

The majority of contracting firms seem to approve of bid depositories because they regulate the timing and flow of sub-bids and at least reduce the amount of bid peddling. But some owners will not permit the use of bid depositories on their jobs because they believe that bid depositories do restrict competition.

The term subcontractor comes from the need to distinguish between a contractor who has a contract with an owner and those *specialist contracting companies*[G] that indirectly do work for an owner through a subcontract with a contractor. In other contractual arrangements, such as management contracts, the specialist firms have contracts directly with the owner and are contractors in their own right; and their estimating techniques and procedures are essentially the same as those of the general contractor. So, although the methods of contracting may be changing, and traditional stipulated sum contracts with a general contractor now are sometimes replaced by management contracts, the essential relationship between an owner and those who do construction work for him remains the same as always, and estimates of construction costs are as essential as ever to construction contracts.

DESIGNER'S ESTIMATE

A designer's estimate, which is made at any time before the contractor's estimate and bid is made, is an effort by the designer to anticipate the contract amount for which the work will be done by the contractor. This preliminary estimating is frequently done (in part or in whole) by one or more of a *designer's consultants*,[G] either by the engineering consultants, who usually estimate only the costs of those parts of the work that they design, or by a *quantity surveyor*[G] or other *cost consultant*[G] who specializes in providing such services to designers and owners.

These preliminary estimates are made without the full information required for a contractor's estimate, and the earliest estimates are frequently made from rough design sketches, with dimensions and few details, and from an outline specification and a schedule of space requirements. This *conceptual estimating*[G] requires not only a knowledge and understanding of estimating as done by contractors; also it requires: a broad knowledge of construction materials, methods, and trade practices; an understanding of building design; a knowledge of comparative costs and economics; and the ability to perceive construction details within the broad lines of design sketches—ideally, from past experience with a particular designer—so that the estimator knows how the designer's sketches will be translated into working drawings and specifications. Preliminary estimates by a skilled practitioner often can be made to within 5 percent of the arithmetical mean of the bids subsequently made for the work by contracting companies, and consequently they make it possible for the costs of the building to be planned as well as its functional parts.

Cost planning[G] should be part of the design process for all building developments, because a proper designer's estimate provides the designer with information about the work that he will need to administer and supervise the contract properly. It is, as well, often an important part of the services the designer provides to his client, the owner.[7] It enables the designer to design the building within the financial limits set by the owner, and sometimes saves the designer from expensive and distasteful redesigning that might otherwise be necessary if bids submitted for the work are much higher than the amount of the budget.

The techniques used in making a designer's estimate cannot be fully explained here, but a brief outline of some of the methods used is given under the following headings:

1. *Cost per place* (per room; per bed; per seat)
2. *Cost per cubic foot* (of building volume)
3. *Cost per square foot* (of building area on ground floor or of building area on all floors)
4. *Cost per story-enclosure*[8] (areas of all floor and roof decks and of all enclosing walls, with applied factors for building height, in stories)

---

[7] See William Dudley Hunt, Jr. (ed.), *Comprehensive Architectural Services–General Principles and Practices*, prepared by the American Institute of Architects (New York: McGraw-Hill Book Company, 1965).

[8] See Douglas J. Ferry, ARICS, *Cost Planning of Buildings* (London: Crosby Lockwood & Son, Ltd., 1964) for explanations of the Story-Enclosure Method and Elemental Estimating, both of which were developed in Britain by chartered quantity surveyors about 1954.

5. *Cost per element* (cost of element expressed in terms of the building area and cost of element in terms of its unit prices; i.e., total cost of element divided by its quantity)

6. *Cost per approximate quantities* (cost of items of work obtained from quantity × unit price, as in a contractor's estimate, but with quantities and prices more or less approximate, depending on available information).

These methods are listed in the order of efficacy for most estimates, and they are briefly described here.

Cost per place: useful only for cost planning of a general nature and on a broad base, such as in a school district on the basis of average cost per pupil. It is suitable for budgeting finances, but not for estimating the costs of individual projects.

Cost per cubic foot: can be very unreliable unless virtually identical buildings are compared. There is not much relationship between the volume of a building and its costs. Costs come primarily from the walls and decks that enclose a building's volume, and there is no constant relationship between the areas of walls and decks and the enclosed volume.

Cost per square foot: often used to indicate the approximate costs of an owner's requirements in the early stages when only the building area is known. More costs are related to a building's plan area than to a building's volume, and properly applied this method is more reliable than the last.

Cost per story-enclosure: realistically takes account of those things that create costs: the areas of the horizontal and vertical planes of a building; the decks and the walls. Also, factors are used to take account of a building's height. It has been largely superseded by the next method.

Cost per element: analyzes buildings into basic parts, such as exterior walls and roof decks, and prices each element separately on the basis of the unit prices of the elements. It approaches the next method in detail and efficacy.

Cost per approximate quantities: the most reliable and the most time consuming method as it comes closest to the estimation methods used by contractors and subcontractors. By measuring approximate quantities, a quantity surveyor can prepare accurate estimates for owners and designers in an acceptable period of time and for a reasonable fee.

The methods used in making a designer's estimate may include several of the above methods for different parts of the work, depending on the information available and on the person doing the estimate. A preliminary estimate might be made by a quantity surveyor on the basis of "cost per unit area," with a conceptual estimate made later (before working drawings and specifications are prepared) on the basis of "cost per element" or "cost per approximate quantities." This practice gives a designer an opportunity to design within the budget and to tell the owner the costs of specific building requirements.

As working drawings and specifications are prepared the quantity surveyor should periodically review his estimate; and ideally he should be retained to prepare a more detailed estimate from the working drawings and specifications before they are completed, so that the costs of the work can be planned as between the various parts of the work and within the budget.

A quantity surveyor's fees depend on the nature of the project and the extent to which his services are required. A single preliminary estimate might cost a few hundred dollars, and comprehensive cost planning services for a complex project might cost up to 1/2 of 1 percent of the cost of the work. Scales of fees are published by national institutes of quantity surveyors.

Since the purpose of a designer's estimate is to anticipate and predict the amounts of the contractors' bids, it follows that a cost consultant (or a designer) must be familiar with the techniques and procedures of estimating in construction firms to prepare realistic preliminary and conceptual estimates. Consequently, the precepts and techniques explained later are fundamental to making estimates of construction costs of all kinds and for all purposes.

OWNER-DEVELOPER'S ESTIMATE

A distinction is made here between an owner-developer's estimate and a designer's estimate because they may differ in both form and function; although they may be one and the same. An owner-developer may have an estimate made—often for a *feasibility study*[G]— before he retains the services of a designer. A feasibility study is made to examine, among other things, the economic feasibility of a project by estimating the costs of the work, and the probable costs in use[G] of the building development. The probable gross income from the development is also estimated, and from all of this data the net income and the net return on the investment can be estimated.[9]

It has been shown that in some cases the costs of the work can have a very significant effect upon the return on investment yielded by a commercial

---

[9] See Keith Collier, *Estimating Construction Costs: A Conceptual Approach*, (Reston, Va.: Reston Publishing Company, 1984), for more on this subject.

development.[10] On the other hand, it has been shown elsewhere that the costs of constructing institutional buildings are not so significant when they are considered with the total *costs in use*[G] over the life of the building.

Feasibility studies often make it necessary to estimate the costs of work without preliminary design sketches, and with only a list of space requirements. In making such estimates, cost and design data from previous jobs are used; but, inevitably, some assumptions have to be made about the form and nature of the building in a preliminary estimate. And once these assumptions become part of the study, they may impose unintended restrictions on the designer and the building's design. Ideally, therefore, the designer should participate in a feasibility study from the outset.

ESTIMATES

The object of all estimates is to supply more information about work; not only the probable costs but also the relative costs of the various parts and how long it will take to construct them. An owner wants to know how much he should spend on the building, and what return he can expect. The designer wants to know that his design can be built within the owner's budget. The contractor wants to know what the work will probably cost so that he can make a bid to do the work for a stipulated sum, or a fee. If proper estimates are not made, a contractor may find himself contractually bound to do work at a financial loss. Or a designer may be obliged to redesign work at no extra fee. Or an owner may find that he has raised a development that is not financially sound and is a poor investment. Estimates and the information they provide are, therefore, essential to property development and to the construction industry, particularly in times of a universal shortage of capital for development and of rising costs.

THE ESTIMATOR

Above all, an estimator must have an extensive knowledge of construction, a knowledge of construction materials and methods, and a knowledge of construction practices and contracts. An estimator should be able to read and write bidding documents, and he should be able to design and sketch construction details. He must be able to communicate graphically and verbally. He should have a facility with measuring techniques

and mathematics, and he requires a general knowledge of economics and business.

An estimator must be able to visualize what is not apparent, and for this he requires imagination. He must be able to think in abstract terms. He must be analytical and critical. An estimator should be able to see the fundamental form through prolific detail. His work consists of translating graphic and verbal information in bidding documents into probable costs in the light of experience. This is not a direct and mechanical process; it is creative, and it demands a high level of skill, concentration, and mental effort.

An estimator must be able to work alone and to make unilateral decisions on matters that are often nebulous. This requires an ability to make decisions in the light of whatever information is available, and later to be able to say that the decision was made because those were the known facts, and that this was the best decision in the light of those facts. It can be a lonely job, and it requires an integrity that makes for honesty with self and with others, and a desire to seek and know the truth of things. It requires common sense, and an ability to work for a goal that is not always achieved. On the other hand, it sometimes produces obsessive secrecy and a reluctance to commit a company's cost information to record.

Some estimators are engineers and architects who have come to specialize in construction costs and contracts. Some are immigrants trained elsewhere as quantity surveyors,[G] particularly in Britain, Australia, and other Commonwealth countries. Others have become proficient estimators by starting work in a construction trade and then entering the estimating office as a trainee. In the past, such trade experience was not unusual and was invaluable. Today, the traditional trades are changing and disappearing, whereas new materials and methods of construction are proliferating. Today, perhaps, the full knowledge of one trade is less preferable than a general knowledge of many, except possibly in the case of a subtrade estimator.

Formal training in construction estimating is not available everywhere, but is offered in some universities, colleges, and institutes, and new programs are continually being developed. In some countries, construction economics[G] and quantity surveying[G] are offered as degree-level courses in universities and institutes of technology. Construction cost research programs have been initiated by professional bodies and governments so that a body of knowledge and techniques is growing and is being disseminated. But the research is too little and the dissemination generally too sparse. Construction economics should be part of the education of every architect, engineer, and of every superintendent, manager, and foreman in the construction industry.

---

[10] Larry Smith, *"Principles of Feasibility for Revenue-Producing Real Estate,"* in Hunt (ed.), *Comprehensive Architectural Services— General Principles and Practice.*

QUESTIONS AND TOPICS FOR DISCUSSION

1. Define an *estimate* and identify the two primary parts of estimating.

2. Explain the purpose of calculating the *unit prices* of completed *work*, and explain by a formula how it is done.

3. Explain how *standard forms of contract* should be used and modified for a particular construction project, and explain why.

4. What is the primary purpose of a *bid depository*, and explain briefly how one operates.

5. Why is "cost per cubic foot" not a good method of making a preliminary estimate?

6. Why is a *designer's estimate* usually required?

7. What are the most valid and useful information and data for estimating, and why?

8. To what other uses can the information contained in an estimate be put by a contractor?

9. What are the several distinct parts of a *contractor's estimate*, and which parts of the *work* do they usually include?

10. If a contractor intends to build an office building on his own property, for his own use and occupancy, would it be necessary for him to make any kind of estimate of the costs of the work? Explain your answer.

11. Describe the main shortcomings inherent in the following *estimating methods*: (a) cost per place, (b) cost per cubic foot, (c) cost per square foot, (d) cost per story-enclosure, and (e) cost per element.

12. Explain the usefulness and shortcomings of *unit prices*.

13. List and explain the advantages and difficulties inherent in a *unit price contract* for: (a) a contractor, and (b) an owner.

14. Discuss the need in the United States for a profession primarily concerned with *building* construction costs and economics.

3

CONSTRUCTION COSTS

In this chapter, some aspects of construction economics and costs related to a building's design are examined. Also, those more tangible aspects of costs primarily related to the competitive market, to the contractor, and his subcontractors are covered. At present estimating is not a science if by a science we mean "a branch of knowledge or study dealing with a body of facts or truths systematically arranged and showing the operation of general laws."[1] Building construction is based on science, and measurement is scientific; but in construction estimating there is no "body of facts or truths systematically arranged and showing the operation of general laws." Among all the estimators in all the construction companies there is a great reservoir of facts and an abundance of knowledge and practical experience; but this information is not systematically arranged and until it is we shall see few general laws in operation. There is a great need for research and dissemination of facts about construction economics.

In her book, *Economic Philosophy*, Joan Robinson refers to economics as "a vehicle for the ruling ideology of each period as well as partly a method of scientific investigation," and goes on to say: "All along it [economics] has been striving to escape from sentiment and to win for itself the status of a science."[2] If this can be said of economics with its impressive array of thinkers, writers, experts, and schools, and with its established places in society and government, what can be said for construction economics?

Since the Second World War, statistics and statistical methods have been used increasingly in many fields. This same period also has witnessed great developments in electronic data processing (EDP) and computers which have stimulated the use of statistical methods in questions of probability because of the ability of computers to deal with huge quantities of information.

It seems that construction estimating has not yet been widely affected by the use of statistical methods and computers, but important developments have occurred, such as described in Chapter 4.[3] Construction is a basic industry, producing a big part of the gross national product, and the complexities of the estimating

---

[1] *The Random House Dictionary of the English Language* (New York: Random House, Inc., 1966).

[2] Joan Robinson, *Economic Philosophy* (Harmondsworth, Middlesex, England: Penguin Books, 1964), pp. 7, 25.

[3] For some other developments see Chapter 5.

and cost accounting process appear to make it an ideal subject for computers.

We do not really know what buildings cost, and why they cost what they do. Indeed, there is no precise definition of cost. Precisely what effect do building regulations, the season, the climate, the design, the designer, and the present methods of bidding and arranging contracts have on construction costs? No one really knows. Some fundamentals appear obvious, but have they been tested? Some research is done, but it appears insignificant considering the general lack of knowledge of design and construction economics.

One fact is clear; the interrelation between Time and Cost in construction. Time is of the essence of a contract, and time is also money. Interim financing is a major construction expense; and the risks arising out of having to predict costs over extended periods often cause higher costs for an owner or losses for construction firms. It has become obvious to many that the traditional methods of designing and constructing buildings are not always effective.

AN EFFICIENT INDUSTRY?

The design of each building is more or less original because of the requirements of owner and site. But, many buildings could be constructed almost entirely of standard components, except for the use of certain plastic materials such as concrete and waterproofing in substructures. Nevertheless, in many designers' offices, draftsmen are employed to draw and redraw building components and details that are essentially the same in function and appearance from one project to the next. Often the details in the drawings and the descriptions in the specifications are copied from manufacturers' catalogues or from previous jobs, thus creating the illusion of originality. This practice is still taught in some architectural and engineering schools and technical institutes; as a result: modular construction is not common; the use of standard components is not always widespread; standard drawing practices are hardly used; and specifications are too often ponderous conglomerates of jargon and misapplied standards.

Considered objectively, there appears to be no reason why design and construction should be separated, as they so often are in English-speaking countries. There may have been advantages to this separation in the past, but do they still exist? And if they do, can we say that they are paramount and are not outweighed by the advantages that could be obtained by integrating design and construction?

What were the advantages to society of a profession specializing in design and with no commercial interest in construction? Has the last century and a half clearly demonstrated the success of this concept? Could not professionalism have been nurtured in construction if professionalism was the means of attaining better buildings and a better environment? And has professionalism brought us to this goal? Or, has it led us away from the ideal of a profession of master builders with a responsibility to society to both design and build that which is sound, commodious, and delightful? We cannot underrate the importance of the built environment to man's well-being, and the special responsibility to society of those given the privilege to shape it. Rather, we should ask if a better environment has been achieved by separating the function of the designer from that of the builder. This is not to say that all the skills required could be found in the members of some kind of super-profession of designer-builders. But then we do not expect any of our professionals to be universal supermen, and some specialization is necessary in all professions.

In the balance, it does seem that separating the functions of designing and constructing has caused problems that are still with us. By isolating and exalting one, the other has not been lifted up. Looking back, we respect the accomplishments of designers and builders. Looking forward, we see the need for change.

The present method of estimating and bidding for stipulated sum contracts has not radically changed in the last 100 years. But in that time construction methods have changed. In the nineteenth century, cast-iron columns and beams were first used in a building frame for a seven-story mill designed by two engineers, Boulton and Watt; the last named the same Watt who invented the steam engine.[4] New buildings appeared as products of the industrial revolution owing little to the past. Since then, building construction has been stimulated and changed by wars and technology, but design and contracting methods have not kept pace. Drafting techniques are often still essentially the same as they were a generation ago. Specification writing is just beginning to appear as a learned skill, but still not taught in many schools.

Many modern buildings are built under new contractual arrangements and by new systems; but most are still built by a contracting system that relies on inadequate methods of planning and communication and a wasteful method of making contracts.

---

[4] See S. Giedion, *Space, Time and Architecture* (Cambridge, Mass.: Harvard University Press; London: Oxford University Press, third edition, 1954), Part III, *"The Evolution of New Potentialities,"* for an account and illustrations of this and other construction developments in the nineteenth century.

Some approximate figures (which cannot be called statistics) indicate one area for research. Estimators have shown that the cost of bidding for stipulated sum contracts is about one- to two-tenths of 1 percent of the total job cost for each general bidder. The sub-bidders' estimating costs are additional. The contractor usually does about 25 percent of the total job with his own forces. The other 75 percent is done by subcontractors. By direct proportion, the subcontractors' total bidding costs would be about three times those of the contractor. But the contractor has the additional responsibility for assembling the total estimate and bid, including the sub-trades. To be conservative, we will assume all the subcontractors' bidding costs are 1½ times as much as the contractor's bidding costs. There are usually several bidders, so let us assume that there are six general bidders and an average of three bidders for each subtrade on a project estimated to cost $1 million.

COST OF BIDDING FOR A $1 MILLION BUILDING PROJECT

General bidders:	$1 million × 0.002 × 6 bidders = $12,000.00
Subtrade bidders:	$1 million × 0.003 × 3 bidders = 9,000.00
Estimated total costs of bidding	$21,000.00

Although based on several assumptions, this figure indicates total bidding costs of from 1 to 2 percent of the total costs of the work.[5] Of the total costs above, only $5,000.00 spent by the successful bidders is productive. The other $16,000.00 spent by the unsuccessful bidders is wasted. Nevertheless, it has to be paid, and it must be included in the total overhead costs added by all bidders to their estimates. It is, therefore, paid for by the customers of the construction industry.

Another disadvantage of the present system of contracting is the military-like chain of communication from owner-design to contractor, and from contractor to subcontractors. This arrangement may have been adequate when designers were generally knowledgeable about all the trades, and most of the construction methods and details were traditional and well known. But today, construction is too complex for the de-signer—even with a team of consultants to help him—to make all the decisions and to prescribe all the materials and methods before the contractor is selected and can be consulted.

Designers and developers, generally, do not appear to have changed their perceptions of buildings if present building designs and developments are evidence. Most buildings are still designed and built for a single limited use as an office block, a school, or a church. And each of these uses is exclusive of other uses and is limited to eight, six, or even two hours a day, depending on a building's function and the denomination of its users. Of all the plant and equipment and fabricated resources of a society, none is used less efficiently than buildings.

Buildings contain few moving parts; doors, window vents, and some fans and pumps. Normally they do not suffer from vibration, overheating, and worn bearings like machinery, and depreciation is not a major expense. The greatest expense and the economic failure of most buildings (and their sites) appears to stem from the fact that they are not used enough before they become obsolete. To owners and designers, a building has only one use, and urban areas are still planned for the nineteenth century and organized according to rural timetables.

The construction industry is so conservative not so much because it is opposed to change, but because it is fettered by obsolete laws and regulations and driven by designers who cannot experiment, by trade unions that are divisive, and by contractors who are conservative because they are not innovators. Research and experimentation is essential, yet is is practically non-existent in the construction industry which is second only to agriculture in its importance. There are building research institutes but presumably with small budgets and less influence, to judge from their effect on the average construction company.

Almost anyone can become a contractor. The primary requirement is to stay in business for the first five years or so. Many do not survive. About 50 percent of all construction business failures occur in the first five years of operation, and most are due to lack of experience or incompetence.

Perhaps more than from anything else, the industry has suffered from the absence of a professional approach to building construction. Much of the knowledge necessary for operating a successful construction business, particularly of construction costs and economics, has not been formalized and passed on by education as in other professions. The professionals in construction have, for the most part, concerned themselves with design and have left execution to contractors, as though the idea and the act can be separated without loss.

---

[5] Some other estimates of bidding costs are much higher, but comparisons are difficult without precise definitions. A general contractor's estimator can often put together a bid for $1 million job in less than four weeks, and several estimators have each consistently bid from $12 million to $20 million worth of work a year, including subtrade work. But, the required time and bidding costs for subcontractors and for smaller projects is often much greater. And in a buyer's market the number of bidders increases, so the total costs of bidding also increase.

Thus, a design always dies a little after its birth. Design is essentially an individual act, and it seems that designers generally are not able to disseminate their knowledge and skill in the manner of other professionals. Finally, the design and construction industry suffers, everyone suffers, from the practice of awarding public contracts to the lowest bidder regardless of whether or not the bidders have been selected or approved by the owner and the designer and irrespective of their qualifications and experience.

The common reaction to such criticism is to point to the construction works that have been designed and built and to say that the criticism is unwarranted in the light of the industry's achievements. But it is not to detract from past achievements to say that the next 100 years will be different, and that we must change and adopt and use new methods of designing, contracting, and constructing buildings now and in the future.

Much of what was learned in the past is of value today and will be of value tomorrow. In the past, builders and estimators were not unaware of the probabilities and risks involved in estimating and planning a project. It was simply that there were so many there was neither the time nor the techniques to deal with more than the most immediate and obvious. Human intuition has always played a major part in estimating and planning and its value cannot be overstated; it will never be entirely replaced. But now intuition can be raised up and given full scope by computers that can handle immense quantities of data in microseconds, and faster:

> The advent of transistorized computers (second generation, starting in 1958), increased processing speeds to microseconds (millionth of a second), and the present-day, solid-state, printed-circuit computers (third generation, starting approximately in 1963) are operating in nanoseconds (billionth of a second).[6]

Computers, new information and communication systems, and new techniques such as systems building and the mass production of building components, are changing the design and construction industry, particularly in its contracting and management methods. Now we should be able to collect and systematically arrange a vast body of facts about the economics of a construction project and to observe the effects of

laws that are still theories and assumptions and that for the most part are still unrecognized.

The greatest advances appear to have been made in industrial and heavy construction wherein professional engineers have used their traditional and practical tool, mathematics, to rationalize construction economics.

COSTS AND ECONOMICS OF CONSTRUCTION

The economics of construction cannot be examined in isolation because they are a part of general economics. But certain simple fundamentals of construction economics stand out, and these are reviewed here.

Construction costs have two origins:

1. The owner-designer, through the owner's requirements and the design
2. The contractor and subcontractors, through the competitive market and their own organizations.

These origins cannot always be separated because one is in part dependent on the other, and a contractor's costs always depend in large part on the design. At the same time, there are aspects of construction costs beyond the control of the owner-designer that are determined in the construction market. Therefore, it is expedient to examine construction costs from these two aspects: (1) design, and (2) the construction market.

COSTS THROUGH DESIGN

Primarily it is the owner who originates the costs of construction through his construction requirements and his ability to pay for them; although at first he may not always know exactly what his requirements are, he will probably have a clear idea of his financial limitations. Therefore, it is important that the designer or one of his consultants be competent to advise the owner on construction costs as well as design.

The ways in which the design can affect costs of a building are practically innumerable. Some of the principal ways include shape and size, materials and methods of construction, and design style.

Shape and Size

These factors must be considered together because they are two aspects of the same thing; the three-dimensional nature of the building, its form and its

---

[6] James A. Saxon and Wesley W. Steyer, *Basic Principles of Data Processing* (Englewood Cliffs, N.J.: Prentice-Hall, Inc., 1967), pp. 181, 182.

mass. Buildings have volume and they have surface area. The volume is the enclosed space, which is the building's reason for existence. The enclosure—the exterior walls, roof, and floor—has surface area. Under present circumstances, spherical buildings are generally less practical than buildings consisting of horizontal and vertical planes, although Buckminster Fuller may have started a minor movement toward hemispherical buildings with his geodesic dome.[7] Therefore, the cubic building is usually still the most economical shape if volume is the primary consideration (see Fig. 3-1).

A square has the lowest ratio of perimeter to area for rectangles, and the surface area of exterior walls is a function of the perimeter. Therefore, the closer a building's plan approaches a square, and the closer its shape approaches a cube, the more economical the enclosed building space, all other things being equal. Unfortunately, few buildings work well as a cube, but the principle can be applied to obtain the most economical shape commensurate with other needs.

In buildings straight lines and planes are usually cheaper than curved and irregular lines and planes. Right angles are cheaper than irregular angles, and rectangles are cheaper than circles and irregular shapes. These facts are not invariable, and building technology may change them. For example, a thin-shell, reinforced concrete barrel-vault roof can sometimes be more economical than a flat roof; and geodesic domes are an economical shape to enclose spaces for certain purposes.

Higher buildings cost more to build than lower buildings of equal capacity because of the extra costs of a structure required to resist winds and earthquakes, as well as to support its own weight. There are also extra costs involved in hoisting up men and materials, in safety requirements, and in limited working spaces in high buildings. High buildings also require additional services, such as elevators and pumps. The exterior walls of high buildings must be designed to withstand higher wind pressures which distort the components and enable dust, air, and water to infiltrate. Heat losses at higher elevations are usually greater because of greater temperature differences, and the exposure to which a high building is subjected requires special design considerations for other conditions, including: thermal movement, anticorrosion, lightning protection, and cleaning and maintenance. All of these features make high buildings more costly.

Both shape and size affect costs, and smaller buildings are more expensive per unit area. It is not the enclosed volume of space in a building that costs money, but rather the surface area and quality of the enclosure (the horizontal and vertical planes that are the walls, roofs, and floors), and the environmental services, such as plumbing, heating, ventilating, air conditioning and lighting.

Materials and Methods of Construction

These costs are partially determined by the owner-designer and are partially determined by external factors, such as:

1. Climate (heat, humidity, salinity, etc.)
2. Availability of material and labor
3. Laws, codes, and regulations
4. Attitudes of people toward buildings.

These factors affect construction costs through their influence on the building's design and on the materials and methods of construction.

Climate, particularly rainfall and temperature, should be a primary consideration in selecting materials and construction methods. Because of advances in building technology, climate is often ignored or defied; sometimes to an owner's discomfort and loss. Fashion may dictate the design and overrule local customs based on climate. Because of climate, houses in Florida, for example, generally cost less per square foot than similar houses in northern states because of differences in building design and heating requirements. Climate also influences costs through its effect on the efficiency of labor at the construction site.

Availability of materials and labor affects local construction costs. Structural steel made in North America may be more expensive in the state of Washington and in the province of British Columbia than it is in the state of New York and in the province of Quebec because of the high freight costs for shipping steel from eastern steel mills. Consequently, reinforced concrete structures are more common than steel structures in the West. But imported steel and a shorter erection time sometimes prevail.

During periods of intense construction activity the costs of certain trade work may increase because of a shortage of skilled tradesmen and the necessity of employing whoever is available, including less skilled and less productive workers. Also, supply and demand affects the costs of construction, the same as every other product, and has great effect on costs.

Laws, codes, and regulations affect building design and construction costs through local building codes, by-laws, fire regulations, and other ordinances. Un-

---

[7] Buckminster Fuller, "Preview of Building," Chapter 11 in Robert W. Marks (ed.), *Ideas and Integrities* (New York: Collier Books, 1969).

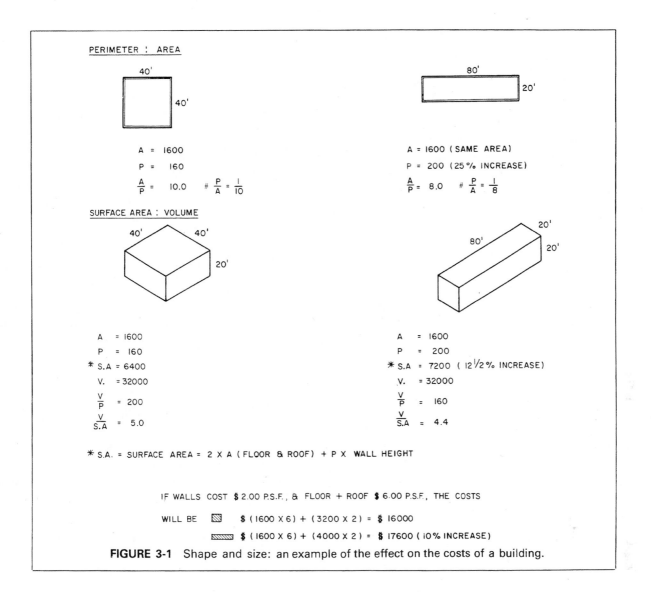

PERIMETER : AREA

A = 1600
P = 160
$\frac{A}{P}$ = 10.0   # $\frac{P}{A}$ = $\frac{1}{10}$

A = 1600 (SAME AREA)
P = 200 (25 % INCREASE)
$\frac{A}{P}$ = 8.0   # $\frac{P}{A}$ = $\frac{1}{8}$

SURFACE AREA : VOLUME

A   = 1600
P   = 160
* S.A = 6400
V. = 32000
$\frac{V}{P}$ = 200
$\frac{V}{S.A}$ = 5.0

A   = 1600
P   = 200
* S.A = 7200 (12 $\frac{1}{2}$ % INCREASE)
V. = 32000
$\frac{V}{P}$ = 160
$\frac{V}{S.A}$ = 4.4

* S.A. = SURFACE AREA = 2 X A (FLOOR & ROOF) + P X WALL HEIGHT

IF WALLS COST $ 2.00 P.S.F., & FLOOR + ROOF $ 6.00 P.S.F., THE COSTS

WILL BE $ (1600 X 6) + (3200 X 2) = $ 16000

$ (1600 X 6) + (4000 X 2) = $ 17600 (10 % INCREASE)

FIGURE 3-1 Shape and size: an example of the effect on the costs of a building.

fortunately, some codes are obsolescent and are not entirely applicable to modern construction. Building codes often vary from place to place without good reason, and consequently North America is covered with a patchwork of different building jurisdictions. Although Canada has made progress toward the widespread use of a national building code there is still resistance. One solution is to give designers more responsibility to ensure that the buildings they design fulfill certain performance specifications. A designer is usually better qualified than an official who is enforcing a code. It is not usual to have an official from city hall watch a surgeon operate on a patient. Why not let the construction industry's professionals bear an equivalent responsibility?

Attitudes of people, such as customers and neighbors, toward a building's design and appearance may greatly influence the design and the choice of materials

and methods of construction, and thereby affect the building's cost. This is particularly true in the case of residences and of retail buildings in which appearance is a means of attracting customers. Contractors' and subcontractors' attitudes toward owners and designers also affect construction costs. There is evidence that in certain instances the owner and the sources of his finances also affect the price level of construction.

Some owners and designers have reputations as tough customers. One designer had such a reputation with local painting contractors, and it was claimed that this caused a cost increase of 10 percent on all contracts under that designer's supervision. It was never quite clear whether this meant that the owner simply had to pay for what he got, or whether the 10 percent was truly a premium. Some designers apply the letter the contract they have written in supervising work and judging its performance, whereas others are less demanding. Construction work is always performed under the terms of a contract; contracts are made among persons; and personal attitudes and relationships always affect costs.

In selecting materials and methods of construction an owner will be more or less guided by his designer, and since selection involves the opinions of two persons and the finances of one, there are several considerations involved. Some considerations primarily involve economy and two aspects of costs:

1. Initial costs of work
2. Subsequent costs in use.

Initial costs of work are those costs incurred in the first instance by an owner in having the work done. These include the costs of materials, labor, equipment, overheads, and profit, which are examined in more detail in the next chapter, and the cost of design services.

Subsequent costs in use are those costs incurred by an owner that arise out of his ownership and use of a building. For example, the costs in use of a metal and glass entrance during the life of a well-used building might include:

1. Washing the glass three times each week
2. Cleaning the metal four times a year
3. Overhauling and oiling the hinges and closers once a month
4. Repairing hinges, closers, and handles once a year
5. Replacing handles every three years
6. Replacing closers every five years
7. Replacing doors every ten years
8. Replacing complete metal and glass entrance after thirty years.

In many cases, the *costs in use* are greater than the *initial costs of the work*; and in some cases, higher initial costs would result in lesser costs in use and an overall saving. If the owner intends to retain ownership, both the *costs of work* and the *costs in use* should be estimated when the building is designed, because only in this way can the true economics of the building be determined and the most prudent decisions be made. But if the owner is speculating and intends to sell the building as soon as possible, his attitude may be different. Life-cycle costing[G] is an important service to building owners provided by construction economists.

Design Style

This element includes the other features and characteristics of a building in addition to size and shape; the less obvious and more subtle details that are not usually apparent but which when taken together have an immediate effect on the costs of construction, and sometimes also a continuing effect on the costs in use.

Formwork and finishing for exposed concrete might be used as an example. A designer might specify that a certain type of form shall be used, that it will be erected with no joints closer together than 4 feet, that all joints will be laid out symmetrically about the center lines of walls, that all construction joints will be made on formwork joint lines, and that on stripping the forms the concrete surfaces will be treated to produce a rough textured finish. These specific requirements, if properly fulfilled, may greatly improve the appearance of the concrete walls, but also they will increase the cost of the work. On the other hand, the treated wall surfaces may not require paint, and the costs in use may thereby be reduced.

Details such as finishes cut to a line, or held back from abutting on another surface, and the absence of trim to cover joints that must be made clean and true when left exposed are some of the innumerable minor details that make a difference in initial construction costs. Anything unusual, original, and untried will cost more, because innovations reduce productivity, and the ultimate benefits, if any, are later gained by others.

There are countless items of work that may increase the costs of a job unnecessarily, such as items included without any real consideration of their importance to a job, and items of a quality far above that which is necessary. Gold door knobs and faucets are not commonplace, but other items are: fine surface treatments on virtually concealed surfaces, expensive metals and metallic coatings used where cheaper ones would do; high-grade lumber used in concealed places; imported hardwoods instead of cheaper domestic woods; polished plate glass installed where undistorted vision is not essential instead of heavy sheet which may be stronger; unsuitable finishes that require continuous maintenance or early replacement; heating and cooling systems designed for extremes of temperature likely to occur only once or twice a year; access doors and cover plates for mechanical valves and controls that are gems of nonferrous metal workmanship. The list is a long one.

To say that certain construction details and items are costly is not to say that they should not be used; only that everyone concerned should know what and where the costs of the work are, and then decide. Either the designer must have an awareness of construction costs and economics, or a cost consultant should be employed to assist the designer in planning and controlling the costs of the work.

The costs of a construction component are often as important as its physical characteristics, because costs are often one of the decisive factors in choosing a particular material or component. And if *cost* is important to the owner, it should embrace both the *initial costs of the work* and the *costs in use*. The function and purpose of many buildings are directly related to investment, costs, and income; and, in any case, in one way or another, all buildings have their economic considerations: in their design and function, in their construction, and in their relationship to land space. The words "economics" and "ecology" are both derived from the same Greek word *oikus* (house), and through this fundamental relationship we can see that construction economics is another means of dealing with some of the problems that beset us.

To be able to measure a thing is to know it, and to begin to understand it, and to be able to describe it; and it is not an exaggeration to say that the techniques of analysis and synthesis and the organization and use of data fundamental to estimating have a much wider application in judging and evaluating other things.

COSTS THROUGH THE CONSTRUCTION MARKET

After the owner's requirements have been translated by the designer into drawings and specifications (which will be the main part of the contract documents), the costs of work have to be determined by the bidders who will make offers (bids) to do the work or otherwise negotiate and arrange to do the work for the owner.

The costs of work always have to be established for each job in a particular place as of a particular period of time; and the costs are subject to all those economic conditions that may affect the prices of all things at all times and in all places. Those conditions are countless, but there are certain things that help to reduce the complexity of estimating their effects on thousands of items of work.

The risk in making an offer to do work and doing that work for a fixed price under certain conditions is not usually carried by one person. Not only is the risk shared by the contractor and his subcontractors, but each subcontractor will usually pass on part of his share of the risk (and potential profit) to others, namely the sub-subcontractors and suppliers.

Each person sharing in the performance of a job has also shared in determining the total costs of the work to the owner by making some of the decisions, estimates, offers, and agreements that constitute a primary construction contract with its subcontracts and sub-subcontracts. To see how these decisions are reached and how the estimates and contracts are made it is necessary to analyze the costs of work and to classify the parts in an attempt to comprehend the whole.

Costs of work may be classified as follows:

1. Material costs
2. Labor costs
3. Equipment costs
4. Overhead costs
5. Profit.

The primary value of these classifications is that they help us examine and analyze construction costs. If a cost does not fit into one of the classifications, the classifications are not necessarily wrong; there simply might be more of them. But fewer classifications are more manageable and too many defeat their purpose.

Material Costs

At times, unusual conditions vividly illustrate that prices can be extremely variable. In the Cariboo region of central British Columbia, vast grazing lands are tracked over each autumn by hundreds of hunters from the cities. Driving conditions become bad when snow falls and many hunters are ill-prepared to face such weather. Gasoline is not readily available once the blacktop is left behind, and extra supplies must be carried. Lack of experience leads many hunters to underestimate their needs, and ground conditions increase gasoline consumption. Consequently, the few isolated ranches are often visited, usually after dark, by many hunters seeking out gasoline. Even traditional hospitality is sometimes overtaxed. One old gas pump bore a rancher's handwritten sign: "*After 7:00 p.m.—first gallon costs $5.00.*" If the usual price were $1.00 per gallon at that place, a night's purchase of 2 gallons would average $3.00 per gallon; and a purchase of 6 gallons would average $1.67 per gallon.

Price[8] is subject to supply and demand and is affected by many other things, including:

---

[8] **Price** and **cost** are commonly interchanged. But "price" is used mainly with objects offered for sale, whereas "cost" is a much more general term. **Price** and **value** are often not interchangeable, for the most valuable things are priceless.

1. Quality
2. Quantity
3. Time
4. Place
5. Buyer
6. Seller.

Most estimators have been asked such questions as "What is the price of a yard of concrete?" To answer this, it is necessary to ask questions in return:

What type and quality concrete is required?

How much concrete do you want to buy?

When do you want it delivered?

Where do you want it delivered?

From whom do you want to purchase the concrete?

What is your relationship with the supplier?

All these questions must be answered before the original question can be answered with any accuracy.

Quality affects price, because a higher quality usually means a higher price. Is 3000 p.s.i. concrete or 4000 p.s.i. concrete required? Higher strength is achieved by adding more portland cement, and cement costs ten times more than stone and sand. So, a higher price is usually required for higher strength concrete, for example.

Quantity affects price, because usually the larger the quantity purchased, the lower the price. Seven cubic yards of ready-mixed concrete may cost $50.00 per cubic yard, delivered. Seventy yards may cost $49.50 per cubic yard, whereas 3 cubic yards may cost as much as $85.00 per cubic yard. A larger quantity of material may mean that certain fixed marketing costs are spread thinner, and freight costs may be reduced by using a larger and more economical carrier. Thus, a supplier can pass on some of the savings to the purchaser of large quantities through a lower selling price.

Time often affects price in several ways, because it affects the production and delivery of a product. If concrete is required at a certain time outside of normal business hours, the supplier may have to pay overtime rates to his employees and increase the price accordingly. Some products are cheaper or more expensive at different times of the year, particularly if there is a seasonal demand, or if weather affects production or delivery. Time affects costs, because of changing markets, fluctuating supply and demand, inflation, and other economic factors. Price is, therefore, invariably tied to a specific date or at least to a specific period of time.

Place and location usually affect price through the means and distance of delivery and the accessibility of the site. Handling goods is costly, and changes in methods of delivery from factory to site affect the final cost to the buyer. Freight costs are also determined by the type of goods and by the quantity delivered. Unforeseen costs of handling, unloading, and getting materials into store or to the job site are not uncommon. Contracts for supplying materials and building components are not always explicit about these things, and the estimator must anticipate and allow for all such costs.

The buyer affects price through his creditability as a customer, through the quantity he purchases, and by the marketing level at which he is able to purchase. **The supplier** affects the price because he, too, is a buyer as well as a seller of materials and services. Similarly, the relationship between a lessor and a lessee affect the rates at which plant and equipment are rented.

There is no such thing as a "fixed price" for anything. Products bear labels saying *"Suggested Retail Price. . .,"* which are often disregarded; and the price of gold goes up and down. Some basic construction materials are notoriously variable in price, and copper prices fluctuate frequently. In 1969, in British Columbia, one of the world's largest producers of softwood lumber, the local price of construction lumber rose from about $100.00 to almost $200.00 per thousand board feet, and then fell back again to the lower price within a period of about a year. In the lumber market, other things between buyer and seller also affect price, including: duties, tariffs, subsidies, corporate ownership, and economic survival.

List prices are usually not the prices at which goods are sold, but are simply a datum, or price level, established as a basis for selling. Selling prices are frequently quoted by percentage adjustments to list prices. This facilitates price quotation and adjustment. One customer may be quoted a price of, *"List less 10 percent."* Another customer may be quoted a price of, *"List less 10 percent, less 5 percent"* for the same goods. The second quotation is not the same as, *"List less 15 percent."* *"List less 10 percent"* may indicate a current and general price adjustment. *"List less 10, less 5"* may indicate an additional special discount of 5 percent below the general price level for a large order or a special customer. These discounts are generally known as *trade discounts*.[G] If the "List less 10 percent" price level remains valid for some time, a new price list may be issued containing all the prices listed at 10 percent below the former list prices.

In some cases, the list price may be a retail price, and the prices to another class of purchaser, such as contractors, may be list price less a discount. At the same time, a third class of purchasers, say, large contracting firms, may get a larger discount. Quotations to supply goods in large quantities for a particular project may be based on yet another price specially discounted even further below list price. Generally, list prices do not mean very much; it is the discounts that are significant.

Discounts can be confusing, and maybe they are meant to be. But they are essential as a means of setting different price levels. A manufacturer may sell large quantities of his product to distributors who have extensive storage facilities and maintain large stocks. They in turn may sell to suppliers with smaller facilities and stocks, who in turn may sell to retailers. At each marketing level the same functions exist—"selling, buying, transporting, storing, risk-bearing, standardizing and grading, financing, and providing market information."[9] All of these marketing functions create costs, and thereby create different prices at different marketing levels. This explains why the home handyman buying lumber from the retail store pays twice the price, or more, paid by the construction company for large quantities delivered to a job site.

An estimator may keep current price lists of materials for reference and obtain revisions as they are issued but for basic materials or products that represent a significant part of the total costs of a project, an estimator usually obtains specific quotations from manufacturers or suppliers for a particular project. If the quantity is large, a quotation may be obtained from a manufacturer. In other cases, it may be necessary to deal with a supplier, depending on the marketing policies of the manufacturer. With some products, manufacturers may bypass suppliers and sell directly to contracting firms; particularly when the order is large enough to eliminate the need for handling and storage at an intermediate level.

Other types of discounts include *cash discounts*[G] for early payment before the due date and discounts for volume of business. Most prices are quoted on the basis of a certain credit period allowed between the time the goods are shipped and the time when payment for the goods is to be made. This period varies, and it may be for thirty days (or less), sixty days, ninety days, or whatever period is agreed. If payment is made earlier, the cost of using money decreases, and the

[9] Vernon A. Musselman and John H. Jackson, *Introduction to Modern Business*, 4th ed. (Englewood Cliffs, N.J.: Prentice-Hall, Inc., 1984), p. 423.

seller can share some of the resultant savings in the cost of credit with the purchaser in the form of a cash discount.

A further type of discount is that given periodically by a supplier to a customer on the basis of the total volume of business done between them over a certain period. This discount, or rebate, is similar to a trade discount, but it does not relate to any particular order or job, and usually it does not show on invoices and statements. This makes it difficult for owner and designer to ascertain actual material costs in cost-plus-fee contracts, in which (according to the standard forms of contract) the owner undertakes to pay the cost of materials after all trade discounts and rebates have been deducted.

Transportation and handling costs are a part of the costs of materials, and an estimator must ascertain what transportation and handling will be necessary so that provision can be made for these costs, either in quotations from suppliers, or in subcontractors' bids, or in his own estimate of costs. These costs may include not only freightage and cartage from factory or supply house to the site but also handling costs of loading and unloading and any hoisting to levels above ground. This includes not only man-hours in handling, but also the costs of using hoists or elevators. In the case of materials like sand and gravel, cartage is often the major part of the cost, and the distance from source to site is a primary consideration. Sometimes, quotations and bids do not specify what is included in the way of handling and hoisting, and this omission sometimes leads to misunderstandings and unexpected costs. An estimator should try to avoid these snares by carefully describing his requirements and closly scrutinizing all quotations and bids.

Suppliers' and subcontractors' bids should make it clear if a bid is made on the assumption that another's elevator, hoist, or other equipment and men will be available for use at the site for unloading and handling, and there should be proper mutual agreement about any related charges to be made.

Storage is another part of the cost of materials. This may involve risk of damage and loss during storage, or the costs of insurance, protection, and security. Some of these costs, such as temporary storage buildings at the site and general security provisions, are better classified and estimated under overhead costs, as described later in this chapter.

Taxes, particularly sales taxes, are another part of the cost of materials. An estimator must ascertain whether or not quoted prices include all appropriate taxes, because not all price lists and quotations make this clear. The usual practice is for local sales taxes not to be included in listed prices, because the price list is often used in several states and provinces, each with different tax rates, or with none at all.

When we speak of *material costs* we refer to the costs at the site to the contractor, and to the owner; and it appears that these costs will become an increasingly larger part of the total costs as fewer materials requiring site labor and more factory-made, standard components are used in construction. Other changes will consequently occur. Purchasing will become more important, and the skilled tradesman less so.[10] Detail design will be done more and more by the manufacturers of components, and entire buildings will be designed by manufacturers. Manufacturers may diversify by incorporating construction companies to create markets for their own products; and in some cases the designing, manufacturing, erecting and servicing of buildings will be done by one corporation which will manufacture, lease, erect, dismantle, scrap, and reconstitute its products.

Labor Costs

These costs may be examined from two aspects:

1. *Labor rates:*[G] the hourly rates of employing workmen, based on total labor costs divided by the total number of hours worked
2. *Productivity:* the rates of production by workmen employed; the amounts of work done in specific periods of time.

Labor rates include all labor costs, both the direct and indirect costs. *Direct labor costs*[G] are wages and other payments made to workmen. *Indirect labor costs*[G] are other payments made by a contractor on the employee's behalf, and these include fringe benefits (according to wage agreements) and statutory payments (according to law). The *wage rate*[G] is the direct cost per hour. The *labor rate*[G] is the total of direct and indirect costs per hour.

Time worked over the standard day (of 7, 7½, or 8 hours, depending on location and wage agreement) is paid for as overtime at rates usually one and one-half or two times the basic wage rate. In addition, "travel time" may also be paid for, in addition to a guaranteed minimum number of hours per day, or per week, especially on out-of-town jobs in remote lo-

cations. For example, on an out-of-town job:

Guaranteed minimum week, say,	60 hours
Standard week, (7½ hours × 5 days)	37½ hours
Overtime hours	22½ hours

If the first 5 hours of overtime are paid at one and one-half times the basic rate, and the balance at two times the basic rate of, say, $16.00 per hour, the effective wage rate will be $21.34 per hour.[11]

Standard week: 37½ hr	@ $16.00	= $ 600.00
Overtime: first 5 hr	@ $24.00	= $ 120.00
balance 17½ hr	@ $32.00	= $ 560.00
$Total 60 hr	@ $21.34	= $1280.00

This is in effect an increase of one-third in the wage rate; and additional costs on out-of-town jobs may include subsistence allowances for board and lodging and traveling costs to and from the job site at start and finish, and sometimes during the job.

A guaranteed minimum day, or "show up time," is paid in some cases to workmen who show up for work at the site but cannot work because of weather, or another reason. This kind of payment is sometimes also required for workmen hired from a union hall who, if found to be unsuitable, are discharged soon after arrival at the site. Premium rates are usually payable for unusual conditions; for work at high levels, dirty work, underground work, work in water, work under water, and work in compressed air (as in caissons).

Fringe benefits, which are part of indirect labor costs, may include paid vacations (holiday with pay), pension fund payments, group insurance premiums, payments to funds for the health and welfare of employees, and payments to funds for apprentices, training and trade promotion. These payments may be based on time worked or on a proportion of wages or they may be levied as a lump sum.

Wage rates and fringe benefits are generally established through negotiations (sometimes preceded by strikes or lockouts) and agreements between employers and the various trade unions in the construction industry. Despite the interdependency of the construction trades, and the fact that their cooperation and coordination are essential to construction jobs, there is often not much cooperation and coordination among construction trade unions off the site. Each local union

[10] The rising costs of tradesmen at job sites and the attitudes of unions are two of the things that will revolutionize the construction industry by diminishing the amount of work done on sites, and by increasing the use of factory-made, standard components in buildings.

[11] Because *wage rates* vary so much according to time and place, different rates are used in examples.

usually negotiates a separate and individual wage agreement with employers, often at a different time and often for a different period from other local unions. There are a few national agreements. Wage rates and fringe benefits consequently vary greatly among trades and localities.[12]

Statutory payments, which are indirect labor costs, are paid by employers to the government on their employees' behalf, according to the appropriate statutes. In the United States these payments include contributions to Social Security and Medicare, unemployment insurance, and workers' compensation insurance. In Canada the payments are similar, except that payments are made to the Canada Pension Plan instead of to Social Security.

To summarize, wage rates are total payments paid to employees (direct costs) divided by the total hours worked, whereas labor rates are all labor costs (direct and indirect) divided by the total hours worked. Wage rates can be established from payrolls, but labor rates are usually best calculated on a weekly or two-week period, or on the basis of some other pay period.

Some estimators use *wage rates* in calculating unit prices[G] and in pricing labor costs in estimates, in which case *indirect labor costs* are added to total *direct labor costs* as a percentage, usually between 20 and 30 percent, according to the trades involved. Other estimators calculate and use *labor rates* to price labor costs in estimates. The choice of method depends on the various trades and rates involved, the type of estimate and contract, the company's accounting methods, and individual preferences.

Productivity is the estimator's greatest challenge. How many man-hours are required to complete each item of work? The variables of productivity are innumerable, and it is one of the major factors in all construction costs. Yet, considering its importance not much research has been done on this subject. The main obstacles to research appear to be the size and diversity of the industry, the large number of small construction companies and the small number of large companies, and the reluctance of most companies to share information.

Construction companies must know the costs of the work that they do. This requirement appears obvious; yet many do not always know what their costs are. Even if they practice some kind of cost accounting they do not always know, because on their own the results are often inadequate to provide a company with all the information it needs. Therefore, most construc-

tion companies need other sources of information, which is why so many estimators buy published cost data.

Pooling and sharing cost information and data sounds to some like socialism and a denial of the free enterprise system; but this is because they misunderstand. It is not necessary for construction companies to disclose their discounts, their overhead and profit, and their unit prices. It is not necessary that they give away anything that would reduce proper competition. All that is involved is that they share certain factual information and data about such things as the effects of season, weather, design, productivity, and other economic factors. This could be done through local construction associations so that no individual source of information could be identified, and all those participating would benefit.

We are now at a time when information gathering and processing is a basic industry. But information about the design and construction industry is, for the most part, still dispersed, raw, and unprocessed, and the time has come when we need to systematically collect and analyze and use this information. An example of the kind of research needed is the Study on Manpower Utilization referred to in Chapter 4, which pointed to one of the major deficiencies of the construction industry when it concluded that: "There is a lack of detailed cost information available to most contractors."[13]

The first reaction to the Study is said to have been vigorous; possibly because it said that it found workmen were "idle for no apparent reason" for about 17½ percent of their total work day. The average total "idle time," including time spent waiting for men, materials, and equipment, was observed to be about 25 percent of the carpenters' work day, on the sites where the study was carried out. *The Study's conclusions, however, placed almost the entire blame for this inefficiency with construction management.*

Generally, the conclusions were that there was a lack of good management and that this resulted in inefficiency, poor utilization of labor, and "involuntary idleness" on the part of workers. The Study should be read in its entirety to understand all of its implications and limitations. One portion of a study does not make an irrefutable case; but its findings and conclusions are supported in part by statistics from other sources, such as Dun and Bradstreet Ltd., whose business information systems, services, and sciences provide "publications and services for management needs."

---

[12] For comparative labor rates see *Building Construction Cost Data* (published annually) (Kingston, Mass.: Robert Snow Means Company, Inc.,) and construction periodicals.

[13] David Aird, *Manpower Utilization in the Canadian Construction Industry*, National Research Council, Division of Building Research, Technical Paper No. 156 (Ottawa, Canada, 1963), p. 38.

These items include annual "Key Business Ratios" and "Failure Records" for various industries which show each year that most business failures can be traced to incompetent management.

Productivity is fundamental to the economics of construction. The estimator, as part of management, has to relate past productivity and past costs to future jobs through cost accounting. But an estimator should not simply be a surveyor and user of data. The estimator can assist in achieving higher productivity: by pointing out those situations wherein cost data indicate that productivity has fallen below the median, or norm; by making economic comparisons of the use of different materials and methods of construction; by comparing productivity in one branch, or company, with that in other branches, or other companies; and by providing data for use in scheduling and controlling construction work. To manage well, it is necessary to know exactly what a company is doing. The greatest obstacle to good management is ignorance and a lack of information.

Productivity is essentially variable, and the variables exist in: (1) the workers, and (2) the workers' surroundings, equipment, and tools. The variables of the worker include:

> anatomy, brawn, contentment, creed, earning power, experience, fatigue, habits, size of man, skill, temperament, and training. The other variables include: appliances, clothes, colors, entertainment, ventilation, lighting, quality of material, reward and punishment, size of unit moved, special fatigue-eliminating devices, surroundings, tools, union rules, and weight of unit moved.[14]

These variables indicate the problem of productivity. Each case consists of a different set of variables, and those construction estimating texts that use the term "labor constants" to identify productivity rates are guilty of creating a false impression of constancy. Similarly, those handbooks and texts that publish construction productivity rates in terms of man-hours expressed to two and three decimal places are also misleading. The published data may have been analyzed and presented in good faith, and the results may be mathematically correct averages, or medians; but, to say that framing and erecting stud walls requires 29.1 carpenter man-hours per thousand board feet of 2 × 4 lumber creates a false impression of accuracy. We should ask how the figure of 29.1 man-hours was obtained. If, as is probable, it is an average figure from

several framing jobs, we should ask how many jobs were analyzed. For example, suppose the figures obtained were as follows:

Job Number	Production Rate (man-hours)
1	35.33
2	34.82
3	31.01
4	29.76
5	29.30
6	28.99
7	28.34
8	27.30
9	23.81
10	22.34
	10)291.00
Average (for 10 jobs)	29.10

Looking at these production rates for ten different jobs it is apparent that if the average were based on more or less jobs the average would be different. There are not enough data to plot a "distribution curve" but if there were data from 100 jobs available, it might be possible and we might get a better picture from the statistics. A mean, or average, can be distorted by one unusual figure, and the median, or the mode, is often a better guide. Better yet would be the ability to mathematically predict the probabilities of variations from medians for all major items of an estimate, and to indicate their probable effects on the total estimated costs of work.

Equipment Costs

A more complete title for this section would be "plant and equipment costs," to identify the two kinds:

1. *Plant*: those things that are "planted" in position, such as a concrete-mixing plant
2. *Equipment*: those things that are mobile, such as a bulldozer.

This distinction is not always made, but in the interest of greater precision such distinctions are to be encouraged.

Once again, a reminder that classifications are only a convenience that do not change the reality of things one bit. Things are what they are, no matter what we call them. We may give names to groups of things for our own convenience and thereby may deceive ourselves if we come to think of the names as the reality.

The economics of plant and equipment are discussed and examined in many publications, and one

---

[14] Frank G. Gilbreth, *Motion Study* (New York: D. Van Nostrand Company, Inc., 1911).

of the primary questions is whether to own or to rent equipment. In estimating, it makes no essential difference whether plant and equipment are owned or rented, because in either case the estimator should allow for all plant and equipment costs in his estimate at realistic rental rates.

If plant or equipment is rented, the rental rate is established by offer and acceptance, as in any other contract. If the plant or equipment is self-owned, an economically realistic rental rate should be established for use within the company, and that rate should take into account all the economic facts of owning and using the plant or equipment.

If such an accounting is not made, one of two conditions will probably result. Either the plant or equipment will be charged for in the estimate at an inflated rate, the total estimated cost of the work will thereby be inflated, and to that extent the estimate will not be competitive; or the plant or equipment will be charged for in the estimate at a deflated rate, and, to that extent, the estimate will be too low, the owner will receive something for nothing and the contractor will suffer a loss. *Owned plant and equipment must be charged out at economical rates just as if it were rented at competitive rates.*

Money invested in plant and equipment should produce an income, the same as any other investment. The amount of income that should be produced varies in the market; but obviously, to show a profit, the amount should be greater than the premium the company has to pay to borrow money from the bank. The income is the net income produced by the plant and equipment after all costs are deducted. These costs are of two classes:

1. *Owning costs*: the costs of owning plant and equipment
2. *Operating costs*: the costs of using the plant and equipment over and above the owning costs.

All plant and equipment costs can be put under one of these two headings; but in some cases the distinction is not always clear because some costs are not always obviously in one class or the other. This condition exists because for the sake of simplicity we have only two cost classifications. We could have a third heading for those costs that relate to both owning and operating, but then some of the advantages in classifying the costs would be lost.[15]

---

[15] An explanatory example of the method of estimating the owning costs and the operating costs of plant and equipment is given in Chapter 10, *Pricing Work: General.*

Owning Costs. These may be identified as:

1. *Depreciation*: loss in value from any cause
2. *Maintenance*: major repairs and replacement of parts
3. *Investment*: costs arising from investment and ownership.

Depreciation is usually the biggest single cost. It arises out of wear and tear (that is, physical depreciation) and obsolescence. As the plant or equipment is superseded by better designed, more efficient, and more desirable plant or equipment, it becomes obsolescent and it loses value.

There are several classical methods of calculating depreciation, and each method gives a slightly different result. This does not necessarily mean that one method and one result is right and the others are wrong. The different methods of calculating depreciation enable accountants to record and keep accounts of different assets that decline in value because of depreciation, and different methods are better suited to different situations. Of course, for the owner's edification, the method used should, if possible, more or less reflect the value of the plant and equipment at different times of life. Depreciation rates for deductible allowances in calculating income tax are laid down by the tax authorities, but these rates may be determined by temporary economic and political strategies rather than by observable facts.

The most common and the most easily understood method of calculating depreciation is known as the "straight-line method." For example:

1. Original cost of equipment delivered, including taxes	$120,000.00
2. Less salvage value after 5 years working life	$ 20,000.00
3. Total depreciation over 5 years working life	$100,000.00
4. Average annual depreciation over 5 years working life	$ 20,000.00

"Original cost" must include all attributable costs, including taxes and freight. "Salvage value" may be only "scrap value" or nothing at all if the equipment is used and dumped at an isolated location. An "average annual depreciaton" of $20,000.00 does not mean that at age 2½ years the equipment will be worth precisely $70,000.00. However, its value at that age should be approximately $70,000.00, depending on the amount of maintenance required and done, the use and abuse of the equipment, and any new developments in this type of equipment that might make the older model more difficult to sell. You can probably relate this to your own automobile, which also depreciates.

Two other classical methods of calculating depreciation explained in many books on business and accounting are: (1) *declining balance method*, and (2) *sum of digits method*. These are less straightforward than straight-line depreciation. The first method depreciates the item by the same percentage amount applied to the undepreciated balance each year, and so, in theory, the item never fully depreciates but does eventually reach a practical salvage value. The "sum of digits" method is not unlike the "declining balance" method; but instead of a constant percentage deduction, a declining fraction of the total costs is deducted each year.[16]

Maintenance costs vary with the type of plant and equipment and with the type of work done. Mobile equipment doing heavy work, such as a crawler-tractor, might have total maintenance costs equal to the total depreciation costs over the equipment's working life. That is to say, if the total depreciation of the equipment is $100,000.00, the equipment owner can expect to pay $100,000.00 in maintenance costs over its working life. At the other end of the scale, the maintenance costs for equipment such as cranes might be from 10 percent down to as low as 5 percent of the total depreciation. Maintenance costs are usually indicated as a proportion of the depreciation because there is a logical relationship between these costs and the working life. Consider how much it costs to maintain your own automobile compared with the annual depreciation.

Investment costs include:

1. *Interest* on investment
2. *Insurances and taxes* on plant and equipment
3. *Storage costs* arising from land and buildings used to store equipment.

You can relate all of these expenses to your own car. (Do not forget the property taxes on your garage, or carport, if you have one.)

Interest on investment may be either interest paid by purchaser to a finance company, or to the seller if the equipment is bought on credit. Or, if the equipment is bought for cash, it is the interest that would have been received if the cash had been invested. This cost of money should also include an allowance for inflation. If inflation is not accounted for, apparent profit may not actually exist.

Insurances for the plant and equipment are necessary to protect its owner against loss, and the premiums will depend on the type of plant and equipment. Plant will usually cost less to insure than mobile equipment. Tax levies vary according to location and regulations, and in some places, only plant affixed to land is taxed.

Storage costs include the use of land and any buildings used to store and protect the equipment when not in use. In some cases, these may be classed as overhead costs. The costs of a storage and maintenance building for equipment would also include costs similar to those arising from owning plant and equipment; namely, depreciation, maintenance, and investment costs.

Operating costs.   These costs may be identified as:

1. *Fuel*: includes lubricants and additives
2. *Running repairs*: includes minor repairs and replacement of small parts
3. *Transportation*: includes transporting to and from site; setting up and dismantling
4. *Operator*: includes wages and fringe benefits.

Once again, relating these expenses to the operating of your own automobile will help you to understand them better. *Fuel* (diesel oil and gasoline) is used at hourly consumption rates related to the "brake horsepower" of loaded equipment. Running repairs depend on the plant and equipment and its use, and there is some connection between this item and the cost of maintenance. Consumable items, the use of which is directly proportional to the amount and weight of work done, are better included under running repairs. These items include such things as fan belts, cables, hoses, cutting edges, and the like. Rubber tires are a large expense, and on rented equipment they may be classed separately as a maintenance cost.

Transportation to and from the site may involve the use of other equipment to carry equipment with

---

[16] With the *declining balance method*, up to twice the percentage annual depreciation found by the straight-line method is deducted from the declining balance each year until the estimated salvage value is reached. Thus, for an estimated 5-year life (and 20 percent straight line depreciation) deduct up to 40 percent of the declining balance each year.

With the *sum of digits method*, the total depreciation is found by first deducting any estimated salvage value from the original cost (total investment); and depreciation is deducted from the declining balance each year as a fraction calculated from the sum of the digits obtained from the estimated life in years. Thus, for a 5-year life the sum is 15 (= 1 + 2 + 3 + 4 + 5), and in the first year, 5/15 of the depreciation is deducted; in the second year, 4/15 of the balance is deducted; and in the fifth year, 1/15 of the balance is deducted, leaving only the salvage value.

tracks that is not allowed on highways, and it also includes the costs of any scout cars required to lead and follow large equipment traveling on highways. Setting up and dismantling plant or equipment, such as a tower crane, can be a major expense and may require the use of a large mobile crane, and its costs too must be estimated.

The costs of the equipment's *operator* are similar to those labor costs previously examined in this chapter. An estimator should also consider the cost of *additional labor* working in conjunction with plant and equipment. For example, excavation equipment and cranes frequently require a man working on the ground in front of the equipment to assist the operator by signaling to him or to do minor handwork with a shovel, and the labor costs should be attributed to the use of the equipment and to the appropriate items of work performed.

Overhead Costs

These are construction costs of any kind that cannot be attributed to any specific item of work. If costs can be attributed to an item of work, they should be, and these costs will then come under one of the classifications already discussed; namely, material costs, labor costs, or equipment costs. Otherwise, they are overhead costs.

Overhead costs can be classified by applying an extension of the same reasoning by which we define overhead costs. That is, if costs can be attributed to a specific job site because the costs arise only out of that particular job, those costs are *job overhead costs*.[G] If costs cannot be attributed to any particular job, they are *operating overhead costs*.[G] The scope and content of these two classifications vary with the conditions and requirements of the contract. That is to say, certain *job overhead costs* on one job (or in one company) may be classified as *operating overhead costs* on another job (or in another company). Once again, the purpose and artificiality of classifications should be remembered.

Job Overhead Costs. These costs can often be estimated in the same way as other costs of the work, because they include material costs, labor costs, or plant and equipment costs, but they are of a general nature. Many job overhead costs are specifically referred to in a contract, whereas others are not and must be anticipated by an estimator. There are two primary contractual sources for these costs:

1. The articles of the contract (the general conditions and the agreement)

2. The general requirements[17] of the contract.

Some of the requirements in a contract are of a general nature only insofar as they are required for some specific items of work, and therefore they should be related to the costs of those specific items, rather than to the job as a whole, as job overhead costs.

Articles of a contract may give rise to the following job overhead costs:

1. *Liquidated damages*: a risk to be priced by a bidder
2. *Taxes and duties*: when not for specific items of work
3. *Legal fees and costs*: related to the bid and the contract
4. *Consultants' fees and costs*: where required to be paid for surveying, building layout, testing, etc.
5. *Contract documents*: extra copies to be copied or purchased
6. *Site staff*: salaries and allowances; offices and accommodation
7. *Personnel expenses*: related to staff
8. *Fees and premiums*: for permits, bonds, and insurances
9. *Protection of life, work, and property*: temporary work required
10. *Contingencies*: for delays, damage, emergencies, inefficiency, and the like
11. *Financing*: short term, as required by the work.

Liquidated damages are predetermined money damages payable to the owner should the contractor cause him to suffer damages (loss) through failure to substantially complete the work by a completion date stated in the contract. These damages are "liquidated" (i.e., settled in advance) and are made part of the terms of the construction contract to create an incentive for the contractor to perform the contract and to complete the work on time, and to make immediate and direct restitution to the owner for damages should the contractor default by not completing on time. The owner could sue the contractor for breach of contract and for actual damages incurred through late completion of the work. But in order to avoid a court action and its attendant costs in time and money, liquidated damages are calculated and agreed in the contract, in ad-

---

[17] General requirements are Division 1 of the *Masterformat* (see the Bibliography).

vance, so that, should it be necessary, the owner can obtain restitution through the contract instead of through the courts. Liquidated damages are, in fact, properly related to the actual damages suffered by the owner. That is to say, liquidated damages are not a penalty for late completion. There is a legal distinction between liquidated damages and a penalty. A penalty is not particularly related to actual damages and may not be valid unless equitably balanced in a contract by a bonus for early completion. A bonus is not necessary in a contract with liquidated damages. If liquidated damages are prescribed in a contract, a bidder must consider:

1. The desirability of bidding for a contract requiring liquidated damages for late completion, rather than bidding for other work that may be available
2. The probabilities that the work of the contract can, or cannot, be completed within the period of time stated in the agreement
3. The amount (if any) to be included in the estimate and bid to offset the risk of having to pay liquidated damages.

Taxes and duties are usually attributable to specific items of work, in which case, they are part of those items' costs. Otherwise, they are a job overhead cost.

Legal fees and costs may arise from legal services in respect of a specific contract; for example, fees for a legal opinion on an unusual term of a contract. Otherwise, legal fees are probably an operating overhead cost; e.g., a retainer paid by a construction company to its legal adviser.

Consultants' fees and costs might arise from design and testing services required to be provided by the contractor. In that case, the fees and costs should be ascertained and included in the estimate. If they are attributable to specific items of work, they should be part of the costs of those items. Fees may be paid to a professional surveyor for surveying a site or for laying out a building, and in such cases they would be part of job overhead costs.

Contract documents may have to be copied or purchased by the contractor, particularly if he requires more copies than the number specified in the contract to be provided by the designer.

Site staff may include the following:

1. Project managers and engineers
2. Superintendents
3. Quantity surveyors
4. Cost accountants
5. Timekeepers and first-aid men
6. Purchasing agents and expediters
7. Storemen, watchmen, etc.

The question to be answered is, Can all or part of a staff member's salary, or wages, or expenses be properly charged to a particular job? If a staff member, such as a purchasing agent, is at the construction company's head office and his salary cannot be charged to specific jobs, then it is an *operating overhead cost*. The size and location of the job usually determines the size and scope of the site staff, and the job overhead costs. Larger jobs and jobs that are not close to the head office usually entail larger job overhead costs because they require more site staff.

Personnel expenses might include such things as transportation, supplies, and equipment, and might also include camp costs and catering costs for staff on out-of-town jobs. Overseas jobs often require personnel expenses for medical treatment, air fares, and special payments of income taxes and bonuses.

Fees and premiums include fees for building permits, bid bonds, performance bonds, payments bonds, and the like, as well as premiums for builder's risk insurance and public liability insurance. All of these costs are directly related to the job. Some insurance premiums may be part of operating overhead costs, because a construction company often has general insurance coverage for the usual risks, and the general premiums do not relate to any one job.

Protection of life, work, and property includes such items as the costs of safety measures; the risk and costs of having to protect, or repair and make good the owner's property at the site, or the property of others, because of disturbance or damage resulting from the work. Such costs cannot always be charged to specific items of work and are, therefore, a job overhead cost, unlike the costs of protecting specific items of work such as newly laid masonry or concrete which can be charged as part of the costs of those items.

Contingencies may be allowed in an estimate for any number of probabilities and risks. For an out-of-town job on which local labor will be employed, the estimator may price the items of work as usual, and then make an estimated allowance of, say, 10 percent on the labor costs to allow for the expected lower productivity of local labor. An estimated allowance may be made for probable delays due to weather conditions, or late deliveries. If work is halted at a site, certain job overhead costs will continue. In alteration work, there may be a risk of damage to existing work that should be allowed for in the bid. Blasting, for example, may weaken or damage nearby structures. The extent of contingencies required in an estimate for any such items depends on the type of contract and the job conditions.

Financing is an important cost because the contractor is paid in arrears for work done, usually at the end of each month during the course of the contract. This means that in most contracts, the contractor must have money available to perform the work. Most contracts also provide for the owner to hold back a percentage of the costs of the completed work each month to provide for the requirements of lien statutes, or to provide security for the owner, or to create an incentive for the contractor to perform the contract. In times of tight money, the cost of financing a job often becomes critical, especially for smaller construction companies. In all contracts in which the contractor has an investment there is a cost of financing that is a job overhead cost.

Financing a contract sometimes gives rise to a practice known as "front end loading," or an "unbalanced bid." This practice gives a contractor the opportunity to try to get overpayments from the owner in the first months of the contract, so that the owner is effectively financing his job and the contractor has to put in less of his own money. This loading is incorporated in a stipulated sum contract by submitting a schedule of values[18] to the designer before the first interim payment for work is made, with the earlier items of work over-valued and the later items undervalued. In a unit price contract, the unit prices for the earlier terms of work are inflated, and unit prices for later items are deflated, so that the total estimated cost is still competitive. Many designers are aware of these practices, and try to circumvent them by not approving schedules of values that contain items of work that are over-valued. This means that a designer must have reliable cost information about the costs of the work in a contract, such as an accurate estimate prepared by himself or by a cost consultant, to guard against front end loading.

A contractor has to allow for the cost of some financing on most jobs, and so do the subcontractors and sub-subcontractors. In fact, the contractor does not carry all the financing costs, only those costs relative and proportionate to the cost of those parts of the job done by the contractor's own forces. The rest of the financing costs are incurred by the subcontractors and their sub-subcontractors, each according to the value

of his subcontract. And in some contracts the subcontractors may have proportionately higher financing costs than the contractor, simply because they receive their payments through the contractor, who may find reasons and excuses to hold onto their money. Likewise, sub-subcontractors may suffer at the hands of subcontractors. Some prime contracts (between owner and contractor) contain provisions to ensure proper and timely payments to subcontractors, because it is usually in the owner's interests that the subcontractors be fairly treated.

It should be pointed out that a large proportion of the interim financing required during most construction jobs comes from the suppliers who extend credit to the general and specialist construction companies who are their customers. The cost of this credit is included in the prices of the materials supplied, and it is, therefore, passed on to the owner.

Finally, we must not overlook the effective interim financing contributed on every job by the workmen, who are also paid in arrears.

General Requirements include:

1. Schedules and reports
2. Samples
3. Shop drawings
4. Temporary facilities
5. Cleaning up
6. Closing out.

Sometimes these requirements duplicate some of those in the general conditions and some refer to costs that are attributable to specific items of work rather than to job overhead costs.

Schedules and reports may include: critical path schedules, sometimes prepared by specialist consultants; site photographs periodically taken to record progress and work to be covered and concealed; and inspection reports of completed work obtained and paid for by the contractor.

Samples and shop drawings are usually required for specific items of work and are, therefore, part of their costs. They are usually for work done by subcontractors, who therefore provide them.

Temporary facilities may be any number of different things to be provided by a contractor for performing the work, and might include:

1. Temporary offices, stores, and facilities for staff and workmen
2. Temporary means of communication, such as telephone, telex, and electronic devices

---

[18] The "schedule of values" is an analysis of the contract sum showing the value (costs) of the various parts of the work and is submitted by the contractor to the designer for his approval before the first contractual payment for work is made.

3. Temporary services, including water, electric power, gas, and drainage; also, temporary heating and ventilation for the building while work is in progress

4. Temporary roads and site drainage

5. Temporary building enclosures for winter work

6. Temporary screens, fences, walkways, and signs

7. Temporary security and safety precautions, such as barricades, lights, and security services

8. Temporary parking and access facilities on the adjoining property of others.

Temporary offices, sheds, and other structures may be either owned or rented by the contractor. Either way, they should be charged to the job in much the same way as any other item of plant. Similarly, the means of communication, and such things as temporary fences, screens, barricades, and heaters, may be either rented or owned. They are usually charged to the job on a "time basis" and include the costs of transporting them to and from the site and of erecting and dismantling them. Costs for these items can be established in the same way as plant and equipment costs.

Temporary services, such as water and electric power, are charged according to current consumption rates, plus costs of permits, installing, and removing meters, pipelines, wiring, and the like. Heating and lighting a building during construction, either by temporary heaters and lights or by using the building's permanent services once they are installed, can constitute a large job overhead cost that is not always easy to estimate because it depends on variable climatic conditions. Experience from previous jobs done under winter conditions, preferably in the same locality, is invaluable to the estimator in these cases.

Cleaning up the site and the building and disposing of rubbish is a continuing expense. Costs may include: labor; rental of bins from a disposal company; and rental of rubbish chutes, incinerators, and other plant and equipment, such as hoists and trucks. It is not uncommon for these costs to be underestimated or overlooked in an estimate.

The costs of cutting and patching to make it possible to integrate the work of subcontractors might be included in this classification. To a large extent, this work is made the responsibility of the various subcontractors, but it is not always possible for the contractor to delegate it all.

Closing out costs might include: drawings and diagrams of services and concealed work as executed by the contractor, permanent bench marks, boundary marks, survey monuments, and similar items; also, the costs of repairs, correcting defects, and any maintenance work required by the contract might be included. Final cleaning of the building, preparatory to occupation by the owner, is included in the general requirements in some specifications. A better practice is to make this work, which is often done by janitorial and maintenance firms, the subject of a separate section of the specifications and a subcontract.

Because job overhead costs are usually referred to in the articles of the agreement and the general conditions of a contract, and in the general requirements of the specifications, it is important that an estimator should carefully read and understand these parts of the bidding documents, as well as the trade sections of the specifications and the drawings. A common fault is to assume that these contractual requirements are always typical and the same as were required for previous jobs. Also, it should be remembered that contract documents do not indicate all general requirements for the work. Usually, only those of direct interest to the owner and to the designer are specified, and the contractor must decide for himself what other things may be necessary. For example, general requirements for winter work may not be explicit in a contract; but, they may be implicit, in that the performance and completion of the work according to the contract's requirements may make temporary enclosures and heaters essential.

Operating overhead costs. Operating overhead costs[G] are those costs that cannot be attributed to any particular job. It is characteristic of these costs that they are incurred by a construction company whether or not it is actually doing construction work. They are often known as "head office overheads;" but this term may be misleading, and the term "operating overhead costs" is more descriptive of the costs of operating a construction business, as distinct from the costs of running specific construction jobs.

The detailed analysis of operating overhead costs is not usually part of an estimator's duties. It is usually the duty of a construction firm's accountant to provide the estimator with the necessary information so that a proper and adequate provision for these costs can be included in each estimate. The accountant has to predict the annual operating overhead costs and the (dollar) volume of work that the company will do in each coming year. These two amounts will then enable him to calculate the theoretical percentage allowance to be made in each estimate to provide for the operating overhead costs. If the company does not do the predicted amount of work, then these costs may have to be taken out of an already diminished profit. For example, if the predicted costs for the next year are:

Operating overhead costs	$ 600,000.00
Volume of work	$20,000,000.00

the percentage allowance for these costs in estimates for projects to be done in the next year would have to be:

$$\frac{\$600,000 \times 100}{\$20,000,000} = 3 \text{ percent}$$

If at the end of the year the company has done only a $15,000,000 volume of work, with all estimates containing a 3 percent allowance for operating overhead costs, only $450,000 may have been obtained toward these costs, and the remaining $150,000 will have to come out of profits. Some firms may apply different percentages to labor costs and material costs to allow for overhead costs in their estimates, because jobs with higher labor costs often require higher overhead costs. Other methods of allowing for operating overhead costs are used, but probably the most common is a percentage addition to the total of all costs of the work.

Operating overhead costs may include:

1. **Management and staff**
   a. Salaries, fringe benefits, and expenses
   b. Transportation (to job sites)
   c. Other expenses attributable to staff and not chargeable to a specific job.
2. **Business offices**
   a. Rent (or depreciation and operating costs of owned premises)
   b. Office furniture and equipment (leasing costs or depreciation allowances)
   c. Office supplies and consumable stores
   d. Other such expenses attributable to the operation of the company but not attributable to a specific construction job.
3. **Communications**
   a. Telephone, telex, and the like
   b. Promotion and advertising.

These overhead costs are not very different from those of any other company in business, and more information about them can be found in many general texts on modern business.

In summary, we have seen that overhead costs are of two basic types: (1) those that are attributable to a specific job, and (2) those that are not; and that the distinction between these two types of overhead costs is not always clear and fixed.

In a stipulated sum contract, the owner is not concerned with the details of these costs, whereas a contractor can usually identify a job overhead cost as a cost arising out of a particular job, as distinct from an operating overhead cost. In a cost-plus-fee contract, the distinction between these two basic types of overhead costs becomes very important to both the owner and the contractor, and a subject for proper definition in the contract. This importance issues from the fact that the job overhead costs are paid directly by the owner as part of "cost;" that is, they are *reimbursable costs*[G] as defined in the contract. The operating overhead costs, on the other hand, are not reimburseable costs and come out of the "fee" paid to the contractor. If "cost" is loosely defined in the contract, the contractor may be able to charge to "cost" (for direct payment by the owner) certain costs that normally should be operating overhead costs payable by the contractor out of his "fee."

"Cost" is generally defined in the standard forms of cost-plus-fee contracts. But, as we have seen, construction jobs produce unique, not standard, products. Therefore, standard forms of contracts without amendments and supplements are not usually suitable for specific projects. Nevertheless, the standard forms do provide a sound basis for most construction contracts, and their use is to be encouraged in the interest of mutual agreement. By proper use of standard forms, the standard and commonplace can be indicated by specific references, and thus the particular and unusual is made more apparent by spelling it out in the bidding documents unencumbered by repetition of the usual.

Profit

Profit[G] is one of the primary motivations of all business, but it is not always the only one. Many small construction companies exist because the principal prefers to work at construction, and as long as he earns the living he needs and expects he counts his business as a success.

An important aspect of profit is that it is one measure of the efficiency and success of a company, but it is not always easy to apply. A "break-even point" is reached when total income reaches total expenditure, and after that point further income is a profit. But how is profit to be measured and expressed?

A distinction must be made between *profit*[G] and *profitability*.[G] Profit is the difference between total income and total expenditure, and is stated in dollars, or in any other currency. Profitability is a better measure of business efficiency and success, and is, perhaps, best stated as a return on investment. It must be emphasized that net profit and profitability are determined by deducting all expenditure from all income. This means, among other things, deducting from income proper salaries for the principals of the company, even if the company is a small one-man operation. Otherwise, the excess of income over expenditure will be false, and a true picture of profit and profitability will not emerge.

Profitability as a return on investment indicates the measure of business success, if we accept the premise that business is undertaken for the purpose of profit. If no investment were made in a business, the available capital could be invested in stocks or bonds to produce a profit. If, instead, the capital is invested in a construction business, then a profit should be produced commensurate with the amount of capital invested and the risk of doing business. How much profit, or what degree of profitabilty, is necessary? Several ratios are used by Dun and Bradstreet, Ltd., business consultants, to examine the economic health of many lines of business, including construction. These ratios include: (1) current assets to current debts; (2) current year profit on tangible net worth; (3) sales to tangible net worth; (4) sales to inventory; (5) fixed assets to tangible net worth; (6) current debt to tangible net worth; and (7) total debt to tangible net worth. The ratio of "current year profit on tangible net worth" is described by Dun and Bradstreet, thus:

> Tangible net worth is the equity of stockholders in the business, as obtained by adding preferred and common stock plus surplus (less deficits) and then deducting intangibles. The ratio is obtained by dividing Profits by Tangible Net Worth. The tendency is to look increasingly to this ratio as a final criterion of profitability. Generally, a relationship of at least 10 percent is regarded as a desirable objective for providing dividends plus funds for future growth.[19]

---

[19] *Key Business Ratios*, Dun and Bradstreet, Ltd.

MARKET CONDITIONS

It would be wrong to give the impression that all estimates and bids for construction work are simply made up of costs of labor, materials, equipment, job overhead costs, and operating overhead costs, all estimated from determined facts and calculated probabilities, and with a profit margin precisely computed according to current economic indicators. In fact, there are other things that at times may have a greater influence on the amount of a bid than any variations of those costs just cited, and the most important of these is the demand for construction work.

There are times when a construction company, having bid for several projects in succession, finds that it has all the work that it needs for the next year, or longer. There are other times when a construction company with an inescapable operating overhead is without work to pay for those costs of being in business. At such times as these, bids are often submitted in ways that appear at the time to be the most expedient under the circumstances.

When work is scarce, bidders may completely omit profit from their estimates, hoping to obtain a contract that will at least help to pay for some of the operating overhead costs and enable the company to avoid the loss of key staff. At such times, owned plant and equipment may not be fully charged for in the estimate in an effort to be competitive, other proper charges may not be made, and greater risks than usual may be taken.

When work is abundant, at least adequate profits are included in bids, and sometimes jobs are obtained despite an unusually high profit margin allowed, because there was little competition. Then, all costs are included in the estimate, and allowances for contingencies that have been included are sometimes found to be unnecessary, thus producing additional profits.

Perhaps the biggest problem for the construction industry is the erratic flow of work—a matter of feast or famine—in part because of the unique nature of the industry and its custom-designed products. Part of the solution, therefore, lies in the development of industrialized building systems and in the prefabrication of more standard building components and whole buildings so as to enable more of the work to be done in factories away from the sites.

QUESTIONS AND TOPICS FOR DISCUSSION

1. Who shares with the *contractor* in determining the costs of the work to the *owner*, and who also shares the risk in doing the work for a stipulated sum? Explain precisely how and why.

2. Name and briefly explain the primary factors that affect the costs of construction materials.

3. Describe a type of discount or rebate, in addition to trade discounts and cash discounts.

4. Explain the meaning of the term *labor rate* and the difference between *labor* rate and *wage* rate.

5. Describe the fundamental difference between the *owning costs* and *operating costs* of construction equipment.

6. What is usually the biggest single cost of equipment? Explain briefly how it can be calculated for estimating purposes.

7. Define *overhead costs*, generally.

8. Explain how and why a *job overhead cost* on one job might be classed as an *operating overhead cost* on another job and give an example to illustrate your answer.

9. Explain the statement "Financing is a job overhead cost."

10. What is the difference between *profit* and *profitability*, and how are they measured?

11. If a contractor bids for twelve jobs before he gets one, who pays for the costs of bidding for the eleven that were not obtained, and how?

12. Which general developments can make estimating more of a science, and why?

13. Who is usually the first to determine the costs of a construction project, and how?

14. Explain briefly how the *shape* and *size* of a building can affect its costs.

15. Explain briefly why higher buildings usually cost more to build than lower buildings of equal capacity.

16. What are the primary external factors that help to determine the materials and methods of construction in a building, beyond the persons directly involved?

17. Explain the significance of *costs in use* to an owner.

18. Compare the costs of painting a concrete wall every 5 years over a building's life of, say, 50 years, to the cost of covering the wall with ceramic tiling when it is first built. What are the advantages and disadvantages of both approaches?

19. Why do some landlords abandon the apartment buildings that they own?

20. Is it good business to have a service garage rotate the tires on your car if the charge is $6.00 per wheel? Explain your answer by calculations. What is an economical price per wheel for tire rotation?

4

WHAT ARE COST ACCOUNTING AND CONSTRUCTION MANAGEMENT?

A study on manpower utilization in the Canadian construction industry concluded:

> There is a lack of detailed cost information available to most contractors. . . . There was a lack of general organizational planning at the job site.[1]

This statement is generally true, not only in Canada but in other countries as well. Yet if the success of a construction company depends on its ability to obtain work in a competitive market and to make a profit, information and good management are essential, and cost accounting (CA) is one of the means. It was explained in Chapter 2 that CA is necessary to estimating in providing information and data from previous jobs. In addition, CA is essential to good construction management in that it provides the other information needed for planning, scheduling, and controlling work.

Cost accounting in construction has one purpose directed toward three primary ends, one of which is immediate, and the other two, in the future. The purpose of CA is to obtain knowledge and information of construction economics. The three primary ends of CA are:

1. To plan, manage, and control the original job (immediate)
2. To make estimates of the costs of other projects (future)
3. To plan, manage, and control other jobs (future).

The second of the three objectives of CA probably is best understood, because it is the logical answer to the inevitable question: From where does an estimator get the cost data to prepare an estimate? There is only one source of valid data for estimating, and that is past jobs; preferably past jobs estimated by the estimator himself or by his colleagues and performed by the construction company for which he is estimating. Failing that, an estimator may seek guidance from the past experience of others, published in handbooks. But he would probably do better by talking to his

---

[1] David Aird, *Manpower Utilization in the Canadian Construction Industry,* National Research Council, Division of Building Research, Technical Paper No. 156 (Ottawa, Canada, 1963), p. 38.

These were the first two of several conclusions reached after work studies were made on several construction jobs in two major Canadian cities. This pilot study is recommended for its content and as an example of the kind of research needed by the construction industry.

company's foremen and superintendents and using their experience.

There is a fundamental difference between cost accounting as applied in other industries to mass production and cost accounting as applied in construction, and the difference stems from the fact that the products are different. Buildings are unique and complex and their construction takes months or years, whereas the products of most other industries are mass produced in a relatively short time. A week's production on a construction site may be hardly perceptible, whereas a week's production of units in a factory may be counted in tens, hundreds, or thousands. But, as construction moves from the site into the factory, so the methods of management, including cost accounting, will need to change. It is work at the construction site that makes construction (and its cost accounting) so different.

FUTURE ESTIMATES THROUGH
COST ACCOUNTING

A simple, hypothetical example explains the application of CA to one item of work by a construction company; and similarly, CA can be applied by a construction company to many items of work in a job to obtain data for future estimates. This may be done by a company's estimator, or it may be done by a cost accountant in the company who will pass on the results of his work to the estimator. It is obvious that if it is done by a cost accountant he must understand estimating and work closely with the estimator.

Looking at the example in Fig. 4-1, and comparing *actual quantities and costs* with *estimated quantities and costs*, the amount of concrete used and placed is more than the estimated amount. This should lead to a check of the estimated amount taken from the contract drawings. If the 600 CY is found to be correct, the next step is to look for a reason at the site. The foreman's explanation may be that such an increase is not unusual, because spillage usually occurs and because forms sometimes bulge and expand. If similar results continue to appear on other jobs done by the company, the estimator must make some allowance for this increase, or waste,[G] in his future estimates. This can be done by adding a percentage allowance to the future measured concrete quantities (e.g., 600 CY + 3% = 618 CY). But the better way is to keep the measured quantity as a ''net quantity'' of 600 CY (the amount required by the contract) and *to add a 3 percent allowance for waste to the unit price*. The prime cost[G] of the concrete of $50.00 per CY is also recorded. In this way, all facts are retained and the

quantities required by the contract are not obscured by estimated allowances for waste. Instead, waste is allowed for in the unit price as a variable to be determined for each job, based on experience.

In the case of actual labor costs, a total of $6,180.00 has been charged for this item of work, which would give a unit price of $10.00 per CY ($6,180.00 ÷ 618 CY), based on a gross quantity of 618 CY. But based on the net quantity of 600 CY (the amount required by the contract), the unit price is $10.30 per cubic yard, and this is the unit price to be recorded for future estimates.

If no conditions or circumstances can be found that might have caused an increase in the labor costs, it must be assumed that the labor costs were underestimated and the actual costs recorded. If similar results are found on other jobs, then it will be necessary to increase unit prices for this item in future estimates.

If the unit prices used in the estimate (in the example) were originally established by CA on several previous jobs, it is unlikely that the unit prices would be changed in future estimates because of higher costs on only one job. But a warning signal has appeared that should be heeded, and special attention should be given to this item on other jobs so that if a change in a unit price is necessary, it is not made too late and after serious losses have occurred.

This example is simply to illustrate the method. Actual unit prices of all major items should be recorded by construction firms, and with sufficient data a mean price can be established together with upper and lower limits (established mathematically by the use of standard deviations) to provide a practical guide for the estimator in pricing. Unit prices and unit rates for labor costs are most important, because labor productivity is the most difficult factor of construction costs to estimate.

Unit rates[G] (calculated from unit prices) are the better form in which to record this data in order to avoid the changing effect of increases in wage rates, as shown in the last example, especially when wage rates are variable. Unit rates are expressed in man-hours per production unit (e.g., 0.75 man-hour per cubic yard of concrete placed in footings).

MANAGEMENT THROUGH COST
ACCOUNTING

Referring again to the example in Fig. 4-1, a more immediate use of CA information can be seen by comparing estimated and actual costs. In the example, the comparison shows a loss on this item of work at completion. This is useful but expensive knowledge, which should be used in the future to avoid a repetition. If

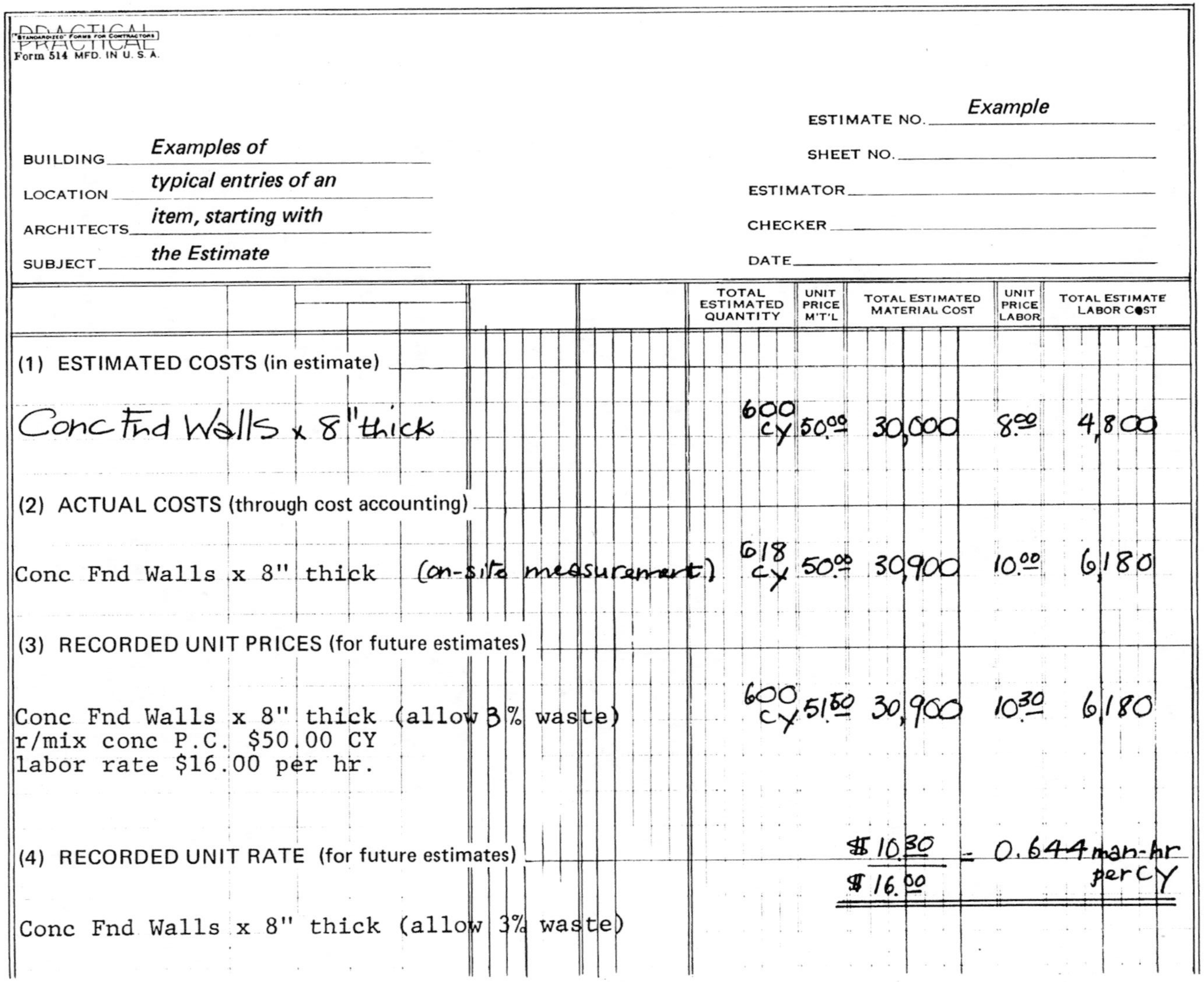

PRACTICAL "Standardized" Forms for Contractors
Form 514 MFD. IN U. S. A.

BUILDING *Examples of*
LOCATION *typical entries of an*
ARCHITECTS *item, starting with*
SUBJECT *the Estimate*

ESTIMATE NO. *Example*
SHEET NO.
ESTIMATOR
CHECKER
DATE

	TOTAL ESTIMATED QUANTITY	UNIT PRICE M'T'L	TOTAL ESTIMATED MATERIAL COST	UNIT PRICE LABOR	TOTAL ESTIMATE LABOR COST
(1) ESTIMATED COSTS (in estimate)					
Conc Fnd Walls x 8" thick	600 CY	50.00	30,000	8.00	4,800
(2) ACTUAL COSTS (through cost accounting)					
Conc Fnd Walls x 8" thick (on-site measurement)	618 CY	50.00	30,900	10.00	6,180
(3) RECORDED UNIT PRICES (for future estimates)					
Conc Fnd Walls x 8" thick (allow 3% waste) r/mix conc P.C. $50.00 CY labor rate $16.00 per hr.	600 CY	51.50	30,900	10.30	6,180
(4) RECORDED UNIT RATE (for future estimates)			$10.30 / $16.00	= 0.644 man-hr per CY	
Conc Fnd Walls x 8" thick (allow 3% waste)					

FIGURE 4-1 Estimated and actual quantities and costs of concrete foundation walls: an example.

a loss is incurred at the outset in placing concrete in foundation walls, it would be better to know before all the concrete is placed so that, if possible, losses might be minimized by reorganizing the work. Costs of major items of work of several days duration can often be controlled in this way so that probable losses are avoided or potential losses reduced, if CA is done on a daily basis. This is only possible with major items because minor items of work are usually completed before any warnings can be heeded. But the major items are the very items most in need of control and attention, because an estimating mistake in those items may cause serious financial loss.

In the above example of concrete foundation walls, if all the concrete is placed over a period of, say, three days, 200 CY may have been placed after the first day. The amount is easily ascertained from delivery tickets.[2] The unit rate for labor placing the 200 CY of concrete can be calculated by dividing the day's labor costs chargeable to this item by the total quantity placed. A resultant unit rate of more than that estimated will indicate that something is wrong, either with the work or the estimate. The work methods should be reviewed by the superintendent immediately, and before the next concrete is placed. The reason for the higher labor costs might be that the labor crew is too large, or that there is a delay between the arrival and departure of ready-mixed concrete delivery trucks, or some other such cause. If no improvement can be made in work methods, the discrepancy must be assumed to be in the estimate. At least, the question has been raised and, if work methods can be improved before more concrete walls are placed, losses might be minimized on this job and eliminated on other jobs, and more competitive bids and larger profits may be possible in the future.

This example illustrates a simple comparison made by a construction firm between the estimated and actual costs of one item of work. But before such a comparison can be made, actual cost data must be obtained; and if the item of work is not complete (and an interim comparison is desired before completion), the amount of work actually done to date must be measured. *This is the substance of construction cost accounting: actual costs properly allocated to the right items of work, and known quantities of work completed for those costs.*

So far, only cost data for estimating and cost control have been discussed. Before work starts, a construction job should be planned and scheduled to achieve the highest possible degree of efficiency; and

whichever planning method is used, information is necessary. Each part of the work must be assessed for its duration; its materials, labor, and equipment requirements; and for its time relationship to other parts of the work. If any part of the work or any activity on the job is critical to completion of the job, this should be known at the outset. It should be given special attention in planning and scheduling, because the start of activities always depend on the completion of certain critical, earlier activities. Hence the development of the *critical path method* (CPM)[G] of scheduling the activities that make up a job. Information required for CPM and for any other planning and scheduling methods can be obtained from the estimate.

For example, in Fig. 4-1, the estimate of the item "conc fnd walls" contains a labor cost of $4,800.00. With a crew of three laborers (placing concrete directly from a ready-mix truck), each man costing $16.00 per hour, the above amount represents a crew time of 100 hours. Obviously, the total time allocated for this item of work in any schedule must be the same as the total time allowed in the estimate. In other words, if the work can be planned so that three such crews (of three laborers) can place concrete foundation walls at the same time, four days should be allowed for this activity in the schedule. But, it is not simply a matter of arithmetic. Nine workers may be too many in a particular location. If three is the practical crew size, then that item of work will require 100 hr (say, 13 days) in the job schedule.

After that example and explanation of cost accounting (CA) it may be incredible to hear that many, perhaps a majority, of contracting companies do little or no formal cost accounting. (By "formal" we mean through an established cost accounting system, but not necessarily computerized.) Some kind of CA is almost always done, as it is not possible to estimate with reason without resorting to some kind of CA; but the kind of CA most often done is "informal," that is, without a proper CA system, often simply by looking at past job estimates as a guide, or even relying on memory for unit prices related to past jobs.

Some say that every project is unique, so it is of little use to attempt CA, as the unit rates and unit prices of one job cannot apply to another. Another argument against formal or systematic CA says that it cannot be justified because the costs of doing CA exceed its value. This is difficult to demonstrate or prove. Both these arguments have some validity, so let us consider each one further.

Every construction project is unique, but in any locality this does not entirely do away with the similarities in productivity and costs among the same basic items of work on different job sites. Certainly there

---

[2] But with one reservation: delivery tickets have been known to be falsified, and periodic verification is necessary.

will be variations among unit rates and unit prices, but often the variations are not so great as to obliterate the similarities. (Briefly, the reasons are clear: in any locality contracting competitors draw their resources from the same sources and compete in the same market.) In any event, how else is an estimator to estimate productivity and such things as waste, shrinkage, and swell? Comparisons among jobs is the only way open; there is no other. This first argument against CA (based on the uniqueness of projects) is fundamentally invalid and contrary to commonsense. Let us look at the next argument against CA.

Given the nature of office systems and bureaucracies generally, there is always a risk that a system such as one for CA will lead to excessive overhead costs so as to outweigh the value of the information and data obtained. Recognizing that risk means that care must be taken to avoid its realization. A CA system must be efficient and effective. To be that, among other things, it must be directed at the proper target and it must be simple, as exemplified in Chapter 12, *Cost Accounting Practices*.

The proper target for CA is the small minority of critical major items of work in any project; the minority of items which bears the greater part of the costs, as indicated by the 80/20 Rule:

> Eighty percent of the costs of a project are created by 20 percent of the items.

(Some may use different figures and call it by another name, such as the 90/10 Rule, but the message is essentially the same.)

The target for CA is that "20 percent" of the total number of items; those that substantially make up a job, and not the multiplicity of minor items whose cost, even when combined, have a much less affect on the job's total costs. Therefore, if we aim at the right target, CA has to deal with only a small minority of items in a job.

The need for simplicity in CA in part derives from the fact that CA is first, a job for a site superintendent, or for foremen under his direction, and from the typical distaste for "paperwork" of most site personnel. Generally and typically, construction site personnel are practical people who have learned and worked in a construction trade; they are artisans who work primarily with their hands. This does not mean, by any means, they are not intelligent or that they cannot use figures; it probably does mean that the use of the written word (or even the written figure in large quantities) is not their choice of occupation; consequently, often they are not comfortable with paperwork; often they share that frequently accurate viewpoint

that clerical work is not very productive. Therefore, in CA there must be, for it to be successful, a minimum of paperwork required, and that paperwork required should be concise and clearly objective. In addition, it is essential to include in the job descriptions for superintendents and foremen that a part of CA is unavoidably part of their responsibility: that done at the site.

The primary ends of CA were stated above: to plan, manage, and control immediate and future jobs, and to make future estimates. Let us examine these in more detail. First, their fundamental requirements are all the same: data and information. (Read the definitions of these two terms in the Glossary. They are not the same thing, except in loose parlance.) Information comes first and it is identifiable with a particular source. When added to other similar information from other sources it becomes data, particularly after it has been analyzed and classified. Both information and data are essential in construction management.

Construction management includes: (1) estimating, (2) planning, and (3) controlling work (see Fig. 5-1). Each of these three main sequential phases of construction requires data and information: (1) estimating, to arrive at costs of work based in part on past cost experience; (2) planning, to get ready to do the work; and (3) controlling the work to ensure that the work is done according to the estimate and the plans made and as required by the construction contract. Aird's Report showed that there was generally a lack of planning on construction sites, and that this arose mainly from a lack of information about the work to be done.

Contract drawings and specifications in a lump-sum contract show much of the information needed for a project to be built, but not all of it. They show only that which the owner and the designer think is necessary. The rest has to be supplied by the contractor. Initially, a contractor has to bring to an estimate a lot of experiential information (information gained through experience). For example, construction drawings may show cast-in-place concrete foundations (footings and walls), their dimensions, extent, and locations. The designer has determined these requirements as part of the design; they are part of the design information. Nothing, however, is shown in the drawings about the formwork required to build the foundations (except the concrete itself); that is left up to the contractor, who must provide it from his experience with formwork; his experiential information about formwork and its costs is needed to add to the design information to complete the entire information needed to perform the contract's requirements.

In a lump-sum (fixed-price) contract, an owner is not concerned with exactly how the work is done and how the contract is performed, provided that the results required by the contract are produced (i.e., the contract is performed). Construction drawings therefore typically show only that with which the owner (and his designer) is concerned: the general design of the building and the work it contains. Construction documents are not exhaustive; they leave a lot to the imagination and experience of the builder.

Estimating involves translating contractual design information (drawings and specifications) into measured and described quantities of work and into items describing job overhead costs; it also involves supplementing that design information provided with the required experiential information, which includes productivity rates and costs. Most of the information created in an estimate will have other uses if the bid derived from the estimate is successful.

Planning work involves further translation of information in an estimate into other useful information for:

1. Planning and scheduling the work
2. Budgeting the contract's finances
3. Obtaining the resources (labor, materials, and equipment) needed to do the work in the amounts and at the times required (purchasing, hiring, renting, and resource scheduling).

Planning and scheduling require items of work in the job estimate to be rearranged (divided or combined) into activities. Activity times are already embodied in the estimate in the form of unit rates, unit prices, and calculated costs of labor and equipment. These costs have to be converted back into hours of labor and equipment time so that the durations of activities in the plan and schedule can be calculated.

Budgeting requires information about time and costs from both the estimate and the schedule to be plotted on a graph that will show month by month during the project's course how much money will be required for the work, and what the income and expenditures will be progressively throughout the project's duration. From this result, the financing needs of the job and the costs of financing the work can be calculated. (This should have been done in an approximate form while making the estimate.)

Obtaining the needed resources first requires a schedule showing the job's need for resources at different times throughout its duration: how much labor of different skills will be needed and when; how much material of different kinds, and how much equipment; each according to the estimate and the schedule.

All of this information must be found in (1) the project's contract documents; (2) the related experience of the contractor and his staff; and (3) the project's estimate. All of these exist before the construction contract is made. All of these constitute the only sources of information to perform the contract. All except the first (the contract documents) are used in cost accounting. Along with the estimate, cost accounting is the basis of construction management.

Construction management is getting construction work done within the particular constraints of contract, time, budget, weather, and all those other things that may hinder performance. Cost accounting (CA) is the link between estimating (that got the job in the first place, and established the primary constraints: time and budget) and construction management. CA is on the other side of the coin from estimating. Some (especially accountants) prefer to call it "job costing" because it involves applying actual costs to a job; but most construction people call it cost accounting, or accounting for costs. In other words, at the end of a job we should know: (1) total income from that job, and (2) total expenditures arising from that same job. The latter is not as obvious as the former, but sometimes even the former is obscure. Consider formwork, for example. (It is often one of the best examples because of its unique nature and its unique relationship to construction.)

Let us suppose that formwork for a multistoried reinforced-concrete building is fabricated from new materials (form ply and lumber) on the building site. The forms are used as the building rises floor by floor. At completion of the concrete work the forms are removed to storage because they can be used again. (Let us suppose that they have generally been used thirteen times, and their potential is for 26 uses; they are 50 percent depreciated.) Properly, the project for which they were originally made should not be charged with all of their fabrication costs (of labor and material), but only with about half of those costs; the exact amount depending on certain other facts not important to our example. The point of the example is to illustrate that cost accounting requires:

1. Actual costs properly accounted and chargeable to a job to be allocated to specific items of work (e.g., labor and material costs and costs of tools and equipment related to fabrication, erecting, stripping, and repairing and cleaning forms);
2. An accurate estimate including measured quantities of work (e.g., contact areas of different kinds of formwork) and estimated costs with which actual costs are to be compared;

3. A knowledge of construction materials and methods (e.g., of formwork) that enables requirements 1 and 2;

4. An understanding of cost accounting and its significance, and an understanding of the economics of cost accounting that makes it possible, effective, and worthwhile.

Given the first three items, the fourth (and perhaps the rarest) is assisted by the use of a microcomputer and suitable software.

QUESTIONS AND TOPICS FOR DISCUSSION

1. What are the primary purposes of *cost accounting*?

2. What is the best form in which to record data of labor productivity for the various *items of work* in a construction job?

3. Explain briefly how *cost accounting* can sometimes help a contractor to avoid or reduce a loss on a construction job.

4. How does an estimate of the *costs of work* directly relate to a schedule for the *work*?

5. Draw a diagram to show the *estimating and cost accounting cycle*, indicating the main construction management functions within the *three* primary phases of the cycle.

6. What is the *initial function* that precedes data processing in construction estimating and management, and why cannot it be done by a computer?

7. What is the primary advantage to an estimator in having a computer system, and why? Is there a disadvantage?

8. If *cost accounting* shows, at the end of a work day, that the first fifty cubic yards of a concrete retaining wall (containing a total of 200 yards) have cost more to place than was allowed in the estimate, what possible conclusions might be drawn?

9. Explain in detail how information from an estimate can be utilized in any one of the essential parts of the management of a construction project.

10. If *cost accounting* accounts for the *costs of work* done, what other information about the *items of work* is essential to make the costs meaningful?

11. Why is cost accounting in the *construction industry* essentially different from cost accounting in most other industries?

12. Discuss the *economics of cost accounting*. How can cost accounting be justified economically?

13. Explain the relationship between a project's *estimate of costs* and its *schedule*.

14. Explain why *cost accounting* can be valuable even though it may be less detailed and less comprehensive than the *estimate* it follows.

5

COMPUTERS IN CONSTRUCTION

This chapter has these primary purposes: (1) to introduce the reader to microcomputers, to computer programs (software) used for estimating and cost accounting, and to the ways in construction in which computers can be used; (2) to help readers who are thinking of using computers for estimating and cost accounting in selecting a way to proceed; and (3) to show that while computer technology has advanced immensely in the last decade the construction industry has yet to make the same kind of progress in using computer systems. To these ends, an example of estimating and cost accounting by computer from the first edition of this book (published in 1974) is included, followed by descriptions of typical currently available computer systems for construction applications.

As to the extent of computer use in construction, without a national survey it is not possible to say. Certainly, we can safely say that in terms of numbers of companies only a minority are using computerized estimating; and probably most that are can be found in the electrical and mechanical trades; especially electrical. There seem to be two main reasons for this last fact: (1) the nature of estimating for these trades, which involves simple measurement (by length and

enumeration), and the making of a schedule of materials as the basis of an estimate; and (2) the relative familiarity of electricians with electronic equipment, so that computers do not intimidate them.

It has been observed that when a contracting company does decide to computerize the first function to be done by a computer is usually general accounting, not estimating. While this is understandable, one must wonder at the logic. General accounting deals with and records a history that was in large part determined by estimating. Estimating, on the other hand, generates work and in part determines profitability; accounting then records it. Logic seems to dictate that the first consideration should be estimating; then cost accounting, as estimating's counterpart; and finally general accounting.

Of computers we may refer to three main classes: (1) mainframe computers (the largest), (2) minicomputers (smaller than the mainframe), and (3) microcomputers (smaller than the minicomputer); but of course somebody will say that these are imprecise terms. The problem is, computer hardware technology is advancing so fast that between writing about it and then reading about it (with about at least a year in between for publication) the written material is more or less out of date. One book, published in 1984, categorizes computers according to size, thus:

> *Microcomputer:* 64k of memory (no longer true)
> *Minicomputer:* from 128k up to more than 1 megabyte of memory (no longer true)
> *Mainframe computer:* more than 4 megabytes of memory.

I have three microcomputers. One (purchased in 1981) has 64k of memory; a true microcomputer. Another purchased a year later of the same make and physical size has 10 megabytes of memory. The third purchased in 1985 has only 640k of memory but the capacity for at least 20 megabytes internally, and an almost unlimited amount externally. Yet all three are undoubtedly microcomputers. So much for definitions. For our present purposes, we can limit our discussion to microcomputers because that is the kind you are most likely to find in a construction office today; simply because microcomputers can store and handle as much or more data than the minis and the mainframes of yesterday; and they are much, much cheaper.

First came the vacuum tube (about 1910), power hungry and heat producing; next the transistor that replaced the tube (in about 1947), a low-power amplifier that was cool; then (about 1960—the exact dates are unimportant to us) came the integrated circuit, small and also cool. In September 1977 it was reported in *Scientific American* (Vol. 237, no. 3, p. 65) that:

> Today's microcomputer, at a cost of perhaps $300, has more computing capacity than the first large electronic computer, ENIAC. It is 20 times faster, has a larger memory, is thousands of times more reliable, consumes the power of a light bulb rather than of a locomotive, occupies 1/30,000 the volume and costs 1/10,000 as much.

Today? Who knows. It is enough to point to the historical facts about computers, because today's comparisons will be outdated and outshone by the time you read them in a textbook. Within the last few years (and in less than a decade) the internal memory of microcomputers has increased ten times at no significant increase in costs. (In 1981 I paid about $1750 for a microcomputer with 64k of memory, and with a lot of software thrown in; in 1985 you can get one with 640k for about the same price.)

So much for the hardware. Do not be overly concerned with it at the outset (technology is boring once you are over the first rush). Software programs are more critical and more exciting because they are the tools that we can use (with a microcomputer as the handle) to do all kinds of things, including estimating and cost accounting.

Software for microcomputers (from now on, simply called here, "computers") that relates to construction estimating and cost accounting is of two main kinds: (1) spreadsheets, and (2) database management systems. Let us examine the fundamental features of each.

Spreadsheets, essentially, consist of nothing more than columns and rows forming a grid of cells (where the columns and rows intersect), just like a sheet of lined paper with columns, and potentially in the same format as an estimating or an accounting sheet with rows and columns; but with an electronic spreadsheet, the widths of the columns are adjustable. The real power and value of a spreadsheet program lies hidden behind the rows and columns: it is the program's ability to manipulate the data put into the spreadsheet's cells by the user. That means the calculating, carrying, analyzing, summarizing, and all the other mathematical functions in estimating. The numbers you put into a spreadsheet can be interrelated in numerous ways. In fact, it was the advent of the first spreadsheet program, VisiCalc, in 1979, that changed the image of the personal computer from a games machine to a business machine. The most common use of spreadsheet programs is generally financial and related to accounting; their potential for estimating has hardly been tapped.

Of electronic spreadsheet programs there are hundreds on the market. The oldest, and still in use in updated versions, is VisiCalc®. The most talked about and perhaps most used is Lotus® 1-2-3®. Of books on spreadsheets there are even more, since each spreadsheet program generates a number of books to supplement the program manuals. Some of these books present the same information found in the manuals but in a different way. Among spreadsheets, the "Big Four" are: Lotus 1-2-3, SuperCalc®, VisiCalc, and Multiplan (each with different versions; seek the most current), but dozens of others may do just as well. It depends on the user's needs and familiarity with computers.

Database management systems (DBMS) are programs designed to store and sort information and to facilitate its retrieval, like an electronic filing system. Again, there are hundreds of these programs available, from the simple "shoebox" type of DBMS to the most famous, dBASE II®, or its updated version, dBASE III®. Some computer users differentiate among DBMSs and call the simple systems simply "filing systems." These store, sort, and let you retrieve. True DBMS, they say, are much more complex and can therefore do many more things under a user's direction.

dBASE III is a relational database, that is, one in which there are relationships among the data stored in the various columns; just as in an estimate. At this point you may wonder: What is the difference between a spreadsheet and a DBMS? They both bear some similarity in potential format to an estimate sheet; what then is the difference?

Spreadsheets are designed primarily to handle figures (amounts; usually of money) and to analyze. Database management systems are designed primarily to handle information (in both words and figures), to organize it, and to enable it to be retrieved in various forms. Both have the ability to produce and print reports. There is some overlapping between spreadsheets and DBMSs. For example, Lotus 1-2-3 has some limited capability as a DBMS, and dBASE III enables calculation so that it can be used for accounting. The differences then are primarily of degree: Lotus 1-2-3 cannot compete with a DBMS such as dBASE III in its ability to be designed in complex ways in order to handle data. Sophisticated DBMSs like dBASE III have built-in programming languages that enable a user to write complex instructions to the DBMS for data handling. Compared to this, Lotus 1-2-3's data management is relatively simple; but it is sophisticated enough to do most ordinary estimating functions. However, it appears (I have no statistics) that most estimating and accounting programs are of the nature of a DBMS (many were written with dBASE II) rather than a spreadsheet; but not all.

Considering estimating using computers, there appear to be the following choices:

1. Buy a dedicated estimating program
2. Write your own estimating program.

Consider the pros and cons: Buy a dedicated estimating program (DEP) and your first problem is, which? Your next problem is learning to use it. To write your own personal estimating program (PEP), you first have to choose a means of writing it, then you have to write it. Let us consider some of the deeper pros and cons, first for a DEP and then for a PEP.

DEDICATED ESTIMATING PROGRAMS

Compared with business accounting programs, there are not many estimating programs available; but then accounting has universal uses while estimating (of our kind) is limited to construction. There are perhaps hundreds of estimating programs available in North America, and hundreds more in other English-speaking countries, especially in England (the original home of the quantity surveying profession). Some are very simple and others are extremely complex. They all appear to have one essential characteristic in common (at least, all that this writer has seen): They emulate the traditional estimating format of the last generation and offer little in the way of innovation arising from the involvement of the computer in a practice for which computers might have been designed. But more about that later.

Among dedicated estimating programs (DEPs) and their origins, there are the following categories: those DEPs that are created with:

1. A computer language (such as BASIC, Pascal, C, or other) and that were written from scratch
2. A DBMS (such as dBASE II or dBASE III) utilizing the inherent programming language of the DBMS (e.g., the Applications Development Language, ADL, of dBASE II)
3. A spreadsheet (such as SuperCalc or 1-2-3 or other) as a template to be used with the proprietary spreadsheet.

Let us consider each of these.

A DEP written in a computer language, probably by an estimator or a cost consultant, with or without the aid of a computer programmer, might be good or bad depending on: who, how, why, and when. Who wrote it? Unless an estimator/cost consultant is also an expert in programming, probably his own DEP will be slow and cumbersome; it may be even practically useless, at least to anybody other than the originator, because it will probably be written in BASIC, and unless compiled (converted to a computer's own machine language) it will be slow. Few estimators/cost consultants are sufficiently expert in programming to do a good job of writing a complex program. Also, it is probable that a purchaser of such a program will have no opportunity to modify the program to his or her own requirements.

A DEP written within a DBMS, on the other hand, may not suffer from the disadvantages just cited. In the first place, it is much easier for a nonprogrammer to learn to write a complex program using a DBMS's own internal language (which is not so far removed from English, and which has the DBMS itself as a foundation). Second, often programs written for special applications (such as accounting, estimating, etc.) are sold for use with a particular DBMS. There are scores, perhaps hundreds, of special-applications programs for use with dBASE II and dBASE III written in the "applications development language" (ADL) of dBASE II and dBASE III, including a number for construction estimating. Also, having written such a program, it is possible to convert the program into the computer language C that will enable the program to operate much more quickly.

Similarly, for estimating, there are programs created to work with spreadsheets, such as 1-2-3 and SuperCalc. They are called templates and consist of a matrix into which have been written the required headings and formulas to provide an estimate format ready to be used. Of course, none of the alternatives discussed so far gives you much more than an outline for an estimate. How could they, considering that which goes into an estimate: descriptions of work, dimensions to be calculated into quantities, and unit prices to be applied to the quantities to give costs of items; all things unique to a particular place and job.

Heck! you may say. Why should I go to all this trouble and expense? I might as well go out and buy a complete estimating program that will do everything. Well, unless your scope of construction work is very limited and you can find a DEP that is specifically designed for that kind of work and contains a comprehensive database (unlikely), you are going to have to do quite a lot of work yourself before you can get a DEP up and running and practically useful. The main reason is, you need a database; and most DEPs do not provide one. At most they usually provide a small and limited model of a database that you can modify for your own needs. Even for house building, the estimating programs that I have seen require considerable modification for several reasons, including: local variations in construction materials and methods across the continent; variations in housing quality and specifications (even in terminology); and variations in the division of work among trades, to name the obvious. And that does not even touch upon the entire area of prices and costs. In other words, buy any kind of DEP and you will have to invest a lot of time in (1) learning it, and (2) creating at least one database for it—more if you deal with a variety of classes of construction work.

Because of the nature of estimating, DEPs generally require the creation of a master file or master estimate (the database) by the user within the framework of the DEP for each major class of work. The master estimate is then used by an estimator like a checklist as items not needed are passed over (and deleted when the estimate is printed) and any new items not already in the master estimate are added. Quantities have to be measured manually, in the old way, and inserted into a modified copy of the master estimate in the computer. When an estimate has been made and used, any new items likely to be used again are included in the original master estimate, which is thus edited every time it is used. Similarly, any items in the original master estimate which are found to be rarely included in job estimates are deleted.

The creation of a master estimate is no light task. For a general contracting company doing a variety of complex nonstandard work a master estimate could cost in time several thousands of dollars to prepare. For a specialist trade contracting company doing mechanical work, the same investment; while for another company doing only drywall work, a master estimate might cost only a few hundred dollars. There is some merit in the concept of a master estimate. The same concept has been used for decades for writing specifications. The master acts as a checklist, thereby helping to eliminate omissions. It grows with use, and can be the basis of, or related to, a cost code used not only in estimating but in cost accounting and other sectors.

A master estimate has another essential use: It naturally becomes the basis for the listing and storage of cost data; the unit rates and unit prices needed to price an estimate, no matter how it is put together. It is here that a master estimate relates to cost accounting through the unit prices and the unit rates derived from them. All of these things should be kept in mind when creating a master estimate. Of course, there is no need to wait until one buys a computer to create a master estimate, or a cost code, or a cost accounting system; and a well-run construction company should already have the basis of these management tools. The question remains: Is a DEP the best choice or is it better to write one's own personal estimating program?

PERSONAL ESTIMATING PROGRAMS

Most will balk at the suggestion that they should write their own estimating program on the grounds of inexpertise with computer systems and a lack of time. Perhaps if they realized the amount of time needed to learn a DEP created by somebody else and to create at least one master estimate to use with it, they might reconsider, especially if they take to heart the following.

Fact: In the last few years, many estimators and cost consultants have written estimating programs without first having any experience of computer systems. Some of these are now being marketed in North America and offshore; others are in limited private use; while many others have not seen the light of a working day. But they were written by novices in computer science.

Fact: One does not have to spend months (years?) learning a comprehensive computer language as if to become a programmer.

The alternative is to use a DBMS such as dBASE II and dBASE III (as have other estimators) and use its internal language (such as ADL in dBASE II and dBASE III). In fact, there are now several supplementary programs that work with such as dBASE II that enable a user to design a format (of an estimate sheet, for example) on a computer screen and to then have the program convert the model on the screen into a program that can be recalled at any time.

Let us not be misled (or misleading) here. There is a lot of time required for a novice to learn enough about a DBMS to write an estimating program that will be useful. But there is a lot of time required whichever way one chooses to computerize the estimating process. The more important questions are: (1) Should you computerize? (2) How should you computerize?

Should you computerize? A difficult question which it is all too easy to answer—wrongly. A glib "yes" or "no" is useless, and considerable thought and research should be given to finding the right answer. The principal (or an officer) of your company first might answer these questions:

1. Do you expect to be in business in five years' time?
2. Do you have to bid competitively for most of your work?
3. Is your work limited to a few main kinds?
4. Is your company employing more than five office staff?
5. Is one of your estimators under 50 years of age?
6. Have you read any books about computers?
7. Is the company prepared to have an employee spend perhaps a total of $10,000 in time to learn to computerize and another $5000 to $10,000 on a microcomputer system?
8. Could you handle more business if it came?
9. Are you dissatisfied with your present estimating and cost accounting methods?
10. Do you or your company possess a library of technical books (no matter how small) that has been added to and used in the past few months?

If you answered "yes" to at least eight questions, you might consider computerization. But the entire subject is really more complicated than can be expressed in a few simple questions, and the answer lies perhaps more in the attitudes of people to change and innovation. Some will resist it, go along in the old way, and survive; others may superficially embrace change, turn to computers and yet never really change their established methods. Sooner or later, computers will be commonplace in all business offices, but computerization is not for everybody, now.

The next question is: How should you computerize? We have all ready set down some of the possibilities, and there are others:

1. Employ a computer consultant (with expertise in construction) to select, customize, and install a system
2. Wait until computerized estimating becomes commonplace, and cheaper.

Employing a consultant may be the most effective way, but not necessarily the most economical. It depends on many things: the quality and costs of the consultant; the alternative abilities (and their costs) within your company; the urgency in your need to computerize; and so on. If you negotiate with a computer consultant: be sure of his ability to set up a system for estimating (accounting experience alone is not enough); do not enter into an open-ended agreement; know your financial commitment, as time required to set up and customize computer systems is more difficult to estimate than time for construction work as there is less experience to call upon.

Software programs for general business accounting vary greatly in quality and cost, and the cheapest, according to reviewers, are not necessarily the lowest in quality. For different accounting functions (general ledger, accounts payable, receivable, etc.) the cost per module for similar capabilities may vary as much as 1000 percent, it appears. Prices for software for such specialized applications are dropping. Many construction software packages still cost thousands of dollars, and while we cannot expect them to match in price those programs for business accounting we can expect better software at lower prices in future. The question is: When? And how long can you afford to wait? Some are still waiting for microcomputers to drop in price and already they are several years behind in their education in computer systems, because the only way to become "computer literate" is to use a computer. Waiting for prices of software or hardware to drop, to save investment money, may not be good business. Compare the figures involved. (The best way to compare them is to use a spreadsheet program!) In the meantime, consider the following information about computer systems and their construction applications.

AN EXAMPLE OF ESTIMATING AND COST ACCOUNTING BY COMPUTER FROM THE SIXTIES

The following description and quotations from a technical brochure entitled, *"Att Databehandla ett Byggnadsprojekt"* (*Using Data Processing on a Building Project*), are given with the permission of the developers of the Quantity Calculator QC-95, the company of Samdata AB, Huvudkontor: Vretenvägen 8, Fack, 171 20 Solna 1, Sweden. This company was formerly known as *Bygg-ADB*, which means in English *Building-ADP* (automatic data processing).

Samdata AB claims that in Sweden many leading contractors use their services and systems, and that they have serviced hundreds of construction jobs. The company has a computer center with divisions for key punching, data processing, programming, systems development, and training. It designs special systems for its clients, and also trains their staffs in the systems. It also provides a key-punching service. The computer center contains an IBM System 360, of the third generation.[1]

Samdata AB explains in its brochure, which is available in English, that:

> Everything is changing. The building industry of the future will look different from that of our time. Computer based systems for building projects (are) today a reality: tomorrow a necessity.
>
> The building industry of tomorrow will require an organization devoted to marketing, prepared to give proposals and offers very quickly. The competition will increase, the bidding periods will be shorter, fast decisions and estimating will be a necessity. The solution is data processing.
>
> Future requirements will be faster deliveries for construction projects, more detailed planning, and more accurate production rates. At the same time, building projects will be more complicated with a greater number of subcontractors, and therefore coordination and more efficient planning will be a necessity.

The lowest price will not always get the contract. In many cases, the construction period will decide the competition. To meet target dates [will be] a necessity. The solution is data processing.

To survive in the building business of tomorrow estimating must be carried out so that it is possible to control the estimates, and so that the project engineers will get faster reports on the progress of the projects; so that any necessary action can be taken. The projects will be larger and more expensive. The risks will increase, and therefore a more advanced technique for cost control will be a necessity. The solution is data processing.

Samdata AB's integrated system is similar to a circle where output data from one routine can be used immediately as input data in the next routine, and where experience from one project is automatically stored and used on future projects.

In the circle [in Fig. 5-1], there are three arrows. If we start at the lower left of the picture, the first arrow represents the estimating phase. The next arrow represents the planning phase, and the third arrow represents the control phase.

Starting with the estimating arrow, the first thing that happens is the quantity survey, which is indicated by the circle lying outside the large circle. All the smaller circles represent programs which Samdata AB uses in its system. The outer circle stands for quantity surveying.[2] The next circle [2] represents the program for pricing the quantities. This program gives, as its output, the final estimate. For cost estimating it is necessary to use stored data on specifications and costs. These data come from the program [1] preceding the circle for cost estimating. This circle is called *"kalkylregister"* (**cost data file**) and represents the programs for updating the standard specifications and standard costs.

In the planning arrow there are four different programs. The first [3], called *"Planeringsunderlag"* (**activity schedule**) represents a technique

---

[1] Remember, this system was operating in the late sixties.

[2] It is significant that the quantity survey is shown outside the "cycle of automatic data processing" and at the beginning. The work of the estimator and the quantity surveyor is interpretive, analytical, and fundamental, and cannot be done by a computer. But the estimator and the quantity surveyor can benefit from the use of tools such as EDP and the quantity calculator to speed up the process of measurement and to record descriptions and measurements of work. (Author's note.)

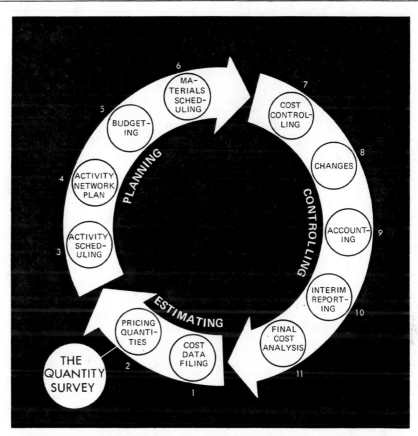

PROGRAMS: (1) COST DATA FILING (Kalkylregister); (2) PRICING QUANTITIES (Kostnads-beräkning); (3) ACTIVITY SCHEDULING (Planerings-underlag); (4) ACTIVITY NETWORK PLAN (Nätverksplan); (5) BUDGETING (Time and Costs) (Tids-ochkostnads-budget); (6) MATERIALS SCHEDULING (Leveransplan); (7) COST CONTROLLING (Littereradförkalkyl); (8) CHANGES IN WORK (Kalkyiandringar); (9) ROUTINE ACCOUNTING (Kostnadsspecification); (10) INTERIM REPORTING (Avstämningsrapport); (11) FINAL COST ANALYSIS (Efterkalkyl).

FIGURE 5-1 Estimating-planning-controlling cycle of construction.

NOTE: The above titles do not appear in the original and have been introduced into this diagram and the text by the author-translator.

for getting production rates and costs for activities in the network diagram which is prepared for the project. The next circle [4] called "*nätverksplan*" (**network plan**) represents the program for network calculations which among many other things, has an advanced technique for resource planning. The two other circles [5 and 6] represent programs for **budgeting** and preparation of **bill of materials.**

Finally, the control arrow consists of five different programs. The first [7] called "*littererad förkalkyl*" is a program for a reorganization of the estimate so that it will fit into the system used for **cost control.** The second program [8] is for **changes in the budget.** The third program [9] is used in cooperation with the **routine accounting** in a con-

tracting company. The fourth circle [10] represents the program for preparing **periodic reports** on the project. And, finally, the last program [11] is for preparing a **cost analysis.** On the basis of this last report the standard costs and standard production rates are updated and entered into the stored register [1] with these data. And so the circle is closed.

Estimating

With the Samdata AB Quantity Calculator QC-95—a unique Swedish product—it is possible to count and measure items directly on the blue-

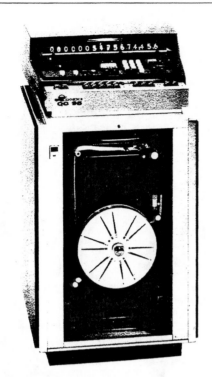

FIGURE 5-2 QC-95 quantity calculator (with paper tape reel).

prints and enter them into a paper tape which then can be fed into a computer for further data processing [see Figs. 5-2 and 5-3].

The Quantity Calculator has many advantages; since the take-off can be speeded up considerably, and most of the handwriting can be eliminated.

Calculations and typing are done automatically by the computer and no extra punching is needed, as this is done by the Quantity Calculator.[3]

With the Quantity Calculator the quantities of a project can be specified into a large number of so-called planning units. This very detailed specification, which can be done in a considerably shorter time than is needed today, makes it possible to use the original estimate for the future planning and control: an important part of the integration idea behind Samdata AB's system. When using the Quantity Calculator for take-off, two pencils are used for counting and measuring the different items on the blue-print. The results of the estimating phase are, first of all, printed

---

[3] "The quantity calculator has three main functions: *measuring, calculating,* and *punching.* These functions can be used together or one at a time.

For the *measuring* there are two special pencils attached directly to the quantity calculator. The first pencil is a sort of tracker with a serrated wheel at the tip and is used to take-off linear distances. The other pencil is used for counting single items and also works as a ballpoint pen so that the items can be marked on the blue-print.

The *calculations* are performed in an electronic desk calculator which can be used either just for calculations, or as a part of the quantity calculator, and, in the latter case, together with the pencils and the punching equipment.

The *punching* is performed by a paper tape punch which also is part of the QC-95. Data to be punched are entered on a special keyboard and the output is an 8-channel paper tape which can then be fed into a computer for further data processing.

To the QC-95 can also be attached a hard copy device so that it is possible to see what is printed on the paper tape."

Nowadays, the calculating function previously done by the QC-95 is performed by a computer without the need for an interfacing hardware device (such as the QC-95) between the input device (electronic pencil, or keyboard) and the computer. Also, the use of paper punch tape has been superseded by hard and floppy disks. The electronic pencil, as described by Samdata AB, is still used today in some systems, but its utility and accuracy is limited and a better device is the sonic digitizer, described on page 63. Nevertheless, the *output* by the Samdata AB system as described here during the sixties is still valid and useful and generally has not been much improved upon, it appears. This indicates that while there have been extensive developments in hardware in the last 20 years there have not been similar developments in software applications for the construction industry. (Author's note.)

FIGURE 5-3 Quantity calculator in use (with electronic pencil).

lists for immediate use; and, second, stored data on magnetic tape for later use in connection with planning and control [see Figs. 5-4 and 5-5].

"Mätprotokollet" is a list showing exactly the **measurements and quantities** registered on the Quantity Calculator.

"Mängd-och kostnadsberäkningen" [**quantity and cost estimate**] is the final estimate for the project, or, if required, a schedule of quantities with the cost figures omitted.

"Kalkylregistret" [**cost data file**] is a document showing all standard specifications and standard costs which are stored on the contractor's tape. It is this document which is used for reference when using the Quantity Calculator. *"Kalkyl-registret"* [**cost data file**] makes it possible to

check and change specifications and prices at any time.

The combination, Quantity Calculator and Data Processing, gives faster take-off and calculations, gives increased accuracy with more reliable prices and more correct calculations, and gives an integration with planning and control through the data stored on the magnetic tape.

Planning

The planning phase is started by drawing up a **Network Diagram** prepared in teamwork by a planning engineer and the foreman on the building site [Fig. 5-6]. In this first phase there are no

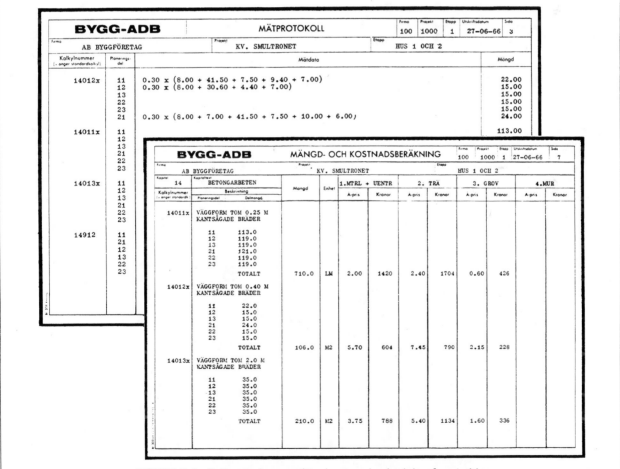

FIGURE 5-4 Estimator's quantity sheet and schedule of quantities sheet.

BYGG-ADB			KALKYLREGISTER FÖR SPECIFIKATIONER OCH SNABBKALKYLER			Firma 100	Utskriftsdatum 27–06–66	Sida 8

Firma: AB BYGGFÖRETAG   A - priser

Kalkylnummer	Produktions-metod	Beskrivning	Enhet	Nr 1.MTRL	Nr 2.TRÄ	Nr 3.GROV	Nr 4.MUR	Nr 5.UENTR	Nr	Nr	Nr
14011		VÄGGFORM TOM 0.25 M KANTSÅGADE BRÄDER	LM	2.00	2.40	0.60					
14012		VÄGGFORM TOM 0.40 M KANTSÅGADE BRÄDER	M2	5.70	7.45	2.15					
14013		VÄGGFORM TOM 2.0 M KANTSÅGADE BRÄDER	M2	3.75	5.40	1.60					
14014		VÄGGFORM ÖVER 2.0 M KANTSÅGADE BRÄDER	M2	3.60	5.20	1.60					
14015		PELARFORM H TOM 0.40 M KANTSÅGADE BRÄDER	M2	10.00	8.80	2.10					
14016		PELARFORM H TOM 0.70 M KANTSÅGADE BRÄDER	M2	10.00	8.80	2.10					
14017		PELARFORM H TOM 2.00 M KANTSÅGADE BRÄDER	M2	10.00	8.80	2.10					
14018		3/4x TREKANTLIST	LM	0.45	0.40	0.05					
14019		RUND PELARFORM DIAM 25	LM	11.50	12.00	2.50					
14020		RUND PELARFORM DIAM 35	LM	12.00	12.00	2.50					
14021		RUND PELARFORM DIAM 50	LM	12.50	12.00	2.50					

FIGURE 5-5 Cost data file sheet. "The three lists shown and described contain entries for wall forms (vägform) and column forms (pelarform) of wood boards, and round column forms. Entries include: the dimensions and quantities; unit prices, and costs of materials; carpenters' time, and laborers' time. The units are linear meters (LM) and square meters (M2)."

time-allowances whatsoever in the diagram. When it comes to the use of network technique in building industry Samdata AB has, for a long time, taken the lead. The experience gained from a large number of projects under different circumstances and for different clients has served as the basis when developing the Samdata AB system.

The estimate and network diagram are linked together so that the quantities and costs of the estimate are distributed over the activities in the network diagram. When doing this, the data earlier

FIGURE 5-6 Preliminary network diagram. "The preliminary network diagram, shown in part, indicates how activities are planned manually before the final schedule is produced by computer."

stored on the magnetic tape are used. The output is the so-called *"Planeringsunderlag"* which is used first, for deciding on the durations of the different activities, and, second, as a tool for the foreman on the building site. [*"Planerings-underlag"* could be called an **"Activity Specification,"** showing in detail the amount of work that has to be carried out under the different activities; see Fig 5-7].

The network diagram is run through a computer; which means that the starting and finishing dates of the various activities are calculated under different conditions so that an efficient use of the available resources is achieved.

The advanced technique for resource planning which has been developed by Samdata AB makes it possible to have the computer determine the

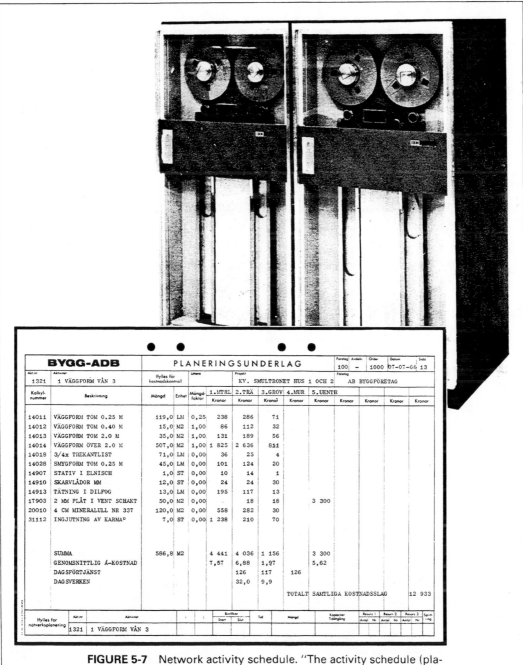

FIGURE 5-7 Network activity schedule. "The activity schedule (planeringsunderlag) shown contains entries for those same items shown in Figs. 5-4 and 5-5, together with other related items of work."

number in the crews on the building site, so that an even manpower level is obtained.

The final network diagram can, in certain cases, be drawn automatically by a lineplotter and gives a very detailed picture of how the planning for the project is carried out [Fig. 5-8].

Control

The collection of data, required for the control of the building project, must be coordinated with the accounting procedures that always exist within a contracting company. A complete integration means that all notations about different data have to be done once only and then are available on the magnetic tapes both for the accounting routines and for the production routines. In the Samdata AB system there are also programs for the accounting routines; but, a description of these is not within the scope of this brochure.

However, . . . Samdata AB has developed . . . programs for invoice handling, machine costs, payrolls and general accounting.

The control results in the so-called *"Avstämningsrapport"* [**periodic report**] which usually is run through the computer once every month. This *"Avstämningsrapport"* gives, for each account, a comparison between estimated and actual costs and also shows completed quantities and actual unit costs and, furthermore, gives a forecast of the expected final costs.

The last *"Avstämningsrapport"* [**periodic report**] for the project is also the final cost analysis. From this report it is possible to get the data about costs and production rates which the contractor wants to enter into his register with standardized specifications and costs.

The circle is thereby closed, and the goal is achieved. This means that, from the existing production, all the necessary information for esti-

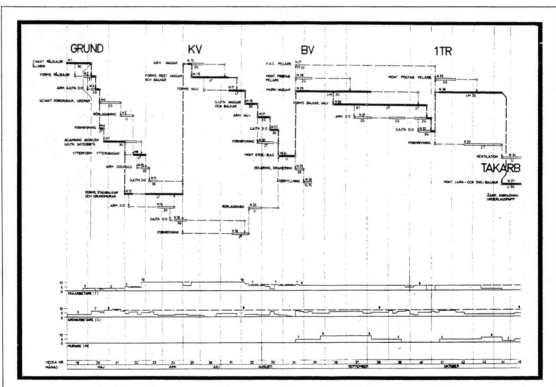

FIGURE 5-8 Final network diagram. "The final network diagram, shown in part, schedules the various work activities, such as forming and pouring concrete walls & beams, and erecting prefabricated columns. It also shows, at the bottom, the scheduled requirements for workmen (carpenters, laborers, and masons), each week, according to the activities."

mating and planning of future projects has been collected.

This description[4] is reproduced because it simply and clearly indicates, even today, over 20 years later, the essential relationships among the several phases of construction management and the importance to construction firms of information and data that can be obtained from estimates and past jobs. But it should not be assumed that this cyclical process of *estimating-planning-controlling* is only possible with the aid of a computer. CPM scheduling, for example, can be done without computers, and much of the facility with which planning and controlling can be carried out depends on the way the estimate has been prepared. Many estimators are aware of this when they measure work in stages (such as floor by floor, for a high-rise building), and an estimate should always be made with other uses beyond the bid in mind.

EXAMPLES OF ESTIMATING AND COST ACCOUNTING BY COMPUTER IN THE EIGHTIES

Most of what we saw above of computer applications to construction, in the example from the sixties, is still up to date in the eighties; but the hardware shown and the medium described (punch tape) is no longer appropriate. Then, it was all that was available: then there were no microcomputers with floppy disks. Now, we can get the same output from microcomputers at a fraction of the cost of the mainframe equipment illustrated. As already indicated, the growth in computer technology over the last decade has been extraordinary; but what of developments in computer applications to construction management? Have they kept up with those of computers? Hardly. We find today that most computer output related to construction management is essentially what was being produced 10 or even 20 years ago. The sole significant exception, computer-aided design (CAD), is unfortunately not directly related to construction management; although it will not be long before microcomputers will be able to automatically convert graphic information (created by CAD) into quantitative information for use in estimating and in management.

In the meantime, progress in developing new estimating systems seems slow. Considering estimating

and its two main parts, (1) measurement and (2) pricing: Almost all computer applications to estimating touch only on pricing, and practically none on measurement, with one promising exception: the sonic digitizer.

The Swedish mainframe hardware illustrated earlier shows an electronic pencil in use for measurement from construction drawings, and such devices have been available for 25 years. They are suitable for linear measurement and for counting, but that is about all. No alternative electronic measurement device for microcomputers has really been successful and popular because of clumsiness and resultant inaccuracy. The sonic digitizer may be the exception. It has, however, one major inhibiting feature.

A sonic digitizer looks like an ordinary pen with a nylon tip, except that it is wired and emits not ink but an electronic "beep" when the point is touched. When set up, the electronic sound is picked up by two elongated microphones fixed at right angles along a horizontal and a vertical edge of a worktable, to which is affixed the construction drawing to be measured. From the location of the digitizer's sound, a "black box" connected to both microphones, the sonic digitizer, and to a microcomputer establishes the "X, Y" coordinates of the point on the drawing touched by the digitizer. When the digitizer touches another point on the drawing, again coordinates are established, and if the digitizer is in a "linear measurement mode," the connected microcomputer prints on its screen the scaled distance between the two points on the drawing.

With the sonic digitizer there is a menu board affixed to the worktable at certain critical coordinates, so that by touching the several grid squares of the menu board an operator can select from various measurement modes, including: counting; linear (point to point); linear tracing (an unstraight line); triangulation (which provides on the screen the measurements of three angles, three sides, and the triangle's area); areas bounded by straight lines; areas bounded by unstraight lines; volumes (areas × depth); and more. From the menu board the operator selects the appropriate scale for the drawing from which measurements are to be taken. There is a function to calibrate between drawing and digitizer to allow for a variation factor in drawing scale due to shrinkage or stretch.

The inhibiting feature of the sonic digitizer is, of course, the need for drawings to be made accurately to scale, as all measurement is scaled from the drawings; which is contrary to customary measurement practice calling for dimensions to be read rather than scaled. Fundamentally, this is not an insurmountable obstacle, as most drawings are reasonably accurate and it would take little significant effort to make and obtain consistently accurate drawings—if the use of sonic digitizers

---

[4] I have not updated or otherwise changed this description of the Swedish system from the sixties, as it is still, in its output, representative of computer applications and output used in some North American construction in the eighties. *Author.*

became widespread. But at present there is no guarantee of such accuracy, especially since reading figured dimensions from drawings is the usual way. The presence of the occasional "not-to-scale" dimension on a drawing is not a problem for the user of a sonic digitizer: To enable the digitizer to measure the correct dimension, he or she simply reads the figured "n.t.s." dimension and touches the appropriate points on a measurement scale (instrument) placed conveniently on the worktable or as part of the menu board.

I have used the sonic digitizer and have found it a useful and sufficiently accurate tool; and undoubtedly refinements have and can be made to it. The question is: Will the construction industry take it to hand and make it a universal tool? If so, its minor shortcomings would rapidly be overcome. At least three makers have integrated and marketed a sonic digitizer with estimating and other construction management software. So far, it appears as the only really workable connection between microcomputers and the most tedious part of estimating: measurement.

Other computer-related tools for measurement include:

1. The electronic digitizer tablet that operates with a low-voltage electric current between a digitizer (not sonic, but connective) and a complex of wiring behind the tablet (work board) to measure scaled distances from a drawing placed on the tablet (i.e., between the digitizer and the wiring)
2. The electronic mouse, or similar device, that is moved horizontally by the user over a drawing to measure scaled distances.

Like the sonic digitizer, both of these devices are connected to a computer system and require accurately scaled drawings from which to measure. The ultimate in computerized estimatng will not require manual measurement at all. But we are not yet ready for that. If perchance further development of CAD produces next week a comprehensive system of automatic measurement from CAD-created drawings by computers, the probability is that the creators of the software will do what all creators of construction software have done so far: emulate the traditional methods of measurement, pricing, etc., instead of finding the new methods that now potentially exist because of computers.

Measurement is the basis of estimating, of translating the graphic (drawings) and verbal (specifications) design information into quantitative information about the owner's requirements for construction work. By definition, it includes proper description of Work (as capitalized and defined in standard construction contract forms), not simply a list of materials. Measurement for estimating needs overhauling and renewing, for it is full of anachronisms, delusion, vagueness, and mindless destruction of information. The way we now measure work is in some respects actually counterproductive. It is essential that ways be found to computerize measurement, and it is essential to adapt the measurement methodology to computers. This is examined and discussed at length in Chapters 7 and 8.

Hardware for a computer system for estimating and cost accounting in this decade should probably have the following features, but none are absolute requirements, as reasonable alternatives exist for each:

1. A desktop microcomputer using either the PC-DOS or the MS-DOS operating system, with a hard disk and one floppy-disk drive. (Other operating systems, such as CP/M and Apple-DOS are not precluded, but for PC- and MS-DOS there is more business software available; a hard disk may not be needed for a small estimating program or can be added later; at least 256k of RAM memory is required)
2. A high-resolution graphics board for basic business graphics (to produce graphs and charts)
3. A sonic digitizer or other measurement device (possibly).

The requirement for a measurement device depends on the kind of work to be measured. For mechanical and electrical work, for example, a device for linear measurement and counting is useful. At present there is not available a wide selection of measurement devices with suitable software that can be integrated with other software. Most sonic digitizers, for example, appear to be sold with complete hardware and software packages. Such software will require customizing for most contracting companies, as everyone has different ideas about the format and contents of estimates.

Estimating software requires certain basic features for all practical programs that should be searched for in selecting software, including:

1. Among the most simple and essential features, a program's ability to allow the user to go back and delete or correct an entry without having to start at the beginning of a phase; a simple feature unfortunately lacking in some programs that are super-

ficially impressive but operationally frustrating and time-wasting

2. The ability to present on screen and in hard copy (printed) all stored data in various complete and abbreviated arrangements (i.e., with or without supporting data from within the system)

3. The ability to sort and isolate specified data for updating by class (e.g., price changes to a class of materials)

4. Adequately detailed descriptions of materials, items of work, overhead items, etc., in a concise and easily handled format that are easily read, learned, and understood

5. A comprehensive, concise, descriptive (preferably mnemonic) coding system accompanying the items' descriptions

6. Time dating of all data stored within the system and of all printed reports

7. The ability to link together selected data by a separate referencing system to provide cost and other information about components, assemblies, elements, and parts of buildings (e.g., the current total cost of a reinforced concrete floor system)

8. The integration of cost summaries into one main, or general, summary

9. An "audit trail" that enables the user or another person to go back into an estimate and trace the trail to an item's origin in the estimate: to carry out the reverse process with an item, to follow that process originally carried out when the item was first inserted into the estimate

10. The ability to easily and quickly create "what-if" alternative forms of an estimate so that the results of alternative input (markup, productivity factors, etc.) can be compared

11. The dual capacity to create an estimate from either an existing master file or estimate, or to begin with a "clean slate"

12. The ability to receive, retain, and reuse sequences of commands within the program for the manipulation of data, including new commands created by the user

13. The ability to perform the following mathematical functions:

    a. Loan amortizations
    b. Depreciation by several methods
    c. Discounting cash flow
    d. Calculating internal rates of return
    e. Forecasting cash flows
    f. Interest and loan drawdown calculations and other business accounting functions needed in estimating, bidding, and cost accounting.

When considering software for estimating and cost accounting, do not assume that the only proprietory software that can be of practical use is among the "big names," or that you need an expensive custom-made software program. It depends on your needs. For some, estimates are not extremely complex and need only contain up to a few hundred different items of work, a few thousand prices, and only require limited descriptions; such as those estimates typically made by thousands of smaller specialist contracting companies for the work of only one or two trades. On the market, there are scores of good, simple, and inexpensive programs that may be adaptable to your needs, programs typically described as financial planning or financial management programs. For example, one such program is Microplan®. Its manual describes it as a "financial modeling tool." The table of contents does not mention estimating but it includes:

1. An electronic spreadsheet
2. Built-in commands for simple and complex mathematical functions (all that you would need for ordinary estimating) shown in an on-screen menu ready for selection, with the program's ability to save specified sequences of commands to repeat required functions in calculating and handling data
3. A report generator for customized reports
4. The ability to work with more than one spreadsheet table at a time; to perform table consolidations; to do variance analysis; and to develop cash flow and income statements and balance sheets.

Such a program obviously does not have the great scope and flexibility that have made spreadsheet programs like Lotus 1-2-3 and SuperCalc famous, but that is not the point: Programs such as Microplan are suitable for some. They are not expensive and they are relatively easy to learn and use. They do not have the capacity in one spreadsheet possessed by the giants, but do you need thousands upon thousands of records? And if you do, do you need them all in one spreadsheet at the same time?

Typically, an estimate of construction costs consists of a number of subestimates, one for each trade, or for each part of a project; one for equipment and another for job overhead costs; with all of these sub-estimates finally summarized in a final, general summary of estimated costs. Each subestimate is the natural content of a single spreadsheet, with its own format and content. Each, if necessary, could be on a separate disk. There is much talk and hype about speed of computers and like-lightning access to data, but unless you are working with immense databases and very complex programs, you may not need a racing car; maybe just a truck; or several trucks for different jobs.

Finally, a few words about the all-important manual that comes with every software program. Before you buy, study the manual at length. If possible, buy a copy with a demonstration disk of the program before investing hundreds of dollars in cash and possibly thousands of dollars in time and energy. Some good software comes with bad manuals, and vice versa; but there is a good chance that a poor-quality manual represents a poor-quality program. Few learn to use a program solely from the manual. Most read parts of the manual and then try the program. When they get stuck, they go back to the manual, and so on. But with most programs if there is not a good, clear, concise, simply written, and well-illustrated manual to which to refer, a novice will have problems and frustrations.

Above all, if you are even only just thinking about computers, get yourself an education in computers; there is no way in which you can stay in business and avoid them, eventually. There are several ways of getting an education:

1. Take an introductory, hands-on course in a local college or high school.
2. Subscribe to one or two popular computer magazines.

3. Frequent the magazine racks of bookstores that carry computer magazines and regularly check the table of contents of a few other magazines (to which you do not subscribe), and when you find an interesting article and it looks worthwhile, buy the magazine.
4. Buy some of the books listed in the Bibliography.
5. Join a microcomputer users' group (even if you have not yet bought a computer); listen and learn; such groups are rich mines of information.

The results of such education will at least open new doors and at best may revolutionize your work and business practices.

There are two parts to computerization of construction management, including that of estimating and cost accounting, and they are:

1. The acquisition of a computer system (both hardware and software) suitable for the purpose
2. The reformation of management systems, such as estimating and cost accounting, to take the greatest advantage of computerization.

In this chapter we have discussed primarily the first of these: a computer system. In future chapters, particularly Chapters 7 and 8, we deal with the second part: estimating and cost accounting and their adaptation to and development by computers.

QUESTIONS AND TOPICS FOR DISCUSSION

1. Describe briefly the *three* main classes of computers.
2. Describe briefly the *two* main kinds of computer software that are relevant to estimating and cost accounting.
3. List the *pros* and *cons* of (a) a dedicated estimating program that can be purchased, and (b) one that is written by an estimator for his or her own use.
4. Obtain published information about several spreadsheet programs and tabulate and compare their features with particular regard to estimating.
5. Obtain published information about several database management programs and tabulate and compare their features with particular regard to estimating.
6. Discuss the advantages and disadvantages of a *master estimate* (as described herein) as it relates to an estimating program.

7. Survey a number of construction companies selected at random to determine (a) whether they use computers, (b) what their computers are used for, (c) the extent of their use, and (d) the configurations of their computer systems.
8. Survey a number of sets of construction drawings to determine their accuracy with a view to measurement with a computer device.
9. Make a list of features in a *computer program for estimating* that you consider essential. Then survey a number of programs (spreadsheet and database management) to find which contain such features. Tabulate your results.
10. Obtain copies of *manuals and demonstration diskettes of a number of estimating programs* and tabulate and

compare their features, with special regard to (a) size and capacity, (b) hardware requirements, (c) user-friendliness of the manuals and the software programs, (d) flexibility of the programs in use, (e) efficacy of the manual and (f) preparation time required before the program is operational (in setting up a master estimate, or database, or both, and in learning).

11. Write a critique of a *dedicated estimating program* with particular regard to those features listed in Question 10 and to other features that are *innovative in estimating*.

12. Make an estimate of the costs involved for a construction company in *computerizing its estimating*, with particular regard to (a) education of staff, (b) a hardware system suitable for the needs of the particular company, (c) a software program, or programs, for estimating suitable to that particular company's needs, and (d) the existence of other computer applications within that company.

6

PRECEPTS OF ESTIMATING AND COST ACCOUNTING

The systematic measurement and pricing of building construction work has a history that goes back at least 300 years. During the last 100 years the construction industry has been stimulated by growth and industrialization and nurtured by some professional bodies.[1] A few principles and precepts have gained general if not universal recognition, and although the term "principle" has been used by some institutes for the present it may be prudent to call them precepts.

PRECEPTS OF ESTIMATING

Five precepts have been entitled: (1) Precept of Purpose, (2) Precept of Veracity, (3) Precept of Verification, (4) Precept of Measurement, and (5) Precept of Accuracy. Each of these is explained below, and its main applications are examined. In subsequent chapters these precepts are followed in the examples and enlarged on in the explanations.

The Precept of Purpose in Estimating

1. The primary purpose of estimating is to make a profit by obtaining and performing construction work by the most efficient means available, and this requires that costs be estimated.[2]

2. The specific purposes of estimating are to calculate the costs of construction work and its attendant risks on the basis of probabilities, and to obtain and to record information about work for management purposes.

The Precept of Veracity in Estimating. All costs of the work should be properly accounted for in an estimate insofar as is practical by allocating all foreseeable costs to the proper items of work, or to overhead items, or to specified contingencies.

The Precept of Verification in Estimating. All estimated costs and other data in an estimate subsequently should be compared with the actual costs and data obtained by cost accounting and, insofar as is practical, the estimated costs and other data should be either verified or corrected.

---

[1] But not noticeably by any organization constituted primarily by construction estimators.

[2] A fundamental purpose is, of course, to provide something that society requires, but this consideration enters into questions that are beyond the scope of a text on estimating.

The Precept of Measurement in Estimating

1. All work should be measured "net in place" (as installed) as required by the contract, and waste[G] should be allowed for in the unit prices of the estimate.[3]

2. No item of work[G] should be measured in place of another item of work.

3. No item of work should be measured in combination with another item of work so as to obscure the quantities or costs of either.

4. All work should be measured in an estimate so as to make its pricing and its subsequent verification as practical and accurate as possible.

The Precept of Accuracy in Estimating

1. All work should be measured and priced as accurately as is practically possible commensurate with the type of work and the units of measurement used.

2. Delusions of accuracy should be avoided by using an appropriate degree of accuracy in estimating and in cost accounting.

These five precepts are explained in greater detail in the sections that follow, and some illustrations are presented. The precepts also are demonstrated later in the estimating examples in Chapter 9.

Purpose in Estimating

Profit should not be more important than producing the things that society needs, but the two: profit and production, are interdependent and each is necessary to the other. Profit is a desirable and necessary motivation. It creates a challenge, and it is a measure of efficiency. (Profit is excess of income over expenditure and in order to know the amount of profit all costs must be known and accounted for and deducted from income.)

The given purposes of estimating are valid for all kinds of estimates, whether they are made by designers or by contractors, even though the methods of estimating may vary. The purposes of planning and controlling the work by using information from the estimate make a construction estimate necessary for all work, whether or not it is the subject of competitive bidding. Estimates are not made solely for the purpose of bidding, but also as a means of efficient execution of the work.

Veracity in Estimating

Unless each item of work bears all the costs attributable to it, its true cost and the true cost of other items cannot be determined, and false costs may be applied to similar items of work in other estimates. An estimate should represent the best possible effort to calculate all the *probable costs* and to come as close as possible to the *actual costs*, which will not be known until the completion of the work.

An estimate should also provide as much information about the project as is possible and necessary for proper management, including information for planning the work and controlling the costs while the job[G] is in progress. To show such things, an estimate must be properly organized and laid out, with: adequate supporting calculations and descriptive notes to make it clear how the items of work have been measured;[G] what assumptions (if any) have been made; and what factors have been allowed for such things as swell and shrinkage, waste, laps,[4] and the like, so that the logic of the estimate can be followed and applied.

The precept of veracity in estimating applies to all the different kinds of estimates described in Chapter 2. However, since preliminary estimates are usually required and prepared before all the information about the design of the work is available, such estimates are invariably made from incomplete information and a number of assumptions. These assumptions should be stated in the written estimate.

Preliminary estimates made by a designer, or by a designer's consultant, or by any other person, must make clear the assumptions on which they are based. As the assumptions become facts, or are changed, the estimate must be revised accordingly.

Preliminary estimates should develop into intermediate estimates, and from these into final estimates as design decisions are made and as the bidding documents are prepared.

An estimate should be true to the facts, such as are known, at all times. Any assumptions that are substituted for facts should be made clear in the estimate and pointed out to the owner to avoid trouble later. This procedure will also draw attention to those parts of the work that still require decisions. Questioning an assumption will sometimes produce a decision and, from the decision, a result. However, if this precept is not applied, a preliminary estimate will probably become a false estimate as the design proceeds.

---

[3] Some estimators disagree with this precept and arguments for it presented here. However, many accept it as a general precept conducive to greater accuracy in estimating and better cost control.

[4] All described in the Glossary.

Verification in Estimating

It is imperative that costs and other information in an estimate are compared with the actual costs and data obtained during the course of the work. This enables the estimate and information to be verified, and corrected if necessary, as the work proceeds. In this way, valid information is available for immediate use on the job for planning and scheduling the work and controlling the costs, and for later use in making other estimates. This is the *cyclical process of estimating and cost accounting,* shown diagramatically and explained in Chapters 2 and 4.

Measurement in Estimating

Work[G] should be measured net in place and as required by the contract, because this is the only unchanging, reliable basis for the quantities of work.[G] The alternative is to measure work including extra material for waste. But the amount of waste is always a variable, and it varies among all items of work, among all jobs, and among contractors. Waste[G] is an aspect of material costs related to the material and its installation that must be estimated. But it is better to allow for it in the unit price, and not in the measured quantities of the estimate so as to distinguish it as a variable to be estimated, or at least considered, each time and for each job.

Waste is material that is not required by the contract to be installed as part of the work, even though it is often a necessary part of doing the work. In a stipulated sum contract the owner is not concerned with waste. It concerns only the contractor who has to do the work for the stipulated sum and who has some control over the amount of waste. The contractor should be concerned with the amounts of waste in all contracts in order to control it and to be able to estimate the waste in future jobs. The amounts of wasted materials should be checked while the work is in progress so that unnecessary waste can be avoided and estimated allowance for waste verified or modified for use in future estimates.

If work has not been measured net, it is necessary to deduct the estimated waste from the measured quantities (which include waste) to find the net quantity, so that a relationship between *net quantity* and *actual waste* can be established. It is impossible to verify the amounts of waste without knowing the net quantities.

There are times when the gross quantities of materials should also be measured, particularly if expensive materials are being used. The amount of waste in certain types of work may be very small; in some cases, virtually a constant factor that has been verified and established by experience. In such cases it may be sufficiently accurate to include the waste in the measured quantities of work. But the actual amount of waste can only be verified by measuring the net quantity installed, and by comparing this quantity with the gross quantity supplied to the job. And this procedure should be followed from time to time with all established allowances for waste so as to check them.

Waste should not be confused with *laps,*[G] which are material parts of the work required by the contract specifications, the nature of the work, and by proper construction practices. *Laps should be measured and included in the quantities* of an estimate as part of the work whenever the laps are not an invariable and integral part of the work being measured. However, when the laps are an invariable and integral part of the work, such as the laps in a roofing system, the laps are not measured; only the net area covered by the work. The measurement of laps and the treatment of laps and waste are shown in several of the examples in Chapter 9.

The practice of measuring one item of work in place of another is not uncommon, but it should not be done except in preliminary estimates.[G] In such estimates, it is not usually necessary to know the costs of particular items of the work, or the costs of work performed by particular trades. The sole object of a preliminary estimate is to find the total costs of the work, or the costs of the major parts, such as the structure, finishes, and the mechanical and electrical systems. Therefore, substituting one item for another may be acceptable in preliminary estimates simply as an expedience. However, in an estimate that is to be the basis of a bid, the practice of measuring one item in place of another will only cause confusion, and it may make cost accounting impossible. Different items of work should each be measured separately, even though they may exist only in combination. For example, plaster is usually applied to a base, such as concrete or masonry; but unless the base is one constructed by the plasterer, such as lathing, it should be measured and priced separately.

In *preliminary estimates* it is quite usual to measure certain items of work in combination. For example, reinforced concrete may be measured in cubic yards, including the steel reinforcing bars, and sometimes even the formwork. The quantities of steel can be estimated quite accurately in this way if previous jobs have been analyzed. There is a logical relationship between the quantities of steel reinforcing bars and the quantities of reinforced concrete in a structure, through the structural design. There is much less and often no such relationship between the contact area of formwork and the quantity of concrete, because there is no constant relationship between the surface area and the volume of concrete components.

In preliminary estimates measuring items of work in combination may be carried still further, and the work may be measured and priced as elements of a building. For example, an external cladding element might consist of a concrete wall with rigid, plastic foam insulation adhered to the inner face and covered with painted hardwall plaster. The outer face of the concrete wall might be covered with a clay brick veneer. All of these different items are combined to make the external cladding element, which can be priced by a combination of the appropriate unit prices, as shown below.

EXTERNAL CLADDING ELEMENT

Descriptions of Items	Price per SF
8″ thick reinf conc wall, incl forms and steel	8.00
Rigid insulation, inside	1.00
Hardwall plaster, inside	1.20
Two coats paint, inside	0.50
4″ thick clay brick veneer, outside	5.00
Unit Price of Element	$15.70

If properly based on valid, historical cost data, *estimating by elements* can be used by construction firms to produce maximum cost figures for maximum cost-plus-fee contracts, explained in Chapter 1. It is generally the best method for making the earliest preliminary estimates.

Measurement and *pricing* are the two complementary parts of estimating, and since measurement precedes pricing measurement must be done so as to make accurate pricing possible. An estimator must consider the item of work being measured, its costs, and how it will be priced; and he must measure the work accordingly. This approach will help an estimator to avoid measuring in ways and in units that obscure the costs of an item and make accurate estimating and cost accounting impossible. This procedure is further explained in Chapter 8, *Measuring Work: Particular.*

In addition to measuring for the purpose of pricing an estimate, an estimator should measure for subsequent cost accounting, because it is through cost accounting that he will obtain data for construction management and for future estimates. Cost accounting usually requires the use of a code to identify the items of work so that costs can be segregated and charged to the appropriate items. An estimator should, therefore, measure items of work in an estimate according to the cost code. Cost codes are discussed further in Chapter 12, *Cost Accounting Practices.*

Generally, there is no need for an estimator to measure work in greater detail than is needed for cost accounting purposes, because the measured details of the estimated work can never be verified, or, if necessary, corrected. There are, however, some important exceptions to this general rule. For example, in measuring formwork to a concrete wall in which there are formed offsets and recesses, the extra labor and material used in forming the offsets and recesses should be measured and priced. However, building the wall forms and forming the recesses is one operation and, therefore, it may not be possible to isolate the extra costs of forming the offsets and recesses (see Fig. 6-1). Obviously, the offset and recessed wall shown in the figure will cost more to build than the plain wall. But how much more? The estimator may never really know. Nevertheless, the extra cost cannot be ignored, and an estimator should price the work of "forming offsets and recesses" by theoretical analysis and experience. The estimator's judgment of the probabilities of costs may never be fully tested in such cases, because the usual cost accounting methods cannot segregate the costs of forming offsets and recesses from the total cost of forming walls because of the integrated nature of the work. If costs of such items must be accurately determined, it would be necessary to use work study methods employing techniques that are beyond the scope of normal cost accounting and that may not always be expedient or desirable.

With the accumulation of cost information on forming walls it may be possible to more or less establish the extra cost of forming walls with offsets and recesses, as compared with forming plain walls; but, this will never be entirely conclusive. Consequently, some estimators wrongly make this a justification for ignoring analysis of costs of such items and may only guess at an allowance for such extra costs. A practical approach to this kind of problem is discussed later.

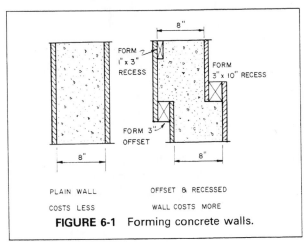

FIGURE 6-1 Forming concrete walls.

Accuracy in Estimating

This is the passion of the estimator, and it is both his goal and his nemesis. He tries to estimate the actual costs of work, and he knows he cannot completely achieve it. Accuracy is often illusory, as when the total estimated costs equal the total actual costs and a detailed comparison shows that they are equal only because of compensating differences. Or accuracy may be a delusion because an estimator does not really understand accuracy in estimating.

An estimator must strive for accuracy; but accuracy is always relative, and the degree of accuracy must be modified according to the items of work, the units of measurement, the quantities of work, the unit prices, and the type of estimate.

A candy bar may be casually divided into halves, and only two children might quarrel over their shares. A gold bar must be precisely measured and weighed to divide it equally. It is useless to measure excavation work to the nearest inch, or to measure concrete to a fraction of a cubic foot, and to then round off the total quantities to the nearest cubic yard. Similarly, it is a delusion of accuracy to price each item of work in an estimate to the nearest cent, or to make a bid of $341,935.69 (three hundred and forty-one thousand, nine hundred and thirty-five dollars, and sixty-nine cents). In both cases, the estimator has not stopped to consider how accurate his measurements can be and need to be. He believes in accuracy, and may pursue it blindly without thought. Pedantry in estimating shows that accuracy is not properly understood. One of the difficulties for the beginner in estimating is to decide how accurate his estimate should be. No estimator can make an estimate more accurate than the information from which he works. The required degree of accuracy is determined by the quantity and the kind of work, and the estimator must decide on the necessary degree of accuracy for each item of work in an estimate.

For example, an estimate may include #3 steel bars as ties around vertical reinf bars in conc columns, as in Fig. 6-2. These ties may cost $.18 per linear foot, (about $.54 per pound), for the costs of material and labor in supplying, bending, and installing the ties. The beginner is often unsure about how to measure the lengths of ties from the structural drawings which show the sizes of the columns but which often only indicate the ties diagramatically, or simply by a note on the drawings. In his difficulty, he may not stop to consider the significance of the problem. First he should ask himself: How many columns and approximately how many ties are required? If there are only a few columns, he may measure the length of the ties directly from the column sizes, because the perimeter of a

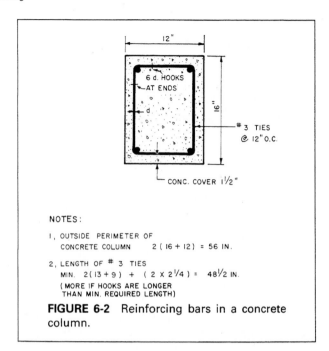

NOTES:

1, OUTSIDE PERIMETER OF
   CONCRETE COLUMN   2 (16 + 12) = 56 IN.

2, LENGTH OF # 3 TIES
   MIN. 2(13 + 9) + (2 x 2¼) = 48½ IN.
   (MORE IF HOOKS ARE LONGER
   THAN MIN. REQUIRED LENGTH)

FIGURE 6-2 Reinforcing bars in a concrete column.

column's cross-section will approximately equal the length of the ties in the column.

If there are many ties, this method of measurement may not be sufficiently accurate. But more precise measurement of the tie length will be of little value if the estimator underestimates the number of ties by overlooking the fact that "#3 ties @ 12" o.c." means that the ties shall be spaced at not more than 12 inches apart, and that in some places ties will have to be spaced closer than 12 inches; as in a column 9½ feet high which requires eleven ties. In addition, all the column ties may amount to less than 1 percent of the total steel in a reinforced concrete building.

PRECEPTS OF COST ACCOUNTING

Each of the five precepts of estimating has an equivalent precept in the other part of the system; in cost accounting (CA). Generally, these precepts apply to CA in much the same way as they apply to estimating, but in addition there are some special applications.

The Precept of Purpose in CA

1. The primary purpose is to make a profit by obtaining and doing construction work by the most efficient means available, and this requires an accounting of actual costs.

2. The specific purposes of CA are: to verify and to correct, if necessary, the costs and other information in an estimate; to provide verified data for planning and controlling the

work in the immediate job (and in future jobs); to provide information for other estimates; and to obtain the total of the actual costs of work in order to determine the amount of profit.

The Precept of Veracity in CA

1. Every item of work and every overhead item should carry all the actual costs attributable to that item.
2. All actual costs of work should be accounted for by CA, insofar as is practical, and any costs that cannot be attributed to an item of work should be attributed to an appropriate and specific overhead item.

The Precept of Verification in CA. All actual costs and other data in a cost accounting should be compared with the costs and assumptions made in the estimate, so that, insofar as is practical, the estimate can be verified or corrected.

The Precept of Measurement in CA

1. All work done should be measured *net in place* as required by the contract, and any difference between the material quantity of an item of work required by the contract and the material quantity of that item of work actually used should be classed as waste.[5]
2. No item of work should be measured in place of another item of work (unless a change has been required by the contract and is so identified).
3. No item of work done should be measured in combination with another item of work, except where justifiably so measured in the estimate.
4. All work should be segregated and measured in CA as it is segregated and measured in the estimate, in order to verify and correct the estimate and to provide information and data for other estimates.

The Precept of Accuracy in CA

1. All work should be measured and costed as accurately as possible, commensurate with

the type of work and the units of measurement used.
2. Delusions of accuracy in CA should be avoided by using an appropriate degree of accuracy in CA and in estimating.

These five precepts are explained below, insofar as their application to CA differs from their application to Estimating.

Purpose in CA

The purposes of CA have been explained before, in the first three chapters. CA cannot be examined in isolation but only as part of the total construction management process, along with estimating. CA is a means of acquiring knowledge about construction work as it is actually done; particularly knowledge about the costs of work as it is actually done. Without a CA system, a contractor may be able to obtain some limited knowledge of completed work and its total costs. At least, a contractor usually wants to know whether a job made a profit or a loss. But some companies do not even know whether they have made or lost money because their records are incomplete, or do not exist. Without CA, a contractor may have some ideas about the job and about its successes and failures; where money was made and where it was lost. But without CA, it is unlikely that any facts will be recorded that would be useful to an estimator in the future. Without CA, a contractor may not know if an item of work or a complete job is losing money until it is completed. The purpose of CA is to provide facts. It may not be enough to justify CA by saying that knowledge is always better than ignorance and more specific reasons may be needed. They are: (1) to have information in order to manage the job in hand, (2) to make other estimates, and (3) to manage other jobs in the future.

Veracity in CA

Cost accounting is useless if it does not deal with facts. The first argument against CA is usually that superintendents and foremen cannot always be relied on to provide the facts, that often they only provide information which will enhance themselves, and that they sometimes manipulate cost figures for their own ends. Of course, that happens. But if we are convinced of its value that is not enough to reject the use of CA.

Construction staff who cannot do what is reasonably required of them are in the same position as other incompetent staff. Many construction foremen and superintendents are convinced of the value of CA and cooperate in making it work. But some will not,

---

[5] This does not refer to changes in quantity resulting from a contractual change in the work ordered by the owner or the designer. Extra work ordered in accordance with the general conditions of a contract becomes part of the work of the contract.

Swell and shrinkage of excavated and fill materials are dealt with here in the same way as waste.

and often they will not stay. Having been hired to supervise a job, they charge costs to the wrong items of work or to those items that are actually costing less than was estimated in order to doctor those items that are costing more than was estimated. They may even charge the costs of one job to another in order to make a losing job look better. When exposed, their argument may be that they are not dishonest, because in any event all the costs are chargeable to that job or to that company. But in a sense there is theft involved, apart from the negligence and dishonesty. There is theft in the sense that the company's estimators may be misled by false information, and as a result the company may suffer a loss.

It is an essential part of the duties of foremen and superintendents to report on the progress, productivity, and the costs of the jobs on which they are employed; and if a foreman or a superintendent cannot report properly, he should not be employed in that position. Many superintendents and foremen have not received adequate training in CA and in other aspects of management and this may explain why some do not perform as they should. In such cases, education about the need for CA and the importance of accurate reporting by site staff may be worthwhile.[6]

Verification in CA

This is one of the primary purposes of CA; to verify the costs and other information in an estimate, or otherwise to correct them in the light of the facts.

Measurement in CA

Work done at a site and measured for CA—for progress reports, interim payment applications, and the like—should be measured in the same way that it has been measured in the estimate; otherwise, valid comparisons cannot be made between the estimate and the CA. As already stated, the primary rules of measurement are: to measure work net in place, and to measure each item of work separately. Work at a site can be measured more easily from the drawings, and by checking its actual dimensions. If an item of work, such as masonry walls, is still largely incomplete, it may be necessary to actually measure each portion of completed work in place. If, on the other hand, the same item is largely completed, with only a small part of the work yet to be done, it will be easier to check the dimensions and to measure the work that is not yet done, and to deduct this amount from the total amount of the item in the estimate. Of course, if there is any doubt about the accuracy of the amount of work in an estimate, the estimated amount should be checked, and the amount of work actually done should be measured. By measuring work at the site from the drawings, rather than measuring every dimension from the actual work, the risk of confusion rising out of differences between dimensions on the contract drawings and actual but incorrect dimensions of work is avoided.

For example, drawings may show concrete footings 24 inches wide by 12 inches deep, whereas the actual width of the footings in place may be 24½ inches. The half-inch of extra width should be ignored in measurements because it is not required by the contract. The footings should be measured as 24 inches wide as required by the contract. To put it another way, only that work required by and paid for in the contract should be measured in CA. This does not mean that extra material used in the work is not accounted for. The actual quantities of materials delivered to the site are to be recorded and eventually compared with the amounts required by the contract and measured in the estimate. If there have been no changes required in the contract, any increase in the amount of material used over the amount required in the contract should be classed as waste and recorded accordingly.[7] If there is persistent waste associated with the use of a particular material, the estimator should know of it, and so should the superintendent because he may be able to reduce or eliminate the waste in future jobs. The general rule of measurement for CA is to measure work by the same methods and units as are used in the estimate.

Accuracy in CA

What has been said about accuracy in estimating applies equally to CA, because one is the reflection of the other. Attempts to be very accurate and highly analytical

---

[6] Some observers have pointed out that the construction industry is unusual in that it recruits some management staff from workmen who are trade union members, and that these superintendents must sometimes face a dilemma in properly carrying out management duties, considering their relationship with their union and its members. Some construction firms now recruit superintendents who have had formal training as engineers or technologists, and preferably some business training, rather than promoting tradesmen in the field. Nevertheless, practical trade experience is invaluable to a superintendent, and obviously the ideal foreman or superintendent would be a tradesman who had returned to college for technical and management training.

---

[7] No matter the type of contract, oversized concrete footings are essentially waste, caused by the method of construction. The owner should not have to pay for any unrequired work unless, of course, it is done deliberately to effect a tangible saving, such as eliminating formwork to the footings.

in CA may eventually result in a failure to achieve anything, an eventuality that is discussed further in Chapter 12.

To be able to measure something is to know something about it, and these precepts of estimating and cost accounting will help estimators and cost ac-

countants to know something more about the construction work they have to deal with. That is why the purposes and objectives of their work must be properly understood, and that is why accuracy, veracity, and verification are so important. Otherwise, mistakes and errors may be perpetuated.

QUESTIONS AND TOPICS FOR DISCUSSION

1. Briefly explain the purposes of estimating.

2. Why is it important that each *item of work* should bear all the costs attributable to it?

3. Why is it important that all the *costs of the work* in a construction job should be properly accounted for?

4. Why measure *work* net in place when it is apparent that more material must be used than has to be installed?

5. Explain the difference between *waste* and *laps* in construction materials.

6. Discuss the statement: *"Generally, there is no need for an estimator to measure work in greater detail than is needed for cost accounting purposes."* Is this always so, and why?

7. What are the most important qualifications of accuracy in estimating and why?

8. Briefly explain the purposes of *cost accounting* relative to estimating.

9. Who is the person most important to proper *cost accounting*, and why?

10. State briefly the primary rules for measuring *work* done on a construction site for purposes of *cost accounting*.

11. Discuss the proposition that there is no need to account for the *costs of every item* in a completed project.

12. Discuss the differences between the precepts of estimating and those of cost accounting.

13. Discover and explain additional *precepts of purpose* in estimating with respect to different kinds of construction contracts.

14. Discuss the *precepts of measurement* given in this chapter with respect to computer applications to estimating and cost accounting.

7

MEASURING WORK: GENERAL

The object of measuring work is to know and to price the quantities of the work in order to estimate their costs. Measurement leads to pricing, and all measurement should be done so as to make accurate pricing possible. Measurement is not an end in itself, and matters of measurement, such as accuracy and tolerances, can only be determined in the light of pricing and costs.

Measuring work in an estimate consists of three visible parts:

1. *Descriptions* of each item of work
2. *Dimensions* of each item of work
3. *Quantities* of each item of work.

These parts are examined in the following sections.

DESCRIPTIONS OF WORK

When both measurement and pricing in an estimate are done by the same estimator, it is possible, but not necessarily desirable, for the estimator to enter very brief descriptions of items in the estimate. The estimator then relies on his memory for a fuller description of

each item when he prices the estimate. This practice may be acceptable for common items of work, but it is not suitable for uncommon items and for complex estimates. Considering the purposes of estimating and cost accounting (explained in the preceding chapters), an estimate should contain as much useful information as is possible and practical. Descriptions should be explicit and definitive, and the precise meaning and scope of each item of work should be clearly indicated in the estimate so that each item can be accurately priced. This requirement does not call for verbose descriptions, and it is possible to write brief and effective descriptions of items of work. Inadequate descriptions, however, are one of the most common faults in estimates.

Descriptions of the work originate in the bidding documents, and it is essential that the estimator study and refer to these documents while estimating. Some estimators do not, and specifications are sometimes almost completely ignored after an initial perusal. Some designers' specifications are too long or badly written, despite the standard formats and guide specifications produced by specification institutes with which all estimators should be familiar. Nevertheless, they must be read.

Estimators take a chance in not paying enough

attention to specifications and in not using them as they should. Some estimators do not recognize or cannot accept the full responsibilities of an estimator's position and have to look to others for guidance and instructions about contractual matters. A qualified and competent estimator should have a good working knowledge of contracts and contract documents and be able to use that knowledge effectively.

An estimator's first reading of specifications should be a quick but complete survey of the entire document. He should use the techniques of "rapid reading," and a course in this subject is an advantage to most.[1] In the initial survey, the estimator should attempt to reduce the scope and content of the entire project to its essentials by studying the "table of contents" at the beginning of the document. After the initial survey, the estimator should then go through the appropriate *sections*[G] of the specifications for the work he is estimating, either marking the document or making separate notes to pick out those requirements that are neither standard, obvious, nor inevitable. Most specification clauses, however, are standard, obvious, and inevitable, because most buildings are for the most part built with commonplace materials and systems.

For example, an estimator sees *concrete footings* shown on the drawings. He reads the *concrete section* of the specifications and sees that it includes a general reference to an ASTM specification for concrete with which he is familiar. He also sees that concrete in footings must have a compressive strength at 28 days of 3500 pounds per square inch, that the maximum size for the aggregate in the concrete is 1½ inches, and that sulphate-resistant portland cement is to be used. This information gives him the required description of the item in the estimate, and it might be written:

> *"conc ftgs 3500 psi (max 1½″ agg) with SR p. cmt."* ("Concrete footings; compressive strength at 28 days 3500 pounds per square-inch (maximum size of aggregate, 1½″), with sulphate-resistant portland cement").

Certain sections of specifications always require extra detailed study and more notes and references than others because they usually deal with special conditions and requirements. Concrete footings are placed under most buildings, and a normal type portland cement concrete is generally used. On the other hand, concrete

piles are not common, and any specification section on piling requires careful reading and interpretation. Obviously, an estimator must have an extensive knowledge of construction materials and methods as well as the ability to read and understand drawings and specifications.

An estimator should also examine and read other specification sections related to the work that he is estimating in order to be sure that he understands the scope of the work for which he will bid. If it is *drainage work,* he should read the sections on *excavation* and *plumbing*; but it is unlikely that he would have to read the section on painting.

Some of the information needed to describe items of work in an estimate is not found in the bidding documents, and it must come from the estimator through his understanding of construction work. For example, formwork for cast-in-place concrete is not usually shown on drawings, and often it is specified in the most general way. An estimator measures from the drawings those surface areas of concrete that will be in contact with formwork (the *contact area*), and he measures any special features formed in the concrete surfaces. The rest of the information required for estimating the costs of formwork must come from the estimator himself. This illustrates that an estimator must know and understand the construction work that he measures and prices; and he must be able to describe the items of work from his own knowledge and in such ways as will enable the items to be accurately priced. (Specific examples are given in Chapter 9.)

Generally, bidding documents[G] do not indicate the procedure and the sequence of work, nor do most construction contracts. The designer illustrates the arrangement and specifies the quality of the work, and also may prescribe how some or all of it will be done. The organization and the sequence of the work, however, is generally the responsibility of the contractor; although there are sometimes contractual exceptions to this rule. Organization of work affects its costs and, therefore, an estimator will have to consider job organization, procedures, and work sequences in making an estimate.

In the case of a standard construction project consisting of more or less common items of work, the question of procedure and sequence of work may not be a problem for an estimator because he should know the usual procedures and sequences involved. When dealing with a project requiring unusual construction materials and methods, however, an estimator may need advice and assistance. It may be necessary for the estimator to work with other members of the contractor's staff, such as engineers and superintendents, to decide on how the work will be done before an

---

[1] The rapid reading techniques taught by one international school do not require any mechanical devices, and have proven to be an asset to many in the reading of documents. Different writings and different documents require different reading techniques.

estimate can be made. Similarly, a standard construction project, but one involving unusual site conditions and circumstances that may greatly affect the costs of the work, may require that an economical method of construction be found before an estimate and a competitive bid can be made. Even in the most straightforward projects there are many costs that are not indicated or referred to in the bidding documents (particularly job overhead items) that an estimator must know about and include.

For example, the costs of the Westcoast Transmission Building (Fig. 7-1) could not have been estimated until certain techniques and procedures had been considered by the contractor, because of the unusual design that utilizes heavy vertical cables to support the suspended floors. The reinforced-concrete central core was slip-formed, and the last concrete to be placed in the core was pumped to a height of over 200 ft. The steel cables were hung over the beams at the top, down the sides of the central core, and were attached to the steel floor decks as the floors were

FIGURE 7-1 The Westcoast Transmission Building, Vancouver, B.C., Canada. Architects: Rhone and Iredale, Vancouver, B.C.; structural engineer: Bogue B. Babicki, Vancouver, B.C. (Reproduced by permission of the architects.)

erected. The cables were later encased and protected against corrosion, and finally the building was enclosed by the reflective curtain walls. This is not standard construction, and estimators would have had to use their imagination and search for information in making an estimate of its costs.

One of the most common errors in estimating often occurs at the outset, when an estimator spends insufficient time in examining the drawings and making notes from the specifications, as described above. He may begin to measure the work prematurely, because the temptation to get going is hard to resist. Yet time spent at the outset in thinking about the work and in studying the documents is always well spent. Junior estimators often are conscious of their confusion when they first look at the drawings of a new project, and they think that starting the estimate will somehow help to clear their minds. This may be so for experienced estimators, but for the less experienced a deliberate effort must be made at the beginning to analyze and understand work shown on drawings and described in specifications before actually starting an estimate.

This preliminary effort by an estimator is always worthwhile, and can be very rewarding. Sometimes an estimator discovers that he can reduce his work by judicious measurement, because the building has features that are repetitive or symmetrical. Often what appears to be a complex set of drawings can be simplified by initially ignoring the details and minor features and by reducing the building to a simple arrangement of vertical and horizontal planes laid out about one or more axes.

After an estimator has examined the bidding documents and made notes in the appropriate sections, the next step is to make an outline of the estimate, consisting of a list of the items of work to be measured and priced, grouped under section headings. For example:

CAST-IN-PLACE CONCRETE

Ftgs (SR p. cmt) (3000 psi)	Extr walls, 8″ (4000 psi)
Fnd walls, 8″ (3500 psi)	Sill projs to extr walls
Cols and Bms (3500 psi)	Intr walls, 8″, 6″ (3500 psi)
Flat slabs (3500 psi)	Stairs and lndgs (4000 psi)
Slab on grd (3500 psi)	Mach bases (3500 psi), etc. . .

Such an outline may not be necessary for an experienced estimator, but it is essential to the beginner, if only as a means of giving him pause and thought before starting the estimate. It helps an estimator to organize the estimate and to avoid omissions, and it helps him to make concise but adequate descriptions by clarifying how headings should best be used in the estimate. Alternatively, an estimator may choose to use a prepared checklist or a cost code to achieve the same purpose, as explained in Chapter 12.

It should be remembered that descriptions describe *work*, not only materials. All items of work contain labor costs, and some items contain only labor costs. There is often a tendency to emphasize the "materials" aspects of an item, and to minimize or even to forget the "labor" aspects. Plant and equipment costs are also important, and their occurrence should be made clear in the descriptions of items. Measurement precedes and is a preparation for pricing, and all costs of work must be priced. For this reason, all items should include all material costs, labor costs, and plant and equipment costs unless otherwise described (such as "labor only" items).

Labor only items[G] in an estimate indicate an experienced estimator, while their absence probably indicates inaccuracy. Their use is the only way to account for certain costs of work.

All descriptions in an estimate are assumed to describe a positive item; but often it is necessary to enter a negative item—that is, an omission, better described as a *deduction*.[G] For example, in measuring the exterior walls of a building, it may be necessary to deduct the areas of doors, windows, and other openings. Such openings are called *voids*[G] when within the boundaries of the measured areas, as in Fig. 7-2. The term *want*[G] is usually used to identify a deduction made to adjust a deliberate over-measurement, as in Fig. 7-3, in which the area is first measured by the overall dimensions and the over-measurement is then adjusted by deducting the *want*. This method of measuring areas is recommended in estimating because it simplifies the measurement of complex areas and, in the case of an error, it also helps to ensure an over-measurement rather than an under-measurement.

The term *void* is sometimes used to identify a deduction that is made within the boundaries of a measured area because one item of work (in the major area) is displaced by another item of work (in the minor area, or areas); as in Fig. 7-4, in which the major area is, say, one type of flooring, and the minor area is another type of flooring in a particular room or area. The practice of writing negative items (deducts, omissions) in a different color is obsolete now that photocopies of estimates are frequently made which do not show different colors.

One way of shortening descriptions of items in estimates is to use *abbreviations*, such as those to be found in this book. At present, there are no standard abbreviations for construction, but some abbreviations are widely used and readily recognized. Omitting vowels and dropping the last syllable (or syllables) are the most usual ways of abbreviating words in descriptions of work. Standardization of terminology becomes more necessary as computers are used and as computer software is developed for construction. In some countries dictionaries of standard construction terminology are published for this purpose.

Another means of abbreviation is the use of a code, usually numerical or alphabetical or a mixture of both, as described in Chapter 12. Such a code is used primarily to identify and segregate costs in cost accounting; but the same code can be used in estimates, thus eliminating the need for verbal descriptions. There is some reluctance to use only a code for describing items in estimates because of the risk of error and misinterpretation. In an estimate such an error could be serious. A similar error in a cost account does not

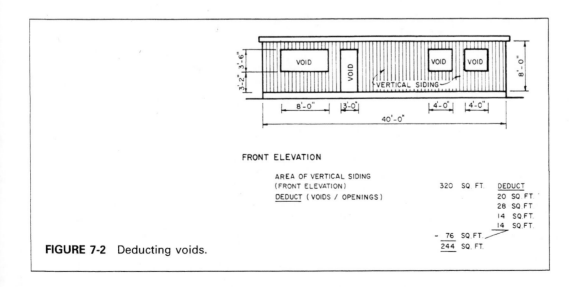

FIGURE 7-2   Deducting voids.

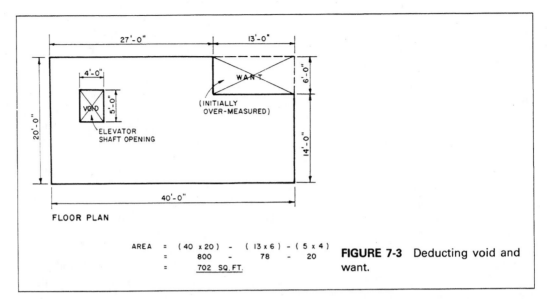

AREA = (40 x 20) - (13 x 6) - (5 x 4)
      =   800   -   78   -   20
      =   702   SQ. FT.

FIGURE 7-3 Deducting void and want.

have the same immediacy and effect, although it might cause a future loss. A practical alternative is to use a code *and* a brief verbal description.

Other aspects of the description of items come from the *Precepts of Measurement in Estimating*, in Chapter 6. The application of these precepts requires that descriptions of the content and scope of each item of work be precise and clear. Loose and careless descriptions result in bad measurement practices and inaccurate estimates.

Descriptions of items usually contain dimensions, because not all dimensions are entered in the three

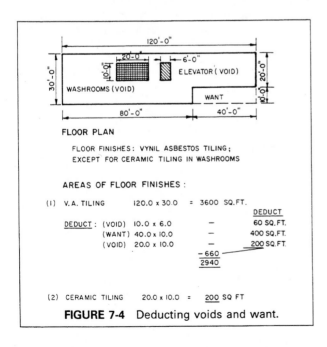

FIGURE 7-4 Deducting voids and want.

dimension columns of an estimate sheet. Entering dimensions in an estimate is discussed below. For the moment it is sufficient to point out that descriptions usually do contain dimensions, and that *dimensions in descriptions* are written as they appear on the drawings, unlike those that are entered in the dimension columns (see Fig. 7-5).

In the figure, the example shows several items with none, or some, or all of their dimensions entered in the description instead of in the dimension columns adjoining. For example, no dimensions for the first item, '*Cont Ftgs*' (*Continuous Footings*), are in the description; all three are in the dimension columns. For the next item '*Isolated Ftgs* (*less than one cy ea*) *size 4' × 4' × 1'3'*'' all three dimensions are in the description and none are in the dimension columns, only the number of isolated footings. For the last item '*12" Fnd Walls* (*below Main Floor*)', one of its three dimensions is retained in the description until the total area of the 12-in. walls has been calculated. Then the third dimension (the thickness) is transferred from the description and applied to the total area to give the total volume of the 12-in. walls.

DIMENSIONS OF WORK

We live in a three-dimensional world, and all three dimensions of each item of work must be in an estimate, either explicitly or implicitly. Usually the dimensions are explicit in the item's description, or in one or more of the three dimension columns of the estimate sheet. Or one or more of the dimensions may be implicit in

PRACTICAL "STANDARDIZED" FORMS FOR CONTRACTORS
Form 514 MFD. IN U. S. A.

GENERAL ESTIMATE

BUILDING Sandown School
LOCATION Sandown IW
ARCHITECTS Charlesworth
SUBJECT WORK BELOW MAIN FLOOR

ESTIMATE NO. 1
SHEET NO. 2 OF 27
ESTIMATOR KC
CHECKER JB
DATE June '84

FRANK R. WALKER CO., PUBLISHERS, CHICAGO

DESCRIPTION OF WORK	NO. PIECES	DIMENSIONS	EXTENSIONS	EXTENSIONS	TOTAL ESTIMATED QUANTITY	UNIT PRICE M'T'L	TOTAL ESTIMATED MATERIAL COST	UNIT PRICE LABOR	TOTAL ESTIMATE LABOR COST
REINF CONC (3500 psi x 3/4") (R/mix Conc @ P.C. $60.00/cy delvd)									
Cont Ftgs									
8'-10' below grade	1/	600.00 x 2.00 x 1.00	1200						
(allow 2% WASTE)	2/	20.50 x 2.00 x 1.00	82						
			1282		47½ cy				
						@ 61.20	2,910	@ 10.00	475
Isolated Ftgs (less than 1 cy ea)									
size 4' x 4' x 1'3"	5/	4	20		20 NO				
(= 20 cf/each)						@ 50.00	1,000	15.00	300
(allow 10% WASTE)									
Isolated Ftgs (more than 1 cy ea)	4/	5.00 x 5.00	100						
x 1'3" deep	1/	6.00 x 5.00	30						
(allow 10% WASTE)			130						
		(Cube)	x 1.25						
			163	(5 NO)	6 cy				
						@ 66.00	400	20.00 EA	100
Fnd Walls									
x 12" thick	1/	600.00 x 4.00	2400						
below Main Floor	2/	20.50 x 4.00	164						
(allow 5% WASTE)			2564						
		(Cube)	x 1.00						
			2564		95 cy				
						@ 63.00	5,985	13.00	1,235
			Sub-totals (page 2/27)			$	10,295	$	2,110

FIGURE 7-5 An example of items of work entered on an estimate sheet.

an item's description (see Fig. 7-6). In this example, for the first item (conc ftgs) all three dimensions are in the dimension columns, because the item measures volume, or is a cube[G] item. For the next item, the 8-inch thick wall, there is one dimension in the description and two in the dimension columns. Although this item is subsequently measured as a cube item, it is expedient to measure it first as a superficial item, that is, as a super,[G] to obtain the area of the wall and thus to obtain the measurements of other related items, such as the wall forms. If the 8-inch thickness dimension were placed in the dimension column, the area of the wall would not appear in the estimate for future use. However, the three dimensions of the concrete wall are explicit as between the description and the dimension columns.

This is not so in the next item, 'bush-hammer wall surf.' Here, the two *super dimensions* of this tooled finish to concrete are explicit in the dimension columns, but the third dimension is not explicit. It is implicit in the description. The specifications may describe this item in detail, and it may be specified that the bush-hammering (in which a pneumatic tool with a special chisel-head is used to chip away the surface of the concrete to expose the aggregate) "*shall remove from between 1/8 inch and 1/4 inch of the concrete wall surface.*" The third dimension is therefore implicit in the specified depth of the bush-hammering.

Similarly, for painting work, two dimensions are usually entered in the dimension columns; the third dimension is implicit in the description. There, the third dimension is more obvious, since the description should state the number of coats of paint.

Thus, the three dimensions of each and every item are required in an estimate, either explicitly or implicitly. If any are omitted, the estimate is incomplete and accurate pricing is not possible. In this way, both the "description" and the "dimensions" are equal in describing an item of work in an estimate so that it may be priced as accurately as possible.

The style of dimensions in descriptions has already been mentioned. It should be as it is in the drawings, with diacritical signs (above the figures) for feet and inches. For metric dimensions it is only necessary to write them in the standard format as shown in examples later. The style of writing dimensions in the dimension columns should be different from that in the descriptions. Dimensions in the dimension columns may be written as decimal fractions of a foot, or, more easily, simply as feet and inches (duodecimals[G]) without the diacritical signs, as in the following table. In the case of metric measurements, it is even simpler, as we shall see.

DIMENSIONS

In Descriptions (as on drawings)	In Dimension Columns	
	Decimal Fractions	feet-inches
2' 0"	2.00	2–0
2' 3"	2.25	2–3
3' 10½"	3.875	3–10½
18' 1"	18.083	18–1

Obviously, the simplest way is to enter dimensions in the columns as feet-inches. But, some students fear that such entries may be confused with decimal fractions of a foot. However, in practice there is generally no problem because decimal fractions of a foot are immediately recognizable, because they all should be carried to at least two decimal places (except for 6 in.). If an electric calculator is to be used for calculating quantities, feet-inches can be converted to decimal fractions of a foot as they are entered into the calculator. In this way an estimator's task of entering dimensions is made easier, and the estimate sheets are simpler and easier to read.

Before calculators, quantities were often calculated manually by junior assistants using duodecimals. But the advent of calculators no longer makes their use necessary. However, as long as we continue to use feet and inches a knowledge of duodecimals is useful.

In examples in this book, the dimensions are entered in feet-inches in the dimension columns (with the exception of those in metric and some in Fig. 7-6), and in the descriptions of items the dimensions are shown as they appear on the drawings. Metric examples should cause no problem or confusion.

Many dimensions required by an estimator are not shown on the drawings and must be calculated from those dimensions that are shown. These calculations must be shown in the estimate, either at the beginning as preliminary calculations or in the description column close to the description of the related item (see the examples in Chapter 9).

Nothing is more exasperating to a cost accountant, or to any other person who has to use an estimate compiled by another person, than finding dimensions in an estimate that are not on the drawings and for which there is no explanation in the estimate. Some estimators seem unable to grasp this fact, probably because of their limited view of an estimate as simply a means to a bid. If an estimator knows and understands that his estimate may be used by others for other purposes, he will probably be more helpful in explaining how he has arrived at the assumptions, conclusions,

PRACTICAL STANDARDIZED FORMS FOR CONTRACTORS
Form 514 MFD. IN U.S.A.

GENERAL ESTIMATE

BUILDING: Sandown School
LOCATION: Sandown IW
ARCHITECTS: Charlesworth
SUBJECT: WORK BELOW MAIN FLOOR -

ESTIMATE NO.: 1
SHEET NO.: 3 of 27
ESTIMATOR: KC
CHECKER: JB
DATE: June '87

FRANK R. WALKER CO., PUBLISHERS, CHICAGO

DESCRIPTION OF WORK	NO. PIECES	DIMENSIONS	EXTENSIONS	EXTENSIONS	TOTAL ESTIMATED QUANTITY	UNIT PRICE M'T'L	TOTAL ESTIMATED MATERIAL COST	UNIT PRICE LABOR	TOTAL ESTIMATE LABOR COST
REINF CONC (3500 psi x 3/4") (R/mix conc @ P.C. $60.00/cy delv'd.)									
Conc Ftgs cont (allow 2% waste)									
	2/	40.00 x 2.00 x 1.00	160						
	2/	31.33 x 2.00 x 1.00	125						
			285		11 cy	61.36	673	12.00	132
Fnd Walls x 8" (allow 5% waste)									
	2/	40.00 x 4.25	340	DDT					
DDT: (openings)	2/	3.33 x 2.00	–	13					
	2/	2.00 x 2.00	–	8					
			−21						
		(Wall Area) =	319 SF						
			x0.67 =	214	8 cy	63.00	504	20.00	160
Bush-hammer Finish to Conc (as Spec. 03.11.10)									
		(Wall Area) =	319						
DDT: (below grade)	2/	40.00 x 1.25	−100 =	219	220 SF	10¢	22	2.10	462
ALTERNATIVELY: enter feet & inches:-									
Conc Ftgs, cont (allow 2% waste)									
	2/	40-0 x 2-0 x 1-0	160						
	2/	31-4 x 2-0 x 1-0	125 =	285	11 cy				
ALTERNATIVELY: enter in metric:-									
Conc Ftgs, cont (allow 2% waste)									
	2/	12 190 x 600 x 300	4388						
	2/	9 550 x 600 x 300	3438 =	7826	8 m³				

FIGURE 7-6 An example of dimensions entered on an estimate sheet in different ways.

and dimensions in the estimate that are not obvious from the bidding documents.

An estimator must make his estimate understandable to others by supplementing it with brief notes and explanatory calculations. Frequently, these calculations are simple enough to be done mentally by the estimator, and as a result too often they are omitted.

The use of electric calculators also tends to cause estimators to neglect to enter calculations and subtotals in their estimates, much to the frustration of the users of the estimates. An estimator will find that such notes and calculations often help him to check an estimate and avoid errors, but primarily they are necessary to explain the estimate to others. All calculations that are obvious (even though they may be too long or complex for mental calculation) and that contribute nothing to explaining the reasoning in an estimate *should not be shown.* For example, in Fig. 7-7, the concrete footing length of 132 feet is not shown on the drawings, so it has to be calculated from the dimensions. *This calculation should be shown in the estimate.* No other calculations need to be shown, other than the extensions and the total quantity. Calculations that cannot be done mentally should be done by calculator or on a note pad, but no parts of calculating processes (such as multiplication, division, etc.) should appear in an estimate. The essential need in an estimate is for an "audit trail," a path along which a reader (auditor) can go and follow the estimate's meaning.

By carefully examining the drawings and specifications before starting an estimate, an estimator is often able to reduce and simplify his work by grouping together similar items with common dimensions, by calculating averages and totals, and by tabulating information. This step is better done at the beginning of an estimate, and in doing preliminary calculations the estimator usually ignores the printed columns and column headings of the estimate sheet. Student estimators often have trouble with the printed columns on an estimate sheet. Some ignore them completely, whereas others use them scrupulously. The columns are intended to be an aid, not an obstacle. Without them, most estimates would be a confusion, and student estimators should make an effort to use them properly. On the other hand, they should learn to ignore the printed columns when it is desirable.

The column between the *"Description"* and the *"Dimensions"* is headed *"No. of Pieces"* in the estimate sheets used in the examples. It is sometimes called the "timesing column" because the dimensions are "times" (multiplied by) the numbers entered there. Many estimators use a "timesing stroke" to separate a "timesing number" from the dimensions; thus: 2/ 2.0 × 4.0. Mathematically, this means 2 × 2 × 4;

but in an estimate, 2/ 2.0 × 4.0 indicates something more. The entry 2/ 2.0 × 4.0 shows that there are two equal areas, both 2 ft × 4 ft. Otherwise, 2.0 × 2.0 × 4.0 indicates a volume, 2 ft × 2 ft × 4 ft. Similarly, the timesing stroke is used in side calculations and in preliminary calculations to indicate multiplicity rather than multiplication.

Timesing can be used effectively to convey information. For example, in measuring the doors in an apartment block of forty suites, with an entrance door to each suite, and ten suites on each of four floors, it is better to enter the dimension for entrance doors as 4/ 10/1 = 40, because this notation immediately conveys a picture to the reader of one entrance door × ten suites × four floors. Of course, the estimator could mentally calculate the total and enter it directly without showing the figures. But this defeats one of the purposes of the estimate: to convey information.

Other examples of descriptive entries of dimensions are:

(1) 2/ ½/18.0 × 9.0 = 162 SF
(Two triangular areas, each with a base of 18 ft × a perpendicular height of 9 ft.)

(2) 1/ 3½/8.0 × 8.0 = 201 SF
(Area of a circle, 16 ft in diameter.)

(3) 3/ 3½/16.0 = 151 LF
(Three times the circumference of a circle 16 feet in diameter.)

Simple fractions such as ½ must be written carefully so as to avoid confusion with 1/ 2/ (once times, twice times . . .).

You may ask, Why times a dimension by 1? Yet there are occasions when "once times" is significant, if only to indicate that the dimension should not be timesed by any other figure, particularly if other items, before and after, are timesed by other figures. The "once times," properly used, also can convey information that might not otherwise be known. This is the purpose of all the conventions and techniques of entering dimensions: to convey information.

Sometimes it is necessary to go back to an item in an estimate and to repeat an entry. This can be done by timesing the dimensions (if not already timesed) or by adding onto the timesing figure—thus, 2.3/3½/16.0 (Originally, three times; now, 3 plus 2, or five times the perimeter of a circle 16 feet in diameter.) Rarely is there a risk of confusion once the convention is known and expected. The 3/ times might have been erased and replaced by a 5/ times when the additional two items were found. But erasures are not always convenient or desirable, and sometimes

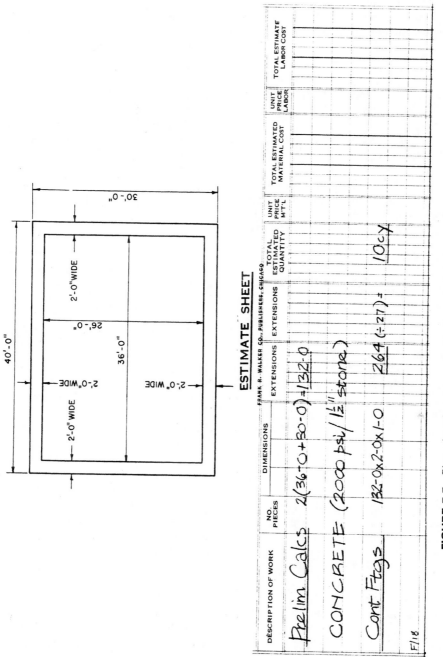

FIGURE 7-7 Plan showing concrete footings and their entry in the estimate.

the "3 plus 2" tells more than "5." This is called "dotting on," but if there is any risk of confusion, do not use it; or use a plus sign.

It is a useful practice to always enter dimensions in this order: horizontal dimensions first; vertical dimensions last. The third dimension in cube items should always be the vertical dimension of height/ depth/ thickness, as the case may be. Again, the use of a simple convention will convey more information.[2] Students of estimating with some knowledge of computer languages and programs will be less conservative about using symbols in estimates; and when computers are used more in estimating more symbols will have to be created. (Examples of estimating done with computers appear in Chapter 4.)

Having entered dimensions in the dimension column, and in the description column when required, the next logical step is to enter the extension, or calculation result in the first extension column to the right of the three dimension columns. Extensions should be in whole numbers. If the dimensions are in feet and inches, the extensions are in feet. It is not usually necessary to enter fractions in extensions, and "rounding off" (up or down) to the nearest unit is usually satisfactory. With several extensions to an item, the extensions will usually more or less compensate. In using metric dimensions, however, because the meter is larger than a foot, with some items it may be desirable to use decimal fractions in extensions. In some cases, there is yet another calculation required to arrive at the "total estimated quantity" of an item that also requires "rounding off," and that obviously affects the degree of accuracy required in the extensions preceding it.

In practice, the extensions are better left until all the work, or a major section of the work, has been taken off (measured) to avoid interrupting the estimator's train of thought. It is important for an estimator to have as few interruptions as possible while taking off[G] quantities. This aspect of an estimator's work is the least understood.

Estimating requires great concentration and a lively imagination, and measuring work need not be the detailed drudgery that some say it must be. The "taker off" constructs the work in his mind as he measures it, and at the same time he analyzes the work drawn by the designer and visualizes the cir-cumstances and conditions affecting it. From this mental process he describes the items of work and enters their dimensions. He has translated the bidding documents into a concise, verbal, and numerical account. Some other person may do the extensions, for this imaginative process should not be interrupted by such routine tasks. Thus, measurement of work by a skilled taker off is a creative act of interpretation.

QUANTITIES OF WORK

The unit of measurement in which an item of work is priced in an estimate depends on several things, including:

1. Materials used in the item of work
2. Labor, plant, and equipment used in the item of work
3. Trade practices related to the item of work
4. Relative cost of a unit of the item of work
5. Appropriate *standard methods of measurement*[G]
6. Functions of computers in estimating.

But, above all, the unit of measurement used for the total estimated quantity of an item should be that unit that most readily facilitates accurate pricing of the item in the estimate.

The common units of measurement of many items are the same units in which the primary material of the item is bought and sold. For example, clay bricks are sold by the thousand, so clay brickwork often is measured in square feet and then converted into units of a thousand bricks by a factor that varies according to the size of the brick, the width of the joint, and the number of bricks in a square foot area of wall of a stated thickness. Others prefer to simply measure brickwork in square feet (or meters), stating the thickness, the size of the brick, and the joint width in the description, leaving the further step of computing the total number of bricks until they are ordered for purchase, at which time an allowance for waste is added.

If one unit of measurement (U_2) is the product of another unit of measurement (U_1) and a factor (f), and $U_2 = U_1 \times f$, mathematically it does not matter which unit of measurement is used in an estimate (U_1 or U_2), if all the required information is given, including the factor (f). The various units of measurement for the most common items of work are given in Chapter 8.

Measuring items of work in the same units of measurement as are used for the basic material may be satisfactory if different unit prices are used for

---

[2] This is the common precept in measuring work. Some manufacturers give different orders of dimensions for their products to draw attention to the most critical (the variable) dimension of their product by stating it first. For example, in the case of concrete blocks with standard face dimensions of 16 inches long by 8 inches high, the variable third dimension (the thickness in the wall) is stated first.

similar items of different dimensions. For example, the unit price "per thousand bricks" for 4-in.-thick brick walls should be higher than the unit price for 8-in.-thick brick walls, all else being equal. There does appear to be some risk of overlooking this requirement when using the unit of measurement of the material rather than a superficial unit (say, square foot of wall area) with which the description of the wall's thickness becomes a much more obvious requirement. With an experienced estimator, either unit, per "thousand bricks" or per "square foot of wall area," will serve equally well; but since the area measurement has to be obtained first to calculate the number of bricks, and since the area measurement better describes the item of work, the original area unit of measurement is preferable in an estimate.

The original area unit of measurement for masonry walls represents the work much more clearly in the mind of an estimator. To speak of 100 SF of 8-in.-thick concrete block wall conveys a clearer idea of the quantity of work than to speak of 112½ concrete blocks (of 16-in. × 8-in. nominal face size with 3/8-in.-wide joints). This is because the *work* consists of concrete blocks that, when built into the wall, lose their identity as separate units. The same argument about using or not using original units of measurement can be made for and illustrated with any other item of work for which the unit of measurement is that of its primary material, such as: wood framed construction measured in units of a thousand board feet; steel framed construction measured in weight-units of tons, hundredweights, or pounds; and reinforced concrete measured in units of a cubic yard. These items of work and their units of measurement are discussed further in Chapter 8.

It may be said in light of the preceding that generally the most rational unit of measurement for any item of work is that unit in which the item is first measured from the drawings. That unit usually is the one that most aptly describes and represents the item in the minds of estimators and others using the estimate.[3] The use of these units usually requires that one or more dimensions be given in the item's description to provide complete information about the item in the estimate.

As we shall see, trade practices and customs, and methods of measurement based on them, do not always call for work to be measured in the most rational units; due, in part, to compromises with the past, and the past emphasis on materials and their costs rather than on labor. But now research into the rationality of measurement and logical programming of construction management systems is underway, which means that there will have to be changes made in the methods of measurement. The advent of industrialized construction that began in the nineteenth century with the mass production of building components and the development of systems building[G] requires estimators to examine their methods and to replace some with new methods of measuring and estimating costs.

The costs of today's mass-produced building components are not of the same nature as the costs of similar components made by hand or by earlier production methods.

In the past, when most doors were specially made, standard methods of measurement[4] called for doors to be measured in square feet. Now, doors are enumerated and described. For example, a flush door, size 1'6" × 6'8", may cost $20.00, and a similar but larger door, size 3'0" × 6'8", may cost $30.00. The smaller door therefore costs $2.00 per SF, and the larger door costs $1.50 per SF. Also, the installation costs of preparing and hanging a door bears slight relationship to the door's size. This illustrates a fact about measuring and pricing doors and other such stock items; namely, that they should be and usually are enumerated and fully described. To measure them and price them in square feet leads to inaccurate pricing.

But not all methods of measurement are so rational. Present standard methods of measurement require formwork for most cast-in-place concrete to be measured by area, the measurements to be those of the actual surfaces of formwork in contact with concrete. Consider the case of formwork for the cast-in-place reinforced concrete stairs shown at (A) in Fig. 7-8. Suppose that the time required to build the forms for the stairs in (A) is 30 man-hours (say, 2 carpenters for 15 hours). What time will be required to build the forms for the stairs at (B), which are 50 percent wider than the stairs in (A)? Surely, they will not require 50 percent more time. The only extra labor required for (B) is in the erection of formwork. The labor costs of layout and cutting the material should be about the same in both cases. And erection of the wider stairs should not require 50 percent more time.

---

[3] If we escape from the limited concept of an estimate as simply a means to a bid and see it as the building's design in another format—as work to be done for the owner—then we may see that the rational units of measurement of this work are not necessarily the same units used to measure and purchase the basic materials. Because in doing the work the materials are arranged and changed by skill, labor, and tools, and it is the *work* to be done that is to be measured and priced, not simply the materials.

[4] Two standard methods of measurement currently published and in use are referred to in Chapter 8.

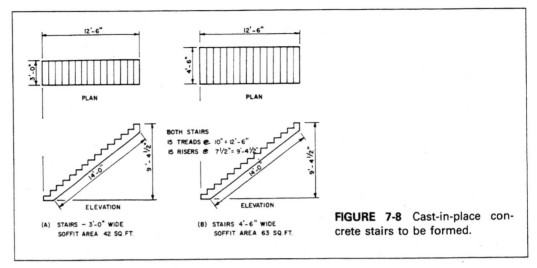

FIGURE 7-8 Cast-in-place concrete stairs to be formed.

This means that unit prices obtained through cost accounting for forming stairs 3′0″ wide cannot properly be used to price the formwork for stairs 4′6″ wide if measurement is by area. But if the unit of measurement is, "*one staircase, 3′0″ wide by 12′6″ going × 10′0″ rise,*" the estimator can use the unit price for forming of, say, $420.00 each (30 hours @ $14.00 per hour) to estimate the cost of forming for a similar but wider staircase (which is 4′6″ wide) of, say, $460.00 each. An increase in cost of about 10 percent appears to be reasonable. An increase of 50 percent does not appear as reasonable.

You may ask, Why then do the standard methods of measurement require such formwork to be measured by area instead of being described and enumerated? It seems that in the past it was necessary to measure all work in standard units (e.g., feet and yards, as cubes, supers, and runs) to combine and manually handle the many items of work in one job. By combining the quantities of similar items of work the number of individual items was reduced; the reasoning being that the cost differences between similar items were too small to be significant.

For example, floor tiling installed in a number of rooms of various sizes and proportions of a project was and still is usually measured as one super item; the total of all the rooms' floor areas. This total quantity of floor tiling and the accompanying description of the item, "*1/8 in. thick marbleized vinyl asbestos floor tiling,*" does not indicate either the room sizes and their proportions (length/breadth) or the straight cutting of floor tile usually required at the perimeters, all of which affect the costs of supplying and laying the floor tiling. The total amount of straight cutting would be a useful indication of certain costs; but straight cutting generally is not measured (usually its measurement is not required by the standard methods of measurement),

and it is allowed for in the main item of work. Obviously, the way to price floor tiling accurately is to measure and price the work, including the straight cutting, in each room separately.[5] But this requires considerably more effort by the estimator, more paperwork and more calculating. The extra accuracy has not been considered to be worth the extra effort when other more indeterminable parts of the estimate are of greater significance. Now, computers and electronic data processing potentially have changed all this.

Quantities in an estimate are usually rounded-off, according to the nature of the item and the unit of measurement. There is no general rule other than common sense. Delusions of accuracy sometimes cause estimators to measure total quantities of work to two or three decimal places. There is a practical hazard in this because a decimal point can be easily overlooked thereby causing a major error. Generally, we are better off without fractions in an estimate. They are rarely necessary, because generally the cost of units of work are not high, and the tolerances of accuracy are usually sufficiently wide.

The need to use fractions depends on the costs of the item and the unit of measurement. If a fraction

---

[5] A common trade practice is to measure areas of finishes "gross" by taking the actual dimensions of rooms up to the nearest multiple of the dimension of the product (tile, sheet) to be installed. This allows for waste material, but it does not necessarily allow for the labor cost of straight cutting at perimeters. An allowance for this labor cost may be made by pricing the gross quantity measured at a unit price for both the material costs and labor costs; but this is not necessarily accurate because straight cutting and waste depend on job and product dimensions, and the differences between them, which are always random and variable. Of course, the experienced estimator can usually make a reasonable judgement, but measuring net quantities and an item of straight cutting in each area is more rational and produces more useful information.

is necessary, use a simple fraction rather than a decimal fraction. The figures 19½ CY are unmistakable, but 19.5 CY can easily be mistaken for 195 CY. It seems that many are misled by a mystical belief that, somehow, decimals must be more accurate, probably because they are often harder to use manually. But, again, computers can change things.

Computers can overcome some of the obstacles that in the past have kept us from estimating in greater detail and with greater accuracy; particularly in handling the large volume of data and calculations involved. If a computer can do the calculations and print out a copy of the estimate in a matter of minutes, why should we not estimate in greater detail? Computer results can be more accurate, because more data can be utilized and stored for future use. The only question remaining without a clear and positive answer: Is the use of computers in estimating economically feasible? This is a difficult question, and an answer cannot be given without research. Probably, at present, under the traditional system of competitive bidding for lump sum contracts,[G] computers would save time and money, particularly since the bidding system itself is uneconomical in that most estimating is non-productive.

Two things are happening: (1) a tendency to move away from the traditional system of competitive bidding for stipulated sum contracts, and (2) the continuing development of small computers. When building components were handmade by craftsmen, the methods of measurement reflected the materials and the labor used. When building components were first mass produced in factories, the methods of measuring those items changed (or should have changed) to suit the new products. This is still going on, and soon it will be accelerated by the widespread use of computers.

MENSURATION OF WORK

Mensuration means measurement and the computation of measurements, and the student of estimating must have a knowledge of and a facility with mensuration, at least as advanced as it is taught in high school. In addition, he needs some algebra, geometry, and trigonometry, and he should develop a practical comprehension of measurements and quantities. This ability comes with practice; but a conscious effort should be made to acquire it as early as possible.

Much of an estimator's work requires imagination to visualize construction work being done so that it can be described and measured in an estimate. It is also necessary to visualize quantities of materials and work. For example, can you visualize a cubic yard: an excavated pit $3'0'' \times 3'0'' \times 3'0''$; a cubic yard of

gravel in a pile (about 6 ft across the base and about 3 ft high); a stack of twenty-seven bags of portland cement; or a stack of about 700 standard clay bricks? Can you visualize 1000 board feet of lumber: one-hundred $2'' \times 6''$ joists, each 10 feet long; 2000 linear feet of $1'' \times 6''$ boards; or twenty-five $2'' \times 12''$ boards, each 20 ft long? It is less difficult to visualize quantities of materials in a heap or a stack. It is much more difficult to visualize them as installed work and incorporated into a building; such as the bricks in a wall, and the joists in a framed floor or roof.

The ability to visualize quantities of work comes in part from an ability to do mental computations; and the mind can learn to compute rapidly and without much apparent effort. In fact, in mental calculation a strained effort can be an obstacle, and it is often better to relax. Also, it appears that complete reliance on mechanical means deprives the mind of a training that has value beyond doing simple computations.

Here, we shall not make a general review of mensuration practices, but rather shall look at some methods that are of special interest and importance to estimators. Integrating dimensions is one of these. An estimator should bring together as many dimensions and parts of the same item of work as possible so that there is only one total dimension to be used. For example, in measuring partition walls, all the lengths of similar walls of the same height should be integrated into one total length as in the following example:

Length	Description	Dimensions	Quantity
20.0	6" Std conc		
60.0	blk ptns		
20.0	(two flrs)		
17.6			
8.6			
126.0		2/126.0 × 8.0 = 2,016 SF	

Note that all dimensions are entered here in feet-inches, or duodecimals.

It is not unusual to see experienced estimators enter dimensions as follows:

$$
Cont\ Conc\ Ftgs
\begin{cases}
200.0 \times 2.0 \times 1.6 = 600 \text{ CF} \\
132.0 \times 2.0 \times 1.6 = 396 \\
200.0 \times 2.0 \times 1.6 = 600 \\
132.0 \times 2.0 \times 1.6 = 396 \\
50.0 \times 2.0 \times 1.6 = 150 \\
34.0 \times 2.0 \times 1.6 = 102 \\
50.0 \times 2.0 \times 1.6 = 150 \\
4.0 \times 2.0 \times 1.6 = 12 \\
2.0 \times 2.0 \times 1.6 = 6 \\
\end{cases}
$$
$$\overline{2412 \text{ CF}}$$

and so on, and on, and on, with each length of concrete footings measured separately and entered in a mechanical and thoughtless way. No wonder some think estimating is tedious. By first collecting the lengths on the estimate sheet (not on a scratch pad) and by obtaining the total length of concrete footings, the dimensions may be entered thus:

Cont Conc Ftgs 804.0 × 2.0 × 1.6 = 2412 CF

Or, if there is a reason for separate measurements, such as for two buildings or for two distinct parts of a building shown on the drawings, the estimator might enter two totals, thus:

$$
\begin{array}{cc}
200.0 & 50.0 \\
\underline{132.0} & \underline{34.0} \\
332.0 & 50.0 \\
\underline{\times 2} & \underline{4.0} \\
664.0 & 2.0 \\
 & \underline{140.0}
\end{array}
$$

$$
\text{\textit{Conc Ftgs}} \begin{cases} 664.0 \times 2.0 \times 1.6 = 1992 \\ 140.0 \times 2.0 \times 1.6 = \underline{\ 420} \\ \qquad\qquad\qquad\quad\ \underline{2412} \text{ CF} \end{cases}
$$

The object is to simplify the estimate by brevity and to reduce the number of computations required to obtain the total quantity of the item without obscuring useful information. Only items of work with two of their three dimensions identical can be integrated by the addition of the varying third dimensions. The previous 6-in.-thick concrete block partitions are all 8 ft high, and their various lengths can be collected. The above footings are all 2 ft wide × 1½ ft deep, and their various lengths, too, can be collected. Of course, all such collections must be carefully checked.

Averages are helpful, but they are often misunderstood and abused. For example, Fig. 7-9 shows the elevation of a concrete retaining wall.

The area of the wall is measured in feet-inches

thus:

$$
\begin{array}{lll}
\text{(A)} & 12.0 \times 4.5 = & 53 \text{ SF} \\
\text{(B)} & 22.6 \times 8.0 = & 180 \\
\text{(C)} & 3.6 \times 14.0 = & 49 \\
\text{(D)} & 12.0 \times 18.6 = & 222 \\
\text{(E)} & \underline{\ 8.0} \times 24.0 = & \underline{192} \\
& (58.0) & = \underline{696} \text{ SF}
\end{array}
$$

Area = Length × Height $(A = L \times H)$; then $H = A/L$

Average height = Area ÷ Length

$$
= \frac{696.0}{58.0} = 12 \text{ ft (average height)}
$$

Note that the average height cannot be calculated without including the varying section-lengths. This average height may be used for measuring other items of work in the reinforced concrete retaining wall; for example, the vertical steel rebars (reinforcing bars) may be measured as averaging 12 feet in length. The average number of rows of horizontal rebars can be calculated by dividing the average height of the wall by the spacing of the horizontal bars and adding an extra bar, because there is always one more bar than spaces. The formwork to the sides of the wall can be measured directly from the surface area of 696 SF already computed. The formwork quantity is 2/696 SF = 1392 SF plus formwork to the ends, which average 14.2½ high (not 12.0).

Some may try to measure the wall area thus:

$$
\begin{array}{lll}
4.5 & 12.0 & 58.0 \text{ (total length)} \\
8.0 & 22.6 & \underline{\times 13.9\frac{1}{2}} \text{ (average height)} \\
14.0 & 3.6 & (799.11) \\
18.6 & 12.0 & \underline{800.0} \text{ SF} \\
\underline{24.0} & \underline{8.0} & \\
5) \ \underline{68.11} & 58.0 \text{ (total length)} \\
13.9\tfrac{1}{2} \text{ (average height)}
\end{array}
$$

This measurement is not correct, because the average

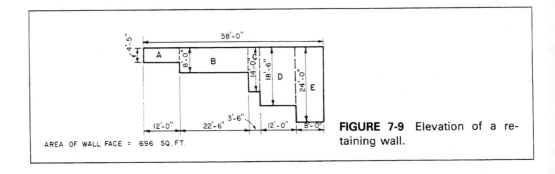

AREA OF WALL FACE = 696 SQ. FT.

FIGURE 7-9 Elevation of a retaining wall.

height is not 13 ft 9½ in., but 12 ft. The error is large (about 15 percent) and unacceptable.

If the wall's elevation were as in Fig. 7-10, the wall's area could be computed by first obtaining the average height, thus:

```
     4.0
     8.0
    12.0
    24.0              58.0 (total length)
 4) 48.0          ×   12.0 (average height)
    12.0 (average height)   696.0 SF
```

because in this case the four section lengths are all the same, and all the bays have two identical dimensions: the wall thickness and the bay length of 14 ft 6 ins.

Perimeters are often used to measure work in buildings, and the accurate computation of perimeters sometimes causes trouble. First, a simple example of a 2-ft-wide concrete footing. The total length of the 2-ft-wide concrete footing in Fig. 7-11 is 132 ft. This can be obtained in several ways, thus:

```
40.0        40.0         30.0        30.0         40.0
40.0 (or)   26.0 (or)    30.0 (or)   36.0 (or)    30.0
26.0        66.0         36.0        66.0         70.0
26.0        × 2          36.0        × 2          × 2
132.0       132.0        132.0       132.0        140.0
                              (less: 4/2.0 = ) − 8.0
                                                 132.0
```

These computations are all basically the same. In the last computation, the outside perimeter is computed first and 4/2.0 = 8.0 is deducted to obtain the true length of the footings. This is the best method.

The first four computations appear be more simple and logical, and you might ask, Why first calculate the outside perimeter (140.0) and then make a deduction? There are reasons that require explanation.

Many building plans are not simple rectangles, and computing their perimeters is not so obvious as it is in the above example. Also, the outside perimeter

is often a useful dimension to have, and it is convenient to compute it while computing the length of the footings. The length of the footings in Fig. 7-11 is 132 LF, and this is the length of the mean perimeter of the footings; that is, the perimeter at the centerline of the footings as shown in Fig. 7-12. In Fig. 7-11, the outer perimeter length is 140 LF; the inner perimeter length is 124 LF; and the mean perimeter length is 132 LF, which is the average (mean) of the other two perimeter lengths. The footings' mean perimeter (and true length) is also the true length of any other items symmetrical about the same mean perimeter line, such as the wall in Fig. 7-13. Since the 8″ foundation wall is centered on the footing, they both have the same mean perimeter and the same length.

Figure 7-14 shows a typical corner (in plan), and a 2-ft-wide concrete footing. It also shows that the inner dimensions (ID) are each less than the outer dimensions (OD) by the width of the footing, and that the difference between the outer and inner perimeters is twice times the footing width at each of four corners. From this it can be seen (and calculated) that the difference between the *mean perimeter* and either the inner or the outer perimeter is (plus or minus) *twice times half the footing width at each of four corners.* This is because there are two dimensions to be adjusted at every corner, each by half the width difference between the inside and the outside perimeters, to arrive at the mean perimeter.

Notice that most building plans do not show the dimensions of footings; only the dimensions of the exterior walls are shown. In such cases, the perimeters can be calculated from wall dimensions in exactly the same way, and the mean perimeter thus calculated can be used to measure the footings, as indicated in Fig. 7-13.

A less simple foundation plan, as in Fig. 7-15, can be approached in the same way, and the mean perimeter may be computed thus:

$$2(40.0 + 30.0 + 5.0) - (4. \times 2.0) = 142 \text{ LF}$$

Notice that re-entrant corners, such as those indicated

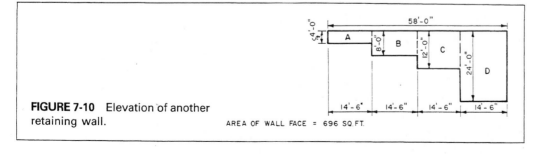

FIGURE 7-10 Elevation of another retaining wall.

AREA OF WALL FACE = 696 SQ.FT.

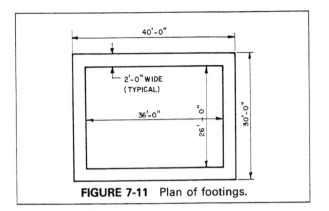

FIGURE 7-11 Plan of footings.

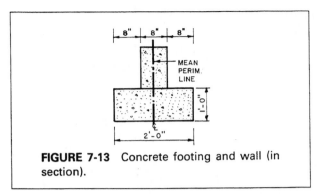

FIGURE 7-13 Concrete footing and wall (in section).

in Fig. 7-15, do not affect the length of a perimeter. However, the presence of a recess, such as is shown in Fig. 7-15 (size 12'0" × 5'0"), does increase the length of a perimeter. Without the recess, the mean perimeter in Fig. 7-15 would be 132 LF, the same as in Fig. 7-11, despite the difference in shape. But the 5'0"-deep recess increases the mean perimeter by 2 × 5.0 = 10 feet. The rule for computing perimeters can be simply expressed:

> **Ignore all re-entrant corners, and add the overall length to the overall width of the building; add the depth of each recess, if any, and multiply the sum by 2. The result is the outside perimeter.**
>
> **To adjust an outside (inside) perimeter to give the mean perimeter, deduct (add) four times the width of the footing, (or the thickness of the wall, as the case may be). The result is the mean perimeter.**

Notice that the adjustment is always *four times* the width or thickness: once for each 90-degree corner, since the perimeter always passes through 360 degrees (= 4 × 90 degrees). This fact is not affected by re-entrant corners and recesses. If a building's inside perimeter is calculated first, the adjustment of four

times the width or thickness is *added* to give the mean perimeter.

It is often useful to be able to compute the length of other perimeters in addition to that of the mean perimeter. Looking at a section through a building's foundations and exterior walls indicates how the adjustment of perimeters can be simply used and expressed. (See Fig. 7-16.)

> **The difference in length between two perimeters is always four times, twice times, the horizontal distance between the perimeter lines.**

In Fig. 7-11, the mean perimeter is 132 LF. The horizontal distance between the *mean perimeter line* and the line of the outer perimeter is 1 foot. Applying the above adjustment: 4 × 2 × horizontal distance of 1 foot = 8 LF; and (132 + 8) = 140 LF, the length of the *outer perimeter*. The length of the *inner perimeter* is, by the same adjustment (132 − 8) = 124 LF. The same adjustment is added or deducted, depending on whether the required perimeter is inside (shorter than), or outside (longer than), the original perimeter. This

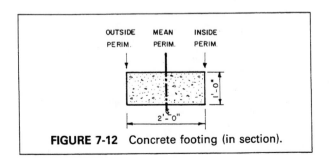

FIGURE 7-12 Concrete footing (in section).

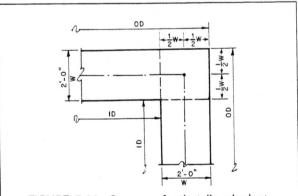

FIGURE 7-14 Concrete footing (in plan) at typical corner.

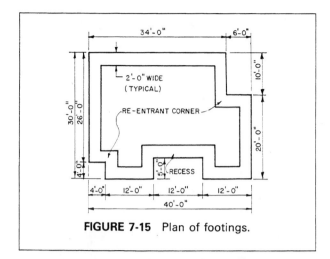

FIGURE 7-15 Plan of footings.

adjustment rule conforms with the general rule for computing perimeters given above.

Consider the exterior wall section of a building and the number of items of work whose lengths are related to the building's perimeter. In Fig. 7-16, many such items have been indicated to show their number. The true length (perimeter) of each one of these items can be easily computed by making one adjustment (an addition or deduction) to a perimeter length.

Volumes of earthworks such as excavations and fillings are required for most estimates, and the accuracy of the measurements and the volumes depends on the quality and amount of available information, as well as the estimator's skill. It is easy to have delusions of accuracy in measuring earthworks, and an estimator should keep in mind the object of the measurement— to estimate the costs of the work—as well as the practical accuracy of the measurements, and the relative importance of the quantities involved compared with other economic and physical conditions affecting the costs of the work.

Measured quantities probably are least significant in estimating the costs of earthworks, because there are so many other factors that are more important. These include:

1. Type and moisture content of the soil, which will determine the type and productivity of the excavating equipment and the degree of swell and shrinkage (increase and decrease in volume) that will occur when earth is excavated and later backfilled

2. Climate, location, and accessibility of the site, which will affect the type of equipment that can be used and the handling and disposal of excavated material on and off the site

3. Size and topography of the site, which will also affect the type and productivity of the excavating equipment as well as the amount of work to be done and material to be handled

4. Type and depth of excavation, which will also affect the type and productivity of equipment and the amount of work to be done and material to be handled.

These and other factors are often more important to the costs of the work of excavating than precisely measured quantities. Nevertheless, most estimators will not try to estimate the costs of earthworks without measured quantities, and many make two estimates of costs: one by pricing quantities, and another by estimating the equipment time and costs required to do the work.

Other considerations in measuring and pricing earthworks are, the working space allowances to be made for other work in excavations, and the provisions to be made for work in stabilizing excavations.[6] The allowances for *shrinkage and swell*[G] caused by excavating and consolidating backfilled materials should be included in the unit prices, according to the Precept of Measurement to measure work net in place, as explained in Chapter 6. This leaves the actual measurement of the volumes of earthworks to simple solid geometry, in the first instance.

Excavations in trenches, basements, and the like, are measured simply by multiplying length times breadth times depth. Excavations in banks[7] are measured by multiplying the cross-section area by the length, if the cross section is more or less constant throughout the length. When the volume to be excavated is enclosed by sides that are not parallel, the *Prismoidal Formula*[8] may be used, as illustrated in Fig. 7-17. In some cases the volume of a prismoid can be calculated to sufficient accuracy by $L \times C$, which in Fig. 7-17(B) gives a volume of 90 cubic feet instead of the $93\frac{1}{3}$ cubic feet computed with the formula. For small works, the first would be sufficiently accurate. The prismoidal formula may be used to measure the volume of excavation over a sloping site or area, as in Fig. 7-18, where excavating is to extend down to level + 1.00 over the site. Assuming even and regular slopes, we may in-

---

[6] These allowances and provisions for excavations are referred to in Chapter 8, *Measuring Work: Particular.*

[7] A bank refers to the face of an excavation at a change in level between two more or less horizontal planes, not to a financial institution.

[8] The Appendix contains explanations of this and other formulas for measuring areas and volumes.

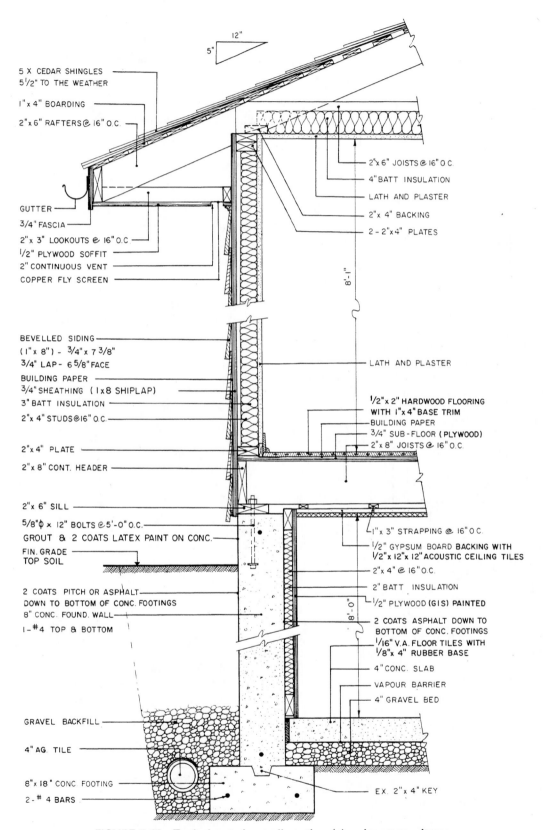

5 X CEDAR SHINGLES
5 1/2" TO THE WEATHER

1" x 4" BOARDING

2"x 6" RAFTERS @ 16" O.C.

GUTTER
3/4" FASCIA
2" x 3" LOOKOUTS @ 16" O.C
1/2" PLYWOOD SOFFIT
2" CONTINUOUS VENT
COPPER FLY SCREEN

BEVELLED SIDING
(1" x 8") - 3/4" x 7 3/8"
3/4" LAP - 6 5/8" FACE
BUILDING PAPER
3/4" SHEATHING (1 x 8 SHIPLAP)
3" BATT INSULATION
2" x 4" STUDS @ 16" O.C.

2" x 4" PLATE
2" x 8" CONT. HEADER

2" x 6" SILL
5/8" φ x 12" BOLTS @ 5'-0" O.C.
GROUT & 2 COATS LATEX PAINT ON CONC.
FIN. GRADE
TOP SOIL

2 COATS PITCH OR ASPHALT
DOWN TO BOTTOM OF CONC. FOOTINGS
8" CONC. FOUND. WALL
1 - #4 TOP & BOTTOM

GRAVEL BACKFILL

4" AG. TILE

8"x 18" CONC. FOOTING
2 - #4 BARS

2"x 6" JOISTS @ 16" O.C.
4" BATT INSULATION
LATH AND PLASTER
2" x 4" BACKING
2 - 2"x 4" PLATES

8'-1"

LATH AND PLASTER

1/2" x 2" HARDWOOD FLOORING
WITH 1"x 4" BASE TRIM
BUILDING PAPER
3/4" SUB-FLOOR (PLYWOOD)
2"x 8" JOISTS @ 16" O.C.

1"x 3" STRAPPING @ 16" O.C.
1/2" GYPSUM BOARD BACKING WITH
1/2"x 12"x 12" ACOUSTIC CEILING TILES
2"x 4" @ 16" O.C.
2" BATT INSULATION
1/2" PLYWOOD (GIS) PAINTED
2 COATS ASPHALT DOWN TO
BOTTOM OF CONC. FOOTINGS
1/16" V.A. FLOOR TILES WITH
1/8"x 4" RUBBER BASE
4" CONC. SLAB
VAPOUR BARRIER
4" GRAVEL BED

8'-0"

EX. 2"x 4" KEY

FIGURE 7-16   Typical exterior wall section (showing many items that can be measured by using an adjusted perimeter length). *Note: This section drawing complements the residence plans included.*

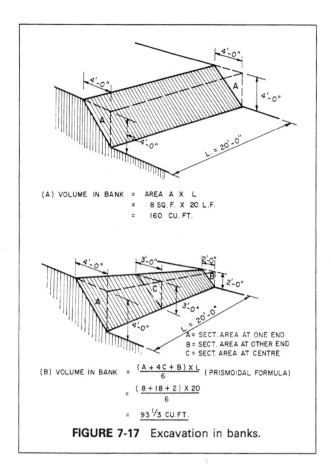

(A) VOLUME IN BANK = AREA A X L
= 8 SQ.F. X 20 L.F.
= 160 CU. FT.

A = SECT. AREA AT ONE END
B = SECT. AREA AT OTHER END
C = SECT. AREA AT CENTRE

(B) VOLUME IN BANK = $\frac{(A + 4C + B) \times L}{6}$ (PRISMOIDAL FORMULA)

= $\frac{(8 + 18 + 2) \times 20}{6}$

= 93 1/3 CU.FT.

FIGURE 7-17 Excavation in banks.

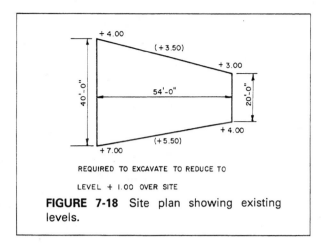

REQUIRED TO EXCAVATE TO REDUCE TO

LEVEL + 1.00 OVER SITE

FIGURE 7-18 Site plan showing existing levels.

terpolate the levels at the centers (in brackets). Using the prismoidal formula,

$$V = \frac{(A + 4C + B) \times L}{6}$$

$$A = 40 \times \frac{3 + 6}{2} = 180 \text{ SF}$$

$$B = 20 \times \frac{2 + 3}{2} = 50 \text{ SF}$$

$$C = 30 \times \frac{2.5 + 4.5}{2} = 105 \text{ SF}$$

Then,

$$V = \frac{(180 + 420 + 50) \times 54}{6} = 5850 \text{ CF}$$

If, as is commonly done, an average of the existing levels at the four corners is taken, the result would

be slightly different:

$$
\begin{array}{r}
4.0 \\
7.0 \\
3.0 \\
\underline{4.0} \\
4)\underline{18.0} = \quad 4.5 \text{ (Average existing level)} \\
-1.0 \text{ (Reduced level required)} \\
\underline{3.5} \text{ (Average depth of excav)}
\end{array}
$$

$$V = 54.0 \times 30.0 \times 3.5 = \underline{5670} \text{ CF}$$

The difference is not large, about 3 percent, and this second method may be used for a small site or with each of the grid squares over a larger site, as explained below.

If a site has no parallel sides, it will be necessary to draw a "compensating line" parallel to another side in order to use the prismoidal formula, as in Fig. 7-19, Site "X."

The areas of irregularly-shaped sites with boundaries that are not straight lines can be calculated by first drawing compensating lines, as in Fig. 7-19, Site "Y," and then by dividing the equivalent area into triangles to calculate the area. The volume of earthworks can then be calculated by averaging the depths of excavation, as above, or, if two sides are more or less parallel, by using the prismoidal formula.

Some degree of approximation depending on the position of compensating lines is inevitable, but these methods can be sufficiently accurate for measuring earthworks and siteworks for which the unit prices are not high. The compensating lines are usually easily drawn in the optimum locations by using a transparent rule or square to keep the plan visible and to facilitate visual equalization of the compensating areas on either side of the line. A transparent plastic sheet with a

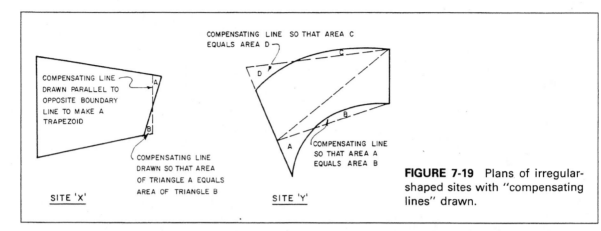

FIGURE 7-19 Plans of irregular-shaped sites with "compensating lines" drawn.

printed grid of small squares makes equalization much easier. The squares and part-squares on either side of each compensating line are counted and balanced. Likewise, an irregular area can also be measured by counting all the squares and part-squares within its boundaries.

In Fig. 7-20, a more precise method of measuring irregular areas is shown. The site plan shows a parcel bounded on the west by a road, on the east by a river, on the south by a creek, and on the north by a boundary line that is not straight. Over the plan have been laid strips of a selected equal width. The area of the site can be found by measuring to scale, from the plan, the average length of each strip inside the boundaries and by multiplying the total length of the strips by the standard width. Irregular areas must be added or deducted as necessary, and as indicated. These irregular areas can sometimes be measured by using compensating lines, and by triangulation, or by dividing the area into smaller strips in the same way. Alternatively, and instead of using strips, grid squares can be drawn on the plan and used to measure areas, as indicated and described above. Measurements are made more accurate by using narrower strips or smaller grid

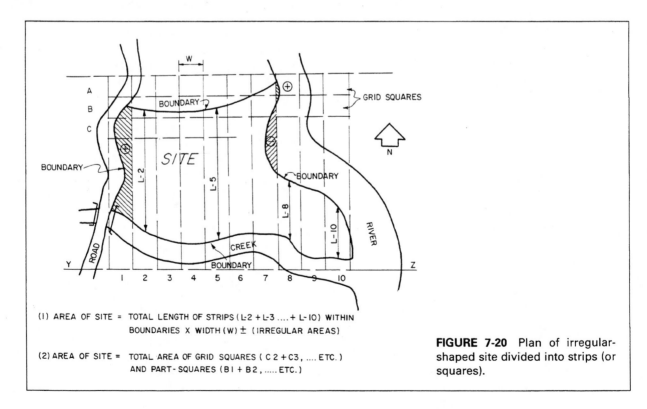

(1) AREA OF SITE = TOTAL LENGTH OF STRIPS (L-2 + L-3 .... + L-10) WITHIN
BOUNDARIES X WIDTH (W) ± (IRREGULAR AREAS)

(2) AREA OF SITE = TOTAL AREA OF GRID SQUARES (C 2 + C3, ... ETC.)
AND PART-SQUARES (B1 + B2, ... ETC.)

FIGURE 7-20 Plan of irregular-shaped site divided into strips (or squares).

squares, the dimensions of which are selected for suitability and convenience.

METHODS OF MEASUREMENT

Methods of measurement vary from place to place according to local custom and practice, and while there is general agreement on the units of measurement for most basic items of work (such as concrete footings in cubic yards, for example), for many items there are no standards of measurement; especially for complex work like wood framing and items that reflect mainly labor costs (labor only items[G]). As a result, in North America, even among localities, there are differences and inconsistencies in measurement practices.

There has been a national standard method of measurement in Canada since 1962, and in this book's first edition (1974) it was, along with the British equivalent document, the basis of Chapter 8, dealing with the particulars of measurement. But since that first edition, in the last decade or so, something came to revolutionize construction measurement for estimating and other contractual purposes: namely, the microcomputer. Consequently, it would be wrong to rewrite for this second edition by referring only to national standard methods of measurement and without paying heed to that more significant fact: the advent of the microcomputer and the effect it has on construction management generally and on estimating and cost accounting in particular.

Computers will not change the principles of estimating and cost accounting. Measurement will always require a human mind to translate design information into quantitative information for estimating purposes—until traditional construction drawings are replaced by design information in an electronic form. Nevertheless, computers are already changing the ways in which we perceive estimates and their contents. Therefore, in this and the next chapter, we shall look at measurement methods as they exist today and how they might exist tomorrow, while recognizing that some estimators have already taken steps toward electronic estimating.

It is recommended that students examine and understand the published standard methods of measurement because they represent decades (centuries, even) of measurement tradition and current practices in construction industries. But equally if not more important, students should know the customary methods of measurement used by the best practitioners in their own areas, and critically compare these with the published methods, and with the revised methods suggested here. All measurement methods are now open for criticism and revision because of computerization.

Today's students will remake current measurement practices.

There is one other reason in this and the next chapter to depart from the format and content of the first edition; another development in the last decade: the adoption in Canada of the Système International d'Unités (the SI system); that is, the metric system, as reflected in the fourth edition of the Canadian Institute of Quantity Surveyors' Method of Measurement of Construction Works (MM-CIQS). Also, let us acknowledge that it is only a question of time before the United States turns to the metric system.

Which is better, the older English method of yards, feet, and inches or the newer SI system? It is a pointless question. It is only a matter of time before the United States finds itself where Canada is today—still using both systems, and still in a process of change that moves imperceptibly. But it is only a matter of time before the old system is defunct everywhere; even though it may be a long time.

Using meters and millimeters (instead of yards, feet, and inches) ultimately does affect measurement and calculation. For those born to the older system, the meter seems too large for some items and too small for others. The yard and the foot were useful; cheaper items could be measured by the yard. Roofing even had its own unit, the square (100 square feet), and one wonders why the square was not more widely used; for painting work for example. But no doubt we can adapt and make the SI as workable as any other system of measurement. There is no reason why a unit of 10 square meters, for example, could not be used for cheaper items, instead of the 100-foot square.

General Principles of Measurement

Decades ago, British standard methods of measurement established general principles that have since been adopted in other countries, such as Canada; and those principles found in the current Canadian document (MM-CIQS) are here reproduced (Fig. 7-21) along with those more extensive "General Rules" at the head of the British document (Fig. 7-22). The former, shorter and simpler, reflects the Canadian situation with construction measurement, but this standard Canadian document is still, after two decades, not widely used in the Canadian construction industry. The British document (SMM-RICS), on the other hand, is the result of agreement between two potent institutions, The Royal Institution of Chartered Surveyors and The National Federation of Building Trades Employers, and is widely used in a country in which contracts with quantities are the rule rather than the exception. But the Canadian document exists and is used; and it is the only standard method of measurement published by a professional institute in North America.

What of these published general principles and rules of measurement, and how do they apply to us in North America? Are they valid for us, here, today—and for tomorrow? I believe that the general principles (in MM-CIQS) do apply; but some of the general rules in the British document while possibly useful today are, nevertheless, somewhat arbitrary and may need to be changed. We shall see. (For example, the "grouping of sizes" indicated in the SMM-RICS is practical, but some of the actual size limits may prove to be otherwise.)

If all construction contracts were for fixed prices, it would not matter how contracting companies measured and estimated costs; except that changes are common in fixed-price contracts, and some of those changes may be valued by unit prices. And once unit prices are to be used between contracting parties it is necessary to have an understanding of methods of measurement.

Ideally, and to avoid disagreements about measurement practices and about the nature and composition of unit prices in contracts, contracts should contain all the descriptive and quantitative information about contract work. This becomes totally feasible and practical by using computer systems. Then both owner's agent (consultant) and contractor must and can use the same methods of measurement and pricing.

Today's students are tomorrow's practitioners and they may find it more effective to measure with computer systems, and that will change some of the principles and rules of measurement. Let us consider briefly measurement, in the past, in the present, and presumptuously, in the future, with computers.

As we have seen, computer applications to estimating so far have not radically changed the methods of measurement. Current published standard methods (Canadian and British) and current informal methods widely used in the United States and Canada generally do not reflect the existence and use of computers by estimators. The measurement methods of today are essentially the same as those of yesterday. The introduction of the SI system (metric) is the only significant change in measurement methods in decades, if not centuries, and that change is not radical: It does not go to the root of measurement principles.

When all estimating (take-off from drawings and related calculations) was done manually and without mechanical (or electronic) aids, it was necessary for measurers to group together like items of work; for to do otherwise was to create too many separate items to handle conveniently. Consequently, we find in all published methods of measurement stipulated groups of items; for example, two classes of concrete blockwork in "walls and partitions" (in MM-CIQS), or the grouping together (in SMM-RICS) of steel reinforcement in concrete beams and columns.

Where no publications of standards exist to guide estimators, most create their own groups of items. We may view those groups of items stipulated in the published methods as an aid to more accurate estimating because otherwise there might have been just one larger group of similar items. Groups of items, large or small, are a concession to the estimator and his inability to deal manually with a multitude of individual and different items: different in details but generally alike; so the multitude is reduced to a manageable number of groups of similar items of work.

In grouping items, smaller groups are less effective in reducing numbers of items but are conducive to greater accuracy, while larger groups have the opposite effect; they reduce the numbers of items but at the same time they also reduce accuracy. For example, consider concrete footings, their measurement and their costs. Isolated footings (bases) are properly measured separately from continuous footings, such as those at a building's perimeter. But can all the isolated footings in a building be grouped together? Even if some of the footings each contain only a few cubic feet of concrete while others contain several cubic yards? Or should the isolated footings be measured in groups, with a total volume for each group? That seems more reasonable than grouping small footings with large footings. But what are proper limits for the groups? (The MM-CIQS says nothing about such groups; the SMM-RICS does.) Or, should each isolated footing be measured separately, thus putting the number of items in this category at a maximum?

Common sense seems to say, group similar items together. Why? To keep an estimate shorter and simpler. But now that we have computers, do we need to keep estimates shorter and simpler? And on the other hand, may it not be possible to make more accurate estimates by keeping each item separate so as to be able to attribute to it all of its probable costs? Not only does size of a concrete column base affect its cost, but so does its location. On the same site, some bases may be accessible by ready-mix truck, others by crane, while others may require concrete to be manhandled, depending on location.

Theoretically, at least, a computer makes it possible for an estimator to consider much more the things that affect the costs of an item of work, and a computer removes the necessity for grouping together items that are only superficially similar. But is there something to be gained by creating much more detail and many more items in estimates? Until it is tried and tested,

METHOD OF MEASUREMENT

GENERAL PRINCIPLES

1. Schedules of Quantities shall briefly describe materials and workmanship, but shall accurately represent the quantities of work to be executed.

2. The Method of Measurement, whilst it aims at providing uniform units of measurement, is a definition of principle rather than inflexible document. In particular and exceptional cases the Surveyor is expected to use his discretion and to adopt special methods, provided the principles of measurement are laid down are observed and the intention is made clear to the estimator. If it is in the interest of accurate and practical estimating, he may give more detailed information than is demanded by strict adherence to the document.

3. Unless otherwise stated, all work shall be measured net as fixed in place.

4. In giving dimensions the order should be consistent, and generally in the sequence of length, width and height.

    Each item of a Schedule of Quantities shall, unless otherwise stated, be held to include conveyance and delivery, unloading, hoisting, all labour setting, fitting and fixing in position, lapping of materials and straight cutting and waste.

    Circular work, shall be given separately; the term "circular" shall be deemed to include any form of curve.

    All work executed in or under water shall be given separately, stating whether canal, river or sea water work, and giving the levels of high and low water where applicable. Any work required to be carried out in compressed air shall be given separately.

FIGURE 7-21   Reproduction from The Method of Measurement of Construction Works, 4th edition, published by The Canadian Institute of Quantity Surveyors, Toronto, Canada, 1978.

SECTION A

General rules

A.1 Introduction

This Standard Method of Measurement provides a uniform basis for measuring building works and embodies the essentials of good practice but more detailed information than is required by this document shall be given where necessary in order to define the precise nature and extent of the required work. This Standard Method of Measurement shall apply equally to both proposed and executed works.

A.2 Bills of quantities

1. Bills of quantities shall fully describe and accurately represent the quantity and quality of the works to be carried out. Work which cannot be measured shall be given as a provisional sum. Work the extent of which is not known shall be described as provisional or given in a bill of approximate quantities.
2. Rules of measurement adopted for little used forms of construction or not covered elsewhere in this document shall be stated.

A.3 Measurement

1. Unless the term metre used in this document is preceded by the words square or cubic it shall be deemed to be linear.
2. Work shall be measured net as fixed in position and each measurement shall be taken to the nearest 10 mm (i.e. 5 mm and over shall be regarded as 10 mm and less than 5 mm shall be disregarded). This rule shall not apply to any dimensions stated in descriptions.
3. Where minimum deductions of voids are dealt with in this document they shall refer only to openings or wants which are within the boundaries of measured areas. Openings or wants which are at the boundaries of measured areas shall always be the subject of deduction irrespective of size.
4. Where classification is given in this document as being between two limiting dimensions then the interpretation shall be as exceeding the first dimension and not exceeding the second.

A.4 Descriptions

1. The order of stating dimensions in descriptions shall be consistent and generally in the sequence of length, width and height. Where that sequence is not appropriate or where ambiguity could arise, the dimensions shall be specifically identified.
2. Unless otherwise specifically stated in the bill or herein, the following shall be deemed to be included with all items:
   a. Labour and all costs in connection therewith.
   b. Materials, goods and all costs in connection therewith.
   c. Fitting and fixing materials and goods in position.
   d. Plant and all costs in connection therewith.
   e. Waste of materials.
   f. Square cutting.
   g. Establishment charges, overhead charges and profit.
3. Junctions between straight and curved work shall in all cases be deemed to be included with the work in which they occur.
4. Notwithstanding the provisions in this document for labours to be given as linear items, such labours may be given in the description of any linear items of work on which they occur.
5. Notwithstanding the provisions in this document for labours to be enumerated, such labours may be given in the description of any enumerated item of work on which they occur.

FIGURE 7-22(a) Reproduction from The Standard Method of Measurement of Building Works, 6th edition, published by The Royal Institution of Chartered Surveyors and The National Federation of Building Trades Employers, London, England, 1979.

A.5 Drawn information

1. Drawn information where required to be provided for the full implementation of this document is defined as follows:
   a. Location drawings
      i. Block plan. To identify site and outline of building in relation to Town Plan or other wider context.
      ii. Site plan. To locate the position of buildings in relation to setting out point, means of access and general layout of site.
      iii. General location drawing. To show the position occupied by the various spaces in a building and the general construction and location of principal elements.
   b. Component details. To show all the information necessary for the manufacture and assembly of the component.
   c. Bill diagram. To be drawn information which may be provided with the bills of quantities to aid the description of the item. Information by way of dimensions or detail may be indicated, alternatively such information shall be included in the relevant description that accompanies the bill diagram.
2. The requirements of this document for detailed descriptions shall be deemed to have been complied with if drawn information is provided and such information indicates fully the items required to be described.

A.6 Standard products

The requirements of this document shall be deemed to have been complied with if the item concerned is a product details of which have been published and to which reference has been made in the description.

A.7 Quantities

1. Where the unit of billing is the metre, quantities shall be billed to the nearest whole unit. Fractions of a unit less than half shall be disregarded and all other fractions shall be regarded as a whole unit.
2. Where the unit of billing is the tonne quantities shall be billed to the nearest two places of decimals.
3. Where the application of clauses A.7.1 and 2 would cause an entire item to be eliminated, such item shall be enumerated stating the size or weight as appropriate.

A.8 Provisional or prime cost sums

1. Where this document requires provisional or prime cost sums to be given in accordance with this clause, the choice of terms shall be made in conformity with the following definitions unless otherwise provided in the conditions of contract:
   a. The term "provisional sum" is defined as a sum provided for work or for costs which cannot be entirely foreseen, defined or detailed at the time the tendering documents are issued.
   b. The term "prime cost sum" is defined as a sum provided for work or services to be executed by a nominated sub-contractor, a statutory authority or a public undertaking or for materials or goods to be obtained from a nominated supplier. Such sum shall be deemed to be exclusive of any profit required by the general contractor and provision shall be made for the addition thereof.

A.9 Work in special conditions

1. Alterations and work in existing buildings shall be so described. Handling materials and getting them in or out of such buildings shall be deemed to be included with the items. Labours on existing work shall be so described.
2. Work carried out in or under water shall be so described stating whether canal, river or sea water and (where applicable) the mean spring levels of high and low water.
3. Work carried out in compressed air shall be so described stating the pressure and the method of entry and exit.

FIGURE 7-22(b) Reproduction from The Standard Method of Measurement of Building Works, 6th edition, published by The Royal Institution of Chartered Surveyors and The National Federation of Building Trades Employers, London, England, 1979.

nobody really knows; there are only opinions. Some say there is nothing to be gained from estimating in greater detail than one can use in a cost account; and usually cost accounting cannot recognize costs allocated to individual and separate items (such as a single isolated column base). But we really do not know what might be possible if computerized cost accounting became one side of a coin with estimating on the other. We need to discover the possibilities. We need new and additional general principles of measurement.

New principles and rules of measurement, in addition to the old, should be made and applied in the light of computer usage and its development, and because computer usage in estimating is still in its first years any new principles are only tentative, yet to be tried and tested. Below, some proposals are offered with that intention.

Proposed New Principles of Measurement

1. Descriptions of items of work shall be adequate to distinguish different items, and for accurate pricing, and where necessary for pricing they shall refer to estimated allowances for waste, shrinkage, swell, laps (where not normally measured), and other important conditions bearing on the quantities and costs of materials and work.

    Commentary: In addition to requiring net measurement (an established principle), this principle requires a measurer to estimate and state allowances for those phenomena that affect quantity and costs so that proper allowances can be made in the pricing. The measurer is in a better position to do this than somebody else. These stipulated allowances should be verified or corrected later by cost accounting.

2. Three dimensions shall be given for each and every item of work, either in an item's description or in its measurement in an estimate. Generally and preferably, dimensions shall be given in the description, and quantities shall be calculated from the smallest number of dimensions that will produce a usable quantity. In order of preference, therefore, the units of measurement are:

    a. Enumeration (with all three dimensions given in the description)

    b. Linear (with at least two dimensions given in the description)

    c. Superficial area (with at least one dimension given in the description)

    d. Volume (with no dimensions necessarily given in the description).

    Commentary: The effect of this principle is to keep individual items separate (by noting their differences) rather than to group them together, and to retain in an estimate as much useful information as possible. The insertion in a description of dimensions used in calculating each item's quantity is preferred wherever such insertion will assist in pricing the work.

3. Descriptions of items of work shall, whenever practicable, contain a reference to a unique location.

    Commentary: The purpose of this principle is obvious; it is to retain in an estimate as much information as possible about each individual item of work. However, at this early stage in the application of new principles, this principle should be applied only when it can be done with ease and without excessive description. (Full implementation of this principle requires a universal system of referencing in three dimensions; something akin to a grid system, but "open" rather than "closed" as with the present grid referencing systems. Such an open system is described elsewhere.[9]

4. All work done under special conditions, including that in alterations, repairs, in connection with existing work, work in small or isolated quantities, in cramped or difficult conditions, under water, underground, in compressed air, or in any other condition or circumstance that is abnormal or likely to increase costs shall be so described and measured and kept separate.

    Commentary: This is an elaboration of an existing principle.

5. When measuring an item of work by volume, consideration should be given to the need to measure any related ancillary items by area; similarly, when measuring an item by area, the need to measure any ancillary items by length; and likewise for items measured by length, to consider any ancillary items to be enumerated.

    Commentary: This new principle is dif-

[9] Keith Collier, *Estimating Construction Costs: A Conceptual Approach* (Reston, Virginia: Reston Publishing Company, 1984), Fig. 3.1, p. 229.

ficult to express simply and in a few words. Many items, because they are measured by volume, require a related item to be measured by area which, had the primary item been measured by area, might have been part of the primary item. For example, with bulk excavation (by volume) it is often necessary to measure an item of trimming and grading (by area) that cannot be included with the volume of excavation. Or, with a concrete-block partition wall (by area), there are usually subsidary items to be measured linearly at the partition's boundaries (e.g., cutting and connections to structural frame at ends, and cutting and fitting the top course up to a slab soffit). Or, with a linear item, such as a pipeline, there are in its length bends of various angles to be enumerated. This principle stems from the use of particular units of measurement (volume, area, length, enumeration) for different items of work and the need *not* to obscure quantitative information about the work. It also works as a general formula to lead us from primary items to subsidiary items.

Measurement for Pricing

In measuring construction work for an estimate the purpose of measurement must be remembered. It is to obtain quantities and information so that the costs can be estimated. Much measurement of work, even that done according to the published national standard methods, is not always entirely rational or appropriate because traditional methods of measurement are used without question; methods that no longer apply because construction methods have changed or because construction costs are no longer constituted as they were.

Measurement should be and can be much simpler (by enumeration) but much more detailed (by description). There has been a trend in this direction for decades. Computers now make it feasible and desirable to take this direction to the ultimate goal: measurement only by enumeration and classification—and by full description of the work. But full description requires standard terminology; that is, a common language for construction.

There is another side to this subject of computerized estimating. It is the side that deals not with more detailed *quantifying* but with more detailed *qualifying*. It is the use of computer systems and large databases containing information about seasonal weather conditions, micro-economics of locations, of different human populations, of all those things that are within the scope of the study of work and productivity, and information about the effects of management, unions, macro-economics, politics, and a thousand other things. Any or all of these may have greater bearing on construction costs than many quantitative differences. But nobody really knows what is more or less important. Much research is needed; but in the meantime we can do something; we can tackle the quantitative; we can measure work and describe work better.

In this chapter, we have examined measurement in general. In the next two chapters we are ready to move on to the measurement of particular work of the various trades and sections of construction specifications. As you read these chapters and study the examples of measurement, keep in mind what was said about the precepts and principles of measurement—both old and new. Keep in mind that we are in times of change, that the traditional ways and means of measurement of construction work have been used for centuries, and that now the advent of computers has changed many of the ground rules of measurement and has swept away many of the reasons for doing things in measurement that have existed since such measurement began. Therefore, you should look at the traditional methods shown here in a critical way and question their reasons. At the same time, also question the new principles and methods proposed here, because they have not yet been tested extensively in the field and the entire subject is still open. Nevertheless, if you learn the traditional methods and consider the new principles and methods proposed, you will be in a good position to measure construction work effectively, and to propose new methods yourself.

QUESTIONS AND TOPICS FOR DISCUSSION

1. What are the primary criteria for accuracy in measuring construction work?
2. What are the characteristics of construction work that must be included in the descriptions of work in an estimate?
3. Differentiate between *voids* and *wants* in measuring work.
4. Describe how an estimator can make his estimate more understandable to others, and why he should do so.
5. What are the primary factors that usually determine the units used in measuring work, and what criteria govern

the selection of the most suitable units of measurement for all kinds of estimates?

6. Select and criticize the unit and method of measurement of one major class of construction work, according to the answer to the previous question.

7. Explain why the rule for adjusting one perimeter length to another perimeter length (for the same building) is always plus (or minus) four times, two times, the horizontal distance between the perimeter lines.

8. State and explain the primary reasons behind the statement: It is in estimating the costs of *earthworks* that measured quantities are of the least significance.

9. Explain in detail why, in measuring cutting and filling over a site, the size of the overlaid grid squares should be selected according to the site's topography.

10. Discuss why, in the *prismoidal formula*, four times the cross section at the center is used.

11. Define (a) a *contour line*, and (b) a *cut-and-fill line*.

12. Discuss ways of *quantifying* the effects of the following phenomena on *construction labor costs*: (a) weather, (b) temperature, (c) humidity, (d) under-employment (scarcity of work), and (e) an abundance of work.

8

MEASURING WORK: PARTICULAR

In Chapter 7 we examined general principles of measurement, both existing and proposed. In this chapter we go to specific divisions, sections, and items of work to apply and to discuss those principles and some current practices too that may or may not accord with stated general principles. Our purpose is to understand existing practices and principles and also the need for new principles in the light of developments over the last few years: principally, the advent, and adoption by some in the construction industry of microcomputers, and their inevitable use in the future.

Below, measurement practice notes that often go beyond current practice and the published methods of measurement (MM-CIQS and SMM-RICS) are offered. Measurers and estimators are urged to make use of the published methods as guides to better practice. These practice notes are offered in the light of:

1. A specific stated principle in the published standard methods: that more detailed information may be given (in estimates and bills of quantities) than is specified by the publication
2. The new, proposed measurement principles expounded in this text
3. Computer applications.

In this chapter, in examining measurement methods for specific divisions and sections of work, examples are offered to illustrate the validity of the new measurement principles expounded. The reader is urged to endeavor to apply the principles illustrated to classes of work other than those cited in the examples. Finally, although this chapter is about measurement of work there is frequent mention of the pricing of work, enlarged upon in Chapter 11. Again, the reader is urged to keep in mind that the primary purpose of measurement in an estimate is to price the measured quantities, and that this purpose supersedes all others, such as ordering materials.

MEASUREMENT OF GENERAL REQUIREMENTS (DIVISION 1)

For work of this division there are no special methods of measurement. Items such as those described in Chapter 5 as job overhead items which are generally found in this Division 1 either require no measurement (e.g., costs of permits and bonds) or, in the case of tangible works (e.g., temporary fences and services), they are measured as described in the later divisions of work.

MEASUREMENT OF SITE WORK (DIVISION 2)

Demolitions and Alterations

Adequate descriptions of the site conditions and the existing work are essential to proper estimating of the costs of these kinds of work. The estimator should do much of his work on the site. Specifications for these kinds of work, especially work in alterations and renovations, need to be written by competent practitioners who can write effectively and who understand the needs of estimators and bidders. The use of precisely defined terms in specifications for this work can be effective for brevity and precision.

Descriptions are especially important here because demolished work is always unique and quantities of work in demolitions and alterations are not easily measured. The importance of adequate descriptions generally cannot be overstated. This does not necessarily mean long, wordy descriptions, as explained in Chapter 7.

Check for the following and similar things that affect costs:

1. Legal restrictions (e.g., on blasting, burning, etc.), and a need for special permits and times for working
2. The locating, removal, and termination of existing utilities and services
3. A need to underpin or otherwise support and shore up adjoining property (land and buildings)
4. Specific requirements for the removal, or otherwise, of existing substructures and services below ground
5. Preservation or disposal of existing materials and building parts on the site
6. The effects of regulations that apply to buildings once alterations are made or are begun.

Clearing and Grubbing

Consider the following:

1. Separate disposal of organic and inorganic materials from the site, haulage, and permit payments for dumping
2. Tree stumps to be removed and roots of trees and shrubs to be grubbed up (to a specific depth below ground surface)
3. Restrictions on burning

4. Trees and other things to be protected and preserved on site
5. Groundwater level and its effects on the work
6. Requirements for retaining walls and drywells (such as around remaining trees) due to changes in grades
7. Unusual soil and other conditions (such as the presence of garbage fill, sand, peat, ravines, caves, watercourses) that affect the work and the use of equipment.

Excavating and Backfilling

With such work, measured quantities are often hypothetical and of limited significance. Location, soil types, topography, time, weather, season, timing, and conditions such as those of moisture content of soil are often more important to costs. Estimators require a knowledge and understanding of soils and of construction equipment to estimate the costs of this class of work. Nevertheless, measured quantities are needed to enable an alternative method of estimating costs. The other method relies solely on an estimator's judgement of equipment time and efficiency.

Descriptions of this work should include: soil type, expected weather conditions, proposed equipment types, and areas and depths (in stages). Volumes alone are insufficient.

Volume measurement (for anything) is the least illustrative because it obscures the most information: the dimensions used in calculating the volume. Classification according to increments of average depth of excavation (as in SMM-RICS; in stages of 1.5 m, or 5 ft) helps to convey information needed in pricing; but then, why not measure excavation by area and state an average depth in the item's description? Successive depth stages can still be used. Then no information useful for pricing the work is lost. (A total volume for each item can also be included.)

Manual labor is usually required in conjunction with site work by equipment. This may be costed by man-day (or man-hour) without reference to actual quantities, depending on the work. Hand excavation work, as such, must be adequately described and measured.

Beyond the obvious lines and planes of excavation (determined by other work, such as concrete foundations), allowances are often needed in excavations to provide work spaces for the installation or removal of other work (forms, waterproofing to foundation walls, etc.). Also, allowances (i.e., extra excavation) are usually needed for creation of banks (sloping sides to excavations) for stability, or for the installation and removal of temporary shoring and supports to sides of excavations. Further, allowances may be needed to get excavation equipment in and out. An estimator has to design a work procedure before measuring excavation work. Usually, bidding documents (drawings and specifications) are of little help. MM-CIQS proposes allowances as follows:

1. At footing faces: 150 mm (about 6 in.) width to allow for form removal

2. At foundation (or basement) wall faces where the excavation has been measured to a vertical plane: 600 mm (about 24 in.) width for form removal, waterproofing work, etc.

3. Slope allowances for banks where excavation shoring is not measured, as follows:

Rock, shale, hardpan	None
Stiff clay	4:1
Clay	3:1
Earth	2:1
Sand	1:1

Loose soil (sand) requires a sloped bank at a 45-degree angle (1:1 slope). Other soils can be excavated to steeper slopes.

Allowances for shrinkage and swell (as percentages) should be stated as part of the descriptions of excavation and fill items, so that (1) the work is measured net, in bank, as explained previously; and (2) such allowances can be made in calculating the unit prices for items.

Work in excavating trenches, usually measured by volume (cubic yards or cubic meters), requires the measurer to determine the dimensions. These dimensions may depend on what is in the trench, or on the kind and size of excavating equipment to be used. Allow room to install and remove formwork to concrete foundations. (MM-CIQS: 150 mm/6 in. width at footing faces; 600 mm/24 in. working space at foundation walls.) Trenches for pipe lines may be better measured linearly stating the depth; trench volume is not always the critical factor; often the equipment is. All trenches might be measured in that same way. It is simpler and more descriptive. Volume measurement always obscures information.

Temporary shoring in trenches is better measured linearly, stating the depth of trench. The more common superficial (contact) area measurement obscures information.

Bulk machine excavation (as in a basement) is commonly measured by volume. Consider measuring it by plan area and state the average depth. Depths are better classified in stages (say, down to 4 ft/1200

mm; 4 to 8 ft/1200 to 2400 mm; and so on). In this way, information about the work is not lost in an estimate.

With all machine excavation work, we should assume that usually some kind of superficial work, often by hand, is also necessary. This includes, for example, hand trimming and grading (or compacting and grading) at the bottoms of trenches and of bulk excavations (as for a basement). If the grading is to required fall, or slope, the labor costs will be higher than if the grading is to be level. The *estimating rule* here is: If it is different, keep it separate.

Backfilling means returning excavated native material into, say, a trench or around foundations. If imported fill is used, because the native material is unsuitable, it is better not to call it "backfill" but "imported fill." It appears at first difficult to measure fill other than by volume. But most specifications require fill to be placed in layers (typically, 12 in. thick) and consolidated to a specific density, thereby making superficial measurement of fill appropriate: indeed, more appropriate than volume measurement. Thus, we see that often the traditional modes of measurement that we have inherited from the labor-intensive days of the last century are now not always appropriate, and many have not been for a long time.

Simpler measurement, and for calculating with the minimum possible number of dimensions, is easier and better because it retains more information about the work measured. If it creates more items of work in an estimate, we do not mind if we are using a computer, and we have the opportunity to make a better estimate as a result.

Work in excavating pits (perhaps, for isolated concrete bases, for example) is best measured by description and enumeration (e.g., machine-excavated pit, 36 in. × 36 in. × 48 in.). The size stated is the minimum size as required by the work in the pit (e.g., a concrete base, size 24 in. × 24 in., allowing 6 in. around for removing forms). The depth depends on job elevations. To measure excavation in pits by volume and to aggregate their volumes into one total volume obscures most of the needed information. Small pits may have to be dug by hand, larger pits by machine. The difference is significant, as is the total number of pits of various sizes.

In all excavation estimates, there must be a calculation of the total amount of excavations of all kinds; a totaling of backfilling and of imported fill used; and the differences indicate the amount of surplus excavated material to be disposed of (possibly by trucking off the site to a dump, probably an expensive item), or an amount of imported material needed if native material is unusable. Here, volumes are needed. A computer's estimating program can give them to us, even though the items described above have been measured by area or by length. Thus, an estimator needs, has, and uses all the information about the work.

Excavation and fill work are among the most difficult to measure effectively, and if we can depart from traditional modes and units of measurement for this work, as described here, it should be easier to do the same with other classes of construction work, as we shall see below.[1]

In Chapter 7 we were introduced to the prismoidal formula, used in the measurement of volumes. Now we take that subject further into the measurement of earthworks by methods related to that formula.

Earthworks to finish the ground over large areas to specified levels and slopes by "cutting down the hills and filling in the valleys" requires other means of measurement based on those already described. The primary means is a grid laid over the site plan to artificially divide up the site into small and manageable areas. The grid may be on a transparent overlay sheet, or it may be drawn on the plan as previously explained. The size of the squares in the grid should be selected to ensure optimum accuracy, as explained below.

All measurements of earthworks by solid geometry are based on an essential assumption—*that all the lines and planes are straight*—because the solid geometry employed is based on volumes bounded by straight lines and planes. The use of grids also involves the same application of solid geometry, and the same assumption is made. In Fig. 8-1 this assumption is illustrated together with conditions that might actually exist. If the topography is gently rolling, a large grid square can be used; but if the topography is rough and broken, a smaller grid square should be used. If, in Fig. 8-1, a grid square of half the size were used, the actual profiles within the smaller grid squares would come much closer to the assumption that surface slopes with a grid square are straight slopes. The same applies to areas to be filled. The more variations and topographical features there are to affect the accuracy of excavation and filling measurements (cut and fill), the smaller must be the grid squares to enable more levels and dimensions to be used in computing the volumes of cut and fill.

Having selected the appropriate size of grid, and having overlaid the site plan with the grid, the estimator may apply one of several methods to calculate the volumes of cut and fill. If there are both cut and fill to be measured, it is first necessary to distinguish the areas of each on the site plan. This is done by plotting and drawing cut-and-fill lines.[G] A cut-and-fill line is a contour line, and a contour line is a line joining points on a plan that are at the same elevation. Thus, a cut-and-fill line is a contour line that joins those points on a plan at which elevation neither cut nor fill is required, because that particular elevation is the required finished elevation.

Cut-and-fill lines are, therefore, the boundaries between those areas requiring excavation and those areas requiring fill, and in some grid squares (through which cut-and-fill lines pass) there will be some cut and some fill. Because of the shallow depths of cut and fill in the proximity of cut-and-fill lines, it is usually accurate enough to take part-squares (created by cut-and-fill lines) to the nearest half of a square, and more than three quarters of a square can be counted as a whole square in measuring areas of cut and fill.

The following compares three apparently different methods of measuring cut and fill over a grid square, or a site. The so-called "Four-point method" uses a formula (the proof of which is given) that is useful when dealing with a large site and with several cut-and-fill lines, for it enables the estimator to simply collect the sum of the cuts and the sum of the fills and to apply the formula to these two totals. The formula is based on the necessary assumption stated earlier, that the slopes within grid squares are straight and even.

Earthwork Volumes, by:

   I.   Prismoidal formula

  II.   Four-point method

 III.   Center-square method.

I. Prismoidal Formula

$$V = \frac{L(A_1 + 4A_m + A_2)}{6}$$

where V   = volume in cubic feet

        L   = perpendicular distance between end planes (A_1 and A_2) in feet

     A_1 = area, one end plane, in square feet

     A_2 = area, other end plane, in square feet

    A_m = area, middle plane, in square feet

(Note: see application of formula below for an understanding of the above terms.)

---

[1] The preceding refers to excavation and fill in building construction. In heavy engineering projects measurement requirements may be different. An earth dam, for example, may consist almost entirely of earth-fill material from close locations and transported by trucks to the dam site. Volume measurement in such a case is still the most obvious and useful, and no information about the work is lost by measuring and pricing by volume. This demonstrates that we cannot make absolute rules for estimating; we can only make and apply principles. Above all else, an estimator must apply common sense and knowledge of construction.

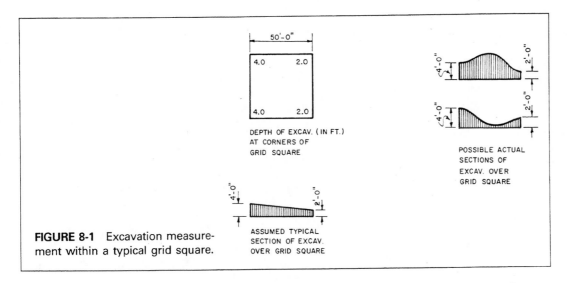

FIGURE 8-1 Excavation measurement within a typical grid square.

II. Four-Point Method.

Use the following formulas (all measurements in feet) to calculate volumes of Cut and Fill in those grid squares divided by a cut and fill line:

$$V_C = \frac{L^2 \times H_C^2}{108 \times (H_C + H_f)} \quad \text{and}$$

$$V_f = \frac{L^2 \times H_f^2}{108 \times (H_C + H_f)}$$

where V_C = volume of cut in cubic yards

H_C = sum of cuts on four corners of grid squares

V_f = volume of fill in cubic yards

H_f = sum of fills on four corners of grid squares

L = length of side of grid squares (in feet)

108 = 4 × 27: (4 × for four corners: and × 27 for cubic feet per cubic yard)

(Note: See application of the formula and also the proof of the formula below.)

Applying the Prismoidal Formula.

Consider a typical grid square, 100′ × 100′, with C = cuts, and F = fills, as shown (in ft), L = 100′; L^2 = 10,000 SF.

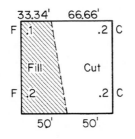

We must assume an even fall across grid square; then, proportion of C/F will be indicated by Cut/Fill line plotted as shown:

$$\text{Area of Fill} = \frac{50.00 + 33.34}{2} \times 100 = 4,167 \text{ SF}$$

$$\text{Area of Cut} = \frac{50.00 + 66.66}{2} \times 100 = 5,833 \text{ SF}$$

$$\text{Total Area} = 10,000 \text{ SF}$$

Volume of fill: Consider end-planes A_1 and A_2 also, middle-plane A_m:

$$A_1 = \frac{33.34 \times .1}{2} = 1.6670$$

$$A_2 = \frac{50.00 \times .2}{2} = 5.000$$

$$A_m = \frac{41.67 \times .15}{2} = 3.12525$$

substituting in $V = \dfrac{L_1(A_1 + 4A_m + A_2)}{6}$

$$V = \frac{100(1.6670 + 4 \times 3.12525 + 5.000)}{6}$$

$$= 319.5 \text{ CF} = \underline{11.83 \text{ CY of Fill}}$$

Volume of cut: (as for Fill)

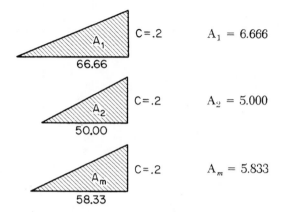

$C = .2$ $A_1 = 6.666$

$C = .2$ $A_2 = 5.000$

$C = .2$ $A_m = 5.833$

Substituting as above:

$$V = \frac{100(6.666 + 4 \times 5.833 + 5.000)}{6}$$

$$= \underline{\underline{21.60 \text{ CY of Cut}}}$$

Applying the Four-Point Method. Substituting into formulas:

$$V_f = \frac{10,000(.3^2)}{108(.4 + .3)} = \underline{\underline{11.90 \text{ CY of Fill}}}$$

$$V_c = \frac{10,000(.4^2)}{108(.4 + .3)} = \underline{\underline{21.16 \text{ CY of Cut}}}$$

Applying the Center-Square Method

Area of Fill = 4,167 SF (as above)
Area of Cut = 5,833   (as above)

                  10,000 SF Total Area

Volume of fill: Calculate average depth of fill, thus:

$$0.1 + 0.2 + 0.0 + 0.0 = 0.3 \text{ feet}$$

$$\frac{0.3}{4} = \underline{0.075 \text{ feet average depth}}$$

Volume = 4,167 SF × 0.075 = 312.5 CF

$$= \underline{\underline{11.57 \text{ CY of Fill}}}$$

Volume of cut: As above:

$$0.2 + 0.2 + 0.0 + .0.0 = 0.4 \text{ feet}$$

$$\frac{0.4}{4} = \underline{0.10 \text{ feet average depth}}$$

Volume = 5,833 SF × 0.10 = 583.3 CF

$$= \underline{\underline{21.60 \text{ CY of Cut}}}$$

Note: Most grid squares would be either 'cut' or 'fill', and only one calculation per square would be necessary. The average depth of 'cut' and 'fill' are better separately tabulated and totaled; and the total depths multiplied by the total area of the squares, to give the total volumes in both cases.

Proof of Four-Point Method Formulas

$$\text{Taking } V_C = \frac{L^2}{108} \times \frac{H_C^2}{H_C + H_f};$$

applied to the same grid square on page 109: $L^2 = 10,000$ SF.

$$H_C + H_f = (0.2 + 0.2) + (0.1 + 0.2) = 0.7$$

Since location of Cut/Fill line in grid square (shown above) divides two sides of square proportionately, in each case, to the elevations at the corners (and again, this assumes a uniform slope at each side): a proportionate division of square's area (10,000 SF) may be made as follows:

$$H_C + H_f = 0.7$$

$$\frac{10,000}{7} = 1,428.57$$

and by proportion,

Area of Cut = 4 × 1,428.5 = 5,714.0 SF approx.
Area of Fill = 3 × 1,428.5 = 4,286.0 SF approx.
       Total Area C/F = 10,000.0 SF

[N.B.: Comparable Areas calculated for I above.]

$$\text{i.e., Area of Cut} = 10,000 \times \frac{H_C}{H_C + H_f}$$

$$\left[\text{Area of Fill} = 10,000 \times \frac{H_f}{H_C + H_f} \right]$$

$$\therefore V_C \text{ (in CF)} = 10,000 \times \frac{H_C}{H_C + H_f} \times \frac{H_C}{4}$$

$$\therefore V_C \text{ (in CY)} = 10,000 \times \frac{H_C}{H_C + H_f} \times \frac{H_C}{4 \times 27}$$

$$V_C = \frac{10,000}{108} \times \frac{H_C^2}{H_C + H_f}; \text{ and substituting:}$$

$$V_c = \frac{L^2}{108} \times \frac{H_c^2}{H_c + H_f}; \text{ and, similarly,}$$

$$V_f = \frac{L^2}{108} \times \frac{H_f^2}{H_c + H_f}$$

For a first trial application of these formulae to grading work (cutting and filling with equipment), the site of the Warehouse, shown in the Warehouse drawings herein, might be used. It is instructive to also measure the cut and fill on the same site using the four-point method, or the center-square method, or both, without using the formulae. Tabulate the estimated cut and fill depths at the gridline intersections, or at the center of each square, after identifying all the squares alphanumerically (A1, A2, . . . B1, B2, . . .), and wherever a partial square occurs call it either a quarter-square, a half-square, or a three-quarter-square. For those partial squares, tabulate only a proportion of the estimated depth accordingly: e.g., for a half-square, enter only half the estimated depth. In this manner, you can then simply add all the estimated depths of cut, and of fill, and then multiply the two totals by the appropriate number of grid squares to obtain the measured volume each of cut and of fill.

Asphalt Paving

Blacktop work is traditionally measured by the ton, because the material is sold by the ton. Delivery slips show the tonnage, and that makes it easy. (How do you check the tonnage and ensure that you are getting true quantities?) But accurate estimating and cost accounting call for measurement by area as well, because area affects the placing costs. Once again, measurement with fewer dimensions proves to be better measurement because it retains, not loses, information.

MEASUREMENT OF CAST-IN-PLACE CONCRETE (DIVISION 3)

Cast-in-place concrete work is usually measured by volume (cubic yards/meters), and as with all volume measurement valuable information about work is obscured as a result. Similarly, almost all formwork is measured by contact area, and again valuable information is often thrown away in estimates. Again, measurement is better when it is simpler; when most concrete work is measured by area or length, and when most formwork is measured linearly or by enumeration.

The MM-CIQS calls for measurement of concrete by volume because it reflects common industry practice. But that practice is old-fashioned and ineffective. It is dated from the times when labor costs were less

significant to total costs of construction work, and when material costs dominated. That many who write about estimating use terms like "materials' take-off" and a "schedule of materials" instead of referring to the contractual and more precise term "work" indicates an attitude that is oriented to "materials" rather than to "labor" and to "work" (as defined in standard forms of contracts).

The argument that work should be measured according to the units in which the basic material (i.e., concrete) is sold in order to enable the material to be ordered from quantities in the estimate is spurious. The first job of an estimate is to estimate costs, all costs, as accurately and as effectively as possible. Then, if the bid that came from the estimate is effective and a contract and a job is gained, then we can go back to the estimate and quickly calculate quantities of materials to be ordered. Or, with an effective estimating program in our computer we can have the needed information even more quickly.

Almost all concrete work, except beds and slabs and isolated bases, is better measured linearly, stating the cross-sectional dimensions in each item's description. That method produces more items in an estimate; but it also produces more information to help in more accurate pricing. Concrete beds (on grade) and suspended slabs (of all kinds) are better measured by areas, with thicknesses stated in the items' descriptions. (A computer program can give us volumes with little time and effort.)

Should all beams in cast-in-place concrete structures be measured by lengths and be kept as separate and individual items, and only grouped when their cross-sectional dimensions are the same? The answer is, Yes—unless we decide to limit groups of beams to specific floors or other specific locations (particularly to each floor in high buildings), such as to the perimeters as distinct from the inner area of buildings. The same can be said for concrete columns. In a large building structure, if there are many different sizes of beams (and most designers try to limit size variations for economy in formwork), an estimator might consider creating groups according to sizes of cross sections (e.g., not exceeding 72 square inches/0.05 square meter; over 72/0.05 but not exceeding 144 square inches/0.10 square meter; and so on).

The general estimating rule again is: If it is different, keep it separate; unless there is reason to create groups of items.

Similarly, concrete column bases measured by enumeration and description of size and location may be grouped for convenience if it is reckoned that no useful information is lost by doing so. And the same applies to other items of cast-in-place concrete work, such as stair flights and landings.

Concrete walls are better measured linearly according to thickness and height. Walls of the same thickness and height might be grouped, or they might be kept separate if they are at different elevations (on different floors). It depends on the conditions of each job.

Concrete work should be measured separately according to:

1. *Mix design:* compressive strength, maximum aggregate size
2. *Location:* footings, foundation walls, outside/inside columns, slabs, etc.
3. *Method of placing:* bucket, pump, etc.
4. *Quantity:* small quantities separate
5. *Special requirements and conditions:* entrained air, continuous pours, etc.

Often it is easier and better to measure concrete material (according to mix design) separate from its placing, which may vary even for concrete of the same mix but to be placed in different locations. This is especially so for estimates of costs of larger projects.

MEASUREMENT OF PRECAST CONCRETE (DIVISION 3)

Precast concrete work is easily measured: All pieces by enumeration and full description, including location. Economy of forms will probably ensure that there are not too many pieces of different sizes for an estimator or an estimating program to handle. Precast concrete and structural steel represent the kinds of products that increasingly predominate in buildings, as opposed to the use of the traditional raw materials. This increasing use of more completely finished products made elsewhere and brought to a construction site only for assembly is one of the reasons for a new and more detailed method of measurement. Other reasons include the advent of the microcomputer and the proportionate increase in labor costs.

Precast concrete components include all formwork and reinforcing steel, both of which for cast-in-place concrete are measured separately. The occasional practice of measuring and pricing formwork and/or steel rebar combined (by description) with cast-in-place concrete only leads to inaccurate estimates of costs. Even for precast concrete, somebody has to measure and price separately all the ingredients and components, including the formwork and the steel rebar, and that person is the precast concrete maker's estimator.

MEASUREMENT OF FORMWORK FOR CAST-IN-PLACE CONCRETE (DIVISION 3)

In estimating costs of a reinforced concrete structure, formwork often is the sticker; the main source of estimating problems. Formwork accounts for about 30 to 35 percent of the total costs of such a structure, sometimes more; about equal to the costs of the cast-in-place concrete, with the costs of the reinforcing steel somewhat less. In construction economics, formwork is, however, best viewed and treated not as materials and labor (it is not incorporated into the work), but as equipment.

Construction equipment is brought to a site and set up ready for use (mobilization); it is used, and wear and tear (depreciation) occurs; repairs during its use may be necessary; parts may need replacing and oil is used as a lubricant; and after use it is dismantled, cleaned, and returned to the yard to await further use on another job site (demobilization). These are the facts of construction equipment costs. The same facts apply to formwork.

Universally, construction economists and estimators estimate formwork costs by measuring the contact area; the actual surfaces of the finished concrete structure to be supported by forms during the placing of the concrete. (A significant exception: on the Pacific coast, a wood-frame apartment building built over a reinforced concrete parking structure for which the formwork utilizes the lumber and plywood subsequently used in building the wood-frame structure. In such cases, the forms are not prefabricated units but are built the same as the wood-frame structure and then dismantled. The plywood and lumber is then cleaned and stacked ready as materials for building the superstructure.)

Formwork is the work associated with forming concrete, and its costs are mostly labor costs. Material costs of forms are usually a small proportion of total costs, in part because of their reuse: often 20 or more uses if the building design makes it possible. This is why measurement of the concrete surfaces in contact with forms is acceptable; there is no better measurement to represent formwork costs. Yet there is no reason why almost all formwork should be measured by area.

Consider formwork to beam sides and soffits, to footings, ground beams, columns, and even to stair and landing soffits. All the formwork of these building components is better measured linearly with the width/depth dimension stated in the item's description. By measuring such formwork by area critical information affecting costs is lost. (Notice that the word "information" has for its root the word "form," meaning to give shape to; to describe.) Again, the principle of simpler measurement by using fewer dimensions to calculate quantities gives better results: more descriptive quantities of work leading to more accurate pricing.

The significance of length to the costs of formwork to beams and columns is obvious, but what about forms for concrete walls; are they better measured by area, or is length more significant for walls too? In fact, even though the common practice is to measure wall formwork by area, some contracting companies have developed from past jobs tables of data for wall formwork based on wall heights. Why? Because height more than any other dimension affects the design and costs of wall forms. (As height increases so the pressure of wet concrete in the forms increases, thereby requiring stronger and more expensive forms.) By measuring wall formwork by length and, therefore, including in the formwork's description its critical dimension, height, more precise estimating and cost accounting are made possible.

Where then should formwork be measured by area? About the only place appears to be at slab soffits where one horizontal dimension is no more significant than the other. But is that always so, or are there cases in which one dimension has more significance, and therefore linear measurement is preferable to preserve that dimension?

Depending on the physical arrangement of the formwork, a pan-joist slab is an example in which one dimension is more significant. Consider now a flat slab such as in a multistory (high-rise) apartment building for which flying forms are designed, constructed, and used over and over. Is there anything gained by measuring that formwork in the traditional manner, by simple area? Of course the slab's area is significant to its formwork costs, but is that the only significant feature and measurement? Is this not a case in which cost estimating calls for measurement by enumeration and description (including contact area)?

Consider also formwork to footings, let us say, 9 in. high in one place and 12 in. high in another. Measurement by area would probably lead to the total areas of these two formwork items being combined into one, with resultant inaccuracies in pricing. Yet, given that most costs of formwork are labor costs, it is clear that while the cost per linear foot for each of these two items cannot be far apart, the cost per square foot for the 9-in. form would be greater than the cost of the 12-in form.

For example, if a 12-in. form costs (for labor and material) $2.40 per linear foot, a 9-in. form should cost about $2.30 per linear foot; or, $2.40 and $3.07 per square foot, respectively.

Applying one of our new general principles of measurement: wherever vertical formwork (such as to walls) is measured by area, we should measure an ancillary item; a linear leveling strip up to which the concrete behind the form will be poured; an item that might otherwise be part of the main item if the formwork were measured by length.

Many formwork items can only be measured properly by enumeration and full description: e.g., "Formwork to column base (located at perimeter) size 36 in. × 36 in. × 24 in." Anything else is less effective.

Often location of a form is more significant to its costs than its size. For example, column forms located at the external perimeter of a building's floor may, because of their supports, be more expensive to install and remove than those within the floor's area.

Descriptions of formwork in estimates normally are deemed to include:

1. Fabrication (if required)
2. Transportation
3. Erection
4. Oiling
5. Stripping and cleaning
6. All required form hardware
7. Supports, falsework, walkways, and related work.

All of these are allowed for in the pricing of formwork. Only the contact surfaces are measured as the basis for pricing. However, it is often necessary for accurate pricing for an estimator to measure in detail everything necessary to a typical unit of formwork (a standard panel, a specially designed flying form) in order to arrive at an accurate unit price; but such detailed measurement is not usual.

MEASUREMENT OF REINFORCING STEEL IN CAST-IN-PLACE CONCRETE (DIVISION 3)

Probably, nobody would think of measuring steel rebar other than by weight, but to calculate the weight it is necessary first to measure the lengths. By calculating the weights of the bars of various sizes we forget the lengths. But why not measure and price rebar by length? After all, the rebar contractor eventually prepares a bending schedule with the length of each bar given as a critical dimension. If length is important in fabricating, why should it not be used in estimating the costs? Again, historically, the estimator has been influenced mostly by the material, for which weight is the basis for buying and selling. Length is critical for the fabricated steel bar installed in the work. Both weight and length should be used in estimating costs. Using a computer system will remove any difficulty in handling the extra information.

The MM-CIQS classifies rebar for measurement according to:

1. Bar size
2. Bar length
3. Number of bends in each bar.

In MM-CIQS, some bar sizes are grouped (20 to 35 mm, and 45 and 55 mm), and all lengths (up to 1 m, 1 to 2 m, 2 to 3 m, 3 to 9 m, 9 to 20 m, 20 to 25 m, and 25 m and over), but these groupings appear to be regional and variable. The classifications "light bending" and "heavy bending" are not used. An alternative to such groupings is to keep all kinds of bars separate and identifiable.

To save on labor costs, modern structural design has simplified rebar so that more straight bars and simpler bending is now used than in the past. This simplifies measurement. The locations of rebar (in foundations, bases, beds, roads and pavings, floors and slabs of various types, walls, beams, columns, lintels, stairs, and the like) should each be stated in the descriptions, as this affects fabrication and placing costs.

A knowledge of construction practice is necessary for measurement since construction drawings are not pictures of the work; they are diagrammatic and symbolic. Drawings do not show everything required. Together with the specifications, the drawings should give an estimator all the design information needed. But design information is only part of the information needed to estimate costs and to build. In addition, experiential information is necessary to supplement the design information, and without that an estimator will not be able to measure all the work. This is true of all construction work of all trades.

With rebar, a designer usually indicates only the truly structural bars, those essential to the structural design. The nonstructural (but still essential) carrying bars, spacing bars, the chairs, bolsters and spacers, and all the other accessories are not shown on drawings. But they must be recognized and allowed for by an estimator. Some, including tie wire, are allowed for in the unit prices, while others are measured.

Wire mesh reinforcement may be measured by area, stating the locations. But by selecting a suitable width of mesh an estimator can measure by length and better determine the most economical arrangement. Weights of mesh are given in descriptions. Total weight also should be given.

For each project, or part thereof, the estimator should, for his or her own knowledge and future use, calculate the average weight of steel per unit volume of structural reinforced concrete. This will vary according to the type of structure, the loads it will support, and the design.

Generally, with concrete work, perhaps most estimators prefer to measure concrete and formwork together, at the same time. There is, however, merit in measuring all concrete (of at least a major part of a structure) and then going back over the concrete measurements to extract the formwork measurements. This has the advantage of giving a chance to review and check concrete measurement. By measuring concrete work other than by volume it is not difficult to have a computer program extract quantities of formwork from those of concrete. This is not possible if concrete is measured by volume.

Reinforcing steel (rebar) should always be measured separately. Despite its apparent complexity to the novice, rebar is easily measured—even by enumeration—from structural drawings, in part because the structural designer thinks and annotates in terms of numbers of bars of specific lengths.

MEASUREMENT OF IN SITU PRESTRESSED CONCRETE WORK (DIVISION 3)

The basic ingredients of concrete, formwork, and steel rebar can be measured as described above, while the unique items are each fully described and dealt with as follows:

1. Cables and tubes, measured linearly
2. Anchors, enumerated
3. For initial tensioning of cables, for pressure grouting, and for any additional tensioning if needed, a lump sum for each item
4. For grouting prestressing tendons, by enumeration.

That which cannot be measured, such as tensioning, requires fully detailed description for accurate pricing.

MEASUREMENT OF UNIT MASONRY WORK (DIVISION 4)

Masonry work, as measured and described in an estimate, usually includes scaffolding and mortar; which means that these are not separately measured and are allowed for in the masonry's unit prices. But many masonry contractors prefer to measure quantities of mortar, to be ready for ordering. They measure, in fact, a list of materials, with the masonry units enumerated, mortar by volume, and they add for scaffolding and labor costs.

Here we find a typical example of the difference in approach to estimating costs by trade contractors on the one hand and by quantity surveyors, construction economists, and other cost consultants on the other hand. The contractor thinks in terms of materials, labor, equipment (i.e., scaffolding, in this trade): the cost consultant, in terms of the finished work. The differences, however, are not great. The areas of walls have to be measured before numbers of masonry units can be calculated. One person needs the information in this format: another needs it in that. If they both use the same suitable computer program for estimating both could have what they need and attain better understanding as a bonus.

In measuring masonry work each class is kept separate according to type and size of masonry unit, purpose and location of the work. The MM-CIQS says cutting is deemed included (not measured separately). The SMM-RICS requires cutting to be measured. More detail is better. Cutting of masonry units can be expensive and may make a significant difference. (The cost of cutting a concrete block, for example, may be as much as the cost of the block itself.) Measurement is the only reasonable way to attempt to take cutting into account. But some cutting is not apparent and never measured. For example, hollow concrete blockwork in partitions in a primary school building may involve little cutting; similar partitions in a high school that has laboratories and extensive piping concealed in the hollow blockwork may involve much cutting, thus increasing the costs of the blockwork significantly. Accurate measurement of such cutting may be virtually impossible, but an attempt should be made in order to establish some productivity information about this kind of work. Also, blockwork in partitions that contains more or less cutting should be so described and kept separate in an estimate (by stating a percentage of blocks cut) so that reasonable comparisons of productivity rates and costs can be made.

The estimator who measures a list of materials, prices it, and then adds the estimated labor costs (at so much a block, or 100 bricks, or for so many days of crew time) will possibly not allow for variations in the amount of cutting required, or for other items of work that involve mostly or all labor and which are not represented by tangible materials already measured. Work (as defined) includes materials, labor, and equipment, or any combination of these. Therefore, proper estimating requires the measurement and pricing of items that include no material portion: only labor, or only labor and equipment costs.

Mortar is used and wasted (dropped) in variable amounts and its accurate measurement is practically impossible. It is expedient therefore, and as accurate, not to measure mortar but to allow for it in an estimate in the pricing.

Horizontal masonry reinforcement is relatively cheap, and if it is to be laid in the mortar joints at every third course (for example) it is as well to allow for it in the pricing also. Vertical rebar reinforcement in masonry with concrete filling around the rebar is more easily measured as a linear item with the quantities of materials taken into account in the synthesis of a unit price. This is the better and easier method for all such subsidiary items of work in which labor costs are a major part. The theoretically precise measurement of concrete in the voids of hollow concrete blocks and around vertical steel bars adds nothing to the accuracy of the estimate.

Unit masonry work should be separated and measured according to:

1. Type and size of masonry unit, usually stating nominal sizes, and prime cost[G] of specific products (e.g., facing bricks)
2. Type and width of mortar joint, including composition of mortar and any special method (e.g., face-shell bedding of blocks; tooled joints)
3. Type of bond in which units are to be laid (e.g., running or stretcher bond)
4. Thickness of wall or veneer, usually nominal
5. Type of masonry construction, such as veneer, exterior wall, partition, combination wall (of two kinds of masonry combined, each showing on one face), piers, columns, chimney stacks, flue linings, fire protection to structural steel or other work, arches, decorative work (each kind kept separate)
6. Location of masonry work, such as exterior, interior, at ground level or at elevated levels, or raised up on beams (therefore requiring additional scaffolding below)
7. Type of reinforcement (if any) in masonry, and whether supplied and installed or installed only
8. Requirements for tying back or bonding masonry to a backing or to other work behind the masonry
9. Surface treatment on masonry, including treatment of joints and any requirements for

selecting particular units and for the workmanship at exposed faces, and any requirements for cleaning, treating, or coating exposed masonry surfaces.

In addition to measuring unit masonry work, proper pricing and proper cost accounting both subsequently require that other less obvious items, sometimes known as labor items[G] (or labors), be recognized, described, and measured for pricing so that the complexity of the work and the amount of labor required can be more accurately estimated. Often, such items are not measured and are allowed for (if at all) in an estimate by a subjective increase in the labor amounts allowed. But the better way is to estimate labor costs from measured quantities. These quantities in an estimate provide a record and a means of comparing jobs, their respective labor requirements, and the ultimate productivity. Measured quantities are the only way to consistently assess and price the less tangible and more variable items in masonry work. Such items include:

1. Cutting (rough or fair, for concealed and exposed locations, respectively) where masonry abuts up or joins to another kind of masonry or other work (such as reinforced concrete) at soffits, walls, columns, girders, arches, and control joints
2. Cutting (rough or fair) at square and rebated reveals, at regular and irregular corners (not right angles)
3. Cutting (rough or fair) to form horizontal and vertical chases (recesses)
4. Cutting and bonding new masonry to old work
5. Forming cavities (in cavity walls, or against other work), including cleaning out and metal ties.

The SMM-RICS describes measurement methods for masonry in detail, but says that cutting at square angles (corners) should be deemed to be included with the masonry work (i.e., not measured as a separate item). There appears to be no valid reason for this (other than custom), and given the relatively high costs of labor it is better to measure and price all such items.

Many secondary masonry items are conveniently measured and priced as extra-over items.[G] Items such as columns and pilasters are best measured linearly. Pilasters (attached to walls) may be described as "extra over" to facilitate pricing without having to decide where a wall ends and a pilaster begins, as one is bonded to the other.

Could general masonry work be measured, according to our newly proposed principles, by enumeration (and detailed description)? At first, the question seems ridiculous. Masonry work: measured by enumeration? How? Why? But consider; in fact, masonry work already is measured by enumeration: by enumeration of masonry units, as just explained. But could it practically and efficiently be measured by enumeration in bigger units of measurement?

One development in masonry work has been the prefabrication of masonry panels, later transported to a site and installed like precast concrete. Obviously, prefabricated masonry can better be measured and priced by the enumerated unit. Why not, then, the built-in-place masonry unit: a wall or a column? Suppose that one project required an item described thus, under a heading:

> Concrete blockwork (spec: 042291)
> 08 × 2050 × 2000; extr wall; wi vert ctrl jont;
> wi 2 botm cors fild sold wi conc; wi 1 bond beam;
> at glvl

(This description with dimensions is written in a special programmable language called Context® devised for computer applications for construction that can readily be written and understood by any construction person who has read the few rules of grammar for that language.)

From that description, a computer program can extract all the information required to price the work for an estimate, and store the priced item in a library for use in future estimates.

MEASUREMENT OF STRUCTURAL STEELWORK (DIVISION 5)

Commonly, steelwork is measured by length and converted to weight; often, similar sections are grouped by weight class (e.g., not exceeding 10 kg per m; over 10 and not exceeding 20 or 25 kg per m—depending on whether one refers to SMM-RICS or the MM-CIQS—and so on). Length measurements are made to and from centerlines on the steelwork drawings.

The measurement principles for steelwork are simple: Describe the grade of steel, the method of fabrication and type of site connection (i.e., bolted, riveted, or welded), and each steel member; if an item is different, keep it separate (except where weight groups are used); finally, convert all items (including bolts, rivets, and welds) to a weight. But is that enough?

Alternatively, the MM-CIQS says, each piece of

steelwork may be enumerated and described in detail as to size, length, and mass; and that is the better way. The total weight of all steelwork should also be calculated and given in an estimate. The SMM-RICS also makes a useful contribution. It says that "unframed steelwork" should be separated from "framed steelwork." Framed steelwork refers to that which constitutes a framed structure, as distinct from that steelwork not generally and accurately jointed together to act as a structural frame. Clearly, framed steelwork is generally handled and erected differently. This is a useful distinction which emphasizes the cost differences between the two main kinds of steelwork.

The SMM-RICS says no allowances shall be made "for rolling margin or the weight of weld-metal." The MM-CIQS implies that welds shall be weighted out and included.

The national steel institutes in the United States and in Canada both publish better literature about their products than many manufacturers, and they also provide information about methods of measurement. These methods of industry should be part of the measurement rules used by estimators and cost consultants.

If the superior method of measurement by enumeration and detailed description of each piece of steel is followed, labors such as holes in steel members can be included; otherwise, they should be measured separately.

Painting and galvanizing is usually measured by stating the steelwork's total weight and description. Again, enumeration of pieces is more useful than simply giving a total weight; although it undoubtedly makes the painting estimator's job more complex; and probably makes for a better estimate of painting costs.

Special estimating forms for steelwork are used. Their column headings should include: (a) code number; (b) number of pieces; (c) material/grade; (d) weight in lb/ft or kg/m; (e) length in feet or meters; (f) total weight [product of (d) and (e)]; and (g) description or class of item. If pricing is done on the same sheet, there should be extra columns for unit prices and calculated costs.

Unframed items of steelwork, such as beams and columns in conjunction with wood-framed or masonry structures should be described in detail, including all steelwork fittings (e.g., bases, caps, brackets, bolts, welds, and the like). The total weight also should be given.

The measurement of steelwork by enumeration and description is a good example of the general method of measurement proposed here for all kinds of building construction work. With steelwork, enumeration of members is usually simple because of the relatively small number of different items, even in a large structure, because of a principle of economic structural design: to limit costs by as much standardization of components as possible. Steel-framed structures are functional and utilitarian; therefore, in most steel structures there is a reasonably constant relationship between steelwork quantity and the structure's function of supporting loads over spans. In some kinds of construction work that are less functional and less utilitarian such relationships may not exist, or they may exist to a lesser and varying degree. Consequently, with such work, unlike structural steelwork, there may be less standardization and relatively many more items to be enumerated and described. However, with computers this should not be a big problem.

MEASUREMENT OF ROUGH CARPENTRY WORK (DIVISION 6)

Here we have another kind of structural framing; with wood members instead of steel. The present and most common method of measurement uses the traditional unit of measurement for framing lumber: the board foot. Yet at a lumber supplier's office yard framing lumber is usually itemized and enumerated: so many 12-foot 2 by 10 joists, and so on.

To measure framing properly it is first necessary to itemize and enumerate framing members and then to calculate the quantity in board feet. There is therefore no good reason not to identify, describe, and enumerate each and every wood member, to retain the information in an estimate, and to calculate the quantities in board feet as a basis for payment: no reason other than a multiplicity of items. Enumeration and description of each and every wood framing member makes for more careful and more accurate measurement.

In a typical wood-framed building, plates are described as of "random lengths" unless specific lengths are obvious. Studs are a class of their own. Joists should be described according to the lengths required (up to the nearest 2-foot increment, as made and sold). Lumber for lintels and the like may be in random lengths unless specific lengths are obvious. The primary problem with measuring framing is that much of the material needed in a building is not shown on the drawings. Other than the obvious framing members, only a person who knows framing knows what to measure.

Wood framing is not common in the United Kingdom, so the SMM-RICS is not much help with this work. The MM-CIQS in its current metric edition says that all lumber shall be measured in meters, or in cubic meters. It goes on to say that lumber shall be kept separate according to: (1) dimensions,

(2) dressing, (3) grade, and (4) species. Lumber measurement varies with the locality, and generally it is desirable to follow local measurement practices, provided that they are not conducive to inaccuracy. The board-foot unit of measurement probably comes under that category: conducive to inaccuracy in estimating. Also, the minor problem of standard lengths remains. It is better to follow the basic rule: Measure all work net, in place. Yet, most of us follow custom and measure lengths up to the next 2-foot increment. There is no good reason for this, and it is unique to framing lumber.

Board-foot quantities can be misleading in estimating. Less labor is required in framing 1000 board feet of 2×12 joists than for 2×10 joists, and 1×4 strapping requires almost twice as much labor per thousand board feet as 2×4 strapping at the same spacing. Enumeration or linear measurement of members removes all such anomalies.

Lumber costs increase as lengths and cross sections increase, and larger sections and lengths over 14 feet are more expensive. Roof framing is more expensive than framing walls and floors, and supporting partitions with short studs in attics and crawl spaces are more expensive in labor than ordinary framed partitions. So each class and member must be kept separate to be priced differently.

Items such as bridging, girts, fire-stopping, and the like (with high proportions of labor costs) should be measured by length over the joists or studs between which their parts are installed, or enumerated.

Sheathing and decking are better measured by area as installed (in square feet, or square meters) and not converted to board feet. The laps and waste of the materials are then allowed for in the pricing. Plywood sheathing is measured in the same way. Methods of jointing, fixing, and supporting edges must be described.

Prefabricated components should be enumerated and fully described. Complex items are better described using a heading, such as:

The following in one prefabricated roof truss Type A, 24 ft span × 8 ft rise:

followed by detailed measurement of the parts of the truss. The same approach can be used to isolate and estimate in detail the costs of any part of a building that requires special attention.

Measurement of rough carpentry work is not difficult once all its parts and members can be identified and adequately described, but if that first step is not done well, the quantities will be short.

MEASUREMENT OF FINISH CARPENTRY WORK (DIVISION 6)

Finish carpentry is better measured either by length or by enumeration and it always requires full description. It often includes many items not of wood (e.g., plastic laminates, metal trim and finish hardware). In some residential construction finish carpenters install no natural wood products at all.

Paneling is measured by area, net in place. Square, raking, and circular cutting should be measured linearly. In some cases, expensive paneling should be measured both net and gross so that the waste due to cutting can be accurately calculated. Traditionally straight cutting is not measured and assumed to be part of each item of work. But with computerization its measurement is recommended. All other labor items should be measured, either linearly or by enumeration.

Few finish carpentry items are better measured by area than by length. Rarely is there a good reason to prefer the former, and usually the latter is feasible and more descriptive. If paneling is to be of a constant height, it is better measured linearly and the height stated in the description. The same applies to eaves, soffits, shelving, and similar items: they are better measured by length with the width described.

MEASUREMENT OF CABINETWORK AND MILLWORK (DIVISION 6)

Custom woodwork made in a mill, or shop, is problematic for cost estimators. Even millwork firms have difficulties estimating its costs. Each product requires analysis and a cutting list that shows each component required. Machine time is estimated for each piece, and time for assembly and finishing is also estimated. The basis is the cutting list. Labor costs may be added as a percentage of the material costs, but often that is not accurate because there is no direct or constant relationship between the costs of labor and materials. The only way to get accurate costs is through cost accounting related to the cutting list.

MEASUREMENT OF GLUED-LAMINATED TIMBERS (DIVISION 6)

Usually these are specified in a separate section of Division 6—Woodwork. Glued-laminated timbers are measured by manufacturers either by weight or by volume: in cubic feet or meters, or in board feet (actually a unit of volume). Weight measurement is becoming more common.

To measure these timbers by board-feet measure, first ascertain the number of $1\frac{5}{8}$-in. or $1\frac{1}{2}$-in. laminations in the section. Usually a cross section's dimensions show which size laminations have been used ($19\frac{1}{2}$ in. is divisible by both $1\frac{1}{2}$ and $1\frac{5}{8}$ in.) From the number of laminations and the lamination's nominal size, calculate the total lumber content in board-feet; add 20 percent for trimming and jointing.

For example, a 9-in. × 39-in. beam, 24 ft long, would require 1250 board feet of 2 × 10 lumber: 26 laminations size $1\frac{1}{2}$ × 9 in. (nominal 2 × 10) × 24 ft long. Or, if it were of $1\frac{5}{8}$-in. laminations, it would require a total of 1150 board feet to the nearest 10 BF.

Glulam timbers are specified according to:

1. *Form:* straight, tapered, curved, or other
2. *Function:* simple beam or purlin; cantilevered beam; arch (e.g., two-hinged foundation arch and tied arch; three-hinged parabolic arch); truss; rigid frame; and posts
3. *Section size:* may be variable, as in tapered members
4. *Strength grade:* according to function (e.g., 24f for bending, 18c for compression, and 26t for tension members)
5. *Service condition:* dry or wet, and the type of glue required
6. *Appearance quality:* industrial, paint finish, and architectural finish showing the natural wood surfaces
7. *Protection requirements:* including sealing, wrapping, and preservative treatment.

For transportation and erection, size and weight are critical and each member must be so described, and the same applies to steel hardware for connections between glulam members.

MEASUREMENT OF MOISTURE PROTECTION (DIVISION 7)

The measurement of areas of various kinds of work in this division, including dampproofing (without membranes), waterproofing (with membranes), built-up and single-ply roofing systems, and roofing of many kinds (shingles, shakes, tiles, etc.) is straightfoward if measurements are made of the actual areas covered by the work.

The areas of roof slopes are measured from eaves lengths and the lengths of slopes. Slope lengths are often measured short because the exact location of the vertical cut at the end of rafters is not correctly determined from a detail drawing. Other necessary measurements are those often ignored: those at the boundaries of the general areas of work where additional work (labor and/or materials) occurs that often makes the difference in the complexity and costs of jobs. For example:

1. At corners and edges of waterproofing, siding, and similar work
2. At eaves, parapets and other abutments, and at changes in level in so-called "flat" (slightly sloping) roofs
3. At eaves, verges, ridges, hips, valleys, and at abutments in sloped roofs
4. At and around other work passing through protection work (e.g., around stacks)

and at all similar locations that create work and extra costs.

All roofing of any kind, from simple single-ply systems to complex built-up systems, including multiply roofing units such as shakes and tiles, is installed according to a number of roofing principles that involve:

1. Size of basic roofing unit (including size of shake, or tile, or roll-roofing width)
2. Fixing location (near edge or center of material)
3. Number of plies required in the roofing installation
4. Resultant gauge (or margin; the spacing from edge to edge) at which the units are installed on a roof surface
5. Resultant lap, or weather.

With most systems an additional ply is required at the eaves where the installation begins, and that needs measuring. Also, at upper edges (where an installation ends) there is extra work, if only cutting. And there is extra work to be measured at all other edges or boundaries; in fact, wherever the general area of work is interrupted. It is this work, often not properly accounted for, that makes an estimate inaccurate. Because of the variety of work and specifications, it is necessary that such items be accurately described to ensure accurate pricing.

Most subsidary items of work are better measured by length, or enumerated.

MEASUREMENT OF SHEET-METAL WORK (DIVISION 7)

Flashings are measured linearly or by enumeration, and again proper description is essential. Descriptions must include:

1. Type and gauge (thickness) of metal
2. Girth of each flashing; that is, the width of sheet metal required to make the flashing before it is bent to the required profile
3. Number of breaks (bends) to form the profile
4. Flashing's location and the type of work with which it is associated
5. Presence of joints, fixing clips, underlayment, caulking, and other features.

Alternatively, all flashings might be enumerated, with continuous flashings in specified lengths between joints. As explained before, all work can be measured by enumeration—and by adequate descriptions. Enumeration is quite straightforward for work such as sheet-metal flashings.

For sheet-metal roofing over areas, enumeration can be of the standard unit designed and developed for a roof, depending on:

1. The type of sheet metal and the dimensions of the roofing unit employed
2. The roof area's dimensions and the frequency of joints.

The same method of measurement might be applied to any other kind of roofing. Or specific roofing areas (e.g., a roof slope) might be enumerated and described. Why measure work in this way, particularly in view of the fact that to describe a roof slope it is necessary to measure its area? Because as explained, by this method an estimate retains all information about work instead of losing it in the calculation of quantities.

MEASUREMENT OF DOORS, WINDOWS, AND GLASS (DIVISION 8)

Most estimators expect only to enumerate doors and windows and to get prices from specialist companies for their supply, or for their supply and installation; but somebody at some point has to estimate in detail the costs of every item incorporated into a building. It is not sufficient to say: "That is the work of a subcontractor and I'll get a price from him."

A subcontracting company has to make a detailed estimate of the costs of their products before they can make a bid for work, and here we are as interested in the work normally done by specialists as we are in the work of general contracting companies, who in fact are themselves specialist contractors who do work in building structures. We cannot ignore the cost analysis of the work of subcontracting companies, and there is good reason why a general estimator should have a knowledge of such work and its costs. There will be occasions when prices and bids from specialists, for such items as doors and windows and finishing work, cannot be obtained just when they are needed; a general estimator needs to be able to produce his own valid prices.

Every part of a building at some point in the process of manufacturing and of construction at a site has to be measured and priced, and in essentially the same way: both factory-made products and those components made on site, such as concrete foundations. And all estimators need to understand the measurement and costing of all classes of items, especially as more and more building components are made in factories.

Chapter 11, *Pricing Work: Particular*, contains an example of the costing of aluminum windows that is included to show how such costs are arrived at and the kind of measurement of component parts (frames, vents, glass and glazing) required. Actual measurement of components[G] is simple enough once the parts are properly identified.

For the measurement of glass and similar items (e.g., plastic and metal panels) we can emulate the measurement practices of the various makers and suppliers of these products, such as those of glass, as reflected in the nationally published methods of measurement (MM-CIQS; SMM-RICS), but is that adequate? Measurement practices vary from place to place. Is it not better then for estimators to ensure that their estimates contain all the information about work that could possibly be needed?

The standard methods of measurement classify glass according to kind, type, thickness, function, location installed, and size (area of light, or pane) in varying dimensional increments: e.g., MM-CIQS says, 20-mm increments for single and 40-mm increments for double-glazed sealed units. SMM-RICS says, areas of panes not exceeding 0.10 square meter, from over 0.10 to 0.50, from 0.50 to 1.00, and over 1 square meter).

Is this use of increments necessary? Why not measure lights (panes) by full description (including actual size) and enumeration? The only reason not to do so is the slightly longer time it takes and the multiplicity of items created; but this should no longer be critical with a computer.

The window and glass trade uses united inches as one mode of measuring their products. (Add together the two dimensions of a window in inches to express its size in united inches.) But this method assumes some fairly constant proportions among window dimensions for it to be useful; and today with nontraditional designs this is not necessarily so. Look, for example, at some of the windows in the Residence illustrated in this book. To compare the costs based on united inches of such tall and narrow windows with those of windows of traditional proportions would be very misleading. Also, to cut and handle glass for such tall and narrow windows would be relatively expensive.

In describing and costing glazed work (windows, curtain walls, etc.) it is important to indicate whether glazing is done at site or factory, and if at site whether from the inside or the outside. Required scaffolding and other temporary facilities should also be indicated.

Glazing methods are many and various both in kind and cost; from simple mastic (putty-like compounds) to complex combinations of mastic polymers and preformed glazing materials; proper description by the measurer is essential. In some instances, it may be desirable to measure the glazing by length and separately from the glass.

MEASUREMENT OF FINISH HARDWARE (DIVISION 10)

Factory-installed hardware such as that on windows is part of the window; but that hardware installed at a site, as on doors, is often the subject of a cash allowance[G] in bidding documents. Usually such a cash allowance covers only the supply, and the installation costs have to be estimated. Often this is difficult unless the finish hardware is for a building of a kind with which the estimator is familiar. To have to estimate installation of finish hardware knowing only the hardware's total cost may be unreasonable, especially if the hardware consists of a high proportion of small relatively cheap items (e.g., door numerals) or of unusual items (e.g., a new-model concealed door closer). Past experience, if any, may be the only guide; or an estimator might ask the designer for an addendum to the bidding documents that will indicate the type and range of hardware items to be installed.

MEASUREMENT OF FINISHES (DIVISION 9)

Finishes generally are not difficult to measure. Most require measurement by net area, with subsidiary items (labors and trim, for example) measured linearly. If the reader wonders how the proposed new approach to measurement introduced here applies to finishes, consider a basic item of work (as defined in the Glossary) as a unique area of floor finish.

For example, under a section heading:

Resilient flooring, 9 in. × 9 in. × 1/8 in. commercial vinyl-asbestos tiling (followed by a specific description of the work)

there might appear:

Flooring to Room 108/2, size 30.5 ft × 15.0 ft (458 SF; 91 LF perim) on concrete

For a particular project, instead of measuring a major finish item in the usual manner, with, say, one total area of resilient flooring to be priced for the entire building, and with all straight cutting unmeasured and priced together with the main basic item of work (as advocated by current published methods of measurement), there would be a separate item for each room and each recognizable area (hallways, etc.). For a large institutional building, therefore, there might be several hundred such items. But is that bad? It might be considered bad by a flooring estimator who had to measure and price so many items for an estimate that is already overdue—if he had no computer. But with a computer and a flooring program a flooring company's estimator would have no cause to be daunted by a multiplicity of such items, and could surely produce a much more accurate estimate much more efficiently.

Such a flooring program (just mentioned) would compute each room's area and perimeter, adjust stored basic unit prices according to job conditions (i.e., site, room sizes, shapes, floor elevations, etc.), and price both the basic flooring item (by area) and the subsidiary labor and base-trim items (by length). For sheet goods it could also show graphically alternative seam (joint) layouts for each room and area and indicate the economics of each alternative.

Finishing work generally has many common characteristics to be recognized and accounted for in estimating its costs. Therefore, it is not necessary to discuss the work of each trade separately, as in the published methods of measurement. Instead, we can create and apply some principles for the measurement of finishes:

1. Separate areas of finishes shall be given separately, identified, and described if not rectangular.

2. Perimeters of each area of finish shall be given.

3. Finishes applied in narrow widths (to be categorized for each trade; generally and traditionally, but not necessarily, to be less than 12 in. (300 mm) wide) are to be measured by length and to include any related subsidiary items (cutting, beads, trim, etc.).

4. Finishes applied in small areas (to be categorized for each trade) shall be so described.

5. Finishing work done under specific conditions shall be so described, including work done:
    a. From scaffolding (when this is not usual)
    b. Overhand (on a surface not facing toward the worker)
    c. On old surfaces (describing any preparatory work)
    d. In more than one color or texture (with the pattern adequately described)
    e. On curved surfaces (describing the type of curve and the radius or radii)
    f. Under any other conditions affecting productivity and costs.

Traditionally, for all finish work the following rules of measurement apply:

1. Horizontal work and vertical work are measured separately.

2. Measurements of work are of the area of the base surface covered by the finish.

3. Rough cutting (i.e., unexposed) to straight lines is deemed included with the main item of work and not measured separately. (This is the traditional rule; it is proposed here that all cutting be measured by length.)

4. Rough cutting to other than straight lines is measured separately by length.

5. Fair cutting (exposed to view) is described (straight, curved to radius, etc.) and measured by length.

6. Temporary rules, screeds, supports, templates, and similar essential items are deemed included with the basic item of work.

All of these rules still apply in our new measurement method, except for the fourth: all kinds of cutting are now to be measured separately. This is proposed here as a new general principle. It is important not only in itself but because the amount of cutting is a characteristic of the work's complexity and distribution. A few large areas have less cutting and less layout, setup, and moving time involved than a larger number of smaller areas with the equivalent total area. This fact is important to costs and is it is not quantified in traditional measurement methods.

Additional features of different kinds of finish work that affect costs and which need to be described or measured are indicated later under Finishes in Chapter 11, *Pricing Work: Particular*. Lest error be overlooked, let us condemn outright any measurement practices that depart radically from the principles and rules of measurement set out here (both traditional and new) and that lead to confusion.

Some Bad Measurement Practices

1. Measurement of stucco and plaster in height increments of, typically, 5 ft, or one scaffolding lift, with the effect of rounding-off height dimensions (from which areas of work are measured) and thereby creating fictitious quantities of work.

2. Measurement of work over all openings (not deducted) because, it is argued, by not deducting openings the extra work measured allows for the extra labor required to work up to and around openings and in the narrow widths often created between openings.

3. Measurement of one item in place of another, so that the quantities of work measured are fictitious.

4. Nonmeasurement of subsidiary items (e.g., work at corners, edges, angles, etc.).

As with other work (such as masonry, for example) an estimator on measuring the primary item of finish work (by area; or by enumeration and description of an area) should then consider the need to measure secondary items related to the primary item; particularly those items of work at the boundaries of an area of finish work, since that is where most secondary items occur, including:

1. Beads, trim, and the like, at exposed and abutting edges (such as at plaster, stucco, drywall, flooring, and ceiling installations)

2. Self-finished edging (such as ceramic rounded-edge tiles)

3. Cutting to lines (such as in painting and other applied coatings).

There are many such secondary items which of themselves cost little but which by their presence indicate the complexity of work and the possibilities of other related higher costs. Therefore, all such items must be measured to enable an estimator to estimate more accurately the costs of the primary item.

An argument is made by some against the measurement of such secondary items: It says that as such items cannot be identified and have true costs allocated to them through cost accounting, there is no reason to measure these minor items; that they cannot be accurately priced because their true costs cannot be known; and that the only way such items can be allowed for in an estimate is by the estimator's judgment and adjustment of the unit prices for the major items of work, depending on their complexity (on the amount of secondary items they include).

There is truth in this argument, especially if it is applied to one project, in isolation. But if an estimator regularly measures and prices secondary items, even though their prices are in the beginning theoretical, over a number of projects, and by comparing their costs, it should be possible for that estimator to progressively increase the accuracy of the unit costs applied to secondary items, and therefore the general accuracy of his estimates. This is especially true for estimators with specialist trade contracting companies who deal with the work of one trade; especially now that they can use a computer to handle and store the measurements and related information. By creating information and data about work it will be possible eventually to estimate costs with less effort and detail, because from the data it will be possible to establish relationships among the physical and economic characteristics of work which can then be used to simplify measurement and to enable computers to calculate and show the probabilities of construction costs. Fifth-generation computers that can emulate the mental processes of experts in making decisions should be able to give estimators a tool that embodies the expertise and experience of the best in their profession. But estimating first has a long way to go.

Measurement of Waste

Among the finishing trades, gypsum drywall is one of the most common and important now that it has displaced lath and plaster as the most common interior finish. (That commonplace drywall is an inferior finish material when compared to lath and plaster is a matter of economics, and regret.) The MM-CIQS calls for drywall to be measured net (under the general rule) and in square meters, but commonly in the trade it is measured gross, by the board. Yet unless it is measured both net and gross the waste due to cutting to job dimensions cannot be known. For example, a room

size 12 ft 6 in. × 10 ft, with an 8-ft-high ceiling, and with wallboards installed horizontally, might require:

Gross area of boards:

Walls:	4 boards, 4 ft × 13 ft =	208 SF
	4 boards, 4 ft × 10 ft =	160 SF
Ceiling:	3 boards, 4 ft × 13 ft =	156 SF
Total gross area		= 524 SF

The net area of drywall installed would be:

Walls:	45 ft × 8 ft =	360 SF
Ceiling:	12.5 ft × 10 ft =	125 SF
Total net area installed		= 485 SF

The difference between the net and gross measurements is about 8 percent of the net area: the amount of waste. More waste probably would occur from cutting around door and window openings.

How can a person estimate costs of drywall work, and make bids to do drywall work, and not know the probable amount of waste of material that will be caused by cutting to job dimensions? How can a contracting company do business successfully and not know the waste on each and every job? How can an estimator continue to do estimates and not want to know everything that can be known about the trade he works with and the jobs for which bids are made? And having done a job, how can a company not want to know as accurately as possible what the real costs of the job were, and exactly how much profit was made, or not? Yet none of this information can be found unless the work is measured both ways, both net and gross.

With drywall (among other, similar kinds of work) we have an anomaly; here more obvious because of the nature and dimensions of the material. On the one hand, there are published methods of measurement that call for net measurement of work, and on the other hand, drywall companies that often measure only the gross amount of material. Neither way gives all the information, particularly the amount of waste and the amount of filling and taping to be done. Obviously we need *all* the information, including both net and gross measurements, and the total length of joints, to be able to estimate costs accurately. And it is not a satisfactory response to say: There is a limit to practical accuracy, and other indeterminate facts of construction and sites outweigh in importance such minor things as waste.

There are other things related to a job that may affect its costs to a greater degree than variations in the amount of waste and of joints; although how can we be sure until we have actually measured and priced all items of work and have really analyzed all the costs and the features of the work that give rise to costs? But, assuming that generally the statement is true, is there still any good reason not to measure both ways, and all items, and to know as much about every job as is feasible? Especially if we can use a computer to assist us and to remove the drudgery? Of course there is not. And the amount of waste alone in some cases is sufficient reason.

MEASUREMENT OF SPECIALTIES AND SIMILAR WORK (DIVISIONS 10, 11, 12, 13, AND 14)

With these divisions we are dealing with work that has something in common: Generally, most of the work has been done elsewhere, prior to the delivery of the "materials" (products) to a construction site for assembly and installation. Finish hardware (Division 8) is similar, and that which was said previously about it generally applies here. As with finish hardware, work in these divisions often is the subject of a cash allowance in a contract. Generally, measurement is simply enumeration and extensive description (based on the contract specifications); and pricing (by the specialist contracting companies that do these kinds of work) is largely dependent on:

1. A major proportion of costs for materials (for the factory-made products installed)
2. The costs of packaging, handling, delivery, unloading, and getting into position for installation
3. The costs of labor for assembly, installation, and testing; often including expenses to send workers out of town
4. Other incidental costs for such as: insurances, storage, protection, and security. The provision of as-built drawings, operating and maintenance manuals, and training and extensive warranties (including periodic maintenance) may be part of a contract and the costs of the work.

For a contractor with subcontractors doing work in these divisions, there is related work and costs to be estimated. These might include:

1. Provision of temporary services and facilities at the site, including site office and storage space; water, power, and telephone use
2. Use of lifting and hoisting equipment (crane, hoist)
3. Provision of accurately located (in other work) holes, chases, anchors, hangers, concrete beds, and other related "builder's work."

Within these five divisions of work (10 through 14) there is great variety of work and requirements. Typical examples include:

Division 10—Specialties

Bathroom, toilet, and laundry fixtures and equipment

Chalkboards, tackboards, and similar educational equipment

Toilet and shower compartments

Demountable partitions

Storage shelving

Division 11—Equipment

Food service equipment

Laboratory equipment

Division 12—Furnishings

Blinds and shades

Draperies and curtains

Carpets and mats

Division 13—Special Construction

Radiation protection

Photographic dark rooms

Coolers and freezers

Division 14—Conveying Systems

Elevators

Escalators

Moving sidewalks

Among these, elevators are one of the most common and more complex, requiring extensive provision of related work (hoistways and beams, machine rooms, pits, and door openings). In Division 14 only the provision and installation of the elevators proper is included. All other related work is included elsewhere in appropriate divisions and sections of work; yet all the related work must be priced in the context of the elevator specialist's work and schedule. This means, for example, that forming for a concrete elevator shaft with door openings may cost more per unit of contact area than other, similar formwork.

MEASUREMENT OF MECHANICAL WORK (DIVISION 15)

With this and the next division of work (Electrical) we enter a different field of estimating (measurement and pricing) because in these trades: (1) the greatest part of total costs is for materials, and (2) measurement is, therefore, closer to how some erroneously characterize all measurement of work: a listing of materials.

In all trades, items of work consist of material and labor (and tools or equipment); but some items may include no material. In the case of a material like concrete, for example, the labor associated with it varies greatly. With the materials used in mechanical work, such as steel pipe for example, the related labor varies less because it is always essentially the same (i.e., to make a joint) even though it varies according to job conditions. Therefore, with mechanical (and electrical) work we can usually reckon on a much more constant relationship between material and labor costs. Consequently, we can relate labor costs more directly to material costs in mechanical work than in many other trades. Measurement of mechanical work, therefore, is basically measurement of installed material. Also, there are in this trade fewer labor only items to be measured (e.g., testing or balancing systems).

Typically, all mechanical (and electrical) work is measured linearly and by the enumeration of such things as fittings, fixtures, boilers, and equipment. Adequate descriptions of systems, services, materials, and locations are essential.

Plumbing and drainage should be measured with each system separated under appropriate headings, such as are found in MM-CIQS:

> Outside services
> Inside buried pipe
> Wastes and vents above ground
> Water piping, etc.

Services connections are enumerated and kept separate. Piping is measured by length, and fittings are enumerated. MM-CIQS says, "No deduction shall be made in pipe lengths for fittings under 250 mm (1 in.) in diameter," which is reasonable considering practical accuracy. Even for larger diameters no deductions for fittings might be made and the fitting items described as "Extra over piping for bend . . ."[2] or whatever the type of fitting. Full descriptions of all

work sufficient for accurate pricing are essential, as always. Descriptions need to include locations of piping, whether it is above or below ground, hung on hangers (described) below floors, in pipe ducts, or wherever, as location affects installation costs.

Outside services are usually measured from property lines up to an imaginary perimeter line around and from 3 to 5 ft (as stated; 1.5 m in MM-CIQS) outside the building. Inside buried piping is then measured from that same perimeter line to the bases of waste stacks, for example.

Sheet-metal ductwork traditionally has been often measured by weight because that is how the sheet metal is bought and sold. (MM-CIQS calls for linear measurement of ductwork and its fittings.) Weight measurement of ductwork is an example of the traditionally dominating influence on measurers and measurement of materials and their commmercial units of measurement.

Most mechanical systems can be divided for measurement purposes into two main parts:

1. The linear systems (e.g., vertical stacks, horizontal mains, and branches from stacks and mains to terminal units, such as fixtures)
2. The terminal units (e.g., plumbing and other fixtures; equipment, for such systems as plumbing, heating, cooling, etc.; and other terminal units; e.g., registers, grilles, sprinkler heads, etc.).

Linear systems include fittings, hangers, brackets, and related items. By subdividing systems (e.g., into stacks, mains, and branches) measurement is simplified and accuracy of pricing can be increased because cost information can be obtained and allocated to these parts of the work. It is not feasible to obtain actual labor costs for specific individual lengths of pipe and fittings, but it is feasible to allocate labor costs to subsystems such as stacks and branches within systems. (Average costs of pipe lengths can then be calculated to provide unit prices applicable to enumerated quantities in an estimate.)

Among linear systems, branches may be enumerated (instead of measured by length) and grouped according to incremental lengths (e.g., up to 5 ft, over 5 and up to 10 ft, etc.) to simplify measurement and improve the accuracy of pricing. Indeed, it is but a short step to the enumeration of all mechanical work in its many parts (pipe lengths included) which is the ultimate simplification of all measurement and (with computers) the beginning of greater accuracy in estimating costs.

---

[2] See *extra-over item* in the Glossary.

MEASUREMENT OF ELECTRICAL WORK (DIVISION 16)

Generally, that which has just been said about the measurement of mechanical work applies equally to electrical, and even more so because of the relative cheapness of electrical systems per unit of length. For example, in electrical work not only branches but entire circuits might be enumerated in groups according to lengths.

Both electrical and mechanical work require that an estimator have a good knowledge of the design fundamentals of the systems to be measured, as bidding documents (drawings and specifications) are often only in outline and usually drawings of systems are only diagrammatic. Mechanical and electrical work is more regulated than most, and consequently bidding documents and contracts rely heavily on this fact to establish contractual requirements. Therefore, estimators of the costs of mechanical and electrical work must be able to design in their minds the detailed requirements for the work often shown only in diagrammatic outline. This is of course true for all construction work, but it is especially so for mechanical and electrical work.

MEASUREMENT AND PRICING WORK: A DIFFERENT APPROACH

In pricing work of any kind in an estimate of costs, the best approach used by many if not most estimators is to treat each major item of work as a discrete job to be undertaken by a crew of suitable qualifications and size and with the necessary tools and equipment. First, the quantity of work is measured and the crew type and size established. Next, the estimator estimates the total crew-time to do the job, and from this a labor cost for the job is calculated. Material costs are estimated in the normal manner.

In this way, almost any kind of construction work may have its costs estimated: a basement excavation, a concrete floor slab, or a wood roof-deck. Having estimated the total costs of labor, materials, and equipment for such discrete jobs, an estimator can then calculate the *unit cost*[G] by dividing the total costs (of labor, materials, and equipment) by the total measured quantity of work for the job. Such unit costs enable an estimator to compare the costs of one job with those of other similar jobs. Often jobs have their costs estimated by the application of unit costs from similar jobs.

Unit costs (and unit prices) are average costs (and average prices), and it is recognized that they are affected by many things, including (besides the ob-

vious market prices for materials, labor, etc.) the quantity of work, the conditions at the site of the work, and numerous other things. Nevertheless, unit costs and unit prices are important means of expressing costs and prices in most kinds of construction contracts, and not only unit price contracts, despite the limitations affecting the accuracy of unit costs.

Computers and databases provide us with the means to make cost estimates more accurate and more effective. Instead of having to use unit costs (as just described) as the medium of construction economics, an estimator now can use the discrete job. For example, a contracting company building houses with basements might create data on basement costs and store in its computer database the costs of hundreds of individual basement jobs, each one a discrete job involving layout, excavation, temporary supports to sides, trimming bottoms, and so on. The information stored for each job would include, of course, all information that traditionally an estimator would create and use, including the volume of material removed. In addition, the information would include plan size, location, soil conditions, weather, and whatever else proves to be relevant as determined by sensitivity analyses and cost accounting. From such information and data stored in a large database, estimated costs could be obtained that reflect the effects on costs of all the information stored.

Eventually, much of an estimator's work could be done by using databases in computer systems. Much of the intuitive estimating of experienced estimators that is so often critical because present techniques and information resources are not adequate could be done more rapidly, more efficiently, and more confidently. In fact, with this approach to estimating, the details of measured work would be of decreasing importance as the databases grew and became more powerful. Eventually, in this approach to costs, detailed measurement generally becomes unnecessary. We would reach the antithesis of that which has been proposed so far: the multiplication of unique items of work instead of the traditional methods of measurement and the grouping of more or less similar items.

But this attainment of the antithesis of a proposed method of measurement and estimating is not a reason for not proceeding with the development of either or both. They do not eliminate each other. They complement each other. Instead of estimating costs by only one method or the other, by either a refinement of the present method involving detailed measurement, or by a refinement of a method that applies costs to larger units (discrete jobs, elements, floor area, etc.), we estimate costs by both methods simultaneously. Using computer systems and software that includes spreadsheets and database managers, that elusive *probable cost of a project* is reached from two opposite directions: the microscopic approach on the one hand, and the macroscopic approach on the other. The es-

timator's task will be to bring the two approaches into alignment on the target. And similarly, in project cost controls, the same dual approach is used: the micro- and macroscopic.

QUESTIONS AND TOPICS FOR DISCUSSION

1. If *trenches for foundations* are to be excavated by equipment, explain why measurement of trench excavation *by volume* is not the most appropriate method, and suggest a more suitable alternative method of measurement.

2. Explain why *formwork to concrete walls* is better measured *by length*, stating the wall height in the formwork's description.

3. If *cutting of concrete blocks* with a masonry saw is necessary for blockwork in partitions, and if the amount of cutting substantially affects the labor costs of the blockwork, describe how you might deal with cutting in an estimate of masonry costs.

4. Which is the better way to measure *structural steelwork* for an estimate of costs? Explain your answer.

5. Describe *a method of measurement for wood framing* in buildings that is conducive to more accurate estimating of costs.

6. Describe *the common physical features of roof coverings* of all kinds that affect the amount of roofing materials installed, and also the labor costs.

7. List at least *ten rules for the measurement of finishes* that are conducive to more accurate estimates.

8. Discuss the proposition that estimators should measure and price *secondary items of work*, even though it is recognized that in cost accounting such items cannot be isolated from the primary items, nor can such items have accurate costs allocated to them through cost accounting.

9. Present arguments for and against the proposition that the measurement of work such as *gypsum drywall finish* should include both *net* and *gross measurements* of the work.

10. Present arguments for and against the proposition that plumbing work can be measured *by enumeration only*.

11. Using *single-family dwelling costs* as an example, discuss the proposition that costs can be better estimated by using *two estimating methods in conjunction*: (1) using detailed measured quantities of work, and (2) using comprehensive costs related to building floor area (per square foot).

12. Outline the contents of *software programs* suitable for use in estimating construction costs by the *two estimating approaches* discussed: (1) using *detailed quantities*, and (2) using *the building's floor area*.

9

MEASUREMENT EXAMPLES AND EXERCISES

The examples in this chapter are based on three sets of drawings contained in this text; namely, the: 1. Preliminary drawings, 2. Residence drawings, and 3. Warehouse drawings.

These sets of drawings were selected and arranged so that the examples and exercises taken from them are progressively more complicated, and so that there is a wide variety of construction work included. Additional measurement exercises may be taken from all three sets of drawings; and if the examples from earlier drawings have been studied and understood, exercises from the later drawings should not be too difficult.

Each one of the Preliminary Examples is taken from a Preliminary Drawing, and each of these examples is complete in itself in that it includes all the work illustrated. However, the Residence Examples embrace only part of the total work shown in the Residence Drawings; and it is the same with the Warehouse Examples. This means that the remaining work in the Residence and Warehouse not already measured in the examples can be measured as measurement exercises, and examples of most of the types of work in these exercises can be found in earlier examples.

For example, the measurement of cast-in-place concrete and formwork is shown in all the Preliminary

Examples, and steel rebar is included in some of them. The concrete work in the Residence and the Warehouse can be measured in exercises; and each is increasingly complex. Similarly, some wood framing is measured in a Preliminary Example followed by a larger framing example from the Residence.

Teaching experience shows that one of the best ways to learn and to practice the measurement of work is to first study a measurement example, then to measure the work without reference to the example, and finally to compare the completed measurement exercise with the measurement example. Studying the examples without actually measuring the work is not very fruitful; neither is simply copying the examples.

Most work can be measured in more than one way, and the methods used in the examples should be compared with other proposed methods. All the measurement examples should be reworked by the student, and examples and exercises should be priced using local and current unit prices. In this way, two things will be accomplished; (1) the significance of the methods of measurement and the degrees of accuracy used should become clearer; and (2) a familiarity with representative costs of work will develop.

With a growing knowledge and understanding of

estimating and cost accounting precepts and practices, there will come to the student an understanding of the limitations of learning estimating from a book. The hypothetical construction job illustrated and used in an example or an exercise is always limited by an absence of some facts.

The Preliminary Examples have been contrived to show certain estimating methods and techniques, some of which cannot be demonstrated in their full value to the estimator because of the short and limited examples necessary to a textbook. For example, the technique of measuring the work in cast-in-place concrete walls (whereby the wall's thickness is indicated in the item's description and is finally applied to the total wall area to obtain the volume of concrete, and the total wall area is then used to measure the forms) is particularly useful with large projects for which there will be many sets of concrete wall dimensions to be entered in an estimate. In estimates for large projects this technique can save much time and effort; but this may not be apparent from a brief example.

However, examples and exercises are essential to learning measurement, and if the dimensions are changed, the examples given can provide an almost unlimited supply of practice exercises. At the end of some examples alternative dimensions are provided so that the examples can be reworked with the different dimensions to give different quantities of work. Since it is impossible to present complete information for hypothetical examples and their measurement, a few general observations and assumptions are made below.

Excavation and fill (and other site work), more than most other types of work, require specific information from the site for estimating the costs of work. The type of ground, the soil conditions, the types of local fill material available, the locations for the disposal of spoil; these are a few of the critical facts that must be known, and that cannot be provided for each example and exercise. Even the method of measuring excavation is affected by such things; and in those examples that include such work, more or less normal conditions have been assumed, if such exist. And unless otherwise indicated, a site may be assumed to be flat, and the soil and ground conditions ordinary.

Concrete is specified for strength and maximum aggregate size, and these details are given in the examples.

Formwork presents no measurement problems, because only the *contact area* is measured and most of the problems occur in the pricing. Formwork is required at construction joints (joints required by stopping and starting concrete pouring) where continuous

concrete placing is not possible, as is usual on large jobs. Because small jobs are shown in the examples, generally no such forms have been measured; but they should be measured in the exercises.

Steel rebar has many possible variations in design and quality, and consequently there can be as many variations in its measurement. In all the examples, the following is assumed to apply, unless otherwise indicated:

Grade of steel	No. 60
Maximum length of bars	30 ft
Length of splices (laps)	36 × bar dia
Concrete cover to steel, generally	1½ in.
Concrete cover in concrete footings	3 in.

These allowances are sometimes increased or decreased by small amounts to "round-off" a dimension in some measurement examples.

For large projects it is necessary to measure all the carrying bars, chairs, and other rebar accessories required. In smaller and simpler projects, few special accessories may be required, and the minor costs of any such items may be covered by a small cost allowance in the estimate.

Bending of rebar is described as "light" (*L. Bending*) or "heavy" (*H. Bending*), as explained in Chapter 8. Bending should be measured as an *extra-over item*[G]; i.e., the extra cost of bending over and above the costs of supplying and installing the rebar.

Finally, experience shows that everyone will estimate a project differently, because estimating deals in probabilities not only of costs and productivity, but also of work methods and procedures. There is really only one ultimate test: How close is an estimate of costs to the actual costs? All the facts are never available to an estimator, for if they were it would not be a question of probabilities but of certainties. Therefore, to some extent estimating is always a matter of opinions and differences. But experience also shows that if a project (such as those in the following examples) is measured and priced according to the precepts and practices of good estimating, and with the same basic cost information, the results of any number of estimates will usually be sufficiently close to assure those who made them that their results are generally satisfactory. In most cases any exceptions will result either from an obvious mistake or from a very different point of view concerning how the work might be done, which might nevertheless be quite valid.

PRELIMINARY EXAMPLES AND EXERCISES

The Preliminary Drawings, unlike the others, are not taken from actual construction jobs. Instead, they were specially contrived for instruction and to illustrate certain precepts and practices of estimating. They do not necessarily represent good design and construction practice; and, in a few instances, unusual designs and drawing practices have been used to better illustrate an estimating practice. These aberrations are indicated and explained in the commentaries.

For brevity's sake, the commentaries do not usually repeat explanations, and consequently, the earlier commentaries contain more explanations and are longer than the later ones. These first estimating examples are simple and brief; but generally they do illustrate measurement techniques that are more effective when used for larger and more complex projects. It will help to understand why certain things are done if this is remembered. *It is necessary to use simple examples to illustrate estimating techniques in a text, even though the techniques are most useful when applied to more complex cases.* Therefore, the first impression on looking at some of these examples may be that they contain too much information in the form of explanatory calculations and notes. However, we are first concerned with good estimating practices and their general application. Besides, rules cannot be broken until they have been learned.

Foundations

Estimating Forms. There are many types of forms available. The "General Estimate" forms used here are ideal for small jobs with only a few sets of dims[1] to be entered against each item in the estimate. For larger jobs, in which items may have many sets of dims, the "Quantity Sheets" used in later examples are preferable, because with only one or two items per sheet "pricing columns" cannot be fully utilized and it is better to use the "Recapitulation Sheets" to which the "total quantities" of items of work are transferred from the "Quantity Sheet."[2] All of these estimating forms, and many others, may be obtained from the Frank R. Walker Company, 5030 N. Harlem Avenue, Chicago, IL 60656, whose estimating publi-

cations are listed in the Bibliography. Similar forms are also published by the Robert Snow Means Company, Inc., whose annual publication, *Building Construction Cost Data*, is also listed in the Bibliography.

Each page of an estimate should carry the job title and other information, as indicated by the printed headings; because confusion later can be disastrous (when, perhaps, an estimate contains fifty or a hundred pages, and some parts have been estimated twice to compare costs).

Entries on estimating forms must be neat, clear, and free from superfluity. If a pen is used, mistakes must be crossed out and a new entry made. Generally, it is better to use a pencil, preferably a propelling pencil with an HB lead to ensure a reasonably consistent dark line.

Dims in descriptions are written as they appear on the dwgs, but *dims in the dim cols* are written as decimals or feet-inches, but without the diacritical signs for feet and inches. All entries are in feet (and fractions of a foot) and need no further identification except the total estimated quantities that are identified (for pricing) as cube, super, run, or number items. Otherwise, use letter abbreviations for units of measurement elsewhere in the estimate (i.e., SF, CY) only if there is a risk of confusion.

Prelim Calcs. Check the dims on each side of plans to eliminate any errors made by the draftsman. Calculate MP (mean perim) of conc ftgs and fnd walls by first finding the "outside perim" from the dims shown. (Usually wall dims are given, not dims for conc ftgs. Here the conc ftgs are dimensioned to simplify the use of the MP.) The MP is calculated by the rule given in Chapter 7; that is, by deducting 4 times the conc ftg width from the outside perim, which is the same as applying the rule for the adjustment of perimeters; i.e., deduct (or add) $4 \times 2 \times$ the horizontal distance between the perimeters; in this case, $4 \times 2 \times (\frac{1}{2} \times 2$ ft), which equals 4 times the conc ftg's width of 2 ft.

Since the conc slab dims are not shown in the dwg, they are calculated together with the length of the *want*[G] from the slab (its width is 4 ft, as shown).

Any calcs can be performed at the outset in this way if the estimator can anticipate needing them; and, in particular, dims that have a general application and dims that require several calculations are better obtained by prelim calcs. The cols of the estimating form can be ignored when it is convenient to do so, such as for prelim calcs. But do not calculate dims and quantities of specific items except at the location of the specific items in the estimate.

---

[1] Abbreviations are mostly found in the *List of Abbreviations* just before Chapter 1. Their use here reflects their use in estimates.

[2] Many of the examples in this chapter have been done on Quantity Sheets in order to make the slightly reduced reproductions easier to read. However, in practice, General Estimate Sheets would be more suitable because the quantities can be measured and priced on the same sheets.

GENERAL ESTIMATE

BUILDING _PRELIMINARY EXAMPLE_

LOCATION _____

ARCHITECTS _____

SUBJECT _FOUNDATION_

ESTIMATE NO. _P-1_

SHEET NO. _1 OF 2_

ESTIMATOR _KC_

CHECKER _____

DATE _1987_

DESCRIPTION OF WORK	NO. PIECES	DIMENSIONS L B D/H	EXTENSIONS	EXTENSIONS	TOTAL ESTIMATED QUANTITY	UNIT PRICE M'T'L	TOTAL ESTIMATED MATERIAL COST	UNIT PRICE LABOR	TOTAL ESTIMATE LABOR COST
PRELIM. CALCS.				SLAB DIMS:			BLDG AREA:		
	55-0			55-0 × 30-0					
	30-0	3/2/8" =		-2-8 -2-8			55-0 X 30-0 = 1650 SF		
	4-0			52-4 × 27-4			DDT 15-0		
	2/89-0: 178-0						X10-0 = -150		
LESS: 4/2/1-0 = -8-0							11-4		
	M.P. = 170-0						4-0 = -45		
							1455 SF		
CONCRETE (2500 psi × 3/4" stone)									
Ftgs, cont	1/170-0 × 2-0 × 1-0		340			13 CY 63.00	819	12.00	156
Fnd Walls × 8"	1/170-0 × 4-0		680 × 8" =			17 CY 63.00	1,071	16.00	272
Slab OG × 4"	1/52-4 × 27-4		1430 DDT						
DDT. 15-0 × 10-0				150					
DDT. 12-8 × 4-0				51					
				-201					
				1229 SF × 4" =		15 CY 60.00	900	16.00	240
FORMS (ERECT AND STRIP)									
Form Ftgs × 12"	2/170-0					340 LF 75¢	255	1.00	340
Form Key, 2×4	1/170-0					170 LF 20¢	34	50¢	85
Form Fnd Walls	3/680 SF					1360 SFCA 20¢	272	50¢	680
Slab Screeds × 4"	3/27-4		82						
	2/23-4		47						
	2/17-4		35			164 LF 10¢	17	40¢	66
				SUB-TOTALS: carry fwd $			3,368	$	1,839

PRELIMINARY EXAMPLE **GENERAL ESTIMATE**

BUILDING

LOCATION _____

ARCHITECTS _____

SUBJECT __FOUNDATION (cont.)__

ESTIMATE NO. _P-1_

SHEET NO. _2 of 2_

ESTIMATOR _KC_

CHECKER _____

DATE _1987_

FRANK R. WALKER CO., PUBLISHERS, CHICAGO

DESCRIPTION OF WORK	NO. PIECES	L	DIMENSIONS B	D/H	EXTENSIONS	EXTENSIONS	TOTAL ESTIMATED QUANTITY	UNIT PRICE M'T'L	TOTAL ESTIMATED MATERIAL COST	UNIT PRICE LABOR	TOTAL ESTIMATE LABOR COST
REBAR (Grade #60)											
#4 in Ftgs	4/	178-0			712						
(36/½"=1-6)⁴ (laps)	4/	1-6			6 = 718		480				
					x.668¹ᵇ		LB 36ᶜ		173	12ᶜ	58
CONCRETE SUNDRIES											
Steel Trowel Slab (Slab Area)= 1229 sf							1230 SF 1ᶜ		12	11ᶜ	134
Cure Slab							1230 SF 1ᶜ		12	2ᶜ	25
Wpf Membrane					1229						
u/slab (inc. laps)					(+15%) 185		1420 SF 8ᶜ		114	5ᶜ	71
Clear Gravel Bed u/Slab x 5" (allow 20% Shrinkage)											
(Gravel P.C. $6⁰⁰ CY. del'd.)											
(Slab Area)= 1230											
DDT. (want @ Ftgs) 164-8x0-8=	110= 1120						17 CY 7²⁰		122	7⁵⁰	128
					x 0-5 =						
Tamp & Blind Gvl Bed Surface							1230 SF 1ᶜ		12	5ᶜ	62
(w/ sand fill)											

COST ANALYSES

$\dfrac{\$6,130}{1455 sf} = \$4.21/sf$ BLDG AREA

$\dfrac{\$6,130}{45 cy} = \$136.25 per CY.$ CONCRETE

Sub-totals: p. 2	$ 445	$ 478
p. 1	3,368	1,839
	3,813	2,317
		3,813
TOTAL COST	$	6,130

PRACTICAL
Form 516 MFD IN U S A

STANDARDIZED FORMS FOR CONTRACTORS

PROJECT **PRELIMINARY EXAMPLE**   ESTIMATOR **KC**   ESTIMATE NO. **P-1 (M)**

LOCATION   EXTENSIONS   SHEET NO. **1 of 2**

ARCHITECT ENGINEER   CHECKED   DATE **1987**

CLASSIFICATION **FOUNDATIONS**

DESCRIPTION	NO.	L	B	D/H			ESTIMATED QUANTITY	UNIT
Prelim Calcs:	MEAN PERIMETER:					Slab Dims:		
3/4570 = 13710	16 765					16 765 x 9 150		
3055	9 150				2/2/200 =	800 800		
16765	1 220					15 965 x 8 350		
	3/ 27 135 =	54 270						
	LESS: 4/600 =	−2 400			2/2/200 =	3 055		
		51 870				+ 800		
						3 855		
CONCRETE (18 MPa x 25mm Stone)								
Ftgs, cont	51 870 x 600 x 300	9340					9.340	m³
Fnd Walls x200	51 870 x	1220	63 280 m²					
			x 200 = 12 660				12.660	m³
Slab OG x 100	15 965 x	8 350	133 310	DDT				
	4 570 x	3 050	−	13 940				
	3 855 x	1 220	−	4 700				
			18 640					
			114 670					
			x 100 = 11 467				11.500	m³
FORMS (erect and strip)								
Form Ftgs x300	2/51 870	103 740					104	m
Form Fnd Walls	2/63 280	126 560					127	m²
Form Key 38 x 89	1/51 870	51 870					52	m
Slab Screeds x 100	(Slab Area) = 114 670						115	m²

FRANK R. WALKER CO., PUBLISHERS, CHICAGO

PRACTICAL
STANDARDIZED FORMS FOR CONTRACTORS
Form 516 MFD IN U S A

PROJECT **PRELIMINARY EXAMPLE** ESTIMATOR **KC** ESTIMATE NO. **P-1 (M)**

LOCATION   EXTENSIONS   SHEET NO. **2 OF 2**

ARCHITECT ENGINEER   CHECKED   DATE **1987**

CLASSIFICATION **FOUNDATIONS**

DESCRIPTION	NO.	DIMENSIONS				ESTIMATED QUANTITY	UNIT
REBAR (grade #60)							
#12.7mm Bars in Ftgs (hot metric standard size bars)							
36/12.7 (laps)	4/54270	217080					
	4/ 500	2000					
		219080 x .994 Kg				218	Kg
CONCRETE SUNDRIES							
Steel Trowel Slab		(Slab Area) = 114670				115	m²
Cure Slab		(Slab Area) = 114670				115	m²
Wpf Membrane		(Slab Area) = 114670					
(laps)		+15% 17200				132	m²
Gravel Bed w/Slab x 125 (allow 20% Shrinkage)							
		(Slab Area) - 114670					
DDT: (want @ Ftg. proj)	1/ 50270 x 200 - 10050					
MP = 51870		104620					
4/3/200 = -1600		x 125				13	m³
50270							

Concrete. This heading is used so that conc items can be grouped beneath it, and their descriptions can be shortened. Grouping similar items of work also facilitates pricing.

Ftgs, cont. The volume of the continuous conc ftgs is found from the length (MP) × width × thickness, as shown. The measured quantity is the net actual quantity required as shown on the dwgs. Any allowance required for *waste* (from spillage, enlarged formwork, etc.) *will be made in the unit price for materials.* The measured quantity of 340 CF is divided by 27, and the result is taken up to the nearest cubic yard.

Fnd Walls. These are described as 8 in. thick so that the total wall area can first be calculated for future use. This practice also reduces the amount of calculation required if there are many sets of such dims in an estimate.

Slab on Grd. As for walls, the super quantity is found first, and the cube quantity later. The *wants* are deducted (DDT) by totaling all deductions in the second extension column to the right of the dims under a heading "DDT." Some estimators use *"Omit"* instead of *"Deduct."*

Forms. Again, a heading is used over a group of like items. Only the *contact area* (area of conc surfaces in contact with form faces) is measured, and allowances for the use and waste of materials are made in the unit prices. *Labor costs are the major factor in pricing formwork,* and it is not necessary to measure in detail such items as form sheeting, support lumber, ties, and form hardware, as explained in Chapter 8.

Most formwork dims can be taken directly from the dims for conc, and for this reason many estimators measure each item of formwork immediately following the related item of conc work. This practice may save a little time, but this minor advantage may be lost during pricing. It is easier to price like items together and not have to alternate from conc work to formwork.

Slab Screeds. Slab screeds are not really formwork, but they are similar in use and cost because they are temporary and, like formwork, are placed before conc is placed. Conc slabs are struck off level with the tops of the screeds installed for this purpose using a straight-edged board, or a length of steel pipe. Screeds for conc slabs on grd may be lengths of dimension lumber supported on wooden pegs driven into the fill beneath the conc slab, and spaced about 10 ft apart. Alternatively, screeds may be lengths of steel pipe temporarily set down on pegs or chairs that have

been fixed and leveled. The screeds are moved as required, and the pegs or chairs are pulled out, or left embedded in the slab. Their locations must be assumed by the estimator. The material costs are minor, and most of the costs involve labor for installing and leveling the screeds. Most estimators prefer to relate the cost of this item of work to the slab area, and do not measure the screed lengths.

Edge forms are required for some conc slabs, both at the slab's perim and at intermediate construction joints in the case of large conc slabs that are poured and placed in alternate panels. These edge forms (which are sometimes of steel and shaped to form a tongue-and-groove joint) are different from slab screeds which are solely for leveling.

Control joints in which vertical strips of joint filling material are installed at a slab's perim, and sometimes at intermediate lines in the slab (to enable the slab to move and to control the cracks that usually occur in a slab soon after placing) are also different from both screeds and edge forms. Each should be measured separately. Sometimes, the control joint strips at a slab's perim can be installed and leveled and used as a screed. This technique is shown in a later example.

Form Key. This item does not require a deduction for conc ftgs, as it is filled with conc when the fnd walls above are placed. The labor costs (as with all formwork) are the largest element in pricing keys; the size of the key does not affect its cost very much. It is often a 2 × 4, beveled to facilitate removal.

Rebar. The bars are measured at the *outside perim* of the conc ftgs to allow for crossing at corners. (The outside perim has not been reduced here by the few inches of conc cover required over the ends of the bars.) *Laps* have been measured for the one ftg length in excess of 30 ft, according to the assumptions about rebar stated above. The total length is multiplied by the weight per foot, and the total quantity is taken up to the nearest 10 lb. No bending is required or measured.

Conc Sundries. Conc sundries include all other items of work related to cast-in-place conc, including curing and finishing. Some estimators also include here such items as gravel beds, whereas others include beds with excav and fill.

Curing. Curing conc slabs is an item of work, and as such it should be measured (and cost accounted) separately.

Wpf Membrane under Slab. This item includes about 10 percent for laps at edges (4 in. for every 36 in. width), and about 5 percent for turned-up edges at the conc slab's perim. Alternatively, the simpler method (recommended by MM-CIQS) would be to measure it net, using the slab area, with an allowance for the laps in the unit price. However, the necessary allowances will vary slightly from job to job. In a larger job this item would be measured elsewhere, such as under *Moisture Protection*.

Gravel Bed. The deduction here is for that part displaced by the inner projection of the conc ftgs, the length of which is calculated from the MP (170.0) less 4 × 2 × the horizontal distance from the perim (center) line of the projection to the MP line (according to the rule given). The estimator makes an allowance in the unit price (and in ordering the gravel) for shrinkage owing to consolidation; and the quantities are measured net, as explained before.

Some estimators measure a separate super item for the compacting of gravel beds and measure the gravel in CY because the cost of compaction relates more directly to the *area* of a bed rather than to its *volume* (i.e., a 6-in.-thick gravel bed would not require 20 percent more compaction than a 5-in.-thick bed). Similarly, finishing a conc slab is measured separately from the conc placing.

This first example has been priced to show the complete method and use of the estimating form. No equipment costs and no overhead costs and profit have been added. Each page is totaled and a summary of page totals is made so that any errors are not carried from page to page.

Suggested outline plans with dims for measurement exercises based on this example are shown in Fig. 9-1. As in the example, dims are to outside faces of footings.

Foundations and Framing

Slab on Grd. The dims on the dwg are used, and the over-measurement is deducted as a want; i.e., a strip 16 in. wide, the length of which is calculated from the MP, Alternatively, the slab can be measured as in the last example by first calculating its actual dims.

Slab Screeds. Slab screeds are measured here by the slab area, unlike in the previous example. The better method is the one that yields the most valid unit price. A run item is better for pricing the material costs. But the labor costs are the greater. If screeds are usually spaced about the same distance apart, there will be a relationship between the run and super quantities; and the super item is certainly easier to measure.

Thus, an estimator must decide how to measure items to ensure accurate pricing and cost accounting.

Exp Joint and Seal. This joint is really a "separation joint" and is commonly misnamed because the filler material used is commonly referred to as "expansion joint material." This type of joint is not usually found in residential construction, but such work at any slab perim would be measured in the same way. The unit price should include both the joint filler strip and the sealing compound poured into place at the top edge. The space for the compound may be formed by a ½ in. × ½ in. removable wood strip fixed over the top edge of the filler strip, and this strip used as a slab screed at the perim.

Dpf Fnds. Dampproofing the conc fnd walls and ftgs is described as requiring 1 gallon of asphalt per coat per square (Sq) (of 100 sq ft) to enable the item to be priced.

Wpf Membrane. This time the turned-up edges are measured, since the perim dim is readily available; and only the laps are added as a percentage. By slightly varying the methods of measurement, the validity of allowances for laps and the like can be periodically checked and confirmed, and revised if necessary. Too often, estimators look for, find, and forever and without question employ allowances and formulas and "rules of thumb." Alternatively, the membrane could be measured net, as explained before, and laps allowed for in the unit price.

Framing. This heading is used, as before, to group like items and to shorten their descriptions.

Stud Walls. The 2 × 4 lumber[3] is measured in LF and converted to BF. Some estimators leave the quantity in LF, which is simpler and adequate. It depends on local custom. The single 2 × 4 sill at the bottom and the double 2 × 4 plates at the top are often measured together with the studs (measured as 4 ft. because probably two will be cut from one 8-ft stud). The plates and studs combined are measured here as one item of work, but there is additional labor required between the conc fnd walls and the bottom 2 × 4 sill. This is measured here as an *extra-over item* to allow for the labor costs of squaring and leveling. Alternatively, the sill (wall plate) and the studs can

---

[3] This is the nominal size of the lumber: 2 in. by 4 in. The actual size after planing used to be 1⅝ in. by 3⅝ in. Now the standard actual size is 1½ in. by 3½ in. when surfaced (by planer) and dried. The standard sizes were revised in 1971. Standard metric dims are: 38 mm by 89 mm.

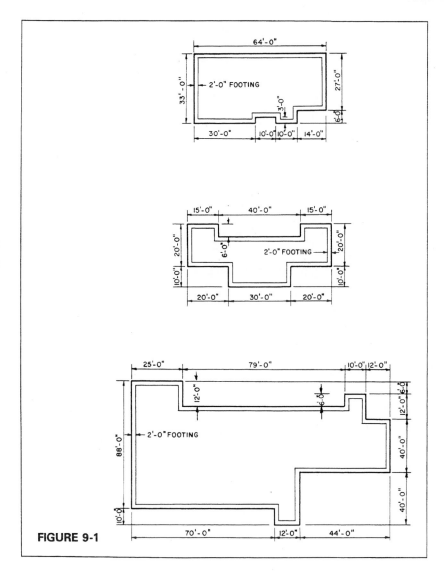

FIGURE 9-1

be measured separately (as required by MM-CIQS), with short studs separated from longer studs; this latter procedure should be followed for a larger project.

The number of studs (at 16 in. spacing) is calculated by dividing the total length of the walls by the spacing, to which are added *three additional studs* for each of the fourteen corners. If the length of a wall is not a multiple of the spacing, an extra stud is required; so, on this basis, all three studs at each corner are added, assuming that none has already been allowed for at the corners by dividing the wall length by the stud spacing. This procedure may cause a slight over-measurement if some wall lengths are in fact exact multiples of the spacing; but usually in framing some extra studs are required. It should be remembered that specified spacings are always the *maximum spacings* permitted, and that closer spacing is permitted and, indeed, is frequently required by the work. Additional

studs (and lintels) would also be required for any openings.

A common "rule of thumb" in measuring residential-type framing is, "allow one stud per foot of wall-length, for studs at 16 inches over centers." This rule is fairly accurate for ordinary house design and construction in which the houses do not have more than six corners. The studs measured in this way provide for additional studs at corners and at openings, but the rule cannot be applied to other frame construction. Such rules are useful only if properly applied. The trouble is that novices think that these rules are among the secrets of the estimating trade, and they abuse them. The only valuable rules are those found and proven by the estimator who uses them. Estimating has many gimmicks and short cuts, and none of them are worth much. Only those rules and precepts that have proven to be consistently valid within a certain

GENERAL ESTIMATE

BUILDING _PRELIMINARY_

LOCATION _EXAMPLE_

ARCHITECTS _____

SUBJECT _FOUNDATIONS & FRAMING_

ESTIMATE NO. _P-2_

SHEET NO. _1 of 4_

ESTIMATOR _KC_

CHECKER _AB_

DATE _1987_

FRANK R. WALKER CO., PUBLISHERS, CHICAGO

DESCRIPTION OF WORK	NO. PIECES	DIMENSIONS		EXTENSIONS	EXTENSIONS	TOTAL ESTIMATED QUANTITY	UNIT PRICE M'T'L	TOTAL ESTIMATED MATERIAL COST	UNIT PRICE LABOR	TOTAL ESTIMATE LABOR COST
prelim calcs	28-0 5-0 4-0 ——— 37-0	3/ 33-0 4-0 ——— 37-0		24-0 2-0 ——— 26-0	7-0 6-0 13-0 ——— 26-0	37-0 26-0 2-0 2/65-0 = 130-0 less 4/2-0 = -8-0 MP = 122-0		Fnd Wall Ht — 3-4 + 0-8 ——— 4-0		
CONCRETE (2500 psi - ¾" stone unless o/wise indicated)										
Ftgs cont (1½" stone)		122-0 x 2-0 x 0-9		183			7 CY			
Fnd Walls x 8"		122-0 x 4-0		488 (wall area) x 0-8 = 325			12 CY			
Slab o/grd x 4"		37-0 x 26-0		962	DDT					
DDT (wants)		5-0 x 7-0		—	35					
		4-0 x 13-0		—	52					
		11-0 x 2-0		—	22					
2/8" = 1-4 (122-0 + 4/2/4") = 124-8		4-0 x 2-0 124-8 x 1-4		— —	8 166 -283					
(slab area) =					679 x 0-4 = 226		9 CY			
FORMS (erect and Strip)										
Form Ftgs		2/122-0 x 0-9		(Better linear)			183 SFCA			
Form Fnd Walls		2/488 SF (wall area)		(Better linear)			976 SFCA			
Form Small Rebate		1/124-8					125 LF			
Slab Screeds x 4" (slab area) =							680 SF			

(As this item SCREEDS is primarily a labor item, it is better measured by area, unless screeds are installed to a regular pattern, as for large-area concrete slabs.)

NOTE: For computer input, all items on this sheet are better measured linearly.

GENERAL ESTIMATE

BUILDING **PRELIMINARY**

LOCATION **EXAMPLE**

ARCHITECTS

SUBJECT **FOUNDATIONS & FRAMING**

ESTIMATE NO. **P-2**

SHEET NO. **2 of 4**

ESTIMATOR **KC**

CHECKER **AB**

DATE **1987**

FRANK R. WALKER CO., PUBLISHERS, CHICAGO

DESCRIPTION OF WORK	NO. PIECES	DIMENSIONS	EXTENSIONS	EXTENSIONS	TOTAL ESTIMATED QUANTITY	UNIT PRICE M'T'L	TOTAL ESTIMATED MATERIAL COST	UNIT PRICE LABOR	TOTAL ESTIMATE LABOR COST
CONCRETE SUNDRIES		4/2¼" 122-0 / -2-8 / 119-4							
Exp Joint & Seal (as detail/specs page -)					120 LF				
Steel Trowel Slab (slab area) =					680 SF				
Cure Slab (slab area) =					680 SF				
Dpf Fnds wi 2 cts Asphalt (1 gall per ct / per Sq)									
124-8 / 130-0		1/ 124-8 × 3-4	416						
		1/ 130-0 × 0-9	98						
2) 254-8 = 127-4		1/ 127-4 × 0-8	85 = 599		600 SF				
Wpf Membrane u/Slab (slab area) = 679									
ADD (edges)		1/ 120-0 × 0-4	40						
ADD (laps)		10% × 720 SF	72 = 791		800 SF				
FRAMING (D fir "Construction" grade)									
2×4 Stud Walls (4'0" high approx)									
124-0 / 1-4 = 93 (plates) 3/ 124-0			372						
+14/3=135 135/ 4-0			540						
			912 × ⅔ BF		600 BF				
NOTE: For computer input, STUD WALLS better measured linearly.									
Extra Lab to Wall Plates					124 LF				
½" ∅ Anchor Bolts set in Conc (124-0/6-0 + 7)					28 No.				
1×8 Shiplap Shthg diagonal on Walls (allow 5% waste)									
4-4 +0-1		1/ 124-8 × 4-5	551						
ADD (laps)		12½% × 551 SF	+ 69 x/BF		620 BF				
NOTE: Better measured linearly, with height stated in the description.									

GENERAL ESTIMATE

BUILDING _PRELIMINARY_

LOCATION _EXAMPLE_

ARCHITECTS _____

SUBJECT _FOUNDATIONS & FRAMING_

ESTIMATE NO. _P-2_

SHEET NO. _3 of 4_

ESTIMATOR _KC_

CHECKER _AB_

DATE _1987_

FRANK R. WALKER CO., PUBLISHERS, CHICAGO

DESCRIPTION OF WORK	NO. PIECES	DIMENSIONS	EXTENSIONS	EXTENSIONS	TOTAL ESTIMATED QUANTITY	UNIT PRICE M'T'L	TOTAL ESTIMATED MATERIAL COST	UNIT PRICE LABOR	TOTAL ESTIMATED LABOR COST
EXCAV & DRAINS									
Remove Topsoil avg 12"dp & stockpile on site									
37-0 x 26-0 2/1-6= +3-0 +3-0 40-0 x 29-0			40-0x29-0x1-0	1160	43 CY				
Machine Bulk Excav Bmt x 2'10"dp			40-0 x 29-0	1160 DDT					
DDT (wants) +3-4 -1-0 +0-9 -0-3 2-10 dp			5-0 x 7-0 — 4-0 x 13-0 — (excav area)=	35 52 -87 1073					
			x 2-10 = 3040		113 CY				
Hand Excav Trench Bottom									
(1-6+2-0+0-6)=4-0			122-0x4-0x0-3	122	5 CY				
Trim Trench Bottom Level									
			122-0 x 4-0	488	490 SF				
Trim under Gravel Bed									
(122-0 - 4/3/8")=116-8			(slab area)=	679					
DDT (want @ perim)			116-8 x 0-8	-78 = 601	600 SF				
Gravel Bed w/slab x 6" (allow 20% shrinkage)									
4/2/1-3= 122-0 -10-0 112-0			(trim area) =	601 x 0-6 300					
ADD (extra @ inside ftgs)			112-0x0-6x0-3	+14 = 314	12 CY				

NOTE: For computer input EXCAV and GRAVEL BED items better measured by area, with depths stated in descriptions.

GENERAL ESTIMATE

BUILDING _PRELIMINARY_

LOCATION _EXAMPLE_

ARCHITECTS_____

SUBJECT _FOUNDATIONS & FRAMING_

ESTIMATE NO. _P-2_

SHEET NO. _4 of 4_

ESTIMATOR _KC_

CHECKER _AB_

DATE _1987_

FRANK R. WALKER CO., PUBLISHERS, CHICAGO

DESCRIPTION OF WORK	NO. PIECES	DIMENSIONS	EXTENSIONS	EXTENSIONS	TOTAL ESTIMATED QUANTITY	UNIT PRICE M'T'L	TOTAL ESTIMATED MATERIAL COST	UNIT PRICE LABOR	TOTAL ESTIMATED LABOR COST
EXCAV & DRAINS (cont)									
4" ⌀ Agric Drain Tile @ Ftgs					134 LF				
(130-0 + 4/2/6") 1/134-0									
Extra 4" Bends (90°) 14/1					14 No.				
Drainage Rock over D. Tile (allow 15% shrinkage)									
		134-0 x 1-6 x 0-9	151						
		134-0 x 2-2 x 0-9	218						
			369		14 cy				
Backfill @ Ftgs (allow 20% shrinkage)					17 cy				
(4-1 − 1-6 + 1-0) = 1-7		134-0 x 2-2 x 1-7	460						
(1-6 + 0-8) = 2-2									
Backfill topsoil avg 12" dp (allow 25% shrinkage)									
		134-0 x 2-2	290						
		5-0 x 7-0	35						
		4-0 x 13-0	52						
		4-0 x 2-0	8						
		8-0 x 2-0	16						
			401						
		x 1-0 =	401		15 cy				
Remove Surplus Excav Native Mat (allow 30% swell)									
		Amount Mach Excav = 113 cy							
		Amount Backfill = −17			96 cy				
[NB: assumes that balance of topsoil remains on site for landscaping.]									

PRACTICAL
Form 516 "MFD IN U S A

PROJECT PRELIMINARY EXAMPLE   ESTIMATOR KC   ESTIMATE NO. P-2 (M)
LOCATION   EXTENSIONS   SHEET NO. 1 OF 4
ARCHITECT ENGINEER   CHECKED   DATE 1987

CLASSIFICATION FOUNDATIONS & FRAMING

DESCRIPTION	NO.	DIMENSIONS				ESTIMATED QUANTITY	UNIT
Prelim Calcs:							
8535 7315	10 050	11 280					
1525 610	1 230	7925					
1220 7925	11 280	610					
11 280 3960		2/19 815 =	39 630				
1830		LESS: 4/600	−2400				
2135		MP =	37 230				
7925							
CONCRETE (18 MPa x 20mm stone, unless %wise shown)							
Ftgs, cont (x 40mm stone)							
		37230 x 600 x 230	5140			5.140	m³
Fnd Walls x 200	37230 x	1215	45235 m²				
1015 +200 1215		x 200	9047			9.050	m³
Slab OG x 100	11280 x	7925	89394	DDT			
DDT: (wants)	1525 x	2135	−	3255			
2135	1220 x	3965	−	4837			
1830	3350 x	610	−	2043			
3965	1230 x	610	−	750			
37230	38030 x	400	−	15212			
4/= +800 (@perim)			26097				
38030		(Slab Area) =	63297				
			x 100			6.330	m³
FORMS (erect & strip)							
Form Ftgs x 230	2/37 230		74460			75	m
Form Fnd Walls	2/45 235		90470			91	m²
Form Small Rebate (20 x 40)							
	1/38 030		38030			38	m
Slab Screeds x 100		(Slab Area)	63297			64	m²

QUANTITY SHEET

PROJECT *PRELIMINARY EXAMPLE*			ESTIMATOR *KC*			ESTIMATE NO. *P-2(M)*				
LOCATION			EXTENSIONS			SHEET NO. *2 of 4*				
ARCHITECT ENGINEER			CHECKED			DATE *1987*				

CLASSIFICATION *FOUNDATIONS & FRAMING*

DESCRIPTION	NO.	DIMENSIONS L	B	D/H						ESTIMATED QUANTITY	UNIT
CONCRETE SUNDRIES											
Exp Joint & Seal (as Spec. 03.11.25)											
4/2/= 37230 −800		1/36430								37	m
Steel Trowel Slab (Slab Area)										64	m²
Cure Slab (Slab Area)										64	m²
Dpf Ends w/ 2cts Asphalt (1 gall per ct/per square)											
walls) 37230 +800		1/38030 ×	1015	38600							
ftgs) 200 230		39630 ×	430	17040 55640						56	m²
Wpf Membrane U/Slab (incl laps)		63297 +15%								73	m²
FRAMING (D.Fir "Constr" grade)											
38×89 Plates (random lengths) incl. bedding											
		3/38030		114090						114	m
38×89 Studs (1200mm @ 400 %c)											
38030 95 400 14/3:42		137/1200		164400						165	m
13mm φ Anchor Bolts in Conc											
38030 −1800 = 21(+7)										28	NO
19×184 Shiplap Sheathing to Walls (allow 5% waste)											
1320 +25		1/38030 ×	1345	51150							
ADD: (for laps)			+12½%	57550						58	m²

PRACTICAL
PRACTICAL
Form 516 MFD IN U S A

CLASSIFICATION *FOUNDATIONS & FRAMING*

DESCRIPTION	NO.	L	B	D/H			ESTIMATED QUANTITY	UNIT

EXCAV & DRAINS

Remove Topsoil avg 300mm dp & stockpile on site

11 280 × 7925								
³/= +900 +900		12 180 × 8 825 107 500						
12 180 8 825				× 300			33	m³

Machine Bulk Excav Bmt × avg 870 mm depth

		12 180 × 8825 107 500		DDT				
DDT: (wants)		1 525 × 2 135 —		3 255				
1015 3350		1 220 × 3 965 —		4 837				
-300 ³/= 900		1 230 × 610 —		750				
+230 2450		2 450 × 610 —		1 495				
- 75 (recess)				10 337				
870				97 163 m²				
				× 870 84 530			85	m³

Hand Excav Trench Bottoms × 75 mm dp

³/= 450		37 230 ×1200 (×075) 44 676 m²						
600				× 075 3 350			3½	m³
180								
1200								

Trim Level Trench Bottoms

				44 676			45	m²

Trim Level u/ Gravel Bed

		(Slab Area)		63 297				
DDT: (want e/ftgs)		35 630 × 200 —		7 126 56 171			56	m²
⁴/= 37 230								
³/= 1600								
35630								

Gravel Bed u/Slab × 150 mm dp (allow 20% shrinkage)

		(Trim Area - above)		56 171				
				× 150				
				8 425				
ADD: (extra depth @ inside ftgs)								
		34 230 ×150×075		385				
				8 810			9	m³

PRACTICAL
Form 516   MFD IN U.S.A.

PROJECT	PRELIMINARY EXAMPLE	ESTIMATOR	KC	ESTIMATE NO.	P-2(M)
LOCATION		EXTENSIONS		SHEET NO.	4 OF 4
ARCHITECT ENGINEER		CHECKED		DATE	1987

CLASSIFICATION FOUNDATIONS & FRAMING

DESCRIPTION	NO.	DIMENSIONS L	B	D/H								ESTIMATED QUANTITY	UNIT
EXCAV & DRAINS (cont'd.)													
100 mm Ø Agric Tile Drains @ Ftgs													
4/ 39630													
2/= 1200 =	1/	40830										41	m
Extra for Bends (90°) 14/1												14	NO.
Drain Rock over Drains (allow 15% shrinkage)													
		41 000 x 450 x 230		4245									
		41 000 x 650 x 230		6130 · 10375								11	m³
Backfill @ Ends (allow 20% shrinkage)													
1015 = 1245		41 000 X 650 X 495		13190									
+230 = -750													
495													
Backfill Topsoil x 300mm deep (allow 25% shrinkage)													
		(Remove topsoil area) = 107 500 m² DDT											
DDT: (Bldg area)		(Slab Area) =		—	63 297								
		(wall plan area) 37 230 x 200			7446								
				-70 743									
				36 757 m²									
				x 300 · 11 027								11	m³
Remove Surplus Excav Native Material													
(allow 30% swell)													
		(Machine Excav) =		85 m³									
		(Backfill) =		-13								72	m³
[NB: Assumes that balance of													
topsoil (22 m³) remains on													
site for landscaping.]													

set of conditions should be used. It is a matter of testing and proving by cost accounting.

Shiplap Shthg. This sheathing is measured net over the area to be covered, with an allowance made for laps and for the loss in width in dressing the board when measuring in BF. The nominal width of the boards is 8 in.; but the actual overall width is 7½ in., which includes a ⅜-in. rebate to make the lap. This leaves an effective width of 7⅛ in. out of the original 8 in. on which the board measure is based. The difference between 7⅛ in. and 8 in. is about 12½ percent, which is the amount allowed in the measurement for laps in converting to a board measure. For a shiplap board 6 in. wide, the allowance should be about 16 percent. An allowance for waste of about 5 to 10 percent should be made for end-cutting in the unit price. It is simpler, however, to measure sheathing net in SF (according to MM-CIQS) and to add for both laps and waste in the unit price.

Excav and Drains. The tendency is to measure this work first, because it is performed first at the site. But there are several advantages in measuring it last. The amount of excav for a building is determined in part by the sizes and depths of the conc fnds and ftgs, and these quantities are known better after the conc work has been measured. Sometimes an estimator cannot inspect a site before starting an estimate, and he has to wait for information from test holes and the like before he knows how the excav work should be measured. So he has to begin by measuring other work.

Remove Topsoil. Topsoil (also called loam and vegetable soil) is usually handled and measured separately from other soil because of its value in landscaping. The item in the example assumes that the topsoil is removed from over the building area (without the wants considered) and piled on the site for future use, part of which will be backfilled around the building later.

Machine Bulk Excav. Machine Bulk Excav is measured here down to the underside of the gravel bed, which is 3 in. above the bottom of the conc ftgs. The calculation of the depth (2.10) is shown. The area of the excav allows a working space 2 ft wide outside the conc fnd walls (actually 2 ft 2 in., in going to the nearest foot). The dwg shows the limit of the excav in the typical section, but this limit is not normally shown on dwgs. Only the major wants are deducted from the area of the excav. The area and method of excav would in fact depend on the soil and ground

conditions. In hard ground, a minimum amount would be taken out; in soft ground, the soil at the re-entrant corners might collapse and have to be removed.

Hand Excav Trench Bottom. The additional depth of 3 in. under the conc ftgs and the drains is assumed to require removal by hand, to finish to an accurate level under the conc ftgs and to accurate grades under the drains. The width of 4 ft includes an allowance of 6 in. for the installation and removal of the inner forms to conc ftgs. The hand work under the conc ftgs and the drains would be done at different times, and might be measured as separate items. The same applies to the next item below, which is directly related; but as the quantity here is small, combining the similar work under the conc ftgs and the drains in this case will not reduce the accuracy of the estimate.

Trim Trench Bottom Level. Most excav work requires additional labor at the newly exposed surfaces, and the method of measurement (MM-CIQS) calls for:

An item of trimming and grading [to be] measured in square feet (meters) under the following headings:

(a) Trimming to bottoms of excavation.
(b) Trimming to vertical face of excavation. (If required when excavated face is vertical.)
(c) Trimming and grading to form sloping banks.
(d) Trimming to all faces of rock shall be kept separate.

Trim Under Gravel Bed. This item is similar to the preceding one, but is performed for a different reason, and probably at a different cost. This item involves finishing off after the machine excavates to a rough grade so that the gravel bed will be of the proper thickness. Since the trimming will probably be done by hand, it might not be practical to always treat it as an item separate from hand excav, and the two might be combined in one item. Some estimators usually measure the bottom few inches of depth as "*hand excav, including trimming.*" But in some ground the trimming may, in fact, involve compaction using a pneumatic tool. Once again, measurement of excav work depends on the ground and the soil conditions and the way in which the work is done; and again it is clear that measured quantities of excav work are of limited value to an estimator when it comes to pricing.

Gravel Bed. Additional gravel is measured against the inner face of the conc ftgs where the excav allowance for formwork was made. If work on the surface of the gravel bed is required to be measured separately, an item such as that shown might be measured.

Drain Tile. The length is found by using the rule for adjusting perimeters with the known perimeter.

Extra (for) Bends. Drain tile is not deducted where bends are measured because the bends are measured as an *extra-over item*. This is the usual way of measuring (and pricing) fittings in small-diameter pipes of all kinds.

Drainage Rock. This item (over drains) is usually washed and screened material containing no fine material that would block the drain, and it is different from and much more expensive than ordinary gravel fill which is often used as taken straight from the pit or river bed.

Remove Surplus Excav Native Mat. The MM-CIQS says:

All excavation items are deemed to include for dumping on site in spoil heaps. When all excavation and backfill quantities are known and equated the excess excavation shall constitute an item of disposal of spoil. If the backfill and grading exceed the excavation quantities, then an item of borrow fill shall be taken, the type of which shall be specified.

This procedure has not been followed here with the topsoil on the assumption that the balance will be used later for landscaping on the site.

Suggested outline plans with dims for measurement exercises based on this example are given in Fig. 9-2. As in the example, dims are to outside faces of footings in the first plan; but in the others, dims are to outside faces of conc fnd walls, which is the more common practice.

Swimming Pool

Prelim Calcs. These include calculating the MP of the pool walls, the avg wall hts at the sides and at the two ends, and the lengths of the three sections of the bottom slab. These are each represented by the hypotenuse of a right-angle triangle, each with a 20-ft base and with varying perpendicular heights (H). The length (L) of the hypotenuse is calculated by $L^2 = 20^2 + H^2$ (to the nearest inch), and the avg length (L) of the three sections is found so that one set of

slab dims can be "timesed" (multiplied) by three. Similarly, the end walls have an avg ht, and the dims are twice "timesed" (multiplied by 2).[4] If a drawing is accurate (and many prints are not), sometimes dims may be scaled. However, calculation is preferable, with scaling used only as an approximate means of checking the calculation.

Forms. It is assumed that the forms of the slab perim will also be used as slab screeds, and only intermediate slab screeds have been measured. Forms for conc walls are measured as before, and item of *raking cutting and waste*[G] (R C & W) is also measured to allow for the additional costs of labor and waste in cutting the bottom edges of wall forms to slopes on both sides of both the side walls.

Many estimators do not know how to deal with R C & W, even though they recognize that it must involve extra costs for labor and materials. Some ignore it, whereas others add an approximate allowance; but it should be measured, and a unit price should be analyzed for each item.

The forming of the gutter recess, the small recess (for perim paving), and the projection are each measured as *extra-over items*; primarily as a basis for the additional *labor costs*, and also for the additional use and waste of lumber inserted to form the recesses and used as supports for the projection. They are measured as run items because their lengths are the most significant dims for the labor costs, as explained before. No adjustment to the volume of conc walls has been made for these features, because the projection almost balances with the recess and a precise deduction would be only about 3 CF, which can be ignored.

Rebar. First, some prelim calcs have to be made to determine the *avg conc wall ht for all four sides*. This average can be found by dividing the conc wall area by the length (the MP), and the result can be used to calculate the avg length of the vertical rebars and the avg number of horizontal rebars in the four sides.

The *avg length of vertical rebars* is found by deducting the top conc cover of 1½ in., adding 3 in. into the slab at the bottom, and adding 6 in. and 24 in. for the top and bottom hooks, respectively. The number of vertical bars is calculated by dividing the

---

[4] The term "to times" (to multiply), as in "timesed by three," is used by many estimators to express a useful convention: e.g., "3/20.6 × 31.4," in which a distinction is made between multiplying dimensions by other dimensions and multiplying dimensions by a number (in the "Number of Pieces" column to the left of the dimension column) in the estimate sheet. The use and value of this convention in estimating was explained in Chapter 7.

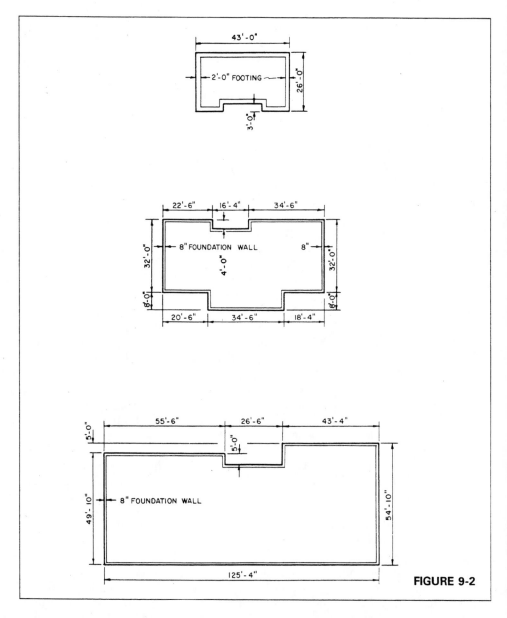

FIGURE 9-2

MP by the spacing (6 in.) and adding additional bars for the corners (one each) and for the wall lengths (one each), similar to the way wall studs were measured. Remember that indicated spacings are always *maximum spacings*, and that extra members (bars) are required for less than maximum spaces (caused by job dims that are not multiples of the spacing) and at corners and ends.

The *length of horizontal rebars* in the four sides is calculated by adjusting the MP to obtain a perim length which is 2 in. inside the outer faces of the walls, for conc cover. This gives the *maximum length*, as obviously some horizontal bars are shorter than others because of the sloping bottom. But, this perim length multiplied by the average number of horizontal bars

in the four sides will yield a sufficiently accurate result, and the avg number of horizontal bars is found by dividing the *avg wall ht* (6.10½) by *the spacing* (12 in.) plus one bar extra (over the number of spaces). Laps have been measured; two per bar in the long sides, and one per bar in the ends, assuming a maximum bar length of 30 ft, as previously stated.

The lengths of rebar in the slab are measured by allowing one lap in the shorter bars less 3 in. cover at each end, and two laps in the longer bars less 3 in. cover at each end. The numbers of bars in both directions are found by dividing the slab dims (less 2 × 3 in. for conc cover at edges) by the rebar spacing of 9 in. in both cases. Because the bars are equally spaced in both directions, the total length of the longer

PRACTICAL
Standardized Forms for Contractors
Form 514 MFD. IN U.S.A.

GENERAL ESTIMATE

BUILDING _PRELIMINARY_

LOCATION _EXAMPLE_

ARCHITECTS _____

SUBJECT _SWIM POOL_

ESTIMATE NO. _P-3_

SHEET NO. _1 of 3_

ESTIMATOR _KC_

CHECKER _AB_

DATE _1987_

FRANK R. WALKER CO., PUBLISHERS, CHICAGO

DESCRIPTION OF WORK	NO. PIECES	DIMENSIONS	EXTENSIONS	EXTENSIONS	TOTAL ESTIMATED QUANTITY	UNIT PRICE M'T'L	TOTAL ESTIMATED MATERIAL COST	UNIT PRICE LABOR	TOTAL ESTIMATE LABOR COST

prelim calcs

		Pool side walls 10-0	Pool end walls	Sloping Slab Lengths 20-3
61-4				
31-4		11-6 11-6 4-6	8-0	8-6	3 [L/20] [L/20] 7 [L/20] 1 21-2
2/ 92-8 = 185-4		8-6 4-6 3-6	4-0	3-6	20-0
less 4/8" = -2-8	2/20-0 16-0 8-0	3)22-0	2)20-0	L= 20-3 = 21-2 =20-0 3)61-5
MP = 182-8	10-0 8-0 4-0	7-4	6-0 (avg)	L= 20-6 (avg)

NOTE: Side walls & end walls - averaged separately.

NOTE: Equal lengths can have heights averaged.

CONCRETE (3500 psi - 3/4" stone)

Pool Slab % Grd (ZERO SLUMP) x 6"

	3/20-6 x 31-4	1927		
(@ under end walls)	2/0-8 x 31-4	42		
	(slab area) =	1969		
	x0-6 =	985	37 CY	

Pool Walls x 8"

	2/3/20-0 x 7-4	880		
	2/31-4 x 6-0	376		
	(wall area) =	1256		
	x0-8 =	837	31 CY	

NOTE: For computer input, better to measure CONC items by area.

FORMS (erect and strip)

Form Slab Edges x 6" 2/3/20-6

		123		
2/31-4		63		
2/2/0-8		3 = 189	190 LF	

Slab Screeds x 6"

5/31-4		157		
2/3/20-6		123		
2/2/0-8		3 = 283	280 LF	

NOTE: Alternatively, measure SCREEDS by slab area.

Form Pool Walls 2/1256 SF (wall area)   2510 SFCA

NOTE: For computer input, better measured linearly stating average heights.

RC & W on last item 4 2/3/20-6   246   250 LF

NOTE: RAKING CUTTING item provides descriptive information about FORMWORK.

GENERAL ESTIMATE

BUILDING _PRELIMINARY_

LOCATION _EXAMPLE_

ARCHITECTS_____

SUBJECT _SWIM POOL_

ESTIMATE NO. _P-3_

SHEET NO. _2 of 3_

ESTIMATOR _KC_

CHECKER _AB_

DATE _1972_

FRANK R. WALKER CO., PUBLISHERS, CHICAGO

DESCRIPTION OF WORK	NO. PIECES	DIMENSIONS	EXTENSIONS	EXTENSIONS	TOTAL ESTIMATED QUANTITY	UNIT PRICE M'T'L	TOTAL ESTIMATED MATERIAL COST	UNIT PRICE LABOR	TOTAL ESTIMATE LABOR COST
FORMS (cont)				$4/\frac{3}{16}\frac{2}{2}"$ 185-4 -4-4					
Extra Lab & Mat to Form in Walls:-				181-0					
Recess $1\frac{1}{2}" \times 6"$	1/181-0			181 LF					
Recess $1\frac{1}{2}" \times 1\frac{1}{2}"$	1/186-0			186 LF					
Projection $1\frac{1}{2}" \times 4\frac{1}{2}"$	1/186-0			186 LF					

NOTE: These are primarily Labor items, and linear measurement is most suitable.

REBAR (grade #60)

Avg Wall Ht = $\frac{Area}{MP}$ = $\frac{1256\,SF}{182-8}$ = $6-10\frac{1}{2}$ (AVG)

#3 Bars in Slab

$(31-4 - \frac{2}{3}") + 1\cdot2 = 32-0$
$\frac{62-4}{0-9} = 83$ $+1 = 84$ 84/32-0 (str)   2688

$(62-4 + 31-2) = 64-8$
$\frac{30-10}{0-9} = 41$ $+1 = 42$ 42/64-8 (str)   2719 = 5407

#3 Bars in Walls

$(6-10\frac{1}{2} - 0-1\frac{1}{2} + 0-3 + 0-6 + 2-0) = 9-6$ 2/373/9-6 (Vert Bent)   7087

$\frac{182-8}{0-6} = 365 (+4+4) = 373$

$(182-8 + 4/\frac{2}{2}") = 184-0$ 2/8/184-0 (Horiz str)   2944

$\frac{6-10\frac{1}{2}}{1-0} = 7$ $+1 = 8$

$(36 \times 3/8")$ (laps)   2/8/6/1-2 (Horiz str)   112 = 10,143
15,550

TOTAL #3 Bars in Pool   X 0.376 = $\frac{5850}{lb}$

Extra L. Bending 2/373/9-6   7087 X 0.376 = $\frac{2670}{lb}$

NOTE: For computer input, REBAR is better measured and input linearly and described by: size, unit weight, and whether bent. Computer calculates total weights.

[NB: NO "CONCRETE SUNDRIES" included here.]

GENERAL ESTIMATE

BUILDING _PRELIMINARY_

LOCATION _EXAMPLE_

ARCHITECTS_____

SUBJECT _SWIM POOL_

ESTIMATE NO. _P-3_

SHEET NO. _3 of 3_

ESTIMATOR _KC_

CHECKER _AB_

DATE _1987_

FRANK R. WALKER CO., PUBLISHERS, CHICAGO

DESCRIPTION OF WORK	NO. PIECES	DIMENSIONS	EXTENSIONS	EXTENSIONS	TOTAL ESTIMATED QUANTITY	UNIT PRICE M'T'L	TOTAL ESTIMATED MATERIAL COST	UNIT PRICE LABOR	TOTAL ESTIMATE LABOR COST
EXCAV & FILL					2/ 2-0	61-4 x 31-4 +4-0 +4-0	AVG HT LONG SIDES·74		
						65-4 x 35-4	SLAB = +06 7-10		
Remove Topsoil (NIL) (assumed none present)									
Machine Excav Pool									
65-4 x 35-4 x 7-10 18,083					670 CY				
NOTE: Better measured by area, stating average depth.									
Remove Excav Mat off Site (allow 25% swell)					670 CY				
(none backfilled)									
Hand Trim & Ram Bottom to Slopes (slab area) =					1970 SF				
Temp Shoring to Sides Excav avg 7'10"dp									
2x(65-4 + 35-4) 1/ 201-4 x 7-0					1580 SF				
Ditto, 12" Extra Ht at Top *									
(above ground) 1/ 201-4					200 LF				
NOTE: For computer input, last two SHORING items are better combined and measured linearly, stating average height.									
Fill Imported Pit Run Gravel around Pool Walls, &									
Ram in 12" layers, as spec (allow 20% shrinkage)									
4/2/ 201-4 1/-0 -8-0 193-4		193-4 x 2-0 x 7-10 3029			112 CY				
NOTE: For computer input, despite existing conventions, such a FILL item is better measured by area and described as, "in 12 in. layers," with computer providing total volume for ordering materials.									
[NB: No gravel bed under conc slab required.]									

*This SHORING item is included to conform to requirements of the Canadian Method of Measurement, but here measured linearly to retain useful information in estimate about the SHORING work.

PRACTICAL
Form 516 MFD IN U S A

PROJECT _PRELIMINARY EXERCISE_   ESTIMATOR _KC_   ESTIMATE NO. _P-3(M)_

LOCATION   EXTENSIONS   SHEET NO. _1 of 3_

ARCHITECT
ENGINEER   CHECKED   DATE _1987_

CLASSIFICATION _R CONC POOL (METRIC)_

DESCRIPTION	NO.	DIMENSIONS L B D/H			ESTIMATED QUANTITY	UNIT
PRELIM CALCS:		MEAN PERIMETER				
30 000 x 15 000		30 000				
2/ 600 600		15 000				
30 600 x 15 600		2/ 45 000 = 90 000				
		4/ 300 = 1 200				
		91 200				
REINF CONCRETE (25 MPa/20 mm Aggregate) CAST IN PLACE						
Pool Slab, to slopes, x 150						
		30 600 x 15 600				
(allow for slopes)						
a= 15 200		80 x 15 600				
b= 1 600						
c= 15 280						
(remainder of slopes)		20 x 15 660 (approx.)				
		30 700 x 15 600 = 478 920 m²				
		x 150	= 71 838		72	m³
Pool Walls x 300						
3·450						
(@ ends) 2·250	2/ 15 600	x 2850	88 920			
= 2·850 AVG						
(@ sides)	2/ 3 600	x 3750	27 000			
	2/ 3 200	x 4050	25 920			
	2/ 15 200	x 3250	98 800			
	2/ 8 000	x 2350	37 600			
(= 2/ 91 200)			278 240 m²			
		x 300	= 83 472		84	m³
Paving, to slopes, x 100						
30 000 x 15 000						
2/ 6 800 6 800		105 200 x 3000	315 600			
36 800 x 21 800		x 100	= 31 560		32	m³
36 800						
21 800		(= 186 870 net)				
2/ 58 600 = 117 200						
4/ 3000 = -12 000						
MP = 105 200						
			TOTAL CONCRETE =		188	m³

PRACTICAL
Form 516 MFD IN U.S.A.

PROJECT *PRELIMINARY EXERCISE*	ESTIMATOR *KC*	ESTIMATE NO. *P-3(M)*
LOCATION	EXTENSIONS	SHEET NO. *2 of 3*
ARCHITECT ENGINEER	CHECKED	DATE *1987*

CLASSIFICATION *R. CONC POOL (METRIC)*

DESCRIPTION	NO.	DIMENSIONS		ESTIMATED QUANTITY	UNIT
FORMWORK (erect & strip) to:-					
Pool Walls x 300 3/278 240 m² (3/ wall area) =				557	m²
Extra Labor & Materials forming RECESS 100 x 450 (for inside gutter) (30 + 15 M)	2/ 45 m			90	m
Extra L & M forming RECESS 100 x 100 (for pavings)	2/ 45 600			91	m
Extra L & M forming PROJECTION x 100 (outside)	2/ 45 600			91	m
Slab Edges x 150 (30 600 + 15 600)	2/ 46 200			93	m
Paving Edges x 100 (@ outside)	1/ 117 200			118	m
Slab Screeds, to various slopes, x 150 (Slab Area) =				479	m²
(End of Formwork)					
Expansion Joints x 100 (as Spec. 03.10.21)					
4/ 91 200 = 1 200					
(@ perim)	1/ 92 400		93		
(@ across pavings)	22/ 3000		66	159	m
CHECK POOL WALLS / FORMWORK AREA:					

30 000 =	2/ 15 000	x	2 400	72 000	
7 200 =	2/ 3 600	x	3 300	23 760	
6 400 =	2/ 3 200	x	3 600	23 040	
30 400 =	2/ 15 200	x	2 800	85 120	
16 000 =	2/ 8 000	x	1 900	30 400	
1 200 =	2/ 2/ 300	x	2 400	2 880	
91 200 =	1/ 91 200	x	450	41 040	
		TOTAL W'L AREA =		278 240	

PRACTICAL
PRACTICAL
Form 516 MFD IN U.S.A

PROJECT	*PRELIMINARY EXERCISE*	ESTIMATOR KC	ESTIMATE NO. P-3 (M)
LOCATION		EXTENSIONS	SHEET NO. 3 of 3
ARCHITECT ENGINEER		CHECKED	DATE 1987

CLASSIFICATION R CONC POOL (METRIC)

DESCRIPTION	NO.	DIMENSIONS	ESTIMATED QUANTITY	UNIT

REBAR (x 400 MPa) (fabricate & install):

PRELIM [pool wall area = mean perim x avg.wall height] OR $A = \dfrac{MP}{H_{avg}}$

CALCS: ∴ $H_{avg} = \dfrac{278\,240\,m^2}{91\,200\,m} = 3\,050\,m$

TO CALC NUMBER $\dfrac{91\,200}{210(spacing)} = 434$
OF VERTICAL BARS: $\underline{+\ 8}$ (@ corners)
                            $\underline{442}$

LENGTH   3050 (avg. wl. ht)
VERT BARS: $\underline{-\ 050}$ (cover)
                 3000
              $+\ 75$ (in slab)
              $+600$ " "
              $\underline{+175}$ (top hook)
                 3850

TO CALC NUMBER $\dfrac{3050\,(a\,vght)}{430\,(spacing)} = 7$
OF HORIZ BARS: $\underline{+1}$ (extra @ top)
                          $\underline{8}$

#10 Rebar in Walls (metric standard deformed bars)

$\left.\begin{array}{l}91\,200\\ \tfrac{10}{300}=3000\\ \overline{94\,200}\end{array}\right\}$ (vert) (horiz)	442/3850 8/94200	1701700 753600		
		2455300		
	(for 2 FACES)	$\times 2 = 4910\,600$ (x .785 Kg/M)	TOTAL QUANT. 3.855	METRIC TONNE

WIRE MESH 150 x 150 x 9/9 Ga. in Pool Slab

(Slab Area) = 479 m²
(laps: +5%) = $\underline{24}$ 503 m²

[NB: "CONCRETE FINISHES" not measured here.]

[REBAR/CONC RATIO: $\dfrac{4910.600 \times .785\,Kg}{83.472\,m^3\,(walls)} = 46.181\,kg/m^3$]

bars (2719 LF) is almost the same as the total length of the shorter bars (2688 LF) in the other direction. *If bar spacings are identical both ways, the total lengths of bars each way should be the same*, except for minor differences resulting from laps and from dims that are not exact multiples of the spacing.

If the slab rebar is measured by "bar length per unit area," the result is similar, thus: With bars at 9 in. spacing both ways there are 2⅔ LF of bar per SF of slab area.

$$\text{Slab Area} \times 2\tfrac{2}{3} \text{ LF} = 1969 \times 2\tfrac{2}{3} \text{ LF}$$
$$= 5251 \text{ LF}$$

To which must be added an extra bar at two adjacent edges:

$$
\begin{array}{r}
5251 \\
(32.0 + 64.8 = 96.8) = +\ \ 97 \\
\hline
= 5348 \text{ LF}
\end{array}
$$

To which must be added an allowance for laps (at every 30 ft):

$$
\begin{array}{r}
5348 \\
(5348 \div 30) \times 14 \text{ in.} = +\ 208 \\
\hline
= 5556 \text{ LF}
\end{array}
$$

This quantity is about 150 LF (= 50 lb) greater than that in the estimate, primarily because no adjustment has been made for conc cover at slab edges. This method of measuring rebar by "bar length per unit area" is useful and accurate *if the extra bars at two adjacent edges are added* (because there is always one more bar than the number of spaces); and the method can just as easily be used when the spacings are not the same both ways. (In some instances it is convenient to use a unit area of more than 1 SF, which is also a multiple of the two spacing dims.) Measurement by this method and measurement by the other (calculating bar lengths and numbers of bars) generally produce results within 2 or 3 percent of each other; these differences in quantities arise from differences between job dims and multiples of the spacing dims and from the absence of adjustments to areas for the conc cover to rebar, as indicated above.

Extra L. Bending. This type of bending (light) is measured "extra over" for the bent vertical bars in the conc walls, the assumption being that the conc slab is placed first and that the vertical rebar in the walls is bent and placed before the slab is poured. Alternatively, cranked bars would have to be placed in the slab with about 15 in. upstanding, and the vertical

rebars would have to be spliced to the cranked bars. This procedure would probably prove to be more expensive because of the laps, although there would then be less steel to be handled in the light bending. Often, one finds that the costs of two reasonable but different ways of doing the same thing are about the same; which means that if an estimator selects one good method for his estimate, the costs will usually be valid even if the method is eventually changed. Not all estimators measure rebar bending in this way. It is simpler to keep bars separate according to size and whether straight or bent.

Excav and Fill. The prelim calcs add a working space 2 ft wide around the outside of the pool to obtain the dims of the excav. It is assumed that all excav mat is removed and that imported gravel fill is to be used. The absence of topsoil is noted to indicate that it has not been overlooked by the estimator.

Temp Shoring. This work is measured when extra excav to form sloping banks is not measured. The measured quantity is a basis for pricing the costs of supporting the sides of the excav, or it provides a contingency for any extra excav work required if shoring is not done and a collapse occurs. The MM-CIQS requires an additional foot to be added to allow for the shoring to project at the top. By measuring this additional 12 in. of height as a separate run item, more information about the work is available from the estimate, i.e., the actual face area of excav to be shored and the length and avg depth of the excav. Information that would be otherwise obscured by adding the extra ht to the general area of shoring and timbering is thereby retained.

The MM-CIQS requires that shoring and timbering be measured only to depths of more than 4 ft, and then only if extra excav to form sloping banks is not measured. As with conc formwork, only the contact areas (supported faces) are measured for shoring, because the costs are mostly *labor costs* and (like formwork) the use and waste of lumber are calculated and allowed for in the unit price.

An exercise may be done from the dwg of this example, but with inside dims as shown in Fig. 9-3. In addition, a dwg is included (with the dwg for the example) for an entirely different pool for a measurement exercise. An example in metric is also provided.

Concrete Pan Joist Slab

Concrete. Although the perim beams and the slab will be placed at the same time so that they are monolithic, the beams and the slab are measured sep-

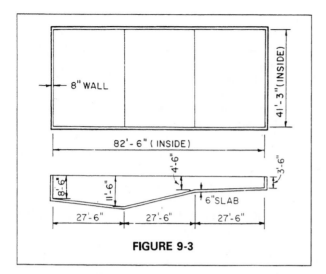

FIGURE 9-3

arately, as required by the methods of measurement (MM-CIQS and SMM-RICS).

This provides an opportunity to obtain cost information and to price the two items—beams and slab—at different unit prices for labor, if such differences can and have been established. Some estimators claim that such distinctions are impractical and unnecessary, because separate and different unit prices for two such closely related items of work cannot be substantiated. But if the distinction between such items is not made in estimates, more accurate costs never will be obtained. Measuring such items separately ensures better cost accounting results and cost analyses.

Pan Joist Slab

Many students see this item as a thin conc slab supported by conc joists and think that it should be measured that way. But structurally, and for a better view of the work to be measured, it should be seen as a *15-in.-thick conc slab with the structurally superfluous concrete displaced by pans.*[5] The volume displaced by the pans is given, and similar figures for standard steel pans of different sizes can be obtained from manufacturer's tables and some estimating handbooks. However, as pans are used and dented their displacement may vary, and cost accounting will show how much.

Form Beam Soffits.   Although the dwg shows masonry below the beam, it is unlikely that the conc would be placed on the masonry, and therefore soffit

---

[5] From the measured quantities, it can be seen that the 15-in. pan joist slab shown contains less concrete than a 6-in.-thick flat slab of the same area. But by increasing the effective depth of the slab, and by using a thinner floor slab on joists, the concrete and the steel rebar are used more efficiently in the structure.

forms are required. The standard methods of measurement call for formwork for sides and soffits of beams to be measured together as a super item. But many estimators prefer to measure soffits separately, because soffits have to be reshored after the forms are stripped, or else the forms for soffits are left in place for several days after the forms for the sides have been stripped. Either way, there is an additional cost for forming soffits. However, it is a general principle of standard methods of measurement that they are not inflexible, and that providing the method of measurement is made clear in the estimate, estimators and quantity surveyors may measure in greater detail and adopt special methods of measurement which are not even standard to better enable the costs of work to be estimated. With this in mind, soffits are better measured separately from beam sides. A simpler alternative construction method has the pans placed on a formply deck.

Form Beam Sides.   There are some complications involved in measuring and estimating this item, because of the junction between beams and slab. The first question is, Should there be a deduction of formwork at the inner side of the beam, at the 15-in.-deep slab? According to usual practice (and SMM-RICS), formwork is *not* deducted at intersections of beams with walls or columns or other beams. But in this case a deduction is justified. It can also be argued that a contact area does not directly reflect the costs of formwork for the perim beams, and that it would be more realistic to measure and price all the work as a run item; i.e., "*form perim beam sides (two) average 32 in. (with no deduction for adjoining 15-in.-deep slab; with soffit measured separately).*" Cost accounting will probably show that formwork costs (per linear foot) do not vary significantly with minor variations in beam depths. It can be argued that the presence of the adjoining slab would not decrease the costs of forming the beam sides (by displacing a portion of the beam forms) and that, therefore, no deduction of side forms is necessary. This illustrates a fundamental fact of estimating:

Work should be measured so that the quantities of work can be priced, and methods of measurement should be determined primarily by the measurements that can best be used to account for the costs of work.

In the example, the formwork to the beam sides has been separated between outer and inner faces, and inner faces have been measured as runs. But such work cannot be accurately priced without considering the locations of the work. For example, forming the 7-in.-high face should cost less than the 9-in.-high face below the slab, not because of the minor difference in height but because of the location.

Form Joist Soffits. Similarly, this item is better measured as a *run item.* Joist soffits 8 in. wide would not cost one-third more (per linear foot) than joist soffits 6 in. wide. These forms and their supports are often erected and stripped by the contractor, whereas the next item of work is often done by a subcontractor.

Form Joists wi Pans. Some estimators measure the gross slab area overall (excluding any slab beams), whereas others measure only the actual plan area of the pans (15/21.6 × 2.6), and still others measure the pans as a run item, stating the pan width. Although the first method is common, the other two are preferable, particularly the last method, for the reasons already given for measuring such work as run items. *In no case is the two-dimensional contact area of the pans measured* (i.e., the actual pan surface in contact with concrete), which in fact is contrary to the previously stated general principle for measuring formwork. The reason for this is that measurement of the pans' contact area would be complicated and the result would not increase the accuracy of estimating. This is significant, and it raises other questions about the validity of other methods of measurement and units of work that are commonly used. Only by questioning them shall we improve them.

Rebar. Rebar is often more easily measured for a large project than for a small project, because for large projects the structural engineer often annotates or schedules every structural rebar by size, length, and location on the dwgs, whereas for smaller jobs the information is often sparse. Problems incurred in measuring rebar arise from requirements not shown on the dwgs, although they are often implicit in the contract through a reference to a standard or a code of practice. Therefore, an estimator must know of all the usual requirements for rebars, including such items as non-structural carrying bars that are not usually shown on the dwgs but are required for installing repetitive structural bars wired at the required spacing to the carrying bars for secured placing and support.

In the example, the conc joists against the perim beams (at the two shorter sides) are not required to be reinforced, according to the CRSI Code of Practice. There are, therefore, fourteen No. 7 bars in conc joists with 6 in. at each end into the perim beam. There are also fourteen No. 8 bars (bent) in joists. In the perim beams the No. 8 bars (straight) are the MP length (average), and one lap is measured for each of the two longer sides (× 4 bars). At corners, No. 8 bars for corner splices (bent to 90 degrees) are measured at twice the lap length. Alternatively, and according to the Code, the continuous bars may themselves be bent to 90 degrees to splice at corners, but the separate splice bars as measured here would probably be easier and cheaper. The No. 5 bars in the perim beams are similarly measured.

The No. 4 stirrups are measured as 1.9 deep × 0.9 wide and with two 4½-in. hooks at the top.[6] The 2.9 long cranked No. 4 bars are in conjunction with the stirrups. The No. 4 bars in the slab are measured 6 in. into the beams at each end. The total length of No. 4 bars 46.6 long is higher than the total length of No. 4 bars 22.9 long, because whereas 46.6 is a multiple of the 18-in. spacing, 22.9 is not; and an additional bar 46.6 long must be allowed for the part space of 3 in. If the slab steel is calculated on the basis of "bar length per unit area," as follows, the result is almost the same.

Taking a square yard (36 in. × 36 in.) as the unit area, it would contain four bars each 36 in long; a total of 12 LF, which equals 1⅓ LF per SF.

$$\text{Reinf Area} \times 1\tfrac{1}{3} \text{ LF} = (46.6 \times 22.9) \times 1\tfrac{1}{3} \text{ LF}$$
$$= 1058 \text{ SF} \times 1\tfrac{1}{3} \text{ LF}$$
$$= 1411 \text{ LF}$$

add: extra bars at two edges   +69
add: extra bar one way (for one dim
     not multiple of spacing)   +47
         Total: 1527 LF

The total measured by the other method in the estimate is 1519 LF. The longer bars are assumed to require one lap per bar. If in fact they are in one length (of 46½ ft) the extra length measured will help to offset the higher handling costs.

Extra for Bending. The weights of bent bars are measured so that the additional cost of bending may be estimated. *Heavy bending* (the cheaper of the two) includes all the bent bars in this example except the stirrups, which are always classed as *light bending.* It is helpful to describe all bars according to whether they are bent or straight when they are measured, and in larger projects all bars are better separated as different items to avoid confusion and to simplify the measurement of rebar and bending.

The MM-CIQS requires bars to be grouped according to length and the number of bends per bar. It also says that bars larger than No. 6 shall not be separated according to bar size; but the increasing use of large bars (No. 14 and No. 18) makes it desirable to do so, as recommended by the CRSI Code. The differences between the two methods of measurement

---

[6] *Stirrups* are usually measured in width and height as 3 in. less than the outside width and height of the conc beam. *Column ties* are similarly measured. For other standard practices, see Chapter 8 and the CRSI Code of Practice.

PRACTICAL
STANDARDIZED FORMS FOR CONTRACTORS
Form 514 MFD. IN U.S.A.

GENERAL ESTIMATE

BUILDING **PRELIMINARY**

LOCATION **EXAMPLE**

ARCHITECTS

SUBJECT **PAN JOIST SLAB**

ESTIMATE NO. **P-4**

SHEET NO. **1 of 2**

ESTIMATOR **KC**

CHECKER **AB**

DATE **1987**

FRANK R. WALKER CO., PUBLISHERS, CHICAGO

DESCRIPTION OF WORK	NO. PIECES	DIMENSIONS	EXTENSIONS	EXTENSIONS	TOTAL ESTIMATED QUANTITY	UNIT PRICE M'T'L	TOTAL ESTIMATED MATERIAL COST	UNIT PRICE LABOR	TOTAL ESTIMATE LABOR COST
Prelim Calcs MP(Beams) = 2(45-6 + 21-9) + 4/1-0 = 138-6						Avg Depth Beams $\frac{2\cdot9 + 2\cdot7}{2}$ = 2·8 (avg)			
CONCRETE (3500 psi - ¾" Stone)									
Perim Beams 138-6 × 1-0 × 2-8			369			$\frac{14}{CY}$			
Pan Joist Slab × 15" 45-6 × 21-9			989½						
			×1-3 = 1237						
DOT (@ pans) ¹⁵/21-6 (× 2·45 CF/LF)			= −790			$\frac{17}{CY}$			
			447						
FORMS (erect and strip) btwn 10 & 15 ft above deck									
Form Beam Soffits 1/138-6 × 1-0						$\frac{139}{SFCA}$			
Form Beam Sides (out) 1/142-6 × 2-9						$\frac{392}{SFCA}$			
138-6 + 4/2/0-6 = 142-6									
Form Beam Sides × 7" (In) 1/134-6						$\frac{135}{LF}$			
Ditto × 9" (In) 1/134-6						$\frac{135}{LF}$			
Form Joist Soffits × 6" ¹⁶/21-6						$\frac{344}{LF}$			
Form Soffits × 1½" ²/45-6 (next perim beams)						$\frac{91}{LF}$			
Form Pan Joists wi 30" × 12" Pans									
¹⁵/21-6						$\frac{323}{LF}$			
Extra for End Pans ²/15						$\frac{30}{NO}$			
Slab Screeds × 3" (slab area) =						$\frac{990}{SF}$			

NOTE: For computer input, CONCRETE and FORMWORK items are better measured linearly, stating other dimensions in descriptions.

GENERAL ESTIMATE

BUILDING PRELIMINARY

LOCATION EXAMPLE

ARCHITECTS

SUBJECT PAN JOIST SLAB

FRANK R. WALKER CO., PUBLISHERS, CHICAGO

ESTIMATE NO. P-4

SHEET NO. 2 of 2

ESTIMATOR KC

CHECKER AB

DATE 1987

DESCRIPTION OF WORK	NO. PIECES	DIMENSIONS	EXTENSIONS	EXTENSIONS	TOTAL ESTIMATED QUANTITY	UNIT PRICE M'T'L	TOTAL ESTIMATED MATERIAL COST	UNIT PRICE LABOR	TOTAL ESTIMATE LABOR COST
REBAR (grade #60) up to 30 ft lengths									
#7 Bars (in JI)	14/22-9	(str)	319 × 2·044 lb		650 lb				
#8 Bars (in JI)	14/25-6	(bnt)✓	357						
(in BI)	4/138-6	(str)	554						
36×1"=3·0 (laps)	4/2/3-0	(")	24						
3l/3 =6·0 (corner splices)	4/4/6-0	(bnt)✓	96						
			1031 × 2·670 lb		2755 lb				
#5 Bars (in BI)	2/138-6	(str)	277						
36×5/8"=2·0 (laps)	2/2/2-0	(")	8						
2 L/2 =4·0 (corner splices)	4/2/4-0	(bnt)✓	32						
			317 × 1·043 lb		330 lb				

138-6 / 1-6 = 92   2(1·9+0·4½)+0·9 = 5·0
(+4+4) = 100

#4 Bars (in BI)	100/5-0	(stirrups)✓	500						
9√24	100/2-9	(bnt)✓	275						
(46-6/1-6 = 31 +1=32)	32/22-9	(str)	728						
(22-9/1-6 = 16 +1=17)	17/46-6	(")	791						
36×½"=1-6 (laps)	17/1-6	(")	26						
			2320 × 0·668 lb		1550 lb				
Extra for Bending:-									
H. Bending	14/25-6 × 2·670 lb		953						
	4/4/6-0 × 2·670		256						
	4/2/4-0 × 1·043		33						
	100/2-9 × 0·668		184		1430 lb				
L. Bending	100/5-0 × 0·668				340 lb				
Allow for Conc Blk Bar Supports					Item				
[N.B: NO "CONCRETE SUNDRIES" taken here.]									

are not great. The important thing is that the method of measurement used is clear and appropriate to the work and the locality; and the clearest method is to measure separately every bar that is different in bar size and bending and to group them according to lengths.

Bar supports, such as steel bolsters and chairs, are usually measured as number items, except continuous chairs, and the like, which are measured as run items in 5 ft and 10 ft lengths. If such items are required by the work, they should be specified and indicated by standard symbols (see CRSI Code). Alternatively, plastic or precast cone bar supports are used, either plain, or with wires, or with dowels of rebar, particularly in smaller projects; and it is assumed that these are to be used in these Preliminary Examples.

Costs for plastic or conc supports are not high, and they can be established by cost accounting according to the type of job and the rebar quantities. Therefore, these accessories need not be measured in detail and can be priced by allowing a suitable sum.

Exercises may be done from the dwg of the example but with the different dims shown in Fig. 9-4.

Concrete Building

Prelim Calcs. Preliminary calculations include the MP and the wall ht, which is taken up to the underside of the roof slab because the wall would probably be placed that way. The avg ht of the plinth, sill, and fascia projs is calculated so that they can be

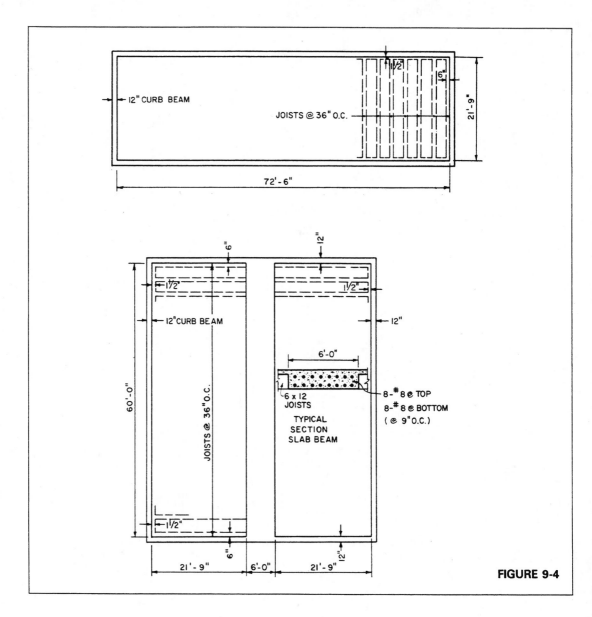

FIGURE 9-4

grouped and measured together. The slab dims are also calculated here, which is usually necessary even when the dims are shown for walls rather than for ftgs, as in the example.

Extra Lab and Mat in Projs to Walls. These items are measured separately so that they can be priced at a higher unit price than the general conc wall item. There is undoubtedly additional time and effort required in ensuring that the cast-in-place conc does fill the forms of the projs. If it does not, there will be some patching to do when the proj forms are stripped, and this risk should be allowed for. In addition, the precept is to measure and price *basic items of work*[G] whenever possible because cost data for basic items is more likely to be available. By measuring these projs separately, the 8-in conc walls are retained as a basic item of work, whereas the projs are not basic items.

An alternative method of construction for the two projections below the windows, which, of course, requires different measurements, is to form a 4-in. recess (with a framed insert) in a 12-in thick wall above and below the plinth projection.

Susp Roof Slab. This is measured as extending over the conc walls as it would probably be placed monolithic with the fascia proj so that there would be no construction joint within the fascia. With all structural conc the separation of different parts of monolithic walls, slabs, and beams for purposes of measurement is somewhat arbitrary, but the effect is not significant.

Roof Beams. These are better measured as a run item at first, with the volume calculated later from the total length. (The value of this procedure is less obvious when the beam is 12 in. × 12 in.) The total length of beams (and columns) of the same size can be used for measuring forms and (when adjusted) for rebar.

Form Walls. The additional quantity (71 SF) at slab edges is a quantity required to theoretically extend the wall forms up to the top of the slab and behind the fascia proj so that the forming of the fascia proj can be measured and priced as an *extra-over item*, as is the forming of the other projs. No deduction is made from the forms for the openings. (The MM-CIQS calls for no deductions for openings of 100 SF or less.)

Extra Lab and Mat to Form Wall Projections. These are measured as run items and described, because to measure them as super items (length × girth), and to combine them into one super item would make accurate pricing impossible. (MM-CIQS calls for such items to be measured as super items if over 24 in. in girth.) The labor costs of these items will not vary in proportion to their girth, but rather in proportion to their length. The material costs will be affected by the girth, but not much, because most of the material costs are in the top and bottom (and in the external supports), and it is only the form sheathing between that will vary with the vertical dim of the projection. If the walls below the windows are assumed to be 12 in. thick, instead of this item a similar item for forming recesses is needed.

Form Openings. These openings are measured as number[G] items to more accurately estimate the labor costs. Variations in opening sizes affect the costs slightly; more important are the number and the types of openings.

Slab Screeds. Slab screeds are required on grade, but suspended slabs (placed on leveled forms) require only movable screeds, such as a length of steel pipe laid on chairs, which do not require laborious installation with pegs, and leveling. The costs of these is therefore almost negligible and can be included with the tools and equipment used for placing the concrete.

Concrete Sundries. These items of work on conc surfaces are inadequately described in the example for accurate pricing, and the job specs would have to be referred to again by the estimator. Spec page references might be included in the descriptions. No deductions have been made for openings, but if they were, the work on reveals (jambs) should be measured; and if the openings were numerous, it would be better to deduct for openings and to measure them. Corners and arrises often require special care and attention, particularly with bush-hammering; which may be another good reason for measuring reveals and deducting openings.

Rebar. The No. 4 bars in the conc ftgs are measured at the outside perim of the ftgs, assuming they cross at the corners. The conc wall ht is divided by the spacing to give thirteen horizontal rows of bars. These are assumed to be spliced by bent No. 4 bars at corners, as in the last example. The length of the vertical bars in walls is equal to the wall ht (11.6), and their number is calculated by dividing the MP by the bar spacing, to which are added twelve extra bars for the number of wall lengths, plus an addition of twelve extra bars at corners. There is an equal number of dowels in conc ftgs, joined to the vertical bars in the walls above. It is not possible to measure exactly

GENERAL ESTIMATE

BUILDING _PRELIMINARY_

LOCATION _EXAMPLE_

ARCHITECTS_____

SUBJECT _CONCRETE BUILDING_

ESTIMATE NO. _P-5_

SHEET NO. _1 of 7_

ESTIMATOR _KC_

CHECKER _AB_

DATE _1987_

FRANK R. WALKER CO., PUBLISHERS, CHICAGO

DESCRIPTION OF WORK	NO. PIECES	DIMENSIONS		EXTENSIONS	EXTENSIONS	TOTAL ESTIMATED QUANTITY	UNIT PRICE M'T'L	TOTAL ESTIMATED MATERIAL COST	UNIT PRICE LABOR	TOTAL ESTIMATE LABOR COST
Prelim calcs		Wall Ht	Wall Projs					slab dims		slab perim
6-0	40-0	8-0						40-0 x 30-0		37-4
20-0 20-0	30-0	0-6	plinth 15"			less 2/1-4=		-2-8 -2-8		27-4
14-0 10-0	4-0	0-6	sill 3					37-4 x 27-4		4-0
40-0 30-0	2/74-0=148-0	3-6	fascia 12							68-8
less 4/2/1-0 = -8-0		12-6		3) 30=10"avg						x2
		1-0		+½"(slope)						137-4
MP= 140-0	11-6 High			10½"(AVG HT.)						

CONCRETE (3000 psi - ¾" stone - except as noted)

Ftgs cont (1½" stone) 140-0 x 2-0 x 1-0   280   10½ cy

Walls x 8"   140-0 x 11-6   1610   DDT

DDT (openings)   5/ 5-0 x 4-0   —   100

1/ 3-0 x 7-0   —   21

4/ 140-0   -121

3/6": +4-0   (net wall area)= 1489 x 0-8 = 993   37 cy

144-0

Extra Lab & Mat

in Projs to Walls   3/ 44-0 x 0-4 x 0-10½   126   5 cy

Slab/Grd x 6"   37-4 x 27-4   1021   DDT

DDT (wants)   14-0 x 10-0   —   140

6-0 x 10-0   60

(10-0 + 2/1-4)=12-8   12-8 x 4-0   —   51

-251

(slab area)= 770 x 0-6 = 385   14 cy

Susp Roof Slab x 6"   (slab area)= 770

ADD (@ over walls)   140-0 x 0-8   93

(roof slab area)= 863 x 0-6 = 432   16 cy

Roof Beams 12" x 12"   1/ 37-4   37

(20-0 - 2/1-4)=17-4   1/ 17-4   18

55 x 1-0

x 1-0 = 55   2 cy

NOTE: All the above items could be measured linearly.

PRACTICAL
Form 514 MFD. IN U.S.A.

GENERAL ESTIMATE

FRANK R. WALKER CO., PUBLISHERS, CHICAGO

BUILDING _PRELIMINARY_

LOCATION _EXAMPLE_

ARCHITECTS _____

SUBJECT _CONCRETE BUILDING_

ESTIMATE NO. _P-5_

SHEET NO. _2 of 7_

ESTIMATOR _KC_

CHECKER _AB_

DATE _1987_

DESCRIPTION OF WORK	NO. PIECES	DIMENSIONS	EXTENSIONS	EXTENSIONS	TOTAL ESTIMATED QUANTITY	UNIT PRICE M'T'L	TOTAL ESTIMATED MATERIAL COST	UNIT PRICE LABOR	TOTAL ESTIMA LABOR COS
FORMS (erect and strip)									
Form Ftgs	2/	140-0 × 1-0		280	280 SFCA				
Form Key 2×4	1/	140-0			140 LF				
Form Walls	2/	1610 SF (wall area) gross	3220						
(140-0 + 4/¾"@slab edges)	1/	142-8 × 0-6	71						
			3291		3290 SFCA				
(140-0 + 4/¾") = 144-0									
Extra Lab & Mat to Form Wall Projections									
Plinth 4"×15"	1/	144-0			144 LF				
Sill 4"×3"	1/	144-0			144 LF				
Fascia 4"×12"	1/	144-0			144 LF				
Form Wdw Openings (5'×4')	5/1				5 NO				
Form Door Openg (3'×7')	1/1				1 NO				
Form Beam Sides	2/	55-0 × 1-0			110 SFCA				
Form Beam Soffits	1/	55-0 × 1-0			55 SFCA				
Form Susp Slab (<10'h) (slab % grd area) =			770						
DDT (@ Beam Soffits)			-55		715 SFCA				
Slab Screeds ×6"	1/	137-4	138						
(20-0 − ¾'-4)	2·1/	17-4	52						
(16-0 − ¾'-4)	3/	13-4	27						
			217		220 LF				
[NB: Slab screeds for Roof not incl.]									

NOTE: All CONCRETE & FORMWORK can be measured
either linearly or by enumeration, with other dims
included in items' descriptions; especially for
computer input.

	GENERAL ESTIMATE		
BUILDING **PRELIMINARY**		ESTIMATE NO. **P-5**	
LOCATION **EXAMPLE**		SHEET NO. **3 of 7**	
ARCHITECTS		ESTIMATOR **KC**	
		CHECKER **AB**	
SUBJECT **CONCRETE BUILDING**		DATE **1987**	

FRANK R. WALKER CO. PUBLISHERS, CHICAGO

DESCRIPTION OF WORK	NO. PIECES	DIMENSIONS / EXTENSIONS	EXTENSIONS	TOTAL ESTIMATED QUANTITY	UNIT PRICE M'T'L	TOTAL ESTIMATED MATERIAL COST	UNIT PRICE LABOR	TOTAL ESTIMATE LABOR COST
CONCRETE SUNDRIES								
Cut Back Ties & Grout Holes Flush				3290 SF				
(as specs page —) (form walls area)								
(140-0 – 2¾") = 137-4								
Sack-rub finish Walls (above grd)(as specs s.p—)								
(inside)	1/	137-4 × 8-0	1099					
(outside on projs)								
(1-0+0-3+0-5) = 1-8	3/	44-0 × 0-4	96					
(144-0 + 1½") = 145-4	1/	145-4 × 1-8	242					
			1437	1440 SF				
Bush hammer finish Walls (above grd)(as specs p—)								
(8-6 – (1-1 + 0-4)) = 7-1	1/	142-8 × 7-1	1011	1010 SF				
Wood Float finish Slab (roof slab area) =				860 SF				
Steel Trowel finish Slab (flr slab area) =				770 SF				
Ditto, Sloping tops Projs × 4" wide								
(not sack-rubbed)	3/	144-0	432	430 LF				
Cure Slabs		(roof slab area) =	860					
		(flr slab area) =	770	1630 SF				
Control Joints & Seal (c slab perim)(as specs p—)								
	1/	137-4		140 LF				
Gravel Bed 4" Slab × 6" (allow for 20% shrinkage)								
		(flr slab area) =	770					
		× 0-6 =	385	14 CY				

GENERAL ESTIMATE

BUILDING _PRELIMINARY_

LOCATION _EXAMPLE_

ARCHITECTS _____

SUBJECT _CONCRETE BUILDING_

ESTIMATE NO. _P-5_

SHEET NO. _4 of 7_

ESTIMATOR _KC_

CHECKER _AB_

DATE _1987_

FRANK R. WALKER CO., PUBLISHERS, CHICAGO

DESCRIPTION OF WORK	NO. PIECES	DIMENSIONS	EXTENSIONS	EXTENSIONS	TOTAL ESTIMATED QUANTITY	UNIT PRICE M'T'L	TOTAL ESTIMATED MATERIAL COST	UNIT PRICE LABOR	TOTAL ESTIMATED LABOR COST
REBAR (grade #60) up to 30' lengths									
#4 Bars (in Ftgs)	5/148-0 (str)		740 × 0.668 lb		500 lb				
#4 Bars (in Walls)	2/13/142-0 (str)		3692						
	2/118/11-6 "		2714						
			6406						
9|²⁴ dowels in ftgs/walls	2/118/2-9 (bnt)		649						
18|18 corner splices (outside only)	12/1/13/3-0 "		468						
DDT (e openings)			7523	DDT					
	5/2/4/5-0		—	200					
	5/2/3/4-0		—	120					
	1/2/7/3-0		—	42					
	1/2/2/7-0		—	28					
			−390						
			7133 × 0.668 lb		4770 lb				
#4 Bars (in Rf Slab) (slab area 863 sf × 3⅓ lf/sf) = 2877									
18-8 (extra @ edges) (slab perim)		(str)	= 145						
4-0 14-8 = 10 (laps)	11/1-6 "		17						
148 1-6 +1			3039 × 0.668 lb		2030 lb				
11									
#5 Bars (in Walls)									
2(5-6+4-6) = 20-0 (arnd openings)	5/2/20-0 (str)		200						
2(7-6) + 3-6 = 18-6	1/2/18-6 "		37						
			237 × 1.043 lb		250 lb				
#5 Bars (in Beams)									
¾ 37-4 38-4	2/57-0 (str)		114 × 1.043 lb		120 lb				
1-0 17-0									
38-4 1-0									
56-4									

GENERAL ESTIMATE

				ESTIMATE NO.	P-5
BUILDING	PRELIMINARY			SHEET NO.	5 of 7
LOCATION	EXAMPLE			ESTIMATOR	KC
ARCHITECTS				CHECKER	AB
SUBJECT	CONCRETE BUILDING			DATE	1987

FRANK R. WALKER CO., PUBLISHERS, CHICAGO

DESCRIPTION OF WORK	NO. PIECES	DIMENSIONS	EXTENSIONS	EXTENSIONS	TOTAL ESTIMATED QUANTITY	UNIT PRICE M'T'L	TOTAL ESTIMATED MATERIAL COST	UNIT PRICE LABOR	TOTAL ESTIMATE LABOR COST
REBAR (cont.) up to 30' lengths									
#7 Bars (in Beams)	3/	57-0 (str)	171						
37-4 + 2 (0-5 + 0-10 hook) {	2/	40-0 (bnt)	80 }						
17-4 + 2 (0-5 + 0-10 hook) {	2/	20-0 (")	40 }						
			291 × 2·044 lb		600 lb				
#3 Bars (stirrups)									
37-4/16 = 25 / +1 =	1/	26 (bnt)	26						
17-4/16 = 12 / +1 =	1/	13 "	13						
(extra c ends)	2/2/2	"	8						
2(15+4)+9 = 47" (say) 4-0 long (No stirrups)=		47							
		× 4-0 long							
			188 × 0·376 lb		70 lb				
Extra for Bending :-									
		LF	lb/FT						
H Bending		649 } 468 }	× 0·668 } × " }	= 746					
		80 } 40 }	× 2·044 } × " }	= 245 / 991		1000 lb				
L Bending		188	× 0·376 =		70 lb				
6" × 6" × 10/10 Gauge WWF in Slab %grd									
		(slab area) =	770						
ADD (laps)		5% × 770 sf =	+38 =		810 SF				
Allow for Bar Supports					Item				

GENERAL ESTIMATE

BUILDING _PRELIMINARY_

LOCATION _EXAMPLE_

ARCHITECTS _____

SUBJECT _CONCRETE BUILDING_

ESTIMATE NO. _P-5_

SHEET NO. _6 of 7_

ESTIMATOR _KC_

CHECKER _AB_

DATE _1987_

FRANK R. WALKER CO., PUBLISHERS, CHICAGO

DESCRIPTION OF WORK	NO. PIECES	DIMENSIONS			EXTENSIONS	EXTENSIONS	TOTAL ESTIMATED QUANTITY	UNIT PRICE M'T'L	TOTAL ESTIMATED MATERIAL COST	UNIT PRICE LABOR	TOTAL ESTIMATE LABOR COST
MOISTURE PROTECTION											
Dpf Conc Below Grd wi 2cts Asphalt (1gall per ct per Sq.)											
$(140-0 + 4/2/4") =$	1/	142-8	×	2-2	309						
$(140-0 + 4/2/8") =$	1/	145-4	×	0-8	97						
$(140-0 + 4/2/12") =$	1/	148-0	×	1-0	148		550 SF				
Wpf Membrane u/slab (slab area) =					770						
(laps) 10% × 770 SF =					77						
(edges) 1/137-4 × 0-6 =					68		920 SF				
SITE WORK (2/6 = 40-0 × 30-0 +3-0 +3-0 43-0 × 33-0)											
Excav to Remove Topsoil, avg 6" dp & stockpile on site											
43-0 × 33-0 1419 × 0-6 = 710							26 CY				
Excav Trenches at Surface											
$(140-0 + 4/2/5") =$ 143-4 × 3-10 × 3-6					1925		71 CY				
(2-0 + 0-6 + 1-4) = 3-10											
Temp Shoring to Trench Sides											
2/143-4 × 3-6					1003						
(@ 6" topsoil Remvd) 1/143-4 × 0-6					72		1075 SF				
Ditto, 12" Extra H't at Top											
(above ground) 2/143-4					287		290 LF				
Hand Trim Trench Bottom under Ftgs											
1/140-0 × 2-0							280 SF				
[NB: trimming under Drain taken with that item.]											
Hand trim under Gravel Bed (G. bed area) =							770 SF				

167

GENERAL ESTIMATE

BUILDING _PRELIMINARY_

LOCATION _EXAMPLE_

ARCHITECTS _____

SUBJECT _CONCRETE BUILDING_

ESTIMATE NO. _P-5_

SHEET NO. _7 of 7_

ESTIMATOR _KC_

CHECKER _AB_

DATE _1987_

FRANK R. WALKER CO., PUBLISHERS, CHICAGO

DESCRIPTION OF WORK	NO. PIECES	DIMENSIONS	EXTENSIONS	EXTENSIONS	TOTAL ESTIMATED QUANTITY	UNIT PRICE M'T'L	TOTAL ESTIMATED MATERIAL COST	UNIT PRICE LABOR	TOTAL ESTIMATE LABOR COST

SITE WORK (cont.)

4"⌀ Agric Drain Tile @ Ftgs incl trimming under to slopes
(148-0 + 4/2/9") = 1/154-0   154 LF

Extra 4" Bends (90°) 12/1   12 No

1" Drain Gravel over D.Tile (allow 15% shrinkage)
1/154-0 x 1-4 x 1-0   205   8 CY

Backfill Trenches @ Ftgs (allow 20% shrinkage)
                    (trench excav) = 1925   DDT
DDT (wants)(ftgs)   (conc ftgs)   —   280
        (fnd walls) 140-0 x 0-8 x 2-6   —   233
        (plinth)   144-0 x 0-4 x 0-3   —   12
        D.Tile
        (gravel)   (D. gravel) =   205
                                -730
                                1195   44 CY

Remove Spoil from Site (allow 30% swell)
44 + 27 = 71 cy (Excav) (amount not Backfill) = 730 CF   27 CY

Backfill Topsoil avg 6" dp (allow 25% shrinkage)
                    (area removed) = 1419 SF DDT
DDT (wants)   (roof slab area) =   —   863
    (@ plinth)   1/144-0 x 0-4   —   48
                                -911
                                508
                                x 0-6 = 254   10 CY

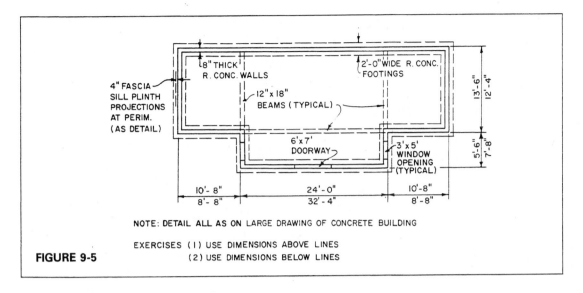

NOTE: DETAIL ALL AS ON LARGE DRAWING OF CONCRETE BUILDING

EXERCISES (1) USE DIMENSIONS ABOVE LINES
(2) USE DIMENSIONS BELOW LINES

FIGURE 9-5

how many bars are eliminated by the openings, so the minimum number is deducted and the usual No. 5 bars around openings are measured.

The No. 4 bars in the roof are measured "per unit area," as explained previously, and laps are measured for the few bars that are over 30 ft long. (This is to be consistent with the assumption made regarding the maximum bar length; in fact, bars 40 ft long would probably be used.)[7]

The rebar in beams is taken 6 in. into the supporting walls. The two beam lengths are added for convenience. The cranked No. 7 bars are measured by adding an additional 5 in. to each of the bar lengths (for the portions at 45 degrees), plus 10 in. at each end for a hook; two such bars are in each beam. No laps are allowed for, as noted. Stirrups are measured as 3 in. less than the beam dims, plus 4 in. hooks at the ends. Heavy and light bending are identified and measured as before.

The welded wire fabric (WWF) in the conc slab on grd requires a side-lap of at least 2 in. and an endlap of at least 8 in. (one mesh + 2 in.). Since, however, it may be cheaper to make bigger laps than to cut the WWF, the amount for laps varies slightly. The unit price for this item is quite low, and this influences the degree of accuracy required.

---

[7] The MM-CIQS has not always been strictly followed here. For example, the MM-CIQS calls for rebar to be classified by lengths, as stated therein; and for brevity and simplicity this has not been done here. The larger and the more complex the work being measured, the more useful further classifications become. However, these examples of quantity surveys are intended to reflect some of the methods in general use as well as published standard methods; and, in some cases, alternatives to both of these.

Excav Trenches. This item is described as "*at surface*" to indicate the level at which excav starts. Some use the description "*surface trenches*" (or "*basement trenches*," as the case may be.) The trenches are excav to 24 in. outside the conc fnd walls for the working space, and 6 in. inside the conc ftgs for ftg forms.

Temp Shoring to Trench Sides. This item is similar to the item measured in the example of the swimming pool, and the need for it here depends on ground conditions. The extra 12-in. height above ground is measured separately as a run item, as before.

Hand Trim Trench Bottom under Ftgs. This item is measured as the width of the ftgs, for the work can be done between the erected ftg forms. The trimming (to falls) under the tile drains is usually done when the drains are laid and may therefore be included with the drains in one item of work. This is another way of measuring these items, which were measured differently in the second example, above.

Backfill Trenches. Backfill trenches is measured by applying an important precept of measurement; i.e., to measure work overall and to correct the over-measurement by deducting the wants. The quantities of backfill and removal of spoil (surplus excav material) should equal the quantity of trench excav because they are all net quantities by bank measure;[G] the shrinkage and swell[G] allowances are to be made in the unit prices.

Exercises may be done from the dwg of this example but with different dims, as shown in Fig. 9-5.

RESIDENCE EXAMPLE

The Residence Drawings are of a house designed by its first owner, an architect, Mr. E. Kuckein of Vancouver, B.C. This house was chosen because of the excellence and simplicity of the design and the dwgs, and because the house contains the kinds of work required for examples and exercises. The dwgs reproduced here are essentially as they were when the construction contract was made and when the work was done.

The house is shown in Fig. 9-6, and the designer described it as follows:

The lot size of 50 feet by 120 feet, the setback requirements, and the orientation dictated the general form of the house. No attempt was made to adhere to accepted standards of design or of construction. The problem was to design a one-family house of high aesthetic value at minimum cost, in an area where none of the existing houses had to be considered. The most economical finish materials were chosen: gypsum wall board for the interior, and stucco for the exterior. For this reason, balloon framing with wood joists and studs was selected and the house was designed to eliminate the effects of wood shrinkage. As a result, three years after completion no cracking in the finish materials is apparent.

The measurement examples of the Residence generally involve different kinds of work from those measured in previous examples, which means that the site work, excavation, and concrete work of the Residence should be measured as exercises.

Although the following examples are set down

FIGURE 9-6

in standard specifications order, which is approximately the same as the order in which the work would be executed, estimators often measure in a different order. Many find it is better to first measure the major finishes such as stucco, drywall, floor coverings and painting. In this way, the estimator soon gets a knowledge of the building's layout and main features, which later helps him to measure the structure of the building behind the finishes. Therefore, the later examples of the Residence might be studied first, leaving the measurement examples involving framing and metals until later.

Masonry (Chimney Stack)

The amount of masonry in the Residence is small, but masonry chimney stacks often present a measurement problem because of the voids in the stack and because of the usually different exposed and concealed masonry work. Often, too, dwgs of stacks are vague and incomplete, showing the exposed masonry, the fireplace, and the stack above the roof, but nothing in between to explain how the stack size is reduced, how the flue location is changed as the stack goes up, and how the throat is to be formed over the fireplace.

The measurement of masonry in chimneys was the subject of some early construction disputes, and formalized methods of measurement subsequently appeared. One measurer wrote in the seventeenth century that "the truest way was to measure [chimneys] as a Solid, and deduct the Vacancies"—meaning the voids,[8] which appears to be perfectly simple and logical. But, it seems, there are good arguments for other methods that are used.

The MM-CIQS requires masonry in chimney stacks to be measured separately, the masonry units being enumerated (bricks, per thousand). The SMM-RICS requires much the same, except that brickwork is required to be measured in square yards, stating the thickness; but "brickwork of two-brick thickness and over . . . shall be reduced to one-brick and given separately in square yards." which would generally be the case with chimney stacks. The SMM-RICS also says that no deductions shall be made for flues wherein the voids and the *work displaced* (by flues) do not together exceed 3 square feet in sectional area; the MM-CIQS avoids any mention of deductions for flues. Obviously, anyone measuring chimney stacks must go

carefully, and it seems that the seventeenth-century measurer had the simplest and clearest idea: Measure that which is solid, and deduct the voids. It could be argued, however, that an even simpler method would be to measure the stack as a run item (in LF), describing the flues and stating their sizes and the overall size of the stack. There does not appear to be much advantage in following the published standard methods, for chimney stacks are not usually numerous in any project and it would be much easier to cost account for a run item.[9]

Work of this nature should be placed under a descriptive heading so that it may be priced as such; i.e., *one brick masonry chimney stack and fireplace.* A sub-heading describes the basic material to be used: the facing bricks, which have had a prime cost (per thousand) applied to them in the contract by the designer, so as to leave his choice within that price range open. The mortar, the joints, and the bond must also be fully described.

Prelim calcs are for the o/a ht, the ht above fireplace, and the ht above fireplace and below ceiling, since there is a different plan section at each level. The perim is calculated at each of the three levels.

The bkwk of facings is measured in SF, indicating thickness and finish. The attached piers are more easily priced as a run item. Both quantities can easily be converted to the number of bricks, as shown. The conversion factor varies with the size of the bricks.

The bkwk of firebricks in the fireplace is measured likewise, followed by the supply and installation of the prefabricated steel throat and damper unit described in the specifications. This installation requires some additional masonry work around and above the throat, the costs of which are mostly labor costs and the material costs of which are not large and are fairly constant, according to the size of the unit. Consequently, this work is best included and priced with the damper unit. Attempting to measure this part of the work more accurately in order to price the masonry materials more precisely would only give the appearance of accuracy.

The flue liners start above the smoke chamber (above the damper unit) and extend up through the precast conc chimney cap, measured later. Common bkwk (not of facing bricks) is measured to three sides, the fourth side of facings having already been measured.

If bkwk is measured as a super (or run) item, the cost of mortar is usually allowed for in the unit price. If bkwk is measured by the number of masonry

[8] F. M. L. Thompson, *Chartered Surveyors: The Growth of a Profession* (London: Routledge & Kegan Paul Ltd., 1968). Chapter Four, "The Origins of Quantity Surveying," refers to Venterus Mandey's *Marrow of Measuring*, of 1682, in which the author, a professional measurer, is "much exercised by chimneys."

[9] Or for another alternative method of measurement that applies in principle to any and all construction work, see the alternative item described on page 173, and also Chapter 7.

PROJECT	*RESIDENCE*		ESTIMATOR	KC	ESTIMATE NO.	R-1
LOCATION			EXTENSIONS	KC	SHEET NO.	1 of 2
ARCHITECT ENGINEER	*Kuckein*		CHECKED		DATE	1987

CLASSIFICATION **MASONRY (CHMNY STACK)-1**

DESCRIPTION	NO.	DIMENSIONS			ESTIMATED QUANTITY	UNIT

The Following Work in One Brick Masonry Stack & Fireplace:

```
4" BK ⎫ 4-0        4" BK ⎫   4-0  (or)  9-4     4" BK ⎫4/ 1-9  7-0     Bk Stack Height
perim ⎬ 2-8        perim ⎬2/= 3-4      2/=2-0    perim ⎬4/  4"=1-4       Bk pavg = 0-1 ⎤ 20-4½
@ Floor⎭ 6-8       @above ⎭   7-4          7-4    @above ⎭    5-8        Flr H't   8-7½⎭    -2-6 openg
         ×2         Opening                        Roof                  "  "      7-6       17-10½
       13-4                                                              Roof =    1-2       -4-0 above
less: 4/4"  1-4                                                          Above =   3-0            ceil'g
       12-0                                                             (carry fwd) 20-4½ 4   13-10½
less: openg- 2-8
      perim = 9-4
```

Selected FACING BRICKS (P.C. $300.°°/M delv'd.) nominal standard size
8×2¼×3¾in. (=6⅓ units per SF.) wi ½in concave tooled joints, as Specs.
(ref. page 04-1) (ALLOW 3% for WASTE); incl mortar & scaffolding:

4 in. Bkwk pointed one side

```
                    1/ 9-4   ×   2-6          23
                    1/ 7-4   ×   13-10½       102
above Clg = 4-0     1/ 5-8   ×   3-8          21
less: cap   -0-4                             146 SF × 6⅓ bks =                    925 bks
            3-8
```

8×8 in Bk Piers (attached) at corners pointed 3 sides; plumbed @ 2 angles

```
                    2/ 13-10½                 28 × 9 bks =                         250 bks
```

COMMON BRICKS (P.C. $200.°°/M, delv'd) as above but not pointed;
(ALLOW 5% for WASTE); incl mortar & scaffolding:

4 in. Bkwk wi raked joints (as key for stucco)

```
                    1/ 2-8   ×   13-10½       37 SF × 6⅓ bks =                    235 bks
```

```
 13"                                        2-8       1-10½ avg. 3/= 3-3    13-10½
  ↕                                         1-1       2/=2-2     2/= 0-8    -1-10½
        ↑22½"                               3-9       3/= 0-8       3-11    12-0
   ←  →  ↓      INTERNAL DIMS              1-10½ avg. 0-8
 32" ↗          SHOWN (N.T.S.)                       4-8½ avg.
```

4 in. Bkwk around Smoke Chamber & 13"×13" Flue (at 3 sides):

```
                    1/ 4-9   ×   1-10½        9
                    1/ 3-11  ×   12-0         47
                                             56 SF × 6⅓ bks =                    355 bks
```

PRACTICAL
Form 516 MFD IN U.S.A.

PROJECT	RESIDENCE			ESTIMATOR	KC	ESTIMATE NO.	R-1
LOCATION				EXTENSIONS	KC	SHEET NO.	2 of 2
ARCHITECT ENGINEER	Kuckein			CHECKED		DATE	1987

CLASSIFICATION MASONRY (CHMNY STACK) - 2

DESCRIPTION	NO.	L	DIMENSIONS B	D/H		ESTIMATED QUANTITY	UNIT
<u>Work in Bk Stack & Fireplace</u> (cont.) :							
4 in Std. Fire Bks in F'place wi ½" flush joints of fireclay mrtr							
(as Specs). (ALLOW 3% WASTE) :-							
@ hearth)	1/	3-4	x	2-0	7		
@ sides) }	1/	6-8	x	2-6	17		
((2/2-0)+2-8) }				24 SF × 6½/3 bks =		155 bks	
Steel Throat & Damper Unit, 38½ × 13 × 4½ in. high %all (as specs); built in, incl rough bk filling to form smoke shelf; incl parging smoke chamber above wi P.cmt-lime mrtr. about ½ in. thick:							
	1/	Item				1 NO	
2½ × 2½ × ¼ in M. Steel Lintel × 3'4" long built in over F'place opening:							
	1/					1 NO	
13 × 13 in (O/all size) Terra cotta Flue Liners set in mrtr:							
(20-4½) - (2-6+1-10½) = 1/16-0						16 LF	
4 in. thick Precast Conc. Chmny Cap, size 1'9" × 1'9" w weathered top surface & one 13 × 13 in flue hole; & set on top Stack:							
	1/	Item				1 NO	

[ALTERNATIVE ITEM DESCRIPTION :)

The following Work in ONE CLAY BK CHMNY STACK containing: —
  ONE F'PLACE OPENING approx 3'4" × 2'0" × 2'6" high
  ONE STEEL THROAT & DAMPER UNIT 3'2½" × 1'1" × 4½"
  ONE 13" × 13" TC LINED CHMNY FLUE × 16'0" high
  ONE P.C.CONC CHMNY CAP, 1'9" SQ × 4" thick, w thrd top, 13 flue
  2000 (approx) FACING BKS (P.C. $300.00/M, delvd)*
   200 "   STD FIRECLAY BKS (P.C. $600.00/M, delvd)
   20'-4½" (approx) O/all Bkwk Height (above conc ftg, m/s)
   Fair pointed joint finish to all exposed bk surfaces
   Complete wi inner Parging (Stucco extr. finish m/s)

   (End of One Chmny Stack & F'place)

* Assumes no common bricks and all facings

units, the mortar can still be allowed for in the same way. But MM-CIQS calls for masonry mortar to be measured separately, with the net quantity required (no allowance for waste to be made in the measured quantities) in cubic yards. The quantity of mortar can be calculated according to the type and quantity of masonry units from the same data that would be used to calculate the mortar costs for the unit price. Considering the relatively minor costs of mortar, and the very large and variable amount of waste usually incurred, it would seem simpler and adequate *not* to measure masonry mortar separately. Scaffolding for masonry work is not always measured, and the costs are often allowed for in the pricing. Yet in some kinds of masonry, the costs of scaffolding are as much as the costs of mortar.

Metals: Miscellaneous and Structural

In such a small job, all metals can be measured together. The measurement is simple, but full descriptions of the work are essential for proper pricing. Each item is enumerated and described; but with many more items, some similar items might be grouped together and measured by weight, stating the number of items in each group.

Each item is described as installed; but in some estimates, such as that of a miscellaneous metals subcontractor, the items would be "supply only," and installation would have to be estimated separately by the contractor or by other subcontractors.

The steel beam is measured first, followed by the ancillary items: the drift pins, brackets, and bolts to connect the beam and the wood frame. The dwg detail of the steel beam to column connection indicates a pair of brackets to "every 4th floor joist," which does not exactly indicate how many are required. Since the beam is pinned to the wood columns at one end, three pair would appear to be adequate; but the designer might argue for four. Each pair requires four bolts, which in this case are more easily measured separately instead of with the brackets.

Flat bar anchors are shown in *Detail "F"*, and here the bolts can be easily measured with the item. (Take note that *Detail "F"* shows a typical elevation of a projecting wing wall, either at the front or back of the house. The flat bar anchors are between wall studs in the wing wall.)

The 2″ × 3″ steel channels bolted between two studs at the ends of the free-standing partition (on the GF) also are to be set in the conc (suitably thickened) to give rigidity to framing.

Weights are needed to price the material costs of these items, and it is useful to remember that steel plate ¼ in. thick weighs 10.2 lb per SF, from which weight the weights of most steel flats, angles, and plates can be calculated with sufficient accuracy for most items.

Other metal items required for this job should be included in other sections of work. Rough and finish hardware for carpentry are measured with the carpentry items. Reinforcement is measured with concrete or masonry, wherever it occurs. Misc metals generally include only custom-made metal items, and not standard products. Structural metals are generally of standard sections cut to the specific lengths as required by the job, with the necessary connections.

Rough Carpentry Framing

Rough carpentry frmg usually includes sheathing to walls and decks, and it is usually better to begin by measuring the sheathing and then to measure the wood frmg beneath. In this way, the estimator becomes familiar with the layout and the dims he will use in measuring the more complicated frmg later.

Because of this building's design, there is little or no advantage in calculating and using a wall perimeter to measure the frmg, and so the total length of extr walls is collected from the dims. Sheathing to walls, floor, and roof deck are each measured separately. The number of exposed ends of walls makes measuring the sheathing to these ends (in n.w.'s, as a run item) worthwhile. Likewise, the n.w.'s of sheathing behind parapets is measured as a run item. Usually such items can be described as less than 3 in. wide, 3 to 6 in. wide, 6 to 9 in. wide, and less than 12 in. wide because exact width is not significant to cost and in this way similar widths can be conveniently grouped together. Cants and sheathing paper, both attached to the plywood sheathing, are measured next.

The distinction between "rough" and "finish" carpentry is not always clear; so items that are left out of one section to be measured in the other are sometimes overlooked. Therefore, it is wise to make notes about such items as the exposed ½ in. ply cladding. Rough carpentry is taken here to be *rough, concealed work*; and all woodwork that is exposed and finished is taken as finish carpentry. Nevertheless, exterior siding is sometimes classified as rough carpentry. (Siding should be in Div. 7.)

The lengths of extr and intr walls are collected, and the numbers of studs calculated by dividing by the stud-spacing (16 in.) and by adding extra studs: for each wall length (one); for short returned lengths of extr wall (four, assuming that a maximum of seven are needed and that three have already been measured); for corners (three); and for junctions (two extra studs in extr walls, and one extra stud in intr walls). Framing methods and the numbers of studs used at such locations vary; for example, four studs are sometimes used at corners in extr walls.

Extr wall frmg is measured separately because the extr walls are often constructed differently from intr walls. One bottom plate and a double top plate require three times the extr wall length. Intr walls require two or three times the wall length for plates, depending on a single or double top plate. Here, double top plates have been measured. Extra intr wall studs are measured at doorways, and extra material is also measured at the bathtub. Intr finishes and fixtures always require some extra frmg material for supports and this must be allowed.

Fixing plates to conc is measured as a separate item. Girths in stud walls are also measured separately because of their relatively high labor cost.

The MM-CIQS calls for all frmg lumber to be measured separately if over 14 ft long, and to be grouped in 2-ft stages. Studs are required to be grouped separately in lengths less than 8 ft and in lengths 8 to 12 ft. These categories relate to lumber costs, but their rigid application is not always practical or necessary, and in small jobs separation as shown in the example is adequate.

Estimated total quantities of frmg are shown in LF, and (in parentheses) in BF. Usually, one or the other unit of measurement is used, and the linear unit is preferable for reasons already given.

The 2 × 3 frmg material at the stairs and kitchen cabinets is similarly measured, as is the isolated 2 × 4 frmg for the ext ply panels on the north elevation. This kind of frmg requires more material per unit area than ordinary walls, and adequate quantities must be measured. Also, both these items should be priced higher than ordinary wall frmg because of the arrangements and locations of this work. No frmg details are indicated here, and it has been assumed that the 2 × 4 wall frmg for ply siding panels would be prefabricated frames. An estimator often has to make such assumptions before he can measure work that is not fully detailed.

The numbers of floor and roof joists required are calculated from the dims divided by the joist spacing, with extra joists added for double joists and for trimming around stairwell and stack. The joist lengths are taken up to the nearest even dim (20 ft), with the knowledge that offcuts can be used for solid blockings between joists. Two additional 20-ft lengths are included for solid blocking that cannot be obtained from offcuts, although they may not be required; but it is easy to under-measure. Additional labors on ends of joists and trimming are described and enumerated.

Cross-bridging can be measured as a run item, or enumerated in sets, one set per space, *but never in BF*. Ledgers are described as *"set into studs"* to remind the estimator of the labor involved when pricing. Likewise, locations of blockings are indicated to facilitate pricing later. Fixing blockings to a steel beam is very different from fixing them to a wood frmg member.

Rough hardware for carpentry includes nails, screws, spikes, joist hangers, and the like. Usually, it is not necessary to measure quantities of rough hardware, because the common items are better allowed for in the unit prices, as shown in Chapter 11.

Finish Carpentry

The exposed plywood cladding in panels to extr walls would be regarded by some estimators as rough carpentry; but the fact that it is exposed and that the joints have to be properly laid out and carefully made means that it requires finish, and that it should be priced accordingly and differently from plywood sheathing. The intr work is similarly measured, but kept separate.

Drilling vent holes is described on the dwgs *"as directed,"* which means "as directed by the designer at the site," and that the estimator cannot measure the work. In the case of a major item so described, the designer should be asked by bidders for more information. If it is not available, they can make an allowance to cover the probable costs or refuse to submit a bid. If, as in this case, it is a minor item, an estimator can make an allowance without too much risk.

The hardwood ply paneling is shown with no horizontal joints, which means that about two thirds of the paneling will require sheets 12 ft long; more expensive than the standard 8-ft-long sheets.

Raking cutting and waste[G] is measured as a basis for pricing the additional costs. Another way would be to measure the material gross (instead of net) and to measure and price the *extra labor cutting* to the required angle. Cutting slots in the hardwood ply for the concealed tread angles is an expensive labor item that must be included.

The hardwood ply paneling in the kitchen cabinets is similar to the paneling by the stairs, and both items could be grouped together because the extra labor items in each case have been identified and measured separately. Thus, the paneling in the cabinets requires mitred corners (not required at the stairs) which is measured separately; the extra labor involved in making the serving hatch door is also measured separately.

The Douglas fir finish material is described as

PRACTICAL "STANDARDIZED" FORMS FOR CONTRACTORS
Form 516 MFD IN U.S.A.

QUANTITY SHEET

PROJECT RESIDENCE ESTIMATOR KC ESTIMATE NO. R-1

LOCATION EXTENSIONS KC SHEET NO. 1 of 2

ARCHITECT ENGINEER CHECKED DATE 1987

CLASSIFICATION METALS: MISCELLANEOUS & STRUCTURAL

DESCRIPTION	NO.	DIMENSIONS	ESTIMATED QUANTITY	UNIT
THE FOLLOWING IN STEEL BEAM WITH CONNECTIONS:—				
10 WF 45 × 17'6" long (=787½ lb) Beam installed in wood framed upper floor —		(1/17-6 × 45 lb = 787½ lb)	(lb 787½)	1 No.
3/4" φ × 10" long m.s Drift Pins welded to beam flanges at ends		2/1 (× 1¼ lb)	(2½)	2 No.
1/4" × 4" × 6" × 4" long m.s Angle Brackets 3/drilled (for 3/8" φ bolts m/s)		4/2 (× 3 lb)	(24)	8 No.
3/8" φ m.s Bolts × 6" long with head, nut, & washers (for brackets m/s)		4/4 (× 1/4 lb)	(4) (818)	16 No.
Drill Web of 10 WF 45 Beam (for 3/8" φ bolts m/s)		4/2		8 No.
Drill Flanges of 10 WF 45 Beam (for r/carp lag-bolts to plates m/s)		4/2		8 No.
(End of Steel Beam)		approx total weight (820 lb)		
3/4" φ × 10" long ms Drift Pin a.b (installed in conc slab for 6x8 wood post over)		1/ (× 1¼ lb)	(1 lb)	1 No.

FRANK R. WALKER CO., PUBLISHERS, CHICAGO

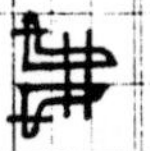

PRACTICAL
Form 516 MFD IN U.S.A

PROJECT RESIDENCE	ESTIMATOR KC	ESTIMATE NO. R-1
LOCATION	EXTENSIONS KC	SHEET NO. 2 of 2
ARCHITECT ENGINEER	CHECKED	DATE 1987

CLASSIFICATION **METALS (cont)**

DESCRIPTION	NO.	DIMENSIONS	b-fwd ($\frac{lb}{1}$)	ESTIMATED QUANTITY	UNIT
$\frac{3}{8}$" x 3$\frac{1}{2}$" m.s Flat Bar Anchors x 3'6" long hooked (180°) one end & 4/ drilled for & incl 3$\frac{3}{8}$" φ x 6" long m.s bolts w/ head, nut & washers; set in conc fnd & bolted to wood framing (as specs and Detail "F.")	5/2 (x 17 lb)		($\frac{lb}{170}$)	10 No.	
2" x 3" (x 6 lb) Steel Channel Stiffeners x 7'0" long 3/ drilled for & incl 3$\frac{3}{8}$" φ x 8" long m.s bolts w/ head, nut & washers; set in conc flr slab & bolted btwn partn studs (at ends of free-standing partn)	2/1 (x 43 lb)		(85)	2 No.	
$\frac{1}{4}$" x 1" x 1" m.s Angle Supports x 10" long for wood Stair Treads 4/ drilled for wood screws	2/12 (x 1$\frac{1}{2}$ lb)		(40) (296)	24 No.	
(End of Misc. Metals)		approx total weight	(295) lb		

[NB: Steel Chimney Throat & Damper Unit & lintel taken with Masonry.]

NOTE: The above measured items (enumerated and described) show by example how much construction work may be measured for computer input, with the computer calculating weights and costs.

PRACTICAL
Form 516 MFD IN U.S.A.

PROJECT	RESIDENCE	ESTIMATOR	KC	ESTIMATE NO.	R-1
LOCATION		EXTENSIONS	KC	SHEET NO.	1 of 6
ARCHITECT ENGINEER		CHECKED		DATE	1987

CLASSIFICATION **ROUGH CARPENTRY FRAMING (SHEATHING)**

DESCRIPTION	NO.	DIMENSIONS				ESTIMATED QUANTITY	UNIT

Prelim calcs

Dims - U. Floor   Roof   Ext Walls (collection)   13-6   Height

(W)13-6 (N) 5-8 ¼ 15-2 (E) 22-0 (S) 15-2 (N) 5-8   and Roof   30-0 √133-0   8-4   8-7½ L Flr
  8-4   8-4   ¾ 0-2   8-0   10-10   8-4   13-4   14-0 ⁴/₌ 8-0 1-0 21-10   7-6 U. Flr
 21-6   ¾ 4-8   15-4   30-0   5-4   14-0   1-8   2-0 ²/₂/₌12-0 0-2 1-2   1-2, Roof
 43-4   18-8✓ 2-0   -5-0   31-4   8-0   23-0 ²/₂/₌10-0 20-8   0-8½ Parapt
¾-0-8 ¾=-0-8 17-4   25-0   3-0   2-6   23-0   21-8   163-0   18-0
 42-8✓   18-0✓   ½=-0-4   0-4   0-4   21-6   21-8
                                24-8   3-4   2-10 ½/0-2   20-8
                                                    ¾/21-8   133-0

DOUGLAS FIR PLYWOOD SHEATHING (EXTERIOR GRADE)

½" Select Sheathing (t&G) to Floor   (allow 10% Waste)

	1/ 42-8	×	18-0	768		
	1/ 17-4	×	8-4	144		
				912		

DDT (@ S/well) 1/ 8-9 × 3-0 − 26 DDT
886   890 SF

½" Select Sheathing (T&G) to Roof   (allow 10% Waste)

	1/ 42-8	×	18-0	768
	1/ 24-8	×	17-4	428
	1/ 14-0	×	2-10	40
	1/ 31-4	×	3-4	104
				1340

1340 SF

5/16" Standard Sheathing to Extr Walls (allow 7½% Waste)

	1/ 163-0	×	18-0	2934
(@ Garage door jambs)	3/ 0-4	×	6-6	4
				2938

2940 SF

NOTE: All above items can be measured linearly (x 4 ft wide.)

5/16" Ditto in N.W <6" wide (wall ends)

| | 1 ∙ 4/18-0 | | | 90 |

90 LF

5/16" Ditto in N.W <9" wide (parapets)

(42-8+2-10+3-4)	2/ 48-10			98
(18-0 +17-4)	2/ 35-4			70
	2/ 3-0			6
				174

DDT (want) (31-4+17-0+14-0) 1/ 62-4 − 62 DDT   112 LF

PRACTICAL
Form 516 MFD IN U.S.A

PROJECT	RESIDENCE	ESTIMATOR KC	ESTIMATE NO. R-1
LOCATION		EXTENSIONS KC	SHEET NO. 2 of 6
ARCHITECT ENGINEER		CHECKED	DATE 1987

CLASSIFICATION **ROUGH CARPENTRY FRAMING (SHEATHING)**

DESCRIPTION	NO.	DIMENSIONS			ESTIMATED QUANTITY	UNIT

4x4 D.fir 'Constr' grade Roof Cants (on sheathing) (allow 5% Waste)

		(Length of parapets) =	112		
ADD (@ E. overhangs)	1/ 62-4		62		
(@ and c. stack)	1/ 9-4		10		184 LF

Standard (black) Building Paper to Extr Wall Sheathing (Laps measd)

(allow 10% Waste)	(area ply wall shtg) =		2938		
ADD (@ N.W's)	1/ 90-0 × 0-6		45		
	1/ 112-0 × 0-9		84		
2-3	1/ 14-0 × 7-1		99		
4-10 (@ ply siding-N)					
7-1 ✓	1/ 17-0 × 3-4		57		
2-3					
1-1 (@ ditto - S)	1/ 31-4 × 3-4		104		
3-4 ✓			3327		
ADD (laps) approx 20% × 3327 sf	=		673		4000 SF

1"x2" Thickener planted on 4/5 proj ply shtg at top stair tread approx 4' long		1 No

[NB: ½" Ply Siding (exposed) meas'd
as 'Finish Carpentry .']

W. RED CEDAR 'CONSTRUCTION' GRADE

2x4 Framing for planting pots supports (N. Elev) in 16' lengths (Waste meas'd)

8/ 14-0		112	
5/ 2-0		10	128 LF

1x6 Bevel Siding as parapet capping (allow 5% Waste)

(Length of parapets)		112 LF

NOTE: Most items measured above by area
can be measured for computer input
linearly, with other dims included
in the descriptions; even such as
"building paper" (3ft wide).

PRACTICAL
Form 516 MFD IN U.S.A.

PROJECT	*RESIDENCE*		ESTIMATOR *KC*	ESTIMATE NO. *R-1*	
LOCATION			EXTENSIONS *KC*	SHEET NO. *3 of 6*	
ARCHITECT ENGINEER			CHECKED	DATE *1987*	

CLASSIFICATION *ROUGH CARPENTRY FRAMING (WALLS)*

DESCRIPTION	NO.	DIMENSIONS		ESTIMATED QUANTITY	UNIT

Prelim Calcs   *Extr Wall Perim   No Studs*   *Int Walls (collect) No Studs*

Extr Dims
(E) 30-0 $\frac{129-4}{1-4}$ = 97   (GF) 3/ 36-0 (e-w) 5$\frac{7-0}{1-4}$=43   (UF) 2/= 36-0 (e-w)

(E) 22-0+8-0 = 30-0   (N) 13-4   w. lengths = 13   3/ 15-0 (n-s)   w. lengths = 8   2/= 3-0 "

(N) 14-0 - ¾" = 13-4   (E) 21-8   s. lengths 5/4 = 20   1/= 3-0 (@Furnace) junc = 7   1/= 7-0 "

(E) 21-6+2¼" = 21-8   (W) 43-4   corners 6/3 = 18   2/= 3-0 (@HW Tank)   2/= 26-0 (n-s)

(W) 13-8+3-10 ⌉   2/2/2-0=8-0   junctns 5/2 = 10   57-0   Total 60 No   1/= 8-0 "

  +5-4+20-6 ⌋ = 43-4   2/3-0= 6-0   window 1/2 = 2 (GF-6½ Wall)   1/= 21-0 "

   2/2-6= 5-0   Total 160 No   28-6 $\frac{24-0}{1-4}$=17   2/= 5-0 (closets)

   1/2-0 = 2-0   (stack) -4-0   4/2 = 8   Total 106-0

    (1294)   (24-6)   25 No   No Studs

  Total (say) 130-0   25-0 $\frac{106-0}{1-4}$ = 80

            wall lengths 9/ = 11

            junctions 9/ = 9

            corners 4/3 = 12

            (112)

D. FIR "CONSTRUCTION" GRADE   Total 110 No

NOTE THE LINEAR MEASUREMENT OF FRAMING MEMBERS!

2x4 Extr Wall Frmg in 18' & 20' lengths (Waste incl.)

   (plates)   3/ 130-0   390

   (studs)   160/ 18-0   2880

      3270 (x⅔ BF)   3300 LF

         (2200 BF)

2x4 Girths btwn extr wall studs (Waste incl.)

(2/3-0 + 2/2-6 + 1/2-0)   1/ 13-0   13 LF

2x4 Intr Wall Frmg in 18' lengths (Waste incl.)

   (GF plates)   3/ 57-0   171

      "   3/ 25-0   75

   (UF plates)   3/ 106-0   318

   (@ Gallery Balust)   3/ 12-0   36

      600 (x⅔ BF)   600 LF

         (400 BF)

2x4 Intr Wall Frmg in 8' lengths (Waste incl.)

@25 for 6½ wall (GF studs)   25 0 60 85/ 8-0   680

(extra for GF col @ Beam)   6/ 8-0   48

   (UF studs)   110/ 8-0   880

(extra @ B. Tub)   4/ 8-0   32

(extra @ Doorways)   15/2/ 8-0   240

(extra @ top plates for   2/3/ 36-0   144

drywall ceilings)   1·1/2/ 8-0   32

      2056 (x⅔ BF)   2050 LF

         (1370 BF)

EXTRA (PARALLEL TO JOISTS)

PRACTICAL
Standardized Forms for Contractors
Form 516 MFD IN U S A

PROJECT	RESIDENCE	ESTIMATOR KC ESTIMATE NO. R-1
LOCATION		EXTENSIONS KC SHEET NO. 4 of 6
ARCHITECT ENGINEER		CHECKED DATE 1987

CLASSIFICATION **ROUGH CARPENTRY FRAMING (WALLS)(FIXTURES)**

DESCRIPTION	NO.	DIMENSIONS		ESTIMATED QUANTITY	UNIT
D.FIR "CONSTRUCTION" GRADE					
Extra Lab & Mat Fastening 2x4 Wall Plates to conc w/ & incl ½"⌀ A. Bolts @ 6' %c					
	1/130-0			130	LF
Ditto 2x4 Plates to conc slab w/ & incl Power Fasteners @ 4' %c					
(57-0 + 25-0)	1/82-0			80	LF
2x4 Extr Wall Frmg in Panels (for ½" Ply Siding m/s) in 14' lengths (Waste incl)					
	2/4/14-0		112		
	14/5-0		70		
	14/2-0		28		
			210 (x⅔ BF)	210	LF
				(140	BF)
2x3 Intr Wall Frmg at Stairs in 10' & 12' lengths (Waste incl)					
	2/3/10-0		60		
	2/8/12-0		192		
	2/2/12-0		48		
			300 (x½ BF)	300	LF
				(150	BF)
2x3 Ditto at Kitchen Cabinets & Fixtures in 12' lengths (Waste incl)					
(W. Elev plates)	6/12-0		72		
(" studs)	22/6-0		132		
(" hatch)	3/2/4-0		24		
(@ Range & Frig)	2/6/2-0		24		
(" " studs)	2/4/6-0		48		
			300 (x½ BF)	300	LF
				(150	BF)
2x8 (full ht) Frmg in Bases to K. Cabinets (Waste incl)					
(8-0 + 12-0)	1/20-0		20 (x1⅓ BF)	20	LF
				(30	BF)
2x12 (full ht) Frmg in Tops to K. Cabinets (Waste incl)					
	2/12-0		24 (x2 BF)	25	LF
				(50	BF)
3x12 Frmd Stairs Stringers in 12' lengths (Waste incl) incl ends to slope					
	2/12-0		24 (x3 BF)	25	LF
				(75	BF)
2x12 "C & Better" V.G Stepping in Stairs Treads in 6' lengths (on Brkts m/s)					
	12/3-0		36 (x2 BF)	36	LF
				(72	BF)
Extra Lab Selecting & Installing Clear Exposed 2x4 Studs at Doorways (as detail)					
(both jambs meas'd)	15/2			30	No
[NB: Exposed Wood Posts & Mullions meas'd as "Finish Carpentry."]					

QUANTITY SHEET

PROJECT	RESIDENCE	ESTIMATOR	KC	ESTIMATE NO.	R-1
LOCATION		EXTENSIONS	KC	SHEET NO.	5 of 6
ARCHITECT ENGINEER		CHECKED		DATE	1987

CLASSIFICATION ROUGH CARPENTRY FRAMING (DECKS)

DESCRIPTION	NO.	DIMENSIONS				ESTIMATED QUANTITY	UNIT

U.Floor No Joists   Roof 25-0 / 1-4 = 19   Joist Length

13-6   43-4 / 1-4 = 33   8-8 / 1-4 = 7   30-0 ↑ +1   38

8-4   ↑ +1   8-4 ↑ +1 38   -5-0 (extra) +3 23

21-6 ↑ (extra) +4   2/4 = 0-4 (extra) +4   12   25-0   23

43-4 /   38   8-8   12   50 No Joists   61 No Joists

D.FIR "CONSTRUCTION" GRADE

NOTE THE LINEAR MEASUREMENT OF FRAMING!

2-4
5-8
8-4
2-4
(18-8)
20-0 long

__2x12 Floor Joists in 20' lengths (Waste incl)__

50/20-0   1000 (x2 BF)   1000 LF
                                   (2000 BF)

__2x12 Roof Joists in 20' lengths (Waste incl)__

61/20-0   1220

(@ S.Overhang) 3/2/20-0   120

(@ N.Overhang) 3/1/20-0   60

(Lam.beams-roof) 3/20-0   60

(extra for blockings) 2/20-0   40

                 1500 (x2 BF)   1500 LF
                                  (3000 BF)

__Extra Lab (only) in Solid 2x12 Blockings to btwn ends of joists (using offcuts)__

(flr and roof) 2/2/43-0   172

(roof overhangs) 2/2/3-0   12

(ditto)   1/2/2-6   5

(@ Steel Beam - N. end) 2/4-0 8

                 197   200 LF

__Extra Lab Cutting & Fitting 2x12 Joists' Ends to Steel Beam__

17-6 / 1-4 = 13 +1 = 14   30 @ 14 / 1   17   17 NO

__Extra Lab & Joist Hangers Trimming 2x12 Joists at Lam.Beams (%s measd)__

(10-0 + 6-0)   2/16-0   32   32 LF

__Ditto Trimming at Stairwell, 9' x 3'   1/__   1 NO

__Ditto Trimming at Stack, 4' x 2'8"   1/__   1 NO

__X-Bridging to 2x12 Joists at 16" %c (measd over joists)__

(43-4 + 8-0)(Floor) 2/51-4   103

(43-4 + 3-0 + 2-6)(Roof) 2/48-10   98

(30-0 - 5-0) + 3-0 (") 2/28-0   56

                 257   260 LF

PROJECT	RESIDENCE	ESTIMATOR KC	ESTIMATE NO. R-1
LOCATION		EXTENSIONS KC	SHEET NO. 6 of 6
ARCHITECT ENGINEER		CHECKED	DATE 1987

CLASSIFICATION ROUGH CARPENTRY FRAMING (SUNDRIES)

DESCRIPTION	NO.	DIMENSIONS		ESTIMATED QUANTITY	UNIT

D. FIR "CONSTRUCTION" GRADE

1x6 Ledger Boards set flush into studs @ 16" ⁰⁄c for joists (Waste 5%)

(flr and roof)	2/2/43-0	172	
(roof overhangs)	2/2/ 3-0	12	
(ditto)	1/2/ 2-6	5	
		189 (x ½ BF)	190 LF
			(95 BF)

Ex-2x12 Headers behind fascias in 16' & 18' lengths (Waste incl.)

| (16-0 + 18-0) (N&S) | 2/34-0 | 68 (x 2 BF) | 70 LF |
| | | | (140 BF) |

2x12 Blockings btwn mullions in 16' & 18' lengths (Waste incl.)

(S)	2/32-0	64	
(N)	2/18-0	36	
		100 (x 2 BF)	100 LF
			(200 BF)

2x10 Headers behind valances in 16' & 18' lengths (Waste incl.)

| (N&S) | 2/2/34-0 | 136 (x 1⅔ BF) | 140 LF |
| | | | (230 BF) |

2x4 Blockings on u/sides {blockings} headers in 16' & 18' lengths (Waste incl.)

(32-0 + 18-0)(on 2x12)	1/50-0	50	
(on 2x10)	2/2/34-0	136	
		186 (x ⅔ BF)	190 LF
			(125 BF)

2x4 Frmd Furrings to eaves soffites in short lengths (Waste incl.)

| 2x(31-0/1-4) = 48 | 60/2-6 | 150 (x ⅔ BF) | 150 LF |
| 1⅓/2 = +8 (say) 60 | | | (100 BF) |

2x4 Blockings lag-bolted to drilled steel beam in 14' lengths (Waste incl.)

| | 2/14-0 | 28 (x ⅔ BF) | 30 LF |
| | | | (20 BF) |

1x3 Blocking/Furring on tower 2x4 (Waste incl.)

| 1x3 | 1/14-0 | 14 (x ¼ BF) | 15 LF |
| | | | (4 BF) |

2x6 Blockings in valances in 18' lengths (Waste incl.)

(S)	2/36-0	72	
(N)	2/18-0	36	
		108 (x 1 BF)	110 LF
			(110 BF)

Rough Hardware (include with items of work) —

FRANK R. WALKER CO., PUBLISHERS, CHICAGO

PRACTICAL
Form 516. MFD IN U.S.A.

PROJECT	RESIDENCE			ESTIMATOR	KC	ESTIMATE NO.	R-1
LOCATION				EXTENSIONS	KC	SHEET NO.	1 of 7
ARCHITECT ENGINEER				CHECKED		DATE	1987

CLASSIFICATION **FINISH CARPENTRY (PLYWOOD)**

DESCRIPTION	NO.	DIMENSIONS					ESTIMATED QUANTITY	UNIT

D.FIR PLYWOOD (EXTERIOR GRADE) GOOD ONE SIDE (G1S) _unless otherwise shown_

½" Ply Panels to Extr Walls (Fascias & Siding) wi exposed vertical 'veed' joints as indicated in Elevations (& as in Details #1/3 & #2/3) (allow Waste 25% on net quantity)

SHEETS (4'x8')

(15-2+10-10+5-4)=31-4 (S)	1/31-4	×	2-3	71 }	4		
(4+11½+9½+2")= 2-3	1/31-4	×	1-1	34 }			
(5-8+8-4)=14-0 (N)	1/14-0	×	2-3	32 }	4		
(*dim scaled)(14-0+5-0)	1/14-0	×	4-10*	68 }			
(ASSUME CONCEALED =17-0	1/17-0	×	2-3	38 }	2		
JOINTS IN PANELS OVER	1/17-0	×	1-1	19 }			
8FT LONG)				262 (10)			262 SF

(Better measured linearly)

½" Ply Panel (as above) 14" x 27" over Window (west) 1/ | | | | | | | 1 NO

Extra Lab making concealed x-tongued vert joints in ½" Ply Panels

(S)⊙	(N)	1/2-3			2¼			
	(N) 10	1/1-1			2¼ LF		(3 NO) 4½ LF	

½" Ply Intr Wall Panels wi concealed x-tongued vert joints (Waste 12½%)

(as Detail #3/3) (S)	1/31-4	×	1-2	37		
(N)	1/17-0	×	1-2	20		
				57 (2)		57 SF

(Better measured linearly)

½" Ply (Good/Solid grade) in Valances x 11" wide wi x-tngd jts (Waste 12½%)

(as Detail #1/3) (S)	1/35-4		36		
(N)	1/18-0		18		
			54		54 SF

½" Ply Eaves Soffites (on 2x4 furr'g m/s) (Waste 15%)

(as Detail #1/3) (S)	1/31-4	×	2-9	86		
(N)	1/17-0	×	2-9	47		
(N)	1/14-0	×	2-3	32		
				165		165 SF

(Better measured linearly)

Extra Lab Drilling Vent Holes in ½ Ply Eaves "as directed" | | | | | | | Item

[NB: ½" Ply Panel in Window (west) supplied with Window (in Div. 8).]

QUANTITY SHEET

PROJECT	RESIDENCE		ESTIMATOR	KC	ESTIMATE NO.	R-1
LOCATION			EXTENSIONS	KC	SHEET NO.	2 of 7
ARCHITECT ENGINEER			CHECKED		DATE	1987

CLASSIFICATION   FINISH CARPENTRY (PLYWOOD)

DESCRIPTION	NO.	DIMENSIONS			ESTIMATED QUANTITY	UNIT
AMERICAN BLACK WALNUT PLYWOOD ("CUSTOM" GRADE) as specs						
½" Walnut Ply Panelling (at Stairs) (ex-4'x12' sheets) w/ exposed vertical "Veed" joints as indicated (Waste 20% on net) *(67% of net area)*						
(7-6+1-1+3-0) = 11-7 2/2/ 8-8 ×			11-7	402	SHEETS	
DDT (wants) 2/3/½/ 7-6 ×			7-6	—	DDT (4'x8') = 4 113 (4'x12') 4	
(@ flr joists) 2/ 8-8 ×			1-0	17		
				−130		
				272		272 SF
Extra Lab in X-tongued end-matched joints in ½" Ply × 7½" long						
2/1						2 No
Extra Lab in cutting slots in ½" Ply for 2×12 Treads & Sinkings for ¼" thick Steel Angle brackets behind 2/12						24 No
RC & W on ½" Walnut Ply (@ btm edges to slope)						
2/2/ 10-9				43		43 LF
½" Walnut Ply Panelling at Kitchen Cabinets & Fixtures (as Details) (Waste 50%)						
(2-1+1-5+2-4)=(5-10) 6-0 1/ 8-0 ×			6-0	48		
2/2/ 1-3 ×			6-0	30		
2/2/ 0-4 ×			6-0	8		
2/2/ 0-4 ×			2-0	3		
2/2/ 0-4 ×			1-3	2		
				91		91 SF
Extra Lab to Mitered Corners in ½" Ply Panelling						
4 06/6-0				60		60 LF
Extra Lab Cutting Finishing & Hanging Hatch Door Panel 4'x1'6" incl Brass Piano Hinge & Ball Catch & Finger Pull 1/						1 No
1×2 Walnut Edge Trim (to match) Hatch Door						
3/ 4-0				8		
2/ 1-6				3		11 LF
½" D. FIR PLY (G15) at Bases & Tops of K. Cabinets w/ mitered corners						
× 8" & 12" wide 2/2/ 10-3				41		41 LF

QUANTITY SHEET

PROJECT	RESIDENCE		ESTIMATOR	KC	ESTIMATE NO.	R-1
LOCATION			EXTENSIONS	KC	SHEET NO.	3 of 7
ARCHITECT ENGINEER			CHECKED		DATE	1987

CLASSIFICATION FINISH CARPENTRY (TRIM)

DESCRIPTION	NO.	DIMENSIONS										ESTIMATED QUANTITY	UNIT

D. FIR FINISH (" C " V.G. GRADE)

2x8 Handrails (on brackets m/s) incl shaped ends (Waste nil)
　　　　　　　2/12-0　　　　　24　　　　　24 LF

3x8 Rail (at Stairwell) framed in at ends (Waste incl)
　　　　　1/4-0　　　　　4　　　　　4 LF

3/4" x 5 1/4" Double Dressed Cap (at Stairwell) incl miters & ends (Waste 4%)
(8-9+10-9+11-7 1/2 +4-1 1/2)　2/35-3　　　71　　　71 LF

1/2" x 1 1/2" Base Trim (at floors/walls) incl miters & ends (Waste incl)
(length extr walls)　2/130-0　　260
("　intr "　)　2/57-0　　114
("　"　"　)　2/106-0　　212
(31-0+14-0+14-0)(@wans)　2/59-0　　118
　　　　　　　　　　　　　　704　DDT

DDT (Wants)(@ pool)　2/24-0　　—　　48　　　DDT
　　(@ Garage)　2/38-0　　—　　76
(@ S. Lengths)　2/3-0　　—　　6
(　"　)　2/2-6　　—　　5
(@ L Room)　2/13-0　　—　　26
(@ Doorways)　(Nil)　　-161
　　　　　　　　　543　　　550 LF

NOTE: PLYWOOD items on previous page can
be measured linearly (with widths
stated in descriptions) to retain more
information about the work in the
estimate. The resultant increase in
the number of items is not a problem
with a computer.

FRANK R. WALKER CO., PUBLISHERS, CHICAGO

PRACTICAL
Form 516 MFD IN U.S.A.

PROJECT	RESIDENCE	ESTIMATOR	KC	ESTIMATE NO. R-1
LOCATION		EXTENSIONS	KC	SHEET NO. 4 of 7
ARCHITECT ENGINEER		CHECKED		DATE 1987

CLASSIFICATION FINISH CARPENTRY (WINDOW WALLS)

DESCRIPTION	NO.	DIMENSIONS				ESTIMATED QUANTITY	UNIT
DOUGLAS FIR (GRADES AS INDICATED)							
6x8 Structural grade Posts in 8' lengths (Waste incl)							
(8-7½+7-6)-(0-10+0-7½) (s) 2/8-0			16			16	LF
2x6 Structural grade Mullions in 16' lengths (Waste incl)							
(8-7½+7-6)-0-7½ (s) 4/16-0			64				
(N) 2/16-0			32				
			96			96	LF
2x4 Structural grade Frames in 16' lengths at walls (Waste incl)							
(N&S) 2/2/16-0			64			64	LF
2x2 Structural grade Trim in 16' lengths planted on posts & mullions (Waste incl)							
2.4.1/16-0			112			112	LF
½"x1¾" "C" V.G. Stops in 6' & 8' lengths planted on (Waste incl)							
(@ Doors) (N) 0 (s) 1.4/2/8-0			80				
1.4/1/3-0			15			95	LF
¾"x1¾" Ditto in 8' lengths planted on (Waste incl)							
(@ Glass) (jambs only) (N&S) 10/2/2/8-0			320			320	LF
¾"x1¾" Ditto in 16' & 18' lengths planted on (Waste incl)							
(@ Glass) (sills & heads) (N&S) 3/2/32-0			192				
3/2/18-0			108				
			300			300	LF
½"x2½" Trim in 18' lengths planted on inside (Waste incl)							
(@ wdw heads & valences) (s) 1/36-0			36				
(N) 2/18-0			36			72	LF
½"x2¼" Door Stops in 8' lengths planted on at intr doorways (Waste incl)							
(jambs only) 2.15/2/8-0			272			272	LF

PRACTICAL
Form 516 MFD IN U.S.A.

PROJECT	RESIDENCE	ESTIMATOR	KC	ESTIMATE NO.	R-1

LOCATION	EXTENSIONS KC	SHEET NO. 5 of 7
ARCHITECT ENGINEER	CHECKED	DATE 1987

CLASSIFICATION **FINISH CARPENTRY (WDW WALLS) (INSTALLATION)**

DESCRIPTION	NO.	DIMENSIONS					ESTIMATED QUANTITY	UNIT
D. FIR FINISH ("C" V.G GRADE)								
1⅝"×5¼" Sill (as Detail #3/3) in 16'& 18' lengths framed to mullions (Waste incl)								
	(S)	1/32-0		32				
	(N)	1/18-0		18				50 LF
1⅝"×7¼" Sill (as Detail #3/3) ditto (ditto)								
	(S)	1/32-0		32				
	(N)	1/18-0		18				50 LF
1⅝×7¼×14" long ditto (ditto)								
(@ W. Wdw)	1/1							1 NO
¾"×3½" Wdw Stool, in 14' length (Waste incl)								
	(N)	1/14-0		14				14 LF
INSTALLATION OF WOOD WINDOWS & DOORS (SUPPLY IN DIV.8)								
Install Wood Windows in 5 lights 14'0"×3'10" %a (N)								1 NO
Ditto 1'1"×15'6" %a (W)								1 NO
Hang Wood Doors with hardware to wood frames as follows:—								
(NB: Intr Doors have matching transom panels over)								
Door (A) 3'0"×7'4"×1¾" Solid 1/1 (entrance)				1				1 NO
" & Panel (B) 2'8"× 6'8"×1⅜" Hollow 5/1 (intr)				5				5 NO
Door (C) 3'0"×7'4"×1¾" Glazed 4/1 (patio)				4				4 NO
" & Panel (D) 2'6"× 6'8"×1⅜" Hollow 4/1 (intr)				4				4 NO
" " (E) 2'0"× 6'8"×1⅜" " 3/1 (")				3				3 NO
" " (F) 3'0"× 6'8"×1⅜" " 2/1 (")				2				2 NO
" " (G) 2'0"× 6'8"×1¾" Solid 2/1 (")				2				2 NO
" " (HWT) 1'6"× 6'8"×1¾" " 1/1 (")				1				1 NO
O/Head Garage Door 14'0"×6'6"×1¾" Solid				1				1 NO
Install Glass Louvres in Alum Frames (Supply in Div.8) to wood frames								
single lights each 3'0"×6'8" %a								3 NO

FRANK R. WALKER CO., PUBLISHERS, CHICAGO

PRACTICAL
Form 516 MFD IN U.S.A.

PROJECT: *RESIDENCE*   ESTIMATOR: KC   ESTIMATE NO. R-1

LOCATION: EXTENSIONS: KC   SHEET NO. 6 of 7

ARCHITECT ENGINEER: CHECKED: DATE: 1987

CLASSIFICATION: FINISH CARPENTRY (INSTALLATION)

DESCRIPTION	NO.	DIMENSIONS	ESTIMATED QUANTITY	UNIT
Install Millwork Cabinets (supplied by Millwork Subcontractor)				
Sink Counter 8'0" x 2'1" x 2'4" %a inc 17"h Splashback w/ returned ends (to frmd walls & panels m/s)			1	No
Upper Wall Cbb'ds (over sink) 8'0" x 1'0" x 2'1" %a (ditto)			1	No
Ditto (over frig & stove m/s) 8'0" x 1'0" x 2'1" %a (ditto)			1	No
Counter Unit (btwn frig & stove) 2'9" x 2'1" x 2'4" %a inc 17"h Splashback (w/ returned end) extending 5'2" long (behind stove)			1	No
Vanity Counter 4'0" x 1'8" x 2'4" %a (in Bathroom)			1	No
Ditto 4'8" x 1'8" x 2'4" %a (in Bathroom)			1	No
Medicine Cabinets approx 2' x 2' %a (in Bathroom)			2	No
Install Bathroom Accessories (supplied by others) incl rough bearers				
Install Toilet Paper Holders (flush type)			3	No
Install Towel Rails			3	No
Install Soap Dish (flush type)			1	No

PRACTICAL
Form 516 MFD IN U.S.A.

PROJECT *RESIDENCE*		ESTIMATOR *KC*	ESTIMATE NO. *R-1*
LOCATION		EXTENSIONS *KC*	SHEET NO. *7 of 7*
ARCHITECT ENGINEER		CHECKED	DATE *1987*

CLASSIFICATION *FINISH CARPENTRY (SHELVING)*

DESCRIPTION	NO.	DIMENSIONS	ESTIMATED QUANTITY	UNIT
¾" D.Fir Ply (Good/Solid) Closet Shelves w⟋ solid clear D.fir Front Edging and 1x2 Wall Bearers (to three edges) and w⟋ Chrome-finish Closet Track w⟋ small Eye Hangers (2 per foot of track-length), as follows:—				
Shelf 1'6" w x 4'6" long	1	(BR #2)	1	N⁰
Shelf 1'6" w x 6'6" long	1	(BR #3)	1	N⁰
Shelf 1'6" w x 7'6" long	1	(BR #1)	1	N⁰
Shelf 1'6" w x 3'0" long	1	(Coats)	1	N⁰
Linen Closet Shelves 1'0" x 2'6" long of ½" x 1" W. Red Cedar Frame and Battens spaced ½" apart on & incl 1" x 2" D.fir Wall Bearers (to three edges) 4/1			4	N⁰
Allowance for Lab & Mat to supply & install minor items of Trim required (and not indicated)				Item

NOTE: The measurement of CARPENTRY work (both Rough and Finish) shows how most construction work of other trades can be measured more simply, but also to provide and retain more information about the work in an estimate.

"C" grade, vertical grain, which means it is kiln dried and of high quality (next to "B" grade, which is the highest). Some estimators would measure an extra labor item for the shaped ends to the 2 × 8 handrails. But in a small job, with a small number of different items, the estimator can sometimes allow for such things in his pricing without fully detailed measurement.

Measurement of base trim (of any kind) can be tedious. The easiest way is to use the total lengths of walls; once times extr walls, and twice times intr walls; and deduct the major wants. Whenever possible other trim should also be measured by utilizing dims of other work to which the trim is attached.

Finish carpentry usually includes the installation (by carpenters) of millwork and other fixtures supplied to the job by a subcontractor or supplier. In this example it is assumed that the wood sash, wood doors, millwork fixtures (cabinet work), and small bathroom fixtures (mirrors, medicine cabinet, and the like) are supplied to the job in this way, and only the installation is measured in this estimate.

Hanging doors includes installing hardware (assumed to be supplied through a cash allowance[G] in the contract), and the cabinetwork is assumed to be supplied with all its finish hardware.

Shelving in this job is simple and probably will be made up on the job. Measurement is equally simple. If it is not more than 12 in. wide, it is to be measured as a run item in the MM–CIQS. It is easier and better to always measure shelving linearly, or to enumerate it.

Moisture Protection

The built-up roofing and the roof insulation is measured from the upper floor plan, from which the o/a dims inside parapets are computed, and from the roof plan shown on the site plan. Measurements are taken of the areas covered by roofing work.

The roofing felts are taken up over the cant strips, up the inside face of parapets, and nailed at the upper edges under the metal flshgs. Such work is better measured as a run item, as in the example. The metal flshgs are fully described, and their girths are stated. The number of breaks (bends) in the girth of each kind of metal flshg is sometimes stated to make more accurate pricing possible, particularly when the flshg is to be formed to an unfamiliar profile. Isolated metal flshgs to vent pipes and the like are described and enumerated.

If the project spec requires moisture protection to be guaranteed, following inspection of the work in progress, or subsequent testing, or both, an item should be noted for pricing the costs.

Finishes

Stucco. The dims are collected and added together in the preliminary calculations and, for clarity, they are identified N, S, E, or W, according to the elevation. The o/a vertical dim is also computed from the dims shown on the dwgs.

The extr stucco is described "*as spec*" (as specified). The full descriptions of all items of work cannot always be entered on estimate sheets because of their length, and in such cases the description should contain the words "as spec" so that the estimator is reminded to look at the specified requirements when pricing the item. The narrow widths of stucco are described according to width, as before, and measured as run items.

Metal beads and expansion joint trim are measured; and although such items are not always indicated or fully described on dwgs, they may be required by the specs or by the class of work.

Drywall. Intr dims for the finishes are computed first, and the perims of the rooms and intr areas are calculated below the items' descriptions, which contain the appropriate wall hts, later multiplied by the aggregated perims to give the areas of drywall finish to walls. In this way the dim entries and calculations are kept to a minimum, and the estimate sheet is uncluttered and easy to read. Sub-totals are entered in an "extension column" to enable the items to be grand-totaled. Deductions are dealt with in the same way.

Narrow widths and metal beads are described and measured as run items, as before. Dims of clgs are calculated so as to measure the finish to clgs over the ptn walls and opngs, and the wants are deducted. To simplify measuring, the clg area over the GF–storage–WC–furnace–coats area is totally deducted (ddt – 18.4 × 5.4), and the actual clg area (17.4 × 5.0) is added to the overall area measured above. The high LR clg (above 14 ft) is measured separately and so described because of additional scaffolding costs. Double wallboard in the garage clg (for fire isolation) is so described and measured separately.

Although designer's dwgs often describe work by using trade names such as "Gyproc," the specs usually make it clear that other equivalent products are acceptable. For this reason, and unless only one particular product is to be used in a job, it is better to avoid the use of trade names.

Measuring the *total gross quantity of drywall* required, in 4-ft-wide boards of the required lengths, will enable the amount of waste to be estimated. Boards installed *vertically* to walls, have a minimum length of 8-ft. Alternatively, the boards are installed *hori-*

PRACTICAL
STANDARDIZED FORMS FOR CONTRACTORS
Form 516 MFD IN U.S.A.

PROJECT	RESIDENCE	ESTIMATOR	KC	ESTIMATE NO. R-1
LOCATION		EXTENSIONS	KC	SHEET NO. 1 of 2
ARCHITECT ENGINEER	MOISTURE PROTECTION	CHECKED		DATE 1987
CLASSIFICATION	(ROOFING & SHEET METAL)			

DESCRIPTION	NO.	DIMENSIONS				ESTIMATED QUANTITY	UNIT

Prelim Calcs - Dims   (Overhangs)   (Want)

(E-W) 15-2 (N-S)   13-6   35-4   5-8   (E-W) 14-0   21-6   4"
           10-10   8-4   ½=-4-0   8-4   3-4   -0-6   2"
    2/   5-4   21-6   31-4   14-0   17-4   21-0
    ½2-0=4-0   43-4   3-0   2-6   -3-0
       35-4   2/0-4=0-8   +0-4   +0-4   18-0
            42-8   3-4   2-10

4 Ply Tar & Gravel B/up Roofing on & incl 1" thick Rigid
Fiberboard Insulation on Vapor Barrier (all as Specs pp —)

	1/ 35-4	×	42-8	1508
(@ S. O/hang)	1/ 31-4	×	3-4	104
(@ N. ")	1/ 14-0	×	2-10	40
				1652

DDT (Want)   1/ 17-4   ×   18-0   — 312   DDT
                                    1340   13½ Sq

4 Ply Ditto on Vertical Faces of Parapet etc. x 8" high above Roof
incl nailing Top Edges   (as Specs p —)

	(E2W)	2/ 42-8	85
	(S. O/hang)	2/ 3-4	7
@ above Entr⊙	(N. O/hangs) 1·2/ 3-4		10
	(")	2/ 2-10	6
(@ returned ends para)	2/ 2/ 2-0		8
	(aro'd chmny)	4/ 1-9	7
			123

123 LF

(NB: 4 Ply Ditto over Cants measd in general Roof Area)

Cut & Fit B/up Roofing to Roof Drains (m/s)
            4/1   4 No

Form 516 MFD IN U.S.A.

PROJECT	RESIDENCE			ESTIMATOR	KC	ESTIMATE NO.	R-1
LOCATION				EXTENSIONS	KC	SHEET NO.	2 of 2
ARCHITECT ENGINEER	MOISTURE PROTECTION			CHECKED		DATE	1987
CLASSIFICATION	(ROOFING & SHEET METAL)						

DESCRIPTION	NO.	DIMENSIONS					ESTIMATED QUANTITY	UNIT
26 Ga GALV STEEL SHEET METAL FLASHINGS (all as Details & Specs)								
Cap Flashings to parapets x 12" girth wi 2-Hemmed Edges & installed wi Clips max 8'0" apart (as Detail #4/3)								
(123-0 –7-0)(As Rfg)	1/	116-0		116				
(corners) 4·4/		0-6		4			120	LF
Counter Flashings to parapets x 9" girth wi Hemmed Btm Edge & Top Edge Nailed & wi Clips a.b (as Ditto)								
(As Cap Flshgs)							120	LF
Ditto to chmny stack x 9" girth wi Ditto & wi Top Edge turned into Bkwk & wi Clips a.b								
	4/	1-9					7	LF
Cant Flashings x 9" girth wi 2-Hemmed Edges & Clips a.b								
(17-4 + 14-0)	2/	31-4					63	LF
Window Head Flashings x 6" girth wi Hemmed Btm Edge & hand to carpenters for installation under Ply (as Detail #3/3)								
(s)	1/	31-4		31				
(N)	1/	17-0		17				
(w)	1/	1-6		2			50	LF
3Lb LEAD SHEET FLASHINGS (as Specs)								
3"∅ Vent Pipe Flashing wi 12"x12" Base & 8" high upstand							1	No
4"∅ Ditto							1	No
Allowance for Roofing Inspection, Testing & Guarantee (as Specs)								Item
[NB: Roof Drains & Pipes in Div. 15]								

PRACTICAL
Form 516   MFD IN U.S.A.

PROJECT	RESIDENCE		ESTIMATOR	KC	ESTIMATE NO.	R-1
LOCATION			EXTENSIONS	KC	SHEET NO.	1 of 1
ARCHITECT ENGINEER	FINISHES		CHECKED		DATE	1987

CLASSIFICATION   STUCCO (EXTR & INTR)

DESCRIPTION	NO.	DIMENSIONS					Height		ESTIMATED QUANTITY	UNIT

Prelim calcs - Dims

(N)(8-0 - 0-4)= 7-8   (E)22-0 (W)13-6   (E) 30-0   ↓132-4   8-7½ (G.Floor)

(14-0 - ⅔/0-4)=13-4   +8-0   +8-4   (N) 14-0   4/2-0 = 8-0   7-6 (U.Floor)

(inside @screen Wl)   1-8   30-0 ✓ 21-10   "   2-0   2/2/3-0= 12-0   1-1½ (Roof)

22-8   (E)21-6   ¹⁻⁰/0-2 = 1-2   "   22-8   2/2/2-6= 10-0   0-8 (Parapet)

½/=-0-2   20-8)   (E) 21-4   TOTAL 1624   17-11

21-4 ✓ 21-6   (W) { 20-8   + 0-1 (@Btm)

½ = +0-2)   21-8   TOTAL 18-0

21-8   132-4↑

Extr Stucco Plaster wi 1"Galv Mesh Reinf & self-furring nails
to walls (as spec)

	1/162-4	x	18-0	2922					
(Reveals@Gar.Door)	2/0-4	x	6-6	4					
				2926 (÷9)					325 SY

Ditto < 3" wide to Reveals

| (@ W.Wdw) | 2/18-0 | | | 36 (÷3) | | | | | 12 LY |

Ditto 3" to 6" wide to N.W's

| (@ Wallends) | 5/18-0 | | | 90 (÷3) | | | | | 30 LY |

Intr Stucco Plaster on Brick Chmny Face Panel in S.Q (as spec)

| | 1/2-8 | x | 13-4 | 36 (÷9) | | | | | 4 SY |

Zinc Alloy Stucco Trim (as spec)

| Expansion Joints | 4/18-0 | | | 72 | | | | | 72 LF |

| Corner Beads | 5/2/18-0 | | | 180 | | | | | |
| (⊙@W.Wdw)(walls) | 2·6/18-0 | | | 144 | | | | | 324 LF |

| Edge Beads (@Btm) | 1/163-0 | | | 163 | | | | | |
| (2-8+13-4+6-6) = | 2/22-6 | | | 45 | | | | | 208 LF |

NOTE: The major item of STUCCO PLASTER might be measured
linearly in 5-foot lifts (or whatever is suitable) to provide
and retain more information about the work in the
estimate.

FRANK R. WALKER CO., PUBLISHERS, CHICAGO

zontally and their lengths vary according to the required job dims. Either way, the total area is the same, but the lengths vary accordingly.

If drywall is measured both net (area covered) and gross (by required board lengths), the waste can be calculated. In the example, waste is unusually high, partly due to the ceiling height (7 ft 6 in.). If, as in the example on page 197, a percentage for waste is calculated and shown in the item's description to be allowed for in the unit-price calculation, then the waste factor is related to the *net quantity*. If the wallboard cost 10 cents per SF, then the unit price for the material would be 10 cents + 25% for waste = 12½ cents per SF, and 3770 SF at 12½ cents = $471.25. Or, if the gross area is used to price the material costs then 4704 SF at 10 cents per SF = $470.40, the small difference being due to the slight inaccuracy in the percentage allowed for waste.

Floor Coverings. Floor coverings are easily measured after the clgs because their dims and quantities are similar, and the quantities used for one serve as a check on the quantities required for the other:

Total clgs area (excluding garage) is 1398 + 221 = 1619 SF; the total area of flr coverings is 630 + 63 + 855 = 1548 SF, which is a difference of 71 SF. This difference is made up of the ddts from the brick flr area of 71 SF (11 + 53 + 7).

Descriptions of the floor items are abbreviated, and reference is made to the specs, as before. These items may have specific requirements in respect to adhesives, cleaning, waxing, and maintenance, which must be accounted for in the pricing. If it is necessary, the estimator should write fuller descriptions in the estimate to ensure that all the costs are included.

Painting (Exterior). Painting and other decoration and coating work is usually measured last so that the dims and quantities of the measured work to be painted can be used. The measurements should be as accurate as the requirements of the items and their unit prices dictate. Most painting (two coats) will cost less than $.50 per SF. Besides, many other factors affect the costs much more than minor variations in quantity.

Where possible, the measured areas of other work such as cladding, paneling, stucco, drywall, and the like, are used to measure the quantities of painting required. Windows and doors are measured overall, with no deductions for glass. Painting on different kinds of surfaces is measured separately, and generally all surfaces are measured as though flat.

Allowances for surfaces that are not flat because of natural variations, applied moldings, and other features, are better calculated in the unit prices, and any allowances established from experience should be indicated in the items' descriptions for this purpose. The MM-CIQS, however, calls for such allowances to be made in the measurements.

Paint to be applied to surfaces of less than 12 in. girth is better measured and priced linearly. Isolated items to be painted are described and enumerated.

Having reviewed the examples for measuring finishes, it might be well to mention again that many estimators and quantity surveyors measure the superficial work such as roof coverings and finishes first, and then measure the structure and frame. This is done to first acquire a knowledge of the building and its layout before measuring the more complex items of work, such as the wood frame.

RESIDENCE EXERCISES

All the work not measured in the examples, including site work, excavation, concrete (including formwork), and interior painting can be measured as exercises. Finally, the entire project might be remeasured and priced (at current and local unit prices) as a complete estimating exercise; and at the same time, variations in cladding and finishes might be made and estimated by first making section-drawings showing the variations. For example, 4-in.-thick brick veneer might be substituted for the exterior stucco finish, or masonry exterior walls might be substituted for framing (each illustrated by a simple section-drawing) to provide more exercises.

WAREHOUSE EXAMPLE

The Warehouse Drawings are of a building that was designed and built for a plywood distributor; and although it has a few features that are peculiar to the site it is generally typical of numerous warehouses with attached offices designed and built for wholesalers and distributors.

The measurement examples taken from the Warehouse Drawings were selected to demonstrate the measurement of types of work not previously shown. The work not measured in the examples, such as the site works, excavation and fill, foundations, miscellaneous metals, framing, finish carpentry, moisture protection, and finishes, can be measured as exercises. Similar work has been measured in previous examples.

QUANTITY SHEET

PROJECT **RESIDENCE**	ESTIMATOR **KC**	ESTIMATE NO. **R-1**
LOCATION	EXTENSIONS **KC**	SHEET NO. **1 of 4**
ARCHITECT ENGINEER **FINISHES**	CHECKED	DATE **1987**
CLASSIFICATION **DRYWALL (WALLS)**		

Prelim calcs Dims

DESCRIPTION				NO.	DIMENSIONS								ESTIMATED QUANTITY	UNIT

(GF) 15-2 22-0 5-4 3-1 14-0 6½' Partn (UF) 10-10 13-6 -13-6 8-4 5-8 Closets
  16-2 ⅞-0-8 ⅞-0-4 ⅞-0-2 ⅞= 4-8 35-4 1-3 -0-6 13-0 2-4 2-4 2/=6-0 =4-0
2-4= 4-8 21-4 5-0 2-11 18-8 -3-0 -3-8 12-1 13-0 -7-10 10-8 8-0 2/-0-2 =0-2
  360 3-11 11-0 20-6 ⅞-0-8 =28-8 ⅞/ 0-4 5-4 5-2 -0-6-3 -0-6-3 6-2 4-2
2/-0-8 ⅞-0-2 ⅞-0-4 -0-6½ 18-0 -4-0 11-9 2-4 21-6 10-2 7-6 35-4 13-6
  35-4 3-9 10-8 20-0 24-8 7-8 -0-6½ -7-6 8-4
  -0-6½ -0-6½ 27-10 21-10
  7-2 21-0 -0-6=⅞
  21-4

½" Gypsum Drywall boards w/ taped & filled joints (as spec)
to Walls (x 7'6" high) (allow 25% Waste)

(GF)   LF   (4'x8' shts)
LR/K. 2(35-4 + 21-4)   1/ 113-4 (x 7-6)   113   2(9+6) =   30 No
WC. 2(3-9 + 5-0)   1/ 17-6   18   2(1+1) =   4
Stor. 2(10-8 + 5-0)   1/ 31-4   31   2(3+1) =   8
Furn. 2(2-11 + 2-6)   1/ 10-10   11   2(1+1) =   4
Clos. 2(2-11 + 2-2)   1/ 10-2   10   2(1+1) =   4
HWT. 2(1-6 + 1-6)   1/ 6-0   6   offcuts =   0
Gar. 2(18-0 + 20-0)   1/ 76-0   76   2(5+5) =   20
(UF)   265   70 No
BR1. 2(11-9 + 13-0)   1/ 49-6   50   2(3+4) =   14
DR. 2(7-2 + 7-6)   1/ 29-4   29   2(2+2) =   8
Bath. 2(7-2 + 5-2)   1/ 24-8   25   2(2+1) =   6
Bath. 2(7-2 + 8-0)   1/ 30-4   30   2(2+2) =   8
Lin. 2(2-6 + 1-3)   1/ 7-6   8   2(1+0) =   2
BR2. 2(21-0 + 10-2)   1/ 62-4   62   2(6+2) =   16
BR3. 2(21-0 + 7-6)   1/ 57-0   57   2(5+2) =   14
Clos. 2(6-2 + 2-0)   1/ 16-4   16   2(2+½) =   5
Clos. 2(4-2 + 2-0)   1/ 12-4   13   2(1+½) =   3
UG.}   1/ 98-4   98   2(7+6) =   26
LR.} 2(27-10 + 21-4)
                                               653 LF   172 No
                                               X 7-6 high
                                               4898 SF

ADD (6½' Partn)   2/ 24-8 x 6-6   321 SF 2(7)   14
  (@ stairwell)   2/ 3-8   x 1-0   8   offcuts = 0
2/=26-0 (extra ht in) 1/ 28-2 x 1-0   28   (use 10' 0 (adjusted
2-2   LR   {2/ 10-6 x 3-0   63} sheets)   later)
  (to balustrade)   {1/ 17-0 x 1-0   17} 2(1½)   3
                        (TOTALS) 5335 SF   TOTAL 189 No
                        (carry forward to next sheet)

PRACTICAL
~~PRACTICAL~~
Form 516 MFD IN U.S.A.

PROJECT	RESIDENCE	ESTIMATOR	KC
		EXTENSIONS	KC
LOCATION			
ARCHITECT ENGINEER	FINISHES	CHECKED	
CLASSIFICATION	DRYWALL (WALLS)		

ESTIMATE NO. R-1
SHEET NO. 2 of 4
DATE 1987

Prelim cales - Dims

15-2	14-0		5-8	
16-2	3-4		8-4	
31-4	17-4		14-0	
2/ 0-4	-0-6 = 4/2	2/2/2" = -0-8		
31-0	16-10		13-4	

DDT ½" Gypsum Drywall a.b (x 7'6" high)   (4'x8' shts)

(GF)	(@ S.Wdws)	1/ 31-0	(x	7-6)	31 LF	7 №
	(@ N.Wdws)	1/ 16-10			17	4
	(@ Int. Doors) 2·³/2/	2-8			27 (2·³/2/2½)=	5
	(@ W. Wdw)	1/ 1-0			1	0
(UF)					76	16 №
	(@ S.Wdws)	1/ 31-0			31	7
	(@ W. Wdw)	1/ 1-0			1	0
	(@ N.Wdw BRs)	1/ 13-4			13	3
	(@ N.Wdw UG)	1/ 16-10			17	4
	(@ Int. Doors)	11/2/ 2-8			59 (11/2/½)	11
					197 LF	41 №
					x 7-6 high	
					1478 SF	
	(Garage Door)	1/ 14-0	x	6-6	91	3
					1569 SF DDT	44 № DDT

(brought forward) TOTAL	5335	TOTAL 189	
	-1569 DDT	-44 DDT	
	3766	145 (incl 8 № 10' sheets)	

**½" Gypsum Drywall boards w/ taped & filled joints. (as spec)
to walls (allow 25% waste)**

3770 SF

(4'x8' sheets 137 №)
(4'x10' sheets 8 №)

sheets   Waste Calcs
137 (4x8') =   4384 SF
  8 (4'x10') =   320 SF
Gross Quantity = 4704
Not   "   = -3766
        Waste = 938 SF
938 x 100 = 25%
3766 ÷ 1

NOTE: As with items of other trades, GYPSUM
DRYWALL work can be measured
linearly (x 4ft wide) to retain more
information in an estimate.

NOTE: Only both NET and GROSS measurement
enable WASTE to be calculated, so both
measurements are required.

PRACTICAL
Form 516 MFD IN U.S.A.

PROJECT	RESIDENCE		ESTIMATOR	KC	ESTIMATE NO.	R-1
LOCATION			EXTENSIONS	KC	SHEET NO.	3 of 4
ARCHITECT ENGINEER	FINISHES		CHECKED		DATE	1987

CLASSIFICATION DRYWALL (WALLS)

DESCRIPTION	NO.	DIMENSIONS			ESTIMATED QUANTITY	UNIT
½" Gypsum Drywall to Walls a.b 3" to 6" wide (Lab only)						
(GF) (top 6½' partn)	1/	24-8		25		
(ends ")	2/	6-6		13		
(reveals W. Wdw)	2/	7-6		15		
(UF)				53		
(reveals W. Wdw)	3/	7-6		15		
(top balustrade)	1/	10-6		11		
	2/2/	3-0		12		
				91	90	LF
Galv Steel Corner Beads to ½" Drywall (as spec)						
(GF) (@ 3"-6" widths)	2/	24-8		49		
"	2/2/	6-6		26		
"	1/2/	7-6		15		
(@ wall corners)	2/	7-6		15		
(@ stairwell)	2/	3-8		7		
(UF)				112		
(@ 3"-6" widths)	1/2/	7-6		15		
"	2/1/	10-6		21		
"	2/2/2/	3-0		24		
(@ wall corners)	4.2.4/	7-6		90		
	1/	1-0		1		
(17+13) (over LR)	1/	30-0		30		
				293	300	LF
Galv Steel Edge Beads to ½" Drywall (as spec)						
(GF) (exposed edges)	6/	7-6		45		
(next chmny stack)	2/2/	6-6		26		
(UF)				71		
(exposed edges)	1.5/	7-6		45		
		1-0		1		
				117	120	LF
Ditto, (ditto) at Door Jambs (as detail Dwg sht. 1)						
(c Int. Doors) 17/	3/2/	7-6		510		
types: B, 5 E, 3	2/	6-6		13	520	LF
D, 4 F, 2						
HWI, 1 G, 2						
[NB: Extra scaffolding for high walls in LR taken later.]						

FRANK R. WALKER CO., PUBLISHERS, CHICAGO

PRACTICAL
Form 516 MFD IN U.S.A.

PROJECT	RESIDENCE					ESTIMATOR	KC		ESTIMATE NO.	R-1
LOCATION						EXTENSIONS	KC		SHEET NO.	4 of 4
ARCHITECT ENGINEER	FINISHES					CHECKED			DATE	1987

CLASSIFICATION DRYWALL (CEILINGS)

DESCRIPTION		NO.	DIMENSIONS								ESTIMATED QUANTITY	UNIT
Prelim Calcs – Dims												
(GF)	13-8 WC	3-9	14-0	22-0	14-0	(UF)13-6	10-10	15-2	13-6		42-8	
15-2	3-10 Storage	10-8	3-4	2/=0-8	2/=4-0	8-4	5-4	2-4	-0-6=½²	2/=36-0		
16-2	5-4 Furn	2-11	17-4	21-4	0-4	21-6	2-4	17-6	13-0	2/=4-8	closets
2/=4-0	22-10	17-4	-0-4	22-4	18-4	43-4	18-6	2½"-0-6		7-2	shower
35-4	-0-6	5-4	17-0	-21-4		2/=-08	-0-6	17-0		1-2	
	22-4	2/=0-4		1-0		428	18-0			91-8	
		5-0									

½" Gypsum Drywall boards wi taped & filled joints (as spec)
to Ceilings ✓ (allow 12% Waste)

4' wide sheets

(GF) (LR, K, etc)	1/35-4	×	22-4	789	(5/14'+4/10'+5/8')=	150
(UF) (BR's, etc)	1/42-8	×	18-0	768	(5/14'+5/12'+4/8')=	210
(U. Gallery)	1/17-4	×	8-4	144	(partially 4/8')=	32
(over Doors)	3·6/3-0	×	0-4	9	(no extra)	—
ADD (Net Area @ Storage, WC, Furn, etc)	1/17-4	×	5-0	87 *	(")	—
				1797		392'

DDT ½" Drywall (Wants)   DDT   ×4'w

(GF) (e. N. Wdw & Entr)	1/17-0	×	1-0		17 *	1568 SF (Gross)
(@ Storage, WC, etc)	1/18-4	×	5-4		98 *	
(over LR)	1/17-0	×	13-0		221	(14'×4' sheets–10 №)
(@ Stairwell)	1/8-9	×	3-8		32	(12'×4' " 5 №)
(UF) (e. Partn Walls)	1/91-8	×	0-4		31	(10'×4' " 4 №)
					-399	(8'×4' " 19 №)
					1398	1400 SF

½" Ditto 16'1½" high above G.Floor incl. extra scaffolding (allow 27% Waste)

| | | | | | | (14'×4' sheets–5 №) |
| | 1/17-0 | × | 13-0 | 221 | (5/14') | 220 SF |

Double ⅜" Gypsum Drywall boards wi exposed joints taped & filled
(as spec) to Ceiling of ✓ Garage (allow 11% Waste)

						(10'×4' sheets–10 №)
	1/20-0	×	18-0	360	(5/3/10')	(10'×4' backing–10 №)
						360 SF

* to deduct Partitions around Storage, WC, Furnace & Coats.

PRACTICAL
Standardized Forms for Contractors
Form 516 MFD IN U.S.A.

PROJECT	RESIDENCE		ESTIMATOR	KC	ESTIMATE NO.	R-1
LOCATION			EXTENSIONS	KC	SHEET NO.	1 of 2
ARCHITECT ENGINEER	FINISHES		CHECKED		DATE	1987

CLASSIFICATION FLOOR COVERINGS

Prelim calcs - Dims

DESCRIPTION	NO.	DIMENSIONS		collect
(GF) 16-2 22-0	13-8	22-4	15-2	Walls
15-2 ¾=0-8	3-10	-21-4	2-0	18-0
¾2-0=4-0 21-4	5-4	1-0	17-2	¾=10-0
35-4	22-10		-0-2	3-0
4"=			17-0	31-0
6"= -0-6	22-4			¾-8-0 (doors)
				23-0

1" thick x 9" x 4½" Brick Paviors bedded & flush jointed in
P cmt mtr on conc floor slab (as spec) (SC & Waste m/s)

(GF - except Garage)	1/35-4	×	22-4	789
				DDT
DDT (Wants @ Entr)	1/17-0	×	1-0	— 17
(@ LR. conc paving)	1/9-0	×	7-0	— 63
(@ chmny stack)	1/4-0	×	2-8	— 11
(@ Storage)	1/10-8	×	5-0	— 53
(@ Furnace)	1/2-11	×	2-6	— 7
(@ Walls)	1/23-0	×	0-4	— 8
				—159
				630

630 SF

Straight Cutting & Waste to 1" Bk Paviors (against walls)

	2/35-4			71
	2/22-4			45
(9-0+7-0)	2/16-0			32
(4-0+2-8)	2/6-8			13
(24-6+3-6+1-0)	2/30-0			60
	2/5-4			11
				232

230 Lf

1" P Cement Fine Topping on conc floor slab steel trwld smooth

| | 1/9-0 | × | 7-0 | 63 |

63 SF

NOTE: Traditionally STRAIGHT CUTTING is not measured, but its
measurement enables more accurate pricing and embodies in
an estimate useful information about the related work and
its form otherwise not recorded.

QUANTITY SHEET

PROJECT	RESIDENCE		ESTIMATOR	KC	ESTIMATE NO.	R-1
LOCATION			EXTENSIONS	KC	SHEET NO.	2 of 2
ARCHITECT ENGINEER	FINISHES		CHECKED		DATE	1987

CLASSIFICATION FLOOR COVERINGS

DESCRIPTION	NO.	DIMENSIONS						ESTIMATED QUANTITY	UNIT
Prelim calcs - Dims									
(UF) 10-10 13-6	15-2	35-4							
5-4 8-4	10-10	-18-0							
2-4 21-6	5-4	17-4							
4" 18-6 43-4 ³/=	4-8	15-2							
2"-0-6 ³/= 0-8	36-0	2-0							
18-0 42-8 ³/=-0-8	0-2								
	35-4	17-4							

0.080" thick Vinyl Asbestos Floor Tiling (one color)
installed on ply subfloor m/s. (allow 10% Waste)

(UF) (B'rms, Baths, etc)	1/	42-8	×	18-0	768				
(u. Gallery)	1/	17-4	×	8-4	144				
(doorways)	6/	3-0	×	0-4	6				
					918				
DDT (Wants)						DDT			
(@ partn. walls)	1/	91-8	×	0-4	—	31			
(@ stairwell)	1/	8-9	×	3-8	—	32			
[NB: no deducts					-63				
made for plumbing					855			860 SF	
fixtures.]									

Extra over last item for Waterproof Adhesive

(Bathrooms)	1/	7-2	×	5-2	37				
	1/	7-2	×	8-0	57				
					94			100 SF	

NOTE: For computer input and estimating, by measuring FLOORING in each room or area separately, together with related STRAIGHT CUTTING (at perimeters, etc.), much more information about the work is recorded and retained by an estimator; thus enabling more accurate pricing and better management of work, especially in projects larger than shown here.

PROJECT	RESIDENCE		ESTIMATOR	KC	ESTIMATE NO.	R-1
LOCATION			EXTENSIONS	KC	SHEET NO.	1 of 2
ARCHITECT ENGINEER	FINISHES		CHECKED		DATE	1987

CLASSIFICATION   PAINTING (EXTERIOR)

DESCRIPTION	NO.	DIMENSIONS						ESTIMATED QUANTITY	UNIT
PRIMER & 2 COATS EXTR OIL PAINT ON PLYWOOD (as spec)									
Isolated Panels / Fascias up to 18' above ground									
(as in FIN CARP p.1) 262 (÷9)								30 SY	
Small Ditto (approx 2sf each) up to ditto									
(as in ditto)		2						2 No	
Eaves Soffites (x 2'3" & 2'9" wide) about 15'6" above ground									
(as in ditto)		165 (÷9)						20 SY	
PRIMER & 2 COATS EXTR OIL PAINT ON WDW & DR FRMS IN WDW WALLS									
Wdw Frms (one edge next glass) 3"–6" wide									
(S) 2/2/ 31-4		125							
(N) 2/2/ 17-4		68							
(Avg Jamb (S) 2/6/2/ 7-0		168							
7' high) (N) 2/3/2/ 7-0		84							
		445	DDT						
DDT (wants) (Wdw Frms <3" wide)		—	130						
(Dr Frms 3"–6" wide)		—	50						
(Dr Frms <3" wide)		—	20						
(Dr Frms 6"–9" wide)		—	15						
		-215						230 LF	
Wdw Frms (one edge next glass) less than 3" wide									
(Heads Frms) (S) 2/ 31-4		63							
(N) 2/ 17-4		35							
(Jambs @ walls)(S & N) 2/2/ 7-0		28							
" (S & N) 1/1/ 7-0		7							
2/= 14·0		133						130 LF	
+3·0									
Dr Frms 3"–6" wide 1·4/ 17-0		85	DDT						
DDT (wants) (Dr Frms <3" wide)			21						
(Dr Frms 6"–9" wide)			14						
		-35						50 LF	
Dr Frms less than 3" wide 1·2/ 7-0		21						20 LF	
(Jambs @ walls)									
Dr Frms 6"–9" wide 2/ 7-0		14						15 LF	
(B/s mullion post)									

FRANK R. WALKER CO., PUBLISHERS, CHICAGO

Form 516 MFD IN U.S.A.
PRACTICAL
STANDARDIZED FORMS FOR CONTRACTORS

PROJECT	RESIDENCE	ESTIMATOR KC	ESTIMATE NO. R-1	
LOCATION		EXTENSIONS KC	SHEET NO. 2 of 2	
ARCHITECT ENGINEER	FINISHES	CHECKED	DATE 1987	
CLASSIFICATION	PAINTING (EXTERIOR)			

DESCRIPTION	NO.	DIMENSIONS			ESTIMATED QUANTITY	UNIT
PRIMER & 2 COATS EXTR OIL PAINT ON WOOD (as spec)						
Flush Extr Doors (extr face only)	1/ 3-0	x	7-4	22 (÷9)	3	sy
Glazed Extr Doors (extr face only) wi single pane (about 14 sf) & meas'd over glass	4/ 3-0	x	7-4	88 (÷9)	10	sy
Flush, Panelled O/head Garage Door wi six panes (about 2 sf each) & meas'd over glass (b/sides meas'd)	2/ 14-0	x	6-6	182 (÷9)	20	sy
PRIMER & 2 COATS EXTR OIL PAINT ON METAL (as spec)						
Parapet Flashings @ 18' above ground (as ROOFING p.2)	1/ 120-0	x	1-9	210 (÷9)	24	sy
Cant Flashings x 6"-9" girth @ 18' above ground (ditto)				63		
Counter Flashings x 6"-9" girth @ 18' above ground (ditto)				7	70	LF
Wdw Head Flashings less than 3" wide @ up to 18' above ground (ditto)				50	50	LF
2 COATS CEMENT PAINT ON ROUGH STUCCO up to 18' above ground						
(Area Stucco)				2926		
(narrow widths)	2/ 18-0	x	0-3	9		
	5/ 18-0	x	0-6	45		
				2980 (÷9)	330	sy

NOTE: ALL PAINTING WORK can be more effectively
measured linearly or by enumeration of items
in the same manner as such work as Stucco
Plaster.

Masonry (Concrete Blockwork)

As explained before, the MM-CIQS follows a common trade practice by stating that unit masonry shall be measured in masonry units: bricks by the thousand and concrete block simply enumerated. Mortar is to be measured separately by volume, and masonry reinforcement is to be measured linearly. But it is questionable whether this is the best method, and the simpler and more descriptive method of measuring masonry as super and run items is used in this example. Nevertheless, if measurement by enumeration is required or preferred, it is a simple step to convert the quantities of super and run items of masonry to numbers of masonry units. A block of nominal 8 in. × 16 in. face dims, including ⅜-in. joints, is ⁸⁄₉ of a square foot. So to convert the area of block walls to number of blocks, add 12½ percent to the number of SF in the wall area, and the result is the equivalent number of 8 in. × 16 in. blocks.

The descriptions of items must be sufficiently detailed to permit accurate pricing; and insofar as the divisions of masonry required by the MM-CIQS are concerned, it is suggested that all masonry work should be identified by general location as well as by type and function. Thus, work in the small wall panels is separated from the warehouse walls, and the 4-in. blockwork at the roof level is so described.

Measuring masonry walls as super items is simplified if features of the walls such as bond beams and lintels (filled and reinforced) are measured as *extra-over items*, as in the example. Alternatively, and especially if the masonry units are to be enumerated from the super and run quantities, such features as require special masonry units can be measured as regular run items (instead of extra-over items), with appropriate deductions from the super item of masonry wall.

If blockwork dims are *not* multiples of the dims of the block units, the estimator should allow for the costs of cutting bocks by measuring run items of "straight cutting and waste." Alternatively, he should enumerate and describe cut blocks. In exposed fair work,[G] the cutting may have to be done with an electric masonry saw, which is expensive, since one cut block costs about as much as two uncut blocks. Where block partitions are built, it is a common practice to conceal electrical conduits and boxes and plumbing pipes within the hollow blocks, and this practice may require a large amount of cutting. It is practically impossible to measure this cutting, and yet it may amount to a significant portion of the total labor costs of the masonry work and cannot be ignored by an estimator. In such cases, it is important that the estimator separately measure and properly describe the masonry work in which this cutting occurs, so that through cost accounting he can obtain cost data for different classes of masonry in different types of buildings. For example, the amount of cutting required for concrete block partitions (with concealed services) would be different in office buildings, schools, and hospitals; and there would probably be a difference between the cutting required in elementary schools and that required in high schools containing laboratories and workshops. However, the amount of cutting in the exterior walls of a warehouse would be insignificant, particularly if modular dims are used. Other job facts and conditions (besides concealed services) may significantly affect the costs of masonry work; for example, a building's size and shape. Consequently, cost data of masonry should always include references to such facts and conditions.

Metals: Structural Steelwork

Measurement in this example is by weight obtained from the measured super and run items and from published unit weights. Alternatively, each piece could be enumerated and described in detail in terms of category, size, and weight. The MM-CIQS includes both of these methods of measurement; and although the latter is preferable for more accurate estimating, the weight method is more common. It is much improved by stating the number of pieces in the total weight of each category of structural metal measured.

The steelwork dwgs, which are part of the bidding documents for a building with a structural steel frame, do not usually show steel columns (and other structural steel components) to the same large scale as they are shown in the Warehouse Drawings, because these dwgs were prepared for the fabricator.[10] Such large-scale dwgs are usually made by the contractor (or his subcontractor) as shop dwgs for fabrication and erection only after a contract has been awarded.

An estimator usually has to measure structural steelwork for a steel framed building from a steel framing plan in which the beams are represented by single lines and the columns by appropriate symbols. Connection details if any may be shown to a larger scale. Hence, the MM-CIQS calls for beams and purlins to be "measured from center to center line of columns," and columns to be "measured from top of base plate to elevation at 'top of steel.'" In this example it is possible to measure the columns to exact lengths because of the large-scale dwgs provided.

---

[10] The steelwork fabricator and the general contractor (who also made the design drawings) were one and the same.

PRACTICAL
Form 516 MFD IN U S A

PROJECT **WAREHOUSE**		ESTIMATOR **KC**		ESTIMATE NO. **W-1**	
LOCATION		EXTENSIONS **KC**		SHEET NO. **1 of 3**	
ARCHITECT ENGINEER		CHECKED		DATE **1987**	

CLASSIFICATION **MASONRY (CONCRETE BLOCKWORK)**

DESCRIPTION	NO.	DIMENSIONS			ESTIMATED QUANTITY	UNIT

HOLLOW LOADBEARING STANDARD WEIGHT CONC BLKWK
OF MODULAR UNITS REINFC'D EVERY 3RD COURSE & WITH
3/8" WIDE MORTAR JOINTS AS SPECS (p —)

8" Extr W'house Walls (allow 2½% Waste)

2/= 100-0 = 98-0 (W)
      -2-0
33/8" = 22-0
(22-0 - 18-0) = 4-0 (ends)

	1/ 98-0	×	22-0	2156
	2/ 1-0	×	4-0	8
				2164

DDT (door opening) 1/ 3-4 × 7-4   − 24 DDT
                                        2140

(Could be measured linearly (x 22ft high)   (x 9/8)

2140 SF
(2410 BLK)

8" Extr Office Walls in Small panels (x10'0" high) (allow 5% Waste)

ELVTN 109-8 = 10-0 (W)
      -99-8

	2/ 4-0	(×	10-0)	8
(W)	1/ 7-4		"	7
(E)	1/ 22-8		"	23
(SE)	1/ 6-8		"	7
				45 LF

(Each panel could be enumerated and
described separately.)   X 10-0 high
                                              450

DDT (door opening) 1/ 3-4 × 7-4   − 24 DDT
                                        426

(x 9/8)

426 SF
(480 BLK)

12" Extr W'house Walls (allow 2½% Waste)

ELVTN 117-8 = 18-0 (N/S)
      -99-8
27/8" = 18-0   (E)
(22-0 - 18-0) = 4-0 (ends)

	2/ 200-0	×	18-0	7200
	1/ 98-0	×	22-0	2156
	2/ 1-0	×	4-0	8
				9364

(Could be two linear items and one enumerated.)

DDT (openings)   DDT
ELVTN 114-0
      -99-8
(opening) 14-4
(Lintel) +1-8 = 16-0

	2/ 16-0	×	16-0	512
	2/ 3-4	×	7-4	49
	1/ 4-0	×	7-4	29
				−590
				8774

(x 9/8)

8774 SF
(9870 BLK)

PRACTICAL
Form 516 MFD IN U.S.A.

PROJECT **WAREHOUSE**   ESTIMATOR **KC**   ESTIMATE NO. **W-1**

LOCATION   EXTENSIONS **KC**   SHEET NO. **2 of 3**

ARCHITECT ENGINEER   CHECKED   DATE **1987**

CLASSIFICATION **MASONRY (CONCRETE BLOCKWORK)**

DESCRIPTION	NO.	DIMENSIONS						ESTIMATED QUANTITY	UNIT
HOLLOW L/BEARING CONC BLKWK (CONT)									
4" Extr W'house Walls at eaves (allow 2½% Waste)									
(on 8"& 12" blk) (E/w)	2/100-0 × 1-4		267 (x 9/8)					267 SF (300 BLK)	
Extra Over for 12"/8" Corner Blks (allow 2½% Waste)									
	2/22-0		44 (x 3/2)					* 44 LF (66 BLK)	
Extra Over for Lab & Mat in Bond Beams (x 8" high) in Blk Walls incl 2-#6 Rebars & conc filling all as specs (p—) (allow 2½% Waste)									
8" Bond Beams	1/100-0		100						
(total office walls)	1/45-0		45						
(over openings)	2/6-0		12						
			157 (x 3/4)					* 157 LF (118 BLK)	
Closed Exposed Ends	1/2		2						
	6/1		6					8 NO	
12" Bond Beams	2/200-0		400						
	1/100-0		100						
(over openings)	2/6-0		12						
"	1/6-8		7						
4/20-0 = 80-0 (next -5-0 (office)	1/75-0		75						
75-0			594 (x 3/4)					* 594 LF (446 BLK)	
Closed Exposed Ends	1·3/2		6					6 NO	
Extra Over for Lab & Mat in Filling Single Isolated 12" Blks Solid wi Conc as Bearing under Joist Ends incl exp metal lath under as specs (p—)									
	26/1							26 NO	

*When ordering, deduct quantities of Special Blks from Standard Blks.

QUANTITY SHEET

PROJECT **WAREHOUSE**	ESTIMATOR **KC**	ESTIMATE NO. **W-1**
LOCATION	EXTENSIONS **KC**	SHEET NO. **3 of 3**
ARCHITECT ENGINEER	CHECKED	DATE **1987**

CLASSIFICATION **MASONRY (CONCRETE BLOCKWORK)**

DESCRIPTION	NO.	DIMENSIONS		ESTIMATED QUANTITY	UNIT
HOLLOW L/BEARING CONC BLKWK (CONT)					
Extra Over for Lap & Mat in Filling w/ Conc & 1-#4 Rebar Vertically in Single Cavity of Conc Blks at Jambs & at Free Ends of Walls, as specs (p-)					
(jambs)	5/2/7-4		73		
"	2/2/14-4		57		
(ends)	6/10-0		60		
			190	190	LF
Extra Over for Lap & Mat in Forming Control Joints incl cutting blks up to steel cols & Sealant, as specs (p-) & as detail (one joint measured at a steel column)					
(w'house 2/3) 4/9/18-0			324	324	LF
8"x16" Blk Piers incl Filling w/ Conc & 2-#5 Rebars, as specs					
(office) (attached to (N) 8" panel walls)	2•10/10-0		120 (x 3/2)	120 (180	LF BLK)
8"x24" Blk Pilasters (attached to 8" Blk Wall) incl Filling w/ Conc & 2-#5 Rebars, as specs (p-)					
(w'house) (W)	7/22-0		154 (x 3/2)	154 (231	LF BLK)
[NB: Cast in place Conc Lintels to be meas'd in Div. 3 - Concrete]					

QUANTITY SHEET

PROJECT **WAREHOUSE**	ESTIMATOR **KC** ESTIMATE NO. **W-1**
LOCATION	EXTENSIONS **KC** SHEET NO. **1 of 4**
ARCHITECT ENGINEER	CHECKED DATE **1987**

CLASSIFICATION **METALS: STRUCTURAL STEELWORK**

DESCRIPTION	NO.	DIMENSIONS							ESTIMATED QUANTITY	UNIT
ASTM-A36 STRUCTURAL STEEL										
FABRICATED SHOP PAINTED & ERECTED AS SPECS (p-)										
Column Bases 3/4" thick Plate										
(MK AI)	9/	0-10	×	0-10	900	SIn.				
(MK BI,CI,DI)	3/	0-7	×	0-8½	179					
(MK EI,FI)	5/	0-8	×	0-8	320					
(MK GI,HI)	2/	0-4	×	0-10	80					
(MK JI)	18/	0-10½	×	0-8	1512					
(TOTAL IN 37 NO B.PLATES)					2991	SIn. ×0.2833 LB ×3/4" =			635	LB
Columns 8WF×31 LB										
(AI)	9/	20-2½			182					
(JI)	18/	20-8½			373					
(= 27 NO)					555	×31 LB		=	17,205	LB
Columns 6WF×25 LB										
(BI,CI)	2/	16-2½			33					
(DI)	1/	16-4⅛			16					
(=3 NO)					49	×25 LB		=	1225	LB
Columns, Pipe										
3½"∅ (4 OD) (EI,FI)	2·3/	10-2½			51	×10 LB	=	510		
3"∅ (3½ OD) (GI,HI)	1·1/	10-2½			21	×8.68 LB	=	183	695	LB
(= 7 NO)										
(TOTAL: 37 NO COLS)										
Beam Seats, 3/4" thick Plate, in Connections to Glulam Beams										
as details (welding m/s)										
(AI)	9/	0-9¼	×	1-6	1499	SIn.				
(BI,DI)	2/	0-5⅜	×	0-10½	113					
(CI)	1/	0-5⅜	×	1-3	81					
(EI)	3/	0-3½	×	0-8½	89					
(FI)	2/	0-5¼	×	0-8½	89					
(GI)	1/	0-3½	×	0-6	21					
(HI)	1/	0-5¼	×	0-6	32					
(JI)	18/	0-9¼	×	0-9	1499					
(TOTAL to 37 NO Cols)					3423	SIn. ×0.2833 LB ×3/4" =			730	LB

PRACTICAL "STANDARDIZED" FORMS FOR CONTRACTORS
Form 516 MFD IN U.S.A.

QUANTITY SHEET

PROJECT WAREHOUSE — ESTIMATOR KC — ESTIMATE NO. W-1

LOCATION — EXTENSIONS KC — SHEET NO. 2 of 4 R

ARCHITECT ENGINEER — CHECKED — DATE 1987

CLASSIFICATION METALS: STRUCTURAL STEELWORK

DESCRIPTION	NO.	DIMENSIONS				ESTIMATED QUANTITY	UNIT
ASTM-A36 STRUCTURAL STEEL (CONT)							
Sides to Beam Seats, 1/4" thick Plate, in Connections to Glulam Beams as details (welding m/s)							
(A1)	9/2/	1-6	x 1-0	27-0 SF			
(B1, D1)	2/2/	0-10½	x 1-6	5-3			
(C1)	1/2/	1-3	x 0-6	1-3			
(E1, F1)	2·3/2/	0-8½	x 0-6	3-6			
(G1, H1)	1·1/2/	0-6	x 0-6	1-0			
(J1)	18/2/	0-9	x 1-0	27-0			
(TOTAL IN 37/2 = 74 No. SIDES)				65-0 SF x 144 x 0.2833 LB x 1/4" =		665	LB
Beam Connections, 1" Plate, (for Glulam to G. Beams) ditto (ditto)							
	10/2/	0-7	x 0-9¼	1295 S In.	x 0.2833 LB x 1" =	370	LB
Ditto 1/4" Plate (ditto) ditto (ditto)							
	10/2/	0-7	x 2-5¼	4095 S In.	x 0.2833 LB x 1/4" =	290	LB
1/4" Shop Fillet Welds (intermittent) btwn Bases & Cols, avg 4" long.							
(A1)	9/4/	0-3	(36 No)	108 L In.			
(B1, C1, D1)	3/4/	0-3	(12)	36			
2 +3 = 5 (Circ E1, F1)	5/3⅞/	0-4	(5)	63			
1 +1 = 2 (Circ G1, H1)	2/3⅞/	0-3½	(2)	22			
(J1)	18/4/	0-4	(72)	288			
(TOTAL TO 37 No BASES)			(127 No)	517 L In.		(127 No) = 517 L In. (43 LF)	
1/4" Ditto (ditto) btwn Cols & Beam Seats, avg 7½" long.							
(A1)	9/2/	0-7¼	(18 No)	131 L In.			
(B1, C1, D1)	3/2/	0-5¼	(6)	32			
(Circ E1, F1)	5/3⅞/	0-4	(5)	63			
(Circ G1, H1)	2/3⅞/	0-3½	(2)	22			
(J1)	18/2/	0-7¼	(36)	261			
(TOTAL TO 37 No SEATS)			(67 No)	509 L In.		(67 No) = 509 L In. (42½ LF)	
1/4" Ditto (continuous) to Beam Connection Plates, 7" long							
	10/2·2/	0-7	(40 No)	280 L In.		(40 No) = 280 L In. (23½ LF)	

FRANK R. WALKER CO., PUBLISHERS, CHICAGO

QUANTITY SHEET

PROJECT	WAREHOUSE	ESTIMATOR KC	ESTIMATE NO. W-1
LOCATION		EXTENSIONS KC	SHEET NO. 3 of 4 R
ARCHITECT ENGINEER		CHECKED	DATE 1987

CLASSIFICATION METALS : STRUCTURAL STEELWORK

DESCRIPTION	NO.	DIMENSIONS		ESTIMATED QUANTITY	UNIT

3/16" Shop Fillet Welds (continuous) to Beam Connection Plates

(A)	9/2/1-6	(18 No)	27-0 LF		
(B1,D1)	2/2/0-10½	(4)	3-6		
(C1)	1/2/1-3	(2)	2-6		
(E1,F1)	5/2/0-8½	(10)	7-0		
(G1,H1)	2/2/0-6	(4)	2-0		
(J1)	18/2/0-9	(36)	27-0		
(TOTAL IN 37 No CONNCTNS)		(74 No)	69-0 LF	(74 No)= 69 LF	
				(828 L In.)	

LABORS TO ASTM-A36 STRUCTURAL STEEL

Machine Ends Cols True & Square :-

8WF (637 LB/AVG)	27/2		54	54 No	
6WF (408 LB/AVG)	3/2		6	6 No	
3½ Ø (102 LB/AVG)	5/2		10	10 No	
3 Ø (92 LB/AVG)	2/2		4	4 No	
(TOTAL 37/2	= TOTAL = 74 No)				

Drill Bolt Holes in Steel Plate :-

1Ø in ¾" Bases	18·3·9/2		60	60 No	
13/16"Ø in ¾" Bases	2·3/4		20		
	2/2		4		
(TOTAL IN 37 No BASES)			24	24 No	

13/16"Ø in ¼" Connectn Sides

(9+3+5)=17	17/2/2		68		
(2+18)=20	20/1/2		40		
(TOTAL IN 37 No CONNCTNS)			108	108 No	

¾"Ø in ¼" Connectn Sides

	10/2/2		40	40 No	
(TOTAL IN 10 No CONNCTNS)					

PRACTICAL
Form 516 MFD IN U S A

QUANTITY SHEET

PROJECT	**WAREHOUSE**	ESTIMATOR	KC	ESTIMATE NO. **W-1**
LOCATION		EXTENSIONS	KC	SHEET NO. **4 of 4** R
ARCHITECT ENGINEER		CHECKED		DATE **1987**

CLASSIFICATION **METALS: STRUCTURAL STEELWORK**

DESCRIPTION	NO.	DIMENSIONS		ESTIMATED QUANTITY	UNIT
ASTM-A325 BOLTS FOR STEELWORK, AS SPECS (p—)					
Anchor Bolts (to be set into conc.) w/ Nuts					
3/4"φ x 12" long	30/2		60		60 NO
5/8"φ x 15" long	5/4		20		
(30+5+2)=37	2/2		4		24 No
(TOTAL IN 84 NO HOLES)				(TOTAL 84 No)	
Connection Bolts (for Glulam Beams) w/ Heads, Nuts, & Washers					
5/8"φ x 12" long	9/2		18		
	18/1		18		36 No
5/8"φ x 8" long	5/2		10		
	1/1		1		11 No
5/8"φ x 6" long	3/2		6		
(9+18+5+1+3+1)=37	1/1		1		7 No
(TOTAL IN 108 NO HOLES)				(TOTAL 54 NO)	
1/2"φ x 12" long	10/2		20		20 No
(TOTAL IN 40 NO. HOLES)					

```
            STEEL WEIGHT SUMMARY
  sht.#1      3/4" Bases =  635 LB
              8 WF Col = 17,205
              6 WF Col = 1225
              Pipe Col =  695
     Connctn  Seats =    730
  sht.#2  "   Sides =    665
   (370+290)= "  (ditto) =  660
 (1306 LF x 0.2 LB)  1/4" Welds = 22
   12
 (64 x 0.15 LB)  3/16" Welds = 1
   12
     158 NO  Bolts = say 162
          TOTAL 22,000 LB = 11 TONS
```

NOTE: For computer input and estimating, input descriptions and lengths of STEELWORK members; computer system to calculate all weights and areas for painting steel.

SHOP-PAINTING STRUCTURAL STEEL, AS SPECS (p—)				11 TONS
ERECTING STRUCTURAL STEEL, AS DWGS & SPECS (p—)				11 TONS

Welds, like steel components, may be measured by weight, or by length, stating the unit weight as in the example. The number of intermittent welds is stated because this indicates their average length, which affects their cost. Labor for machining ends and drilling holes is described and enumerated, as are the anchor bolts and the connection bolts. The fully detailed measurement in the example of welds is included to instruct the student, not necessarily to represent common practice in industry.

Erecting the fabricated components is part of the work; and, as stated in the MM-CIQS, each measured item is held to include "conveyance and delivery, unloading, hoisting, all labor setting, fitting and fixing in position . . ." in its description. Many estimators, however, choose to price the erection of the steel as one separate and inclusive item based on the total weight, the number of pieces, and the time required for an erection crew and equipment. This is why the estimator should indicate the "number of pieces" when measuring steelwork by weight, because weight alone is not sufficient to accurately estimate erection time and costs. And this is why the better method of measuring structural steel is to enumerate and fully describe each piece.

Rough Carpentry: Decking and Beams

Wood decks made up of tongued-and-grooved planks can be measured as super items, or a deck area and thickness can be converted to BF. This conversion requires an allowance to be made for (1) the t & g joints, and (2) for the loss in width caused by the lumber manufacturer's dressing the planks. Board-foot measure is always based on nominal dims, and a t & g plank with a nominal width of 6 in. may have an actual overall-width of 5⅜ in. and, with a tongue ⅜ in. wide, an effective width of 5 in. Therefore, an allowance of 20 percent must be made for this loss in width from the nominal dim. (A plank 8 in. wide would require an allowance of about 15 percent.) A small allowance for waste caused by end cutting and loss should be made in the unit price. If lumber items are measured up to the nearest even dim, they can be described as "*including waste*."

Glued-laminated wood members are best measured by enumerating and fully describing them, the same as steel members. But the manufacturer of glulam products has to measure the lumber content as a basis for pricing, and this is done by calculating the number of BF from the number and nominal dims of the individual laminations (as explained in Chapter 8), or by calculating the beam's volume and weight and pricing

it by means of a unit cost related to the unit of measurement. Although from the contractor's viewpoint the easiest and best way to measure glulam products is by enumeration and description, that method does not lead to a full interpretation of costs. In this example the glulam beams are measured in LF, and the lumber content is calculated in BF. An understanding of prices and costs always requires their resolution into unit prices so that comparisons can be made.

Rough hardware for carpentry work is measured by description and enumeration except for common hardware such as nails and spikes, which can be allowed for in the unit prices.

Special labor required on carpentry items (such as "fire cut ends of joists") are usually described and enumerated as separate items so that the carpentry items themselves (the joists) can be priced as *basic items*.[G] If a special kind of labor comprises a major part of a carpentry item's costs (such as with the "*2 × 12 roof joists shaped to curve at top edge*"), the two may be combined into one particular item for measuring and pricing; because the item is so unusual as to make it unlike any basic item, leaving no advantage to be gained by separating the labor item.

Descriptions of carpentry items of work must always include the grade of material and the method of fixing if other than the usual nailing. As explained before, if length of lumber is a cause of additional material costs (and possibly additional labor costs of handling long lengths), these lengths should be measured separately and so described.

WAREHOUSE EXERCISES

All the work not measured in the examples can be measured in exercises; and as a major estimating exercise the entire project might be measured and priced at current, local unit prices and the total estimated costs compared with local costs of constructing similar warehouses. To provide more exercises and, at the same time, to develop a better understanding of costs, simple drawings of alternative methods of constructing the exterior walls, structural frame, and roof decks might be made, and the work measured and priced therefrom. A clearer understanding of the effects of differences in building dimensions on construction costs can be obtained if change orders[G] are devised and written out, and if the costs of the ordered changes are estimated. For example, it could be vividly demonstrated in this way that a significant change in the height (and volume) of the warehouse does not make a proportionately significant change in total costs of the work.

Although the examples in this chapter involve *measurement of work*, both the examples and the exercises will prove to be more valuable to a student if they are priced. *Pricing quantities of work* leads to a fuller understanding of measurement, even if the unit prices are hypothetical (which they must be), because the purpose of measurement is pricing, and it is pricing that determines the requirements for measuring construction work. *If you want to know how to measure any item of work, find out how it will be priced.*

Most of the examples of measuring work in this chapter have been used many times in estimating classes at the British Columbia Institute of Technology and at Douglas College (more recently), and the earlier examples in this chapter have been used numerous times. Each time a group of students has done one of these examples, some new discovery has been made. Sometimes, errors have been discovered, and even these have given rise to useful discussions that have helped students to learn. Sometimes, new points of view have been expressed by students, indicating that some widely accepted methods of measurement may need changing.

CONCLUSION

Estimating is not a pure science, for subjective judgments are part of it, and it is not entirely a matter of deducing from self-evident truths. And whereas this is particularly true of the pricing part of estimating, it is also true of measurement to a lesser extent. Measurements of quantities are made primarily so that the work measured can be priced; and as an estimator views and understands the pricing of work, so will he measure it. Therefore, there is often room for more than one way of measuring any item of work and, therefore, there will always be different opinions about measurement methods.

However, it is a widely held opinion among quantity surveyors that better results are obtainable if it is *work* that is measured (rather than simply measuring the materials that form a part of it) and if the work is measured *net in place*, and as required by the construction contract, with calculated allowances for such things as waste, laps, swell and shrinkage made in the unit prices that are calculated for the items of work.

Perhaps one of the most illustrative and illuminating items of work that can be studied in its economics and in its measurement and pricing is *formwork for cast-in-place concrete*, and also the reinforced concrete itself. This is why so many examples are based on this kind of work.

Reinforced concrete requires and contains within the measurement and pricing of its three primary parts—formwork, reinforcing steel, and concrete—most of the techniques and principles of all construction estimating. Therefore, it is an ideal subject for most students of estimating, and the measurement and pricing of formwork vividly illustrates that it is work that is measured, not materials alone, and that the purpose of measurement is primarily pricing.

Measuring work is often painful; sometimes tedious at the start, as many students complain. It is painful because it demands a high level of sustained concentration and thought, and nothing is more arduous. But like running and climbing and other activities that cause discomfort when first begun, measurement becomes tolerable with practice, and for some even a source of pleasure and satisfaction. An estimator who has measured the work in a project has built the project within his own head, wall by wall, and floor by floor. He probably knows more about the construction of the project and its details than the designer, and he is probably more aware of any errors and omissions in the drawings and specifications.

Having learned and applied the precepts and techniques of measurement, there is only one thing left to do—practice. Practice is the only way to overcome the initial pain and it is the only way to become proficient in measuring construction work.

Finally, at the end of this chapter on measurement we should have a reasonable comprehension of traditional measurement practices; and let it be noted that this writer has in this chapter consistently pressed a singular point of view about measurement: that the best mode of measurement is the simplest and the most direct. That is to say: When an item is initially (directly and instinctively) measured in a particular unit (by enumeration, linearly, or by area), the item's quantity should be expressed in that same unit and not converted to another. For example, formwork to the side of a continuous concrete footing is first measured in linear feet, or in meters. Leave it as a linear item; do not multiply its length by the height to obtain an area. Instead, include the height in the item's description.

There is a hierarchy of units of measurement best expressed in our own estimating terms:

Numbers ..... with 3 dimensions in the description
Runs .... with 2 dimensions in the description
Supers .... with 1 dimension in the description
Cubes .... with 0 dimensions in the description

The preferred and most effective unit of measurement

PRACTICAL
Form 516 MFD IN U.S.A.

PROJECT **WAREHOUSE**			ESTIMATOR KC	ESTIMATE NO. **W-1**	
LOCATION			EXTENSIONS KC	SHEET NO. **1 of 6**	
ARCHITECT ENGINEER			CHECKED	DATE **1987**	

CLASSIFICATION **ROUGH CARPENTRY: DECKING & BEAMS**

DESCRIPTION	NO.	DIMENSIONS			ESTIMATED QUANTITY	UNIT

DOUGLAS FIR "CONSTRUCTION" GRADE UNLESS OTHERWISE INDICATED

2" thick T&G Decking "STANDARD" grade laid in a "controlled random pattern" on wood joists @ 4'0" o/c (m/s) in Flat Roof Deck as specs (p-) (allow 3% Waste)

200-0   20-0
+20-0   × 11 Bays   ¹/220-0 × 100-0 22000 SF
220-0 ✓ 220-0 ✓   ×2 BF
                                          44000
(allow for T&G & Dressing) +8800 (+20%)
                                          52,800

53000 BF
(22,000 SF)

2×6 T&G

3×14 Roof Joists in 20' lengths (incl Waste)

100-0 = 25   10 Bays
4'   +1   +1 canopy   26/11/20-0   5720 ×3½ BF
      26   20000 BF
      11 N⁰   (5720 LF)

Fire Cut Ends 3×14 Joists   26/1   26   26 N⁰

3×6 Runners (Ledgers) in 20' lengths bolted to Glulam Beams @ 4'0' o/c (bolts m/s) (incl Waste)

                        9/2/100-0   1800
(@ canopy)   1/1/100-0   100
                                         1900 ×1½ BF
                                                      3000 BF
                                                      (1900 LF)

3×4 Joist Seats (Plates) in 20' lengths bolted to Conc Blk Bond Beam @ 4'0" o/c (bolts m/s) (incl Waste)

            (W)   ¹/100-0   100 × 1 BF
                                              100 BF
                                              (100 LF)

3×6 Ditto (incl Waste)

            (E)   ¹/100-0   100 ×1⅓ BF
                                              150 BF
                                              (100 LF)

QUANTITY SHEET

PROJECT	WAREHOUSE			ESTIMATOR	KC		ESTIMATE NO.	W-1
LOCATION				EXTENSIONS	KC		SHEET NO.	2 of 6
ARCHITECT ENGINEER				CHECKED			DATE	1987

CLASSIFICATION ROUGH CARPENTRY: DECKING & BEAMS

DESCRIPTION	NO.	DIMENSIONS							ESTIMATED QUANTITY	UNIT

SUPPLY ONLY D. Fir Glulam Beams "Industrial" grade (for appearance) & "Interior" grade (for service) unless otherwise indicated (including 20% Waste in BF quantities for manufacturing)

9"x27⅝" Beams 50-0-(0-3+9-4)=40-5	9/	40-5			364	×34.0 BF/LF			12,376	BF
9"x29¼" Beams (50-0-0-3)+9-4 = 59-1	9/	59-1			532	×36.0 BF/LF			19,152	BF
5¼"x27⅝" Exterior grade Beam (@ canopy)	1/	40-5			41	×20.4 BF/LF			837	BF
5¼"x29¼" Ditto (@ canopy)	1/	59-1			59	×21.6 BF/LF			1275	BF

ERECT ONLY Glulam Beams onto steel columns (generally about 20'0" high above floor) (connections & bolts m/s)

9"x27⅝" Beams	9/	40-5			364	× 52 LB/LF *		9 NO= 18,928	LB
9"x29¼" Beams	9/	59-1			532	× 55 LB/LF		9 NO= 29,260	LB
5¼"x27⅝" Beam	1/	40-5			41	× 30 LB/LF		1 NO= 1230	LB
5¼"x29¼" Beam	1/	59-1			59	× 32 LB/LF		1 NO= 1888	LB

* At 30 LB/CF

[NB: Glulam Beams to Office Roof measured later.]

NOTE: T&G DECKING (previous page) can also be measured linearly, and for computerized estimating the board measurement is not needed with all lumber items measured by length. Glued-laminated beams, measured like steelwork.

QUANTITY SHEET

PROJECT	WAREHOUSE		ESTIMATOR	KC	ESTIMATE NO.	W-1
LOCATION			EXTENSIONS	KC	SHEET NO.	3 of 6
ARCHITECT ENGINEER			CHECKED		DATE	1987

CLASSIFICATION: ROUGH CARPENTRY: DECKING & BEAMS

DESCRIPTION	NO.	DIMENSIONS	ESTIMATED QUANTITY	UNIT
GALV STEEL ROUGH HARDWARE (all Bolts incl Nuts & Washers)				
3/4"φ x 18" Bolts wi two 2 5/8"φ Split Rings each & Drill 9" Glulam Beam & 2/3" Runners				
(3x6 Runners to Beam)	9/24	216	216	No
3/4"φ x 10" Bolts wi one 2 5/8"φ Split Ring each & Drill 5 1/4" Glulam Beam & 1/3" Runner				
(@ canopy)	1/24	24	24	No
3"x3"x1/4" Angle Clips each 3/nailed to wood joists & to beams				
(@ outside joists)	9/2/2	36		
(ditto, @ Canopy)	1/2/1	2	38	No
1/2"x3/16" Flat (twisted) Joist Ties x 18" long each 3/nailed to joist & set into Conc Blkwk				
(@ ends of joists	26/2	52		
on Conc Blkwk)	26/1	26	78	No
12" Lengths Plumber's Strap each end 3/nailed to joists and beams as Ties				
(@ Canopy)	24/1	24	24	No
(NB: Not @ outside joists wi angle clips)				
24" Lengths Ditto each end 3/nailed to ends of pairs of joists as Ties ✓				
(@ W'house roof joists)	24/9	216	216	No
(NB: Not @ outside joists wi angle clips)				
3/4"φ x 8" Bolts & Drill 3" Joist Seats (Plates) & set into Conc Filling in Bond Beams				
	2/26	52	52	No
[NB: Bolts for Glulam to Steel Connections Taken with Structural Steelwork.]				

QUANTITY SHEET

PROJECT	WAREHOUSE		ESTIMATOR	KC	ESTIMATE NO.	W-1
LOCATION			EXTENSIONS	KC	SHEET NO.	4 of 6
ARCHITECT ENGINEER			CHECKED		DATE	1987

CLASSIFICATION ROUGH CARPENTRY: DECKING & BEAMS — OFFICE

DESCRIPTION	NO.	DIMENSIONS							ESTIMATED QUANTITY	UNIT
DOUGLAS FIR "CONSTRUCTION" GRADE										
2x12 Roof Joists in 14' lengths (incl Waste)										
8'-4 = 67 1'-4 +1 +4(extra)=72	72/14-0			1008	× 2 BF				2000 BF (1000 LF)	
2x12 Ditto in 18' lengths (incl Waste)										
(header)	72/18-0 1/90-0			1296 90 1386	× 2 BF				2800 BF (1400 LF)	
2x12 Ditto in 10' lengths cut to 8'6" lengths & shaped w. Circ Top Edge (to large radius) as shown for vault-shaped office roof bays each notched one end for roof gutter & installed @ 90° across main roof joists, as detail.										
3'-4 -0-4 3'-0 3'-0 = 24 1'-4 +1 25	2/25								50 No	
2x12 (D Dressed) Headers in 16' lengths installed against last joists (incl Waste)										
	2/32-0			64	× 2 BF				130 BF (64 LF)	
2x2 Blockings installed on top edges of joists (incl Waste)										
	2/7/32-0			448	× ⅓ BF				450 LF (150 BF)	
3x8 Runners (Ledgers) in 18' lengths bolted to Conc Blk Bond Beam @ 4' o/c (bolts m/s) (incl Waste)										
(on W'house wall)	1/90-0			90	× 2 BF				90 LF (180 BF)	
4x4 Cant Strips in 16' lengths planted on roof sheathing next headers (incl Waste)	2/32-0			64	× ⅔ BF				64 LF (45 BF)	

QUANTITY SHEET

PROJECT	WAREHOUSE		ESTIMATOR	KC	ESTIMATE NO.	W-1
LOCATION			EXTENSIONS	KC	SHEET NO.	5 of 6
ARCHITECT ENGINEER			CHECKED		DATE	1987

CLASSIFICATION *ROUGH CARPENTRY: DECKING & BEAMS — OFFICE*

DESCRIPTION	NO.	DIMENSIONS			ESTIMATED QUANTITY	UNIT
½" thick D. Fir (Exterior) "Select" grade Sheathing Ply installed on joists in flat roof deck (allow 3% Waste)						
	1/89-4	×	31-4	2799	2800	SF
Extra Lab Nailing ½" Sheathing to Circ top Edges of roof joists						
	2/8-0	×	31-4	501	500	SF
½" Ply Gutter Lining (btm & side) × 8" total girth (use Waste above)						
	2/31-0			62	62	LF
SUPPLY ONLY D. Fir Glulam Beams "Industrial"/"Interior" grades a·b						
5"×16¼" Beam	1/20-0		20 ×12.0 BF/LF		240	BF
(20-8 − 0-8) = 20-0						
3¼"×16¼" Beams	2/28-0		56			
2/14-0 = 28-0	1/12-0		12			
			68 ×8.16 BF/LF		555	BF
89-4 68-0						
2/-1-4=88-0 −56-0						
−20-0 12-0						
68-0						
ERECT ONLY Glulam Beams onto steel columns (about 10'0" above floor) (connections & bolts m/s)						
5"×16¼" Beam	1/20-0		20 × 17 LB/LF	1 NO=	340	LB
3¼"×16¼" Beams	2/28-0		56 × 11 LB/LF	2 NO=	616	LB
3¼"×16¼" Beam	1/12-0		12 × 11 LB/LF	1 NO=	132	LB

NOTE: ROOF SHEATHING (plywood) can be measured linearly (× 4ft wide); The EXTRA LABOR NAILING item is better enumerated; and GLUED-LAMINATED BEAMS are measured best by enumeration; or, if many of same size, they can be measured linearly, stating weights.

QUANTITY SHEET

PROJECT	WAREHOUSE		ESTIMATOR	KC	ESTIMATE NO.	W-1
LOCATION			EXTENSIONS	KC	SHEET NO.	6 of 6
ARCHITECT ENGINEER			CHECKED		DATE	1987

CLASSIFICATION ROUGH CARPENTRY : DECKING & BEAMS — OFFICE

DESCRIPTION	NO.	DIMENSIONS			ESTIMATED QUANTITY	UNIT
GALV STEEL ROUGH HARDWARE, as before						
$\frac{3}{4}"\phi \times 12"$ Bolts & Drill 3" wood runner & side of Hollow Conc Blk Bond Beam & set into Conc Filling (m/s)						
$\begin{array}{l}90-0= 23 \\ 4-0 \ \ +1 \\ \underline{+5} \,(extra) = \underline{29}\end{array}$	29/1		29		29 NO	
24" Lengths Plumber's Strap each end 3/nailed to ends of pairs of joists as ties, as before						
	72/1				72 NO	
Sheet Metal Joist Hangers 2x12 size						
(68-4) =64	64/1				64 NO	
Ditto 4x12 size						
	4/1				4 NO	
[NB: Bolts for Glulam to Steel Connections taken with Structural Steelwork.]						

NOTES: In these estimating examples, descriptions and measurements are generally more detailed and precise than those in many estimates done in industry, because here are examples. Also, descriptions can be shorter when using a cost code and standard items.

The new principles of measurement proposed herein call for greater precision and more detail (and more measured items of work, because there is to be less grouping of items), but using computers should reduce the time and effort of estimators, not only in applying the new principles but also in basic measurement.

The above examples should be reviewed critically in the light of the new principles of measurement proposed, and items and their measurement methods revised accordingly.

for any item is that which requires the largest number of dimensions in the item's description, because obviously it is then more descriptive. You may say: If that is so, why do we not enumerate everything? And the response to that question is that eventually, probably we shall. But not until large databases are commonplace.

QUESTIONS AND TOPICS FOR DISCUSSION

1. In measuring *wood studs*, explain how the number of studs in, say, the framed exterior walls of a house should be measured, with particular reference to the requirements for extra studs for any purpose and reason.

2. Regarding *slab screeds*, (a) what is their purpose, (b) how are they installed, and (c) what is the best way to estimate the costs of slab screeds?

3. *Formwork* is generally measured by the "contact area" in square feet. Explain in detail why this is so, and why formwork is not measured as other work is generally measured. Explain also, by an example, why formwork is sometimes better measured as a linear item.

4. Explain precisely the differences between *light bending* and *heavy bending* of rebar. Which is the more expensive, and why?

5. Explain all the differences between "framed" and "unframed" *structural steelwork*, and why they should be distinguished in an estimate. Also, explain the primary considerations in pricing both these kinds of structural steelwork.

6. Why should carpentry *cross-bridging* be measured as a linear item, or enumerated in sets? Why not measure it in board feet in the same way most rough carpentry work is measured?

7. Explain fully the term *raking cutting and waste*, and explain how it can be measured and priced in an estimate and verified by cost accounting.

8. Discuss the proposition: Most errors in the measurement of *rebar* (apart from arithmetical errors) are *errors of omission*.

9. Compare the two methods of *measuring structural steelwork* described in Chapter 8 as applied to the structural steelwork in the Warehouse. Which is the better method in this case? Which is the better method generally?

10. Compose a *standard method of measurement* for one of the following sections of work: *Formwork for concrete*; *Rough carpentry*; *Structural steelwork*. Assume that in the future all estimating will be done with the aid of computers and that the estimating and cost accounting cycle (as described in Chapter 4) will be applicable.

11. Explain by figured examples how *waste* of gypsum wallboard may be dealt with in an estimate.

12. Discuss methods of measuring *brick chimney stacks* for cost estimating, indicating the advantages and disadvantages of each.

13. Explain how and why you would measure, for cost estimating purposes, the following items: (a) a sheet-lead flashing at the apex of a conical church steeple, and (b) an elaborately turned (by lathe) and decorated newel post of white oak, assuming suitably illustrative dimensions.

14. What is the best way to measure *trenches for foundations*, and why?

10

PRICING WORK: GENERAL

By *pricing work* we mean computing and applying *unit prices*[G] to measured quantities to arrive at an estimate of the probable costs of work. The different classifications of costs were examined in Chapter 3, and they are:[1]

1. *Material costs*
2. *Labor costs*
3. *Equipment costs*
4. *Job overhead costs*
5. *Operating overhead costs*
6. *Profit.*

This chapter, and the next, deals primarily with the first three classifications of costs and their computation by means of unit prices. The last two classifications—operating overhead costs and profit—are not computed by means of unit prices, and their assessment goes beyond practical estimating into the areas of accounting, business, bidding strategy, and management policy.

The first three classifications are called *direct costs*[G] because they are by definition always attributable to the items of work of a specific construction job.

The last two classifications likewise are called *indirect costs*[G] because by definition they cannot be directly attributed to a specific job, as explained later.

The remaining classification, *job overhead costs,*[G] by definition lies between the other two groups of costs, in that although these costs can be attributed to a specific job they cannot be attributed to specific items of work. Thus, they are among the direct costs of a construction job, but they cannot always be priced by unit prices because they do not always relate to specific items of work, but rather to the job as a whole.

Although we are primarily interested here in those direct costs that involve unit prices, a brief review of the indirect costs will be helpful in comprehending all construction costs and their places in estimates. (*Profit* is also included because it is a cost to the owner.) Following a look at some general aspects of costs in this chapter, the next chapter looks at some specific aspects and examples of direct costs.

PROFIT AND OVERHEAD COSTS

Profit is assessed in the light of risk and competition, the supply and demand for construction services, and the need for work. It is usually included in an estimate as a percentage of other costs to arrive at the total

---

[1] All are defined in the Glossary.

estimated cost of the work. It may be calculated as a percentage of the total of all other costs, or it may be based on a certain class of costs—usually labor costs—and the profit on materials may be looked for in discounts. The way in which costs are marked up to allow for profit really depends on the market, the company, and the work it does.

Operating overhead costs are the costs of being in business, whether construction work is being done or not. To include these costs in an estimate, a projection is made of future operating costs and the anticipated volume of work that will be done over, say, the next year. The calculated percentage of *operating costs* to *volume of work* is compared with similar percentages for previous years and, in this way, a percentage is established to be applied to the other, direct costs of work to allow for operating overhead costs.

Profit and operating overhead costs, (or indirect costs), often simply referred to as "*profit and overhead*," are usually the last costs to be included in an estimate because they are related to the total direct costs and to the anticipated total volume of work to be done in the foreseeable future.

Job overhead costs are different from *operating overhead costs* because they can be attributed to a specific job; but they cannot be attributed to any specific items of work of that job. Because these costs are so numerous and various, they are computed in a variety of different ways: by lump sum; by salaries, wages, and rental rates on a time basis; and, in some instances, by unit prices, all depending on the kind of job overhead item. These costs are usually priced before the profit and operating overhead costs are added, and after the measured work has been priced. Figure 10-1 shows the common classifications of costs and the general

order of pricing, ending with operating overhead costs and profit.

Before examining these classifications, it might be pointed out once again that, like all classifications, the common classifications of costs are somewhat arbitrary; they are not completely definitive, and not all costs can always be so precisely classified. Nevertheless, the classifications of costs in Fig. 10–1 are reasonably distinct; *except for job overhead costs* some of which might be classed as direct costs and others, at another time, as indirect costs, depending on the nature of the work and the contract and the organization of the construction company. But as the number of classifications are increased, the less useful the classifications become; so we use as few classifications as possible.

A *unit price*[G] has been defined as the costs of an item of work divided by the number of measured units of that item. As such, it is an *average price* that will vary depending on the number of units and any number of other conditions. Nevertheless, it is a convenient means whereby we can calculate and compare and analyze and price the costs of work.

It is necessary in defining a unit price to be specific about its subject; whether it is for material costs, labor costs, plant and equipment costs, overheads and profit, or for any combination of these. It is usually better to separate the unit prices and costs for each of these categories, but most standard estimating forms have separate columns for material costs and labor costs only. On the other hand, in unit-price contracts,[G] the unit prices are usually combined to include all the direct costs, and sometimes they include all direct and indirect costs, thus providing one comprehensive unit price for each item of work.

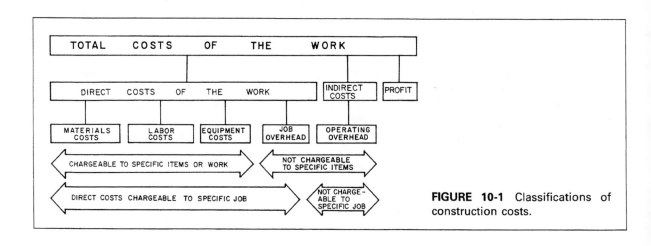

FIGURE 10-1 Classifications of construction costs.

PRICING PLANT AND EQUIPMENT

Plant and equipment costs are dealt with in several ways. In some estimates they are entered against the appropriate items of work and, as often there is not a separate column on an estimate sheet for equipment, they are sometimes entered in the "material costs" column. Primarily, the estimator wants the *total labor costs* separate and distinct; therefore, no other costs can be included with them. The "materials" column is the only other place to enter equipment costs. Alternatively, an estimate form with a separate, third column for equipment costs can be used if they are a major part of the work and if all types of costs are required to be shown separately.

In some estimates, plant and equipment costs are estimated separately at the end of the estimate, just before the final summary. One reason for this is that some plant and equipment is on a site for a long time and is used for many items of work. An overhead crane, for example, might be on site almost from job start to finish, or at least until the building structure is completed, and it might be used for lifting and placing concrete, steelwork, timbers, trusses, pieces of form-work, and loads of other materials. In such cases, the estimator may estimate the period of time the crane is needed on site and compute the costs on a monthly rental basis; plus transportation, setup, and removal costs. Many items, such as excavating equipment, table saws, and other plant, tools, and equipment, which have a number of different uses, are estimated in this way with no direct reference to specific items of work. On the other hand, the costs of specialized equipment, such as that used in pumping concrete, can and should be attributed to one or several specific items and priced together with material costs and labor costs for those specific items and expressed as a separate unit price, if required.

In some estimates, particularly in estimates for projects not requiring a large amount of heavy and expensive equipment, such as a shopping center project with no high buildings, estimators may allow for plant and equipment costs as a percentage of total costs, or as a percentage of labor costs. The assumption is that the plant and equipment costs are about the same proportion of total costs in similar jobs, and cost accounts may show that this proportion is fairly constant. *Small tools*[G] are usually allowed for as a percentage of total labor costs in this way.

Estimating any costs by proportion requires an estimator who can make a proper use of cost data from a series of previous, similar jobs done under similar conditions, with cost accounts of those jobs

showing reasonably constant relationships among the different costs. This method of estimating is contrary to the precepts covered in Chapter 6. It is not recommended for estimates in which more accurate estimating methods can be used, or where they should be used because the equipment costs are a major part of the work; particularly if the estimate is for a bid for a stipulated sum contract.

Equipment costs have to be estimated in the same way as any other costs. If equipment is leased, it means that the lessor has to calculate the rental rate he must charge. If equipment is owned by a bidder making an estimate, it means that he must calculate a realistic rate per day (week, month) before he can estimate the total costs. It is important that the rate be high enough to include all the owning and operating costs of the equipment, and low enough to be competitive in bidding. The elements of these costs were discussed in Chapter 3, and an example of pricing these costs will illustrate the basic method for pricing the costs of any tool, plant, or piece of equipment used in construction.

In Chapter 3 *owning costs* were described as:

1. *Depreciation:* loss in value from any cause
2. *Maintenance:* major repairs and replacement of parts
3. *Investment:* costs arising from investment and ownership.

To price these costs we need three figures as a basis, and they are:

1. *Total investment:* total purchasing and delivery costs of the item to the purchaser less estimated salvage value
2. *Estimated working life:* the number of years, and hours per year, the item is expected to be used and to remain economically usable
3. *Average annual investment:* the average amount of money the purchaser of the item will have invested in the item in each year of its life.

The total investment is made when the item is purchased; but as the item depreciates in value the value of the investment gets progressively less. The older the item (tool, plant, or equipment), usually the less value it has. So over the total working life, the average annual investment is somewhere between 100 percent of the total investment and zero. Common sense tells us that the average annual investment should be about 50 percent of the total investment. Actually, it is rarely calculated at 50 percent because of the accountant's method of calculating.

For a five-year working life, the average annual investment is 60 percent of total investment; and for a ten-year working life, it is 55 percent. The average is calculated thus:

First day of 1st year	100 percent
First day of 2nd year	80
First day of 3rd year	60
First day of 4th year	40
First day of 5th year	20
First day of 6th year	0
5 years)300	= 60 percent, average

It depends on the years of working life, and the greater the number of years the closer the average comes to 50 percent when it is calculated this way.

The average annual investment figure is required as the basis for calculating the investment costs per year for the item.

The estimated working life, as with all estimates, should be based on experience. If not on one's own, then it should be based on the experience of others, such as the guide figures published by equipment makers and associations. The number of hours per year of working life is usually taken at between 1000 and 2000 hours, and again it must be a realistic estimate based on experience. The working life figure is required to calculate both the average annual investment and the average annual depreciation.

The amount of the total investment made in purchasing equipment is understandably the most important figure in all estimates of equipment costs, because the investment, once made, should produce a return; so that at the end of the working life the total investment and a profit (return) on the investment will have been returned to the investor. This principle is fundamental to all investments. To achieve it, depreciation must be allowed for in the equipment rate used to price the use of equipment on a job, as explained in Chapter 3. *The total depreciation* equals the amount of the total investment—the original costs less any salvage value obtained by selling the equipment when it is no longer economical to maintain and operate it. *The average annual depreciation* is calculated from the total investment and the working life, in years, by one of the three methods mentioned in Chapter 3; and for estimating purposes, it is usually calculated by the straight-line method.

For example, a haulage truck for highway use might have a purchase price of $40,000 and an estimated working life of 5 years:

(1) Total Investment		
Purchase price of truck		$ 40,000
Sales tax (say, 5%)		2,000
Delivery costs, say,		800
		= $ 42,800
Less: estimated salvage value		− 2,800
		$ 40,000
(2) Estimated Working Life		
5 years × 1800 hours		= 9000 hours
(3) Average Annual Investment		
60 percent of $40,000		= $ 24,000

ESTIMATE OF OWNING COSTS (per year/hour)

Depreciation

Total Investment (above)	$ 40,000
Less: rubber tires and tubes[a]	$ 4,000
Total depreciation	$ 36,000
Average annual depreciation (20%)	$ 7,200

[a] Because the truck will require more than one set of tires during its life they are dealt with separately. Alternatively, the other, say, two additional sets of tires could be included here in the total depreciation.

Maintenance

Taken as a percentage proportion of the depreciation (as the two are logically related), based on experience and published statistical data.
50 percent of $7,200 average annual depreciation = $ 3,600

Investment

The annual interest rate for money	(percent)
borrowed or invested,[a] say,	10
Insurance and taxes, say,	2
Storage of truck, say,	3
	15 percent
15 percent of $24,000 average annual investment =	$ 3,600

[a] The rate will vary with time, place, and person; but it should not be less than what the equipment owner pays for short-term financing for his business.

Depreciation per year	$ 7,200
Maintenance per year	3,600
Investment per year	3,600
Estimated owning costs (per year)	$ 14,400
(per hour)	$ 8.00

The operating costs of the truck might be calculated as follows. Theoretically, a gasoline engine will consume 0.065 gallon of gasoline per brake horsepower per hour when the equipment is operating fully loaded. Other running costs for oil, filters, and the like, are usually taken as a percentage proportion of the fuel costs based on experience. In some cases, with some equipment, an efficiency factor of less than 100 percent might be applied in calculating the fuel costs, assuming that it would not be operating all the time; but that assumption has not been made here in the case of the truck.

ESTIMATE OF OPERATING COSTS (per year/hour)

Fuel, 150 HP × 0.065 gal
  gasoline @ $1.20 gal × 1800 hr   = $21,060
Lubricants and accessories, say,
  20 percent of fuel costs   =   4,220
Tires, 3 sets @ $4,800 per set (average) = $14,400[a]
                           5 years =   2,880
Tire repairs, say, 14 percent of tire costs   =   400
Running repairs,[b] say,   =   240
       Estimated operating costs (per year) $28,800
                          (per hour) $ 16.00

[a] Tires are sometimes included in owning costs.
[b] Includes only minor items such as fan belts; all other repairs are allowed for under Owning Costs—Maintenance.

Thus, the total charge-out rate for the truck, per hour, would be $8.00 + $16.00 = $24.00 per hour, plus the costs of a driver and overhead and profit.[2]

Whatever costs and unit prices are computed at the outset, they must be regarded as theoretical and tentative, to be checked and validated and revised as necessary by cost accounting in the light of actual experience. Plant and equipment should be a subject of cost accounting, the same as labor. In the past, plant and equipment costs have not received much attention, because they were often only a small part of total costs. Construction companies often do not charge adequate and proper costs for their own plant and equipment, particularly for equipment and plant used on stipulated sum contracts. This practice effectively reduces the profit, so that these construction companies are, in fact, gradually consuming their investment in plant and equipment. When the plant and equipment is worn out, either there is no money to replace it, and more credit is necessary to stay in business, or other liquid assets have to be used if available.

If equipment is to be hired for a contract, competitive bids should be obtained from rental firms as early in the bidding period as possible, and these bids should be dealt with the same as the other bids for the supply of materials and for subcontract work, as explained later. If *owned equipment* is to be used, rental rates quoted by rental firms may be a useful guide to an estimator in estimating the owned equipment costs for a project. However, the rental rates (or charge-

out rates) are simply the costs per hour and, as with labor costs, the other factor to be estimated is the productivity, the amount of work that can be done. Productivity of equipment is discussed in Chapter 11 under *Site Work*.

PRICING MATERIALS

Materials costs are the easiest part of an estimate to price, if the materials are properly described and the work is accurately measured. The greatest possible care and attention should be given to estimating the costs of primary materials (those materials that make up the major part of the total material costs), and an estimator should obtain firm and competitive offers for their supply and delivery.

Requests for offers should be sent out as early as possible to ensure that they are obtained in good time, and the written quotations received should be made a part of the estimate. Some estimators leave spaces in the estimate sheets for the immediate entry of all quoted prices and the suppliers' names next to the items of work as soon as they are received. Actual quotations and sub-bids (or photocopies) and bids received by telephone and immediately entered on a standard form for such verbal bids should be placed with the estimate. All information for an estimate should be put together in one place. This helps to ensure that the estimate is priced on the basis of the most competitive prices, and that no offer is misplaced and overlooked. Time and confusion are great enemies of an estimator, and organization and systematic handling of information and data are essential. Errors are easily made in the rush to submit a bid by a deadline, and sheets of paper are easily misplaced.

Bidding construction firms should always send out requests for quotations and sub-bids, and they should not rely on suppliers and other firms to submit them automatically. Otherwise, a desirable offer may be overlooked. The requests can be in a standard letter or postcard bearing the company's name, and with the title of the project entered; letting it be known that offers are required by the sender for the supply of materials, products, equipment, or for subtrade work.

Offers for the supply of materials should be checked on receipt to see that:

1. They are for the correct material or product, and the correct project; that they refer to the proper specification items; and that descriptions are complete and accurate and conform to all specified requirements.

---

[2] As an approximate guide to "bare rental rates" for equipment (excluding operating costs), it may be noted that the total bare rental rate per month is often between 4 and 5 percent of the total investment, usually closer to 5 percent. In the case of a truck this rate would include tires.

2. They specify delivery to the required location (see reference to unloading and handling, below).

3. They include all sales taxes and all other charges required, or sales taxes are specifically excluded.

4. They specify the correct quantity, because quantity usually affects the offer and the price level.

5. They contain the correct delivery date, for late delivery of certain items may cause expensive delays (this may not be a guarantee of prompt delivery, but it is a start).

6. They are valid offers for a stated and adequate period of time, because it may be some weeks before the contract is awarded, and some months later before the items are required on the site.

7. They include proper discounts and proper credit periods and terms according to those terms that are expected by the contracting firm from its different suppliers.

An estimator must try to ensure that no probable costs are omitted from an estimate. He should ensure that (either in the offers received or in his own estimate) there are allowances for all costs of unloading and handling deliveries, and that any hoisting and storage costs are included.

Allowances for *waste*, for increases and decreases in bulk of excavated and fill materials, and the like, should be stated in the descriptions of the items and included in the unit prices. If an allowance of, say, 25 percent is included in an item's description, the quotations for the supply of the material should be based on the gross quantity; that is, the net quantity measured in the estimate plus 25 percent. But in pricing the item in the estimate, the *quoted unit price*, plus 25 percent, should be entered in the unit price column of the estimate. For example:

Code	Item	Material Unit Price
0204	River sand fill in trenches (allow 25% for shrinkage by consolidation)	$10.00 per CY *(i.e., $8.00 per CY quoted plus 25%)*

Quotations

1. Amazon Co. $8.00 per CY
2. Mississippi Co. $8.20 per CY

In this way, the estimate explicitly records all the necessary data. The quantities in the estimate are net

quantities—the amounts required by the contract documents—and the estimated factors (for *swell, shrinkage, waste,* etc.) are clearly shown and are, therefore, available for validation or revision as required and as determined through cost accounting.

Material costs will usually include sales taxes, and it is often necessary to keep these costs separate so that sales taxes can be readily added or deducted. In some government contracts sales taxes may have to be dealt with in special ways. This is one more reason to separate all the different costs of work and to make every estimate as analytical as possible.

PRICING LABOR

Labor costs are the most difficult part of an estimate to price, because labor productivity is the most difficult thing to predict. The unit prices for labor costs are derived from:

1. *Wage rates* and *labor rates*
2. *Productivity factors.*

(These terms were explained in Chapter 3.)

Some estimators price estimates by using *wage rates* in unit prices for labor, and they allow for all fringe benefits and other related costs in the summary of the estimate, usually as a percentage added to the estimated total of wages. No other costs are added into the "labor column" of the estimate so that an accurate total of wages can be obtained as a basis for calculating the *indirect labor costs.*

Other estimators compute and use *labor rates*[G] in unit prices for labor. These rates are computed by calculating a tradesman's wages for a standard week and adding all other costs (to the employer) in respect to that employee (as explained in Chapter 3), and dividing the total of the *direct* and *indirect labor costs* by the number of hours of work. If the work is for an out-of-town job, or if other special conditions exist, the costs of those conditions are also taken into account in calculating the labor rates. Which is the better method depends on the construction company and the type of work in the estimate. There are arguments for both methods.

If *wage rates* are used in unit prices, the total estimated direct costs of wages can be readily compared with payroll totals periodically and during the course of the work. The *indirect costs* of fringe benefits and statutory payments are then added as a percentage of the *direct costs*; and this percentage varies depending on the mixture of trades, each trade having different fringe benefits. In 1983 indirect labor costs were from about 18 to 33 percent of the direct labor costs for union rates, depending on the trade. For nonunion rates, the additions for benefits are less.

If *labor rates* are used in unit prices, greater accuracy may be obtained by pricing the work of different trades done under different conditions, especially if the conditions are unusual and require the consideration of overtime rates, costs of subsistence, and the like. Also, the full costs of specific items can be seen more readily if this method of pricing labor costs is used.

Productivity factors are the other ingredient of unit prices for labor costs, and they are one of the primary reasons for cost accounting. In pricing the labor costs of an item of work, an estimator's first source of productivity data should be the analyzed cost accounts of his own past jobs. But there are times when suitable data are not available. Estimating and cost accounting have been described as a cyclical process, whereby estimating gives rise to cost accounting, which, in turn, feeds back data for future estimates. It is, therefore, reasonable to ask, How do you start? How is an item priced when no historical cost data are available?

This is a common situation because many firms do no cost accounting at all, and many of the firms that do some cost accounting do not derive much benefit from it. Besides, everyone has to start somewhere. As a result, many estimates are priced by intuition (particularly the labor costs), by guesswork, by references to estimating handbooks, and by a varying mixture of these and other means.

If it is possible to make an estimate of the probable total costs of a construction project by a similar process of analysis and synthesis, it should be possible to make an estimate of any part of the whole, such as the labor costs of an item of work. The work processes in any item of work can be analyzed step by step, and estimates can be made of the time required to carry out each activity until the total time for the complete item has been estimated. This requires the estimator to have a good knowledge of construction, in order to analyze the work processes, and it also requires that he have enough time to apply this "method study" to those items of an estimate that require this technique.[3]

In competitive bidding, an estimator is usually short of time, and it is not suggested that he can analyze the work processes of all items of work for which he does not have historical data to arrive at a unit price. But in most jobs there is usually a relatively small number of important items that account for a large part of the total costs, and it is these items that may require and warrant careful method study and analysis if cost data are not available. For example, in a job costing $2 million, the costs of the reinforced concrete structure might be accounted for as follows:

COST OF A REINFORCED CONCRETE STRUCTURE (1969)

Item	Materials and Other Costs	Labor Costs[a]	Total Costs
1. Concrete (placed)	$100,000	21,500	121,500
2. Equipment Rental	12,500	—	12,500
3. Test and Inspection	3000	—	3000
4. Patching and Rubbing	1000	6000	7000
Concrete (placed)	$116,500	27,500	144,000
5. **Formwork** (erected and removed)	24,000	180,000	204,000
6. **Reinf Steel** (placed)	72,000	29,000	101,000
Total costs (including profit and overhead)	$212,500	236,500	449,000

[a] Including all fringe benefits and other charges.

In the above costs (from an actual job), the labor costs of formwork are just over 40 percent of the total costs of the structure, whereas the labor costs of placing concrete are less than 5 percent (see below). Obviously, the only place where significant savings might be made by the contractor is in the formwork labor; and it is here that the estimator, and others of the contractor's staff, should apply the greatest amount of time and attention both before and after bidding.

COST OF A REINFORCED CONCRETE STRUCTURE (1969)

Item	Materials and Other Costs	Labor Costs[a]	Total Costs
1. Concrete (placed)	22.30	4.80	27.10
2. Equipment Rental	2.75		2.75
3. Test and Inspection	0.65		0.65
4. Patching and Rubbing	0.20	1.35	1.55
Concrete (placed)	25.90	6.15	32.05
5. **Formwork** (erected and removed)	5.40	40.05	45.45
6. **Reinf Steel** (placed)	16.05	6.45	22.50
Total costs (percent) (including profit and overhead)	47.35	52.65	100.00

[a] Including all fringe benefits and other charges.

---

[3] This aspect of an estimator's work may involve "work simplification" and "methods engineering" that at times might necessitate the aid of an expert, although all estimators and superintendents should be familiar with the principles so that they can be applied when necessary and where possible before a bid is made.

An estimator's time and effort should be applied where they are most effective. In most jobs, as in the one above, most of the costs are more or less fixed and minor variations will have little effect on the total costs. For example, the labor costs for placing concrete cannot be reduced so as to make a significant difference in the total costs.

The *quantity of an item of work* has a significant effect on productivity and on the labor costs for two reasons:

1. The startup and finishing time required
2. The learning process at the beginning.

All items of work require a certain time at the beginning for setting out and organizing the work, and at the end a certain time is necessary for dismantling and cleaning up. This startup and finishing time is not proportional to the total amount of work done, and it tends to remain more or less constant despite the quantity of work. This means that smaller quantities require proportionately more time than larger quantities of work.

Each item of work in each job has certain characteristics that are the same in all jobs and other characteristics that are unique to a particular job. No item of work is absolutely and completely the same, or different, on different jobs. To the extent that an item of work varies from one job to another, the tradesmen doing the work have to adapt to the new conditions and to the unique characteristics of the job. This process of adaptation and learning may be so brief as to be practically nonexistent, especially if the workmen have much experience with the particular item of work and are soon working at optimum productivity. Or, the learning process may be much longer because there are new problems to be solved and new conditions to which to adapt, and it may be some hours, or days, before all the snags are unraveled and the work is proceeding well.

Ideally, the effect of *quantity of work* on *labor costs* should be apparent from historical cost data, and with sufficient data it should be possible to establish guidelines for pricing. However, until cost accounting is well established and practiced, there will probably not be enough data to indicate such modes and trends; and in the meantime the estimator has to interpolate and adjust prices according to quantity through his own judgment. The important thing is *to do it*, and to do it consciously and deliberately, and then to try and check the accuracy of what has been done by cost accounting. This should be an estimator's constant attitude: to get to the facts about costs and to pursue them with a positive desire to know them. The person with the contrary attitude can always find reasons and excuses why costs cannot be estimated, and he will justify poor practices, such as careless measurement and pricing, by pointing to the unknowns.

Pricing labor costs in *alteration work*[G] and work in small jobs, such as minor additions to existing buildings, requires special considerations, because the conditions under which this kind of work is usually done usually entail low productivity and high labor costs. There is a big difference between wood framing and gypsum wallboard in extensive partitioning in a new building, and the same kind of work done in small quantities to fill existing openings in an alteration job. In fact, despite their superficial similarities, they are entirely different items from the point of view of labor costs.

Work in alterations and in small jobs for which there is no data can be estimated by the methods study approach mentioned earlier. The only alternatives are guesswork or intuition. An experienced estimator's intuition is sometimes a wonder to behold, but it is not guesswork. Rather, it is the rapid comprehension and working of a mind programmed by experience; and perhaps estimating effort could be less if we understood intuition more.

If, for example, the alterations include an item of work to fill in an existing doorway with framing and gypsum wallboard, the labor costs of the item might be analyzed and estimated as follows:

LABOR COSTS: FILLING EXISTING DOORWAY

Carpenter	Minutes
1. Take out existing door (3' 0" × 7'0") (removal by helper; see below)	5 —
2. Take out existing wood frame and trim (removal by helper; see below)	30 —
3. Cut and install 2 × 4 floor plate in 3'3" opening with two ramset fasteners	10
4. Cut and install two 2 × 4 studs at jambs	10
5. Ditto one 2 × 4 at head	10
6. Ditto two 2 × 4 studs between jambs	10
7. Ditto ½" wallboard sheets (4' × 8') to both sides of opening	30
8. Collect tools and clean up	5
9. Move to next location	10
	120
Allow for 75 percent efficiency $(+\frac{1}{3})$	+40
	60)160

Carpenter: total time $= 2\frac{2}{3}$ hours

Helper (with Carpenter)	Minutes
1. Deliver materials from store to location of work	15
2. Remove existing door to stores	10
3. Remove frame for disposal	10
4. Clean up	5
	40
Allow for 67 percent efficiency ($+\frac{1}{2}$)	+20
	60)60
Helper: total time =	**1 hour**

Carpenter, $2\frac{2}{3}$ hours @ $20.00	= $53.40
Helper, 1 hour @ $15.00	= $15.00
	$68.40
Total Costs, say,	**$70.00** (per doorway)

An efficiency factor is always necessary, because 100 percent efficiency is never achieved; and according to some studies the commonly used factor of 75 percent efficiency might be too high for some jobs. Of course, the factors could be included in the estimates of time required for each step of the operation, but it is easier to apply a factor as in the example.

To estimate labor productivity (labor units[G]) for unusual items of work, estimators might use the formula found in PERT (program evaluation and review technique[G]):

$$t_e = \frac{a + 4m + b}{6}$$

where t_e is the expected time
    a is the optimistic time
    m is the most likely time, the time returned most frequently by those taking part (if such information is available, otherwise it is subject to the estimator's judgment)
    b is the pessimistic time

Sometimes, this is called the "three time estimate," and it is characteristic of PERT; but there is not sufficient space here to examine this subject more completely. Many books on PERT are available and some are relevant to construction.

SUBCONTRACT WORK

A major part of the general estimates made by prime bidders are the *sub-bids*[G] submitted to them by subcontract firms; and a major part of a general estimator's work is to compare and select sub-bids and incorporate the most competitive and favorable (usually the lowest) into the general estimate. Remember, a bid, or a subbid, is an offer, the acceptance of which will lead to a contract, or a sub-contract, if all the other necessary ingredients are present.

Each sub-bid should be in writing, stating precisely and without qualification the scope of the work included in the offer, and the amount of the offer. Frequently, a written bid is dispensed with, at least in the first instance and between parties who have had previous dealings; and a sub-bid is often made by telephone and confirmed later in writing. There is, obviously, some risk attached to this practice, and written confirmation at least is essential. Risk probably arises more from possible misunderstandings of the scope and terms of a verbal offer than from any dishonesty; but, either way, care should be taken to avoid trouble.

The scope and terms of sub-bids are a frequent source of misunderstanding, often leading to incomplete general bids,[G] or to bids with parts of the work included twice (i.e., in more than one sub-bid), thereby causing an inflated general bid. If a general bid is incomplete because of work excluded in error from sub-bids, the general bid will be lower than it should be, and may, therefore, be accepted as the lowest bid. Later, there may be a dispute about who bears the loss because of the exclusion. If a general bid is erroneously inflated by the duplication of work included in sub-bids, it is not likely to be accepted.

One of the common causes of such misunderstanding and error are the bidding documents,[G] particularly specifications. Specifications for stipulated sum contracts are properly directed to primary bidders,[G] one of whom usually becomes the contractor. The specifications form part of the contract documents of the contract between the owner and the contractor, and they must, therefore, be directed to the contractor, who is responsible to the owner for all the work required by the contract documents. The distribution of the greater part of this work among subcontractors (who are responsible to the contractor for its performance) is the responsibility of the contractor, unless the designer has nominated certain work to be done by particular subcontractors who, nevertheless, still have a subcontract with the contractor. An owner looks only to the contractor for performance of a stipulated sum contract.

The scope of each subcontract is generally defined by the *sections*[G] *of the specifications* and by trade practices, and if specification sections and trade practices are compatible no misunderstanding is likely to occur. But the contents of sections depend on the required work, and upon the specification writer. Some writers know and follow local trade practices closely, because they know the sections will be the scope and basis of sub-bids. Other writers do not always know or care and, in the final view, a specification writer is contractually correct when he says that the specifications are ultimately directed to the contractor, who is responsible to the owner for all of the work, and its division among subcontractors is the contractor's concern.

It is apparent to some in the industry that the stipulated sum contract for work that must be done by a large number of specialized subcontractors is sometimes inappropriate, particularly in the matter of contractual responsibility. Hence, the appearance of the management type of contract, in which most of those who do work on a site have a direct contractual responsibility to the owner. Nevertheless, stipulated sum contracts will probably be in use for some time, and a primary bidder must analyze and compare the sub-bids he receives, not only their amount, but also their scope.

For large projects, the sub-bids are best tabulated on a chart as they are received, checked, and if necessary confirmed with the sub-bidders. In some projects there are sub-bids for separate and for combined sections of work, such as plumbing and heating and ventilation work. Some firms may bid for both, and some may bid for only one section; and a sub-bid for plumbing may be less when the plumbing is combined with heating and ventilation than when it is to be done alone. (Usually, this is because of the fixed job overhead costs, which do not increase as the amount of the other direct costs increase.) This can make the selection of sub-bids difficult, but clear bidding documents and tabulation will reduce the difficulty.

A general bidder may have all the work to be done by his own forces estimated well in advance of the "closing time for bids," and yet still be unable to avoid a rush in the last few hours. Bid depositories[G] have helped to eliminate this problem by designating the time available after receiving sub-bids and before submitting bids to the owner to a day or more. Without a bid depository, a general bidder might receive sub-bids up until the last hour, or less, before the general bid has to be submitted to the owner.

To ensure that a proper general bid is submitted, complete with a bid bond and the other prerequisites, it is a common practice, where permitted, to submit a bid and the bond a day or more in advance, and to send a telegram up to within a few hours of the closing time for bids with amendments that reflect lower sub-bids or other information. This procedure is confidential, of course, because a telegram that states, "Reduce

our bid for the Temple Gates Project by $9500.00 (nine thousand five hundred dollars); signed. . . ." is quite meaningless to anyone but the owner who has received the original bid. It is also safe for the bidder because the first bid to be made is a relatively high figure, later reduced. Should something happen to prevent the amendment from being made, the bidder is not likely to find himself with an unwanted contract for a low amount.

UNIT PRICES AND CALCULATIONS

Delusions about accuracy are probably more common in pricing than in measuring work. Somehow, $.05 on a unit price of $6.50 per cubic yard seems much more significant than *"allow 20 percent for shrinkage in consolidation of fill material."* The fill is visualized as a muddy morass, and a 20 percent allowance sounds close enough.

If a labor rate is $18.00 an hour (which is $.30 a minute), may not an estimator round off a price of $6.48 to $6.50 per cubic yard, if there are only a few hundred cubic yards? The multi-million dollar bid that ends with 50 cents and the unit price given to three decimal places are rarely justifiable, even if they do no harm. What is more important is the attitude that these things may indicate; perhaps, a preoccupation with a numerical accuracy that may not be a true reflection of the facts, and which may be a substitute for common sense.

Common sense is the first requirement in all pricing and measurement, and it can save time and prevent trouble for an estimator. Common sense says that the simple is preferable to the complex, and that a hammer is not the best tool to kill a fly. Many unit prices in an estimate can be rounded off to the nearest 5 cents without any loss in accuracy, because they are applicable to relatively small quantities. Other unit prices that are applicable to large quantities may sometimes need to be calculated to a fraction of a cent; but in most cases, a simple fraction (1/4, 1/3, 1/2, etc.) will suffice and will avoid the risk of being misread; always a risk with the decimal fractions.

One way of avoiding the need for fractions in unit prices is to use a larger unit of measurement. The square yard is not so widely used as the square foot, and yet the larger unit is often much more appropriate to many super items of work, such as earthwork, shoring, dampproofing, insulation, drywall, and the like. Many trades customarily do measure their work in units larger than a square foot, usually either in square yards or squares (of 100 square feet); and there appears to be no good reason for the customary use of the square-foot unit in many trades. The "square" is perhaps too large for some items; and one minor disadvantage with the yard is its basis of 3 feet (super) and 9 feet (cube), which does not fit into a decimal monetary system. The use of the metric system changes all that.

Finally, a word about those items in an estimate for which no cost data are available, and on which an estimator must put a price so as to complete his estimate; the kind of item that cannot be found in any data or publication when it is needed. How does an estimator find a reasonable unit price for such an item when time is short?

The first thing to do is to assess the relative importance of the item to the estimate as a whole. It doesn't make sense to agonize over an isolated item or an item whose cost is very small considering the tolerances of accuracy that are acceptable. At the same time, a good estimator does not want to throw away the chance of obtaining the job, or having obtained it, to throw away money because of under-priced items.

Having assessed the importance of the item in question, the estimator should make an appropriate effort to estimate its probable costs, and if the costs are relatively small, he should not spend too much time and effort on it. If the costs are likely to be significant, the estimator should gather whatever relevant data he can and make the best possible effort to estimate the costs. This should be done by stating briefly in the estimate the data used and the basis for the estimate of the costs of that item. There should be some rational basis and some usable data available, no matter how tenuous, to which the estimator can refer. Above all, he should not simply guess and show no rationale, because at some later date he may not be able to remember or explain why he included the costs he did. On the other hand, if he states the data and the basis of his rationale in the estimate, he can refer to it later and say, if necessary, "There is the data that were available at the time and, on that basis, that is what I decided. Can you tell me a better way?" The chances are that most critics cannot. However, there may be times when the risk is great, and then the estimator should make it known to his directors and obtain their advice and instructions.

Estimating publications such as those by Walker and by Means can be of help to an estimator when he is in need of cost data, if he uses the published data intelligently. And one of the more reliable ways of using published cost data is to relate them to personal experience and personal information, as follows.

The word "data" is the plural of "datum," and a datum is often used in construction as a physical reference point, or level, from which other points and levels are established. A similar method can be used to establish probable costs in an estimate from a "cost datum."

Let us suppose that an item of work involves placing steel rebar in sizes No. 10 and No. 11, for which an estimator has no personal cost information. He finds that a publication indicates a unit rate of, say, 13½ man-hours per ton for placing bars of sizes No. 10 and No. 11; and for placing smaller bars of sizes No. 5 and No. 6 (for which he does have his own data) he finds that the publication indicates 18 man-hours per ton. His own cost records indicate a unit rate for placing bars of sizes No. 5 and No. 6 of 20 man-hours per ton.

Applying his own costs to the published data, he finds that there is a difference of 11 percent, or a factor (F) of 1.11 applicable to the published data. Applying the same factor to the other published data, he obtains an estimated unit rate of 15 man-hours (13.50 × 1.11) for the larger bars to use in his estimate. Of course, the factor can only be used in this way if the estimator can foresee that conditions of productivity similar to those that have applied to the rebar work he has done in the past will also apply to future rebar work in which larger bars are placed. Nevertheless, relating personal cost information to published cost data in this way will generally enhance the value of both sets of data. The method can be represented thus:

$$A^e = A^d \times F$$
$$B^e = B^d \times F$$

where A^e = estimator's own information about the item of work, A

A^d = published data for item A

B^d = published data for item B

F = calculated factor

B^e = data required by the estimator about item B

Do not be awed by mathematical symbolism; a great deal of common sense is dressed up in this manner nowadays; but it can be helpful in remembering, as long as we do not come to believe that we are dealing with scientific laws and forget to apply common sense.

Common sense tells us that the published data above were probably derived from jobs in which the workmen were experienced in placing steel bars of larger sizes, whereas we may know that our own workmen have not yet had that experience. So we should apply yet another factor for learning a new kind of work, and allow for a unit rate of, say, 18 manhours per ton (15.00 × 1.20) for this job, and hope that we shall have an opportunity later to test our estimate by cost accounting.

Guessing is not estimating, and often what an experienced estimator may refer to as a guess (or "a guestimate") is a shrewd judgment, modestly clothed. To make such judgments requires experience and an instinct for the costs and prices of construction work that can be acquired and cultivated.

First, an estimator should read a wide selection of publications on the subject, particularly those issued periodically, from which he should make comparisons with his own cost data. He should be inquisitive and curious about costs, so that whenever he comes across cost information he should try to convert it into a unit price so that he can compare and remember it. He should have a general knowledge of costs beyond his own field, such as: the costs of basic materials that are also used in related industries, the rates of different kinds of transportation, and the rental rates for many things from helicopters to hacksaws. At the same time, he should be aware of the many factors that sometimes make a mockery of the scientific approach and that may produce a spread of 100 percent between bids.

Perhaps some of the most valuable experience an estimator can have, if he chooses to acquire and make use of it, is to work as an estimator in another country; preferably in one which is industrially underdeveloped and in which the job conditions are different from those in North America. If not as an estimator, he might work in another part of the local construction industry. In a totally different environment, and lacking the aids usually taken for granted, there is an opportunity to enlarge the imagination and the capacity for ingenuity and to see the economics of construction from another point of view.

In some countries, economic conditions are unusually different from those here at home; labor costs may be almost insignificant, and the use of construction equipment neither politic nor possible; material costs, on the other hand, may be grossly inflated by freight costs, duties, and insurances. Overhead costs in places overseas are often very high because of expatriate staff and great distances between company offices and sites. Such conditions require visiting estimators to reconsider completely their understanding of construction costs and economics.

PRICING AN ESTIMATE

Measurement and pricing is not always done by the same person, which is why it is so important in estimating that we use a standard format and proper

descriptions (or a valid substitute, such as a code); so that all who work with an estimate (both during its creation and later, in management) may fully understand its reasoning and content.

In pricing an estimate, it is important to keep a sense of proportion. Items in an estimate priced to show a total cost for each in dollars and cents appear ludicrous if we think of the facts that lie beneath that cost: facts of material waste, labor productivity, and so on, that belie the apparent accuracy implied by the cents in the total cost. Even more ludicrous then is the total estimated cost of an entire project that includes cents—or even an odd amount of dollars. Surely, for a major project, we may round off a final total to the nearest $100? In the case of individual items of work in an estimate, we may safely round off totals (up or down) to the nearest $10 and the rounding off for each item will more or less cancel out. At the same time, we dispel delusions of accuracy and reduce the amount of computation.

As each section or division of work is priced in an estimate, average unit prices for certain classes of work should be calculated from the total costs to give the estimator a general insight into and check of the estimated costs of the different classes of work. For example, in the case of reinforced concrete, all the costs of concrete work should be divided by the total volume of all concrete in the job, thus:

$$\frac{\$\text{Total costs of Concrete Work}}{\text{(including Formwork and Rebar)}} \Big/ \frac{}{\text{Total Quantity of Concrete}}$$
$$\text{(cubic yards)}$$

$$= \text{Average total Cost per Cubic Yard for Reinforced Concrete}$$

Similarly, the total weight and cost of steel rebar should be divided by the total volume of concrete to provide other useful information. Also, the total contact area and cost of formwork should be related to total volume of concrete. By such simple calculations, an estimator gains two things: (1) a general knowledge of costs as they relate to completed works, and (2) cost figures which, when compared to equivalent cost figures from other jobs, enable the estimator to see if the latest total costs are correct within reason.

With the increasing use of electronic calculators, and now computers, and the resultant reduction in mental involvement in computation for estimates, serious errors (often caused by misplaced decimal points) are an increasing hazard. Therefore, in pricing estimates, it is essential to employ all possible means of checking and cross-checking to find and eliminate errors.

QUESTIONS AND TOPICS FOR DISCUSSION

1. In pricing *equipment costs* for the use of a bidder's own equipment in an estimate, describe briefly *two ways* in which an estimator can establish rates for the equipment.

2. Describe how an estimator should deal with quotations for the *supply of materials* received by telephone, and explain why.

3. State those things that an estimator should look for in checking *offers for the supply of materials* to a construction project.

4. Explain how and why the *quantity of an item of work* often has an effect on labor productivity.

5. Discuss briefly the major factors affecting the scope of work done by subcontractors.

6. Explain why a sub-bidder might offer to do both *plumbing work* and *heating and ventilation work* for a total amount that is less than the total amount of his two separate and simultaneous sub-bids for the same plumbing and for the same heating and ventilation.

7. Show in two ways how a *unit price for steel rebar* (supplied and installed) calculated at $0.4575 per pound might be better written in an estimate.

8. Explain what an estimator should do to estimate the *labor costs of an item of alteration work* with which he has little experience, and for which he has no cost data.

9. Explain briefly the precepts an estimator should follow in estimating the *costs of an item of work* that appear to be relatively important to the estimate but for which he has little data and limited time to estimate the costs.

10. Explain how a bidder can often leave the submission of the *actual amount of his bid* to the very last but, at the same time, ensure that all the bidding requirements are properly met.

11. Describe the differences between *cost information* and *cost data*.

12. Is there such a thing as a *fixed price* for anything? Discuss this question.

13. Is it more economical to rent or to own *construction equipment*? Explain your answer.

14. Describe a general method, applicable to much construction work, whereby *estimators can check their work* and avoid major errors.

11

PRICING WORK: PARTICULAR

Examples of pricing are available in many estimating texts and reference books,[1] and as this book is primarily concerned with fundamentals, precepts, and methods, it does not attempt to be a reference book of factual information as well. Nevertheless, some examples will be useful to illustrate the practical application of the estimating precepts and methods explained in previous chapters and to indicate particular points in pricing work in the various divisions.

The standard divisions *Masterformat* that were followed in Chapter 8, *Measuring Work: Particular*, are also followed in this chapter, which, in addition, refers to Division 1, *General Requirements*; previously mentioned only briefly because general requirements include items creating overhead costs that require no special explanation in terms of measurement.

Readers are urged to obtain current wage rates and labor rates in their own localities and to recalculate all examples using local rates and prices.[2] In this way, the examples will not be used as if they were of valid,

actual unit prices, and students will obtain some idea of local unit prices. It must be emphasized that the examples in this book illustrate only methods and do not reflect actual cost information, although the examples have been made as realistic as possible.

PRICING GENERAL REQUIREMENTS (DIVISION 1)

These general requirements are referred to in Chapter 5, *Construction Costs*, under *Job Overhead Costs*, where some of the costs that arise out of the articles and conditions of the contract are listed. Most of these overhead costs are easily priced.

Supervision and staff salaries and expenses are usually straightforward; but the provision of construction camp facilities for staff and workmen in remote areas is sometimes more difficult to estimate, because costs per man, per day, depend partly on the maximum

---

[1] See Bibliography—*Estimating and Cost Accounting*.

[2] As pointed out before, no attempt has been made here to use any particular wage rates or labor rates. In fact, different rates have been deliberately used in the text to avoid emphasizing any particular

---

rate and to demonstrate that rates do continually change. Also, in construction, costs are rarely hard facts, and a firm offer to supply materials at a stated price is one of the few examples available of a "cost fact," and that only to the purchaser. Costs are always relative.

number of men provided for by the camp facilities, the degree of occupancy, and the duration of the project.

Construction camp facilities and living standards for workmen at remote sites are covered by union agreements in most places. Typical requirements are: 112 square feet of bedroom space for 2 men; room fully furnished, lighted, and heated, with individual thermostats; clean bed linen weekly, and blankets to be laundered every 3 months; 1 shower fixture for every 10 men; 1 washbasin for every 5 men; and toilets provided according to specified requirements related to population. Recreation rooms and canteens are to be provided separately. Food standards generally have to be high, and catering is usually subcontracted to a catering firm. The menus and variety of choice are often superior to many second-class hotels, and they have to be, under the circumstances. Also, higher standards generally seem to follow higher wage rates.

Camp and subsistence costs in British Columbia, Canada, in 1967, were calculated at from $10.00 to $20.00 per man, per day. In 1983, the costs were as high as $85.00 per day in one camp, but more typical costs were from $40.00 to $60.00 per day. These costs were based on contracted catering costs of from $25.00 to $35.00 per man, per day, depending on numbers, quality, and location. They were also based on 100 percent occupancy of the construction camp. At 80 percent occupancy the costs increased by about 10 percent for 25 occupants, and by 7½ percent for 200 occupants. On small jobs the camp and subsistence costs could be as high as 50 percent of the basic wages.

Premiums for construction bonds depend on the location, size, and duration of the project, and on the percentage of the value of the project to be bonded. Typical Canadian rates are given below to show how they are arranged. Rates in the United States are reported to be from 15 to 20 percent higher.

CONSTRUCTION BOND RATES

Bid Bonds. A premium of $10.00 is charged regardless of size for both Bid Bond or Letter Consenting to Surety. This premium will be refunded if the contractor is successful and a Performance Bond is issued.

Performance Bonds

(a) Short-Term Projects

(i) Up to twelve months

Percentage[a]	Rate per Annum	Basis of Premium
1– 10%	$17.50 per $1000	Bond Amount
11– 50%	3.50 per 1000	Full Contract Price
51–100%	5.25 per 1000	Full Contract Price

(ii) Balance of Project Time. If term of project exceeds 12 months a renewal premium at the original rate is charged based on the uncompleted portion of the contract price.

(b) Long-Term Projects

Usually only economical if project cost exceeds $10,000,000 or time exceeds 24 months.

(i) Up to 24 Months. Basis of premium: full contract price.

Percentage	Amount		Rate per Annum
1– 50%	1st	$2,500,000	$5.70 per 1000
	Next	2,500,000	4.50 per 1000
	Next	2,500,000	4.00 per 1000
	Over	7,500,000	4.00 per 1000
51–100%	1st	$2,500,000	7.50 per 1000
	Next	2,500,000	5.75 per 1000
	Next	2,500,000	5.50 per 1000
	Over	7,500,000	5.00 per 1000

(ii) Balance of Project Time. If term of project exceeds 24 months, a renewal premium charge of 1% of the premium per month is made.

(c) Over-Runs and Under-Runs

Additional adjusting premiums will be charged or credited at the same rate as the original premium in the event the contract is increased or decreased. This adjustment is usually ignored unless the adjustment exceeds $50.00.

Payment Bonds

(a) Short-Term Projects

(i) Up to 12 Months. $2.00 per $1000 of the full contract price regardless of bond percentage.

(ii) Balance of Project Time. As per Performance Bond.

(b) Long-Term Projects

Included in Performance Bond rate.

Supply Bonds

Percentage	Rate per Annum	Basis of Premium
1– 50%	$1.75 per $1000	Full Contract Price
51–100%	2.65 per 1000	Full Contract Price

Maintenance Bonds

Percentage	Rate per Annum	Basis of Premium
1– 50%	$1.00 per $1000	Full Contract Price
51–100%	1.60 per 1000	Full Contract Price

[a] Percentage of contract price. Probably the most common bonds are performance bonds for an amount equal to 50 percent of the contract price (amount), on the assumption that the need for a performance bond, should it arise, will most likely occur in the latter stages of the contract when the work is at least 50 percent complete.

As a rough guide, performance bond premium costs are from ½ to 1 percent of projects' total costs. The requirement for payment bonds, supply bonds, and maintenance bonds is not nearly so common as the requirement for a performance bond; and it is becoming common practice to require major subcontractors to provide performance bonds.

Premiums for insurances vary considerably according to job location, type of construction, value of contract, and the types of coverage required. An estimator should always obtain quotations for a project's builder's risk and public liability insurance and include the premium amounts as a *job overhead cost*. Costs of workmen's compensation and employer's liability insurance are better treated as *indirect labor costs,*[G] although some may treat them as a job overhead. Some other insurance premiums may have to be treated as an operating overhead because they provide for general coverage. Builder's risk and public liability insurance premiums may be as low as ½ of 1 percent of the contract amount for a large multi-million dollar contract, and as high as 1 percent on smaller contracts.

Photographs to show work in progress cost about $50 per shot at downtown sites by a professional photographer, and naturally they cost more if traveling costs are involved. Other general requirements are numerous and varied, but once identified and classified they are not usually difficult to price.

Any problem in this division is more likely to involve identifying the need for an overhead item and in estimating its extent or quantity, rather than in pricing it. Toward this end, many estimators use a check list of overhead items and general requirements; and some use a standard estimate summary sheet, designed for their company's needs, on which are listed those overhead items that experience has shown are most likely to be required in the majority of their jobs. Some estimating offices go further and publish a manual for the use of their estimators that contains check lists for most divisions of work and guides and data for estimating the costs of the more common items.

The majority of general requirements can be priced in the same way that similar items in other divisions are priced. For example, fences, screens, and other such temporary work require measuring and pricing in the same way as framing and sheathing; and temporary offices, and the like, are charged for like plant and equipment. The majority of job overhead costs are related to either the site, or to the cost or duration of the work, and knowledge of the site's location and characteristics, and of the total duration and costs for the work is essential.

PRICING SITE WORK (DIVISION 2)

Demolition generally must be priced either at the site or from extensive notes and measurements and sketches made at the site. However, massive demolitions of complete structures are beyond the scope of this text.

Alterations generally involve labor, tools, and equipment; and each item of work should be priced according to the crew required, together with the requisite tools and equipment, by the day or by the hour.

Remembering the well-known principle that "work expands to fill the time available," the estimator should consider estimating most minor items in quarter-day units. (The work day is divided into four quarters by two coffeebreaks and lunch.) Major items should be estimated up to the nearest full day.

A contingency allowance for unforeseen work and contingencies should be included in an estimate of alteration work.[G] The best method is to price the items as they are seen, and to show a contingency as a separate and specific item in the estimate, rather than to allow for contingencies by loosely increasing the crew-times and costs for the items of work. The first method is more rational and permits better cost accounting and checking of the estimate. An estimator should always try to facilitate subsequent cost accounting through his estimates by indicating his reasons for including costs and allowances, which in turn will help to produce more cost information and data to help in making other estimates.

Excavating is done mainly by equipment such as dozers, tractor-shovels, scrapers, trenchers, and the like; and with most kinds of excavating equipment there are certain economic considerations to be taken into account in estimating the equipment costs[G] of doing work. In Chapter 10, the method of estimating rates (per year, hour) for plant and equipment was discussed and illustrated. The other primary consideration is productivity; the amount of time, and therefore the costs, required for a machine to do a certain amount of measured work.

In estimating the productivity of equipment, the basic unit of time is the cycle time: the number of minutes required for a machine to complete a work cycle. In the case of a shovel, for example, cycle time might include loading the shovel with earth, hauling it to a truck (for dumping) or directly to a dump site close at hand, dumping the earth, and returning to load the shovel again to begin another cycle. Most earthwork, such as excavating, is made up of a series of such repetitive cycles that can be observed and timed in operation and that, on the basis of collected data, can be calculated for an estimate and subsequently be validated or corrected by cost accounting.

A cycle time consists of (1) fixed time, and (2) variable time. *Variable time* depends on speed and distance; the distance that the machine has to travel in hauling and returning. *Fixed time* is the balance of a cycle time, and is so-called because it is more or less fixed by the type of machine and its method of operation. Therefore, fixed times can be established by calculation, observation, and experience for different machines of different types, if the times are periodically checked and revised as necessary. Variable times must be calculated for each project according to the job and site conditions, hauling distances, and machine speeds.

Machine manufacturers publish specification data for their machines, including machine speeds in the several gears, both forward and reverse. Variable times are therefore calculated as follows:

$$\text{Variable time} = \frac{\text{Haul Distance (ft)}}{\text{Haul Speed (mph)} \times 88}$$
$$+ \frac{\text{Return Distance (ft)}}{\text{Return Speed (mph)} \times 88}$$

Different gears and speeds are usual for hauling (loaded) and returning (unloaded). The factor 88 is to convert from miles per hour to feet per minute.

Having calculated a variable time, the fixed time is added to produce a cycle time for the particular job; and not much can be done to minimize this cycle time other than to use a suitable machine and to plan the job so that the variable time can be kept to the minimum. Since the basis of equipment costs is time, the next part of an estimate is to calculate the number of trips per hour by dividing the cycle time into 60 minutes and finally to estimate the production by dividing the quantity of earth to be excavated by the amount in each load. However, there are two other factors to be considered as well.

Excavations are properly measured by "bank measure"; that is, the quantity of earth in place (in bank) before it is excavated. But we know that when earth is excavated *swell*[G] occurs, that the earth increases in bulk. Therefore, a *swell factor* must be applied in calculating the production of an excavating machine. This factor will depend on the type of ground and the ground conditions, as previously explained.

The other factor to be applied to an estimate of any machine's productivity and production is commonly referred to as an *efficiency factor*. It is a factor that is applied to allow for inefficiency (and should more precisely be referred to as an "inefficiency factor," but that sounds negative), because no machine can continuously operate for 60 minutes in every hour. Commonly used efficiency factors are: (1) for machines on wheels, 0.75 (45 min/hr); and (2) for machines on tracks, 0.83 (50 min/hr), but these are not necessarily realistic, and must be tested and corrected by cost accounting.

As an example of the application of the above factors and of cycle time to estimating equipment costs: Consider a basement excavation in loamy soil, size 50 ft × 30 ft × 6 ft deep, a total of 333 CY, in which a tractor shovel (1½ CY capacity) is used to bulldoze

earth to both ends of the excavation, as in Fig. 11-1. By this typical method, more earth is moved in each cycle as the bucket of the machine is filled and an additional amount of earth builds up in front of the bucket.

If the machine's travel begins at the center and extends beyond the end of the excavation, the distance forward may be taken as about 35 ft. Then, if the average speed forward is 1.5 mph and 2.0 mph in high reverse:

$$\text{Variable time} = \frac{35 \text{ ft}}{1.5 \times 88} + \frac{35 \text{ ft}}{2.0 \times 88}$$
$$= 0.265 + 0.200 = 0.465 \text{ min}$$
$$= \text{(say), } 0.5 \text{ min per cycle}$$

The fixed time for shifting the machine is, say, 0.25 min per cycle. Cycle Time = (0.5 + 0.25) = 0.75 min. With a 1½ CY shovel used as a dozer to push the earth, and assuming that another ½ CY would build up in front of the machine, 2 CY would be moved in each cycle. The number of cycles per hour would be a maximum of 80 cycles (60 min divided by 0.75 min per cycle), thus moving a maximum of 160 CY per hour (80 cycles × 2 CY each). But the factors for *swell* and *inefficiency* have yet to be applied.

Allowing a factor for swell of 0.80, and allowing an efficiency factor for a tracked machine of 0.83, the estimated maximum amount of earth excavated per hour would be 160 CY × 0.80 × 0.83 = 106 CY. The time required to excavate 333 CY would therefore be 3.14 hr (333 CY divided by 106 CY per hr); and allowing for cleaning up and squaring the excavation,

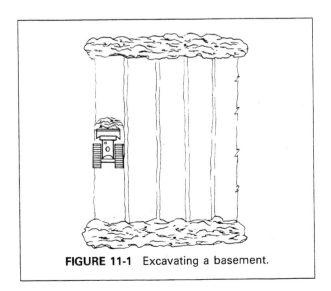

FIGURE 11-1 Excavating a basement.

the estimated minimum total time required would be 4 hours. Time for mobilization and demobilization, transporting to and from the site, and any idle time would be extra.

If the tractor shovel could not be used to push the earth as described, the excavation might take twice as long to complete. The example (based on data from a machine manufacturer) is intended only to illustrate the method of estimating a cycle time and the time required to do a particular job from data obtained from machine manufacturers, equipment associations and, above all, from observation and cost accounting of actual jobs.

Having estimated the total time required for the equipment, including that required for its transportation to and from the job site, the equipment costs can be estimated by applying the rate for owning and operating costs, calculated as explained in Chapter 10, and the labor rate for the operator. In addition, the cost of a flat-bed truck (and driver) to transport a machine on tracks will be required. Finally, any required contingency allowances and overheads and profit will be added to arrive at the total costs.

Temporary shorings for excavations involve mostly labor costs if the lumber is re-used several times. Shoring the sides of a trench 12 ft long × 3 ft wide × 8 ft deep, as shown in Fig. 11-2, might require the lumber as shown here, depending on the soil conditions.

Materials

```
2/3/8  ft  2 × 10 boards =   80 fbm (feet board measure)
6/12   ft  2 ×  8 wales  =   96 fbm
6/3    ft  4 ×  6 braces =   36 fbm
                  Total:    212 fbm @ $0.30 = $63.60
        Divided by number of uses (say) =      ÷ 5
                                        =     12.72
   Divided by area supported (SF) (2/12 × 8 ft)   ÷ 192
          Material/Labor costs (per SF) = $ 0.07
```

Labor

```
Labor installing:   2 men × 2  hr = 4 hr
Labor removing:     2 men × 1½ hr = 3 hr
                  Total:    7 hr @ $18.00 = $126.00
   Divided by area supported (SF) (2/12 × 8 ft)   ÷ 192
          Material/Labor costs (per SF) = $ 0.66
```

This illustrates one method of pricing temporary work in which the materials are re-used, as in concrete formwork. The measurements in the estimate are in "contact feet," and the materials are not measured until the unit prices are analyzed. This simplifies measurement of work in which the number of uses is a major factor in material costs, and material costs are relatively low.

Gravel and sand are used for many things, in-

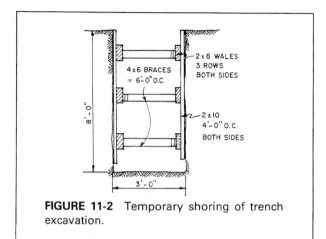

FIGURE 11-2 Temporary shoring of trench excavation.

cluding fill, road bases, and for aggregates. Often the cartage from source to site is as much or more than the cost of the materials at the source; so source and site locations are important. Remember that *moisture content* affects the weight and volume of these materials, and that allowances must be made for *shrinkage*[G] of loose materials that are placed and compacted as fill. These allowances can be approximately calculated from average figures in reference books, but actual figures for local materials should be established from experience. Usually, the costs of different types of gravel and sand from the same source do not vary greatly. The biggest difference in costs is between unwashed materials used for fill and washed and screened materials used for aggregates and other special purposes. Washed sand used in mortar, in concrete, or in plaster will cost several times as much as sand used as fill.

PRICING CONCRETE (DIVISION 3)

In a reinforced concrete building, the complete costs of reinforced concrete per cubic yard in place is about four to six times the cost of ready-mixed concrete, and the following analysis illustrates the approximate distribution of costs:

REINFORCED CONCRETE HI'RISE BUILDING FRAME

	Percentage of Total Costs		
	M & E	+ L[a]	= Total
Concrete, in place[b]	27	+ 8	= 35%
Formwork, erect and strip	8	+ 27	= 35%
Rebar, in place	19	+ 11	= 30%
	54	+ 46	= 100%

[a] M & E, materials and equipment; L, labor, including all benefits and charges.
[b] Including inspection and testing.

These figures are approximate, but indicative of the relative costs of the different parts. The total labor costs (including indirect labor costs) are about 46 percent, and the other 54 percent is in the material costs and equipment costs. Current, national average figures can be obtained from annual publications on construction costs in the United States and Canada.[3]

At a total cost of $220.00 per CY (equals 100 percent) the costs would be:

REINFORCED CONCRETE HI'RISE BUILDING FRAME

	\multicolumn{3}{c}{Costs per CY in Place}
	M & E + L[a]	= Total
Concrete, in place[b]	$ 59.40 + $ 17.60	= $ 77.00
Formwork, erect and strip	17.60 + 59.40	= 77.00
Rebar, in place	41.80 + 24.20	= 66.00
	$118.80 + 101.20	= $220.00

[a] M & E, materials and equipment; L, labor, including all fringe benefits and charges.

[b] Including inspection and testing.

An estimator should have a general knowledge of such cost figures in order to make an approximate check of an estimate and to appreciate the relative importance of the various parts of the work he is measuring and pricing, so that he make reasonably accurate decisions.

Ready-mixed concrete prices depend primarily on the cement content, because the cement is by far the most expensive ingredient, making up about one-third of the total cost. Concrete mixes with aggregate sizes of ¾″ and 1½″ maximum may have the same prices, but concrete with ⅜″ aggregate is often more expensive. Lightweight concretes and semi-lightweight concretes (with natural sand) are also more expensive. Quotations for specific projects and quantities are usually obtained, because prices are affected by location and quantity as well as by specifications.

Some estimators allow up to 5 percent for waste in placing cast-in-place concrete.[4] It appears that *actual quantities placed* are often higher than the net quantities in the estimate; probably because of oversized forms, and some spillage. Reinforcing steel represents about 1 to 2 percent of the total volume of reinforced concrete, which is not usually deducted in measuring (120 pounds of steel equals about ¼ cubic foot, which equals about 1 percent of a cubic yard). In addition five percent waste appears to be excessive, but it depends on the

job and the contractor. Actual waste should be accounted for and recorded for future estimates.

Considerable interest is usually expressed in the *costs of placing concrete*, probably because the actual costs are easily segregated and compared with the estimated costs. But placing costs do not amount to a large and important part of the total costs of concrete work. If the concrete is placed by a chute directly from the mixer-truck—the most economical means—the cost is about ½ man-hour per cubic yard. To place concrete above ground by crane requires about 1 man-hour per cubic yard plus the crane costs.

Formwork costs are a major part of the costs of cast-in-place concrete, and the variations and probabilities of this temporary work are numerous. With form materials, the type and the number of uses involved are the most important items; and before pricing an estimate a decision about these items must be made, depending on the number of stories, the size of the building, and the variations in sizes of concrete members. *Material costs* include the wood sheathing (or rental of steel forms); the support lumber; the hardware, including wedges and bolts; and the consumable items such as form-ties, oil, and nails. Plywood and steel are the most common materials used at the contact surfaces. Lumber boards are not so widely used now, except to produce an architectural concrete finish. Plywood is usually ⅝ in. and ¾ in. thick and comes in sheets usually 4 feet × 8 feet. Special formply, 11/16 in. thick, is available with coatings of resin and other plastics to protect the form's contact surface and to eliminate or reduce the need for oiling prior to each use. Typical numbers of possible uses of sheathing are as follows

Type	Location	Number of Uses	Average Number
Uncoated formply	Slabs	4–6	5
	Walls	6–8	7
	Columns	8–12	10
Coated formply	Slabs	8–12	10
	Walls	12–20	16
	Columns	20–30	25
Fir boards	Slabs	1–3	2
	Walls	1–3	2
	Columns	1–3	2

Excessive cutting and fitting, damage and repairs, and the design of the building may curtail the number of uses. Employing well-made, modular-sized, form panels and careful oiling, stripping and handling may increase the number of uses. Each use usually causes some waste through cutting and overlapping, and an allowance of 10 percent is commonly made for this contingency.

---

[3] See Bibliography—*Estimating and Cost Accounting.*

[4] Some say divide the number of cubic feet in the total measured quantity by 25 (instead of 27) to obtain the number of cubic yards, thereby making a constant allowance of 8 percent for waste. This is a typical example of the kind of thinking and gimmickry that is practiced by some people who call themselves estimators.

The number of uses of fiberglass and steel forms is usually much higher than that for wood, but the higher initial costs may tend to balance out with the number of uses.

Support lumber is usually Construction or Standard grade (No. 1 or 2) S4S fir, or the equivalent, for studs, walers, and light braces. Secondary supports may be Construction-grade rough sawn fir, or patented steel shores and scaffolding, which must be allowed for at proper rental rates. Apart from forms for footings, the costs of using form sheathing and support lumber are about equal. Form panels that have a variety of uses should be designed to withstand handling and moving. As a result, the sizes and quantities of support lumber used may be larger than those required solely for the support of filled forms.

Formwork labor costs vary according to design and site conditions, and actual experience is the only true means of making an accurate estimate. As a rough guide, the following figures are reproduced:

MAN-HOURS PER 100 SF OF CONTACT AREA OF FORMWORK

	Fabricate	Erect	Strip	Clean
Continuous footings	2–3	5–6	1½–2	1½–2½
Isolated footings	6–7	7–9	2–3	2–3
Pedestals and piers	4–6	6–8	2–3	2–3
Grade beams and foundation walls	4–6	4–6	2–2½	1–2
Walls	4–6	2–4	1½–2	1–2
Columns	5–7	4–6	3–4	1½–2½
Flat slab soffit	2–4	2–4	1½–2½	1–2
Beam sides	4–6	3–5	2–3	2–3
Beam soffits	2–4	8–10[a]	2–3	2–3

[a] Includes reshoring time at soffits.

As a guide to pricing formwork two examples are given, and following the same procedure as in the examples it is possible to price any formwork once the basic decisions about design and re-use have been made.

FORMWORK TO FOUNDATION WALLS × 8 FT HIGH, PER 100 SF CONTACT AREA

Materials

	First Use	Re-uses
100 SF 5/8″ formply @ $500.00 MSF	$ 50.00	—
10% waste allowance	5.00	$ 5.00
150 BF lumber @ $300.00 MBF	45.00	—
10% waste allowance	4.50	4.50
Hardware (ties, nails, use of bolts, wedges)	8.50	8.50
	$113.00	$18.00

Labor

		First Use	Re-uses
Fabrication: carpenter (first use)	4 hr @ $18.00	72.00	—
Fabrication: carpenter (re-use)	1 hr @ $18.00	—	18.00
Erection: carpenter	4 hr @ $18.00	72.00	72.00
Stripping: carpenter	2 hr @ $18.00	36.00	36.00
Stripping: helper	1 hr @ $14.00	14.00	14.00
Cleaning and moving: helper	1½ hr @ $14.00	21.00	21.00
Total per 100 SFCA (Labor and Materials)		$328.00	$179.00

With these two figures for "first use" and "re-uses," the average cost of any number of uses can be easily found. For example, assuming seven uses:

$$\frac{\$328.00 + (6 \times \$179.00)}{7} = \frac{\$328.00 + \$1074.00}{7}$$

= $200.00 (average) per 100 SFCA

= $2.00 (average) per SFCA for labor and materials.

In the above example, notice that 10 percent is allowed for waste due from cutting in the first use, and for recutting in subsequent re-uses. Hardware is not measured in detail because it is only about 4 percent of the total costs and practical measurement is not possible. But the allowance for hardware can and should be periodically validated or revised by cost accounting. Initial fabrication assumes that panels are prefabricated so that only adjustment and fitting is required in the re-uses, but this depends on the type of work.

FORMWORK TO PAN JOIST SLAB, PER 100 SF CONTACT AREA (2′6″ × 40′0″)

Materials

150 BF lumber to joist soffits (2 × 6) and beam support under (3 × 10) @ $300.00 MBF ÷ 5 uses	$ 9.00
10% waste allowance for lumber	0.90
Hardware (say)	2.10
	$ 12.00

Labor

Erection of lumber and shores:	carpenter	4 hr @ $18.00	$ 72.00
	helper	2 hr @ $14.00	28.00
Removal of ditto:	helper	1½ hr @ $14.00	21.00
Reshoring joists:	helper	½ hr @ $14.00	7.00
Cleaning and moving lumber:	helper	½ hr @ $14.00	7.00
			$147.00

Equipment

Rental of 3 adjustable shores to 3 × 10 beam (under joists) @ $1.40 each (for 1 month)	$ 4.20
Rental of steel pans, 24 in. wide × 40 ft long, including installation and removal by subcontractor	60.00
	$211.20

Alternatively:	= $2.12 per SFCA
Cost of 2 × 6 joist forms per lin. ft	$3.80
Cost of 24 in.-wide steel pans per lin. ft	$1.50

In the last example, the lumber quantity depends on the width and the spacing of the joists and the need for intermediate support and support at the slab's perimeter. There is no prefabrication required, so each use is essentially the same, unlike in the previous example. The lumber cost is divided by the expected number of uses. In some jobs, some of the lumber intended for rough carpentry can be pre-used for formwork, if this is not prohibited by the contract, in which case the only lumber cost for forms might be an allowance for waste.

Steel pans are often rented and installed and removed by the rental company at a unit price per square foot of slab area (excluding slab beams) or per linear foot of pans. If the contractor owns the steel pans, his costs will be similar and should be charged in the same way. Extra costs for the use of any special end-pans should be allowed.

Other steel forms, such as for walls, are either owned or rented and may be handled by the contractor. But in some cases erection is by the rental company. Either way, the estimator must allow for their costs; largely, depreciation and repairs. Rental rates often include services such as erection drawings and some site supervision. Special forms to fill in to job dimensions can be provided at extra cost if required. Forms for beams (including slab beams in pan joist slabs) and columns are more likely to be specially made, because standard panels are less easily utilized for these members. But the pricing method is the same, with beam soffits requiring shores and reshoring costs.

One of the best ways to understand formwork costs is to view formwork as *plant*, or *equipment*. This is particularly easy to visualize if the forms are hired in prefabricated panels. The formwork costs then can be identified and classified as *owning costs* and *operating costs* (or *using costs*) containing all of those cost elements previously described.

Reinforcing steel bars vary in cost for many reasons, as explained in Chapter 8, and they are usually "shop fabricated" (cut to length and bent) and delivered to the site marked and ready for installation. Site bending is usually more expensive, but it is sometimes necessary. Some contracting companies buy bars in large quantities and fabricate them in their own shops. *Light bending* costs about 100 percent more than *heavy bending* per unit weight. Small quantities of bars can cost up to 50 percent more than large quantities when installed. Placing costs vary considerably, but specialists can usually place steel much more economically than a general contractor.

The Means' cost data book[5] gives a national average bare cost (1983) for grade 60 reinforcing steel of $450 per ton, fabricated and delivered, and $324 per ton for accessories, handling, and placing at site. The same book provides data on other variations for quantity, sizes, lengths, and grades. Accessories for steel bars, such as spacers, tie wire, and the like, are included and priced at about $28.00 per ton of steel, which is about 3½ to 4 percent of the total installed price. It is not always practical nor necessary to the accuracy of an estimate to measure these accessories, unless the design requires the use of chairs and bolsters.

The estimator should check his total costs of reinforced concrete by comparing the *average price per cubic yard*, including formwork and reinforcing steel, with the costs for past jobs. He should also check the estimated quantity of reinforced concrete by dividing the total volume by the total floor area of the building and comparing this ratio with that of past buildings. He might also make further comparisons among the quantities of concrete, formwork, and steel rebar in the several parts of different buildings (such as the slabs, columns, beams and walls) as an accuracy check and to obtain useful data.

PRICING MASONRY (DIVISION 4)

Masonry units come in many kinds, both clay and concrete, with a few composed of less common materials such as glass and gypsum. Waste from breakage depends on the type of masonry unit, and how it is delivered. Packaged units on pallets (wooden platforms) usually cost more, but they are usually more economical because of fewer breakages, perhaps less than 1 percent. Breakages may be 5 percent, or higher, for unpackaged units. Allowances for waste from breakage should be made with all kinds of units, according to experience, unless paid for by the supplier.

Concrete blocks that are not packaged and protected and that get wet from rain are difficult to lay properly, and higher labor costs and lower quality work may be the result. In some areas, particularly those in which clay bricks are not an indigenous material, concrete blocks are produced to high standards of quality. In some areas where clay bricks are widely used, concrete blocks are a second-class product used only in cheap work, and these local circumstances are reflected in the local costs of different kinds of masonry.

Masonry mortar may be delivered ready-mixed, or it may be mixed at the site. The costs are usually about the same, but a better controlled mix is possible

---

[5]See *Bibliography*. All costs cited here are "bare costs," excluding overhead and profit.

with ready-mixed mortar. *Waste of mortar* is high. Mortar joints in hollow concrete blocks are of two kinds: "face shell" joints, and "full" joints. In the more common "face shell" joints, mortar for the bed-joint is placed only along the two faces of the block and not on the cross-webs. In this type of joint, therefore, the amount of mortar does not vary significantly with the thickness of the concrete block and wall.

The costs of *scaffolding and hoists* for masonry are often priced as a "lump sum," and about $15.00 per 100 SF appears to be general. But on large masonry jobs the scaffolding should be designed and priced in detail and charged for like other plant and equipment according to the time required. Isolated work, such as on chimneys and work starting above ground, usually requires more scaffolding.

There are two major considerations associated with *masonry labor costs:* (1) the weather, and (2) the number of helpers required. The weather affects productivity, the quality of the work, and the need to protect both bricklayers and masonry. If wet weather is likely, it may be possible and desirable to allow for temporary shelters. It also may be necessary to allow for lost time because of weather. Work that has been soaked when laid or when still green (fresh) may require more finishing and cleaning because of smeared joints and mortar stains.

From several observations, the usual number of bricklayers to helpers on concrete blockwork such as in warehouse walls appears to be about four or five bricklayers to two helpers. For brickwork, more helpers may be required because more mortar is used. Other factors affecting the number of helpers are the amount of scaffolding, the type and the height of the work, the handling of masonry units, the use of ready-mixed mortar or mortar mixed on site, and union agreements. The relative figures above were obtained from jobs on which ready-mixed mortar was used, and the blocks were delivered packaged on pallets and placed close to the bricklayers. In some areas the number of helpers to bricklayers is reported to be as high as one to one.

The degree and quality of finish of masonry work affects the labor costs, and apprentices are sometimes employed to tool joints and to clean masonry; but it is probably better to price the work as though done by fully trained tradesmen. The physical characteristics of the masonry units may affect labor costs, and units of the same type that vary excessively in size may cause higher costs because of problems in laying out the work and in bonding the masonry units.

Another consideration in masonry costs is the amount of cutting required to conceal conduits, electrical outlets, plumbing, and the like. Extensive cutting up to soffits and other similar items should be measured and priced separately; but detailed cutting cannot

practically be measured and thus must be estimated by cost accounting.

Some examples are given here to illustrate the analysis of masonry unit prices.

6" LIGHTWEIGHT CONCRETE BLOCK PARTITION WALLS, PER 100 BLOCKS/PER BLOCK/PER SF

Materials

100 – 6" × 8" × 16" blocks @ $1.05 each	=	$105.00
2% waste allowance (breakage and cutting)	=	2.10
1/4 CY mortar @ $60.00 per CY	=	15.00
Scaffolding and hoist (allow)	=	15.00
		$137.10

Labor

Bricklayer: 6 hr @ $20.00	=	120.00
Helper: 3 hr @ $16.00	=	48.00
Total per 100 blocks		$305.10
Total per block		$ 3.05
Total per SF[a]		$ 3.43

[a] An 8" × 16" nominal block face (with ⅜-in. joints) has an area of 128 sq. in., which is 8/9 SF.

In the example above, the labor time assumes some detailed cutting of blocks, as this is common in partition walls; but again it must be emphasized that these examples are to illustrate precepts and methods, not to provide factual data about productivity and costs.

EXTRA COST OVER 6" LIGHT WEIGHT CONCRETE BLOCK PARTITION WALL FOR LINTELS, PER 100 LF/PER LF

Materials

75 – 6" × 8" × 16" lintel blocks @ $1.50 each	= $112.50
300 BF lumber for supports @ $300 MBF ÷ 5 uses =	18.00
Concrete fill, 1 CY @ $60.00 per CY	= 60.00
Reinf steel, 2—#4 bars @ $0.20 LF	= 40.00
	$230.50

Labor (extra)

Bricklayer: .8 hr @ $20.00	=	160.00
Helper: 4 hr @ $16.00	=	64.00
		$454.50

Deduct (to obtain "extra costs")

75 standard blocks @ $1.05 each	– 78.75
Total per 100 LF (Extra)	$375.75
Total per LF (Extra)	$ 3.76

In the above example of pricing concrete block lintels, the *extra cost per LF* over the cost of a plain wall has been estimated. The extra cost of the lintel blocks is obtained by deducting the cost of standard blocks. The additional cost of concrete fill and steel bars is included. The *extra labor costs* of placing steel, filling lintels with concrete, and installing and removing temporary supports under the lintels' soffits are included. The small cost of the use and waste of support lumber has been allowed for in the same way as for formwork items. The total cost is an *extra–over cost,*[G] which simplifies measurement. But the lintels could be measured and priced as a complete item of work in the same way as the wall is priced. Equipment may be necessary for concrete filling.

The next example is of clay unit masonry:

CLAY FACE BRICK VENEER, 4″ THICK, COMMON BOND, PER M/PER SF

Materials

1000 face bricks @ $300.00 per M	=	$300.00
2½% waste allowance	=	7.50
½ CY mortar @ $64.00 per CY	=	32.00
Scaffolding and hoist (allow)	=	24.00
		$363.50

Labor

Bricklayer: 16½ hr @ $20.00	=	$330.00
Helper: 12½ hr @ $16.00	=	200.00
Total per 1000 Bricks		$893.50
Total per SF[a]		$ 5.66

[a] $893.50 × 0.00633 bricks.

In this example, the mortar is priced higher, assuming that the brick veneer requires an exterior grade cement mortar instead of a cement-lime mortar (1:1:6) such as is used in partition walls. The allowance for scaffolding is included, at about $.15 per SF. The number of bricklayers to helpers is greater. The unit price may be calculated per thousand bricks or per SF based on 6.33 standard bricks per SF, with ½-inch wide joints.

It should be pointed out that brick prices vary greatly across the continent (by as much as 100 percent for the same item according to one publication)[6] and in some locations common bricks cannot be purchased for the price of face bricks in other locations. Also, there is a great variety of different types of face bricks available, with corresponding variations in face brick prices and in physical characteristics.

Developments in design and changes in building economics over the last fifty years have sparked a return to clay bricks as a major structural material. Reinforced concrete design has reached a high degree of efficiency, but formwork costs are high, and the logic of erecting and removing formwork for cast-in-place concrete is not always sound. The advantages

---

[6]*Building Construction Cost Data*—1983 (Kingston, Mass.: Robert Snow Means Company, Inc.).

of clay bricks over many other materials include lower initial costs, lower maintenance costs, and a better appearance.

Structural clay masonry, which combines clay brickwork and steel reinforcing bars with concrete to unite them, has inherited the advanced design techniques of reinforced concrete; but it does not require expensive formwork. Structural masonry in lintels, beams, and floor systems usually requires some temporary supports, but nothing like the formwork required by cast-in-place concrete. Instead, clay brickwork becomes the permanent form for the concrete and steel in structural clay masonry; it does not need painting, and it matures well.

Pricing structural masonry requires the same considerations given to other masonry, with special attention to the costs of hoists and scaffolding, especially on high buildings. At the same time, the costs of steel rebar, concrete, and temporary supports must be taken into account in much the same way as in reinforced concrete. Recent developments in the design, fabrication, and erection of prefabricated, structural masonry wall panels indicate that some estimating practices for structural clay masonry follow those for precast concrete. This is representative of a general trend in which more building components are produced under the controlled conditions of mass production, and the major construction costs involve erection and installation.

PRICING METALS (DIVISION 5)

Most work in this division is done by specialist subtrades,[G] and the general estimator may have only handling and erection or installation costs to estimate.

Structural steelwork is fabricated in a shop, and this detailed and precise work is sometimes highly automated and should be priced by a steelwork estimator. The pricing of steelwork is deceptively simple, because unit prices are usually quoted per ton for supply, fabrication, and erection, as well as for painting the steel. To give an idea of the distribution of costs, a breakdown of the costs of steelwork for a one-story warehouse building with open web joists supported on trusses on WF columns appears as follows:

STRUCTURAL STEEL FOR WAREHOUSE (1983)

Steel delivered to shop	$ 590	40%
Detailing costs	50	4%
Shop fabrication, priming, and shipping	320	22%
Cost delivered to site	960	66%
Unload and erect 10 hr @ $20.00	200	14%
Rental of equipment	50	3%
Direct costs: erected at site	1210	83%
Indirect costs: Overhead and profit	240	17%
Total cost per ton	$1450	100%

Site painting, if required, would be about $15 per ton extra. Steel (bare) costs in 1983 averaged $550 delivered to shop.[7] The warehouse costs listed above were for the West only, but they do show the typical distribution of steelwork costs.

Unframed steelwork, such as a steel beam over an opening in a masonry wall, would be priced differently. For example:

ONE 10″ × 25.4 LB I-BEAM, 20 FT LONG OVER OPENING

Material

Beam 20 ft × 25.4 lb	=	508	lb
Cost per lb delivered	=	×30	cents
		$152.40	
Cost for one cut	=	7.60	
Delivery to site	=	50.00	
Cost of beam delivered	=	$210.00	

Erection

Crane ½ hr @ $50.00	=	25.00	
Labor 2 hr @ $15.00	=	30.00	
Total cost each	=	$265.00	
Total cost per ton	=	$1043.00	

This unframed steelwork is better priced as a number item, which is in accordance with one of the methods in **MM-CIQS**, described in Chapter 8. The weight measure and the grouping of items are not conducive to accurate pricing of the labor and equipment costs of this kind of work.

PRICING CARPENTRY (DIVISION 6)

Rough framing is not difficult to price if it is properly measured according to the proper classifications of items of work. Some residential framing work is done by "labor only" contracts at a unit price per unit of floor area, with the owner supplying the lumber; it is possible to price the framing of houses and apartment blocks in this way if the estimator has sufficient productivity and cost data available from other similar jobs. However, a detailed estimate is always better, even if several items are eventually priced at the same unit price. The following examples illustrate the methods of pricing framing items in detail.

---

[7]For the South, East, and Midwest. Add $15 per ton for the West. *Building Construction Cost Data—1983* (Kingston, Mass.: Robert Snow Means Company, Inc.).

SILL ON FOUNDATION WALLS, PER MBF/PER LF

Materials

2 × 4 standard grade fir, per MBF	$280.00
5% waste allowance (cutting to lengths)	14.00
250 anchor bolts (½ in.) @ $.30 each[a]	75.00
	$369.00

Labor

Carpenter: 28 hr @ $20.00	$560.00
Helper: 8 hr @ $17.00	136.00
Total per MBF (2 × 4)	$1065.00
Total per LF (2 × 4)	$ 0.71

[a] Bolts are often measured separately.

Sills and plates are often measured with the general framing, in which case the additional labor in laying-out and setting can be measured and priced as an extra-over item.

FRAMED 2 × 4 STUD PARTITIONS, PER MBF

Materials

2 × 4 standard grade fir, per MBF	$280.00
2% waste allowance (cutting)	5.60
Nails, 15 lb @ $0.35 per lb[a]	5.25
	$290.85

Labor

Carpenter: 20 hr @ $20.00	$400.00
Helper: 2 hr @ $17.00	34.00
Total per MBF	$724.85

[a] Nails are often measured separately.

Studs 8 feet long usually cost less than other dimension lumber. Exterior framed walls will require less labor if they are framed on the deck and "tilted up" into position.

FRAMED 2 × 10 FLOOR JOISTS, PER MBF

Materials

2 × 10 standard grade fir, per MBF	$340.00
10% waste allowance (cutting)	34.00
Nails, 8 lb @ $0.35 per lb	2.80
	$376.80

Labor

Carpenter: 15 hr @ $20.00	$300.00
Helper: 3 hr @ $17.00	51.00
Total per MBF	$727.80

Smaller joists would require more labor time per MBF and larger joists slightly less. Waste allowances are not always necessary.

Fir dimension lumber prices vary as much as 100

percent according to location. The lowest prices are in the Northwest where the fir lumber originates. Prices for carload lots of 20 to 35 MBF are about 10 to 20 percent less than for lots of 10 MBF and less. Prices also vary according to size and length, and according to the demand. To illustrate the variation in prices, a synopsis of a typical dimension lumber price list is given below. The prices were about average across the continent in 1969–70. Lumber prices fluctuate greatly, and special quotations are necessary for each project of any size. In 1983, the 1970 prices had roughly doubled, but demand was down.

DOUGLAS FIR DIMENSION LUMBER (1970) (1986)[a]

Standard grade (No. 2 Common) in random lengths of 8 to .20 ft; in carload lots; delivered to site

Size	Price per MBF	Extras
2 × 2	$141	1. For specified lengths, 10 to 20
2 × 3	137	ft, add $5.
2 × 4[b]	130	2. Ditto, 22 to 24 ft add $10–$20.
2 × 4	138	3. For 10 MBF lots add 10
2 × 6	138	percent.
2 × 8	138	4. For smaller lots add 20
2 × 10	143	percent.
2 × 12	143	

[a] prices about doubled in 1986.
[b] 8-foot studs.

Notice that 2 × 4, 2 × 6, and 2 × 8 are the same price; 8-foot studs are less; 2 × 10 and 2 × 12 are more, as are specified lengths. Fir planks and small timbers cost more; for example, 3 × 4 to 6 × 8 timbers cost $152 to $187, and larger timbers (up to 14 × 14) cost about $205 MBF. Larger orders of specified sizes and lengths can be purchased at more competitive prices than list prices. Prices for different grades and sizes fluctuate considerably according to supply and demand in the housing market.

Plywood has generally replaced lumber boarding for sheathing because of the wide selection of types and qualities and lower installation costs. Typical prices in 1970 for unsanded sheathing (standard grade) were: ⅜″ thick, $100.00; ½″ thick, $150.00; ⅝″ thick, $180.00; ¾″, $215.00 MSF. In 1983–4, plywood prices were about double those of 1970. Typical unit prices are analyzed below. If there is not much handling involved, all the work may be done by carpenters. Waste varies considerably with the job.

PLYWOOD WALL SHEATHING, PER MSF/PER SF

Materials

⅜″ ply sheathing, per MSF	$200.00
10% waste allowance	20.00
Nails, 5 lb @ $0.35 per lb	1.80
	$221.80

Labor

Carpenter: 20 hr @ $20.00	$400.00
Total per MSF	$621.80
Total per SF	$ 0.62

PLYWOOD FLAT ROOF SHEATHING, PER MSF/PER SF

Materials

⅝″ ply sheathing, per MSF	$360.00
5% waste allowance	18.00
Nails, 10 lb @ $0.35 per lb	3.50
	$381.50

Labor

Carpenter: 10 hr @ $20.00	$200.00
Helper: 2½ hr @ $17.00	42.50
Total per MSF	$624.00
Total per SF	$ 0.63

This example assumes that intermediate edge supports at right angles to the joists are not required. Edge supports can be provided by: inserting short lengths of 2 × 4 between joists; using H-clips on the plywood edges; and using tongued and grooved plywood sheets; all of which increase the costs. Large deck areas can mean a big reduction in installation costs, and the amount of waste is also less.

Furrings, and the like, where strips of lumber or plywood are fixed to stud walls or masonry to receive and to plumb drywall finishes, should be measured and priced in LF, not in BF. The unit price per LF can be converted to a price per SF for a specified spacing of the material.

FURRING ON FRAMING, PER MLF/PER LF

Materials

1 × 4 standard grade fir @ $240.00 MBF/	
@ $80.00 MLF	$ 80.00
10% waste allowance	8.00
Nails, 10 lb @ $0.35 per lb	3.50
	$ 91.50

Labor

Carpenter: 15 hr @ $20.00	$300.00
Total per MLF	$391.50
Total per LF	$ 0.39

The unit price for 1 × 3 furring would be about $0.37 per LF, the only difference being in the cost of the lumber.

Wood posts and columns are usually more easily measured and priced as run or number items rather than in board feet. The cost of installing a 6″ × 6″ fir post, 8 ft long, cannot be much different from the cost of installing an 8″ × 8″ post 8 ft long; but the number of board feet in one and the other differs by about 80 percent. If rough carpentry items are priced on a board foot basis, *there must be a different unit price for each size of lumber.*

Finish carpentry is generally more difficult to price than rough carpentry, because of the higher proportion of labor costs in finish work and the greater variation in standards of workmanship. Also, the materials and components in finish carpentry are generally more complex or require special treatment.

For example, consider comparatively simple items like exterior wood siding, or interior paneling. Wood siding installation costs depend in part on the treatment at corners: whether rough and covered by trim; or fitted up to a vertical corner trim; or mitred, which is the most expensive method. Similarly, interior paneling costs depend on the treatment at perimeters and corners, and covering them with trim is much cheaper than exposed edges, either set in or scribed, and mitred corners.[8]

With siding and paneling, the laps (between boards) should be measured in BF quantities, and waste from cutting and fitting should be allowed for in the unit price because it is an estimated variable. Instead of measuring this work in BF, it can be better measured by the installed net super area, in which case the laps as well as the waste have to be allowed for in the unit price. Each such allowance should be stated in the item's description.

RED CEDAR PANELING, PER MBF/PER MSF

Description (in estimate):

> 1″ × 8″ Western Red Cedar Paneling, "A" Grade, BCLMA pattern No. 101; secret-nailed vertically to framing with no end joints (estimated waste—15%)

To calculate the unit price of the paneling materials, per MBF (excluding laps, already allowed for in measured quantity):

---

[8]Exterior wood siding and eaves soffits are sometimes classified as rough carpentry work; but if rough carpentry is properly defined as "concealed, and generally structural in nature," siding, soffits, and other exposed work in which appearance is important, and in which edges and joints should be neatly cut and tightly fitted, are more accurately described as finish carpentry, or cladding. Increasingly, installing siding is a specialist's work. In the Northwest, rough carpentry framing (and sheathing) is defined as that required to close-in a building, including installing windows and doors, but excluding siding or other finish.

CEDAR PANELING MATERIALS, PER MBF

Quoted price, delivered, per MBF	$700.00
15% waste allowance	105.00
Nails, 15 lb @ $0.50 per lb	7.50
Cedar shingles (for shimming), say,	2.50
Total per MBF	$815.00
Total per SF (coverage)	$ 0.69

To calculate the unit price of materials per MSF (including laps), the laps are ⅜ in. wide, in a board 7³⁄₁₆ in. in actual width, out of 8 in. in nominal width (Fig. 11-3). This gives an effective covering width of 6¹³⁄₁₆ in., or a loss of about 15 percent from the 8-in. nominal width on which the BF quantity is based. Which means that 1 BF, which *in theory* covers 1 SF (with a nominal 1-in.-thick board), in practice in this case covers only 85 percent of a square foot (with an actual ¾-in.-thick board).

CEDAR PANELING MATERIALS, PER MSF

Quoted price, delivered, MBF	$700.00
17½% lap allowance[a]	122.50
	822.50
15% waste allowance	123.38
Nails, 18 lb @ $0.50 per lb	9.00
Cedar shingles (for shimming), say,	2.92
Total per MSF	$957.80

[a] 850 SF + 17½% = 1000 SF, approx.

The other materials (nails, cedar shingles) are increased by 17½ percent, because they are now required for 1175 BF, not 1000 BF, as before. A paneled wall 12½ ft long × 8 ft high contains 100 SF net area of paneling and requires 117½ BF of materials, plus waste. Either way:

$$117\tfrac{1}{2} \text{ BF @ } \$815.00 \text{ MBF} = \underline{\$95.76}$$

$$100 \text{ SF @ } \$957.80 \text{ MSF} = \underline{\$95.78}$$

A slight difference in results is due to rounding off figures. A bigger and common discrepancy is often made by calculating the loss between 8 in. and 6¹³⁄₁₆ in. as 15 percent, and adding 15 percent instead of 17½ percent for laps. (1000 − 15% = 850; 850 + 17½% = 1000.)

The labor costs of installing the paneling can be calculated either way. If cost accounts show that it requires 24 hours of a carpenter's time to install 1000 BF; then, it will require:

$$\frac{24 \text{ hr}}{1} \times \frac{1000}{850} = 28.23 \text{ hr to install 1000 SF net area.}$$

Either way:

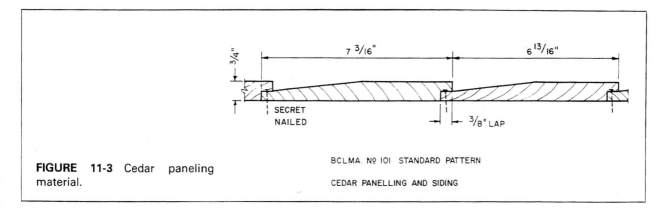

FIGURE 11-3 Cedar paneling material.

BCLMA. Nº 101 STANDARD PATTERN

CEDAR PANELLING AND SIDING

Labor

Carpenter: 24 hr @ $20.00		
Total per MBF	=	$480.00
Carpenter: 28.23 hr @ $20.00		
Total per MSF	=	$564.60
And the labor costs for paneling the wall are:		
117½ BF @ $480.00 MBF	=	$ 56.40
or, 100 SF @ $564.60 MSF	=	$ 56.46

(The small difference results from rounding off.)

Many carpentry items, including shiplap sheathing, siding, interior matching (tongued-and-grooved), and tongued-and-grooved heavy wood decking can be measured and priced in the same ways. In some cases, helpers or laborers are required for handling, and in other cases, such as with horizontal siding, two carpenters may have to work together. These items and their costs cannot be determined without the guidance of historical labor costs and experience with the work.

One reference book for estimators considers labor costs by describing typical work crews for specific items of work and by stating their approximate daily outputs. It is much more helpful and realistic to read the following description, for example:[9]

Placing Wood Chair or Dado Rail. In large rooms, long straight corridors, etc., a carpenter should fit and place 275 to 300 LF of wood chair rails per 8 hr day, at the following labor costs per 100 lin ft:

	Hours
Carpenter	2.8
Laborer	0.5
Cost per 100 LF	3.3

---

[9]*The Building Estimator's Reference Book* (Chicago: Frank R. Walker Company, 1967), pp. 962, 963.

In small kitchens, pantries, closets, bathrooms, etc., a carpenter will place only 160 to 180 LF of chair rail per 8-hr day, at the following labor costs per 100 LF:

	Hours
Carpenter	4.7
Laborer	0.5
Cost per 100 LF	5.2

---

than it is to read that it requires 4.25 man-hours (average) to install 100 LF of rail, without any indication of job conditions. Cost account records should contain qualified cost data, indicating job features and conditions so that the data can be properly used in future estimates.

Finish carpentry and millwork specifications are frequently based on one (or more) of the three standards of woodwork described in standard specifications:

1. **Economy:** wherein price outweighs quality of work
2. **Custom:** for good quality regular work
3. **Premium:** for the finest work, such as in monumental buildings.

The labor costs should be priced accordingly, and recorded cost data should be identified with one of these three standards of woodwork.

It is not uncommon for the labor costs of installing millwork to be priced as a percentage of the total costs of the millwork supplied to the job. The maxim is: *Do what you like, but know what you do*. If an estimator has historical cost data that are pertinent and show that the relationship between labor costs and material costs for a particular class and standard of work has been consistent within a certain limited deviation, he may be in a position to use a percentage of the material costs to estimate the labor costs. Of course, inaccuracies and discrepancies will arise if an estimator has nothing better than a rule of thumb; and a detailed estimate of labor costs is preferable, especially if each of the items of work can be priced separately on the basis of data obtained through cost accounting. But better a general rule of cost proportions supported by experience than a detailed estimate without any such support.

PRICING MOISTURE PROTECTION (DIVISION 7)

This division embraces a great variety of items of work, the most common of which items include bituminous materials and membranes such as waterproofing and built-up roofing.

Built-up roofing prices are simplified by the fact that most of the membrane materials (felts and papers) are sold in rolls containing enough material to cover 4 squares (400 SF). Some of the heavier materials, such as smooth surface roofing, are sold in rolls to cover one square, and some others to cover two squares. Each roll contains 8 percent additional material for edge and end laps, so that in a roll of No. 15 asphalt felt there are 432 SF, and in a roll of the heavier, smooth surface roofing there are 108 SF.

Roofing prices should be analyzed according to job conditions such as: weather; location; building height; accessibility to roof; roof area; degree of slope, or pitch, of the roof; and the number of interruptions in the roof areas caused by changes in slope and level, stacks, mechanical buildings, fixtures on the roof, and the like. In other words, the ideal roofing job is, perhaps, an unobstructed flat roof of over 200 squares, over a single-story warehouse that is located about a mile from the roofer's yard and that at the time of roofing has no exterior walls yet erected, and consequently, no problems with spillage on wall surfaces. In addition, and ideally, the deck is bone-dry, and the roofing work is to be done during a fine and sunny week in May.

Such roofing jobs may be too infrequent, but a good method of pricing any work is to price an ideal job and to use it as a datum for pricing other jobs. This method of pricing from a datum (or base price) established as a basis for pricing specific jobs has been used successfully in estimating and cost accounting in manufacturing industries, and there is no reason why these techniques cannot be adopted by the construction industry. This point is discussed again later in this chapter.

Two other factors to be considered in pricing roofing are the optimum crew size for a job, and the fixed costs of setting up and clearing away at com-

pletion. A certain minimum crew is necessary to tend the kettle (in which the asphalt is heated); to transport and hoist, or pump, the hot asphalt to the place of application; to lay roofing felts; and to apply the asphalt to the felts. Depending on the roofing specifications and the job conditions, a crew of 5 might apply from 15 to 25 squares daily, of from 3- to 5-ply roofing on flat decks. That represents an average of about 2 man-hours per square, which is worthwhile remembering because it appears to be an approximate figure for many built-up roofing applications.

Some examples of the analysis of unit prices for built-up roofing illustrate the pricing method, but the prices of materials and labor are not necessarily current:

5-PLY FELT, ASPHALT, AND GRAVEL ROOFING (UP TO 100 SQUARES) ON FLAT WOOD DECKS, PER SQ.

Materials

No. 2 sheathing paper, 1/4 roll @ $3.20	=	$ 0.80
No. 15 asphalt felt, 1 1/4 rolls[a] @ $7.20	=	9.00
120 lb asphalt @ $6.00 per 100 lb	=	7.20
400 lb gravel, 1/7 CY @ $8.40	=	1.20
Nails, fuel, mops, etc., allow	=	1.00
		$19.20

Labor

Roofer: 2 hr @ $17.00	34.00
Foreman: ½ hr @ $1.00 (extra)	0.50
Total: per Square	$53.70

[a] 1 ¼ rolls × 4 Sq. = 5 Sq. × 1 ply; or 1 Sq. × 5 ply.

In the above example, one ply of sheathing paper is nailed down and covered by two plies of felt over which is mopped 20 lb of asphalt per square. Three additional plies are laid and mopped with 20 lb of asphalt per square under each of them and are covered with a flood coat of 60 lb of asphalt, which is then covered with 400 lb of gravel per square. It is assumed above that one of the crew is a working foreman. For over 100 squares the labor costs might be 10 to 20 percent less. Overhead and profit might be an additional 20 to 30 percent, or more.

INSULATION BOARD (INSTALLATION ONLY) ON 2-PLY FELT AND ASPHALT VAPOR BARRIER (UP TO 100 SQUARES) ON FLAT WOOD DECKS, PER SQ.

Materials (excluding insulation)

No. 2 sheathing paper, 1/4 roll @ $3.20	=	$ 0.80
No. 15 asphalt felt, 1/2 roll @ $7.20	=	3.20
40 lb asphalt @ $6.00 per 100 lb	=	2.40
Nails, fuel, mops, etc. allow	=	0.40
Insulation[a]		$ 7.20

Labor (including laying insulation)

Roofer: 1 hr @ $17.00	=	$17.00
Foreman: 1/4 hr @ $1.00 (extra)	=	0.25
Total per Square	=	$24.45

ª Insulation material varies in type, thickness, and price, and so has not been included above.

Prices for different classes of insulation vary greatly; but if prices are related to the "R factor" of the insulation material, it will be seen that prices increase as the R factor increases, and that different insulation materials of different thicknesses but with the same R factor cost about the same. On concrete decks omit sheathing paper and add asphalt primer under roofing felts.

4-PLY FELT, ASPHALT, AND GRAVEL ROOFING (UP TO 100 SQUARES) ON FLAT CONCRETE DECKS, PER SQ.

Materials

No. 15 asphalt felt, 1 roll @ $7.20	=	$ 7.20
140 lb asphalt @ $6.00 per 100 lb	=	8.40
400 lb gravel, 1/7 CY @ $8.40	=	1.20
Fuel, mops, etc., allow	=	0.80
		$17.60

Labor

Roofer: 1 7/8 hr @ $17.00	=	31.88
Foreman: 3/8 hr @ $1.00 (extra)	=	0.38
Total per Square	=	$49.86

ASPHALT PRIMER TO CONCRETE DECKS, PER SQ.

Material

1 gallon asphalt primer @ $3.00	=	$3.00

Labor

Roofer: 1/10 hr @ $17.00	=	1.70
Foreman: 1/40 hr @ $1.00 (extra)	=	0.02
Total per Square	=	$4.72

On concrete decks there is no need for sheathing paper as there is on wood decks (to stop hot asphalt from dripping through) and no nailing to concrete decks is required. But concrete decks do need priming to ensure adhesion of the asphalt.

5-PLY FELT ASPHALT AND MINERAL SURFACED ROOFING (UP TO 100 SQ.) ON SLOPING WOOD ROOFS, PER SQ.

Materials

No. 2 sheathing paper, 1/4 roll @ $3.20	=	$ 0.80
No. 15 asphalt felt, 3/4 roll @ $7.20	=	5.40
80 lb asphalt @ $6.00 per 100 lb	=	4.80
M. surfaced roofing, 2 rolls (90 lb) @ $10.00	=	20.00
Nails, fuel, mops, etc., allow	=	1.00
		$32.00

Labor

Roofer: 2½ hr @ $17.00	=	42.50
Foreman: 1/2 hr @ $1.00 (extra)	=	0.50
Total per Square	=	$75.00

This specification may be applied to slopes on which surface asphalt and gravel cannot be retained on the roofing. Labor costs are higher because of the heavy sheets and the slope.

Warranties stipulating that the roofing be inspected while it is being installed require from $3.00 to $7.00 per square to be added to the cost of the roof.

Sheet metal flashings in conjunction with built-up roofing on, say, a 200-square warehouse roof may not amount to more than 5 percent of the total roofing costs. On an institutional building wherein some of the sheet metal flashings may be a visible architectural feature, the flashings may cost several thousand dollars and amount to a much larger proportion of the roofing costs.

Sheet metal materials vary considerably in cost, whereas the labor costs of fabricating and installing them tend to vary more with the complexity of the work than with the material. The materials in usual order of comparative cost, with the cheapest first, are:

1. **Galvanized steel** (1¼-oz zinc coating), 26 gauge (GSG) 0.0217 in. thick—$0.30 per SF
2. **Galvanized copper-bearing steel,** (2-oz. zinc coating) 26 gauge (GSG) 0.0217 in. thick—$0.40 per SF
3. **Aluminum sheet,** 24 gauge, 0.020 in. thick—$0.40 per SF
4. **Zinc alloy sheet,** 0.027 in. thick—$1.35 per SF
5. **Stainless steel sheet,** easy formed, 28 gauge, 0.16 in. thick—$2.00 per SF
6. **Copper sheet,** cold rolled, 16 oz per square foot—$2.20 per SF
7. **Lead sheet,** 4 lb per square foot—$3.00 per SF

All of these products are sold by weight, and prices (per 100 lb) must be converted to prices per unit area, or super quantities in the estimate must be converted to the equivalent weights. The above prices are only illustrative and approximate for large quantities, and prices for smaller quantities may be 20 percent higher, or more. The prices shown indicate only general and relative cost levels; some sheet metal costs fluctuate greatly, especially for copper. It is possible to obtain one metal cheaper than another by buying in large quantities, even though it is shown above to be more expensive. Prices also vary not only according to quantity, but according to locality and availability, and to fluctuating metal prices.

Stainless steel of the "Ezeform" type, which is very soft and ductile and easy to bend, may require less labor than galvanized steel. Similarly, sheet lead is easier to form than most other metals. There are many other flashing materials, such as plastics, metal alloys, coated metals (such as stainless steel coated with copper), and aluminum with plastic and enamel coatings, which are cheaper than the traditional copper and lead, and are colored.

Waste will vary according to the required widths and girths of the sheet metal work and the standard sheet sizes. Most sheet metals are available in a variety of sizes, although the most common sheet dimensions are 30- and 36-in. widths and 96- and 120-in. lengths. In galvanized steel, 36-in. widths are standard and 30- and 48-in. widths are slightly more expensive. A supplier's catalogue is necessary to obtain all the information on sizes and prices.

Unit prices for labor on sheet metal should be obtained through cost accounting, in which it is simpler to relate productivity to the length or area of metalwork (describing the kind and thickness), rather than to relate labor to the total weight of the metal. Labor costs depend largely on the amount and complexity of the work and whether or not forming can be done in a shop. Large quantities of flashings of a simple profile and with only two or three "breaks," which can be made on a bench and delivered to the site ready for installation, are the most economical in terms of labor costs.

GALVANIZED (COPPER BEARING) STEEL 26-GAUGE SHEET EAVES FLASHING (IN LENGTHS NOT EXCEEDING 10 FT) × 18 IN. GIRTH, WITH 4 BREAKS AND TWO HEMMED EDGES, PER LF

Materials (for one 10-ft length)

15 SF galv sheet @ $0.40 per SF	=	$ 6.00
Clips, wedges, screws, etc., allow		0.60
		$ 6.60

Labor (for one 10-ft length)

Shop labor, 3/4 hr (fabricating)[a]
Site labor, 3/4 hr (installing)

1 1/2 hr @ $18.00		$27.00
Total 10-ft length		$33.60
Total per LF		$ 3.36
Total per SF		$ 2.24

[a] Includes two men (2 × 3/8 hr) cutting, forming, and back painting.

In the above example, 26-gauge galvanized steel sheet weighs 100 lb per 100 SF, so the conversion is easy. Flashings are often specified with an underlay of roofing felts for which a unit price can be analyzed, as for built-up roofing. Sheet metal roofing is priced in a similar manner to flashings, although more of the labor may be performed at the site.

Many other analyses and explanations of unit prices for work in this division, including: wood, asbestos, and asphalt shingles; slate roofing; sheet metal roofing; and corrugated aluminum, steel, and asbestos cement roofing and siding are to be found in Walker's *The Building Estimator's Reference Book.*

PRICING DOORS, WINDOWS, AND GLASS (DIVISION 8)

Doors are usually standard products, and custom-made wood doors are a millwork item. In either case, they are delivered to the site ready for installation. Consequently, their pricing is relatively simple for the general contractor.

Door installations vary immensely in cost, from about $60 for a single interior door in a light steel frame with a latchset up to $3,000 or more for double doors to a hospital's operating room, with stainless steel frame and hardware, including closers.

Door assemblies, complete with frame and hardware from one supplier, are replacing the traditional system of various doorway parts assembled at the site by a carpenter. Quotations can be obtained for complete door assemblies, and the general estimator has to add only for installation time at the site. For example:

RESIDENTIAL INTERIOR DOOR ASSEMBLY

Comprising:

One 1 3/8" thick hollow, rotary mahogany (stain grade) prefinished flush door, with cedar styles
One 18-gauge pressed steel frame with 4 5/8-in.-wide throat (for wood frame and drywall finished walls) and matching snap-on trim
One latchset-Beverley design-26/D finish, 2 3/4-in. backset with hinges (attached to frame) and door stop (spring type):

Total price of assembly, delivered	$50.00
Labor handling and installing assembly:	
Carpenter: 1/3 hr @ $18.00	$ 6.00
Helper: 1/3 hr @ $15.00	$ 5.00
Total each unit	$61.00

Wood and metal windows, like doors, are easy to price once quotations have been obtained for their supply and delivery. Aluminum windows are an important building component and are widely used. Residential windows are often standard products, delivered from stock; but the heavier and more expensive commercial and institutional windows are usually custom made because of the variations required in their designs.

As an illustration of estimating and pricing this class of custom work, in which most of the work is done in a factory, an example of a price analysis for custom-made commercial aluminum windows follows. The prices and rates used in this example include profit and overhead and were valid for a particular location in 1983. Obviously, they will not apply elsewhere at different times, and the prices shown should be taken for what they are—a means of illustrating an estimating method and an analysis of the costs of the work.

CUSTOM-MADE COMMERCIAL AND INSTITUTIONAL ALUMINUM WINDOWS

Materials (including profit and overheads)

Aluminum windows solid sections, per LF	
Main frame, universal type, 1½″ deep	$0.90
Vent frame, ditto (Ixx = 0.069 in.⁴)	$0.90
Vent frame, ditto (Ixx = 0.167 in.⁴)	$1.10
Tee bar, ditto (Ixx = 0.076 in.⁴)	$0.80
Tee bar, ditto (Ixx = 0.133 in.⁴)	$1.00
Tee bar, ditto (Ixx = 0.596 in.⁴)	$1.40
Glazing bead (extruded section)	$0.20
Drip cap (ditto)	$0.20
5½″ sill (ditto) incl. chairs	$2.70
8″ sill (ditto) ditto	$4.40

Aluminum window tubular sections, per LF	
Vent frame, universal type, (Ixx = 0.121 in.⁴)	$1.50
Tee bar, ditto (Ixx = 0.498 in.⁴)	$2.10
Tee bar, ditto (Ixx = 0.807 in.⁴)	$2.80

In these unit prices sections are cut to length, and a 10 percent waste allowance is included. Prices vary according to weight of section, and whether solid or tubular, and usually amount to about $1.00 to $1.50 per pound from the extrusion manufacturer.

Aluminum finishes to sections, per LF	
Clear anodizing	$0.25
Bronze anodizing	$0.25
Gold anodizing	$0.28
Colored enamel	$0.25

Vent hardware, including stainless steel Anderburg hinges, white bronze fastener, and weatherstripping, per set	$8.50

Sheet glass (B-Quality), including risk, cutting, and waste, per SF

Single strength		
(3/32 in. thick; 18 oz. per SF) (0–10SF)	$0.60
Double strength		
(1/8 in. thick; 24 oz. per SF) (0–10SF)	$0.80
(5/32 in. thick; 32 oz. per SF) (10–15SF)	$1.30
Heavy sheet		
(3/16 in. thick; 40 oz. per SF) (15–20SF)	$1.40
Heavy sheet		
(7/32 in. thick; 45 oz. per SF) (15–20SF)	$1.50

Polished plate, or float, including risk, cutting, and waste, per SF

(1/4 in. thick; 50 oz. per SF) (25–50SF)	$1.50

Glass prices vary greatly according to sizes and the quantity purchased, and they may vary as much as 100 percent between prices for bulk purchases by the carload and the case and prices for panes ex-stock cut to size. The above prices are representative of those charged by a window manufacturer who purchases glass by the case or pallet and who establishes an in-shop price list for use by his own estimator, but who buys glass at continually fluctuating prices at the lowest price possible.

Labor Rate (including profit and overheads)

Factory labor wage rate	=	$12.00 per hr
Factory labor overhead (50%)	=	6.00
Factory labor rate	=	$18.00 per hr
Profit and office overhead (33⅓%)	=	$ 6.00
Factory labor charge-out rate	=	$24.00 per hr

Fabrication (including profit and overheads)

1. Fabrication of main frame, with four arc-welded corners including glazing beads:
   20 min @ $24.00 per hr = $8.00 each
2. Fabrication of vent frame, with four arc-welded corners, including glazing beads and hardware:
   40 min @ $24.00 per hr = $16.00 each
3. Installation of tee bar mullion, with two mechanical joints at ends, including beads:
   3 min @ $24.00 per hr = $1.20 each

Glazing (including profit and overheads)

Labor glazing in factory, per light:
   15 min @ $24.00 per hr = $6.00 each
Site glazing is usually more expensive than shop glazing but it is necessary if the windows have to be transported far and if there is a risk of damaging the glass and glazing in the window after leaving the factory and before installation.

Window Installation (including profit and overheads)

Materials, per LF (of frame)

Elastomeric calking compound $\frac{\$4.00}{25LF}$ per tube	=	$0.16
Plastic foam backing	=	0.06
Plugs and screws, say,	=	0.20
		$0.42

Labor, per LF (of frame)

Installing: 20 LF per hr @ $14.00		=	0.70
Calking: 50 LF per hr @ $14.00		=	0.28
			$1.40
Profit and office overhead (33⅓%)		=	0.46
Total per LF (of frame)			$1.86

This example assumes that scaffolding does not have to be provided by the window subcontractor and that it is available for use at no charge by the general contractor.

Following is an example using the unit prices above.

COMMERCIAL-TYPE ALUMINUM WINDOW, 5 FT WIDE × 4 FT HIGH, WITH SIDE-HUNG CASEMENT VENT, DRIP CAP AND 5½-in. WIDE SILL, AND WITH CLEAR ANODIZED FINISH

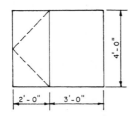

Materials

Main frame, universal type, 1½" deep, 18 LF @ $0.90	=	$ 16.20
Tee bar mullion (I_{xx} = 0.133 in.⁴), 4 LF @ $1.00	=	4.00
Vent frame, universal tubular type (I_{xx} = 0.121 in.⁴), 12 LF @ $1.50	=	18.00
Vent hardware, 1 set @ $17.00 each	=	17.00
Glazing beads (12 + 14 LF) = 26 LF @ $0.20	=	5.20
5½" sill, including chairs, 5 LF @ $2.70	=	13.50
Drip cap 5 LF @ $0.20	=	1.00
Clear anodizing 70 LF @ $0.25	=	17.50
Total		$ 92.40

Labor (as above)

Fabricate main frame, 1 frame @ $8.00	=	8.00
Fabricate vent frame and install hardware, 1 vent @ $16.00	=	16.00
Install mullion, 1 @ $1.20	=	1.20
Total		$117.60

Glass and Glazing to Aluminum Window, 5 ft × 4 ft

Materials

2 lights, 32-oz clear sheet (2.0 × 4.0) + (3.0 × 4.0) = 20 SF @ $1.30 =		$ 26.00
Glazing tape 26 LF @ $0.04 =		1.04
		$ 27.04

Labor

2 lights @ $6.00 each =		12.00
Total		$ 39.04

Window and Installation (Summary)

Fabricated window, as above	=	$117.60
Glass and glazing, as above	=	$ 39.04
Delivery to site, allow	=	2.50
		$159.14

Installation

Window frame, 18 LF @ $1.86	=	33.48
Sill, 5 LF @ $2.60[a]	=	13.00
Drip cap, 5 LF @ $1.86[a]	=	9.30
		($214.92)
Total Cost: Window Installed (including profit and overheads), say,		$215.00[b]

[a] The analysis of the unit price is not shown.

[b] This represents a unit price of $10.75 per SF of window installed, which is a typical price for a commercial window.

The same estimating approach may be used for glass and metal storefronts and entrances to stores, offices, and institutional buildings. This class of work is estimated and done by *specialist contractors,*[G] whose estimators are sometimes required to prepare shop drawings and to do a certain amount of site supervision and general office business, unless the company is quite large. As a result, these estimators become very knowledgeable about the specialty work with which they are dealing, and most construction work is estimated by such estimators.

Finish hardware was described in Chapter 8 as a significant part of the work in a building and which is often included in a contract under a *cash allowance*[G] prescribed by the designer. Many other sections of work may be dealt with in the same way; and whatever can be said here with regard to finish hardware can also be applied to other work, particularly that covered by cash allowances and also some work in divisions 10, 11, 12, 13, and 14.

Cash allowances are used by designers usually because they have to delay making decisions about certain parts of a project, such as selecting specific items of finish hardware. At the same time, the designer wishes to include that part of the work in the contract so that its costs are part of the contract amount. This may be because the items are required to be purchased through and installed by the general contractor; or it may be for another reason, such as the financing from a mortgage company based on the contract amount of a stipulated sum contract.

It follows, therefore, that if a cash allowance is included in a contract by a designer, there will probably be a lack of information about the work it represents. If the designer had all the information required, there would be no need for a cash allowance. Nevertheless, the contractor is, at least, usually required to allow for coordinating the work covered by the cash allowance with the other work in the project; and he may be required to allow in his bid for installing items such as finish hardware and equipment supplied and paid for out of a cash allowance.

A careful study of the wording of the bidding documents is first necessary to establish precisely what is covered by a cash allowance. Whatever is not must be included elsewhere in the estimate. For example, a cash allowance may be for the supply of finish hardware (or equipment) by a firm to be selected later by the designer. But does the allowance also include getting the items into the building that is under construction? If the items are the refrigerators and stoves for an apartment block of 100 suites, the handling costs may be quite high. Even the exact nature of the items supplied may be significant. For example, finish hardware may be described as including door closers. However, there is a difference between installing surface-mounted closers and concealed closers. Also, $100 worth of door hardware may take only one hour of installation time, but $100 worth of plastic door numerals may require many hours to install. The contractor must know what he is required to do so that his estimate of the costs can be reasonably accurate.

In addition to allowing for any handling and installation costs not included in the cash allowance, the contractor's bid must include any other related costs he may require for overhead and profit, and for any other expenses. It is a common practice to allow a lower percentage for overhead and profit on cash allowances than on the costs of other work, but it is probably unrealistic to include no markup on cash allowances on the supposition that there will be no related overhead costs.

PRICING FINISHES (DIVISION 9)

This division includes a great variety of different work that, for pricing purposes, can be grouped as follows:

1. **Drywall work.** Manufactured boards and panels such as plywood, and composition and gypsum wallboards are installed with linear trim at edges and corners (and sometimes at joints) as a finish, sometimes with special fire protective and acoustical qualities.
2. **Tile work.** Ceramic and other tiles, blocks, and slabs of various compositions are adhered to a base surface.
3. **Sheet work.** Flexible sheet goods are applied to base surfaces as resilient, acoustic, and decorative coverings.
4. **Wet finish work.** Plastic materials are mixed and applied to a base surface in such thicknesses as are required to give sufficient strength and density for finishes with various qualities; including durability, imperviousness, and acoustical and decorative qualities.
5. **Coating work.** Plastic materials are applied to a base surface in one or more thin coats to provide a protective and decorative finish.
6. **Beds and wet backing work.** Similar to wet finish work, but preparatory to, and a backing for, finish work.
7. **Lathing and dry backing work.** Supports and backings for finish work are constructed with dry materials, usually either metal lath or gypsym lath board for wet work and backing boards for drywall and tile finishes.
8. **Supporting work.** This includes suspended systems for ceilings and vertical stud systems for partitions, usually of light metal members, designed to be self-supporting and to carry finishes, lathing, or backings.

As before, these classifications are not entirely definite, and some finish work might fall into more than one classification. But by classifying the work in this way it is possible to see common facts and similarities and to discuss the pricing of a great number of different kinds of work without referring to each one separately.

Material costs and labor costs of finishes are affected by: the quantity of work; the sizes and shapes of rooms and areas; the amount of cutting required; and the amount of trimming or other labor done at edges, joints, and corners; consequently, changes in plane increase the costs. The type and quality of the surfaces or supporting work affect costs, because shimming or other treatment or adjustment of the base surface may be necessary. Hoisting and handling materials create additional labor costs, and restricted working space may reduce productivity. Refer to *Finishes*, in Chapter 8, *Measuring Work: Particular*, for further features affecting costs.

Drywall work is usually done by carpenters, who install the boards and panels to the supporting work. Some work, such as acoustic ceilings, is often done by other specialist trades. The material costs include the boards or panels and the fasteners. Waste may be a significant cost, depending on sizes of boards or panels and room dimensions. Trim should be measured and priced separately. Labor costs involve cutting to size and installing the drywall material and installing trim at joints, edges, and corners. Sometimes, trim may not be used, and labors such as fair cutting, scribing, and mitering may be required. These labors are expensive and should be measured and priced separately. In suspended acoustic ceilings, the panels are sometimes simply laid into the supporting grid system, and only cutting at perimeters is required.

Tile work is done by several trades, according to the type of material, whether it be ceramic tiles, precast slabs and blocks, wood and composition blocks, resilient tiles, acoustic tiles, or others. The material costs include the units and the adhesive, or mortar. Waste is not usually a major cost unless areas are small or irregular, or unless the units are easily broken. Waterproof adhesives are expensive, but the cost of ordinary adhesives represents only a few cents a square foot.

Labor costs of tiling are increased by patterns and mixed colors and sizes. Exposed edges requiring fair cutting are expensive, especially for hard materials. Tiling installed with traditional mortar is usually more expensive than that installed with thinner applications of fast-setting adhesives because of the longer time required and because preparatory beds and backings are often required for "mud" (mortar) setting. With thin-set mortars and latex adhesives, the base surfaces must be true and free from irregularities, otherwise some additional preparatory work may be necessary. Beds and backings for tiling should be measured and priced separately.

Sheet work is most common in *floor coverings,* such as linoleum and vinyl plastic sheet goods; but, there are similarities with sheet wall coverings such as vinyl fabrics and wallpapers. Cutting and waste occur at edges and at joints and seams, particularly with patterned goods for which extra cutting is necessary to match patterns at seams. The specific locations of seams may also create additional cutting and waste, particularly with a floor covering in which seams should not be placed across door openings, but parallel to lines of traffic to avoid transverse wear at seams. Good trade practices usually prohibit the use of narrow pieces of trade goods, and this creates more waste of material and additional labor in setting out and cutting.

Wallpapers may be put in this classification for pricing purposes. Papers are usually sold in rolls, or double rolls, containing 36 and 72 square feet, respectively. The waste is usually quite high, from 15 to 20 percent or more with some special types and patterns. Labor costs generally increase as the price and quality of the material increase.

Wet finish work is fundamentally different from the preceding classifications. The materials are mixed with water to produce a wet and plastic mixture (like mortar) which is applied to the base surface in one or more coats. Usually, more than one coat is necessary for soffits and walls because the finish coat is different from the others, and because of the difficulty of applying and curing an adequate thickness of plastic material in one coat. Cement toppings, mastic flooring, and terrazzo are often laid on floors in one application.

Material costs for wet finish work include the dry ingredients and the mixing agent, plus any special additives for color, hardness, and other qualities. Waste is not usually high for applications to floors, but it is high with other applications, in which a large amount of material usually is dropped or spilled during application.

Equipment costs for mixers, sprays, and scaffolding of various kinds are usually incurred for this work, and they should be included.

Labor costs for wet finish work include the costs of erecting and removing scaffolding, mixing the materials, applying the plastic mixture to the base surfaces, curing the applied work, and cleaning up. Patching after other trades is also usually necessary. Applications made in several coats with curing periods between applications increase labor costs, especially if the work is of such quantity or arrangement that it is necessary for workmen to leave the site for periods of several days between applications. *Quantity* is particularly important to costs, and the most economical job is one containing enough work to enable it to be scheduled in a continuous sequence, as in a multi-story building.

Coating work is typified by painting, but also includes other thin, wet, plastic coatings applied by sprays and other means. The materials are usually premixed and delivered in cans or drums ready for application, although some site mixing may be required. Different materials are often used for undercoats and finish coats. The material costs, including consumable items such as brushes and rollers and mixing and cleaning agents, are usually much lower than the labor costs. A painter may apply 2 to 3 gallons of paint in a day with, say, $40.00 worth of materials and $120.00 for labor.

Labor costs of coating work vary according to:

1. **Material applied.** Heavy materials like enamel require more time than thin materials such as stain and varnish.

2. **Type of surface being coated.** Rough and absorbent surfaces require more time than smooth, impervious surfaces.

3. **Means of application.** Spray equipment covers an area faster than brush or roller.

4. **Number of coats.** The later coats go on faster than the first coat.

5. **Area and planes to be coated.** Large flat areas require less time than small broken areas, multi-plane surfaces, and narrow widths; and walls are easier to coat than ceilings.

6. **Amount of "cutting in" required** between contiguous coatings of different colors or types and around openings, and the like.

7. **Number of colors and types of coating applied,**

as in the preceding item, and, in addition, the resultant interruptions and additional cleaning of brushes and equipment required.

Labor costs are also incurred by handling scaffolding and other equipment to provide working access, and equipment costs also must be included.

Beds and wet backing work can be compared to wet finish work for purposes of price analysis. It includes items such as cement plaster and toppings to receive other finish work, such as tile and sheet work.

Lathing and dry backing work can be compared to drywall work when using gypsum board lath and gypsum backing boards to receive finish work, except that both the material costs and the labor costs of lathing and backings are less than for drywall, because there is no need for any special joint treatment and because gypsum lath and backing board does not cost as much as gypsum wallboard. Also, there is less waste, because the location and number of joints are less important in concealed work. In addition to metal beads and other trim, 2″ × 2″ cornerite lath is installed at internal corners, and strip lath, 3 and 4 inches wide, is installed at heads of openings and at certain joints and changes in base surfaces. It is better to measure and price all such minor items of work separately unless the amount involved is very small.

Supporting work done by carpenters, lathers, and other finishing trades to carry finishes is similar to framing carpentry in that it is made up of light members (such as metal tee bars and steel studs) erected in supporting systems. The linear members, together with wire hangers, tie wire, fasteners, and other accessories, may be priced piecemeal as run and number items. Or the material costs of a specific supporting system (with members at specified spacings) may be analyzed and priced as a super item. Similarly, labor costs may be related to the area of the specific system or to the amount of material erected. For simplicity in measurement and pricing, the former is preferable. Scaffolding and other equipment costs must also be included in an estimate.

Other costs of finish work may arise from: inspection and testing requirements, special warranties, provision of samples, extra materials for owners' maintenance, and patching and touching up after other trades have finished their work.

In summary, the pricing of finishes, although materials and methods vary widely, does permit some generalization about the precepts and methods of measuring and pricing. Unit prices and costs of finishes are affected by:

1. Work to floors
2. Work to walls
3. Work to soffits
4. Area sizes and shapes
5. Repetition of similar areas
6. Perimeter/area ratios
7. Total quantities
8. Changes in plane
9. Number of corners
10. Number of openings
11. Quality of finish
12. Sizes of boards, panels, and sheets
13. Installation methods
14. Number of joints
15. Location of joints
16. Treatment of joints
17. Treatment of edges and perimeters
18. Treatment of corners
19. Use and type of trim
20. Type of base surface and adhesive.

These factors, when applicable, should be reflected in the descriptions of the items of work and also in the quantities and methods of measurement employed in the estimate so that they can be taken into account when pricing the work.

PRICING SPECIALTIES AND SIMILAR WORK (DIVISIONS 10, 11, 12, 13, AND 14)

These divisions of work were mentioned in Chapter 8 with regard to their measurement and description in estimates so that items of work can be priced.

Because work in these divisions is, generally, highly specialized and performed by specialist firms, pricing the items of work is not usually a general problem; it is usually done by a specialist firm whose estimator is experienced and specializes in that kind of work. However, there are two areas in which problems do frequently arise for the general contractor and his estimator. These areas include: (1) items from suppliers installed by the general contractor (for example, metal storage shelving), and (2) co-ordinating subcontractors' work in these divisions with other work on the job site (for example, special construction in rooms such as studios, radiation centers, and laboratories).

Pricing the installation of items supplied to the job site can be a problem, as was explained before with respect to finish hardware. So often the estimator does not have enough information, because the specific items have not been selected by the designer and they are to be supplied under a cash allowance in the contract; or the estimator has no experience in dealing with the items. It is a matter of risk to be calculated on the basis of the information available.

Similarly, in the matter of co-ordinating the work, it is a question of information and risk in dealing with uncommon items. All major buildings contain elevators, and all contractors have experience in dealing with this subcontractor's work, so the problems should be few. However, food service equipment and radiation protection may be a different matter. First, a general estimator should obtain all the information available, and he should try to learn as much about the work as he can. This may mean pressing the designer to obtain and pass on all the information he can get from the specialist firm. (The designer has not necessarily included all the information he has in the specifications.) Second, the estimator must carefully examine the related specifications and the sub-bids submitted for the work to ensure that all the work required by the contract is included and properly and clearly allocated among the contractor and his subcontractors. Scheduling is particularly important; and if the contractor has a contract containing an article on liquidated damages, he should minimize his risk by extending a similar contractual obligation to his subcontractors.

Above all, it is a question of information and communication—and scheduling. Which might lead us to consider the possibilities of reducing risks attributable to a lack of design information by doing the work within some contractual arrangement other than a stipulated sum contract.

PRICING MECHANICAL WORK (DIVISION 15)

In some respects, estimating the costs of mechanical work appears to be more straightforward than other estimating, whereas in other respects it appears to be more difficult. It is generally easier to price if certain precepts and methods are followed, and often more difficult to measure. There are many publications written solely for the mechanical estimator, probably because of the distinctive nature of mechanical work and of mechanical systems in buildings. Nevertheless, because of the nature of mechanical work, mechanical estimating (if the term can be used without causing confusion) can be done systematically. For although each mechanical system in a building is unique in its own arrangement and scope, it is still made up of standard manufactured components such as pipes, fittings, valves, fixtures, and mechanical equipment.

The labor costs of installing mechanical systems are always more or less subject to site and job con-

ditions, the same as all labor costs. But, at the same time, they are generally more directly related to the materials installed and somewhat less to site and job conditions than labor costs in many other kinds of construction work. Joining one pipe length to another by means of a pipe fitting is a distinct operation whichever mechanical system it is in, and it is this relationship between materials and labor in mechanical work that makes it easier to rationalize and systematize the estimating of the costs of mechanical work. Each pipe fitting requires two or three or four joints, depending on its type. And each type of pipe requires a certain type of joint and fitting. Consequently, mechanical estimating largely depends on a detailed take-off of all the materials: the pipes, the fittings, the valves, the fixtures, and the items of mechanical equipment; and the labor costs are directly related to the material items, particularly to the pipe fittings (and their joints) and to the fixtures and equipment (and the connections to them). Perhaps only with mechanical (and electrical) work is it correct to refer to a "material take off" for an estimate.

Published *labor units*[G] are available to mechanical estimators,[10] based on a systematic approach to mechanical estimating, together with guidelines for establishing *efficiency factors* related to specific jobs and specific mechanical firms through cost accounting. In other words, there is a published set of data for labor productivity with an explanation of how to adjust and utilize them with efficiency factors for mechanical work.

Earlier in this chapter, reference was made to the use of a datum in pricing. The use of published unit prices as a datum and as a basis for bidding and contracting is not something new. Published schedules of unit prices for construction work are used by some government departments and private companies,[11] and bidders make their offers by quoting percentage additions or deductions required by the bidder to be made to or from the unit prices in a prescribed schedule, leading to unit price contracts in which the work done is measured and paid for at the adjusted unit prices. To make an estimate and a bid for work to be done on this basis, an estimator must be able to compare the published unit prices (the datum) with actual unit prices (established for his company by cost accounting)

---

[10] The *Labor Calculator* published by the National Association of Plumbing, Heating, Cooling Contractors, Washington, DC 20036. This useful publication uses the term "labor units" in reference to the data it contains concerning man-hours required for a wide variety of items of mechanical work. Some other publications use other terms, such as "labor factors" and "labor rates." There is no uniform terminology in this field.

[11] Such as those published by Richardson Engineering Services, Inc., California, and by a number of government departments overseas.

to arrive at a factor for different items, or, more practically, for different sections or systems of work.

A labor unit is also a datum; but whereas a price datum applies to the unit prices of a group of related items of work, a labor unit applies to the labor time (in man-hours) required for a specific item of work. Adjustments to labor units (the data) are made, as required, by efficiency factors calculated for specific projects, or for specific parts of projects such as mechanical systems or subsystems.

A series of labor units for screwed steel water piping with malleable iron fittings might be as follows:

LABOR UNITS X EFFICIENCY FACTORS FOR SCREWED STEEL PIPING

Pipe Size (in.)	Labor Unit (man-hr per Ell Fitting) for Efficiency Factor:										
	0.5	0.6	0.7	0.8	0.9	1.0	1.1	1.2	1.3	1.4	1.5
½	0.30	0.36	0.42	0.48	0.54	0.60	0.66	0.72	0.78	0.84	0.90
¾	0.35	0.42	0.49	0.56	0.63	0.70	0.77	0.84	0.91	0.98	1.05
1	0.40	0.48	0.56	0.64	0.72	0.80	0.88	0.96	1.04	1.12	1.20

For ease of calculating, the above table (shown in part) shows a practical range of efficiency factors and the products of the labor units and the efficiency factors.

The item of work in the table includes cutting and threading two pipe ends and fixing the pipe fitting. The tabulated labor units should be based on wide, actual experience so that average productivity (or the mean) is about equal to that indicated by the labor unit times the ''efficiency factor'' of 1. That is to say, according to the table, a 1-in.-diameter pipe fitting with two pipe joints, on the average should normally require 0.80 man-hour to install. Under certain circumstances it might conceivably require up to 1.20 man-hours, or as little as 0.40 man-hour. The immediate, usual reaction to published labor units is often one of surprise at their magnitude, and in some instances the published figures are undoubtedly higher than practical experience would indicate. On the other hand, most forget (or do not know) that a large part of a workman's time is spent in doing things other than actually working at his trade, as explained in Chapter 3.

Establishing an efficiency factor is critical in using a labor unit, and it is suggested that this can only be done, in the first instance, by considering those things that most affect labor productivity, namely:

1. **Labor availability and skill**
2. **Supervision availability and skill**
3. **Type of mechanical work**
4. **Design and inspection of work**
5. **Job organization**
6. **Site and work conditions**
7. **Delays, deliveries, and details**
8. **Season and weather**
9. **Market supply and demand**
10. **Estimating data.**

These are examined in more detail, since each item has several aspects. In fact, it would be possible to further subdivide each of the above ten items, and so on, ad infinitum; but it would not be practically possible for an estimator to effectively rate the influence on labor productivity of more finely divided factors without the help of a computer and a specially designed program and much information.

Labor availability and skill depend, in part, on the amount of work at hand and a project's location. If the project is far from town, it may be necessary to hire local labor. If the mechanical contracting company is busy, all its regular workers may be employed on other jobs and new and unknown workers may have to be hired, with a possibly lower level of productivity, and certainly with a greater risk.

Supervision availability and skill are affected in the same way as labor availability and skill. The success of a job often is decided by the quality of the site supervision, and individual supervisors might be rated for this purpose. The method of rating would be similar to that under discussion.

Different types of mechanical work may have different labor efficiency factors, and an assessment should be made for each major system in a large project in terms of the probable labor productivity in installing that system. The size of the contract may also be considered here, since small jobs are often less productive than larger jobs.

Design and inspection of work (by the designer or his engineering consultant) often has an effect on labor productivity. The design includes not only the drawings and their effectiveness and practicability, but also the specifications, and the extent to which these may or may not be observed is critical. The effect of bylaws and regulations and their enforcement by officials should also be considered.

Site and work conditions include many factors that affect productivity. The organization of the job as a whole, and the mechanical part in particular, should be considered. A mechanical contractor's work is affected by the general contractor, by the other subcontractors, and by the way in which the various parts of the job are put together. Access, storage and working spaces, hoisting facilities, and facilities for workmen are some of the things to be considered under site conditions and their effect on labor productivity.

The deliveries of materials and equipment, and the timely receipt of design details and additional instructions from the designer, are critical to the good progress of the work, and delays may result in lower productivity.

The season and the weather affect some types of mechanical work more than others, and for this reason it is necessary to review each mechanical system separately. Underground work outside a building may be seriously affected, whereas interior plumbing may remain unaffected by the weather.

The market's supply and demand for construction in an area will have a direct effect on labor productivity and on some of the preceding factors, such as availability of labor and supervision.

Estimating information and data vary in availability and in reliability, and for the more standard types of mechanical systems more is usually available. An estimate is as good as the information and data on which it is based, and this final factor enables an estimator to take some account of the quality of the information and data he is using.

The estimator's assessment for each factor is listed and the average factor is calculated; for example, as follows:

EFFICIENCY FACTOR RATING[a]—PLUMBING SYSTEM

1. Labor availability	1.1
2. Supervision availability	0.8
3. Type of work	1.1
4. Design and inspection	1.2
5. Job organization	0.9
6. Site and work conditions	1.0
7. Delays, deliveries, details	0.9
8. Season and weather	1.2
9. Market supply and demand	1.1
10. Estimating data	1.0
Total	10.3
Average factor	1.03

[a] If the estimator has no opinion on any item he rates that item 1.0 (average).

Once labor units are established and used with efficiency factors established as above, it is essential that the validity of the factors be confirmed or revised by frequently comparing estimated labor costs with actual labor costs through cost accounting.

PRICING ELECTRICAL WORK (DIVISION 16)

Almost everything that has been said about mechanical can be said about electrical work, because similar conditions exist in mechanical and electrical work and the same measurement and pricing methods are applicable. Like mechanical, electrical work can be broken down into systems; and the basis of an estimate is a schedule of materials to which labor units can be related and for which efficiency factors can be assessed, as explained before, for the several systems of work in the project.

In both mechanical and electrical estimating, the measurement (take-off) must be done by an estimator experienced in the design and installation of the systems of work. Then the material items can be priced from published lists, and the labor times can be calculated from published labor units by a junior assistant. When this has been done, the senior estimator can make the estimate ready for completion by applying efficiency factors to the total labor times (in man-hours) for each system, or sub-system, and by applying labor rates to the totals of man-hours adjusted by factors to obtain labor costs. Similarly, the senior estimator can prepare the material costs for calculation by applying quoted discounts to the totals of the list prices for the systems measured in the estimate.

AN ESTIMATING METHOD

This method of estimating, which uses published price lists, quoted discounts, scheduled data, labor units and efficiency factors to adjust varying price and productivity levels has several advantages for bidders and for estimators.

First, it requires that information and data obtained by cost accounting be systematically scheduled, and that produces several benefits. Next, it enables junior estimators to do useful and instructive work under the supervision of a senior estimator. At the same time, it relieves the senior estimator of much of the routine labor of estimating and enables him to handle more estimates and apply his time and experience where they can be most effective. Finally, the adoption of such a systematic method of estimating encourages the standardization of terminology and of estimating methods through the publication of schedules of data on labor productivity by trade associations. This, in turn, encourages the general rationalization of estimating, and the collection of information and the creation of data.

Such an estimating method could be adopted by the members of any trade association for their mutual benefit through the pooling of data and through better estimating without any detrimental disclosures, reduction in competition, or loss of autonomy. It can be adopted by individual firms and operated independently, but there are advantages in pooling productivity information.

There is no suggestion here that we might adopt some European bidding practices such as those in the Netherlands in which bids for construction work are viewed by a committee of representatives of the bidding companies prior to their submission to the bidding authority.[12] Clearly, there are ways in which construction practices involving estimating and bidding might be improved without detracting from the free enterprise system.

As long as "the lowest bid" is the generally acceptable bid, it is desirable to improve the validity of the lowest bid. The inescapable fact is that it is much easier to have the lowest bid, if only by default; and naturally every owner prefers to pay less rather than more. Therefore, it is essential that all bidders be competent to bid as well as to do the work. Education and better methods are needed, therefore, especially in the pricing of work, which is much less straightforward than measurement.

Pricing work effectively requires above all else a system which, in turn, requires information and data. Computer systems are one means; but needed even more than computer systems are persons with the ability to develop and use new techniques for gathering, analyzing and using information and data about construction work, productivity, and costs.

QUESTIONS AND TOPICS FOR DISCUSSION

1. Identify and explain the application of two different factors (stated as percentages) required in analyzing the time for *excavating a basement* with a piece of equipment.

2. In considering economies to be made in the construction of a *reinforced-concrete framed building*, which specific costs of the work offer the greatest possibilities for reductions and why?

3. If a cast-in-place concrete structure cost an average of $200.00 per cubic yard of *reinforced concrete, formed and placed*, indicate the approximate and proportionate costs (per cubic yard) of the concrete, the forms, and the steel rebar, showing the labor costs of each separate from the other costs.

4. Show by an example the analysis of a *unit price* for a *6-in.-thick conc blk ptn wall*, assuming the conc blks cost $1.00 each; the cmt mtr, $60.00 per CY; and the mason, $15.00 per hour.

5. Describe briefly two ways of measuring and pricing *structural steelwork*, and explain why one should be more accurate than the other.

6. Analyze unit prices for *framed floor joists*, sizes 2 × 6 and 2 × 8, for comparison, and explain if and why one should cost more than the other.

7. In accounting for and recording the costs of *built-up roofing* for future estimating, state the main job conditions you would want to record to explain and qualify your cost data.

8. Sketch a *two-light aluminum window with an opening vent*, showing the several dimensions (of your choice), and measure the various items that you as an estimator with a window manufacturer would have to price in detail.

9. Describe the major considerations in estimating the *costs of finish work* generally classified herein as tile work.

10. Describe in detail how the *costs of plumbing work* can be estimated by use of published data on prices and productivity.

11. Estimate the *amount of time required* for a carpenter to do the following job: Cut an opening through the exterior wall of a wood-framed, single-story house (built in 1965), with a wood siding exterior, and a gypsum drywall finish inside, and install a wood casement window, 3 ft × 4 ft in size. Assume a wood lintel is needed. Show all details of your estimate.

12. Estimate *the amount of time required* by a crew of carpenters to frame a hipped roof on a single-story house with an L-shaped plan area of 1000 square feet, and consisting of 3000 FBM of 2 × 6 and 2 × 8 lumber with two hipped ends.

---

[12] Keith Collier, *Construction Contracts*, 2nd ed. (Prentice-Hall, Inc.: Englewood Cliffs, N.J. 1987), Chap. 2.2.

12

COST ACCOUNTING PRACTICES

The purposes and precepts of cost accounting (CA) were explained in Chapter 6, together with the purposes and precepts of estimating, because we believe that cost accounting and estimating cannot be properly understood unless seen as two parts of one function: construction management.

Both information and experience are essential to management, and reports indicate that a lack of these is a major factor in the inefficiencies of and business failures in the construction industry.[1] The estimator must have information and the experience of past construction work in order to estimate the probabilities and the costs of future work. A construction superintendent must be able to oversee the entire project to bring it to successful completion, and at the same time he must know all the details of the work and its costs as they were measured and priced and as they are actually incurred.

Construction is essentially a management function rather than one of investment by a contractor whose investment in the work is usually relatively small and temporary. The so-called construction management

contracts, discussed earlier, came about as a result of the recognition of construction as primarily a management function. This function became more apparent as building construction became more complex, and as proper management became more necessary. The need and the demand for good management was a deathly angel for many general contractors. They could not provide it because they did not know how.

The general contractor often saw himself simply as a contractor for site works and structure; not primarily as a construction manager, but as the first of a group of specialist contractors each responsible for specific parts of the work. He saw himself as a contractor who, in doing the initial parts of the work, was therefore required to see that the other parts fitted together. Of course, this was not true of all, but it was true of many, and it still is true of some.

Now there are construction management companies that were general contractors, who no longer have plant, equipment, and a labor force but who have retained an experienced staff of foremen, supervisors, estimators, managers, and engineers. Many no longer use the title "contractor" because it does not describe their new function. Their assets are management expertise, experience, and information rather than capital, plant, and equipment.

---

[1] In the study on manpower utilization referred to in Chapters 3 and 4, and in the annual reports of business failures by Dun and Bradstreet, Ltd., referred to in Chapter 3.

Data are essential as a basis for inference for estimating probabilities and for making decisions. Information is the stuff of decision-making and of management, and it must be systematically obtained and analyzed and put into usable forms. Contractors often have at hand large amounts of information, but it is in a raw and unusable form because they have no systematic process for handling and analyzing it; and much of it is acquired incidentally and without deliberation through other systems, such as the payroll.

It is not essential to use a computerized estimating—cost accounting—management system, as described in Chapter 4, to obtain and analyze information and data. But it is necessary to have a systematic process; and then, when it becomes economical and desirable, a subsequent change to electronic data processing (EDP) should not be too difficult. The greatest difficulties with CA are usually at the outset, and not primarily with the system but rather with people; and the same can be said about the next stage, computerization.

CA is not usually a popular subject, and for everyone in a company who realizes its value there will be others who will resist it; some, because they are suspicious that it is a waste of time and money, and that it will only lead to more paperwork and a larger overhead; others, because they do not want the additional responsibility; and still others who would prefer not to have someone know as much as they do about the costs of the jobs that they are supervising.

Some of these attitudes are justified, at least in part and at the outset. Some CA is not worth the expense, because data is obtained and never used; and CA has been made an end in itself in some companies. As to the matter of responsibility, it should be understood that CA is an integral part of construction management and supervision, and it is, therefore, part of the normal duties of supervisory staff. Finally, no competent foreman or supervisor need fear anything from CA, because it is an objective extension of the estimating process; primarily, to report on an estimate's validity and to provide data for estimating and management. Perhaps the main reasons for the opposition to CA come from a lack of understanding and knowledge, which is understandable when one sees the lack of training for construction foreman and supervisors, particularly in estimating and cost accounting.

CODES FOR CA

First, it is necessary to have a code for CA whereby items of work are represented by a series of symbols; and at this point it would be worthwhile to review the meaning of the term, item of work.[6] A code is necessary for several reasons, but primarily for brevity, accuracy, and for better communication.

Brevity is obtained by using, say, up to seven numerals or letters to represent the description of an item of work that would otherwise require several or many words. Accuracy and better communication are both obtained by standardizing and codifying the descriptions of items. Coding makes it necessary to first carefully define and describe the items if a code is to have any value. Once coded, the descriptions are crystallized and fixed within the code so that future misinterpretations and misunderstandings are less likely than with original and loose verbal descriptions.

For example, if the code for "labor placing concrete in footings" is 0303, that numerical symbol will always mean that same item of work in the same CA system. A verbal description, on the other hand, would be much longer and might vary slightly with each writer, so that it might not always be clear whether the item included "labor," or "material," or both. Or, the location "in footings" might be omitted, or "footings" and "foundation walls" might be combined in one item.

Many agree that seven numerals or letters are a practical maximum to represent an item of work, and some say that less are enough. It depends on the structure of the code. Four numerals provide for almost 10,000 items (0001 to 9999), which, theoretically, is more than enough. But the divisions and sections of work and the need for flexibility may preclude the use of a large portion of the consecutive numbers from, say, 1 to 9999.

Several books containing cost codes have been published. For example, one uses letters and numbers:

C-40. All labor costs for handling materials, placing and removing runways, mixing, hoisting, placing and consolidating concrete for reinforced concrete construction, or as follows:

C-41. Placing concrete for columns

and so on.[2]

Another published code uses only numbers. For example:

5-12. Column Concrete: together with a list of third-number classifications to be added:

[2] *The "Practical" Construction Cost Schedule* (Chicago: Frank R. Walker Co., 1968).

1. Freight
2. Cartage
3. Unloading

38. Placing
39. Scaffolding
40. Laying out[3] . . . etc.

In this last code, "labor placing concrete for columns" would be "5-12-38." This entry requires seven numerals and signs, which in the opinion of some are too many. Not only is the number of numerals or letters important to the person writing them down at the site, but it is also important in the use of a computer system, which has a limited number of spaces in the width of the paper print-out used for its reports.

Another cost code is published by the Construction Specification Institute within the Masterformat referred to previously. This code is based on the sixteen standard divisions of construction work. Each item requires two digits (from 01 to 16) to identify the standard division, such as (01) General Requirements, (02) Site Works, (03) Concrete, . . . through to (16) Electrical. A further breakdown of items requires at least two or three more digits; and to obtain proper identification, a total of seven or more digits is probably required, which again may be too many. Masterformat endeavors to embrace all kinds of construction work, and consequently it has to use many numbers initially in identifying the divisions and broad-scope classifications, such as "cast-in-place concrete," and "concrete unit masonry." Most contracting firms need to codify a few hundred items in a limited scope of operations, not hundreds and thousands of items over an entire project. Most contractors need a code that will enable a distinction to be made between, say, "placing concrete in foundations," and "placing concrete in columns"; not between "cast-in-place concrete" and "library equipment." They require a code of limited scope, and one of some detail. Or, more precisely, they require a code that can develop the amount of detail that at times may be required.

All construction jobs are in some ways unique, and there are many differences among most jobs. One job may contain 100 cubic yards of cast-in-place concrete below ground level, and none above ground. Another job may have 3,000 cubic yards of concrete between the footings and the fifteenth floor. The "concrete placing" costs on the one job may be less than $1,000, and on the other job more than $40,000. Can the same cost code be used on both jobs? The answer is, yes, if the code has been designed for such flexibility.

There are several ways in which flexibility can be built into a cost code. Numbers that are multiples of 10 can be used to codify the headings of groups of

similar items, as in the first example above, in which C-40 represents "labor handling and placing reinforced concrete"; and "labor handling and placing reinforced concrete in columns" (slabs and beams, and so on), is represented by C-41, (C-42, etc.). In this way, the ten-multiple code number (C-40) can be used for placing all reinforced concrete on small jobs, whereas some or all of the subsidiary numbers (C-41 to C-49) can be used on larger jobs to segregate the costs of placing the various kinds of reinforced concrete.

Another aspect of flexibility in cost codes is the difference between what might be called the *basic* and the *particular items* of a code. The basic items[G] are those that form the body of the code, including the group headings and subheadings, and the items that are to be found in almost all jobs, such as "labor handling and placing concrete in footings." A *particular item*[G] in the concrete division of work might be "labor in heating concrete aggregates for cold-weather concrete work," or an even less common item.

Each cost code should be formulated for a construction company to reflect its activities and basic items of work. Therefore, each original code should contain a specific minimum number of items. As estimates are made, the estimators will, from time to time, come across items that are not among the basic items of the code. Each of these particular items is then given an appropriate code number, according to its type and the heading under which it should be placed in the code; and that will be the code number for that item in that job. If a particular item continually appears, it should be made a basic item and given a permanent number in the code. Similarly, basic items that prove to be rarely used should be dropped from the code to become particular items if and when they are needed.

No cost code can be completely comprehensive, and attempts to produce and use a standard, rigid, and very detailed code are usually doomed. Such a code will probably be too long and inflexible, and eventually it will prove to be incomplete. Better to create an organic code with small beginnings, and with a framework that has the potential for growth, so that with each job the code can grow to suit the work for which it is intended. This means that the estimator must not only use the cost code when estimating, but that he must also work with it in creating new code numbers for particular items; which means that the code cannot be a petrified thing but must be living and malleable. It also means that the site personnel who are allocating workmen's time to items of work each day must refer to a copy of the estimate to discover the code numbers for the particular items of work of that job. This procedure, it follows, helps to overcome

---

[3] George E. Deatherage, P. E., *Construction Office Administration* (New York: McGraw-Hill Book Company, 1964), pp. 209, 225.

the general inclination to ignore the estimate and to codify items according to individual memory or opinion.

REPORTING FOR CA

There is only one person who can do the original reporting for the distribution of labor costs to items of work, and that is the foreman directing the labor. On a small job, it may all be done by the general foreman, or even by the superintendent; but on larger jobs it must be done by the foremen because it is they who know best what the workmen are doing. If the information is recorded by the timekeeper, it is still the foremen's responsibility to divide and distribute the workmen's time to items of work, because they direct the workmen to their various tasks in the first place. This reporting should require not more than 15 to 20 minutes a day of a foreman's time, for what should be one of his primary responsibilities.

There are many printed forms designed for reporting labor distribution to items of work, and samples of the headings and layouts of several forms are shown and explained in Fig. 12-1.

Daily reports have the value of immediacy, and probably greater accuracy, in that foremen do not encounter a delay in completing the distribution of time if reports have to be submitted each day. Daily reports with a separate form for each item of work are probably most effective on large jobs wherein each foreman should not have more than two or three reports to complete, containing up to a maximum total of, say, twenty individual entries daily. If a foreman is in charge of ten men, and if each man works on two different items in one day, that will require twenty entries, which is not too many; and even forty entries should not take more than about 20 minutes to enter.

Any number of variations on a daily report form is possible, according to a company's requirements and the kind of work done. There are two fundamental parts:

1. The daily checking and recording of each man's total time, and the entry of the wage rate and amount for payroll
2. The daily distribution of each man's total time to items of work (represented by code numbers) for CA.

These two items may be completed together on the same form or entered separately. In larger firms and on larger jobs, they are probably better done separately, providing the total time is checked from one form to the other.

Information for both purposes may be entered on a daily time card, which is sent each day to the head office for data processing, with the information entered as shown in Fig. 12-1.

Many standard forms are published and sold for estimating, cost accounting, and bookkeeping by construction firms; and rather than reproduce them here it is suggested that publishers' catalogues containing illustrations of the forms and explanations of their uses be consulted. One of these publishers is the Frank R. Walker Company of Chicago,[4] which also publishes *Practical Accounting and Cost Keeping for Contractors*, an inexpensive book that explains these subjects and the use of the Walker's forms in some detail.

Equipment time and costs should be distributed to items of work when possible, and this can be done by the daily reporting of equipment hours and their distribution in the same way as for labor. "Idle time" should be distributed to items of work *pro rata* to the distributed "working time." Equipment and plant such as hoists and tower cranes, which have many uses, and which, therefore, cannot always have their time distributed to different items, should nevertheless have their *total idle time* and their *working time* reported daily. An effort should be made to distribute the time to types of work, if not to specific items of work; and when a crane is used for such items as placing forms, steel rebar, and concrete the times can and should be segregated and identified. If any information can be obtained without too much effort, the effort should be made and the information obtained.

Materials should be charged to items of work by means of the cost code, and every order, invoice, and delivery ticket should bear both a job name and number, and a code number, for the item of work. With many distinctive materials and components this is easily done. Most problems arise with the ordinary materials, such as ready-mixed concrete and construction lumber, which are used in many items of work and are sometimes also used in job overhead items, such as temporary fences and barriers.

Ready-mixed concrete can usually be accounted for and its costs distributed to items of work because of the delivery tickets and the entries in Daily Reports regarding concrete pours. Delivery tickets should be marked with a job number and a code number, and Daily Reports should indicate the ticket numbers and the amounts and locations of concrete placed. If both are not done daily, it may be that extra yards of concrete required for waste or for extra work cannot be ac-

---

[4] Publishers of standard forms and complete bookkeeping systems for contractors, architects, and engineers, and of several books on estimating. See the Bibliography.

HEADINGS AND LAYOUTS OF SEVERAL FORMS
USED IN REPORTING FOR COST ACCOUNTING

DAILY LABOR DISTRIBUTION REPORT

Job name/number:　　　　　Date:　　　　　Sheet number:

Employees Name/No.	Time In	Time Out	Hours	O/T Hours	Rate $	Amount $	LABOR DISTRIBUTION			
								(code numbers)		
(1)	(2)	(3)	(4)	(5)	(6)	(7)	(8)	(9)	(10)	(Etc.)

(1) Some use only the name, or only a number; but a combination of both is better. (2) Starting time. (3) Finishing time. (4) Hours worked, up to maximum of a standard day, depending on the labor agreement. (5) Overtime hours worked, entered on a separate line to permit entry of a different rate, and its extension. (6) and (7) These entries may be by a timekeeper, or clerk. (8) (9) (10), etc., are for entries to distribute total time in (4) and (5) to different *items of work,* represented by code numbers entered above the columns.

DAILY LABOR DISTRIBUTION REPORT

Job name/number:　　　　　Date:　　　　　Sheet number:

Employees Name/No.	Rate $	Hours									Total Hours
		1	2	3	4	5	6	7	8	O/T	
(1)	(2)	(3)								(4)	(5)

(1) Some use only the name, or only a number; but a combination of both is better. (2) May be entered by timekeeper, or clerk. (3) Each hour (up to 8 hours) of each day is distributed to *items of work* by entering code numbers in columns, in spaces below. (4) Overtime is entered here. (5) Total hours are entered as a check. This form is separate from any payroll functions.

LABOR DISTRIBUTION REPORT

Job name/number:　　　　Date:　　from　　to　　　Report/Sheet number

Work Description	Code No	Hours	O/T Hours	Rate $	Amount $	Total Cost this period	Total Cost to date	Estimated Total Cost	Difference (+ or −)
(1)	(2)	(3)	(4)	(5)	(6)	(7)	(8)	(9)	(10)

(1) Brief verbal description. (2) Matching code number. (3) Hours worked, up to maximum for a standard day. This may show "total hours" for the indicated period; or, it could contain, say, five columns for daily entries in a week. (4) Overtime, entered on a separate line as before. (5) to (9) These entries may be made by a timekeeper or payroll clerk. (10) Shows difference between (8) and (9) to indicate state of job costs.

DAILY LABOR REPORT

Job name/number:　　　　　Date:　　　　　Code number:

Employees Name/No	Work Description	Hours	O/T Hours	Rate $	Amount $
(1)	(2)	(3)	(4)	(5)	(6)

(1) Some use only the name, or only a number; but a combination of both is better. (2) Description should match the code number at top. **A separate Daily Report** is made for *each item of work* by the foremen. (3) Hours worked, up to maximum of standard day. (4) Overtime, entered on a separate line, as before. (5) and (6) These entries may be made by timekeeper, or clerk.

FIGURE 12-1 Headings and layouts of several forms used in reporting for cost accounting.

DAILY TIME CARD

Man No. and Name   Date

Job No.	Job Cost Code	Hours	Rate $	Class
3004	1008	4	6.00	•
3004	1107	4	6.00	•
3004	9089	1	6.00	TT [a]
3004	1107	1	9.00	OT [b]

(1)   (2)   (3)   (4)   (5)

(*1*) Identifies the job, by number. (*2*) Identifies the *item of work*, and other costs such as "travel time". (*3*) Indicates hours distributed. (*4*) Hourly *wage rates*. (*5*) Indicates the times and rates for (*a*) travel time, (*b*) overtime, etc., in (*3*) and (*4*). This example shows only the information that is entered at the site. The extensions and labor distributions done by EDP to produce the printed payroll and cost reports are not shown.

FIGURE 12-1 (*continued*)

curately accounted for. The accuracy of delivery tickets must, however, be verified periodically.

Construction lumber is more difficult to accurately distribute to items of work. It may be on the site some time before it is used, and once used and installed, it is often soon concealed by other work. With this and similar materials, an estimator should try to include in the estimate all quantities of the material required; not forgetting the temporary uses of lumber for forms and supports, which should be made specific items in the estimate, identifiable by description and by code number. Further identification for distribution purposes can sometimes be made in terms of the species and grades of lumber; but it is not unusual for, say, Standard grade (No. 2 common) lumber, in 2 × 4 and 2 × 6 sizes, to be used for several different items of permanent and temporary work. It is also not unusual for 2000 or 3000 board feet of lumber to be unaccounted for on a job, because: (1) it was not allowed for in the estimate; (2) it was used on the job without any attempt to record its use; (3) it was stolen, or borrowed for another job. These reasons should be obviated by: (1) specific and measured quantities in the estimate for all types of work, including temporary work and job overhead items; (2) daily records on the site; (3) the use of proper records for all materials moving on and off site, and to and from stores and suppliers.

If there is no other provision made to account for the use of such materials, notes should be made in the Daily Report about the amount and use, particularly if the material is used for a job overhead item for which there may be costs allowed in the estimate but no specific quantities of materials indicated. If no effort is made to record the use of these basic materials and to allocate them to specific items, the looseness and lack of knowledge concerning them will be per-

petuated, and the misplaced costs of several thousands of board feet of lumber will make attempts at accuracy elsewhere in the estimating and CA rather futile.

It is true that CA, like estimating, cannot be absolutely accurate, but this is not a valid argument against its practice and use. Practical CA is as feasible as practical estimating if the precepts in Chapter 6 are followed.

MEASURING FOR CA

Of those construction companies that do CA, many are not able to make full use of the cost information they obtain because it is incomplete, and above all, *because they lack interim measured quantities of work.* It is of little value to know the labor costs expended on an uncompleted item of work if the quantitites of work done, and yet to be done, are not known. Without these quantities, the costs have little meaning.

It is a common practice simply to look at the items of work and to mentally estimate the amount, proportion, or percentage of work completed. But this procedure is unsatisfactory and often inaccurate for most types of work, and actual measurement is usually necessary to obtain accurate quantities.

The precepts of measurement in estimating and in CA are given in Chapter 6, and some practical advice on measurement in CA is also offered. Here, it is sufficient to stress the fact that CA without the interim measurement of work is, for the most part, valueless.

Interim labor costs may be a by-product of the payroll. Similarly, interim material costs may be a by-product of other normal accounting routines. But a practical CA system must entail *interim measurements of work*, and it is at this point that some firms fail by not periodically recording the quantities of work done. Part of the reason for this failure is a reluctance to employ a person to do the measuring. On many jobs, the measurement can and should be done by foremen; but on other jobs, because of their size or complexity, the job may require a measurer or a surveyor.

As an illustration of practicability, we can refer to a multi-million dollar community complex consisting of many kinds of work, including reinforced concrete high-rise apartment buildings with underground parking and commercial offices and stores, for which all measurement and all segregation and allocation of labor costs and material costs were done at the site by a young woman trained as a building technologist who reported directly to the project engineer.

Cost accounting is possible, but a practical and realistic approach is essential. Cost accounting undoubtedly creates more work, costs money, and must be done by technical staff. It is easy to cheat a CA system; it should objectively report bad news as well as good news, and it will not always produce immediate results. Site staff are, by nature and training, practical and active, and paperwork does not sit well with them. Therefore, the amount of paperwork for CA must be kept to a minimum at the site. Cost accounting is itself the cause of an overhead cost, and it must be economical and simple. If it is expensive it cannot be justified, and if it is complicated it will fail from lack of support by the site staff.

If necessary, foremen and supervisors who are unfamiliar with CA and its relationship to estimating and construction management should be educated in these subjects. Unless they appreciate the value of CA, some may believe that the allocation of costs to the wrong item of work is not serious, because (it will be argued) it is all part of the total job costs. A foreman may lend a hand at a particularly difficult item of work without charging any of his time to the item, and instead charging all of his time to supervision. As a result, it may appear that the costs of the item involved have been over-estimated.

Ideally, most CA should be done by estimating staff, and the best way to train junior estimators is to have them measuring and allocating costs on the site, and calculating and recording unit prices from completed jobs in the office. Sometimes the title, *cost accounting*, misleads the executive, and CA is wrongly made a responsibility of the accounts department. Because most accounting and clerical staff lack the necessary technical knowledge for construction cost accounting—which is different from cost accounting in other businesses and industries—the CA system may be a failure because the costs are not consistently related to measured quantities of the items of work done.

Most of the time, the need for estimating is immediate and obvious whereas the need for CA is not immediate and obvious, and it may not produce immediate and obvious results. An estimate, and a subsequent bid, may produce a contract within a few weeks of starting the estimate, whereas CA at its best produces only information. Yet because estimating and CA are really parts of the same construction management process, the difference between them is more apparent than real; and estimating without CA is not truly estimating, because "calculating the costs of work on the basis of probabilities" requires historical information and data and systematically recorded experience.

COST ALLOCATION FOR CA

We have cited the 80/20 Rule concerning the distribution of costs in construction ("80 percent of total costs are created by 20 percent of the number of items"), and this general rule must be kept in mind while doing CA. Also, an argument has been made for the measurement of minor, subsidiary items of work (e.g., straight cutting at perimeters) even though it is obvious that such items cannot be separately identified and have correct costs allocated to them in CA. How, then, are such subsidiary items to be dealt with in CA?

Let us suppose that we have among the items of work in the job estimate those shown in Fig. 12-2. There is a major, basic item of work (to be installed in several different areas) and there are several related subsidiary items (including cutting, tying to other work, etc.), as shown. When the bricklayers come to build the partition walls and their time is allocated to that work each day, obviously it will not be possible to divide up their time and properly allocate time to all the items involved, main and subsidiary. The foreman, or timekeeper, will only be able to allocate the bricklayers' time to the entire group of items: concrete block partition walls, together with all of the related subsidiary items, as shown. Nevertheless, the allocation of correct costs to this *group of items* tells the company something useful: if the allocated time is close to the estimated time for the entire group of items, then the estimate was reasonably accurate. And if this represents the usual CA practice as each job is completed, and as CA is done on each job for such items as those in this example, the validity of the estimates made will become apparent despite the fact that it is not done separately for each and every item of work.

Again, if this is the way in which costs are allocated in CA (i.e., to groups of items: generally, to

PRACTICAL
STANDARDIZED FORMS FOR CONTRACTORS
Form 516 MFD IN U.S.A.

QUANTITY SHEET

PROJECT PORTSMOUTH COLLEGE ADDITION ESTIMATOR FV ESTIMATE NO. 1

LOCATION PORTSMOUTH EXTENSIONS JB SHEET NO. 04/1/23

ARCHITECT ENGINEER CJ CHECKED LM DATE 1 June 1987

CLASSIFICATION C. BLK. MASONRY: INTR. PARTITIONS

DESCRIPTION	NO.	DIMENSIONS L	×	H			ESTIMATED QUANTITY	UNIT
MODULAR L/W CONC BLOCKWORK (as Spec. 04)								
6" thick partition walls wi fair exposed surfaces, pointed (as Spec. 04.02.13) both sides; incl cutting to conceal piping & conduits (all other labors meas'd. separately)								
(1st Floor)	2/	204-0	×	9-6	3,876			
	2/5/	30-4	×	9-6	2,881			
	2/	3-8	×	9-6	70			
						6,827		
(2nd Floor)	2/	118-0	×	9-6	2,242			
	2/3/	30-4	×	9-6	1,729			
						3,971	10,800	SF
						10,798	(12,150	BLK)
Fair cutting 6" blkwk at u/side conc deck								
(1st Floor)	2/	204-0			408			
	2/5/	30-4			303			
	2/	3-8			8			
						719		
(2nd Floor)	2/	118-0			236			
	2/3/	30-4			182			
						418	1,137	LF
						1,137		
Fair cutting 6" blkwk at conc abutments								
(1st Floor)	10/2/	9-6			190			
(2nd Floor)	8/2/	9-6			152		342	LF

NOTES: Major item is 6 in. partition walls (on two floors); Minor items include: fair cutting of blockwork at underside of concrete deck (or equivalent work); fair cutting at concrete abutments (concrete walls and columns); and other labor items not shown here.

For estimating, major and minor items are each priced separately (on separate pricing sheets in long estimates.) For CA, major and minor items are grouped together and labor costs are allocated to each group for each floor.

FRANK R. WALKER CO., PUBLISHERS, CHICAGO

FIGURE 12-2 Items in an estimate to be grouped together for cost accounting purposes.

a main item with a number of subsidary items grouped with it) the argument may be raised against the measurement in an estimate of the subsidary items because they are superfluous, since costs cannot be allocated to them individually. But the allocation of costs to individual subsidary items is not essential to effective CA, providing costs are properly allocated to appropriate groups of items, as illustrated.

There is no absolute need to attempt to account for every item of work in every job, and in each job a judgement is necessary to decide whether to cost particular items. The normal practice should be to do CA on all significant items; but at times there may be valid reasons to pass over certain items in a job and to not do CA for those items on that job. Valid reasons for this include unusual job conditions affecting certain items and their costs so that they cannot be representative on a particular job, and unusual features within the work itself (an abnormally high number of corners, for example) that make the work unrepresentative and its costs therefore not a useful guide for future estimates.

QUESTIONS AND TOPICS FOR DISCUSSION

1. State three possible arguments *against the institution of cost accounting in a construction company,* and state three counter-arguments for its institution.

2. Present an argument *for the use of cost accounting by a construction company* that obtains most of the work it does by negotiating rather than by competitive bidding.

3. Who should *allocate workmen's time* to the items of work done for cost accounting, and why?

4. Compose a suitable *cost code for concrete work by a general contractor,* briefly indicating and explaining the main features of the code.

5. Explain briefly the differences between *basic items of work* and *particular items of work* as they are included in and affect construction specifications and cost codes.

6. Show the arrangement and column headings of a *daily labor distribution report* suitable for a construction firm doing a great variety of work.

7. Explain briefly *the problems of accounting for framing lumber* on a construction job, and what should be done to make the accounting as accurate as possible.

8. What makes *cost accounting in the construction industry* unique, and what site activities are usually essential to it?

9. Discuss the main features and practices of *cost accounting for plant and equipment costs.*

10. In measuring conc ftgs for cost accounting it is found that, although the drawings show conc ftgs to be 24 in. wide, the actual widths are from 25 to 26 in. State which widths you would record to calculate the amounts of concrete placed, and explain why. Explain how you would determine and deal with the actual quantities of concrete placed.

11. Illustrate and explain by an example the effects of *cutting concrete blocks* on the costs of masonry work and how the costs of cutting blocks are best dealt with in estimating and cost accounting. (State any necessary assumptions.)

12. Devise a method for estimating and accounting for the *labor time required to install various kinds of wood trim* (baseboard, casings, etc.).

GLOSSARY

Construction people often use construction terms loosely—and some incorrectly (such as *plan*)—and, as a result, misunderstandings occur and disputes arise. Certain terms and phrases in the text are shown in the text to be in this Glossary by a [G]; many of them have an ordinary meaning as well as a special meaning in construction, and that is why they are here. The word *work*, for example, has an ordinary meaning and a special, contractual meaning in construction contracts. A few terms in this Glossary, such as *precontractor*, have been specially coined to describe more precisely a person or thing in construction.

This Glossary originated in this book's first edition[1] and was developed in three later books. It provides a useful means of reviewing the main features of the subject and its background; its primary purpose is, however, clearer expression and better understanding.

Abstract estimate   One made with a summation or abstract of unit prices (often totalled and represented by a single unit price) applied to the simple measurements of a building; usually the gross areas at ground level. The easiest, best-

known, and often least-effective kind of estimate of construction costs.[2]

Activities   See Work activities.

Addendum   An addition to bidding documents issued to the bidders.

Advanced purchasing   Purchasing of materials by an owner before awarding contracts for construction work to ensure their timely delivery.

Agent of the owner   A construction technician, usually an architect, an engineer, or a construction manager, who represents an owner before and during a construction contract in which he is named as the owner's agent and advisor (or one of them) and who usually is responsible for or involved in the design of the work of that contract. A quantity surveyor usually is also an agent of an owner; and there are others. An owner often has more than one agent.

AIA   The American Institute of Architects.

Alteration work   New work done to and in conjunction with existing work, other than complete demolition.

Application for payment   Made by a contractor to a designer

---

[1] Published in 1974.

[2] See Keith Collier, *Estimating Construction Costs: A Conceptual Approach* (Reston, Va.: Reston Publishing Company, 1984), for a more complete explanation and example. Other such explanations are noted in this Glossary by the initials *ECC*.

269

according to the terms and conditions of the construction contract, before the certification of payment by the designer to the owner, and based on the contract's schedule of values previously submitted and approved.

Approximate quantities (of work) Measured by using rounded-off dimensions and by not making minor adjustments for voids, wants, and displacements by other kinds of contiguous work; used usually in conceptual estimates and preliminary estimates (*ECC*).

Architect A person registered as such; one mentioned in some standard forms of construction contracts as the representative and agent of the owner; a designer.

Area-perimeter ratio The relationship between a building's gross plan area and the perimeter of that plan expressed as a ratio; for example, for a building 40 ft square and containing 1600 square feet of area, the area-perimeter ratio is 10.0; for a building 20 ft by 100 ft, and 2000 square feet of area, the ratio is 8.33. Typical ratios for apartment buildings range from 10 to 30, and for parking garages, from 30 to 150 (*ECC*).

Bank measure (in-bank measure) The measurement of natural ground to be excavated in place and before excavation, because soil increases in bulk once it is excavated.

Bar chart See Gantt bar chart.

Bare costs The actual direct costs before adding any markup for overhead costs and profit. A term usually in need of particular definition.

Basic element One similar in makeup and usage to a basic item of work; an element commonly found in a particular class of construction, whose historical costs are therefore useful in making elemental estimates. (If necessary an element's unit costs may be reduced to those of a basic element for estimating purposes by deducting the theoretical costs of minor atypical features of the element.)

Basic item (of work) Item of work identified and described in specifications and in cost codes and commonly found in a particular type of construction work, which can therefore be part of a basic cost code or a basic specification for that type of construction, as opposed to a particular item of work; the criterion being an item's practically inevitable occurrence in that type of work (for example, concrete footings in building construction), even though their dimensions and details vary. It is the recurrence of basic items in projects that makes their identification and the use of basic specifications and cost codes possible and effective.

Bid An offer to do construction work for payment, the acceptance of which constitutes a contract between the precontractor who made the bid (i.e., the bidder) and the owner who accepted it. Also known as a proposal (in the United States) and a tender (in Canada and in most other English-speaking countries). Sometimes called a general bid when made by a general contracting company that seeks to become a contractor (or a general contractor) or a sub-bid when made by a specialist contracting company that hopes to become a subcontractor. Also known in legal terminology as an offer.

Bid bond A bond provided by a surety company on behalf of a bidder to guarantee to an owner that the bidder will enter into a construction contract with the owner in accordance with his bid if it is accepted by the owner. The bid bond is forfeited to the owner if the bidder does not enter into a contract when his bid is accepted; or if, alternatively, the bidder does not pay to the owner an amount (by way of damages) equal to the difference between the amount of the defaulting bidder's bid and that of the next largest bid (assuming there is more than one bid); but only up to the face amount of the bid bond, that is, usually not less than 10 percent of the bid amount.

Bid depository A system, usually set up by a contractors' organization, to regulate sub-bidding by receiving, registering, and distributing sub-bids to general bidders as designated by the sub-bidders; usually, the use of a bid depository is authorized or required by the bidding authority. (See also, Plan room.)

Bidder One who makes a bid.

Bidding authority Someone who solicits bids for construction work and provides bidding documents for that purpose; usually an owner (private or public) or an owner's agent such as an architect, an engineer, or a construction manager; the owner/designer seeking bids who, therefore, has the authority to state requirements for bidding.

Bidding documents Issued by an owner or by a designer on an owner's behalf to bidders; the same in content as the subsequent contract documents (assuming that a contract is made) plus certain other documents needed for bidding but not for a construction contract, such as the instructions to bidders.

Bid estimate One made as a basis for a bid for construction work and therefore usually more detailed than a preliminary estimate, but not necessarily so.

Bid peddling See Bid shopping.

Bid shopping The practice of some contracting companies which, having received sub-bids for work, suggest separately to each of the subtrade bidders with the lowest sub-bids that they reconsider their bids and submit new and lower sub-bids because their original sub-bids were, they say, not quite low enough; something like a Dutch auction conducted covertly and with the bidders kept apart.

Bills of materials Lists or schedules of materials required for construction work prepared by a contractor or his subcontractors after a construction contract is made but before and as a means of purchasing. Sometimes prepared by a designer as part of the bidding documents for a construction contract, but not usually in building construction contracts nor as a means to advanced purchasing. (Not the same as bills of quantities.)

Bills of quantities (BOQ) Used in contracts with quantities as bidding documents and as contract documents and containing the terms and conditions (commonly by reference to standard contract documents), specifications, and accurately measured quantities of work (according to a published standard method of measurement), which during bidding are priced by the bidders in the calculation of their bids. BOQs are usually prepared by an agent of the owner such as (in engineering projects) an engineer or (in building projects) a quantity surveyor. BOQs are roughly equivalent to a project manual in North America, except for the insertion, in BOQs, of measured quantities of (the) work and "cash columns" for their pricing by bidders; bills are usually identified by the names of the construction trades represented, hence the use of the plural bills. BOQs are not unlike the schedules of quantities and schedules of unit prices used in some engineering contracts in North America for engineering construction work, but are usually more detailed and specific and based on a national standard method of measurement, particularly when intended for building construction work.

Bonus See Liquidated damages, Penalty.

Builder's work Generally trade work done in conjunction with and subsidiary to the work of mechanical, electrical, or other mechanical installations, such as building equipment that requires a certain amount of cutting and patching of other trade work and minor related trade work (such as excavation and concrete) done in conjunction.

Building (construction) work (as distinct from engineering construction work) Generally custom-designed work for shelter construction or other buildings for use by people, including residential, commercial, institutional, governmental, and industrial buildings; typically involving the work of a large number of trades.

Building density The relative proportion of actual work within a building's inner space, or volume; with particular reference to partition walls, fixtures, and similar work, the precise nature of which depends on the class of building; an important thing to consider when comparing buildings and their costs.

Building element See Element (of construction).

Building equipment Machinery and equipment permanently installed in and as part of a building as distinct from equipment and construction equipment.

CAD (computer-aided design) Design that employs computers for graphic representations and for calculations (for structures, energy conservation, and capacities of mechanical and electrical systems, for example).

Calculated risk In estimating, a risk that is recognized and for which costs are calculated and included in the estimate either by simply making an allowance based on a best estimate or by measurement and calculation of costs (of, say, certain temporary work) and then by including in the estimate a proportion of those calculated costs based on the degree of probability of the risk materializing.

Cash allowance An amount of money specified to be allowed by all bidders in their bids for specific parts of the work of a project for which the owner or an agent of the owner is unable or unwilling at the time of preparing the bidding documents to provide sufficient design information to enable the bidders to estimate the costs of that specific part or parts; which specified amount is the agent's best estimate of the costs. (The contract sum is subsequently adjusted according to the amount of variation between the actual amount instructed [by the agent of the owner] to be expended on the specified parts of the work and the specified amount of the cash allowance.) Also known as a prime cost sum (P.C. sum) or a provisional sum, especially outside the United States.

Cash discount A discount from a written price given by a supplier to a customer for payment for the materials supplied by a stipulated date. (See also Trade discount and Volume discount.)

Certificates of payment Periodically made by the agent of the owner following approval of an application for payment, according to the terms and conditions of the construction contract, to certify to the owner that a specified amount is due for payment to the contractor. A normal prerequisite for payment to a contractor.

Certified cost engineer A member of the American Association of Cost Engineers certified by that body for his experience, ability, and knowledge. (See also Cost engineer.)

Change in (the) work (of a construction contract) Contractually either the subject of a change order or of a minor change in the work (of a construction contract), as defined by the contract, such as the AIA Document A201. Known also (in AIA Document A201) as a modification (a broader term) and in some contracts as a variation.

Change order An order issued by an agent of the owner according to the terms and conditions of a construction contract to the contractor to make a specific change in the work that may result in a change in: the scope of the contract's work, the contract sum, or the contract time; depending on the change order's purpose and substance.

Chartered quantity surveyor A member of the Royal Institution of Chartered Surveyors (RICS), qualified in quantity surveying and entitled to use this title and the designation ARICS (the general appellation) or FRICS (Fellow). (See also Quantity surveyor.)

C.I.Q.S. The Canadian Institute of Quantity Surveyors.

Circular cutting (and waste) Cutting any material or work to a curved line and the resultant waste (offcut), which is usually higher than that due to straight cutting.

Clerk of (the) works An inspector and monitor of construction work employed by an owner, usually under the direction and control of an agent of the owner, sometimes according to a construction contract's terms and conditions. Generally an obsolete term used primarily outside North America.

CM Initials representing Construction Management or construction manager.

CM arrangement (of contracts) One in which an owner has several separate construction contracts with several specialist (trade) contractors for the work of a project.

CM project A project administered by a construction manager, usually with a CM arrangement of contracts.

Component (as distinct from unassembled material, such as yard lumber) A portion of construction work that is classed as material but usually composed (prefabricated) elsewhere and off the site, often in a factory; sometimes, but not necessarily, made according to a special design for a particular project. (See also Products.)

Conceptual estimate One made from rudimentary design information such as a schedule of space requirements, preliminary design sketches, and outline specifications; usually made by a quantity surveyor or other cost consultant; often a preliminary estimate; sometimes a bid estimate (*ECC*).

Conceptual estimating The process of making a conceptual estimate by substituting absent design information (e.g., construction details) with that from the estimator's experience, and by judging a project's design requirements from other criteria (e.g., the class of building; the economic constraints on the work; economic utility; the owner/designer's requirements and predilections); often made by using an elementary cost analysis, or approximate quantities of work.

Conceptual estimator A convenient but improbable term for an estimator who makes a conceptual estimate.

Construction The design and production of construction work.

Construction contracts See Contract with quantities, Cost-plus-fee contract, Maximum cost-plus-fee contract, Stipulated-sum contract, and Unit-price contract.

Construction costs See Costs of construction work.

Construction equipment Mobile machinery used in performing construction work, such as a bulldozer or a crane. (See also Plant, Equipment, Building equipment.)

Construction management In the ordinary and traditional sense, normal management of construction work, usually by a contractor with subcontractors; but in a more recent and specialized sense, Construction Management (CM)—capitalized to distinguish it from the other—involves a contractual arrangement in which an owner employs a construction manager as an agent and has a number of separate construction contracts (instead of one) for the several parts of the work of a project, all arranged, managed, and coordinated by the owner's construction manager, often working with other agents of the owner. (See also Development management, Project management.)

Construction management contract One between an owner or his project manager and a construction manager for the management of a CM project, usually for an agreed fee.

Construction manager A person (corporate or individual) appointed by an owner (or by an owner's project manager) as an agent of the owner to work with other agents of the owner in designing construction work, preparing bidding documents and contract documents, arranging construction contracts, and managing the several contractors to ensure that all of the work of the CM project is completed within the scheduled time and budget, according to the terms and conditions of a construction management contract.

Construction materials See Materials.

Construction work See Work.

Consumable items Those that are used, worn, or consumed by doing work, especially fuel and lubricants, parts of equipment such as fan-belts and sparkplugs, and parts of tools such as saw blades.

Contact-area (of forms) The area of formwork actually in contact with the concrete; commonly used as the primary basis of measurement and pricing of formwork.

Contingency allowance (sum) An amount included in an estimate by the estimator to provide for specific or nonspecific contingencies that may arise during the work (e.g., a snowfall requiring clearing, or the discovery of rock below ground surface requiring blasting and removal). (See also Cash allowance.)

Contract amount See Contract sum.

Contract documents Specifications, drawings, contract agreement, terms and conditions, and other such documents prepared by agents of an owner, initially as bidding documents, that describe and illustrate the work of a construction contract and how it shall be performed and paid for; properly containing nothing that was not part of the initial bidding documents except by mutual consent of the owner and the contractor, as listed in the contract's written agreement and as modified by any subsequent modification (which is also a contract document).

Contract manager One who contracts to manage a project and to advise and to represent the owner. One hired by a contractor to do the same. Not a common title in North America.

Contract sum The total amount of money paid by an owner to the contractor, usually in monthly installments, for construction work done according to the construction contract between them. In stipulated-sum contracts the contract sum is explicit but subject to modification; in other contracts it may be only implicit and not finally determined until the work is completed; also called in some contracts the contract amount.

Contract time The period stipulated in a construction contract for the substantial completion of the work, or the actual time taken for completion if no contract time is stipulated.

Contract with quantities: A construction contract in which the contract documents (and the bidding documents) include bills of quantities prepared by a quantity surveyor employed as an agent by the owner.

Contractor The party (of the second part) to a construction contract who does the work or part of it.

Contractor's estimate One made for purposes of bidding or negotiation for construction work. (See also Conceptual estimate, Bid estimate, Preliminary estimate.)

Cost accounting That part of ordinary construction management by which the actual costs of construction work are segregated and attributed to specific items of work, or groups of items, and to specific items of job overhead costs, after which the cost information is analyzed and the results are combined with other data for use in planning and scheduling, in cost control, and in estimating the costs of other projects.

Cost-benefit analysis A technique for appraising investments in projects that attempts to identify and evaluate all their costs and benefits; not only the purely monetary but also the social benefits; as distinct from other analyses, such as feasibility studies, that deal only in purely business terms; but this is not always easily done. (How does one measure the aesthetic pleasure that may be derived from developing a park, for example?)

Cost code Figures, letters, or words arranged in a systematic code for the representation of items of work and job overhead items; used for speed, ease, and convenience in estimating, cost accounting, and other construction management functions. The Masterformat provides a numerical code, for example. (See also Basic item.)

Cost consultant A general term for a quantity surveyor, construction economist, cost engineer, or other professional person who provides expert advice on construction costs and economics.

Cost control The part of construction management that seeks to ensure during both design and production that construction costs incurred in a project do not exceed, in an owner's case, the budgeted amount, and in a contractor's case, the estimated costs.

Cost engineer One with education and experience in construction and construction economics who uses his knowledge and skills in cost estimates, cost control, construction management, and other areas of construction. (See also Certified cost engineer, Quantity surveyor.)

Cost estimate See Estimate (of construction costs).

Cost information and data See Information, Data.

Cost planning The technique of estimating and accounting for the costs of (construction) work during the design phase (of construction) and of selecting materials and methods and types of construction contracts to ensure the completion of the work of a project within the financial budget and time schedule.

Cost-plus-fee contract One in which the owner agrees to pay the contractor (usually each month) all the actual, direct costs (of construction work) (the reimbursable costs of work), plus a fee—either a lump-sum fee paid in installments pro rata the actual direct costs or a percentage of the actual direct costs—to allow for the indirect costs (the nonreimbursable costs) of the work. Generally this kind of contract is made because an owner or designer is unable to provide bidders with more design information about the required work and because the owner is therefore unable to obtain at an acceptable price another kind of construction contract (such as a lump-sum contract) with less risk for himself.

Costs in use All of the costs incurred by an owner as a result of his ownership of a building (or other development) over and above the initial costs of the (construction) work, including the costs of the land, its development, and the development costs, including depreciation, maintenance, taxes, insurances, the costs of financing, vacancies (of rental properties), management, and all other operating costs.

Costs of (construction) work All of the direct costs and indirect costs (of construction) work; generally classified as labor costs, material costs, plant and equipment costs, job overhead costs, operating overhead costs, and profit.

Cover bid One that is not intended as a genuine bid but is submitted in order to satisfy appearances.

CPM See Critical path method.

Crashing Speeding activities in a construction schedule in order to complete the work in a shorter time. The objective is to "crash" only those activities necessary for an economically optimum solution, since crashing costs more.

Critical items of work Those that determine the minimal duration of a project; those on the critical path.

Critical path The longest irreducible sequence of work activities and events that determines the minimal duration of a project.

Critical path method (CPM) A method of planning and scheduling using a list of work activities that are graphically represented in a critical path network (diagram) in order to discover the critical path.

Critical path network (diagram) A graphic means of determining and demonstrating the critical path of activities in a project. A network consists of arrows representing work activities and nodes (circles) representing events, or vice versa.

Cube (item) An item of work in an estimate whose quantity is expressed as a volume. (See also Super, Run, Number.)

Custom (items, design) Specially designed; not standard.

Cut-and-fill line A line on a site plan joining those imaginary points at which neither cut (excavation) nor fill (placing of fill material) occurs, because at those points the ground's existing elevations are equal to the desired finished elevations; consequently, cut-and-fill lines separate areas of cut from areas of fill.

Data (as distinct from information) Information from several sources analyzed and synthesized to give reference levels of productivity and costs and other things as bases and guides for estimating costs, planning work, and other construction management activities.

Deduction In estimating, a negative quantity required by deliberate overmeasurement (of irregular shapes) and adjustment for a want, or for an opening or void in the work measured.

Density (of a building) See Building density.

Depreciation The lessening in value of tangible assets due to any cause; usually, physical aging, use, wear and tear, and obsolescence.

Design information That information about a project provided to bidders and to contractors by the owner and designer and others (agents of the owner); as distinct from experiential information together with which the design information ideally comprises all of the information needed to perform the construction contracts of the project.

Design phase (of construction) The earlier phase in which the work is designed, usually followed by the production phase. The two phases are sequential in traditional construction, but in CM projects the two phases may more or less overlap, thus enabling fast-track construction.

Designer A party to a contract to provide professional design services to an owner (the other party); usually an architect or an engineer; sometimes a construction manager; sometimes a person (corporate or individual) who performs the design function as part of a package deal, turnkey project, or development project.

Designer's consultant   A party to a contract to provide specialized design services to a designer for building structures, mechanical and electrical services, acoustic treatment, and suchlike. Also, one who provides cost consulting or management services to a designer.

Designer's estimate   An estimate made for an owner by his agent or employee before receiving bids or before entering into negotiations for construction work. Also called a conceptual estimate, preliminary estimate, budget estimate, or approximate estimate.

Developer   A person (corporate or individual) who develops land through construction and who therefore becomes an owner to this end; one who seeks a profit from development of land, either by selling a development or by holding it to reap a return on the investment.

Development costs   All the costs from land assembly and acquisition to the fees paid to real estate agents for selling a developed property of which the construction costs may be a lesser part; often divided into "hard" and "soft" development costs, the former going for tangible things and the latter for intangibles such as advertising and fees.

Development management   Professional services wider in scope and at a higher level of responsibility than either construction management or project management and embracing both of these. The complete management of an investment in real property, including (if necessary) land assembly and acquisition, feasibility studies, design, estimates of construction costs, value engineering, cost control, production of construction work, and possibly property management.

Development management project   One in which the owner is represented by a development manager.

Development manager   A corporation that provides development management services for a fee.

Direct costs (of construction work)   Generally classified as labor costs, material costs, plant and equipment costs, and job overhead costs, all of which are directly attributable to a specific project. (See also Indirect costs [of construction work].)

Direct labor costs   Those paid directly by a contractor to a worker. (See also Indirect labor costs.)

Discount   See Cash discount, Trade discount, Volume discount.

Division (of work)   One of the 17 standard divisions of construction work in the Masterformat. Divisions in specifications are divided into nonstandard sections of work by the specification writer, according to the nature and extent of the work, to facilitate the production of specifications and bidding. The 17 standard divisions are:

Division 0—Contract
Division 1—General Requirements
Division 2—Sitework
Division 3—Concrete
Division 4—Masonry
Division 5—Metals
Division 6—Wood and Plastics
Division 7—Thermal and Moisture Protection
Division 8—Openings (Windows and Doors)
Division 9—Finishes
Division 10—Specialties
Division 11—Equipment
Division 12—Furnishings
Division 13—Special Construction
Division 14—Conveying Systems
Division 15—Mechanical
Division 16—Electrical.

Drawings and specifications   An imprecise but popular term for bidding documents and contract documents.

Duodecimals   A number system based on twelfths used in calculating quantities from dimensions of work given in feet and inches; now generally obsolete but still of value in manual calculations.

Element (of construction)   A part of a structure that always performs the same function in any structure; for estimating purposes, a structure may consist of any number of elements, depending on design, function, estimating limitations, and expediency. A practical minimum number of elements in a building is three, consisting of (1) those items of work mostly related to a building's area, (2) those items mostly related to a building's perimeter, and (3) the remainder. For most elemental estimates more elements are preferable. All building elements consist of at least one item of work and usually more; some consist of dozens of items (*ECC*).

Elemental cost analysis   The allocation of costs of work to elements (*ECC*).

Elemental (cost) estimate   One made by estimating the costs of elements; often a conceptual estimate; sometimes a bid estimate.

Employer   In many English-speaking countries outside North America, an owner in a construction contract.

Engineer (in this text)   A professional engineer registered to work as such in one of the construction-related disciplines, including soils, structural, civil, mechanical, and electrical engineering.

Engineering (construction) work (as distinct from building construction work)   Generally, work other than that done in buildings for shelter, and including highways, heavy construction (dams and such), and industrial construction (refineries, plants, and such).

Entire contract   One in which the entire work of the contract must be performed before any payment for the work is made.

Equipment   Mobile machinery used in the performance of construction work, such as a bulldozer; sometimes called construction equipment to distinguish it from machinery and equipment installed in a building. (See also Building equipment, Machinery, Plant, Plant and equipment costs.)

Equipment costs   See Plant and equipment costs.

Estimate (of construction costs)   At least the calculation of the construction costs of a project; more fully, the measurements and resultant quantities of work, the itemized general requirements, and the estimated costs of (construction) work. (See also Bid estimate, Conceptual estimate, Contractor's estimate, Designer's estimate, Elemental estimate, Preliminary estimate.)

Estimating   The process of making an estimate consisting of two main parts: (1) measurement and (2) pricing. It is reckoned that $M + P = E_c$; that the effort (E) required to produce an accurate and effective estimate is more or less a constant (E_c) for any particular class of estimate, and that, therefore, if the effort put into measurement is less than it might be, then the effort required for pricing must be commensurately greater, and vice versa. The effort required for pricing may be made in part before making a particular estimate by analyzing and synthesizing historical cost (information and data) for future estimates.

Estimator (in this text)   Generally, one who makes estimates, usually for a contracting company, a CM company, a cost consultant, or an owner; also a cost consultant, a cost engineer, or a quantity surveyor.

Event   In CPM an event is the finishing of one or more work activities or the starting of one or more other work activities, usually dependent on the finishing of the former activities; or more usually both the starting and finishing. In one format of CPM, events are indicated by nodes or circles in the diagram to which work activities represented by arrows are diagrammatically connected; in another format of CPM the symbolism is reversed.[3]

Existing work   That which already exists on a particular site when a construction contract is made and which has some physical connection or other relationship with the work of the construction contract in question. (See also Alteration work, New work.)

Experiential information   That information about a project already known by bidders and contractors from their experience; as distinct from design information, which is unique and particular and together with which the experiential information comprises all of the information needed to perform the contracts of the project.

Extra-over (item of work)   Part of, or a particular feature of, an item of work in an estimate, measured and priced separately from the main item to simplify measurement and pricing and to increase effectively the number of basic items and the amount of information related to basic items.

Fair cutting   Cutting of masonry and other trade work that will remain exposed and is therefore required to be executed neatly in a workmanlike manner.

Fair work   That exposed to view and therefore finished to a suitable appearance, according to the class of work.

---

[3] See Keith Collier, *Managing Construction Contracts* for a fuller explanation. Other such explanations are noted in this Glossary by the initials *MCC*.

Fast-track construction   That in which design and production overlap, so as to reduce construction time. (See also Phased construction.)

Feasibility study   A study of the economic feasibility of a project, usually based on a conceptual estimate, development costs, and the estimated costs in use. (See also Cost-benefit analysis.)

Final completion (of work)   Total completion of work and total performance of the construction contract, except possibly for the subsequent making good of any defects in the work. (See also Substantial completion [performance] of work.)

Fixture   A removable item installed and fixed in place in a building in such a way (more or less permanently) that legally it is considered part of the improvements, such as a plumbing fixture or a venetian blind.

Fringe benefits   A popular term for indirect labor costs.

Gantt bar chart   A diagrammatic chart used in scheduling, attributed to Henry L. Gantt and Frederick W. Taylor, in which activities are represented by horizontal bars, the lengths and positions of which indicate the activities' relative order, their duration, and the dates of starting and finishing. In such a chart, usually the horizontal axis shows the weeks, days, and dates, while the vertical axis shows the titles of activities. Probably the most used type of schedule diagram in construction (*MCC*).

General bid   One by a bidder who seeks to become the contractor (or general contractor) for a project; as distinct from a sub-bid.

General bidder   One who makes a general bid.

General condition items   A popular but imprecise term for those items that usually give rise to job overhead costs and which are often cited by the written general conditions of a construction contract, hence the name (e.g., a performance bond). However, many job overhead costs are not mentioned in contract conditions, and some general conditions do not affect construction costs. (See also General requirements.)

General contractor   A popular but noncontractual term for a contractor who has subcontractors. (In the past the term referred to a contractor employing workmen of several different trades who undertook to build with his own forces and financial resources a complete or almost complete building; hence the term is generally obsolete). (See also Primary contractor, Prime contractor, Specialist [trade] contractor.)

General requirements   Those temporary services and facilities and other items provided by a contractor that give rise to job overhead costs and that, because of their general nature, are related to a project as a whole rather than to specific items of work. Properly, specified in construction document in Division 1, General Requirements, of the Masterformat. (Some of these items are commonly referred to in the general conditions of contracts, but Masterformat recommends that general conditions be limited to contractual-legal requirements. Confusion and error may be avoided by references in both parts of a contract.)

GSA   General Services Administration of the United States government; GSA/PBS: General Services Administration, Public Buildings Service.

Heavy construction See Building (construction) work, Engineering (construction) work.

Holdback (money) (also retainage) Those portions of cash amounts due to contractors for completed work held back (retained) by the owner as security and not paid until later, usually at substantial completion (performance) or at final completion of work, according to the terms and conditions of the contract and to any relevant laws (such as a mechanics' lien act).

Idle time For construction equipment, that time spent on a construction site while not in operation.

Improvement A legal term referring to anything erected on and affixed to or growing on land, such as buildings, roads, fences, services, and trees, which legally (but subject to interpretation by local statute) are seen as part of the land.

Independent contractor An individual who has a contract to provide certain services for payment, as distinct from an employee. (Not only related to construction.)

Indirect costs (of construction work) Profit, and those costs of (construction) work generally classified as operating overhead costs which cannot be attributed to specific projects (as distinct from direct costs, which can be entirely attributed to specific projects). Their magnitude is in part determined by the competitive market.

Indirect labor costs Those paid by an employer on an employee's behalf for such things as insurance, Social Security (retirement pensions), and vacations. (See also Direct labor costs.)

Industrial construction See Engineering (construction) work.

Industrial engineering Primarily concerned with the efficiency of industrial processes through time and motion study, work study, planning, and scheduling, and work controls.

Information (as distinct from data) Knowledge about some specific event or thing; here, about particular projects and their work. (See also Design information, Experiential information.)

Instructions to bidders One of the bidding documents that provides bidders with instructions on how and where to make an acceptable bid; one that should not contain anything that would make it necessary to become subsequently part of the contract documents.

Interim payments Those made periodically (usually monthly) to a contractor by the owner during construction, according to the terms and conditions of the construction contract, on the basis of the total proportional value of the work completed to date, less any required holdback, less the total of all previous payments. (In this way the calculation of each interim payment is done anew each time and any errors are not carried forward from payment to payment.)

Item of work A portion of construction work that by its nature can be observed, identified, and separated from the rest of the work for purposes of estimating, cost accounting, construction management, and similar purposes. Direct costs can be allocated to specific items of work. (For example, a masonry wall is composed of one item of work only; the masonry units and the mortar joints are inseparable and constitute one item.) Items of work usually involve only the work of a single trade. (See also Basic item, Particular item.)

Job A popular term for a project or for part of one.

Job overhead costs Those direct costs (of construction work) that because of their general nature cannot be allocated to specific items of work, only to a specific project; as distinct from operating overhead costs. (For example, the costs of temporary facilities on a site, or of a building permit for a project.)

Labor (as distinct from supervision) Workers, the costs of whose work can be allocated to specific items of work as a direct cost; also their work activities.

Labor and materials payment bond See Payment bond.

Labor costs That part of the total costs (of construction work) expended on labor and dependent on the labor rates paid and on productivity, including both direct and indirect labor costs. The costs of work other than material costs, plant and equipment costs, overhead costs, and profit.

Labor item (of work) An item of work the direct costs of which include mainly labor costs and only minor material costs if any. (See also Labors.)

Labor only item See Labor item.

Labor rate The total costs for labor paid to an employee, including all direct and indirect labor costs for a specific period of time (and in a specific place), divided by the total number of hours worked during that period.

Labors Minor items of work consisting almost entirely of labor done for or to or in conjunction with major items (e.g., vertical cutting of brick masonry work where it abuts up to a concrete wall). (See also Labor item.)

Labor unit Productivity expressed in man-hours for a specific quantity (unit) of work (e.g., 0.54 man-hour for one two-joint ell pipe fitting; or, 0.6 man-hour for placing 1 cubic yard of concrete in footings directly from a truck); used in estimating costs of work.

Laps (in construction work) Additional material required by and incorporated into work because of particular dimensions of the work and of the material used and the need for joining by overlapping, tongue-and-groove, shiplap, or other such features.

Lien A legal charge against real property for materials, work, or services supplied for that property (*MCC*).

Liquidated damages (as distinct from damages awarded by a court of law, and from a penalty for late completion) Settled and agreed to (liquidated) damages included in a construction contract's agreement and payable in the event of late completion of the work (*MCC*).

Long-lead procurement The same as advanced purchasing.

Lowest bidder The bidder who has submitted the lowest valid bid.

Lump-sum A fixed and stipulated sum; as in lump-sum contract and lump-sum fee.

Lump-sum contract A popular term for a stipulated-sum contract.

Lump-sum fee (as distinct from a percentage fee) Usually in a cost-plus-fee contract.

Lump-sum items   Those for which the costs are expressed as a total amount without detailed calculation by way of measured quantities and unit prices.

Machinery   One class of material incorporated into construction work. (See also Equipment.)

Management contract   One between an owner and a management contractor.

Management contractor   One who contracts to manage a project, to bring it to timely completion and within an agreed budget, and who participates in the design phase of a project; but who (unlike a construction manager) has subcontracts, although he may not bear any of the risk related to performance.

Market value   That which would be equalled by a selling price arrived at by a seller and a buyer acting prudently and at arm's length in an open market (*ECC*).

Markup   A popular term for the inclusion in an estimate of the operating overhead costs and the profit, often (either singly or jointly) as a percentage of the direct costs, to arrive at the total estimated costs as a basis for a bid or for negotiations leading to a construction contract.

Masterformat   The title in North America of a published system of identification, specification, data filing, and cost accounting based on 17 standard divisions containing nonstandard sections of construction work.

Material costs   Those expended on materials, including the costs of taxes, delivery, handling, storage, and the costs of laps and waste. The costs of work other than the labor costs, plant and equipment costs, overhead costs, and profit.

Materialman   An old, sexist term for a supplier.

Materials   Every tangible thing required to be installed and permanently incorporated in construction work according to a construction contract, including products, components, building equipment, and machinery.

Materials supplier   See Supplier.

Maximum cost-plus-fee contract   One fundamentally the same as a cost-plus-fee contract except that in the former the contractor agrees to complete the work and perform the contract at a total cost not greater than the stipulated maximum cost in the contract agreement. Often this kind of contract contains a ''sharing clause'' whereby the contractor shares in any ''savings'' made by completing the work at a total cost less than the stipulated maximum cost. (Similarly, sometimes the contractor bears a share of any ''loss,'' according to the contract.)

Methods engineering   Primarily concerned with the study of industrial and industrial-construction methods.

Minor change in (the) work (of a construction contract)   Contractually (in AIA standard contracts), the subject of an order by an architect with authority under the construction contract to order minor changes in the work that do not involve an adjustment to the contract sum or the contract time and that are not inconsistent with the intent of the contract. (See also Change in [the] work [of a construction contract], Change order.)

Modification   Defined in the AIA Document A201 as a written amendment to a construction contract signed by both parties

(owner, contractor); a change order; a written interpretation of a construction contract issued by the architect; or a written order for a minor change.

Net, in place   A term used in reference to the recommended method of measuring construction work as set down (outside the United States) in nationally published standard methods of measurement (for construction work); namely, to measure work by the dimensions indicated or, if none are indicated (such as for excavations), according to specific dimensional allowances as laid down, and to make all necessary allowances for shrinkage and swell and waste, as required, in an item's unit price and *not* its measured quantities of work.

New work   Construction work as defined, as distinct from existing work. (These terms are significant in renovations.)

Nominated subcontractor/supplier   One selected and named (nominated) by the owner or agent of the owner in specifications, or subsequently in the designer's instructions to the contractor, with whom the contractor is reasonably required to enter into a subcontract/supply contract, provided the contractor raises no reasonable objection. A nominated subcontractor/supplier is paid for his work and materials from prime cost sums or provisional sums (cash allowances) stipulated in the specifications. The purpose of such nomination is to enable an owner and his agents to delay design decisions about work covered by such sums (allowances), and which are to be performed or supplied by nominated subcontractors or suppliers; to give them greater control over a project's work than otherwise in a stipulated-sum contract. This practice is common in English-speaking countries outside North America.

Nonreimbursable costs (of work)   Those so defined in a cost-plus-fee contract and covered by the contract's fee; usually the indirect costs (of construction work) as defined. (See also Reimbursable costs of work.)

Notice of change   A written notice without real contractual significance issued to a contractor by an owner (usually through his agent) giving notice only of an intention to order a change in the work (of a construction contract); intended to initiate the necessary negotiations for the change without making a commitment.

Number (item)   One for which the quantity is expressed as a number (i.e., by enumeration). (See also Cube, Super, Run.)

Offer   See Bid.

Office overhead costs   A popular but imprecise term synonymous with operating overhead costs that refers to the costs incurred at a contracting company's permanent office (as distinct from those incurred at a temporary site office); sometimes called head-office overhead costs.

Operating costs of equipment   See Owning and operating costs.

Operating overhead costs   Those costs of operating a construction contracting company that, because of their general nature or because they are indistinct or unrelated, cannot be accurately allocated to specific projects as they are incurred and, instead, are charged to projects usually as a percentage of the direct costs by a markup; with profit, the indirect costs (of construction work).

Other contractor A contractual term to describe one who is not a party to the contract in question but who also has a construction contract with the same owner for work at the same site, therefore creating a need for recognition and cooperation among the owner's several contractors at that site.

Overhead and profit A general and imprecise term. See Overhead costs, Profit.

Overhead costs A general term that includes both job overhead costs and operating overhead costs, better replaced by a more specific term.

Owner The first party to a construction contract who pays the contractor (the second party) for the construction work; also the one who owns rights to land on which the work of a contract is done and who therefore owns the work; the client of a designer, construction manager, project manager, or development manager.

Owner-designer A convenient term when referring to an owner in a construction contract who is contractually represented by a designer who at times may act unilaterally on the owner's behalf.

Owner-developer An owner who develops land in order to make a profit from the development.

Owner's agent See Agent of the owner.

Owning and operating costs Total plant and equipment costs. Owning costs that are incurred simply by ownership of plant or equipment and primarily consist of the costs of depreciation, maintenance, and investment, and operating costs that are incurred by actually using and operating plant or equipment (over and above the owning costs) and consisting primarily of the costs of the operator, fuel, lubricants, consumable items, repairs, mobilization, and demobilization.

Package deal Also a "design and construct contract"; one that includes necessary design services for and in addition to the construction work of a project; sometimes a negotiated contract; sometimes a maximum cost-plus-fee contract; sometimes including land acquisition. Some try to make a distinction between a package deal and turnkey project (sometimes called a design and manage contract), but there are many variations and the terminology is loose and unprecise.

Particular item (of work) (as distinct from a basic item) One that requires an original and unique description in specifications and a cost code because it is not a basic item and not part of standard documentation (e.g., standard specifications).

Payment bond One by which a surety company guarantees that the contractor named in the bond will properly pay all legal debts arising from the construction work.

P.C. sum See Prime cost sum.

Penalty (for late completion) A monetary penalty contractually payable by a contractor to an owner for late completion of construction work, often not upheld by the courts (*MCC*).

Performance bond One by which a surety company guarantees to the owner on behalf of the contractor the proper performance of the construction contract (*MCC*).

Performance specification One that specifies the subsequent performance of completed construction work rather than prescribing how the work shall be constituted and installed. (See also Prescriptive specification.) Most construction specifications contain both kinds, often combined.

PERT See Program Evaluation and Review Technique.

Phased construction That in which the design and the production of work more or less overlap, thus shortening the time of a project; this is achieved by creating more than one construction contract for a project; commonly practiced in CM projects; sometimes popularly called fast-track construction.

Physical depreciation That caused by aging, usage, and wear and tear. (See also Depreciation.)

Planning and scheduling Planning includes the listing of all activities in a logical order; scheduling includes calculating the activities' durations and the duration of the entire project and putting dates to their starting times and finishing times. (See also Critical path method.)

Plan room A location (often in the offices of a contractors' organization) at which drawings and specifications as bidding documents are displayed for the use of bidders, often associated with a bid depository.

Plant (as distinct from mobile construction equipment) Static machinery more or less planted and fixed in place (perhaps only for the duration of a project), such as a concrete batching plant.

Plant and equipment costs All of the owning and operating costs of plant and equipment; the costs of (construction) work other than labor costs, material costs, job overhead costs, operating overhead costs and profit, and excepting the costs of small tools, which are similar in nature to plant and equipment costs but usually of less significance.

Points One point is one percent of a mortgage amount charged as a fee or premium by a mortgagee to a mortgagor.

Precontractor (as distinct from a bidder or a contractor) A useful term for one who is actively negotiating with an owner or his agent for work; or one who has submitted a bid that is under consideration but has not yet been accepted and who may be negotiating with the owner over details in the bid or over possible changes in the work.

Preliminary estimate One made during a project's design phase. (See also Conceptual estimate.)

Prescriptive specification (as distinct from a performance specification) One in which the materials and methods are prescribed. (Many items are specified by a mixture of both kinds of specification.)

Primary bid One submitted by a primary bidder for a primary contract.

Primary bidder One who seeks to become a primary contractor.

Primary contract One between an owner and a primary contractor. Also, a prime contract.

Primary contractor A less common but more precise term for a general contractor. Also, a prime contractor.

Prime contract See Primary contract.

Prime contractor   See Primary contractor.

Prime cost   The original costs of materials supplied, or work done, without a markup for the primary contractor. (See also Prime cost sum.)

Prime cost sum   A term used outside North America for a cash allowance. (See also Provisional sum.)

Primordial agreement   The tacit or partly formed agreement that usually exists at the outset and during the early stages of negotiations between an owner and a precontractor, or their agents or representatives, for a construction contract; probably expressed, at least in part, by a large part of the current national standard forms of construction contract with which the negotiators are familiar and containing such things as terms and conditions dealing with methods of payment for work, the provision of bonds and insurances and the supervision of work; those terms and conditions established by custom and usage that are already generally understood and accepted.

Procurement   In construction the procuring and purchasing of materials and other needs.

Production phase (of construction)   In traditional construction the latter phase following the design phase; in CM projects the two phases more or less overlap, as in phased construction.

Production rates   Unit rates of production; the total amount of work done in a given period of time divided by the number of units of time (hours, days); (e.g., placing concrete in continuous footings at ground level at a rate of 0.5 man-hours per cubic yard.)

Products (as distinct from basic materials such as yard lumber and bags of cement)   Construction materials produced and finished away from a construction site that are less complex than components and machinery.

Profit   The excess of income over expenditure for materials, labor, small tools, plant and equipment, and overhead costs; for an owner, a cost of the construction work; for a contractor, a reason for doing work and taking risks.

Profitability   The net return on a business investment often measured by a percentage obtained by dividing profit (times 100) by the business's tangible net worth.

Program evaluation and review technique (PERT)   A method of planning and scheduling when little historical information is available on which to base the estimation of activity and project durations; not widely used in ordinary construction projects. (See also Critical path method.)

Project   An undertaking of which the work of a construction contract may be the whole or a part. In the latter case the several parts of a project may be performed either by other contractors (in the traditional mode) or by specialist (trade) contractors (as in a CM project).

Project management   In an ordinary, looser sense it is practically synonymous with Construction Management. In a more precise sense it refers to an arrangement in which an owner employs a project manager (either as an agent, or as an independent contractor, for a fee, or as an employee) as his representative. It involves services at a higher level of responsibility than Construction Management and often in-cludes the appointment and supervision of a construction manager and a designer, but it is not as comprehensive as development management. (See also Project manager.)

Project manager   A person (corporate or individual) appointed by an owner to act as his representative in a project and to do more or less those things that the owner would otherwise have to do, including (possibly) hiring the designer, construction manager, quantity surveyor, and other agents and employees, making payments for services and for work, and making changes in the work and decisions about other related things.

Project manual   The written parts of bidding documents that become, for the most part, contract documents, as distinct from the drawings; often contained in more than one volume, and often inaccurately referred to as specifications, which are only one part of a project manual.

Proposal   See Bid.

Provisional sum   Similar to a prime cost sum (cash allowance) but included in a contract for work that may or may not be needed (i.e., provisional work) such as work in a substructure, or work required by a contingency, hence also contingency sum.

Quantities of work   Measured quantities of construction work, not simply of materials, in estimates and in bills of quantities.

Quantity surveying   Translating construction drawings into bills of quantities, including specifying the work and the general requirements, measuring and calculating quantities of work and their costs, and making cost estimates. (See also Quantity surveyor, Taking off [quantities].)

Quantity surveyor   One who surveys drawings and measures quantities of work and generally does quantity surveying; one who prepares bills of quantities and other bidding documents and contract documents, arranges for bids and for their review, advises on the selection of contractors, administers the financial aspects of construction contracts and projects, negotiates and agrees with contractors the value of changes in (the) work, checks applications for payment, settles construction accounts, and generally acts as an agent (or an employee) of an owner or of a contractor. Most professional quantity surveyors also undertake feasibility studies and conceptual estimates; they also make surveys, prepare technical reports, and advise on construction contracts and construction economics. They generally perform the functions of cost engineers and construction managers (and to some limited extent those of designers and appraisers) in all fields of construction, but especially in building construction. (See also Chartered quantity surveyor, Cost engineer.)

Raking cutting (and waste)   Cutting material during installation at an angle (or rake) to the lines of the building, or to the lines of the joints in the work, thus creating additional costs of labor and material (through waste).

Reflected dimensions and quantities   Those of work taken from those of other work already measured (e.g., the measured quantities of interior plaster or of gypsum drywall used for painting work).

Reimbursable costs of work   Those so defined in a cost-plus-fee contract; generally the direct costs (of construction work). (See also Nonreimbursable costs [of work].)

Replacement costs The costs of replacing a building (or part of one) with another building (or part) equal in quality and function to the original, but not necessarily identical; the usual basis for assessing the value of a building by the cost approach. (See also Reproduction costs.)

Replacement value Value of improvements based on replacement costs.

Reproduction costs The costs of exactly reproducing an existing building, or a part. (See also Replacement costs.)

Retainage See Holdback.

R.I.C.S. The Royal Institution of Chartered Surveyors.

Rough cutting See Fair cutting, its opposite.

Run (item) One whose quantity is expressed as a linear measurement. (See also Cube, Super, Number.)

Schedule of quantities Similar to a bill of quantities, but whereas the latter is usually only for the work of one trade, and bills of quantities for all trades are part of the bidding documents and contract documents for a contract with quantities, a schedule of quantities often refers to a list of items of work, the unit prices for which are submitted with a bid for a contract, often a unit-price contract. Schedules of quantities are more common in North America than bills of quantities and are used mostly in contracts for engineering construction work.

Schedule of unit prices Similar to a schedule of quantities but often without quantities, as in a lump-sum contract in which the unit prices are intended to be used for the valuation of changes in the work; also used in other kinds of contracts.

Schedule of values (SOV) A breakdown (analysis) of a contract sum, usually required of a contractor in a stipulated-sum contract before submission of the first application for payment for checking and approval by an agent of the owner, after which the SOV is the basis for all future applications for payment in that contract. An SOV usually shows the various sections of work; the names of the contractor, contractors, or subcontractors responsible; and the value (total costs to the owner) of each section or part section, the total of which equals the contract sum. Cash allowances are usually shown separately.

Scheduling See Planning and scheduling.

Section (of a specification) A distinct part of a division with its own title and references that are usually numerical-alphabetical and consist of a standard division number (from 0 to 16) followed by a nonstandard alphabetic letter that varies according to a project's scope and as determined by a specification writer; usually the work in a section of a specification should be:

1. Recognizable as a distinct entity and part of a project's work and consisting of one or more related items of work.

2. Done by only one trade contractor.

3. The subject of not more than one trade's sub-bid so that the scope of all sub-bids contain one or more whole and identifiable sections of work so that no sub-bid need contain only part of the work specified in one section.

The extent to which these requirements are met varies because specification writers cannot determine exactly how a project's work shall be divided among a contractor's subcontractors (unless they are nominated subcontractors); therefore specification writers should create as many valid sections of work as possible in order to facilitate bidding.

Services Water, gas, electrical, drainage, sewerage, and other lines carrying supplies to and wastes from buildings and other structures, and also installed within structures; usually classified as either private services (within a site's boundaries) or public services (within a site's boundaries) or public services.

Shelter construction Generally construction work in buildings to house people; the construction of dwellings of all kinds.

Shop drawings Those made for production purposes by other than a designer.

Shrinkage and swell The increase (swell) and the decrease (shrinkage) in the volume of excavated and imported fill materials that occur when excavation and filling are done. Soils increase in bulk when excavated; fill materials decrease in bulk when placed and consolidated. Proportions of shrinkage and swell vary greatly and depend on the physical nature and moisture content of the material and the manner in which material is handled and treated. Indicative proportions intended as illustrative guidelines only are:

Sand and gravel	Swell 5–20%	Shrinkage 10–15%
Loamy soil	Swell 15–25%	Shrinkage 15–20%
Ordinary soil	Swell 20–30%	Shrinkage 20–25%
Heavy clay	Swell 25–40%	Shrinkage 25–30%
Solid rock	Swell 50–75%	Shrinkage 0%

One cubic yard of ordinary soil in bank measure becomes, say, 1.25 cubic yards when excavated and 1.05 cubic yards, more or less, when backfilled and compacted. (Such figures are only illustrative; actual values should be established by experience for specific local materials with differing moisture contents in different locations.)

Small tools Generally hand tools and small items of equipment (using the term loosely) the costs of which are individually and relatively small and which therefore are normally accounted for and estimated by approximate methods, such as a percentage of labor costs established by experience; as distinct from plant and construction equipment, the individual costs of which are relatively large; although the difference is solely one of degree and the principles involved are the same in both cases. (See also Small tools' costs.)

Small tools' costs See Small tools; the costs vary greatly among projects and for different trades, and different costing methods are needed accordingly; for plumbing work, the costs may be relatively high (depending in part on a contracting company's obligations in management-labor agreements for the supply of tools), while for another trade the costs of small tools may be practically nonexistent. The answers are found by cost accounting.

Source building For estimating purposes, that from which information is obtained. (See also Subject building.)

Specialist contracting company See Specialist (trade) contractor.

Specialist (trade) contract One between an owner and a specialist (trade) contractor; a primary contract in a CM project.

Specialist (trade) contractor A contracting company with a contract to do trade work in a project; usually the work of only one or two trades, hence the term trade (or sometimes subtrade) in the title; often referred to as a subcontractor whether there is in fact a subcontract. Only a subcontractor has a subcontract, and a company doing trade work directly for an owner is a contractor, but not necessarily a primary contractor or a general contractor.

Specifications The major part of a project manual apart from the bidding documents, contract agreement, and the conditions of the contract usually found therein; the written descriptions of work that complement the construction drawings. (See also Performance specification, Prescriptive specification.)

Standard form (of construction contract) One published or endorsed by one or more professional bodies, such as of architects, engineers, contractors, or an association or board made up of representatives of such bodies; usually consisting of a contract agreement and general conditions of the contract. (See the Bibliography.)

Standard method of measurement (for construction work) A document published by an institute of quantity surveyors (or other professional construction body), with or (in some cases) without the cooperation of contracting organizations, or published by a committee of representatives from such bodies, which sets out agreed methods of measurement for construction work, trade by trade, for purposes of standardization and to facilitate and increase the proper understanding and use of bills of quantities, estimates (of construction costs), schedules of quantities, and schedules of unit prices based upon the standard methods.

Statutory law (statute) Written law created by a legislative body; as distinct from case law (common law).

Stipulated sum That stipulated in a bid for a stipulated-sum contract for which the bidder offers to do the work and perform the contract, which stipulated sum becomes the contract sum if the offer is accepted and a contract is made.

Stipulated-sum contract See Stipulated sum.

Sub-bid An offer to a contractor or to a precontractor to do trade work, the acceptance of which constitutes a subcontract between the specialist (trade) contractor (now a subcontractor) who made the sub-bid and the contractor who accepted it; a contract subsidiary to a primary contract between an owner and a contractor. (See also Bid.)

Sub-bidder One who submits a sub-bid.

Subcontract See Sub-bid, Subcontractor.

Subcontractor One who does trade work in a contract subsidary to a primary contract; one defined as such by a primary contract, as distinct from a supplier.

Subject building The one under study; the one the costs of which are to be estimated.

Substantial completion (performance) of work Completion (performance) such that the work is substantially ready and usable for the purpose for which it was constructed, even though some minor items may yet remain to be completed that do not significantly detract from its readiness for use; something less than total completion or final completion; completion so certified by the designer (or other with contractual authority) as substantial completion according to the terms and conditions of the construction contract. Substantial completion is usually more contractually significant than final completion since certain major contractual and other legal matters depend on it.

Sub-sub-bid An offer to a subcontractor (or to one expecting to become a subcontractor) to do trade work, the acceptance of which constitutes a sub-subcontract between the trade contractor who made the offer and the one who accepted it; a trade contract subsidiary to a subcontract. (See also Sub-bid.)

Sub-subcontract See Sub-sub-bid, Sub-subcontractor.

Sub-subcontractor One who does trade work in a contract subsidiary to a subcontract; one defined in a subcontract as a subcontractor to the contracting party of a subcontract.

Subtrade A construction trade, the work of which is usually performed by a specialist (trade) contractor and so called because the work is traditionally performed by a subcontractor; as an apparent contraction of subtrade contractor, often loosely used in referring to a specialist (trade) contractor. In CM projects this work of subtrades is mostly performed by contractors. (See also Trade contractor, Trade work.)

Subtrade bidder One who bids for a subcontract.

Subtrade company One that usually does the work of one or a few subtrades within a subcontract; having such a subcontract, then a subtrade contractor. (See also Specialist [trade] contractor.)

Subtrade contractor (as distinct from a primary contractor) Loosely used in referring to a specialist (trade) contractor, because such persons often are subcontractors.

Subtrade work See Subtrade, Subtrade contractor, Trade work.

Super A popular abbreviation of superintendent.

Super (item) One whose quantity is expressed as a superficial measurement (of area). (See also Cube, Run, Number.)

Superintendent One appointed to represent a contractor on a site, usually according to the requirements of a construction contract, who receives instructions (from an agent of the owner) and generally manages the work for the contractor; one in charge of labor, including foremen, on a site (*MCC*). (See also Supervisor.)

Supervision A contractor's supervisory and managerial staff on a site, as distinct from labor; a distinction made primarily for purposes of estimating and cost accounting.

Supervisor One appointed to represent a construction manager on a site (as distinct from a superintendent, which many supervisors originally were) (*MCC*).

Supplier One who supplies materials for construction work and who is not a subcontractor as defined in the primary contract. (See also Subcontractor, Supply contract.)

Supply bond One given to guarantee proper and timely delivery of ordered materials.

Supply contract One between a supplier and an owner, contractor, subcontractor, or sub-subcontractor, for the supply of materials. (The nature of the materials supplied is often the contractual point on which turns the distinction between a supplier and a subcontractor.)

Swell See Shrinkage and swell.

Systems building (systems construction) The construction of a number of similar buildings for an owner using prefabricated standard building components specially designed for that owner and produced by a system that includes a guarantee by the owner (such as a school board, for example) to build a specified quantity of buildings of the selected design and components within a certain period; the design and fabrication of components that integrate the work of several trades (e.g., wall, floor, and roof components complete with finishes and integrated mechanical and electrical services) and other features intended to give limited standardization, mass production, and resultant cost reductions.

Takeoff (of quantities) The result of taking off (quantities).

Taking off (quantities) Measuring construction work from drawings. (See also Quantity surveying.)

Target figure (contract) Practically the same as a maximum cost-plus-fee contract; one in which a target figure, or maximum amount, is stipulated, beyond which the owner is not obliged to pay, unless the contract provides otherwise; for example, the owner may be obliged to pay only a specific proportion of the costs over and above the target figure. There are many possible variations.[4]

Tender See Bid.

Terminal units Fixtures serviced by a mechanical or electrical system, or both, including plumbing fixtures, air registers, diffusers, and light fixtures; the units that terminate a branch of a service system (*ECC*).

Third party One who is not a party to the contract in question.

Tools, plant, and equipment costs See Plant and equipment costs.

Total completion (of a contract) See Final completion, Substantial completion.

Trade contract One for the work of one trade made with a specialist (trade) contractor; either a contract or a subcontract.

Trade contracting company One that does trade work.

Trade contractor See Specialist (trade) contractor.

Trade discount One allowed by a supplier to a customer

---

who is a contracting company; the amount of the discount is deducted from a list price or from an already discounted price (e.g., list less 30 percent, less 5 percent). (See also Cash discount, Volume discount.)

Trade quantities Quantities of trade work.

Trade work That done by one particular trade according to local custom, trade union agreement, or both; the work of a trade contract.

Turnkey project (also, design and management project) One in which the contract between owner and contractor makes provisions for such things as land acquisition, design of the work, and production, so that an owner can in fact simply pay, turn the key, and walk into a completed building. Similar to a package deal and a development project.

Uniform Construction Index (UCI) The original title form of Masterformat.

Unit cost The unit cost of an item of work is an average cost per unit calculated by dividing total costs of the item by the measured (net) quantity (the number of units). As applicable and needed, unit costs may include material costs, labor costs, plant and equipment costs, job overhead costs, operating overhead costs, and profit. Therefore, the content of unit costs must, to avoid error and misunderstanding, always be made clear. An item may have separate unit costs to include different costs (e.g., in estimates it is usual to at least have separate unit costs for labor); in contracts with quantities, unit costs may include all direct costs and some or all indirect costs. All costs vary, therefore unit costs or similar items in different projects will be different. Nevertheless, unit costs are the only means whereby costs are conveniently compared, and they are the primary source of unit prices.

Unit price Similar to a unit cost but usually consisting of all direct costs and some or all indirect costs, as in a bill of quantities or a schedule of unit prices; usually based on historical unit costs that are based on actual costs.

Unit price contract One in which unit prices for the items of work are stipulated by the bidders and related to the (usually) approximate quantities of the items listed. The actual quantities of work done are later measured and priced at the unit-price contract's unit prices as the basis for payment. (See also Unit cost, Unit price.)

Unit rate See Production rates.

Use and waste Usage (of plant, equipment, forms) and the resultant wear and tear, or depreciation that gives rise to costs.

Value engineering The comparison and economic evaluation of alternative construction methods to produce a required result; an aspect of construction economics.

Variation (to a construction contract) See Change order, Modification.

Void In measuring, a deduction made for an opening or for a minor area (e.g., a stairwell) in a major area. (See also Want.)

Volume discount A discount, or rebate, allowed by a supplier to a regular customer because of a certain minimum volume

---

[4] For more information, see Keith Collier, *Construction Contracts*.

of business transacted between them over a certain period. (See also Cash discount, Trade discount.)

Wage rate The rate per hour for straight wages, exclusive of all fringe benefits and statutory payments for the worker. (See also Labor rate, Direct labor costs, Indirect labor costs.)

Want In measurement, a deduction made for an overmeasurement deliberately made to simplify measurement of an irregularly shaped area. (See also Void.)

Warranty period The specified period (usually one year) immediately following substantial completion during which a contractor undertakes to correct work found not in accordance with the construction contract.

Waste Construction material that is extra to the actual net quantity required by the work, as indicated by a contract, but that is nevertheless required by or used in performing the work, or is somehow lost as a result of doing the work, and therefore contributes to the material costs. (Some waste is usually unavoidable, as in cutting a sheet. Other waste may be caused by careless design and production practices that overlook dimensions of products and the work. Waste is subject to individual efficiency and other contingencies and is therefore essentially variable. It is usually more easily ascertained by cost accounting if it is first estimated and stated in an item's description and thereby kept separate from the net quantity of work and by allowing for waste in the unit price.) (See also Laps, Shrinkage and swell.)

Weasel clause A pejorative term for those clauses in documents that unreasonably pass on to a contractor risks that could be better dealt with by more equitable contractual means; a clause that is an attempt to weasel out of what otherwise would be a responsibility.

Work The substance of a construction contract; consisting of labor, materials, the use of small tools, plant, equipment, and all other services and things required of a contractor by a construction contract, for which the owner pays. (See also Alteration work, Costs of construction work, Existing work, Item of work, New work.)

Work activities A term used in planning and scheduling to indicate the discrete parts into which total work is divided for this purpose. In some projects work activities may be relatively large and may even consist of all the work of one trade; this is common in Gantt bar charts for smaller projects. In large engineering projects, in which there may be large quantities of a relatively small number of items of work, each item of work may be divided for scheduling purposes into a number of separate work activities (e.g., laying a pipeline may be divided into one-mile lengths). In other projects some work activities may be fractions of items while others are groups of items; it is a matter of expediency.

Work study The systematic analysis of work with the intention of achieving greater efficiency from labor and supervision; it involves detailed examination of work in progress and its analysis (*MCC*).

Wrap-up insurance A method of insuring construction work of a project by combining all required insurances for all purposes in one insurance policy, usually arranged and paid for by the owner. The objectives are to ensure that proper and adequate insurances exist for the work and all involved in it, and to reduce the costs of insurance partly by eliminating overlapping policies and by reducing the costs of writing and administering the insurance. Wrap-up insurance is complex and its use requires the services of an insurance consultant-broker.

BIBLIOGRAPHY

The amount of published material related to the subject of this text and available in North America and Europe is immense. This bibliography is limited to a few publications that are particularly relevant and that enlarge on the subject matter.

The following divisions are made for convenience, even though they are not always completely indicative of the listed publications' full contents:

1. Construction contracts and specifications
2. Quantity surveying and construction economics
3. Estimating and cost accounting
4. Construction management
5. Computers
6. Computer software for construction.

CONSTRUCTION CONTRACTS AND SPECIFICATIONS

American Standard Construction Documents, published by the American Institute of Architects, 1735 New York Avenue, N.W., Washington, D.C. 20006.

British Standard Construction Documents, published by RIBA Publications Limited (for the Joint Contracts Tribunal), 66 Portland Place, London, England.

Canadian Standard Contract Documents, published by the Canadian Construction Documents Committee, 85 Albert St., Ottawa, Ontario, K1P 6A6.

COLLIER, KEITH, *Construction Contracts*, 2nd ed., Englewood Cliffs, N.J.: Prentice-Hall, Inc., 1987. Examines the differences among the several kinds of construction contracts, in part by comparisons among the standard forms of contracts used in the United States, Canada, and Britain. One of the few books on construction contracts.

HARDIE, GLENN M., *Construction Contracts and Specifications*, Reston, Va.: Reston Publishing Co., 1981. Part 1 deals with the basics of contracts; Part 2 with specifications; and Part 3 with practical applications, including specifications for the same warehouse building dealt with in this book on fundamentals of estimating.

Masterformat, published jointly by the Construction Specifications Institute, Washington, D.C., and Construction Specifications Canada, Toronto, Ontario. A standard format for specifications, databases, and cost codes in construction, now based on 17 standard divisions (originally 16 divisions), as described in this book's glossary.

QUANTITY SURVEYING AND CONSTRUCTION ECONOMICS

Helyar, Frank, *Construction Estimating and Costing*, Toronto, Ontario: McGraw-Hill Ryerson Limited, 1978.

Method of Measurement of Construction Works, Toronto, Ontario: The Canadian Institute of Quantity Surveyors. Now in the metric mode.

Principles of Measurement (International) for Works of Construction, London, England: The Royal Institution of Chartered Surveyors.

Standard Method of Measurement of Building Works, London, England: The Royal Institution of Chartered Surveyors and the National Federation of Building Trade Employers. (Several editions have been published; commentaries and interpretations are also available. Similar standards are published in some other Commonwealth and European countries).

ESTIMATING AND COST ACCOUNTING

The Building Estimator's Reference Book, Chicago, Ill.: Frank R. Walker Publishing Co. A classic that has gone through many editions, it contains much factual information about construction and many examples of cost analyses.

Capitalized Approach to Budget Estimating, Washington, D.C.: General Services Administration, Public Buildings Service, 1981.

Collier, Keith, *Estimating Construction Costs: A Conceptual Approach*, Reston, Va.: Reston Publishing Co., 1984. Shows and explains through complete examples how estimates may be made quickly and effectively using several different techniques suitable for designers, contractors, cost engineers, and appraisers. A unique and useful book.

Conceptual Estimating Guide, Washington, D.C.: General Services Administration, Public Buildings Service, 1981.

Means, *Building Construction Cost Data* (annually), Kingston, Mass.: Robert Snow Means Co., Inc. One of the best sources of data that can be converted into useful information for both estimator and appraiser. The companion publications cited below are of similar quality. Referred to in this text.

Means, *Mechanical and Electrical Cost Data*. Very detailed information that enables one to make estimates of M & E work following the "tree" format described in this book.

Means, *Square Foot Costs*. Useful to owners, contracting companies, appraisers and others seeking quick approximate estimates. Best used in conjunction with more detailed cost data such as are found in the companion manuals cited above.

CONSTRUCTION MANAGEMENT

Collier, Keith, *Managing Construction Contracts*, Reston, Va.: Reston Publishing Co., 1982. Views this large subject from the standpoint of construction contracts. As a sequel to the author's book on construction contracts, it deals in particular with that relatively new approach to building called Construction Management.

The GSA System for Construction Management, Washington, D.C.: General Services Administration, Public Buildings Service, 1975.

COMPUTERS

BYTE, The Small Systems Journal, Peterborough, N.H.: One of the most informative computer magazines with more advanced contents than some others.

Construction Computer Applications Newsletter, Silver Springs, Md.: Construction Industry Press. Published monthly, with an increased circulation this newsletter should grow into an informative magazine.

INFOWORLD, The Newsweekly for Microcomputer Users, Menlo Park, Ca.: A readable source of computer news and reviews of both hardware and software, and a useful guide for the computer customer.

PC, The Independent Guide to IBM Personal Computers, New York, N.Y.: Readable and useful even if you do not own an IBM computer.

PC WORLD, The Comprehensive Guide to IBM Personal Computers and Compatibles, San Francisco, Ca.: Readable and useful.

PROFILES, The Magazine for Kaypro Users, Solana Beach, Ca.: Slimmer than the former publication, it nevertheless contains much valuable information and is well worth the money.

Sippl, Charles J., with JoAnne Coffman Mayer, *The Essential Computer Dictionary and Speller*, Englewood Cliffs, N.J.: Prentice-Hall, Inc., 1980.

COMPUTER SOFTWARE FOR CONSTRUCTION

CMAC Computer Systems Ltd., New Westminster, BC, Canada.

Means, Robert Snow, Company, Kingston, Mass.

Walker, Frank R., Publishing Co., Chicago.

Appendix

MENSURATION
OF AREAS AND VOLUMES
AND OTHER FORMULAE

AREAS OF REGULAR FIGURES

Triangle

Area = length of one side × ½ altitude (altitude is perpendicular distance to corner opposite the side measured); i.e., $A = z \times \frac{1}{2}a$

Trapezoid

Area = half the sum of the parallel sides × altitude (altitude is perpendicular distance between the parallel sides); i.e., $A = \frac{1}{2}(w + z) \times a$

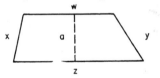

Parallelogram

Area = length of one side × altitude (altitude is perpendicular distance to opposite side); i.e., $A = z \times a$

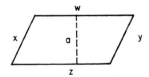

Regular Polygon

Area = ½ sum of all sides × inside radius

Circle

$$\text{Area} = \pi r^2$$
$$= 0.7854 \times \text{diameter}^2$$
$$= 0.0796 \times \text{circumference}^2$$

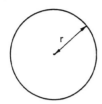

Sector

$$\text{Area} = \text{length of arch} \times \tfrac{1}{2}\ \text{radius}$$
$$= \frac{\alpha°}{360°} \times \pi r^2$$

Ellipse

Area = major axis $\times$ minor axis $\times$ 0.7854; i.e.,
$A = a \times b \times 0.7854$

Parabola

Area = base $\times$ ⅔ altitude; i.e., $A = b \times \tfrac{2}{3}a$

AREA OF AN IRREGULAR FIGURE

Procedure.   Divide the irregular figure into strips of any equal width (d) by equally spaced parallel lines. Measure the length of each of the parallel lines. Apply one of the following rules to calculate the area:

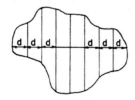

1. Trapezoid Rule.   Add together the lengths of all the parallel lines and deduct ½ the length of the first line and ½ the length of the last line. Multiply the total by the standard distance (d) between the lines. (Usually accurate enough for estimating site work and similar items.)

2. Simpson's Rule.   This rule requires an even number of strips. Add together the lengths of the parallel lines, taking the first and last lines at actual length (1 × value); the second, fourth, six, etc., from each end at 4 × value; the third, fifth, etc., from each end at 2 × value. Multiply the total by one third of the standard distance (1/3d). (Very accurate for figures bounded by smooth curves.)

3. Durand's Rule.   Add together the lengths of the parallel lines, taking the first and last lines at ⁵⁄₁₂ × value; the second from each end at ¹³⁄₁₂ × value; and all the others at full value (1 × value). Multiply the total by the standard distance (d) between the lines.

Notes: The smaller the width of the strips—the standard distance (d)—the more accurate are the results. The areas also can be measured with a planimeter.

SURFACE AREAS AND VOLUMES OF REGULAR SOLIDS

Sphere

$$\text{Volume} = \tfrac{4}{3}\ \pi r^3$$
$$= 0.5236 d^3$$
$$\text{S.Area} = 4\ \pi r^2$$
$$= 3.14159265 d^2$$

Ellipsoid

Volume = ⅙ $\pi\ abc$
S.Area (no simple rule)

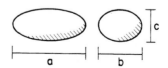

Cylinder

Volume = area circular base × height; i.e., $\pi r^2 \times h$

S.Area = (2 × area circular base (ends)), + (circumference × height)

= $(2 \times \pi r^2) + (2\pi r \times h)$

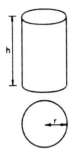

Paraboloid

Volume = area circular base × ½ height; i.e.,

$V = \pi r^2 \times \frac{1}{2}h$

S.Area (no simple rule)

VOLUME OF AN IRREGULAR SOLID

The Prismoidal (Prismatoid) Formula. This formula is reasonably accurate for measuring volumes contained by two parallel planes at the ends connected by planes containing straight lines or smooth curves, as shown.

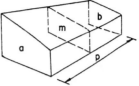

Volume = sum of the areas of the two parallel planes plus 4 × area of the parallel mid-section multiplied by ⅙ of the perpendicular distance between the two parallel ends; i.e., $V = (a + b + 4m) \times \frac{1}{6}p$. The observant may have noticed that the configuration of this prismoidal formula is the same as that for the "three times estimate" related to PERT and cited in Chapter 10.

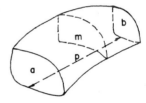

INDEX

CONSTRUCTION DRAWINGS

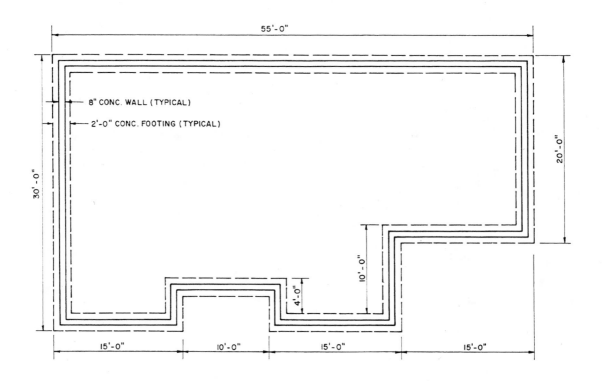

FOUNDATION PLAN

- 55'-0"
- 30'-0"
- 20'-0"
- 10'-0"
- 4'-0"
- 15'-0"
- 10'-0"
- 15'-0"
- 15'-0"
- 8" CONC. WALL (TYPICAL)
- 2'-0" CONC. FOOTING (TYPICAL)

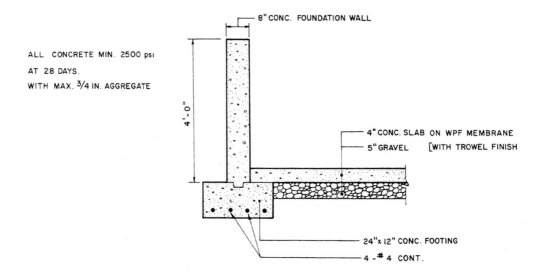

ALL CONCRETE MIN. 2500 psi
AT 28 DAYS.
WITH MAX. 3/4 IN. AGGREGATE

- 8" CONC. FOUNDATION WALL
- 4'-0"
- 4" CONC. SLAB ON WPF MEMBRANE
- 5" GRAVEL [WITH TROWEL FINISH
- 24"x 12" CONC. FOOTING
- 4 -#4 CONT.

TYPICAL SECTION

P-1
FOUNDATIONS

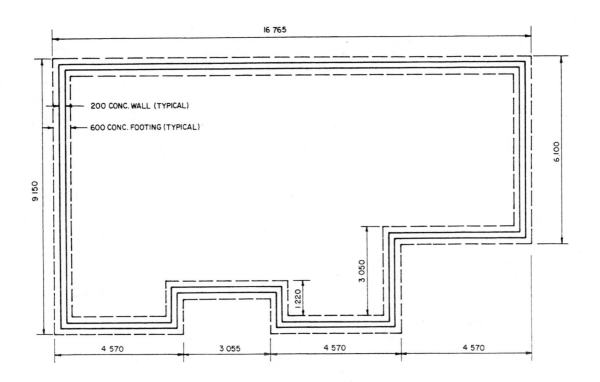

FOUNDATION PLAN

16 765

9 150

6 100

200 CONC. WALL (TYPICAL)

600 CONC. FOOTING (TYPICAL)

3 050

1 220

4 570

3 055

4 570

4 570

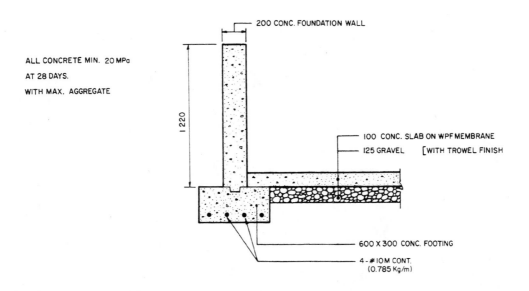

200 CONC. FOUNDATION WALL

ALL CONCRETE MIN. 20 MPa
AT 28 DAYS.
WITH MAX. AGGREGATE

1 220

100 CONC. SLAB ON WPF MEMBRANE

125 GRAVEL   [WITH TROWEL FINISH

600 X 300 CONC. FOOTING

4 - #10M CONT.
(0.785 Kg/m)

TYPICAL SECTION

METRIC P-1
FOUNDATIONS

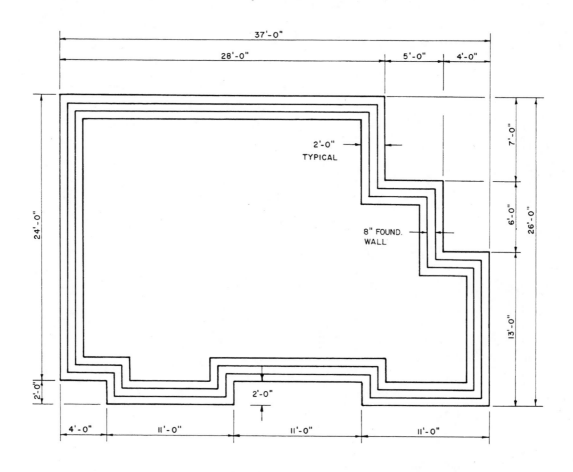

FOUNDATION PLAN

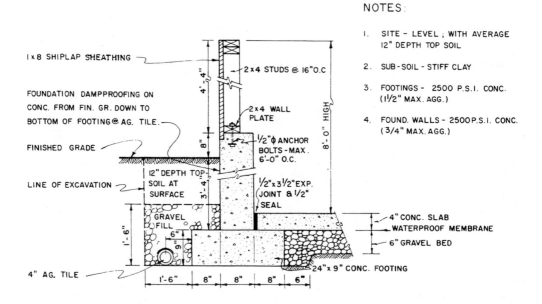

TYPICAL SECTION

NOTES:

1. SITE – LEVEL ; WITH AVERAGE 12" DEPTH TOP SOIL

2. SUB-SOIL - STIFF CLAY

3. FOOTINGS - 2500 P.S.I. CONC. (1 1/2" MAX. AGG.)

4. FOUND. WALLS - 2500 P.S.I. CONC. (3/4" MAX. AGG.)

**P-2
FOUNDATIONS &
FRAMING**

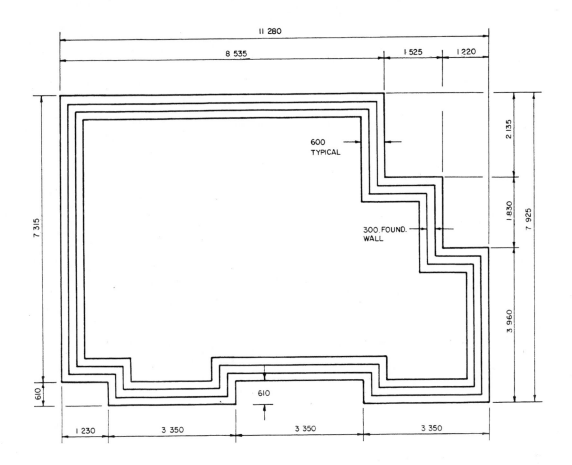

FOUNDATION PLAN

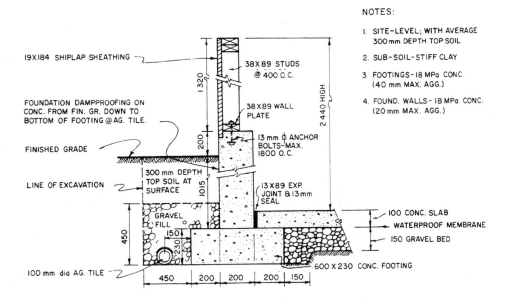

NOTES:

1. SITE-LEVEL; WITH AVERAGE 300 mm DEPTH TOP SOIL

2. SUB-SOIL-STIFF CLAY

3. FOOTINGS-18 MPa CONC. (40 mm MAX. AGG.)

4. FOUND. WALLS-18 MPa CONC. (20 mm MAX. AGG.)

TYPICAL SECTION

METRIC P-2
FOUNDATIONS &
FRAMING

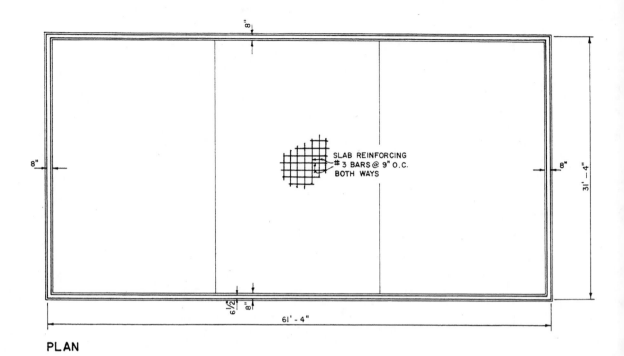

PLAN

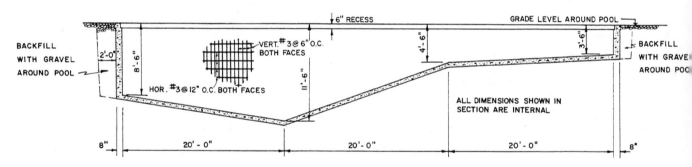

LONGITUDINAL SECTION (NOTE: SHAPE OF POOL SECTION AS SHOWN FOR PURPOSE OF EXAMPLE ONLY)

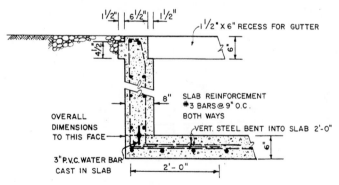

TYPICAL SECTION AT SIDES

(END WALLS SIMILAR)

NOTES

1. 3500 P.S.I. - $3/4$" MAX. AGGREGATE; UNFINISHED CONCRETE.

2. #3 BARS : (0.376 LB. PER LIN. FT.) GRADE 60

3. VERT. BARS BENT 90°, 2'-0" INTO SLAB.

4. CONC. SLAB (ZERO SLUMP) WITH FLOATED FINISH; LAID ON NATURAL GROUND

GROUND CONDITIONS & FILL

1. COMPACTED GRAVEL & CLAY

2. NO TOPSOIL AT SURFACE; SITE LEVEL

3. FILL WITH IMPORTED PIT-RUN GRAVEL AGAINST WALLS

P-3

SWIMMING POOL

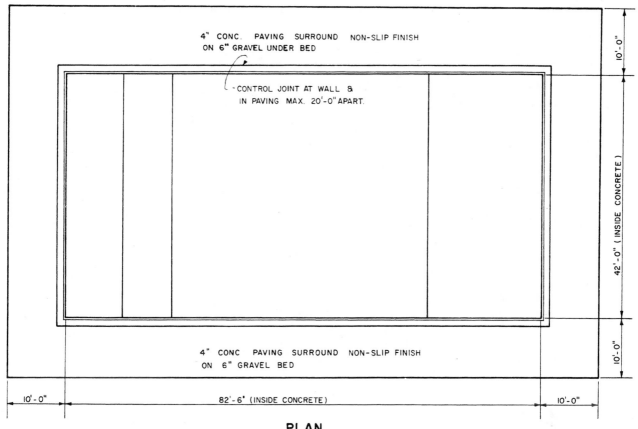

4" CONC. PAVING SURROUND NON-SLIP FINISH
ON 6" GRAVEL UNDER BED

CONTROL JOINT AT WALL &
IN PAVING MAX. 20'-0" APART.

4" CONC PAVING SURROUND NON-SLIP FINISH
ON 6" GRAVEL BED

10'-0"

42'-0" (INSIDE CONCRETE)

10'-0"

10'-0"   82'-6' (INSIDE CONCRETE)   10'-0"

PLAN

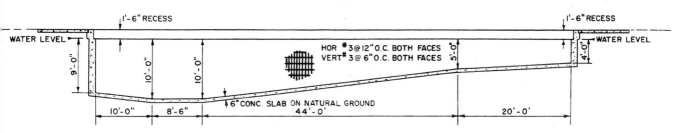

1'-6" RECESS

WATER LEVEL

HOR #3@12"O.C. BOTH FACES
VERT #3@6"O.C. BOTH FACES

5'-0"

1'-6" RECESS

WATER LEVEL

4'-0"

9'-0"   10'-0"   10'-0"

6" CONC. SLAB ON NATURAL GROUND

10'-0"   8'-6"   44'-0'   20'-0'

TYPICAL SECTION

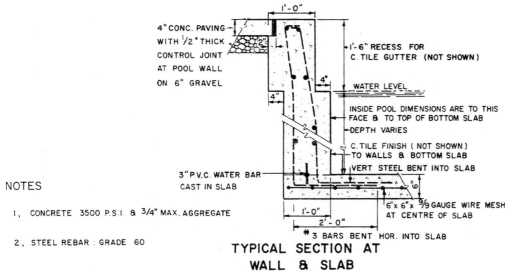

1'-0"

4" CONC. PAVING
WITH 1/2" THICK
CONTROL JOINT
AT POOL WALL
ON 6" GRAVEL

2"

4"

4"

1'-6" RECESS FOR
C. TILE GUTTER (NOT SHOWN)

WATER LEVEL

INSIDE POOL DIMENSIONS ARE TO THIS
FACE & TO TOP OF BOTTOM SLAB
DEPTH VARIES

C. TILE FINISH (NOT SHOWN)
TO WALLS & BOTTOM SLAB

VERT STEEL BENT INTO SLAB

3" P.V.C. WATER BAR
CAST IN SLAB

1'-0"

2'-0"

6"x 6"x 9/9 GAUGE WIRE MESH
AT CENTRE OF SLAB

#3 BARS BENT HOR. INTO SLAB

**TYPICAL SECTION AT
WALL & SLAB**

NOTES

1, CONCRETE 3500 P.S.I. & 3/4" MAX. AGGREGATE

2, STEEL REBAR : GRADE 60

**P–3A
SWIMMING POOL**
(for estimating exercise)

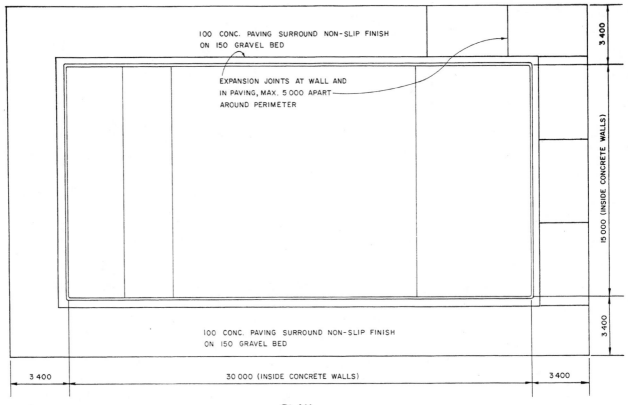

100 CONC. PAVING SURROUND NON-SLIP FINISH
ON 150 GRAVEL BED

EXPANSION JOINTS AT WALL AND
IN PAVING, MAX. 5 000 APART
AROUND PERIMETER

3 400

15 000 (INSIDE CONCRETE WALLS)

3 400

100 CONC. PAVING SURROUND NON-SLIP FINISH
ON 150 GRAVEL BED

3 400

30 000 (INSIDE CONCRETE WALLS)

3 400

PLAN

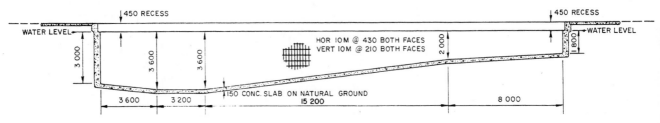

450 RECESS

WATER LEVEL

3 000

3 600

3 600

HOR 10M @ 430 BOTH FACES
VERT 10M @ 210 BOTH FACES

2 000

450 RECESS

WATER LEVEL

1 800

150 CONC. SLAB ON NATURAL GROUND

3 600   3 200   15 200   8 000

TYPICAL SECTION

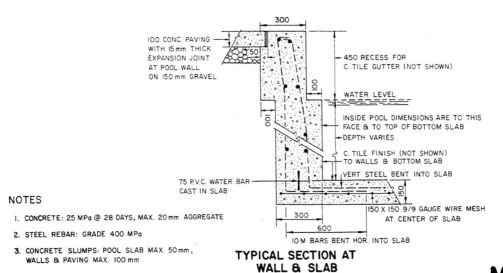

100 CONC. PAVING
WITH 15 mm THICK
EXPANSION JOINT
AT POOL WALL
ON 150 mm GRAVEL

300

50

100

100

450 RECESS FOR
C. TILE GUTTER (NOT SHOWN)

WATER LEVEL

INSIDE POOL DIMENSIONS ARE TO THIS
FACE & TO TOP OF BOTTOM SLAB

DEPTH VARIES

C. TILE FINISH (NOT SHOWN)
TO WALLS & BOTTOM SLAB

VERT STEEL BENT INTO SLAB

75 P.V.C. WATER BAR
CAST IN SLAB

150

300

600

150 X 150 9/9 GAUGE WIRE MESH
AT CENTER OF SLAB

10 M BARS BENT HOR. INTO SLAB

**TYPICAL SECTION AT
WALL & SLAB**

NOTES

1. CONCRETE: 25 MPa @ 28 DAYS, MAX. 20 mm AGGREGATE

2. STEEL REBAR: GRADE 400 MPa

3. CONCRETE SLUMPS: POOL SLAB MAX. 50 mm,
   WALLS & PAVING MAX. 100 mm

METRIC P-3
SWIMMING POOL

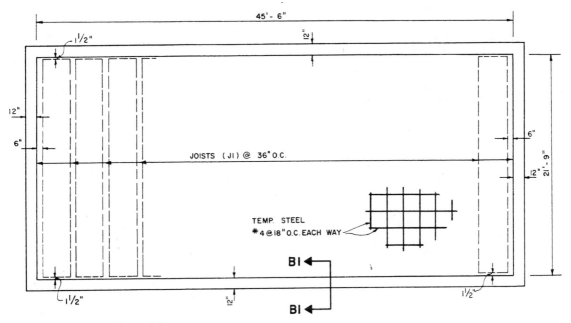

PLAN OF ROOF SLAB

Dimensions shown: 45'-6" (overall width), 21'-9" (overall height), 12", 6", 1½" various callouts

JOISTS (J1) @ 36" O.C.

TEMP. STEEL #4 @ 18" O.C. EACH WAY

B1 B1

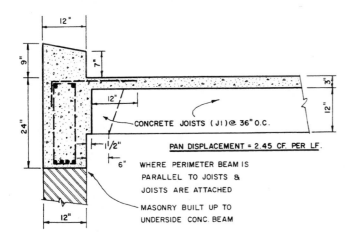

SECTION (B1) TYPICAL PERIMETER BEAM - B1

12", 9", 7", 24", 12", 3", 12"

CONCRETE JOISTS (J1) @ 36" O.C.

PAN DISPLACEMENT = 2.45 CF. PER LF.

WHERE PERIMETER BEAM IS PARALLEL TO JOISTS & JOISTS ARE ATTACHED

MASONRY BUILT UP TO UNDERSIDE CONC. BEAM

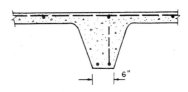

TYPICAL JOIST - J1

6"

SPEC. NOTES:

1. CONCRETE 3500 P.S.I. AT 28 DAYS, 3/4" MAX. SIZE AGGREGATE

2. STEEL GRADE 60, MAX. BAR LENGTH 30 FT, SPLICED LAPS 36 x DIAMETER

REBAR SCHEDULE - JOISTS AND BEAMS

MK.	SECTION	NO	SIZE	LENGTH	NO	SIZE	LENGTH	BENDS	SPACING
			STRAIGHT			BENT			
J1	3 / 12 / 6	1	#7	22-9	1	#8	25-6	4-0 1-4½ 4-0 / 1-0 12-9 1-0	36" O.C.
	NOTE: J1- JOISTS ATTACHED TO PERIM. BEAM ARE NOT REINFORCED								
B1	9 / 24 / 12	4	#8	CONT.	4x4	#8	6-0	3⌐3	SPLICES AT CORNERS
		2	#5	CONT.	4x2	#5	4-0	2⌐2	
					-	#4	5-0	90° STANDARD STIRRUP HOOKS	18" O.C.
					-	#4	2-9	9⌐ 2-0	18" O.C.

WEIGHTS OF REBAR: (PER LIN. FOOT)

#4 - 0.668 LB.   #7 - 2.044 LB.

#5 - 1.043 LB.   #8 - 2.670 LB.

P-4
CONCRETE
PAN JOIST SLAB

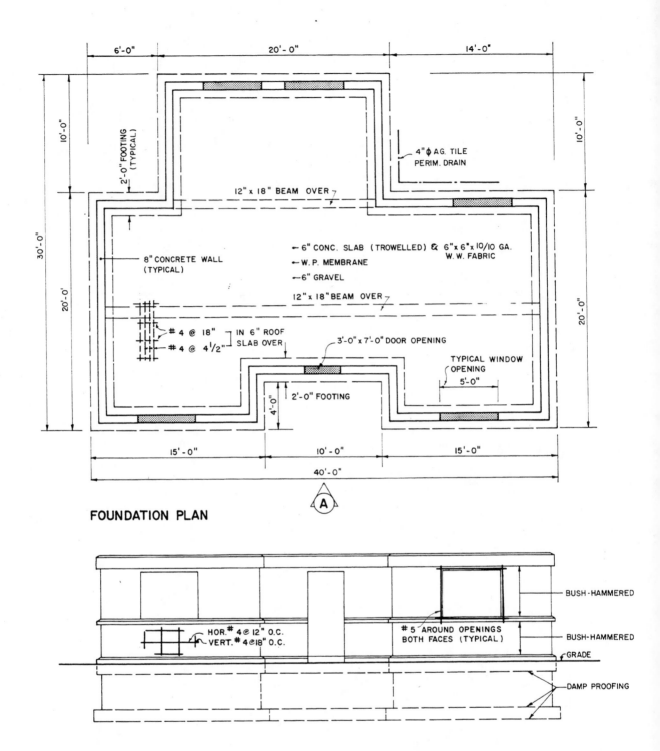

FOUNDATION PLAN

6'-0"   20'-0"   14'-0"

10'-0"   10'-0"

2'-0" FOOTING (TYPICAL)

4"φ AG. TILE PERIM. DRAIN

12" x 18" BEAM OVER

8" CONCRETE WALL (TYPICAL)

← 6" CONC. SLAB (TROWELLED) & 6"x 6"x 10/10 GA. W. W. FABRIC
← W. P. MEMBRANE
← 6" GRAVEL

12" x 18" BEAM OVER

30'-0"

20'-0"

20'-0"

#4 @ 18"
#4 @ 4½" — IN 6" ROOF SLAB OVER

3'-0" x 7'-0" DOOR OPENING

TYPICAL WINDOW OPENING
5'-0"

4'-0"

2'-0" FOOTING

15'-0"   10'-0"   15'-0"

40'-0"

Ⓐ

FOUNDATION PLAN

Ⓐ **FRONT ELEVATION** (OTHERS SIMILAR)

HOR. #4 @ 12" O.C.
VERT. #4 @ 18" O.C.

#5 AROUND OPENINGS BOTH FACES (TYPICAL)

BUSH-HAMMERED

BUSH-HAMMERED

GRADE

DAMP PROOFING

CONCRETE BUILDING —PLAN & ELEVATION

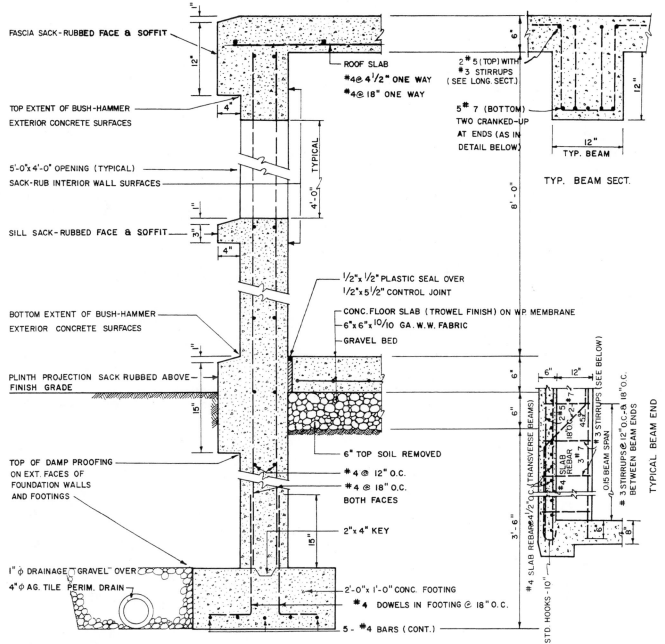

FASCIA SACK-RUBBED **FACE & SOFFIT**

ROOF SLAB
#4 @ 4½" ONE WAY
#4 @ 18" ONE WAY

TOP EXTENT OF BUSH-HAMMER
EXTERIOR CONCRETE SURFACES

5'-0" x 4'-0" OPENING (TYPICAL)
SACK-RUB INTERIOR WALL SURFACES

SILL SACK-RUBBED **FACE & SOFFIT**

BOTTOM EXTENT OF BUSH-HAMMER
EXTERIOR CONCRETE SURFACES

PLINTH PROJECTION SACK RUBBED ABOVE
FINISH GRADE

TOP OF DAMP PROOFING
ON EXT. FACES OF
FOUNDATION WALLS
AND FOOTINGS

1" ⌀ DRAINAGE GRAVEL OVER
4" ⌀ AG. TILE PERIM. DRAIN

½" x ½" PLASTIC SEAL OVER
½" x 5½" CONTROL JOINT

CONC. FLOOR SLAB (TROWEL FINISH) ON W.P. MEMBRANE
6" x 6" x 10/10 GA. W.W. FABRIC
GRAVEL BED

6" TOP SOIL REMOVED

#4 @ 12" O.C.
#4 @ 18" O.C.
BOTH FACES

2" x 4" KEY

2'-0" x 1'-0" CONC. FOOTING
#4 DOWELS IN FOOTING @ 18" O.C.
5 - #4 BARS (CONT.)

2 #5 (TOP) WITH
#3 STIRRUPS
(SEE LONG. SECT.)

5 #7 (BOTTOM)
TWO CRANKED-UP
AT ENDS (AS IN
DETAIL BELOW)

12"
TYP. BEAM

TYP. BEAM SECT.

TYPICAL BEAM END

TYPICAL SECTION

SPECIFICATION NOTES

1, ALL CONCRETE 3000 P.S.I. (1½" MAX. AGG. SIZE IN FOOTINGS, ¾" MAX. ELSEWHERE)

2, BUSH-HAMMER ALL EXTERIOR VERTICAL SURFACES, AS INDICATED.

3, SACK RUB REMAINING VERTICAL SURFACES WHERE EXPOSED & SOFFITS OF SILL & FASCIA (NOT SLAB)

4, STEEL TROWEL FLOOR SLAB. (TO RECEIVE FLOOR TILING) AND SLOPING TOPS OF PROJECTIONS

5, WOOD FLOAT ROOF SLAB (TO RECEIVE INSULATION & ROOFING)

6, DAMP PROOF EXTERIOR SURFACES CONC. WALLS AND FOOTINGS BELOW PLINTH.

7, SITE ASSUMED TO BE LEVEL.

P-5
CONCRETE BUILDING
—TYPICAL WALL SECTION

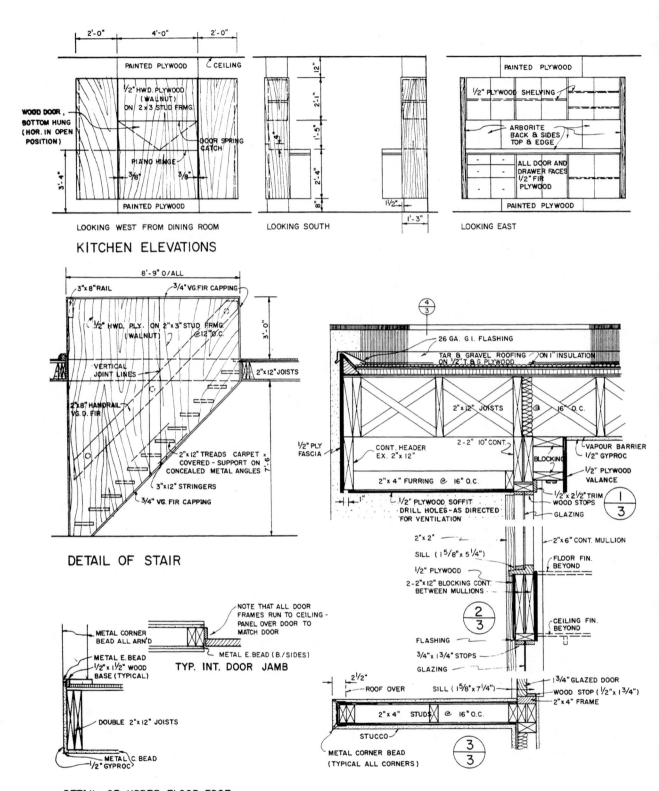

KITCHEN ELEVATIONS

LOOKING WEST FROM DINING ROOM

2'-0" | 4'-0" | 2'-0"

PAINTED PLYWOOD — CEILING
1/2" HWD. PLYWOOD (WALNUT) ON 2 x 3 STUD FRMG.
WOOD DOOR, BOTTOM HUNG (HOR. IN OPEN POSITION)
DOOR SPRING CATCH
PIANO HINGE
3/8" — 3/8"
3'-4"
PAINTED PLYWOOD

LOOKING SOUTH

12" / 2'-1" / 1'-5" / 2'-4" / 8"
1 1/2"
1'-3"

LOOKING EAST

PAINTED PLYWOOD
1/2" PLYWOOD SHELVING
ARBORITE BACK & SIDES TOP & EDGE
ALL DOOR AND DRAWER FACES 1/2" FIR PLYWOOD
PAINTED PLYWOOD

DETAIL OF STAIR

8'-9" O/ALL
3"x 8" RAIL
3/4" V.G. FIR CAPPING
1/2" HWD. PLY. ON 2"x 3" STUD FRMG. (WALNUT) @ 12" O.C.
3'-0"
VERTICAL JOINT LINES
2"x 12" JOISTS
2"x 8" HANDRAIL V.G. D. FIR
2"x 12" TREADS CARPET COVERED - SUPPORT ON CONCEALED METAL ANGLES
7'-6"
3"x 12" STRINGERS
3/4" V.G. FIR CAPPING

TYP. INT. DOOR JAMB

NOTE THAT ALL DOOR FRAMES RUN TO CEILING - PANEL OVER DOOR TO MATCH DOOR
METAL CORNER BEAD ALL ARN'D
METAL E. BEAD
1/2" x 1 1/2" WOOD BASE (TYPICAL)
METAL E. BEAD (B./SIDES)

DETAIL OF UPPER FLOOR EDGE

DOUBLE 2"x 12" JOISTS
METAL C. BEAD
1/2" GYPROC

TYPICAL WALL & ROOF DETAILS

4/3
26 GA. G.I. FLASHING
TAR & GRAVEL ROOFING ON 1" INSULATION ON 1/2" T. & G. PLYWOOD
2"x 12" JOISTS @ 16" O.C.
1/2" PLY FASCIA
CONT. HEADER EX. 2"x 12"
2-2"x 10" CONT.
VAPOUR BARRIER 1/2" GYPROC
BLOCKING
1/2" PLYWOOD VALANCE
2"x 4" FURRING @ 16" O.C.
1/2" PLYWOOD SOFFIT DRILL HOLES - AS DIRECTED FOR VENTILATION
1"
1/2" x 2 1/2" TRIM WOOD STOPS
GLAZING
1/3

2"x 2"
SILL (1 5/8" x 5 1/4")
1/2" PLYWOOD
2-2"x 12" BLOCKING CONT. BETWEEN MULLIONS
2/3
FLASHING
3/4" x 1 3/4" STOPS
GLAZING
2"x 6" CONT. MULLION
FLOOR FIN. BEYOND
CEILING FIN. BEYOND

2 1/2"
ROOF OVER
SILL (1 5/8" x 7 1/4")
2"x 4" STUDS @ 16" O.C.
STUCCO
METAL CORNER BEAD (TYPICAL ALL CORNERS)
1 3/4" GLAZED DOOR
WOOD STOP (1/2" x 1 3/4")
2"x 4" FRAME
3/3

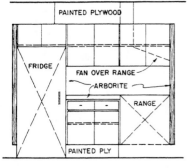

PAINTED PLYWOOD

FRIDGE

FAN OVER RANGE

ARBORITE

RANGE

PAINTED PLY

LOOKING WEST

NOTES

1. ALL WOOD & PLYWOOD D. FIR UNLESS OTHERWISE INDICATED

2. ALL EXPOSED SURFACES PAINTED TWO COATS UNLESS OTHERWISE INDICATED

3. HWD. PLYWOOD SURFACES, OILED & RUBBED FINISH

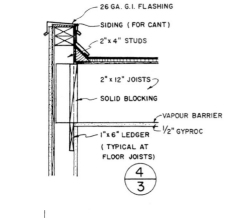

26 GA. G.I. FLASHING

SIDING (FOR CANT)

2" x 4" STUDS

2" x 12" JOISTS

SOLID BLOCKING

VAPOUR BARRIER

1/2" GYPROC

1" x 6" LEDGER (TYPICAL AT FLOOR JOISTS)

4/3

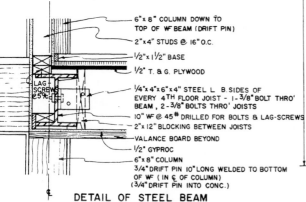

6" x 8" COLUMN DOWN TO TOP OF WF BEAM (DRIFT PIN)

2" x 4" STUDS @ 16" O.C.

1/2" x 1 1/2" BASE

1/2" T. & G. PLYWOOD

1/4" x 4" x 6" x 4" STEEL L. B. SIDES OF EVERY 4TH FLOOR JOIST - 1-3/8" BOLT THRO' BEAM, 2-3/8" BOLTS THRO' JOISTS

10" WF @ 45# DRILLED FOR BOLTS & LAG-SCREWS

2" x 12" BLOCKING BETWEEN JOISTS

VALANCE BOARD BEYOND

1/2" GYPROC

6" x 8" COLUMN

3/4" DRIFT PIN 10" LONG WELDED TO BOTTOM OF WF (IN ¢ OF COLUMN) (3/4" DRIFT PIN INTO CONC.)

LAG-SCREWS @ 5"

DETAIL OF STEEL BEAM
TO COLUMN CONNECTION

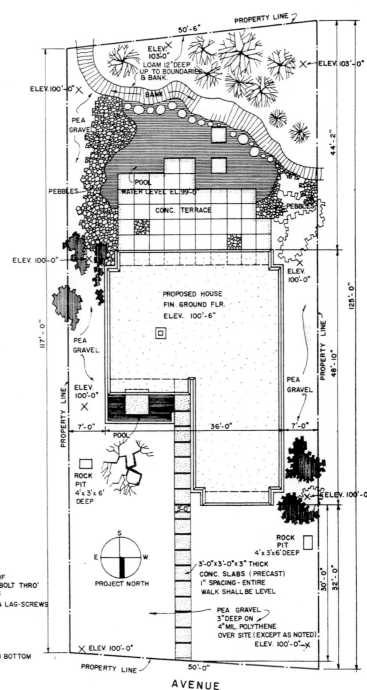

PROPERTY LINE

50'-6"

ELEV. 103'-0"
LOAM 12"DEEP UP TO BOUNDARIES & BANK.

ELEV. 103'-0"

ELEV. 100'-0"

BANK

PEA GRAVEL

POOL
WATER LEVEL EL. 99-0"

CONC. TERRACE

PEBBLES

PEBBLES

44'-2"

ELEV. 100'-0"

ELEV. 100'-0"

117'-0"

PEA GRAVEL

PROPOSED HOUSE
FIN. GROUND FLR.
ELEV. 100'-6"

PROPERTY LINE

125'-0"

PEA GRAVEL

48'-10"

PROPERTY LINE

ELEV. 100'-0"

7'-0"

POOL

36'-0"

7'-0"

ELEV. 100'-0"

ROCK PIT
4' x 3' x 6' DEEP

3'-0"

ROCK PIT
4' x 3' x 6' DEEP

S

E   W

PROJECT NORTH

3'-0" x 3'-0" x 3" THICK CONC. SLABS (PRECAST) 1" SPACING - ENTIRE WALK SHALL BE LEVEL

30'-0"

32'-0"

PEA GRAVEL 3"DEEP ON 4"MIL. POLYTHENE OVER SITE (EXCEPT AS NOTED). ELEV. 100'-0"

ELEV. 100'-0"

PROPERTY LINE

50'-0"

AVENUE

SITE PLAN

RESIDENCE 1

RESIDENCE (1)

SITE PLAN

PROPERTY LINE

ELEV 103'-0"

125'-0"

48'-10"

PROPERTY LINE

32'-0"

44'-2"

ELEV 105'-0"
LOAM 12" DEEP UP TO BOUNDARIES & BANK

50'-6"

ELEV 105'-0"

BANK

PEA GRAVEL

WATER LEVEL EL 99'-0"

CONC. TERRACE

POOL

PROPOSED HOUSE
FIN GROUND FLR.
ELEV 100'-6"

36'-0"

PEA GRAVEL

7'-0"

ELEV 100'-0"

50'-6"

PEA GRAVEL

PEBBLES

ELEV 100'-0"

PEA GRAVEL

ELEV 100'-0"

7'-0"

POOL

117'-0"

PROPERTY LINE

ROCK PIT
4'x3'x6' DEEP

PEA GRAVEL
3' DEEP ON
4 MIL POLYTHENE
OVER SITE (EXCEPT AS NOTED)
ELEV 100'-0"

3'-0"x13'-0"x3" THICK
CONC. SLABS (PRECAST)
1" SPACING - ENTIRE
WALK SHALL BE LEVEL

ROCK PIT
4'x3'x6'
DEEP

PROJECT NORTH

N S E W

ELEV 100'-0"

PROPERTY LINE

AVENUE

50'-0"

KITCHEN ELEVATIONS

PAINTED PLYWOOD

FAN OVER RANGE

ARBORITE

FRIDGE

RANGE

PAINTED PLY

LOOKING WEST

PAINTED PLYWOOD

1/2" PLYWOOD SHELVING

ARBORITE BACK & SIDES, TOP & EDGE

ALL DOOR AND DRAWER FACES 1/2" FIR PLYWOOD

PAINTED PLYWOOD

LOOKING EAST

1'-3"

1/2"

LOOKING SOUTH

2'-0" 4'-0" 2'-0"

CEILING

PAINTED PLYWOOD

1/2" HWD PLYWOOD (WALNUT) ON 2x3 5/8 STUD FRAMING

DOOR SPRING CATCH

PIANO HINGE

WOOD DOOR - BOTTOM HUNG (HOR IN OPEN POSITION)

LOOKING WEST FROM DINING ROOM

NOTES

1. ALL WOOD & PLYWOOD D. FIR UNLESS OTHERWISE INDICATED

2. ALL EXPOSED SURFACES PAINTED TWO COATS UNLESS OTHERWISE INDICATED

3. HWD PLYWOOD SURFACES, OILED & RUBBED FINISH

DETAIL OF STAIR

2"x12" JOISTS

8'-9" O/ALL

3/4" VG FIR CAPPING

2"x12" TREADS CARPET COVERED - SUPPORT ON CONCEALED METAL ANGLES

3"x12" STRINGERS

3/4" VG FIR CAPPING

1/2" HWD PLY ON 2"x3" STUD FRAMING (WALNUT)

VERTICAL JOINT LINES

2'x6" HANDRAIL

TYP. INT. DOOR JAMB

NOTE THAT ALL DOOR FRAMES RUN TO CEILING - PANELS OVER DOOR TO MATCH DOOR

METAL E. BEAD (B/SIDES)

METAL CORNER BEAD ALL AR'D

METAL E BEAD

2"x2"x1/2" WOOD BASE (TYPICAL)

DETAIL OF UPPER FLOOR EDGE

METAL CORNER BEAD

DOUBLE 2"x12" JOISTS

1/2" GYPROC

METAL C BEAD

TYPICAL WALL & ROOF DETAILS

26 GA. G.I. FLASHING

SIDING (FOR CANT)

2"x14" STUDS

SOLID BLOCKING

1"x6" LEDGER (TYPICAL AT FLOOR JOISTS)

2"x12" JOISTS

VAPOUR BARRIER

1/2" GYPROC

4 / 3

VAPOUR BARRIER

1/2" PLYWOOD VALANCE

2"x2"x1/2" TRIM WOOD STOPS

GLAZING

BLOCKING

2"x6" CONT MULLION

1 / 3

TAR & GRAVEL ROOFING ON 1" INSULATION

26 GA. G.I. FLASHING

1/2" O.R.S. PLYWOOD

2"x12" JOISTS

2-2"x10" CONT

CONT HEADER EX 2"x12

2"x4" FURRING @ 16" O.C.

1/2" PLYWOOD SOFFIT DRILL HOLES - AS DIRECTED FOR VENTILATION

FLOOR FIN. BEYOND

SILL (1 5/8"x5 1/4")

1/2" PLYWOOD

2-2"x12" BLOCKING CONT BETWEEN MULLIONS

CEILING FIN BEYOND

FLASHING

3/4"x1 3/4" STOPS

GLAZING

2 / 3

1 3/4" GLAZED DOOR

SILL (1 5/8"x7 1/4")

WOOD STOP (1/2"x1 3/4")

2"x4" FRAME

ROOF OVER

2"x4" STUDS @ 16" O.C.

3 / 3

STUCCO

METAL CORNER BEAD (TYPICAL ALL CORNERS)

1/2" PLY FASCIA

DETAIL OF STEEL BEAM TO COLUMN CONNECTION

6"x6" COLUMN DOWN TO TOP OF W BEAM (DRIFT PIN)

2"x4" STUDS @ 16" O.C.

1/2" T & G PLYWOOD

1/2" T & G PLYWOOD

2"x4" 1 1/2" BASE

1/4"x4"x6"x4" STEEL L B SIDES OF EVERY 4TH FLOOR JOIST - 1 3/8" BOLT THRO' BEAM, 2-3/8" BOLTS THRO' JOISTS

10" W 45 # DRILLED FOR BOLTS & LAG-SCREWS

2"x12" BLOCKING BETWEEN JOISTS

VALANCE BOARD BEYOND

6"x6" COLUMN

LAG SCREWS

3/4" DRIFT PIN 10" LONG WELDED TO BOTTOM OF 6" x 6" COLUMN (3/4" DRIFT PIN INTO CONC.)

TYPICAL WALL & ROOF DETAILS

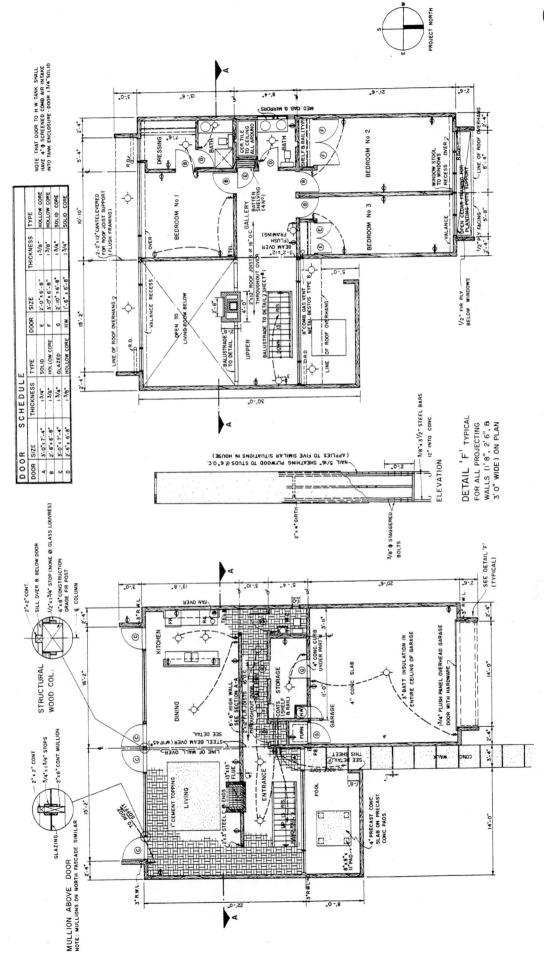

DOOR SCHEDULE

DOOR	SIZE	THICKNESS	TYPE
A	3'-0"x 7'-4"	1 3/4"	SOLID
B	2'-8"x 6'-8"	1 3/4"	HOLLOW CORE
C	3'-0"x 7'-4"	1 3/4"	GLAZED
D	2'-6"x 6'-8"	1 3/8"	HOLLOW CORE

DOOR	SIZE	THICKNESS	TYPE
E	2'-0"x 6'-8"	1 3/8"	HOLLOW CORE
F	3'-0"x 6'-8"	1 3/8"	HOLLOW CORE
G	2'-10"x 6'-8"	1 3/4"	SOLID CORE
HW	1'-6"x 6'-8"	1 3/4"	SOLID CORE

NOTE THAT DOOR TO H W TANK SHALL
HAVE 4" ∅ SCREENED COMB AIR INTAKE
INTO TANK ENCLOSURE- DOOR 1 3/4" SOLID

UPPER FLOOR PLAN

DETAIL 'F' TYPICAL
FOR ALL PROJECTING
WALLS (1'8", 2'6", 8
3'0" WIDE) ON PLAN

ELEVATION

STRUCTURAL
WOOD COL.

MULLION ABOVE DOOR
NOTE: MULLIONS ON NORTH FASCADE SIMILAR

GROUND FLOOR PLAN

RESIDENCE ②

PROJECT NORTH

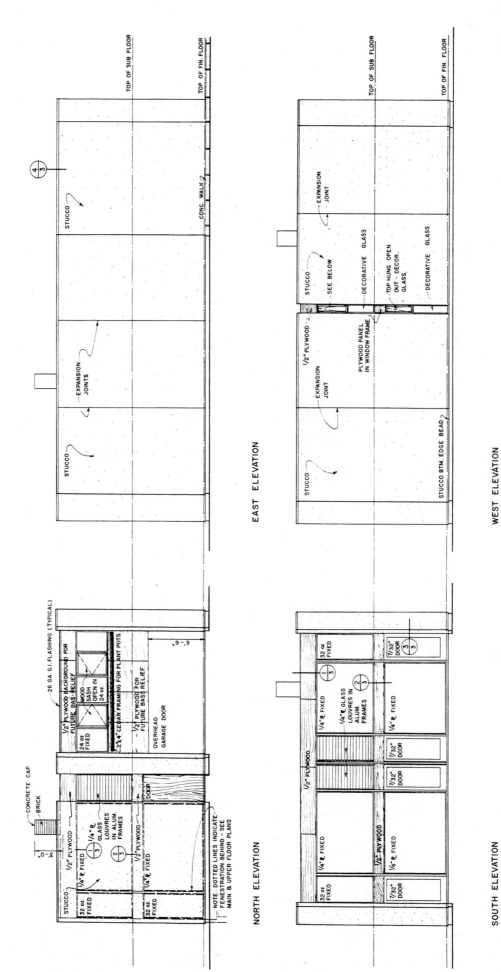

EAST ELEVATION

WEST ELEVATION

NORTH ELEVATION

SOUTH ELEVATION

RESIDENCE ③

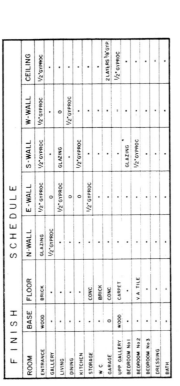

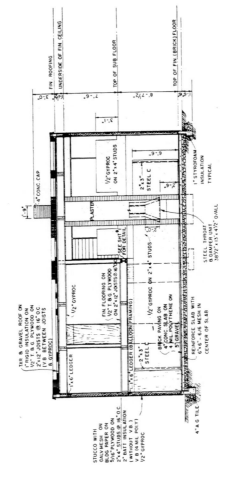

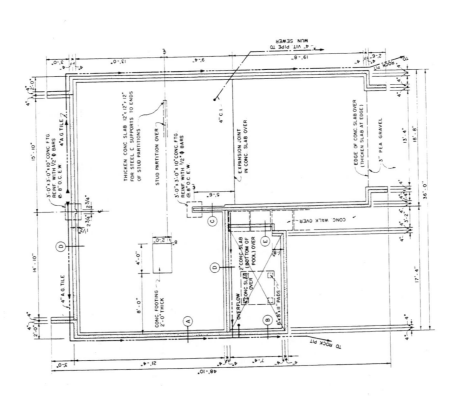

FINISH SCHEDULE

ROOM	BASE	FLOOR	N-WALL	E-WALL	S-WALL	W-WALL	CEILING
ENTRANCE	WOOD	BRICK	GLAZING	½"GYPROC	½"GYPROC	½"GYPROC	½"GYPROC
GALLERY	"	"	½"GYPROC	0	GLAZING	0	"
LIVING	"	"	"	½"GYPROC	GLAZING	½"GYPROC	"
DINING	"	"	"	0	½"GYPROC	0	"
KITCHEN	"	"	"	0	"	"	"
STORAGE	"	CONC	"	½"GYPROC	"	"	"
W C	"	BRICK	"	"	"	"	"
GARAGE	0	CONC	"	"	"	"	2 LAYERS ⅝"GYP
UPP GALLERY	WOOD	CARPET	"	"	"	"	½"GYPROC
BEDROOM No 1	"	"	"	"	GLAZING	"	"
BEDROOM No 2	"	V A TILE	"	"	"	"	"
BEDROOM No 3	"	"	"	"	½"GYPROC	½"GYPROC	"
DRESSING	"	"	"	"	"	"	"
BATH	"	"	"	"	"	"	"

SECTION A - A

FOUNDATION PLAN

RESIDENCE ④

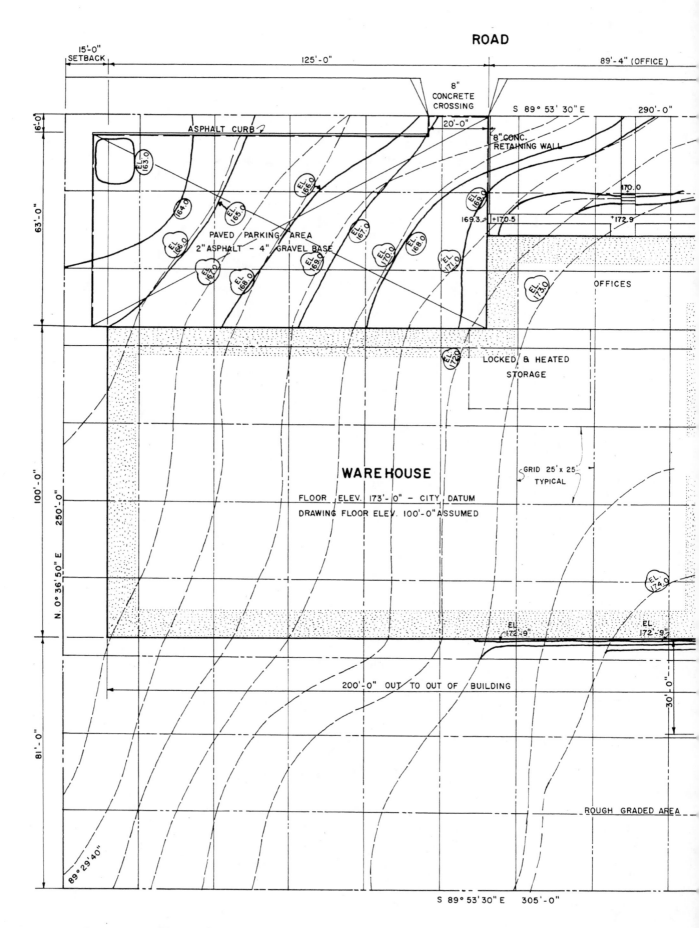

SITE PLAN

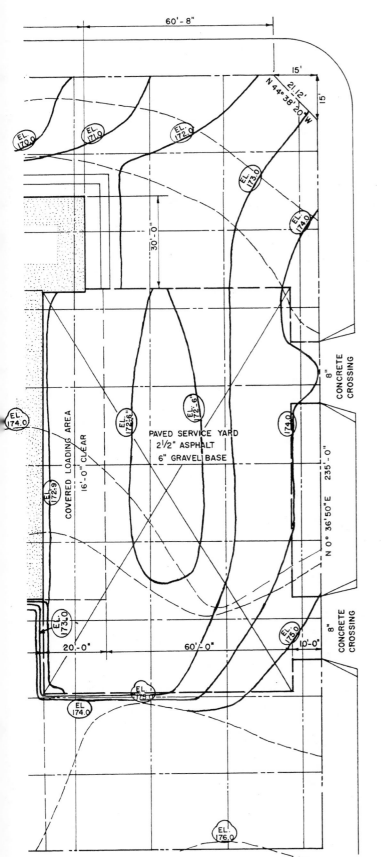

60'- 8"

15'

N 44° 38' 20" W
2½'

15'

30'- 0"

EL. 170.0

EL. 171.0

EL. 172.0

EL. 173.0

EL. 174.0

EL. 174.0

EL. 172'-6"

EL. 172'-6"

EL. 174.0

PAVED SERVICE YARD
2½" ASPHALT
6" GRAVEL BASE

COVERED LOADING AREA
16'-0" CLEAR

EL. 172.9

EL. 173.0

EL. 174.0

EL. 174.0

20'-0"

60'-0"

10'-0"

EL. 175.0

EL. 176.0

8"
CONCRETE CROSSING

8"
CONCRETE CROSSING

N 0° 36' 50" E   235'- 0"

ROAD

NORTH

LEGEND

EXISTING CONTOUR LINE   EL. 174.0

PROPOSED CONTOUR LINE   EL. 173.0

WAREHOUSE   1

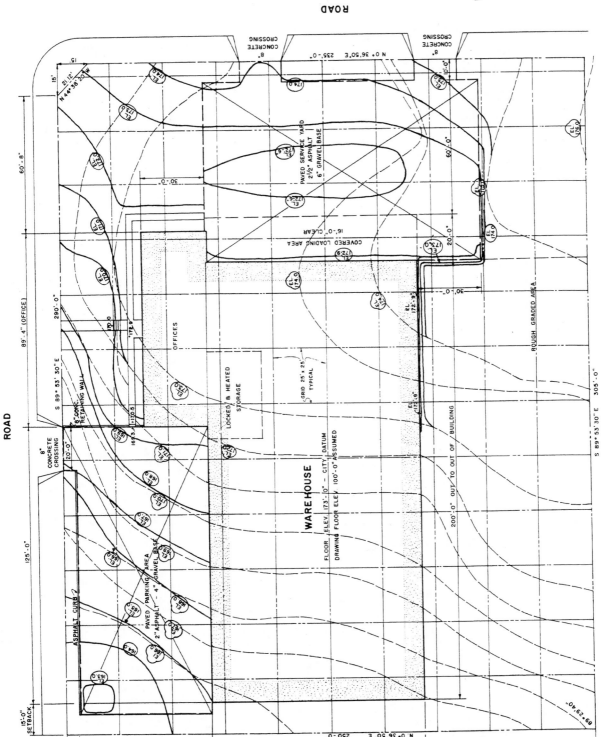

WAREHOUSE

SITE PLAN

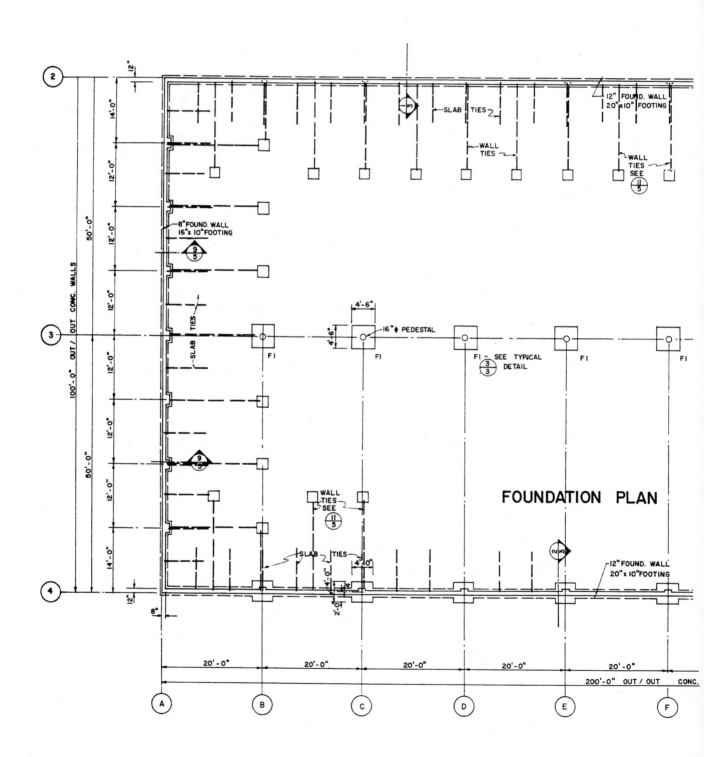

NORTH

FOUNDATION PLAN

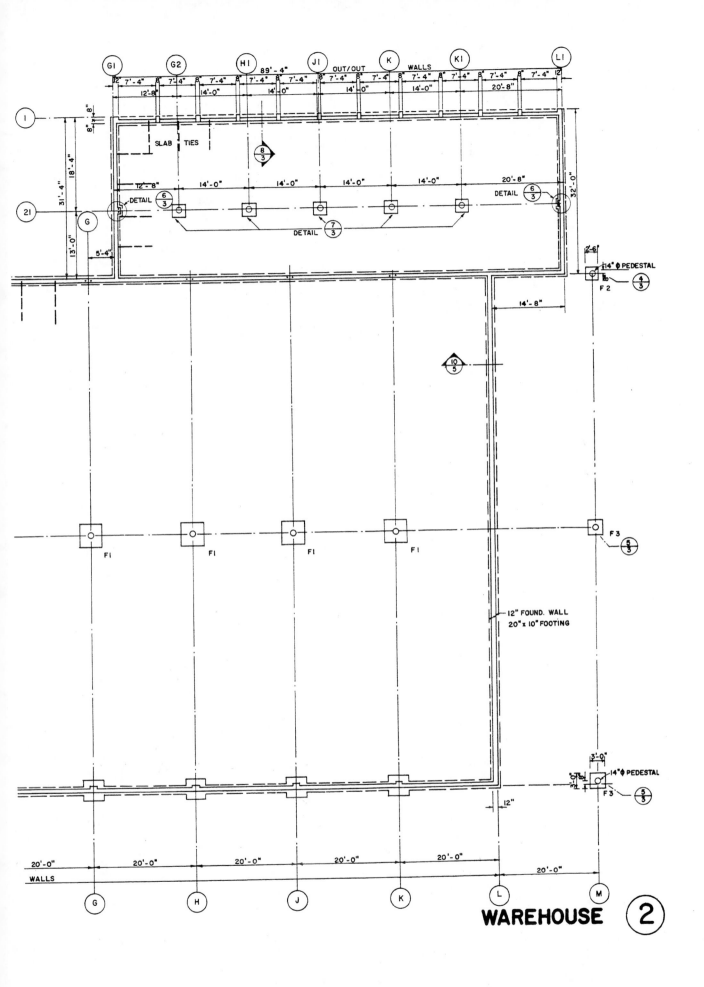

WAREHOUSE ②

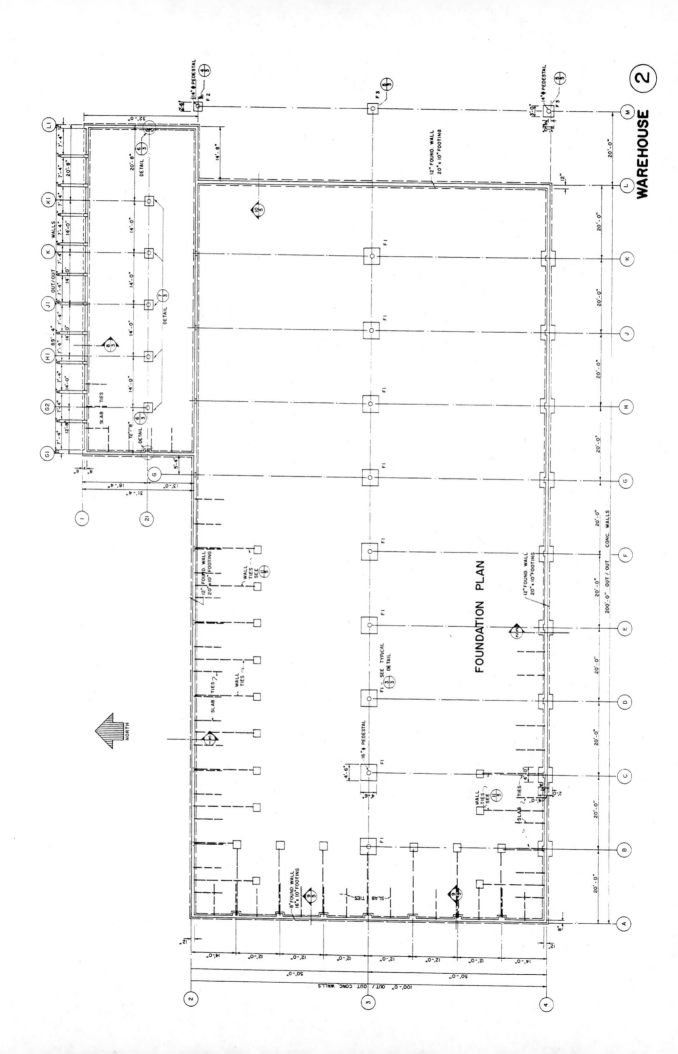

FOUNDATION PLAN

WAREHOUSE ②

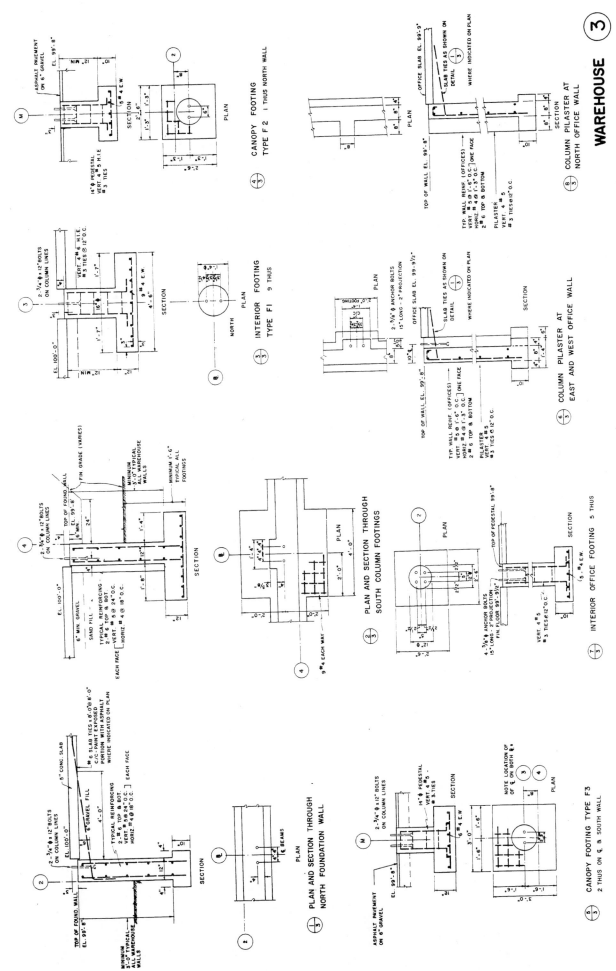

WAREHOUSE (3)

FOOTING DETAILS (SEE OTHERS ON SHEET 5)

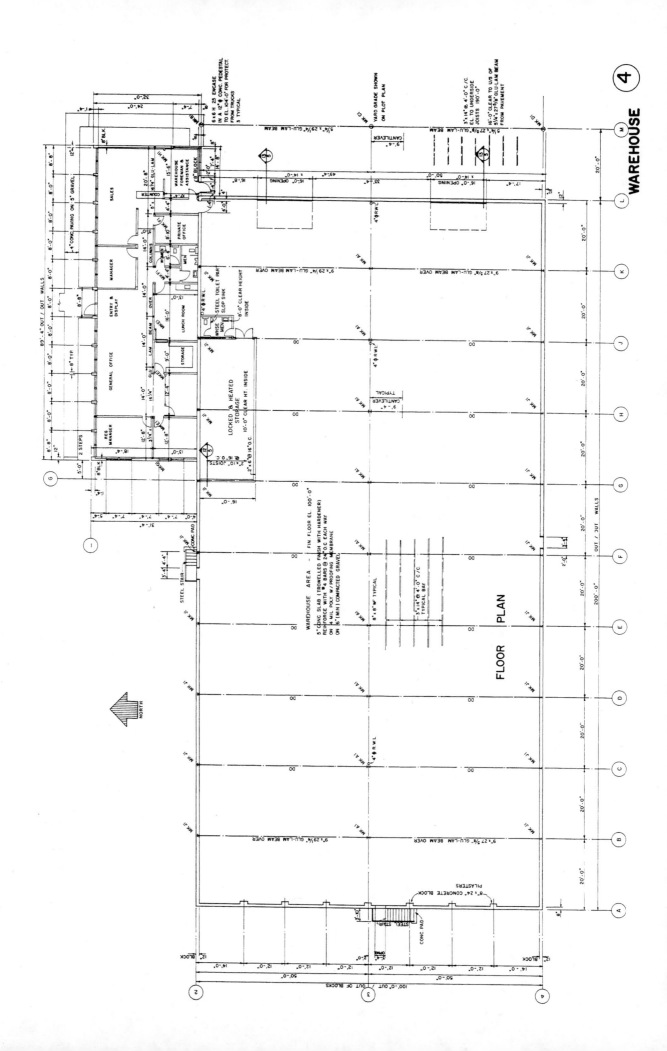

WAREHOUSE

FLOOR PLAN

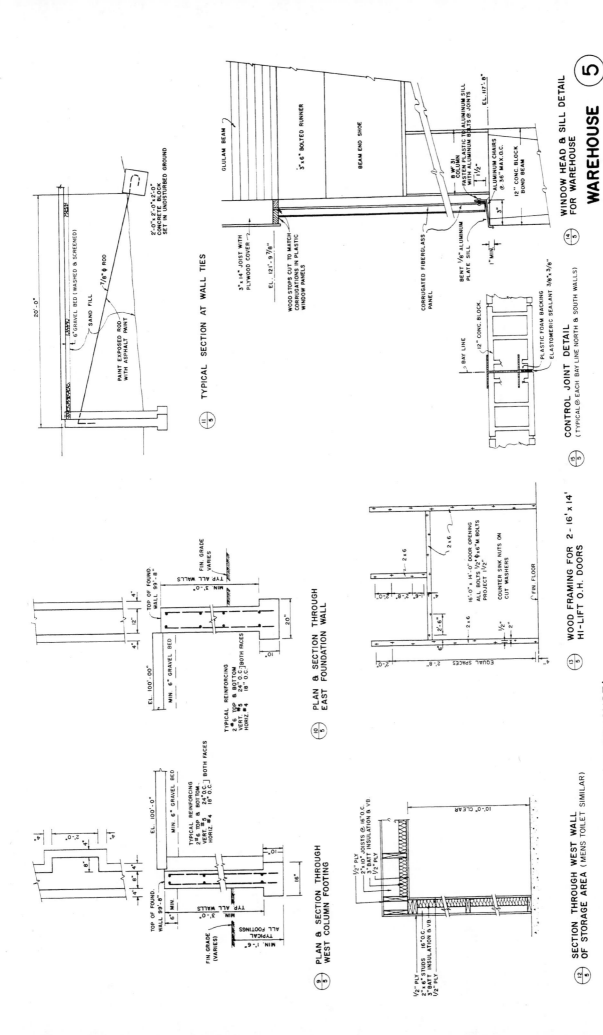

TYPICAL SECTION AT WALL TIES

2'-0"×2'-0"×2'-0"
CONCRETE BLOCK
SET IN UNDISTURBED GROUND

6"GRAVEL BED (WASHED & SCREENED)

SAND FILL

7/8"⌀ ROD

PAINT EXPOSED ROD
WITH ASPHALT PAINT

20'-0"

11 / 5

WINDOW HEAD & SILL DETAIL FOR WAREHOUSE

GLULAM BEAM

3"×6" BOLTED RUNNER

BEAM END SHOE

3"×14" JOIST WITH PLYWOOD COVER

EL. 121'-9 7/8"

WOOD STOPS CUT TO MATCH
CORRUGATIONS IN PLASTIC
WINDOW PANELS

CORRUGATED FIBERGLASS
PANEL

8 WF 31
COLUMN
FASTEN PLASTIC TO ALUMINUM SILL
WITH ALUMINUM BOLTS @ JOINTS

1/2"

ALUMINUM CHAIRS
@ 36" MAX. O.C.

12" CONC. BLOCK
BOND BEAM

EL. 117'-8"

BENT 1/8" ALUMINUM
PLATE SILL

1" MIN.

3"

14 / 5

CONTROL JOINT DETAIL
(TYPICAL @ EACH BAY LINE NORTH & SOUTH WALLS)

BAY LINE

12" CONC. BLOCK.

PLASTIC FOAM BACKING
ELASTOMERIC SEALANT 3/8"×3/8"

15 / 5

PLAN & SECTION THROUGH EAST FOUNDATION WALL

FIN. GRADE
VARIES

TOP OF FOUND.
WALL 99'-8"

MIN 3'-0"
TYP ALL WALLS

EL. 100'-00"

MIN. 6" GRAVEL BED

12"

4"

20"

10"

4"

TYPICAL REINFORCING
2 #6 TOP & BOTTOM.
VERT. #5   24" O.C. BOTH FACES
HORIZ. #4   18" O.C.

10 / 5

PLAN & SECTION THROUGH WEST COLUMN FOOTING

EL. 100'-0"

MIN. 6" GRAVEL BED

TOP OF FOUND.
WALL 99'-8"

MIN 3'-0"
TYP ALL WALLS

TYPICAL
ALL FOOTINGS
MIN. 1'-6"

FIN. GRADE
(VARIES)

4"

2'-0"

4"

8"

8"

4"

8"

4"

16"

10"

6"

TYPICAL REINFORCING
2 #6 TOP & BOTTOM.
VERT. #5   24" O.C. BOTH FACES
HORIZ. #4 18" O.C.

9 / 5

WOOD FRAMING FOR 2 - 16'×14'
HI-LIFT O.H. DOORS

2×6

2×6

2×6

2×6

EQUAL SPACES 2'-8"

2'-0"

4"

2'-6"

4'-6"

8'-0"

2'-0"

16'-0"×14'-0" DOOR OPENING
ALL BOLTS 1/2"⌀×6"M BOLTS
PROJECT 1/2"

COUNTER SINK NUTS ON
CUT WASHERS

FIN FLOOR

1/2"

2"

13 / 5

SECTION THROUGH WEST WALL
OF STORAGE AREA (MENS TOILET SIMILAR)

1/2" PLY
2"×6" STUDS 16"O.C.
3" BATT INSULATION & VB
1/2" PLY

1/2" PLY
2"×10" JOISTS @ 16"O.C.
3" BATT INSULATION & VB
1/2" PLY

10'-0" CLEAR

12 / 5

WALL SECTIONS & DETAILS (WAREHOUSE)

WAREHOUSE 5

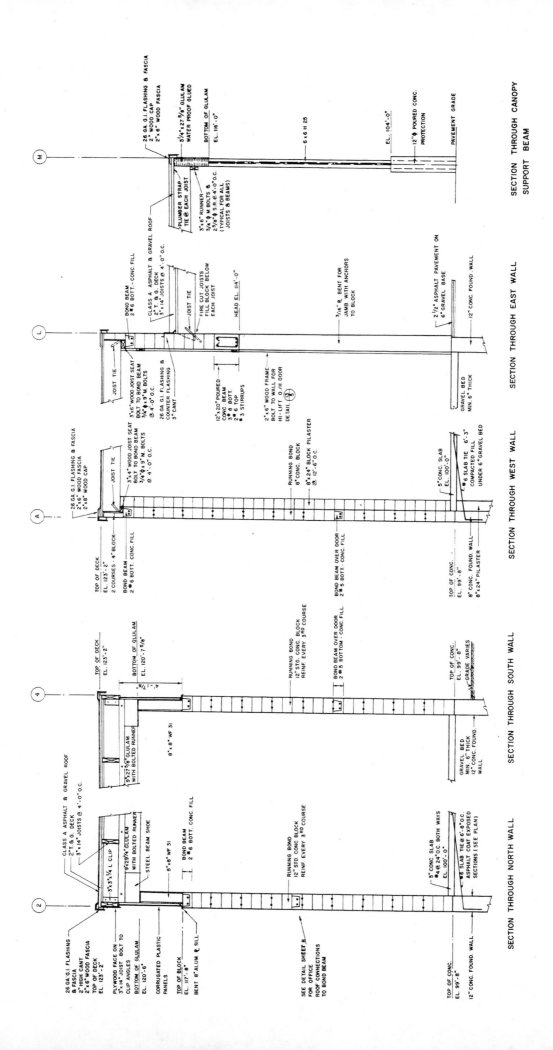

SECTION THROUGH CANOPY
SUPPORT BEAM

SECTION THROUGH EAST WALL

SECTION THROUGH WEST WALL

SECTION THROUGH SOUTH WALL

SECTION THROUGH NORTH WALL

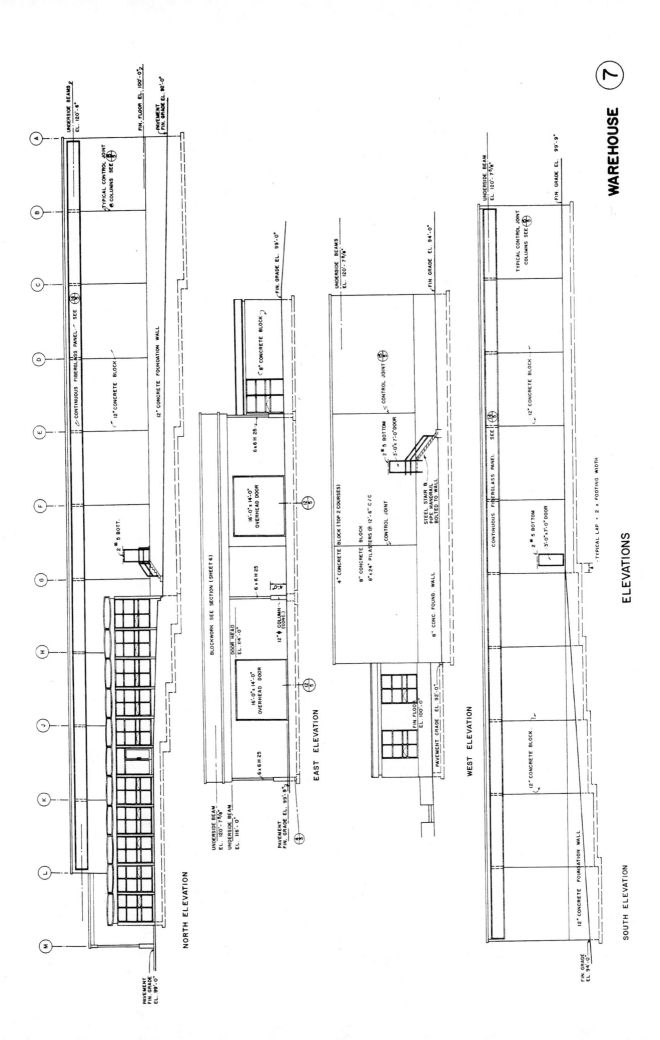

WAREHOUSE ⑦

ELEVATIONS

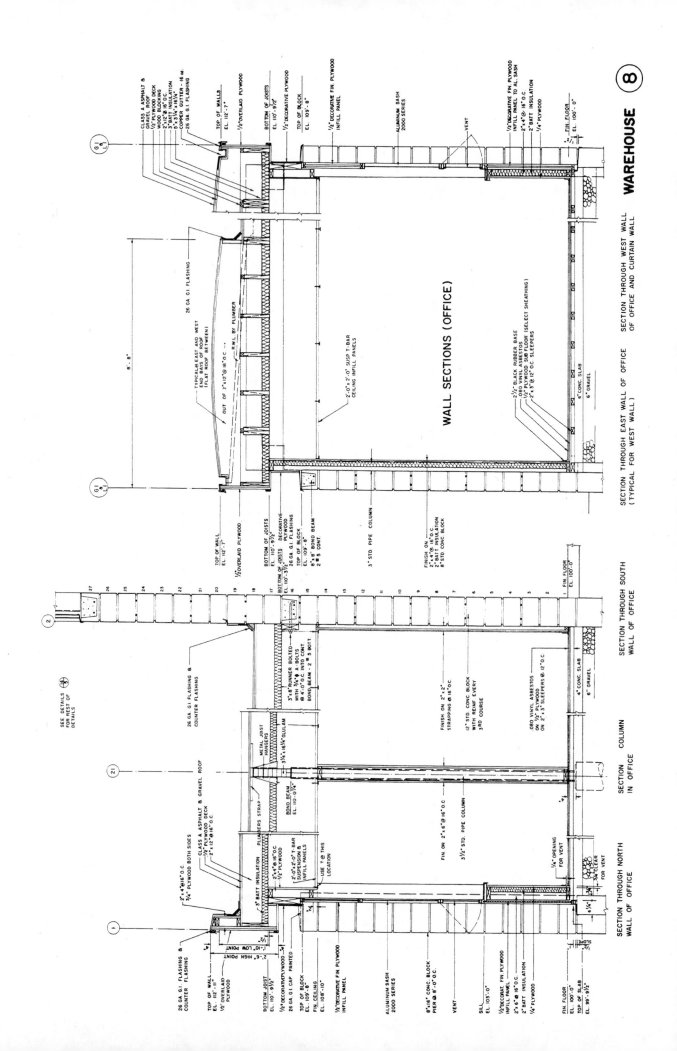

WALL SECTIONS (OFFICE)

SECTION THROUGH EAST WALL OF OFFICE
(TYPICAL FOR WEST WALL)

SECTION THROUGH WEST WALL
OF OFFICE AND CURTAIN WALL

SECTION THROUGH SOUTH
WALL OF OFFICE

SECTION
COLUMN
IN OFFICE

SECTION THROUGH NORTH
WALL OF OFFICE

WAREHOUSE ⑧

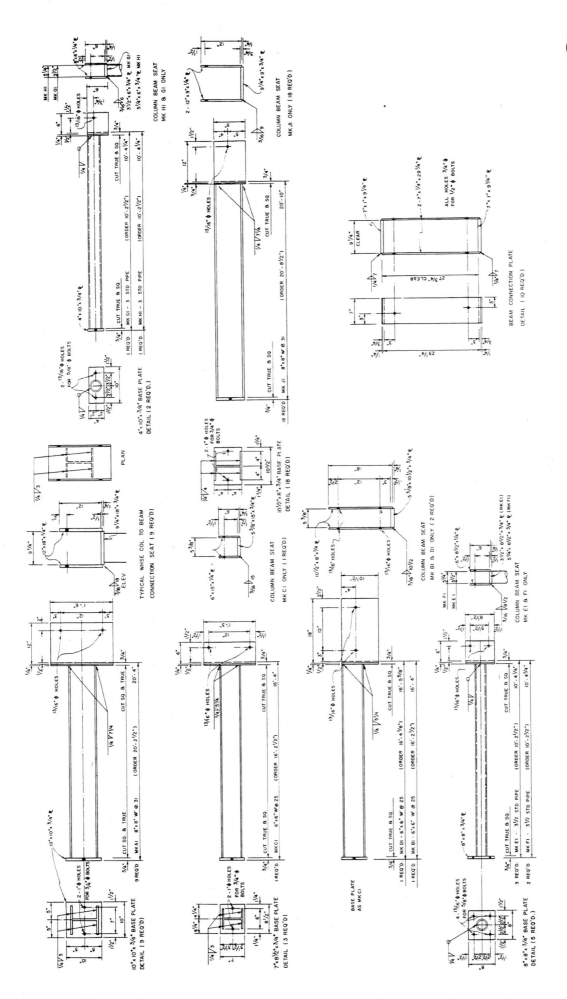

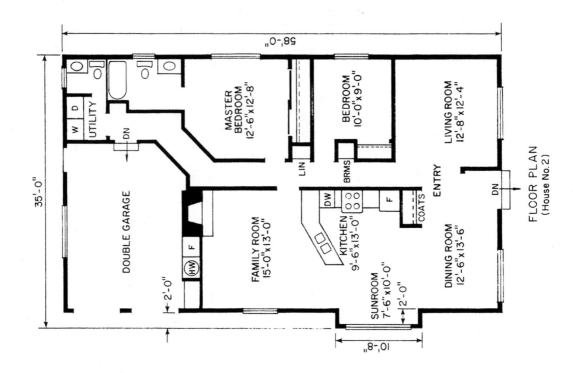

FLOOR PLAN
(House No.2)

MASTER BEDROOM
12'-6"x12'-8"

BEDROOM
10'-0"x9'-0"

LIVING ROOM
12'-8"x12'-4"

DOUBLE GARAGE

UTILITY

W D

DN

FAMILY ROOM
15'-0"x13'-0"

HW F

KITCHEN
9'-6"x13'-0"

DW

F

COATS

ENTRY

DN

SUNROOM
7'-6"x10'-0"

DINING ROOM
12'-6"x13'-6"

LIN

BRMS

58'-0"

35'-0"

2'-0"

10'-8"

2'-0"

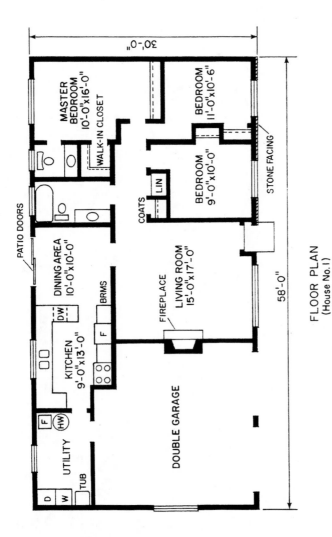

FLOOR PLAN
(House No.1)

MASTER BEDROOM
10'-0"x16'-0"

WALK-IN CLOSET

BEDROOM
11'-0"x10'-6"

STONE FACING

PATIO DOORS

DINING AREA
10'-0"x10'-0"

KITCHEN
9'-0"x13'-0"

DW

BRMS

F

COATS

LIN

BEDROOM
9'-0"x10'-0"

FIREPLACE

LIVING ROOM
15'-0"x17'-0"

DOUBLE GARAGE

UTILITY

F HW

D W

TUB

30'-0"

58'-0"

HOUSE PLANS may be used for measurement exercises in conjunction with Figure 7-16, Typical Exterior Wall Section, on page 94, and with a specification sheet (prepared by the instructor and students) containing window and door sizes and other information.

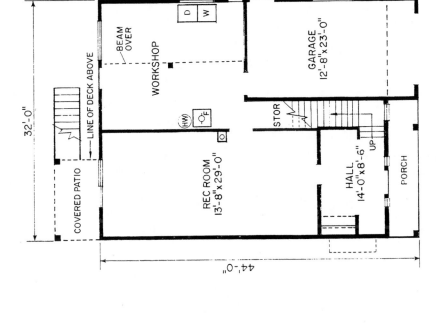

BASEMENT PLAN
(House No. 3)

BEAM OVER

WORKSHOP

D   W

GARAGE
12'-8" x 23'-0"

REC ROOM
13'-8" x 29'-0"

HW   F

STOR

HALL
14'-0" x 8'-6"

UP

PORCH

COVERED PATIO

LINE OF DECK ABOVE

32'-0"

44'-0"

MAIN FLOOR PLAN
(House No. 3)

BEDROOM
10'-0" x 13'-0"

BEDROOM
9'-6" x 10'-6"

TWLS

SH

MASTER BEDROOM
12'-0" x 15'-6"

DN

MORNING RM
10'-0" x 8'-0"

PH DESK

F

KITCHEN
10'-0" x 10'-0"

DW

DINING ROOM
10'-0" x 14'-6"

LIVING ROOM
14'-6" x 15'-0"

FIREPLACE

RAILING

DN

SUNDECK

32'-0"

44'-0"

HOUSE PLANS may be used for measurement exercises in conjunction with Figure 7-16, Typical Exterior Wall Section, on page **94**, and with a specification sheet (prepared by the instructor and students) containing window and door sizes and other information.